The Norsemen in the Viking Age

Eric Christiansen

Blackwell
Publishing

BLACKWELL PUBLISHING
350 Main Street, Malden, MA 02148-5020, USA
9600 Garsington Road, Oxford OX4 2DQ, UK
550 Swanston Street, Carlton, Victoria 3053, Australia

The right of Eric Christiansen to be identified as the Author of this Work has been asserted in accordance with the UK Copyright, Designs, and Patents Act 1988.

First published 2002
First published in paperback 2006 by Blackwell Publishing Ltd

1 2006

Library of Congress Cataloging-in-Publication Data

Christiansen, Eric.
  The Norsemen in the Viking Age / Eric Christiansen.
    p. cm. – (Peoples of Europe)
  Includes bibliographical references and index.
  ISBN 0-631-21677-4 (alk. paper)
  1. Northmen. 2. Vikings. I. Title. II. Series.

DL65.C49 2001
948'.022–dc21   2001025598

  ISBN-13: 978-0-631-21677-3 (alk. paper)
  ISBN-10: 1-4051-4964-7 (paperback)
  ISBN-13: 978-1-4051-4964-8 (paperback)

A catalogue record for this title is available from the British Library.

Set in 10.5 on 12 pt Sabon
by Kolam Information Services Pvt. Ltd, Pondicherry, India
Printed and bound in the United Kingdom
by TJ International Ltd, Padstow, Cornwall

The publisher's policy is to use permanent paper from mills that operate a sustainable forestry policy, and which has been manufactured from pulp processed using acid-free and elementary chlorine-free practices. Furthermore, the publisher ensures that the text paper and cover board used have met acceptable environmental accreditation standards.

For further information on
Blackwell Publishing, visit our website:
www.blackwellpublishing.com

Cover Image

An eighteent[h] [...] eleve [...] e formerly in H[amm]erstad Church on Öland, now lost. I[ts inscriptio]n reads: 'Estrith had this stone erected in memory of [her husba]nd Björn, God help his soul'. It surrounds the image of a l[ong-h]aired lady giving birth (?) to dragons under a canopy, pre-Viking Age in origin: see p.265.

The Peoples of Europe

General Editors
James Campbell and Barry Cunliffe

This series is about the European tribes and peoples from their origins in prehistory to the present day. Drawing upon a wide range of archaeological and historical evidence, each volume presents a fresh and absorbing account of a group's culture, society and usually turbulent history.

Already published

The Etruscans
Graeme Barker and Thomas Rasmussen

The Normans
Marjorie Chibnall

The Norsemen in the Viking Age
Eric Christiansen

The Lombards
Neil Christie

The Serbs
Sima Ćirković

The Basques*
Roger Collins

The English
Geoffrey Elton

The Gypsies
Second edition
Angus Fraser

The Bretons
Patrick Galliou and Michael Jones

The Goths
Peter Heather

The Franks*
Edward James

The Russians
Robin Milner-Gulland

The Mongols
David Morgan

The Armenians
A. E. Redgate

The Britons
Christopher A. Snyder

The Huns
E. A. Thompson

The Early Germans
Second edition
Malcolm Todd

The Illyrians
John Wilkes

In preparation

The Sicilians
David Abulafia

The Irish
Francis John Byrne and Michael Herity

The Byzantines
Averil Cameron

The Spanish
Roger Collins

The Romans
Timothy Cornell

The Scots
Colin Kidd & Dauvit Brown

The Picts
Charles Thomas

The Angles and Saxons
Helana Hamerow

*Denotes title now out of print

Contents

List of Maps   vi

List of Abbreviations   vii

Acknowledgements   xv

Introduction:

    Vikings   Their Age   The Aim   1–9

1 INDIVIDUALS   10
2 FAMILIES   38
3 COMMUNITIES AND ASSOCIATIONS   64
4 DISTRICTS AND TERRITORIES   87
5 PEOPLES   112
6 POLITICS   133
7 WAR   168
8 WORK   189
9 EMIGRATION   214
10 PAST   236
11 PRESENT   251
12 FUTURE   279

Postscript: MODERN RESEARCH   301

Appendixes:
  A DYNASTIC IDENTITIES   325
  B DATES   327
  C WEIGHTS AND MEASURES   333
  D THEGNS   335

References   337

Index   367

Maps

1 Women of some importance   18
2 Big men, *c.*900–*c.*1050   75
3 Hypothetical territories, *c.*750–*c.*1000   90
4 Viking-Age districts   95
5 Scandinavian peoples, 750–1050   113
6 The Danish kingdom under Canute   151
7 Chiefdoms and kingdoms, *c.*800   161
8 Import–export, 800–950   211
9 Migration, 950–1050   234
10 Cults   260
11 Rune-stone regions, *c.*970–1070   277
12 Burial rites, *c.*900–*c.*1000   287

Abbreviations

AA   Acta Archaeologica, Copenhagen.
AAL   Acta Archaeologica Lundensia.
Aarbøger   *Aarbøger for nordisk oldkyndighed og historie*, Copenhagen 1866–.
AB   Adam of Bremen: *Gesta Hammaburgensis Ecclesiæ Pontificum.*
AEW   *Altnordisches etymologisches Wörterbuch*, J. de Vries.
AF   Árbók fornleifafélagsins, Reykjavik 1977–.
Ágrip   *A. af Noregskonungasógum* (ed. and trans. M. J. Driscoll, London 1995).
ANF   Arkiv for nordisk filologi, Lund (Christiania 1883–).
ANS   Anglo-Norman Studies.
AP   Archæologia Polona, Warsaw 1958–.
ARF   *Annales Regni Francorum* (ed. Pertz and Kurze, Hanover 1895).
ASC   Anglo-Saxon Chronicle.
ASB   *The Annals of St Bertin*, trans. J. N. Nelson, Manchester 1991.
ASCEN   *Anglo-Scandinavian England*, ed. J. D. Niles and M. Amodio, Maryland 1989.
ASP   Approaches to Swedish Prehistory, ed. T. B. Larsson and Lundmark.
ASE   *Anglo-Saxon England*, Cambridge 1972–.
ASSAH   Anglo Saxon Studies in Archaeology and History, Oxford 1987–.
ASMA   *Aspects of Maritime Scandinavia*, ed. O. Crumlin-Peterson, Roskilde 1991.
AU   *The Annals of Ulster*, ed. MacAirt and S. MacNiocaill, Dublin 1983.

AUD	*Arkæologiske udgravninger i Danmark 1990*, Copenhagen 1991.
AUSA	The Audience of the Sagas, ed. L. Lönnroth, 2 vols, Gothenburg 1991.
B	*Von Ågedal bis Malt: Die skandinavischen Runeninschriften*, T. Birkman, Berlin 1995.
BAR int	British Archaeological Reports: International Series, Oxford.
BOCO	J. Downes and T. Pollard, *The Loved Body's Corruption*, Glasgow 1999.
BUSO	*Burial and Society*, ed. C. K. Jensen, 1997.
CAJ	*Cambridge Archaeological Journal 1990.*
CCC	*Contact, Continuity and Collapse,* ed. James H. Barrett, Turnhout 2005.
CH	*Celtica Helsingiensia*, ed. A. Ahlqvist et al, Helsinki 1996.
CHRIS	*The Christianization of Scandinavia*, ed. P. Sawyer et al, Alingsås 1987.
CHS	*The Cambridge History of Scandinavia*, ed. Knut Helle, Cambridge 2003.
CEPS	*Centrale platser centrala frågor*, ed. Larsson and Hårdh, Lund 1988.
CM	*Collegium Medievale*, Oslo 1988–.
CONBALT	*Contacts across the Baltic Sea*, ed. A. Hårdh and B. Wyszomirska-Webart, Lund 1992.
CONIL	*A Companion to Old Norsen–Icelandic Literature and Culture*, ed. Rory McTurk, Blackwell 2005.
CSA	*Current Swedish Archaeology*, Stockholm 1993–.
DAB	*Dublin and Beyond the Pale*, ed. Conleth Manning, Bray 1998.
DADA	*Da Danmark blev Danmark*, Peter Sawyer, Copenhagen 1988 and 2002.
DEBU	*Death and Burial*, vol. 4 of York Conference on Medieval Europe, ed. T. Dickinson and B. James, York 1992.
DIP	*Digging into the Past*, ed. S. Hvass and B. Storgaard, Aarhus 1993.
DLU	*Danmarks længste udgravning*, ed. O. Olsen, Copenhagen 1987.
DNM	*Dictionary of Northern Mythology*, Rudolf Simek, trans. A. Hall, Woodbridge 1996.
DR	*Danmarks Runeindskrifter*, ed. L. Jacobsen et al, 2 vols, Copenhagen, 1941–52.
DS	*Danske Studier*, Copenhagen.

DSted	*Danmarks Stednavne* (Institut for Navneforskning), 25 vols, 1992–.
Dudo	*D. of St Quentin: History of the Normans*, trans. E. Christiansen, Woodbridge 1998.
Edda	see SnE and PE.
EE	*Encomium Emmæ Reginæ*, ed. Alistair Campbell, London 1949.
EG	*Etudes germaniques, Lyon / Paris 1946–.*
EHD	*English Historical Documents*, vol. I, ed. D. Whitelock, London 1968.
EHR	*The English Historical Review*, Oxford.
EME	*Early Medieval Europe*, Oxford 1991–.
EUNO	*Europeans or Not?*, ed. N. Blomqvist and S-O. Lindquist, Gotland 1999.
EXTRA	*Exchange and Trade*, vol. V of *Medieval Europe*, ed. Hall, Hodges and Clarke, York 1992–.
EYM	*Excavations at York Minster*, i/2 Derek Phillips and Brenda Heywood, London (HMSO).
FA	Fragmentary Annals: see Radner.
FESTOL	*Festskrift til Olaf Olsen*, ed. J. Steen Jensen, Copenhagen 1988.
FENSO	*Fennoscandia Archaeologica*, Helsinki 1983–.
FIMU	*Finskt Museum*, Helsingfors 1893–.
FKH	*Festskrift til Kristian Hald*, ed. P. Andersen et al., Copenhagen 1974.
FLW	Florence (John) of Worcester.
FMS	*Frühmittelalterliche Studien.*
FRES	*Folke og ressurser i Norden*, ed. J. Sandnes et al., Trondheim 1983.
FROSA	*From Sagas to Society*, ed. G. Pálsson, Enfield 1992.
GEDI	*Germanic Dialects*, ed. B. Brogyany and T. Krömmelbein, Amsterdam/Philadelphia 1986.
GR	*Germanische Religionsgeschichte*, ed. H. Beck, D. Ellmers and K. Schier, Berlin/New York 1992.
Grágás	Ed. K. Karlsson et al., Reykjavik 1992; partly translated as *Grágás: Laws of Early Iceland* by A. Dennis, P. Foote, R. Perkins, vol. i, Winnipeg 1980.
Guta saga	Ed. H. Pipping in *Guta Lag och Guta Saga*, Copenhagen 1905–7.
GUM	*Guld magt og tro: Gold, Power and Belief*, Jørgensen and P. V. Petersen, Copenhagen 1998.
GV	*Gotland vikingaön*, ed. G. Westholm, Länsmuseet på Gotland, Gotländskt Arkiv 2004.

HIHO	*Der historische Horizont*, ed. K. Hauck, Göttingen 1988.
HØKO	*Høvdingesamfund og kongemagt*, ed. P. Mortensen and B. M. Rasmussen, Copenhagen 1991.
Hsk	*Heimskringla*.
HT (D)	*Historisk Tidskrift*, Copenhagen.
HT (N)	*Historisk Tidsskrift*, Oslo.
HUG	*Hugur*, ed. Claude Lacouteux and O. Gruchet, Paris 1997.
IBA (1 and 2)	*Interbaltic Colloquium: Ostseekolloquium*, 1991 and 1992.
IGG	*Idee, Gestalt, Geschichte: Festschrift* to Von See, Odense 1988.
IMPA	*Images of the Past*, ed. N. Roymans and F. Theuws, Amsterdam 1991.
ISCEVA	*Ireland and Scandinavia in the Early Viking Age*, ed. H. Clarke et al., Dublin 1998.
JAR	*Journal of Archaeological Research*.
JBAS	*Journal of the British Archaeological Society*.
JDA	*Journal of Danish Archaeology*.
JEGP	*Journal of English and Germanic Philology*, Illinois.
JEA	*Journal of European Archaeology*, Aldershot 1993–.
JMH	*Journal of Medieval History*, Amsterdam 1974–.
KF	*Kaupang Funnene*, ed. C. Blindheim et al., 2 vols, Oslo 1981 and 1999.
KHL	*Kulturhistorisk Leksikon*, 21 vols, Copenhagen 1956–77.
KICU	*Kings, Currency and Alliances*, ed. M. Blackburn and D. Dumville, 1998.
KIKOT	*Kontinuitet i kult og tro*, ed. B. Nilsson.
Kock	*Den Norsk-Isländska Skaldediktningen*, 2 vols, Lund 1949.
KRIS	*Kristnandet i Sverige*, ed. Bertil Nilsson, Uppsala 1994.
KS	*Knytlinga Saga*
LACON	*Language Contact in the British Isles*, ed. P. S. Ureland and G. Broderick, Tübingen 1991.
LAR	*Lund Archaeological Review*, Lund 1995–.
LB	*Landnámabók: The Book of Settlements* trans H. Pálsson and P. Edwards, Manitoba 1972.
LEAF	*Leather and Fur*, ed. Esther Cameron, Guildford 1998.
M	*Runes and Their Origin*, Erik Moltke, Copenhagen 1985.

MAMMEN	*Mammen: grav, kunst og samfund i vikingetid*, ed. Mette Iversen, and J. Vellev, Højbjerg 1998.
MESCA	*Medieval Scandinavia. An Encyclopaedia*, ed. P. Pulsiano, New York/London 1993.
MGH	*Monumenta Germaniae Historica.*
MIAS	*Military Aspects of Scandinavian Society*, ed. A. Nørgaard Jørgensen and Berthe Clausen, Copenhagen 1997.
MKS	Morkinskinna
MLUHM	*Meddelanden från Lund Universitets historiska museum.*
MOR	*Myte og Ritual*, ed. J. P. Schjødt, Odense 1994.
MS	*Medieval Scandinavia*, Odense 1968–.
MYWO	*Mythological Women*, ed. R. Simek and W. Heizmann, Vienna 2002.
NAA	*Nordic Archaeological Abstracts*, Stavanger, Højbjerg.
NAR	*Norwegian Archaeological Review*, Oslo.
NIY	*Norges Innskrifter med de yngre runer*, ed. M. Olsen, 3 vols, Oslo 1941–54.
NOHED	*Nordisk Hedendom: et symposium*, ed. G. Steinsland, U. Drobin et al, Odense 1991.
NONO	*The Norse of the North Atlantic*, ed. G. Bigelow (AA, lxi), Copehagen 1991.
NOWELE	*North-West European Language Evolution*, Odense 1983–.
NW	*Namenwelten*, ed. A. van Nahl, L. Elmevik and S. Brink, Berlin/New York 2004.
OJA	*Oxford Journal of Archaeology*, Oxford 1982–.
OM	*Olaus Magnus: a Description of the Northern Peoples*, ed. P. Foote, 3 vols, London 1996–8.
ONFRAC	*Old Norse and Finnish Religions and Cultic Place- Names*, ed. T. Ahlbäck, Stockholm 1990.
ONIL	*Old Norse Icelandic Literature: a Critical Guide*, ed. C. Clover and L. Lindow, Ithaca 1985.
Ögld	Östorgötland (SW).
ØPOLIS	*Økonomiske og politiske sentra i Norden*, ed. E. Mikkelsen and J. H. Larsen, Oslo 1992.
OUTU	*Outland Use in Preindustrial Europe*, ed. H. Andersson, Ersgard and E. Svensson, Lund 1998.
OXVIK	*The Oxford Illustrated History of the Vikings*, ed. P. Sawyer, Oxford 1997.
PAC	*Pagans and Christians*, ed. T. Hofstra et al, Groningen 1995.

PAP	*People and Places in N. Europe 500–1600*, ed. I. Wood and N. Lund, Woodbridge 1991.
PE	*The Poetic Edda*, trans. C. Larrington, Oxford 1996.
PISMA	*Poetry in the Scandinavian Middle Ages* (7th International Saga Conference), ed. Teresa Paroli, Spoleto 1990.
PL	Patrologica Latina, ed. Migne.
PONO	*The Population of the Nordic Countries*, ed. E. Iregren and Liljekvist, Lund (*Archaelogical Report*, xlvi) 1993.
PZ	*Praehistorische Zeitschrift*, Berlin / New York 1909–.
RBN	*Rom und Byzanz im Norden*, ed. M. Müller- Wille, Stuttgart 1997.
RER	*Regions and Reflections*, ed. K. Jennbert, L. Larsson et al., Lund 1991.
RG	*Rodulfus Glaber: Opera*, ed. and trans. J. France and N. Bulst, Oxford 1989.
RIBE	*Ribe Excavations 1970–76*, ed. M. Bencard et al., 4 vols, Esbjerg 1980–91.
ROMU	*Aarskrift fra Roskilde Museum*, Roskilde 1980.
RRIM	*Recent Archaeological Research on the Isle of Man*, ed. P. J. Davey, BAR British Ser., cclxxviii, Oxford 1999.
RUQUIF	*Runeninschriften als Quellen interdisziplinärer Forschung*, ed. K. Düwel, Berlin 1998.
SAAR	*Saami Religion*, ed. T. Ahlbäck, Stockholm 1987.
SADO	*Studien zur Archäologie des Ostseeraumes*, ed. Anke Wesse, Neumünster 1998.
SAL	*Settlement and Landscape*, ed. C. Fabech and J. Ringtved, Aarhus 1999.
SANA	*Sakrale Navne*, ed. G. Fellows-Jensen and Holmberg, Uppsala 1992.
SAP	*Social Approaches*, ed. Ross Samson, Glasgow 1991.
SAS	*Studia Anthroponymica Scandinavica*.
SB	*Saga Book of Viking Society*, London 1892–.
SCEU	*Scandinavians and Europe 800–1350*, ed. J. Adams and K. Holman, Turnhout, 2003.
SG	Saxo Grammaticus: SG (FD): *Saxo Grammaticus: History of the Danes*, trans. P. Fisher and H. E. Ellis Davidson, 2 vols, Woodbridge; SG (EC): *Saxo Grammaticus: Danorum Regum Heroumque Historia*, trans. E. Christiansen, BAR Int. Series, lxxxiv, cxviii (i and ii), 1980–81.

SHAS	*The Ship as Symbol*, ed. O. Crumlin Petersen and B. M. Thye, Copenhagen 1995.
SIDK	*Siedlungen im deutschen Küstengebiet*, ed. G. Kossack et al, 2vv, Bonn 1984.
SJH	*Scandinavian Journal of History*, Stockholm 1976–.
Skj(A and B)	*Den norsk-islandske skjaldedigtning*, ed. Finnur Jónsson, 4 vols, Copenhagen 1912–15.
SMEOL	*Structure and Meaning in Old Norse Literature*, ed. J. Lindow, 1986.
SMHD	*Scriptores Minores Historiæ Danicæ*, ed. M. C. Gertz, Copenhagen 1918–22.
SPEN	*Speculum Norroenum*, ed. U. Dronke et al., Odense 1981.
SnE	Snorri Sturluson: *Edda*, trans. A. Faulkes, London 1987.
SS	*Scandinavian Studies*.
SSHB	*Scandinavian Settlement in Northern Britain*, ed. B. Crawford, Leicester 1995.
STN	*Studia Neophilologica*, Oslo/Stockholm, 1928–.
TRHS	*Transactions of the Royal Historical Society*, Cambridge.
TROG	*Tradition og historieskrivning*, ed. K. Hastrup, Aarhus 1987.
TV	*The Vikings*, ed. R. T. Farrell, London-Chichester 1982.
UNHAVE	*Untersuchungen zu Handel und Verkehr der vor- und frühgeschichtlichen Zeit*, pt. iv, ed. K. Düwel, H. Jankuhn et al., Göttingen 1987.
VA	*Viking Artifacts*, J. Graham-Campbell, London 1980.
VACON	*The Viking Age in Caithness, Orkney and the North Atlantic*, ed. C. Batey et al., Edinburgh 1993.
VANO	*Völker an Nord und Ostsee und die Franken*, ed. von Freeden et al, Bonn 1999.
VC 8	*The Proceedings of the Eighth Viking Congress*, ed. P. Foote and O. Olsen, Odense 1981.
VC 10	*Proceedings of the Tenth Viking Congress*, ed. J. E. Knirk (Larkollen 1985), Oslo 1987.
VC 11	*The Proceedings of the Eleventh Viking Congress*, see VACON
VC 12	*The Proceedings of the Twelfth Viking Congress*, ed. B. Ambrosiani and H. Clarke, *Developments Around the Baltic* (Birka Studies iii), Stockholm 1994.

VE	*Viking Empires*, A. Forte, R. Orim and F. Pedersen, Cambridge 2005.
VIK	*The Vikings*, ed. T. Andersson and I. Sandred, Uppsala 1978.
VINAS	*Vikings and the North Atlantic Saga*, ed. W. W. Fitzhugh and E. Ward, New York 2000.
VIPA	*Visions of the Past*, ed. H. Andersson, P. Carelli and L. Ersgård, Stockholm 1997.
VIRE	*Viking Revaluations*, ed. A. Faulkes and R. Perkins, London 1993.
VISO	*Violence and Society in the Early Medieval West*, ed. G. Halsall, Woodbridge 1998.
VS	*Vikingesymposium*, Aarhus, Copenhagen and Odense 1982–.
WA	*World Archaeology*, London 1969–.
WM	William of Malmesbury
WOO	*Words and Objects*, ed. G. Steinsland, Oslo 1986.
WW	*The World of Work*, ed. A. J. Frantzen and D. Moffat, Glasgow 1994.
ZPDB	*Zum Problem der Deutung frühmittelalterlicher Bildinhalt*, ed. H. Roth, Sigmaringen 1986.

Acknowledgements

I thank Arthur Astbury above all, for his vigilant proof-correction which was too late to prevent the many errors of the hardback edition. Then Peter Sawyer, for living up to his name with the lumber he found there, and Jayne Carrol for her patient criticisms.

Most of the references have now been linked to listed sources, or eliminated; the text has been supplemented if not much modified in the light of seven outstanding books on Viking Age topics published from 2001 to 2005.

Introduction

Vikings

'Enough is enough. Something really must be done to stop publishers putting the word "Viking" in the title of all books that have vaguely medieval and faintly Germanic subjects', wrote the author of *Chronicles of the Vikings*,[1] in which, nevertheless, the word means nothing more precise than 'person of Nordic aspect and speech living in Scandinavia and the Norse colonies in the Early Middle Ages'. He was right. Publishers must have their vikings. When Keynes and Lapidge translated Asser for the Penguin *Age of King Alfred*, the firm made them mistranslate *pagani* (which means heathen) as vikings. Asser was careful with his choice of words: but so what? It is one of the most convenient misnomers: 'too well established to be abandoned' according to Gwyn Jones. We slap it on to sea-kings of the ninth century, laborious crofters in the Orkneys, hill-farmers holed up in the Lincolnshire wolds, proto-urban artisans in Ribe and York, and most perversely of all to the colonists of Greenland and part-time Americans right down to their fading away in the fifteenth century, benighted fashion-victims eating their own dogs and failing to become like the Eskimos, for fear of contravening the teachings of the church.[2] Viking has almost become an ethnic term (as if all US citizens were called cowboys), but not quite. No one refers to Nordic slaves as vikings. 'Viking slave' suggests a poor Irishman (see below, p. 26) or Slav, chained up by a speaker of Old

---

1 Page, reviewing Farrell's *Vikings* in SB, xxi, 306. His *Chronicles* were reissued in 2000.
2 McGovern's theory, based on the evident authority and wealth of earlier Greenland bishops; and see now Fitzhugh and Ward 200 (VINAS) 338–9 for 'blame the bishop'. Lesley Abrams' review: 'Why American attempts to appropriate early Scandinavian enterprise are misguided' (*Times Literary Supplement*, 30 June 2000) was timely.

Norse, and the native Norse thrall seems not to qualify – unlike women, children and domestic animals. Why has this miscalling triumphed?

Long before the raids on the West began, the word is found in Anglo-Latin glossaries, where it meant robber, and that is how the Anglo-Saxon chroniclers used it in the tenth century. *Wicingas* were usually coastal marauders, rather than members of the horse-borne land armies of Danes or heathen which roamed over England from 866. A force which camped at Fulham in 879 is described as 'a heap of vikings'; perhaps the army which had made peace with Alfred the year before was supposed not to be. English sources continued to use the word as a synonym for pirate or marauder down to the thirteenth century. Among the Norsemen there was a slightly different emphasis, for poets, at least, were more tolerant. In Skaldic verse it can mean 'us raiders', but usually 'them, the enemy': whether English, Bretons, Wends, or Norsemen. Three rune–stones commend men who went *í víkingu*; 'on viking raids': but that was unusual. Later versifiers praise rulers who hang or drive out such pests. *Víkingar* occurs on a few Danish and Swedish rune-stones to describe both respectable sons raiding overseas, and local nuisances; later on, in Icelandic sagas, vikings are just pirates. The origin of the word has been studied to the point of redundancy, and remains uncertain.[3] Its acceptance as the all-purpose noun for most Nordic people of a certain ill-defined period was partly owing to the lack of any suitable alternative, and partly to the Romantic illusion that marauding by sea was a noble pursuit in those days, foreshadowing the maritime enterprise which had made modern nations great.

Sir Walter Scott did not share this illusion, but his revival of the forgotten *Vi-king* (in *The Pirate*, 1828) came in the nick of time, to mean what everybody else wanted it to mean: a sort of blond barbarian with a mission to invigorate and de-sophisticate. Progress

3 Fell 1986 established the priority of the Anglo-Saxon *Wiceng* over recorded uses of ON *Víkingr*, but the paucity of ON records before the tenth century means that there is no telling who used it first. The Sawyers and Hødnebø 1987 revived the theory that it meant 'person from Viken', and that such persons became archetypical pirates. See now Jesch 2001, 44–68 for how the word was used. Another possibility is that *víkingr* was borrowed from the Anglo-Frisian word for 'camper' (wicing-wítsing); see Grønvik *Víkingr*, ANF CXIX 2004, 5–16. Others point to *vika*, a spell or turn of duty, and Westerdahl proposes that *vika* once meant 'half a crew', so that viking   relay oarsman. There are many *vik*-words to play with, as in Askeberg 1944, 114–83, and the problem is fairly analysed in Coates 1999; he concludes that the OE and ON forms are parallel developments from a common Germanic verb meaning to withdraw, leave or depart (80–3). Parallel parallel developments would strengthen his case.

demanded raw energy. Progress demanded the crushing of the weak and degenerate, even before Darwinists made this into a pseudo-scientific doctrine; and above all, the rough beasts of the nineteenth century needed romantic precursors with similar tendencies to smash, burn, travel, carouse, and scare nuns.[4] The bourgeois of Scandinavia and Normandy could congratulate himself on ancestors prone to frenzy and sexual outrage, but glorified by history rather than wanted by the police. Overworked emigrants could plough Minnesota in the footsteps of imaginary Olafs and Svens who had gone that way in saga-time. Naval patriots of the German empire could grant honorary German citizenship on their remote cousins, the Jomsvikings (on whom see below, chapter 3). Violence never seems to be so naked that it scorns to wear a scrap of history, and the lure of the uninhibited tinkles through advanced consumer-civilizations; as late as the 1950s and '60s, a susceptible French bourgeoisie has succumbed to the 'sulphurous prestige of the fair, naked brute'.[5] What would all these fantasists have done, if they had not been allowed their vikings? And who can blame them for turning these bad men into a historical force, a great civilization, a super-identity for all early medieval Old Norse speakers? It is not surprising that archaeologists have adopted and extended the meaning of the term to cover inanimate objects ('viking pins', etc), and that others write as if there were a race or tribe of this name. Even Randsborg, the Danish archaeologist, put his name to a chapter entitled 'The Viking Nation'.

Since all ethnic names are now interpreted as political constructions of ephemeral or mutable validity, this nation may seem as good as any. Wallerström classifies viking as an ethnic signifier based on occupation – which it may be now, but wasn't then. There is one case in medieval literature of vikings appearing as a people (in the Old English poem *Widsith*) but those *Wicingas* and *Wicinga cynn* were lumped with other groups once native to Jutland (Wenlas, Wernas, Heathobards), not specified as pirates or generalized as pan-Nordic representatives.

In this book, viking will mean only what it meant then: sea-raider, pirate, rover. No distinction of sex or race is made, since speakers of Frisian, Old English, Irish, Finnish and Baltic languages made very

---

4 See Wawn 2000 for an account of Victorian vikingism, which is summed up by Carlyle's question in *The Early Kings of Norway* (1875): 'Who is best man? The Fates forgive much – forgive the wildest, fiercest cruellest experiments – if fairly made for the determination of that.'

5 Boyer 1991, 50; his amusing sketch of French viking delusions is in AUSA 1991, and see *Dragons et Drakkars* (ed. J. M. Levesque, Caen 1996) for more.

good vikings, and king Alfred was quick to learn this skill. The evidence for female sea-rovers is shadowy, but the notion is attractive and not impossible (see below, p. 21). The great majority of Norse speakers will thus be free of that label, and eligible for others, although none is exclusive and most are questionable.

Norse is a linguistic term which is sometimes applied to Norwegians and their colonies, but not to Danes or Swedes. Ditto for Norsemen. Northmen was used at the time, and covers the lot, but may seem to exclude women, and tended to be used for the more northerly Norse, just as Danes became a word for southern Scandinavians in time, but not at first. Scandinavians are a bloodless geopolitical fiction. There is no one satisfactory word for these people at this time, just as there was none for the Anglo-Saxons before the tenth century, except in Bede's imagination. They were all speakers of closely related languages which are now classified as the Old Norse family of tongues, and thus qualify, in theory, as a 'speech community'; they could fight without interpreters. By the tenth century, verse-making in an Icelandic – West Norse dialect was a skill which commanded audiences from Dublin to Novgorod, if no further, but these were retinues recruited from far and wide, receptive to new words and odd accents, less bound by mother tongues than others. The later version of Old Icelandic became the medium for a great literature in which all the Nordic peoples are indeed linked by a common tradition, mythology, and religion or ethic; but that was a literary convention, more eloquent of thirteenth-century Iceland than of the viking age. So the problem remains, and the words Norse will be used for the people, and Nordic for the culture, for want of anything better.

In any case, the plan is to detach these populations from the organizing principles which are often applied to them: the Germanic continuum, the mythology of the North, the formation of states/ethnic identity/urbanization, Viking civilization and so on, with the creaking zeppelin of Europeanization moored overhead. A confused ethnic terminology will be true to this purpose.[6]

Their Age

The age of vikings was invented in Scandinavia to label artifacts, and adopted by those mentioned above who were convinced that vikings, whether as bogey-men or ginger-men, had triggered a decisive moment in the development of Europe and the birth of nations.

6 See below, chapter 5, for more on ethnicity.

They applied the iron law of the *Zeitgeist*, which says that those who live in any historical period must reflect its spirit to be worthy of notice. A room in a museum in Copenhagen became three centuries of Nordic and Northern history,[7] and a whole viking age was born.

But when was it? It has no agreed beginning or end, no obvious geographical boundaries, no defining characteristics; like the Dark Ages or the Heroic Age it is trapped between history and prehistory, a season for all men to construct or construe at will. Sea-borne marauders have always been active all over the world, so that it seems odd to call one epoch after one sequence of raids, especially as contemporary western writers saw them as a mere repeat in the cycle of afflictions by which God chastened those he loved, not as a new departure.[8] Viking raids had pestered the Roman Empire, and would continue in the Baltic to the Reformation, as in the seas off North Britain; shore-dwellers in South Britain were no safer from raids during the Hundred Years' War than they had been in the days of Alfred and Ethelred. Pirates no longer conquered kingdoms, but this was because governments like Edward III's and Henry V's had become better vikings than the old sea-kings. The fourth crusade, which sacked Constantinople in 1204, showed what private enterprise could do in an Age of Faith to exceed the achievements of the vikings.

So it has been claimed that denoting periods 'by loaded terms, ... such as Anglo-Saxon, Norman, Merovingian, Viking...is clearly a redundant and misleading starting point which needs to be abandoned'.[9] Randsborg made a start, for the Danes, by giving them a new set of periods, in which the Age of the Plough-People (*c*.1000 BC–200 AD) is followed by an Age of the Warriors (200–700), and that by the Age of the Sea-Rulers (700–900) and the Age of the Kingdom-Builders (900–1200), each with a distinct social structure, economy and domestic architecture. So the transition to Sea-Ruler time meant more sowing of rye, better ploughs, carts, and ships, bigger houses and many more pigs; so much so that 'never before or since in the history of Denmark has the primary producer had

7 Worsaae used the concept in Copenhagen during the 1840s; du Chaillu's *The Age of the Vikings* (1889) spread it abroad, although with a much wider time-limit; and Sawyer's *The Age of the Vikings* (1962) nailed it to the mast. There is now an *Encyclopedia of the VA* by John Haywood (Thames and Hudson 2000). A Social-Darwinist view of *vikingtid* as a necessary phase of transition from a greater to a lesser state of dependency on natural forces was preached by the Norwegian Alexander Bugge (1870–1929).

8 Lund 1989 and Coupland 1990.

9 Saunders in NAR i.

such good conditions – relatively speaking'.[10] He did not explain why the golden age of the pig-farmer should be called the Age of the Sea-Rulers, and this scheme has not proved popular. Others have stuck to the viking label, but have disagreed about when and what. If it means an age of urbanization, migration, great earth-works and new villages, as Randsborg and Myhre claim, archaeology demands that it begin nearer 700 than 800; but if it is to be an age of mass-production in metal and stone, Clarke and Ambrosiani stand up for *c*.760 as the date of technological change at Birka. To which Sawyer and Roesdahl reply that raids on western Europe are what gave and give the age its name, and as none are recorded before the 790s, a decade when there was a 'change of relationship between between Western Europe and Scandinavia', *c*. 790 is as good a start as any. Besides, 'what distinguished the viking period in European history was not brooches, gripping beasts, or emporia, but vikings'.[11] So it begins with raids to the west, and ends when they end – which is not as reasonable a view as it seems.

It is not obvious why raids on illiterate or pagan peoples (other Northmen, Saxons, Frisians, Slavs and Balts) such as had been common in the eighth century and earlier should belong to a different age from those which hit the record-keepers of Ireland, Britain and Gaul; and it is hard to be sure when these record-keepers were finally safe from raids, since one Norwegian king was plundering Lincolnshire in 1153 and another was invading western Scotland in 1263. Scandinavian scholars are prone to redefine the age in terms of developmental theory, so that when Danish or Norse society reach a certain 'level of political organization' the chiefs go west in longships as part of the plan: this is 'history speaking'(see below, pp. 120, 316). When Sawyer and others noticed differences between the raids of the ninth and those of the late tenth centuries they offered a first and second viking age to rationalize the discrepancy, and so led others to 'draw the dividing line at the appropriate time for each constituent region'.[12] Graham–Campbell cuts it three ways:

> Early: late eighth to late ninth centuries
> Middle: late ninth to second half of tenth century
> Late: second half of tenth to beginning of twelfth century

10   AA, lx, 1989 'The Periods of Danish Antiquity', esp. 187–92, and see below pp. 196–8.
11   Roesdahl 12 VC 106–16, Sawyer 1995[2], Clarke and Ambrosiani in SADO 1998, 37; dissent from Myhre begins ISCEVA (1998) 3–36.
12   So Dumville (1997, I) begins the Second Viking Age in North Britain *c*.925, halfway through Graham-Campbell's Middle, and before the end of Sawyer's First. Irish authors tend to stretch their own VA to 1171.

But Graham Campbell is primarily concerned with the dating of artifacts rather than social evolution or political organization. So he puts the final date quite late, apparently because one style of ornament, the Urnes, was still current in Norway and Ireland after *c.*1100.[13] Swedes who use rune-stones as markers of this age are also obliged to end it late, although recent revisions in style-chronology add further uncertainty. Rune-stones, spear-heads, axe-heads, swords, wood-carvings and the Gotland picture-stones all have their own slightly discordant dates fixed by authorities (Erik Moltke, Jan Petersen, David Wilson, Sune Lindqvist, et al.) on the basis of burial-datings subsequently found inaccurate, or of data now multiplied.[14] Nevertheless, here are the current dating conventions for the viking age (which some include in the Younger, or Later, or Long Iron Age, and some don't):

AD 400 to 550 or 600   Migration Age or Early Germanic Iron Age.
AD 550/600–750/800   Later Germanic Iron Age, Merovingian, Late Migration or (in Sweden) Vendel period.
The Vendel is subdivided into five phases with disputed dates: (a) 550–600/650, (b) 600/650–700/725, (c) 700/25–750, (d) 750–800, (e) 800–850; based on questionable distinctions of style.
AD 700/800–1030/1125   Viking Age, depending on where and who you are. Still later Iron Age, sometimes.

An unfortunate traveller sailing from Bremen to Novgorod shortly after the year 1100 would pass from the Salian period to the Early Medieval to the Late Viking to the Crusading (west Finland) to the Viking again (east Finland) to the Kievan. Does it matter? It wouldn't, if names attached to periods and ages were not taken to be settled verdicts on the nature of those times. Hence the lust for more meaningful labels expressed by those who think they know how and when human societies developed. There are more 'labels' below, but meanwhile it is worth noting that the Icelanders manage very well without a viking age. They call the period from *c.*930 to *c.*1030 the saga age, because of the famous stories associated with it by their thirteenth-century authors; and the sixty years before that

---

13   *Viking Artifacts* (1980) 5–7; but in *The Vikings in Scotland* (1998) Late Viking yields to 'Late Norse' about 1050.
14   For the date-wars between Nordic archaeologists see now J. Hines (ed.), *The Face of Change* (Oxbow 1999) and for the making of the conventions Høilund Nielsen 1991 and 1997 and Hedeager 1992 8–21. For revisions of style-dates in general see Skibsted Klæsøe 1997; of Gotland artifacts, see Thunmark Nylén (*Tor,* xxiii, 1990–1); of spears, Thålin in Christiansson and Hyenstrand *Nordsvensk Forntid* (Umea 1969) and of arrow- heads, Wegraeus in *Birka* (1986) 21–34.

are called the Age of Settlement, because that is what it was. Not that the viking age is a complete misnomer; there were times for raiding by sea (in Ireland 825–85, 910–999; in France 834–890s; in Southern England 840s–910 were the bad times, with a replay for the English 990–1016; the Frisians were hit frequently in the ninth century, the Saxons only rarely, except in the 880s). The habit of piracy for its own sake, rather than raiding as a naval strategy, is difficult to quantify or date. In Scandinavia, raiding by sea had a long history and a bright future, before and after the dates of this age; but, for the sake of convenience, this book will be concerned with the years between 750 and 1050 regardless of any unifying principle or theme.

At present there are five such unifying principles on offer,[15] all of them seen as 'transformations' of Nordic societies, but none of them fitting the conventional dates of the age:

1   from paganism to christianity: 700–1250 would be a realistic time for that, but it wasn't a substitution of one for the other until 1050 or so.
2   centralization of authority; no permanent shift before 1050.
3   non-urban to partly urban settlement: 750 onwards, in places, but see chapter 3 for the limits of this movement: not especially Norse.
4   non-market to market exchange: co-existent *c.*600–*c.*1200?
5   increased productivity, increased surpluses: *c.*600–*c.*1300.

These changes were so slow and variable that it seems perverse to pin them to this age, and vice versa, or to interpret it in terms of their fulfilment.

The Aim

This book presents sketches of Nordic people in viking times less firmly framed than usual. The concepts of transition and development from one state of society to another, or from one political system to another, will not be relied on, or used as explanatory mechanisms in themselves, because they have been too often used with unconvincing results. These populations of farmers and fighters

---

15   The six authors of Barrett 2000 offer a convenient résumé of these changes, and then test them in relation to the history of Orkney (seen as periphery to a Norwegian centre), with courteous devastation; e.g. 'the five characteristics . . . did not occur as a contemporary state-formation package'.

have been hitched to the subjects that interest historians – the discovery of America, the development of Old Norse literature, the evolution of the nations of Scandinavia, the birth of the English state, the tribulations of the Early Christian Irish, the decline of the Carolingian empire, the rise of the Russians, the place-names of the Danelaw, etc. – each of which demands a different sort of viking. Many fine books have been written on those major historical themes, but it seems worth trying to find other approaches: to examine with questions rather than answers, and to disregard the hold of the developmental theories which have been clamped over those occasionally pleasant lands. 'Every apprehension of the past which proposes to understand it better by construing it has only the more thoroughly misunderstood it' wrote John Climacus, alias Søren Kierkegaard, in *Philosophical Fragments* (1843);[16] as true to-day as it was then, but all the same, here goes.

The first five chapters are mainly descriptive, and survey the geography, ecology, social conventions and self-awareness of individuals and groups insofar as they are revealed in contemporary sources. The subjects of chapters 6 to 9 are what seem the important areas of Norse activity: politics, war, work and migration. Chapters 10 to 12 concern Past, Present and Future not because these were of particular interest to Norsemen, but some of their thoughts on these states can be compared with those of more easily approachable peoples, and form some sort of guide to mentalities. Religion is not given its own chapter; it is everywhere.

No consistent principle will be followed in the spelling of personal or place-names, and apologies are offered to all jealous lovers of Normalized Old Norse or Current Usage.

---

16 Trans. Swenson and Hong, (Princeton 1969), 98. But in this context *construere* must mean construct. The developmental approach to the early Scandinavians (Danes in particular) is loud and clear in Chris Wickham *Framing the Early Middle Ages*, (Oxford 2005), 364–76, and in *The Cambridge History of Scandinavia*, vol. 1, ed. Knut Helle (Cambridge 2003), 160–201.

1

Individuals

Now must I, from wood to wood
Creep with small renown;
Who knows if I will not win
Wide acclaim hereafter?

The verses are attributed to the future king Harald Hardrada, slinking from Norway after the defeat and death of his brother Olaf (St Olave) in 1030.[1] They are late, inauthentic, and true to the experience of all hunted nobodies who live to become rich and famous somebodies. They would do for king Alfred, hiding from the Danes in the early spring of 878, already a king but down on his luck, or for the Danish pretender, Sweyn Estrithson, running away to the woods in the 1040s in flight from the invincible king Magnus Olafsson. They epitomize the self-confidence needed by survivors in hard times; and yet this is not a good place to begin.

Two preconceptions dog the idea of individuality in the early medieval period. One is that the very idea was not invented until the twelfth, fifteenth, or eighteenth century. The other is that everyone had a place in the social world and knew what it was. There are reasons for believing both, in some circumstances; but for the time being they can be ignored, or sampled in the incisive survey of Oexle (1999), who traces the doctrine of medieval communitarianism from Novalis to Tönnies to Miegel to Minc. For there is another theory: that viking times were good for relatively unbridled individualism, whether or no the concept existed. Raiding, trading, land-taking and valour in battle were opportunities for men and women to leave the herd, and get somewhere. So Jochens claims that early Iceland was 'like the American West...congenial to the uninhibited exercise of

---

1 Found in the collection of stories about kings and others called Morkinskinna (Mks) 9 verse 45.

traditional heroic qualities', and admirers of the Greenland and Vinland venturers have draped them with the mantle of Columbus,
obsessive loner. Later heroic legends and poems are called in evidence: they 'reflect the would-be heroic individual in life' according
to von See[2] and many others.

A weight of scholarship nevertheless insists that among 'Germanic'
peoples, from start to finish, the collective ruled and shaped the
individual: 'the individual acquires all his value by virtue of his
belonging to the community' and 'the principle of association' ruled
the lives of all but the outlaw, who was the exception that proved the
rule. Genetics and culture reinforced each other through institutions
already old before the first viking raid: the autonomous kin-group, or
ætt; collective responsibility for compensation owed to injured parties outside the kin-group, or by outsiders to its members; and the
heritability of almost everything material and spiritual down patrilinear descents, recited by revered keepers of tradition. The Norseman was named, trained, dressed, equipped, led, entertained and
finally buried or cremated under rules prescribed to maintain social
cohesion, not individual enterprise, and in daily life 'obedience to
strict codes of behaviour is revealed in all records of Germanic
culture'.[3] So runs the Germanist catechism, still dutifully chanted to
fill a silence, as we really know very little about all this. The confident generalizations are distilled from a literature produced before
this period, or after, or elsewhere.

There is some middle ground. Two developments are allowed to
have loosened the hold of the tribal collective, by offering at least
alternative conformities. Colonization was one; and the forming of
war-bands of young warriors the other. But neither really lightened
the preponderance of society over self. Settlers merely created new
communities and families; team-spirit and lordship clamped the warrior even more firmly to his fellows. Christian missions may have
fingered the individual, as morally unique, but up in these parts

2   von See 1981 154–93, and Jochens 1995, 200. Neil Price claims that 'an emphasis
on personal identity' was 'a defining characteristic of the age' (VINAS 2000, 41).
3   Bauschatz 1982, 61; see also the Durkheimer Baetke in *Das Heilige im Germanischen* (1942), and the far more readable Vilhelm Grønbech in *The Culture of
the Teutons*. On Scandinavian law as ancestral custom with religious authority see
Fenger 1983, 57, representative of a deep-rooted legal-historical tradition of dimin-
ishing momentum. Marx and Durkheim disagreed over the collective dynamic: for
Marx 'the collective life-forms are holy, the private structures are alienation and
unreality'; for Durkheim the collective can only be achieved by the consent or
concurrence of wide-awake individuals, even if, once achieved, it becomes holy
(Gustafsson 1972, 20–33). It comes to much the same thing in the viking age,
which would have inherited its collectives from way back.

baptism was viewed as a collective experience, which merged converts into a christian community wholesale. Few would oppose
Steensberger's claim that that creative pioneers are essential to the
maintenance of the viable group, because many assume that social
utility is the standard by which creativity is to be judged; that, or the
endurance of the group through prudent modification or quasi-
biological renewal. The loud *merde* which ensured the glory and
annihilation of the Old Guard at Waterloo – one man's indignation
– is not welcome in this scheme of things.[4]

To judge how thoroughly self and society were integrated in viking
times, it may help to assess the force of the four commonest inhibitors or moderators of individualities in other times:

1   ancestry and kinship, which make one being in theory merely the
    representative of ancestors and descendants, inheritor and trans-
    mitter of status and character and appearance;
2   communal conformity: the custom of the country, how we do, did
    and will do things here;
3   gender;
    and
4   servitude, the person as property.

How far these pressures were resisted, and how easy were solo flights
for the inspired, the powerful, and the deviant, will be considered in
turn, before looking through one of the exits from collectivity usually
open to all individuals: suicide. Were these societies like the Roman,
in which families could be proud of their self-destroyers?

Ancestry and Kin

The usual identity card of the Norse was the plain patronymic, as in
GAUT SON OF BJORN or THORGERD STEINAR'S DAUGHTER,
two of many rune-stone examples, and this habit was exported to
the British Isles and persists all over the world in Johnson and Jensen
and Hansen. But such names were not like modern surnames, a
routine identification passed down the family; Kousgaard Sørensen
established that they were 'primarily a means of emphasizing one's

---

4   Steensberger 1986, 175–7 develops the idea that individuals create culture for
communities to transmit. Wenskus insisted that the *Gefolgschaft* (military retinue)
was friendlier to individual development than the clan; see Bazelmans 1991 on this.
For group conversions see now Cusack 1998: the full collectivist gospel.
5   Kousgaard Sørensen 1982, 12

self-satisfaction by pointing to one's creditable relationship with an eminent, powerful, influential, brave, and in other ways meritorious father'.[5] People with common names (Atsur, Thorgisl, Toki) are no more likely to have patronyms than others with highly distinctive names (Sasgerth, Finulf's daughter: DR 81, Skaern 2). Those who wanted to be known as part of a wider family could in theory sport an ancestor's name with the suffix *-ing* as with the YNGVALDIN-GAR on the Rök stone, but examples of this datable to the viking age are extremely rare, confined to the noblest of kindreds, or the mythical, and not always to be distinguished from *-ing* groupings of a different kind: war-bands, children of one father rather than heirs of a remoter grandparent, or people who come from one place (Falstrings from Falster, Hälsings from Hälsingland).

Runic inscriptions often concern family groups, in the relationship sponsor – the dead – the living, especially in eleventh-century Sweden, but very seldom wider cousinhoods; and among the earlier stones, an individual is sometimes remembered alone. ERIK'S MONUMENT is all it says on the eighth-century Starup stone in South Jutland (DR 17); and in the following century the name HAIR-ULFR was enough for the Øster Løgum stone by the N–S Jutland highway (DR 15; B 354). Monoliths were rarer, less of a craze than they became after *c.* 970, and a carver or sponsor could strike a personal note, as at Gørlev on Zealand (DR 239): THIAUDVI put up a stone to UTHINKAUR, with no stated relationship, only the command MAKE GOOD USE OF THIS MEMORIAL and the words I SET THE RUNES RIGHT, in case anyone objected to the new abbreviated alphabet, and the ambiguous spelling that resulted from it. This tradition begins in Denmark *c.* 750, spreads, diversifies, becomes clamorous and stereotypical, but never quite loses the individual in the formula. Among the Danes, and on thirty Swedish stones, there were those who preferred not to wait for family piety; they put up memorials to themselves, like poet and christian Eskill Sulkason on Lolland (DR 212, Tillitse, post 1025) who:

HAD THIS STONE RAISED TO HIMSELF: EVER WILL STAND – WHILE THIS STONE LIVES – THIS MEMORIAL – WHICH ESKILL MADE.

Such 'boasting stones' were probably not pure egotism; the boasters may have wanted to be known as christians in contrast to pagan relations; examples, therefore, of not entirely collective baptism (B. Sawyer 1991 108–9 discusses). Long before this purely commemorative custom began, sixth-century chiefs had been celebrated in runes on big stones at Stentoften, Gummarp and Istaby in Bleking, but the tallest of all, a granite needle thirteen feet (4 m) tall at Björketorp bears only a grim warning by the technician (DR 360–B 120) which runs, approximately:

> I MASTER OF THE ROW OF RUNES BURIED HERE POTENT RUNES.
> INCESSANTLY ENCUMBERED BY SORCERY...TO DEATH THROUGH MALICE IS HE WHO BREAKS IT

The aim may have been to protect the local dynasty, but the voice is one expert's.

Land was held by families, but not all moveables. The earliest continental runes name individuals on things, and from *c.* 500 come objects scratched with first persons singular: the sword or ring speaks for itself[6] or the owner speaks through the brooch, even anonymously, like EK UNWODIR (I, THE UNENRAGED) of Gårdlosa in Scania. To carve whole sentences on stone was reason for self-congratulation long after that, however social the occasion. In the mid-tenth century the colonial big-wigs on Man paid to advertise themselves on stone crosses, but it was the sculptor who got himself remembered:

> GAUT MADE IT, AND ALL IN MAN
>
> (Michael 2: Kermode 74)

like the Dane Soti, who shortly before had cut runes at Glavendrup for Ragnhildr, at Rønninge for his own brother, and at Tryggevælde for Ragnhildr again (DR 209, 202, 230); and like the four eleventh-century Swedish carvers who can be identified by the idiosyncracies of their work, as well as by their signatures: Opir, Asmund, Livsten and Balli.

Dynasties and families may have repressed individuality, then as now, but the politics of this period suggest that individual ambitions were more likely to repress dynasties; conditions for the routine distribution of wealth and power among members did not exist. Cemeteries apparently shared by one family usually contain one or more graves of exceptional interest, with exotic oriental, Frankish or Anglo-Saxon ornaments that point to the egregious. If there ever had been an egalitarian tribal community, it had broken up in the Migration Age, when the rich began leaving their women, kinsmen and animals in the old longhouse, and moving into big halls, where they could live like lords, among male dependents.[7] Rulers were

---

6 Compare Anglo-Saxon examples in Bredehoft, ASSAH, ix, 1996, 103–9.
7 Herschend 1993, 190–4.

exceptional in this respect. They could assert themselves at the expense of their kin, and discard them more freely in pursuit of personal gain, like their Anglo-Saxon and Frankish contemporaries: king Offa was accused of pruning his family tree to the trunk, and the Danish dynasty seems to have dwindled through internal competition in the ninth century, until extinct. Further down the scale, kin may have counted for more, and asked more of the individual: family solidarity may have been necessary for survival, but families had obvious limits as wealth-increasing and fighting units, and in this period there were alternatives.

One result of this may have been the tendency to bear nick-names: stronger among the Norse than among their neighbours at this period, as rune-stones, place-names and foreign annalists bear witness. 'Pelt-dear' (sugar-daddy?), 'loathsome', 'forest-guest' are very early examples (M 169), and some of these became Viking Age proper names: *Óspakr* (the unruly), *Skeggi* (the bearded), *Styrr* (noisy), and *Knútr* (knot) are examples, with *Stígandr* (strider) and *Sumarliðr* (summer voyager) both beginning in the British Isles among colonists. The names parents gave were improved by the Hairy, the Stooper, the Calm, the Dwarf, the Goblin, the Speckled, the Ugly, the Neck, the Skinny, the Unwashed, the Self-Willed, the Wriggler and the Pugnacious: these were ways of telling Úlfr from Úlfr and Tóki from Tóki away from home. Praise often came by negatives, in litotes: the Un-worthless, the Un-deceitful, the Un-niggardly, the Unafraid, the Unquiet, the Undoomed; others were distinguished by lack, as in the English Danelaw with the Godless, the Foodless, the Shirtless, the Trouserless. If Ivarr, the invader of East Anglia in 869, was really called the Boneless (*Beinlauss*: possibly a later misreading of *exosus*, 'hated' as *exossis* 'boned', but not very likely, considering the rarity of *exossis*) he may have been complimented in a roundabout way for his furious riding. Such names tend to be stereotypical everywhere, and to acquire ironical and in-group meanings; they are not chosen by the bearers, but at least mark them out with secondhand personalities, usually uninherited, and recognizable in the wider world.[8]

8 See VACON (1993) for Fellows Jensen (398–400) and Insley (351–2) Fellows Jensen 1994, 26–7, and Whaley 1991 and 1993 for later practice in Iceland. The largest collection of such names is E.H. Lind *Norsk-isländska personbinamn från medeltiden* (Uppsala 1921) and for saga by-names, Finnur Jónsson 'Tilnavne' Aarbøger 2nd ser., 1907, 161–381.

Custom

The country can be host to many customs, and as Jens Jakob Jensen noticed in 1977, attempts to work out a common viking age system of values are undermined by the ethical discrepancy between the two main sources, Runic inscriptions and Skaldic verse. They present different social norms: what he called '*hirth*-ideals' for the court or retinue, and family values, for the homestead and the farm. In verse, the worthy man was restless, aggressive, intimidating, vindictive, spendthrift, fearless, famous overseas and seldom at home. In runic epigraphy of the later viking age, he is sometimes remembered for having died far from home in pursuit of gold and honour, but he is usually praised for his social status (as lord, *bumann, drengr, thegn, buandi, godi*) or for his association with others (*lagsman, skibari, felagi*) of similar rank, or for his good housekeeping, property and local influence, or for his qualities as a father or husband. The discrepancy is not resolved (as in Jakobsson 1991) by taking the swords and spears found in male graves as mainly symbolic of rank, rather than working weapons; the evidence for real vikings, and for powerful peace-lovers is equally good. In verse, the women are usually on-lookers, admiring the men for their fine ships, glittering array, and valour in battle; in the inscriptions they are pious or lamented widows, rich and respectable, sharing the domestic virtues of their sons and husbands; or else queens in their own right, or patronesses; or, like the men, just 'good'. Jensen's survey[9] included all Danish and Swedish inscriptions of the period 950–1100, and his conclusions may therefore be skewed in favour of Uppland values, and must be in favour of the upper classes. The individual Northman within those categories evidently lived with at least two ethical systems, between which he could move in pursuit of private ends; and those outside these categories cannot be assumed to have lived under a monolithic morality. Geography alone, the sparsity of populations, the diversity of ecologies, argues for ethical variety. Easy communication by sea brought varieties together.

---

9 *De for mandigt fjernet efter guld* by Jens Jakob M. Jensen was published as a pamphlet in Copenhagen in 1977, but the farming-fighting contrast has often been noted. The concentration of runestones in Mälardal enables Herschend (1994b, 102) to trace a shift in the definition of 'good' people *c*.975–*c*.1100 from the socially-beneficial group-enhancers to the well-born landowning group-dominating individuals. But 'good' applied to categories which are not obviously one or the other; see B. Sawyer 2000, 101–11.

Gender

The condition of women in a patriarchal, heroic and warlike world is often assumed to have been submissive, semi-servile if not actually servile; so much so that some attribute the power, wisdom and sexual freedom of certain female archetypes in ON literature (Gudrun, Brynhildr, Sigrid Storrada et al.) to lingering reminiscences of pre-patriarchal days, back in the Bronze Age: memories preserved in folk tales, traduced by christians, and revived in the thirteenth century by a 'miracle' of literary creativeness. This is not only unlikely, but unnecessary. Female independence and consequence were a social fact in the viking age at the level which inspires legend: the top. Thanks to marriage, inheritance and economics, women were valuable, if freeborn, as far down the scale as freedom and property reached.[10] It can be argued that women still had to operate within the strategies of a male-dominated system, as an often overworked instrument of the family or kin-group, condemned by her sex, if she escaped exposure at birth (see p. 39–40) to the stereotyped roles of marriage-pawn (or 'peace-cow' mediating between families), inciter of male valour (nag), howler of lamentations for dead males, and jealous bitch. Such women appear in sagas and soap-operas and real life, but can hardly represent the day-to-day experience of their sisters without corroboration from contemporary sources.

However, the evidence for powerful Nordic women is good, and unsurprising to those familiar with what was going on outside Scandinavia, for the tenth has been called 'the century of women' by Pauline Stafford: she has the lady Ethelflaed of Mercia, Hrotswitha of Gandersheim, Marozia the pope-maker, the empress Theophanu and the Frankish queen Gerberga to back her. The richest Norwegian boat burial, at Oseberg, was that of a woman surrounded by goods and travelling gear and apparently accompanied by her maid, in the beautifully finished ceremonial boat now dated to 834. On Funen, among the Danes, a little later, a man called Guthfrith raised a rune-stone to a woman called Thiodborg (DR 188) who needed no further identification, and before that most of the fifty or so cremation graves at Valsgärde in Sweden were women's, and the highest mound,

10 Heinrichs in SMEOL (1986) 110–40 and Jochens 1996, 132–61, and 162–203 discuss the survival of female archetypes; for Gimbutas on primeval matriarchy see Gilchrist 1999, 25. Jochens derives the modern idea of the 'independent Nordic woman' from the 18th century pioneer Nordicist Mallet (EG, xlvi, 1991, 400–9) but Olaus Magnus the Swede was ahead of him (OM 5, 27–33) in the sixteenth century, and Saxo's fearsome Dane-women are the subject of a study by Mrs Sawyer: Strand 1980.

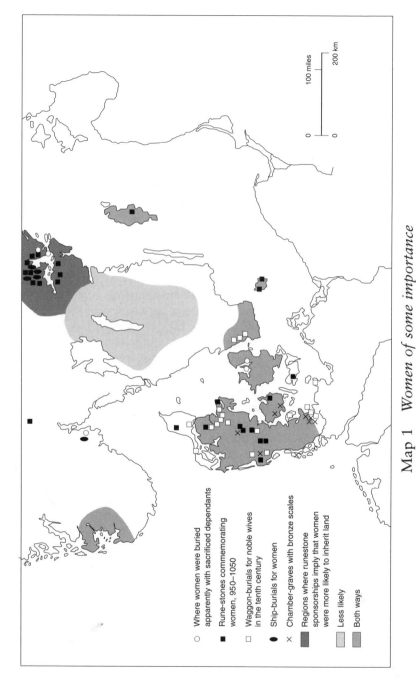

Map 1 *Women of some importance*

(After Eisenschmidt 1994, 55–6 and B. Sawyer 2000) Only 4.2 per cent of all rune-stones commemorate women alone.

Where women were buried
apparently with sacrificed dependants

Rune-stones commemorating
women, 950–1050

Waggon-burials for noble wives
in the tenth century

Ship-burials for women

Chamber-graves with bronze scales

Regions where runestone
sponsorships imply that women
were more likely to inherit land

Less likely

Both ways

0   100 miles

0   200 km

crowning the whole landscape, was raised over a woman. Wall-hangings found at Oseberg and Överhogdal show women as religious leaders and owners of herds and horses.

King Gorm of Jelling and his son Harald Bluetooth both eternalized Thyrwi (Thyra) 'Denmark's Ornament' (or Improvement), and she or another Thyrwi was named as queen by the three men who made her mound (Baekke I: DR 54) and by a dependent or client (Laeborg: DR 26). Her grandson Sweyn Forkbeard's wife, fictionalized as 'Sigrid the Strong-Minded' by the Icelanders, was a player of importance in the Baltic politics of the 990s, if somewhat hard to pin down; but St Olave's widow, Astríðr was the crucial guarantor of her young son Magnus' seizure of Norway in 1034–5, and was praised as such by Sigvatr the poet. She had the treasure, and influence with her father's people in Sweden to make this bastard son of an unpopular king something more than the pawn of a discredited faction. He was not her son, but she got him elected even when his accession meant that his natural mother, Álfhildr, would be a potential rival: and the poet praised her for this.[11] By then, Norwegians had endured four or five years of female rule, when Alfífa (Aelfgifu) of Northampton stood behind the young king Sweyn, son of Canute, who also became king at the age of fifteen or thereabouts. Her regime was remembered for her harshness, as well as the bad harvests, in the twelfth century, by when the whole emergence of a Norwegian kingdom was fabulated in tales of overmighty Danish women: Gytha, Gunnhildr, Sigrid and Alfífa. Such tales show that here as elsewhere in the West and East, high birth and powerful husbands gave women power and esteem, but the evidence of the graves indicates (like the fifth- and sixth-century graves of southern Britain) that this esteem was not confined to the rulers, but went deeper than that.

Many women were buried with pairs of scales; not because they had been traders, as has been suggested (there is no evidence of any female traders), but as symbols of good housekeeping, like the keys found with many more, to look the meal or treasure chest. The magnificent lock found in one of the chests reused as coffins (for Danes?) under York minster in the tenth century was guarding more than meal, and smaller boxes occur elsewhere, in the Fyrkat graves for example. Rule of the household speaks from the Mälardal cremations: men's ashes put into pots, but women burnt with pots, for

11 See P. and B. Sawyer 'Adam and the Eve of Scandinavian History' in *Perceptions of the Past in Twelfth Century Europe*, 37–51 for the tangled tales of Sweyn's wife or wives. For Thyra, B. Sawyer 2000, 158–66. Jesch 1994 discusses these verses, and see Jesch 1990, 156–7. Álfhildr left Norway and lived as an anchoress in England, where her tale was told by William of Malmesbury (*Gesta Pontificum*, 412–15) in lurid but credible terms. He believed she was buried at Malmesbury: another individualist.

future use. As with the post-viking-age lady buried at Fläckebo in SW Västmanland, whose husband Holmgautr of Hassmyra claimed:

WILL COME MISTRESS TO HASSMYRA
NO BETTER THAT HOUSEHOLD TO GOVERN.

Such women had a hold on the moveable goods of the family, if not the full shared ownership (*félag*) of the later laws. The runes of Sweden point to their having an inheritance-right long before it was written down, and Birgit Sawyer relates it to the extent that women share in the sponsorship of memorial stones. Most of all in Uppland (23–24%), less so in Södermanland and Öland (6%), even less in Denmark and Västergötland, hardly at all in Norway, Småland and Gotland. Such inscriptions confirm the impression that wives could not inherit directly from husbands, beyond their share of goods held in common; but among the Swedes (not the Gautar) daughters and sisters inherited from fathers, and were allocated real or notional shares in the property of their own families, at least after *c.* 1000.[12] The unequal distribution of memorials, by place and date, (see map 11) must undo some of the significance of those percentages, but none of her general conclusions jars with the impression given by Anglo-Saxon wills, that whatever the legal situation was, it enabled some women to hold much more property than most men. Which is not to suggest that most women were not relatively poorer and less free than most men; only that female individuality was no more and no less limited up here than in most of Christendom.

The absence of husbands on raids, or their deaths overseas leaving minor heirs, may have contributed to this, more than any primary importance attached to the producing of children in 'frontier' societies: children could be bred from slaves, and in any case many seem to have been killed at birth. The needs to secure family property at home, and to increase wealth by going elsewhere, were better served by partnerships between sexes than by patriarchy; but whether this explains the strong Nordic women, or the women whose sons took metronyms rather than patronyms depends mainly on the interpretation of inscriptions, which are seldom unambiguous. On one of the Ardre stones on Gotland a husband commemorated his wife Rodiauth, who DIED YOUNG, LEAVING AN INFANT. Why her, of the many who met the same fate unrecorded? Because of the child, which would inherit? Inherit what, mother's property or father's? Or

---

12 B. Sawyer 1988, esp. 28–34, and her 'Women as Bridge-Builders' PAP (1991) 211–24. Her *The Viking-Age Rune-Stones* (Oxford 2000) discusses the evidence for women's ownership and inheritance in chs 4 and 5.

because a childless mother's property could be reclaimed by her parents? Or because he missed her?

Apart from their property-rights, Nordic women are sometimes said to have excelled others in their independence as fighters, seeresses, and poets; but only the poetesses stand up to investigation.

Where female soldiers are taken for granted, their choice of arms is not seen as a mark of individuality; but in the viking age it would have been. There are one Norwegian and two Danish examples of women buried with military accoutrements, and these need not be interpreted as amazons: for male artefacts deposited in Swedish womens' graves (outside Birka) see Bolin, CSA xii 2004; the richer, the more differentiated by sex. Conversely, there is no reason why women who fought as men should not have been buried as women;[13] there could have been dozens of temporary hell-cats who ended up as respectable housewives. Later sagas and histories told of 'shield-maidens' in days of old, and the traditions must be based on something. Clover and Clunies Ross have argued that they derive from a social fact of twelfth century Iceland, where the laws refer to a 'ring-lady' (*baugrygr*), who was the only surviving daughter of a sonless father, and so entitled to collect or pay compensation for wrong as if she were a son. This orphaned claimant's masculine role, they claim, begot the warrior-maiden of ON literature;[14] ignoring the objection that even in Iceland vindicating a claim did not necessarily mean hand-to-hand combat in full armour. Jochens is more credible, when she ascribes these stories 'to male fantasy and day-dreaming during war abroad, later recalled for entertainment', during the long winters – but for male fantasy any season will do. Women certainly accompanied the ninth-century armies in the British Isles and the Continent, and the Frankish poet Abbo of St Germain gave the Dane-women at Paris some fine contemptuous hexameters, to drive their men back into battle; but if there were actual fighting units of women, or single swordswomen with the men, they did not attract the attention from foreign observers they merited. The skalds show that scaring women was a routine proof of manliness, as when Valgardr á Velli celebrated king Harald Hardrada's raid on Denmark in 1045/46: Harald *sailed off the Scanian coast*, and he *scared ladies* (brides) *dear to the Danes*, while not far from Roskilde *grieving households dragged themselves silently to the*

---

13 See *Women who became Men* by Antonia Young (London 2000) on the Albanian women who take on men's roles and dress, possibly as substitutes for males killed or in hiding. For Rus warrior women: Price 2002, 332.

14 Clunies Ross 1994, 120–2, but compare the sober and balanced assessment by Præstgaard Andersen in MYWO 291–318, and her *Skjøldmøer-en kvindemyte* (Copenhagen 1982), and Jesch 1990, 105–6.

woods in flight.[15] To frighten the women was to dishonour the men; they were clearly not expected to hit back.

But they might still get the upper hand in scaring, when they became prophetic; at any rate women's primacy as seers and sorceresses, adept in the art of *seiðr*, is often asserted as an inheritance from the shrieking enthusiasts who fired the ancient Germans to do or die. *Seiðr* was described in thirteenth-century Iceland as mediation in trance between this and another world through possession by another being. By that date it was considered diabolical by the clergy, unwholesome and effeminate by the laity, and very convenient for the plots of sagas. It was practised by women, and by men, and had been perfected, along with other forms of magic, by Lapps. How sorcery was conducted in the earlier viking age has been much disputed. Snorri claimed in Ynglinga Saga (chapter 7) that in early times *seiðr* 'could discover men's fates, and things that had not yet happened, and could also bring about men's deaths or misfortunes or bad luck and deprive men of their wits or strength and give these to others':[16] a useful trick for a girl to know, but Snorri derived it from Odin, and contemporary sources refer to both male and female sorcerers, like other accounts down to the present day. Anscar found a male oracle at work in Sweden in the ninth century, and Adam of Bremen wrote of the 'arts of male magicians' in Norway in the eleventh. Jochens' theory that 'the performance of magic was originally reserved for women', and that this was reflected in the generally high status of all women in 'Germanic' societies, runs counter to this kind of evidence, and to the warlocks of the sagas and the laws. She suggests that 'nordic churchmen...could conceive of men only in positions of power and authority, whether good or bad' and so recognized wizards but not witches; moreover, before christianity, *seiðr* had become taboo for males because it meant surrender to another being, and was therefore a sort of spiritual unmanning.[17]

It is not clear what problem such speculation is supposed to solve. All over the world there are, and have been, male and female magi-

15   Skj IB, 360–58, from Snorri's Harald saga, chs 19–21, and from Mks 13 and 14, trans. Gade, 151.
16   trans. Clunies Ross 1994, 200. The job-description would fit the seeress of *Vǫluspá*, but that is a millenarian fiction of late date, not a guide to social reality. Sybilline prophecies circulated freely in medieval christendom, confined to no one social context.
17   Jochens 1996, 72–3, 129–36. And cf. Clunies Ross 1994, 210 and VA ch. 18, AB 4, 30. Göransson 1999 deduces the vital importance of priestesses from images in the Oseberg tapestries. Solli (1997–98) stresses the vital importance of the queer male shaman. For *seiðr* and other images: Price 2002.

cians and seers. It would be surprising if things had been any different among the Norse peoples of this period, and the hints of all-powerful sybils among the ancient Germans are beside the point; there are no such hints in the sources here.[18] Indeed, if women had any kind of exclusive rights to necromancy, it is odd that so many should have been willing to renounce them in favour of christianity, the faith that did not 'allow a witch to live': career opportunities for convert women were few, until very much later, with the founding of the first nunneries in the twelfth century.

Some poetesses rejected the new order. Among them the Icelander Steinunn was remembered for her verses against the priest Thangbrand, who was shipwrecked on leaving the island *c*.985: elegantly translated by Jesch (1990, 166–7). She and two others are tantalizing proof that women could be skalds in the pagan period, but to conclude that their work fitted in to a 'female-dominated cultic environment' is to overlook the strong personal flavour of all verse in that period. The now-common assertion that *Vǫluspá* must be by a woman because the verse is attributed to a sorceress would make great girls of Virgil, Shakespeare, and Racine, who used the same device. Norse poetesses deserve to be treated as individuals, not as spokespersons. A lady called Hildr Hrólfsdóttir was alleged by Snorri to have made verses threatening a king with loss of cattle, if he outlawed a man called Hnef; the poem has been forced into a tale of how king Harald Harfagr got rid of Hrolf Ganger, an evident fiction, but the words are 'genuinely old', according to Jesch (1990, 163–4), and fiery. Jórunn 'the female poet' (*skáldmaer*) is credited with four impressively convoluted stanzas about a reconciliation between that king and one or two of his sons, negotiated by the male poet Guthormr Sindri ('the un-blind'): the context is unclear, but perhaps *c*.940, and remarkable as a tribute to 'the power of poetry' (Jesch) rather than a eulogy of the war-lord, although couched in warlike language. None of the poetesses' verses concern 'typically female preoccupations': their authors were making good in a male-dominated profession. However, the small amount of their surviving work may be due to the fact that eulogy and satire were preferred by later scribes to other genres embraced by women.[19]

---

18 Cf. Jochens 1996, 210, and Lecouteux 1984, 247; in prose sources female necromancy is the exception rather than the rule. Studies of later witchcraft in Iceland and Scandinavia are many, but there was an imported element in later Nordic demonology. On viking age techniques see below, chapter 12, pp. 288–90. On Vǫluspa as finale for seeress-culture see Kress 1988.
19 See Straubhaar in MESCA, 594–6, and Jesch 1993, 168–75 on the difficulty of assessing the female contribution to Eddic verse. On the male-female tension within it, see Judy Quinn 'Women in Old Norse Poetry' CONIL 523–8.

How far men were type-cast by gender is not easy to determine, beyond the broad hints given by their grave-goods. They were not expected to spin or weave; but as women could rule, inherit, own, compose verse, and mediate between gods and mankind, those functions were not exclusively masculine. The 'iron-age good' of which Herschend writes[20] evidently allotted the responsibility of leading, wealth-getting and fighting chiefly to men; but the Gotland picture-stones seem to show some males dressed as women, and it seems that these societies also accepted 'ritual inversion' as normal on some great occasions. There was no doubt as much gender-stereotyping then, as after the conversion; but it clearly ran along somewhat different lines.

Servitude

Servitude means loss of personality and rights in the legal sense, but need not involve the suppression of individuality. In most medieval societies, slaves either possessed a measure of economic freedom, as smallholders living near, but apart from their lords; or the prospect of gaining the lesser dependency of the freedman; or of rising within the household to responsibility for goods and animals.[21] At Hørning in North Jutland a stone was erected soon after 1000 to read: TOKI THE SMITH CUT THE STONE AFTER THURKIL GUTH-MUND'S SON, WHO GAVE HIM GOLD AND FREEDOM – the boast of an ex-slave or ex-captive who could afford the noblest proof of worth. Toki the Smith inscribed another stone for Rifla and his father, at Grensten (DR 91): GOD HELP THEIR SOUL, perhaps because they too had helped him. Thorkil Gudmundsson may have emancipated Toki, as a pious deed, like the great ones of Anglo-Saxon England; perhaps the chances of liberation may have improved with the conversion of the owners, and certainly traditions grew up of much harsher slave-régimes in pagan days. Morkinskinna (chapter 37) has king Harald Hardrada reciting verses to remind a profiteering parvenu of the time when his people were thralls, wearing undyed tunics:

> *Do you recognize this tunic? Cow you must render*
> *To the descendant of kings; And to the descendant of kings*
> *A full-grown ox; Children, and all you gain, you must surrender*
> *To king's descendant, And a pig, and a tame goose....*

20 *The Idea of the Good in Late Iron Age Society* (Uppsala 1998).
21 On viking age slavery within Scandinavia, see Stefan Brink, forthcoming.

Words which belong to the twelfth century, when there were rich men of whom the most terrible words could be uttered: 'There is no information about his pedigree'.

Whether slavery bound the majority in viking age Scandinavia is much debated, and cannot be settled by later anecdotes (e.g. the emancipations of the great chief Erling, described in the Heimskringla *Ólafssaga*), or by reading back from law-codes contrived by such hardliners as the great jurist Andrew Sunesen, archbishop of Lund, who insisted in the Scanian code (chapter 79) that 'wheresoever the lord shall find his runaway slave, be it in the presence of the king or the archbishop, he is rightly allowed to arrest him with violent hands'. Vikings had been zealous slave traders, but they merely profited from long-established systems of slavery in the countries they invaded, or fed the great slave-markets of the Mediterranean and the Middle East; what regimes prevailed within their own lands and colonies is so unclear that they can be described both as enslavers and as emancipators.

'There is no archaeology of bondage': a dictum not much respected by archaeologists. In the Migration Age, they find a small end-room beyond the byre in the remains of Danish and Swedish long-houses, possibly slave-quarters; later on, there are 'accompanied burials' with human remains among the horses and dogs and weapons burnt or interred with the chief, as at Ile de Groix, Balladoole, Hedeby and Oseberg, where the remains are often interpreted as slave-victims, killed for company, as Ibn Fadlan witnessed in Russia.[22] Wamers even deduces 'slave warriors' from the gear of the Hedeby victims, and such men are attested in contemporary Poland and Cordova; but it seems unlikely, with what is known about the recruitment of retinues from the sons of freeholders. Place names with the element *Thrael* (the Trelleborgs are the obvious example) may be reminders of forced labour, rather than slave-gangs; no reconstructions of how Nordic farms were worked either require or rule out the use of slaves. The capture of women by raiders within Scandinavia is well attested, whether for ransom or servitude. That Valgarðr who admired Hardrada's intimidation of women, gloats over what made them afraid:

> *The women were captured. Lock held girl's body. Many women were led by you. Down to the bright ships Fetters bit greedily into the flesh.*

22 Wamers 1995, 156, and Norr 1993 for the little back rooms. Tollin has found from a survey of estates in medieval Småland that from 1050 on, slavery and labour services were characteristic of large (viking-age?) older properties, and smaller farms worked by free family labour appear more recent; *Rågangår, gränshallar och ägoomraden* (English summary), Stockholm 1999. This is like many parts of medieval England.

When it comes to slave hunting and trading outside Scandinavia the sources are abundant, and have been used to good effect by Pelteret (1991 and 1995). Two accounts of what it was like to be caught, the Life of St Findan, and Warner's Satire on Moriuht are especially vivid. Findan was an unlucky pawn in Irish politics. First his sister was taken by vikings, just about the time when they were making a camp at Dublin, as a centre for their sale and blackmail dealings with the Leinstermen. Findan was sent to ransom her, and was himself captured, but the raiders were persuaded to let him go. However, his father fell foul of a local king, and was killed; the king had the son carried off a second time to be rid of him. He was shipped from Leinster to the Orkneys, sold three times en route and then escaped. He had been chained, but he was unshackled when he helped defend his captors' ship in a sea-fight.[23] The complicity of native chiefs and visiting shippers is as stark in this account, as it might be in eighteenth-century West Africa. Findan became a saint; but his fellow-countryman Moriuht escaped from slavery to become a professional poet in Normandy, where his verses earned him the uninhibited contempt of a rival, Warner of Rouen, from whose caustic denigration (of *c*.1000) a poignant picaresque emerges.

He was seized by Danes along with his wife, bound tightly in chains 'like a robber or lunatic', then sent to sea and made to row. His captors beat him; then 'stand round him, admiring the active brute, and pissing on the crown of his bald head. His penis droops, and he is led by his horn, like a goat. He suffers insults, and the part of wife is forced on him, rather than on his wife. Furred like a bear, Moriuht is stripped. You play in front of the sailors, bear, and you score.' The satire lies in the victim's sexual appetite exceeding that of his abusers; he is 'an arse-hole for all, and when penetrated by a penis groans out: Alas! what a poor one!'

They take him overland to Corbridge, the trading station next to Hadrian's Wall. They put him up for sale, under an ivy wreath, and and nuns buy him for only 3d, because of his misshapen figure. But he was expelled from the convent for seducing one sister too many, and sent to sea in an oarless boat, to be captured again by Danes and sold again in Saxony to a widow, for only one bad penny; to start a new life as a sex-machine for both sexes until his emancipation and reunion with his wife and child.[24]

The poem is a more reliable source for the author than for the subject, or butt. On the subject of slavery, or captivity, it suggests:

---

23 *Vita Findani* (MGH SS xv (i) 502–6).
24 Best edition with translation by C.J. McDonough, *Warner of Rouen: Moriuht, a Norman Latin Poem* (Toronto 1995). See van Houts 1999, 18–21.

1 that it was a misfortune, but worse than that: a humiliation which tainted a man for life, whether he escaped or not, in the eyes of the free-born.
2 that it was a fact of life, and a fit subject for comedy. This highly educated Latinist is convulsed with the idea that slavery is too good for the hairy Hibernian sex-maniac.
3 that transit was worse than servitude ashore. It was much better not to be at the mercy of Nordic sailors, then as now, but in Northumbria and Saxony, Moriuht's chief sorrow was separation from his family; and he managed to get the help of a dowager Norman countess in finding them.
4 Servitude never dented his self-esteem, or effaced his personality; this evidently sharpened Warner's spite, but the little victim of it was a survivor. He had gone through a bad patch, but he had won his way to a happy ending: a ticket to inflict bad verse for a good living on gullible Norman patrons, some of them the grandsons of vikings. He had the last laugh, with his Latin.

Four powerful inhibitors of individuality may thus be recognized as social facts, but denied their sway over viking age men and women as conceived of by the hard-shell collectivists. Many threaded their own ways through and between the collectives, either by the sword or their wits. The collectives, and the group-consciousness they generated were not necessarily hostile to individual eccentricity, any more than the schools, monasteries and courts of Christendom. If their members lived by received wisdom and stereotyped models of behaviour, they were like us; not entirely predictable. 'Everywhere the pretence of individuality recurs', says MacNeice (*An Eclogue for Christmas*); and seldom as stridently in any age as in the work of the skalds, or Norse poets.

Poets

Poets made the stereotypes memorable. Their egotism is accepted as a sign of authenticity in the surviving texts (see pp. 308–9) and they have been described by Liberman (following Steblin-Kamensky) as 'the first medieval poets to cross the border of unconscious authorship'[25] whatever that is: evidently a mental affliction which stopped Aldhelm, Cynewulf, Gottschalk and Sedulius Scottus at Immigration. Liberman

25 'Germanic and Scandinavian Poetry', SS, lxxi, 1998, 105, and MESCA 263. Jochens described Egil's *Sonatorrék* as 'the oldest surviving evidence of the subjectivity of a known individual in the third écriture' (1996, 15): same thing?

and many others hold that the skalds composed their praise-poems or satires against a background of lost epic and heroic verse, from which they were escaping. They 'learned to say banalities tied to the current moment' and so 'trivialized the information which poetry had conveyed from time immemorial' (the rage of Achilles, the courage of Hector, the arrogance of Agamemnon: plot, scenery, speech) by applying these themes in a heavily contorted form to chiefs either alive or recently dead; and by intruding their own claims to respect.

I have killed six steel-rain announcers in all

bragged Thormoðr Kolbrunarskald (Skj IB 264), of his victims:

> *I am only just thirty now, and I recall the destroying of men: I caused their heads to be bitten.*

Egill Skalagrímsson, an Icelander like nearly all of them, was later made the hero of a saga (by Snorri himself, it seems), and became the star of this new tenth-century breed, in retrospect. The saga includes verses (whether or not by Egill) which date from that century, or relate to its events and to the mind of a poet with a distinctive diction and high self-esteem, honed by misfortune. When he praises king Eric Bloodaxe of York (died 952) as an artist in battle *heard-of east across the sea* (i.e. in Norway), he aligns Eric's victories with his own, in the verse business; for it is he who *loads praise on to the ship of thought* and *bears timber from the temple of words*. Later in life, he voiced his sorrow at the death of his sons, and evoked a range of feeling as wide of that found in the Carolingian or Irish poets. Kormákr Qgmundarson's adulterous thoughts on the Steingerðr he loved, and his contempt for her husband; Bjǫrn Hítdaelakappa's bitterness over his former betrothed Oddny's married sex-life; Egill's disgust at his own infirmities; show rampant self-regard among the gifted colonials, if they can be relied on as viking-age utterances in their present form.[26] This local flowering of what Lindow calls 'semantically charged word-play' won the Icelanders a hereditary claim to be court-poets off the island, and a political voice as satirists on it and off it. Personality breaks through much of it: dark, morose, Óttarr; uneasy, volatile, outspoken Sigvatr, St Olave's friend; Eyvinðr, the competitive court-vegetable; Hallfreðr, the trouble-maker; emerge from the verses, not only from prose fiction in 'Skald-sagas'.

26 For Steingerðr's ankles (*this yearning will not die from me all my life*), see Turville Petre's trans. (1976, 47), and Faulkes' (Sn.E 70) for Ormr Steinthorisson's hope that *the beer plank's body and mine to one room be brought after death*. Beer-plank, carrier of refreshment woman.

Their job was to celebrate 'institutionalized violence' in stereotypical phrases for the delight of military paymasters and their retinues. Self-awareness was not the result of withdrawal from collective fury or boisterousness, but of sharing it. As the chief bends waves, winds, men, women, and peoples to his will, so the poet wrestles the whole experience into metre, and addresses the chief (at least, until the 1030s) by the second person singular: thou, like an equal. Even when he addresses women, he remembers his importance. 'When he says, *O Lady*, he really means *Notice me. Admire me, adore me, advertise me. Look lady, how good I am at being a man*', as when Thjóðolfr Arnorsson breaks off his praise of the Dano-Norwegian king Magnus (1040s) to boast of his own winnings at the battle of Helganes:

> *I bought home a Götaland shield and a mail-coat as well...that was my allocation...beautiful weapons I got (but I told the tranquil lady that before). I got a helmet there.*[27]

When the chief versifies, vanity soars. If the verses attributed to the Orkney earl Einarr are genuine, and *c.*930 in date, he bragged of his superiority not only over his enemies, but over his brothers, and defied the Rogaland king Harald himself:

> *I shall not fear that; I have hewn a cut in Harald's shield –*

the eloquent bastard claims to be as good as anyone.[28]

The poets also revealed their own feelings about the choice between the gods. In *Sonatorrek*, Egill reviewed his relations with Odin, a family friend who had betrayed him by letting his family perish: *I grew trustful, believing in him, until...the prince of victory broke friendship* and so no longer deserves offerings. Nevertheless, *if I reckon it better*, Odin did give him his poetic skill, and his powers of perception. He is not defied or renounced, any more than the god of Job. The troublesome Hallfreðr (*c.*1000) was also reluctant to ditch One-eye: *all our race has made poems in praise of Odin. I recall the highly-valued practise of people, my ancestors*. Hallfred's patron, Olaf Tryggvason (995–9) was baptized, and so *reluctant I turn my hatred on the first husband of Frigg* (Odin) *because I serve Christ; for*

---

27   Cited in Frank in PISMA, 69, and the Thjóðolfr from Skj IB, 337. See Matiushina 1998 on the aggression in the love-verses.
28   Mundal 1993 accepts these verses as authentic, but they read like the later anti-overlord chip on the Orcadian shoulder. Whoever composed them thought it a suitable brag; Poole (1991, 161–72) argues that the verses were originally a dramatic monologue about Einarr, later attributed to him for narrative purposes.

the rule of Odin pleased the poet well.[29] As Lange put it: 'Hallfreð's christianity was called Olaf'. It went deeper with Sigvatr, poet of the next Olaf, the saint (*c.*1015–28), who spoke of his patron as his daughter's godfather:

> *O Lord, help him who my daughter home (hallowed be thy name)*
> *from heathendom made appear, and gave her the name Tofa.*

After that, the poet was 'implicitly included in the royal family by what for him was a sacred relationship'; Olaf's fall from power and death in battle made no difference, as the king became his friend in heaven, and by then Sigvatr had been on pilgrimage. Despite the inherited diction and vocabulary, saturated with heathenism, despite the special relationship with Odin, inventor of poetry and bringer of inspiration, 'the court scalds seem to have been quick to take to the new religion', according to Fidjestøl: true of the eleventh, not of the tenth century, which makes them rather slow.

How and why this burst of poetic individuality lit up the butchers, buggers and braggarts is unknown. The switch from the celebrating of dead heroes, as in the verses on the Rök stone, *c.*800, to boosting the living can be connected with increased competitiveness among rulers in the more intense and far-reaching raids of the 830s onwards, or with the more contemporary tastes of the retinues which served them. All that survives is a selection of what was preserved orally in Iceland; whether what survives represents the court entertainment of the whole viking age is doubtful. The incentive to egotism is also there in the competitive word-play of the derision (*senna*) and comparison (*mannjafnaðr*): found in Eddic poetry and sagas as literary conventions, they have often been traced by speculation to the firesides of viking chiefs,[30] when the drengs had drunk, or to the meetings of champions at play time. The *Maldon* poet made the raiders of 991 exchange mockery with the English across the water, and one of the first Danes to make an impression on westerners, king Godofred, was given a vaunt or taunt by Charlemagne's biographer, Einhard: 'he was so puffed up with vain hope that he promised himself power over the whole of Germany... he was boasting that he would arrive at Aachen, where the king was holding his court'. The loud mouths of the Danes were notorious; it was easy for the Franks to claim that they had killed another king Godofred at a parley near Cleves in 885

---

29   Trans. Turville Petre 1976, 72; and see Fidjestøl on the *erfidrápa* on Olaf, in VIRE (1993) 111–12: ibid., 114–15 on Sigvat's verses below.
30   Ellis Davidson 1983 for retrospective recreation of flyting; but these were not technical terms, just words for quarrelling and comparing.

because 'he had infuriated them by abuse and scornful words'.[31] The links between this verbal aggressiveness and skaldic verse are tenuous, but not invisible. At any rate, the Franks and Anglo-Saxons had found other forms for their self-assertion, in latin and christian culture.

But what of those who moved outside the collectives, rather than rising to fame within them? Or were moved out, by collective decisions?

The Furious

The most famous lunatics of the viking age are the *berserkir* (probably 'bear-skin dressers'), thought in later times to have formed units of shock-troops in war, and bands of desperadoes in peace. They were a real enough nuisance in twelfth-century Iceland to be mentioned in the laws as men prone to periodic frenzies, for which they were outlawed, along with those who failed to restrain them.[32] In sagas they appear as fighters of sociopathic habit, often solitary, malign, uncanny and gruesome; but what relationship this recognizable, and fairly universal type, bore to the realities of viking times is not known. Airy fantasies have arisen, of Migration Age bear-cult brotherhoods reflected in Sutton Hoo helmet-plates, Torslunda ornaments, names in *bjorn*, mumming masks, epic stereotypes, and any remotely ursine antiquity; but the only reference to viking age *berserkir* which might be contemporary is in the dubious *Haraldskvæði* about Harald Hárfagr (*c*.930?), as a description of one of the warrior bands in his retinue (see pp. 54–5). If there were bands of braves in fur suits, or naked, among the Nordic raiders into Western Europe, it is strange that the annalists and preachers failed to notice them. Dancing in animal skins for luck in hunting and mating is not the same as fighting in delirium, or lycanthropy.[33]

Effeminacy and Homosexuality

Effeminacy and homosexuality appear in the maledictions appended to some rune-stones; as present in sagas and laws of the later period

---

31   *Vita Karoli* ch. 14, and for the killing of Godofrid, the Annals of Fulda (trans. Reuter, 97).

32   *Grágas* ch. 7 (trans. Foote, 39); the penalty was $\frac{1}{2}$ lb silver and 3 yrs exile.

33   Simek 1993, *berserkir* summarizes the warrior-cult theory, which is developed in all directions by H. Blaney in *The Berserkers* (Colorado 1972) and in MESCA 37–38, and see Breen 1997 and 1999, and Price 2002, 78–84, 366–74.

they have been studied by Meulengracht Sørensen in a work translated by Joan Turville Petre as *The Unmanly Man* (Odense 1983); from which it appears that in Iceland, as elsewhere, unmanliness was seen as disgraceful, and was epitomized by the man who passively accepted anal penetration. If the Moriuht poem is anything to go by (see p. 26) this fate could be expected by the less valuable captives, which may account for the contempt earned by those who sought it voluntarily.

RÆTA BE WHOMSOEVER DAMAGES THIS STONE OR DRAGS
IT AWAY TO COMMEMORATE ANOTHER

is written on the huge Glavendrup memorial (DR 209): but whether this refers to the scorn roused by the *raeti* (passive sodomite), or to the fear of being sodomized involuntarily is not clear.[34] The place of the unmanly in everyday life is not shown by these formulae, or by the later sagas and laws. After all, these men were sailors, who spent time together, so that manly-man homosexuality between consenting adults may have been as common as at other periods; not in the least remarkable, and so not remarked upon in sources. It has been asserted that in viking times the warrior reserved his love for other males, and was therefore disinclined to express love for women in verse, hence the heterosexual deficit in Skaldic poems; a chain of reasoning weakened still further by the notion that the later romantic verse (*mannsöngr*) of the Icelanders developed from songs directed at female slaves to humiliate their owners, not to express genuine passion.[35] This is all speculative. Whatever bond there was between males can only be inferred from later or earlier analogies, such as the feeling which in historic times reigned between the Finnish headman (*noita*) and his corps of pure young men sent out to reconnoitre forest with a view to sanctifying the place suitable for burn-beating. As for the unmanly, whether sodomized or not, the seriousness of the accusation would have rallied other males of the family to their defence in law; the accuser might well be found guilty of defamation (*nið*) and made to pay (see pp. 284–5).

34 In one Olaf Tryggvason anecdote, buggery is treated as the sort of mishap that occurs at sea; and Perkins (1999, 199–200) finds in the sealore of Agdanes, the cape at the mouth of Trondheim fjord, traces of a sex-inversion rite to appease the local land-spirit.

35 Jochens in FROSA (1992) and Jesch 1991, 157 on this. *Mannsǫngvar* are usually post-Reformation ballads; see Matiushina 1998, and Tvengsberg 1995, 144 on the Finnish boy scouts. Solli has proposed Odin as a sort of cosmic queer, but given the nature of the evidence, it is hard to disentangle he-men in frocks, nancy-boys, and ritual perverts. See her 'Odin — the queer?' UOÅ 1997–8, 7–42.

Outlaws

It is often said that outlawry was the fullest possible separation of the living individual from the community among all the northern peoples, especially in the pre-christian period. The Nordic evidence is all later than this period. The saga of Grettir the Outlaw, the laws of the Icelanders, and the Danish military law concocted by Sweyn Aggeson in the 1180s[36] relate to other times and places. However, where wrong can only be righted by agreement between interested groups of responsible males, it follows that the irresponsible wrong-doer can expect to be killed out of hand by someone, or excluded from the protection of a group: his family, or kin, in this case. So it was in Iceland down to the 1280s, when the king of Norway became the vindicator of public peace; until then, an unamended wrong led to the perpetrators being outcast as 'wolf', 'wilderness man', 'forest man'. If he stayed on the island he had to avoid settlements, live with beasts and be hunted like them: a civil death, from the collectivist viewpoint. In practice, exclusion meant different things, depending on who had been offended rather than on the obduracy of the offender; on whether the offender's family backed him or the other families; on whether it was worth offending them even if he were outlawed; and if anyone tried hunting the outlaw, they had better outnumber or outfight him. As described in sagas, outlawry was really a way of identifying losers in a competitive society, rather than an irreversible doom on the anti-social. Outlaws were debarred from the courts, but could be recruited by chiefs as hit-men, casual labour, and low-grade clients (*flugumenn*); they could emigrate to Norway or Greenland and start again. This was the situation in one peculiar commonwealth of legalistic freemen at one period of its history; conditions were and had been different everywhere else, and what prevailed in viking-age countries can only be inferred.[37] Three relevant clues emerge:

1 Among both Danes and Swedes, the infliction of capital punishment and penal servitude is well attested: for rapists, robbers, slanderers and adulterers, according to Adam of Bremen (4, 21).

---

36   The workman-like specification of outlawries in e.g. *Baugatal* or ring-payment section of *Grágas* (trans. Foote 1983, 85) can be compared with the fanciful reconstructions of Danish custom in Saxo book 10 and Aggesen: *The Works* trans. E. Christiansen (London 1992) 42–3, 45.

37   Amory 1992 summarizes the way outlaws lived in Iceland, and see Gade in MESCA 116 for later variations elsewhere. Breisch (1994, ch. 4) argued that outlawry in Iceland degenerated from serious expulsion to a mere degradation.

Outlawry was evidently not the ultimate threat of an offended collective in those parts.

2 Being 'outside law' is a relative condition when law can mean local custom, a chief's will or power, a district, or agreement in a specific case (see pp. 256–7). The outlaw differed from the man escaping from a powerful magnate, or kin-group, or from the litigant slow in meeting obligations but not a full defaulter, only by degree. The Anglo-Saxons borrowed the term from the Danes as a convenient way of describing the banned freeman under a system heavily dependent on accountability imposed by royal decree; no such accountability emerged in Scandinavia for centuries, and it may be that full public proscription developed equally late.[38]

3 Until then, the gravity of outlawry can only have reflected the authority of the outlawing bodies; rather restricted geographically, until the development of the five big Norwegian legal jurisdictions (eleventh century?), even if dreadful in the suspension of land-right within the district.

The outlaw cannot have been the least fortunate of outcasts in regions of widespread mobility, where fugitives from hunger, war, slavery and sacrifice padded through the forests.

Suicide

Suicide is not always a matter of individual choice, and no doubt the troop of Norsemen who killed themselves in 925 to avoid being killed by Frankish pursuers[39] included some who died reluctantly; but most would have preferred to avoid the fate of the vikings hanged at Winchester thirty years earlier, after surrendering to king Alfred. A group suicide also appears in the *Landnamabók* legend (chapter 8) of the Irish slaves of the founding colonists, who murdered their master, fled to the Westmanna islands, and were surprised by an avenging posse: 'they jumped over a cliff that has been called after them ever since'. Warrior codes usually condone voluntary self-killing, and the Anglo–Saxon annalist who noted that an apparently

---

38 As in Denmark, where it is difficult to trace before the royal decree of 1200 against obdurate homicides.

39 Flodoard, *Annales*, 925 (PL cxxxv, 435c); deemed a case of 'black-and-white honour' by Alexander Murray in *Suicide in the Middle Ages* i (Oxford 1998), 62. Flodoard suggests that it was not dishonour or defeat they feared, but massacre.

Nordic 'king Sigeferth killed himself' in 964, also reveals that 'his body is buried at Wimborne', the burial place of king Alfred's elder brother; rather than being staked or burnt or tossed into a bog?[40] Later traditions are not unanimous on suicide. When the Norwegian cleric who wrote *Ágrip c.*1180, tells how the great ruler Hákon jarl had made his slave Kark cut his throat for him, while he was hiding from his enemies in a pigsty, he explained the deed with another tale of how one of Hakon's ancestors had renounced kingship so that he would be entitled to hang himself as a plain earl: which he did.[41] But if kings were not meant to kill themselves, legends of how king Jormunrek did so, and how kingly Odin tricked king Dómaldi into hanging himself need some explaining; preferably not by Germanist theory. The supposed pan-Germanic tradition of self-slaughter, (including the suttee of widows and daughters, and the anticipation of fate by the old and useless, and fallen heroes and retainers loyal to slain lords) is unsupported by any reliable evidence of what actually happened in this period and is usually padded out with fiction or anachronistic references to ancient Germans,[42] or later folklore. There is no shortage of that. At Nimwegen in 1679 Sir William Temple was assured by a count Oxenstierna that in Sweden there was a rocky bay called Odin's Hall, where, in former times 'men who were sick of Diseases they esteemed mortal or incurable, or else grown invalid with Age... and fear to die meanly and basely in their Beds, they usually caused themselves to be brought to the nearest Part of these Rocks, and from there threw themselves down into the Sea'.[43] The retainer loyal unto death has sometimes been detected in the 'accompanied burials' of great chiefs, and Ibn Fadlan certainly reported that the 'better men' in the retinue of the Rus kagan were ready to sacrifice themselves for him; but he did not say how, or when. Battle would seem to be the obvious place, as recorded on the Hedeby stones:

KING SWEYN FIXED THIS STONE AFTER SKARTHI HIS RETAINER WHO ... MET DEATH AT HITHABU (DR 3).

40   King Sigeferth had come to Eadred and Edgar's courts with some Welsh rulers; nothing more is known.

41   Trans. Driscoll, 24–7.

42   So Engfield 1972.

43   An example followed by Temple's own son John (William III's secretary at war) off London Bridge ten years later. That actually happened; Odin's Hall, and the myth of Odin's hanging himself and claiming suicide victims belong to imaginary worlds, of unverifiable relevance to viking days.

Agents and Patients

Historians reward the best efforts of the eccentrics and the egoists with a place in the line-up.[44] Only the palaeopathologists get down to irreducible singularity, as in the case of the 'majesty of buried Denmark'. Bones from Jelling church, now supposed to be king Gorm's (c.958), reveal a big-headed, heavy-browed fellow, with 'anomalous dentition', but sound limbs; about 5 foot 8 inches (172 cm) tall, and probably under fifty when he died, despite his later nickname, The Old. The bones of his son Harald and his grandson Sweyn lie so far unmolested, at Roskilde or Lund, and what is left of Canute may lie under the chancel of Winchester cathedral, or in a green box above it; but Canute's sister and her son Sweyn II (1046–75) were dug up at Roskilde and reconstructed by F.C. Hansen in 1914. Estrith (baptized Margaret) was one of the strong ladies who outlived their husbands and promoted their sons: Adam of Bremen says she was married twice, once to a Norman duke, once to 'duke Wolf', and Ulf Jarl drifted into saga and church legend as the hardly innocent victim of Canute's early morning vindictiveness. His widow, some fifty years later, had her grandfather's buck teeth, a lop-sided face, jutting jaw and crooked back that robbed her of $2\frac{1}{2}$ inches; a badly-mended fracture of the upper left arm gave her months of pain. Her tall son ($6\frac{1}{2}$ foot, when the average was below 5 foot 8 inches) bore the marks of his adventures as a self-made king: three broken ribs, an awkward twist to the back, head skewed to the right, reminders of hard fighting. With his big flat head, receding forehead, beetle brow, long nose and slight overbite, he looked majestic if he stood still, but walked knock-kneed and flat-footed – 'not so pronounced that he got a nickname thereby';[45] but in the Harald sagas of Heimskringla and Morkinskinna a rough-tongued farmer's wife calls him 'both lame and cowardly'. Like his mother's, his brain capacity was above the modern average (by over a gill: $150\,\text{cm}^3$) and Adam of Bremen, who knew him, found him an intelligent and persuasive talker. His affability, lechery and wit were written about by Icelanders over a century after his death, and the dynasty kept his memory green in Denmark. He was christened Magnus, tried to conquer Norway and

---

44 There are some, like Erik Ringmar, who attribute even major political events to the fulfilment of the individual's self-imagined identity. But the case he offers, of Gustavus Adolphus, is that of complementary and fairly stereotypical identities driving king and people to war: see *Identity, Interest and Action* (Cambridge 1996).
45 Hansen 1914, 19: a slim outsize folio illustrated with drawings of the remains and reconstructions of the faces.

England, and failed; but he and his mother were generally good friends to the clergy, and he left behind him seven episcopal sees which became the foundation-stones of a post-viking-age kingdom.

For those two, words and even biographies can be fitted to the bones with some confidence; for the rest, it is mostly speculation.[46] As with a Dane who died about fifty or less years before Sweyn, in the new royal town of Lund, where his bones were found in 1990. Not all of them, because this man had been laid on his back with his hands and feet tied to posts, so that they could be severed more neatly with cuts from above. Nevertheless, it took two blows to take off the left hand above the wrist, and two to slice through the right shin. It is not clear whether he was already dead, or died as a result of this treatment. The hands and feet were not present in the grave, and a similar burial nearby lacked the skull, although the lopped limbs were thrown in. The excavator concluded that they had been dishonourably executed, and buried below dung-heaps for some offence against the king: this was 'an early manifestation of royal supremacy at a time when the state was not fully established.'[47] A pat conclusion, since the poets congratulated kings for mutilating plain thieves and vikings; so it is possible to link these deaths to the birth of the Danish state, one way or another, if you must. Whatever they did, they deserve better than to be merged with collective con-sciousnesses and group mentalities congenial to the ant, the bee, and the cultural historian.

46   Arup's 'Kong Svend 2's biografi' Scandia 1931 was the first true source-critical essay on this ruler; now, more and more is being deduced from more and more VA skeletons. Sellevold, Lund Hansen, and Balslev Jørgensen 1984 was a useful survey. Most of the medieval history of Greenland is from skeletons; see Lynnerup in VINAS, 285–93.
47   Carelli 1993–4 offers a careful analysis in English.

2

Families

Unhappy the man who
Bears the limbs of his kinsman's corpse
Down from his house

lamented Egill Skalagrimsson; he called his family his 'kin-stockade' (*frændgarðr*), broken by the sea that drowned his sons,[1] and there is no denying that up here, as almost everywhere else in the pre-modern world, families were the social unit and the emotional centre. If there was anything peculiar about the families of the Nordic world, it was not so much the intensity of their coherence as the lack, or relative underdevelopment of alternative groups: the states, churches, cities and lordships which shared people with families elsewhere. There can be no doubt of the feelings expressed on the rune-stones:

DEATH OF MOTHER...[and father? illegible]...WORST TO A SON

was cut in reverse on the stone at Rimsø, North Jutland, and at Ålum (M 190) Thurvi commemorated her nephew Thorbjorn:

TOWARDS WHOM SHE FELT MORE KINDLY THAN TOWARDS A DEAR SON;

and at Bällsta, fourteen lines of verse in honour of Ulf end:

GYRIDR TOO LOVED HER HUSBAND THEREFORE SHALL SHE HAVE HIM SPOKEN OF IN A LAMENT

---

1 *Sonatorrek* again: Turville Petre 1976, 24–41.

On Gotland, Ardre 4 was put up by four sons to their mother Ailikn in christian times, and they pray:

GOD AND GOD'S MOTHER HAVE MERCY ON HER AND ON THEM THAT MADE THE MEMORIAL – THE BIGGEST THAT MEN CAN SEE

[Gotlands Runinskrifter 114)

Most of the stones in Denmark, and in Sweden the overwhelming majority of stones, commemorate spouses or children or parents or kin by blood or adoption: for Kirkmichael 3 on Man (Kermode 104) no doubt spoke for other parents with:

BETTER IS IT TO LEAVE A GOOD FOSTERSON THAN A BAD SON

Of course, other motives than filial piety or parental love were involved, and Mrs Sawyer has made much of the possibility that many were mere land-right markers; but the emotion comes through.

As elsewhere, families had functions now seen as public or some-body else's business: the armed defence of property and persons, the performance of religious ceremonies, the prosecution of crime at law, and the disposal of its own dead are examples. All economic life rested on production by families, whether through farming, or through farming supplemented by herding and hunting.[2] Power and wealth sat in the enlarged family dwellings called halls; indigence and insignificance had no kin; gods, giants, dwarfs, and elves were conceived of as warring families. But who, or what, was family in viking times?

Birth Control

With so much to do, the family could not be left to nature, to shape at random. Its size, discipline, responsibilities and rights had to be controlled. One control which has roused interest in recent years was by infanticide, or especially by the killing of baby girls through exposure at birth, a normal or occasional practice in most parts of the world down to the twentieth century. The apparent imbalance in the sex-ratios discernible in viking-age cemeteries led Clover to

2 Ringsted 1992, 135–42 summarizes the 'household-economic approach' to medi-eval economies, which will be followed here; also in D. Herlihy: *Medieval House-holds* (London 1985). Svend Nielsen's *The Domestic Mode of Production – and Beyond* (Copenhagen 1999) compares Denmark, Iceland and Egypt.

suggest that some Nordic populations carried baby-killing so far that there was a serious shortage of adult women in Hǫrðaland, Ostfold, Vestfold and Hedeby. Daniell's *Death and Burial in Medieval England* (London 1987) came to a similar conclusion about a society in which infanticide was penalized, and the Icelandic sagas offer data on infant exposure both within, and regardless of, christian law as interpreted in the twelfth and thirteenth centuries. Indeed, Boswell concluded that in Iceland exposure meant informal adoption by passing strangers; and was met with scepticism.

But there was something wrong with those sex-ratios: they apply only to those percentages of inhumation burials which yield bones that can be sexed, and they are contradicted by other Nordic evidence from other places. In the mere 20 per cent of usable bones found at Birka, the proportions are more-or-less equal, while 86 per cent of all Danish inhumation graves have been identified as female. Where the males preponderate, the question of where are the women? need not always be answered by exposure at birth. Some were buried apart, like the ten or a dozen female skeletons of eleventh-century date recently found at Visby, on Gotland; others may have been cremated at later dates than the men, and so be less identifiable. Identifications by what are taken to be characteristically male or female types of ornament are unreliable, where this can be tested, as on Gotland; and Wicker has recently reviewed the evidence[3] to show that most of Clover's case for unusual rates of selective infanticide is insecure. As a result, there is little point in discussing what the causes and consequence of this practice might have been. When it came to culling babies, Norsemen appear to have been driven by considerations like those of Franks and Anglo-Saxons: prudential, religious and sentimental. Sentimental, certainly; this is the period in which childish things appear in children's graves: bronze jingle-bells, little ornaments and mirrors, infant clothing.

The Old

All that emerges from these quasi-demographic conjectures[4] is what was thought likely before: that all round the Baltic, as elsewhere, a

---

3   Wicker 1998, and Hines 1997 for general discussion including Anglo-Saxon England; Clover 1988 for theory, Bennicke 1985 and Sellevold 1984 for Danish evidence; Helgesson and Arcini (1996) 55 found 80/128 child graves at Fjälkinge (Scania).
4   Carlsson 1983 and 1988.

balance had to be kept between family size, as a factor in family survival or prosperity, and the productive capacity of the land. The old could lose out in such an equation, as easily as the newborn, and the superfluous young; there was little comfort in the *Ynglinga Saga* tale, as told by Snorri in the 1230s, of how old king Aun of Uppsala had bought decades of life by the sacrifice of one son for each, until the Swedes said no: 'it was afterwards called Aun's disease, when a man died of old age without any sickness'. In patriarchal societies, old males have the advantage of sex, and in warlike societies, of rarity: few old men's bones have been found in viking age cemeteries or mounds, and the average age at death (another dubious statistic) is usually put below thirty. The folklore of many northern peoples tells of the killing of the old by their families in former times, or in remote places. In Sweden there were traditions of 'family precipices' (*ättes-tupan*) off which they were pushed to avoid Aun's disease; and of 'family cudgels' (*släktklubban*) for knocking them on the head.[5]

Patriarchy

Patriarchy might be expected in Nordic families, and has been freely inferred from the myths and legends as told by Snorri and the Eddic poets in later centuries. There, the masculinity is blatant, in the case of the three main gods: Thor, the serial rapist and pulverizer of giantesses, wielder of the phallic hammer and protector of his own sisters; Odin, the paterfamilias of the privileged gods called Æsir, maker and breaker of the rules by which they live, lord of their great hall, and wily seducer of women; Frey or Niord, carved with a big phallus at Uppsala, according to Adam of Bremen, and starring in a brutal courtship which is the subject of the poem *Skírnismál*. By contrast, Odin's wife Frigg is a hausfrau, Freyja is a promiscuous tease, and the other goddesses are little more than names, for poets to use as kennings. Snorri lets no goddess sit on the high, or lower benches at Ásgard, where Odin holds court and even the degraded trickster Loki can claim a seat. If this mythology reflects viking-age social life, women counted for little within the family; but those who accept this equation[6] ignore a mass of evidence which suggests the

---

5   There was a collection of these at Stockholm; one found in Tidersrum church in 1934 turned out to be a carpenter's mallet; Nordland 1969, 73. They resemble the clubs once shown in the Tower of London as used to massacre Danes on St Brice's day.
6   As apparently do Clunies Ross (1994, 188 and 1949–58) and Jochens 1996, 33–48 and 47–8; the former suggested that men kept women out of myths because their wives bore children who died, while they only procreated. Gimbutas-followers tend to

opposite, as above pp. 17–19. The creation myth in Snorri's Edda denies the human female (not the cow) any part in the first acts of generation; he looks back to a Golden Age of the world 'before it was destroyed by the arrival of the women', and there is little doubt that many of his contemporaries in the schools of western Europe would have enjoyed the myth, since the battle of the sexes was a worn literary theme. Those who took the misogynist line were not trying to keep the whole female sex in servitude, or under male control; they were protesting, often obscenely and derisively, at the fact that women were not keeping quiet and obeying orders, and there was nothing they could do about it. There is no reason to suppose that Snorri was aware of that literature; or that he could, or wanted to, express the actual philosophy of gender which had prevailed in the pre-conversion period.

To set against the men's club atmosphere of Asgard and Valhalla, feminist mythologers have invoked the crucial importance of gian-tesses (not necessarily gigantic) and she-elves (not at all elfin) in founding human dynasties, guarding the landscape, and guiding the lives of favoured families and heroes: the evidence is somewhat ear-lier than Snorri, and may be corroborated by the many little stamped tokens of the pre-viking period, on which male and female figures embrace on equal terms in what has been called the sacral marriage: a theory discussed in chapter 6.

All the same, there is no escaping the emphasis on male descent and patriliny on the rune stones, and in contemporary records of male-dominated dynasties; on male landownership in the place-names, beginning with the pre-viking names in – *lev*, and flowering in the Danelaw combination of personal name + *by*; on the prepon-derance of rich male over rich female graves and memorials; and Adam of Bremen's report on the eleventh-century Swedes:

> Every man has two or three or more women at the same time, according to the extent of his power; the rich and the rulers have more than they can count.

(AB 4, 21)[7]

explain the dethronement of the Mother-goddess and matriarchy by men's acquiring a more accurate understanding of the reproductive system and their part in it. The redating of the Överhogdal wall hangings to this period (*c*.900–1100) enables Eva-Marie Göransson to compare images of men and women woven by women, with those carved by men on the Gotland picture-stones, and to conclude that each sex down-played and simplified the other (*Fornvännen* xc (1995), 129–38), surprise, surprise. The wall-hanging is an amazing muster of animals, possibly representing female wealth.

7 The eleventh-century rune-stones at Täby and Hagby (SW) are taken to be documentary evidence of lawful bigamy in Larsson 1996: Jarlabanki was the son of

Men were the bosses; but since their wellbeing depended largely on the ability of their families to collaborate with others bound to them by the giving and taking of daughters, married females and others had acquired, at least by *c*.1000, restricted and variable but indefeasible inheritance and personal rights similar to those accorded to Frankish and Anglo-Saxon women. These have been deduced from rune-stone inscriptions by Birgit Sawyer, who has found that among the inscribed landowners of Svialand, but not among the Danes or Gautar, brothers and sisters shared inheritances (see map 1). She attributes this difference to political pressure from Danish kings, anxious to keep useful or even taxable estates undivided. Since there is no evidence that such estates were taxed, or that any king could meddle with custom in matters of inheritance before the twelfth century, this explanation is questionable, if not easily replaced by another.

Marriage

Marriage not only started new families; as elsewhere, it was an incident in the history of old ones, at least among the free and property-holders. There was no one word for it, even in the twelfth- and thirteenth-century vernacular speech, only words for stages in the alliance of two families. *Gipting* was the giving away of a woman, not necessarily in marriage. *Mundr* was the bride-price, given by the groom's family, and *mundarmál* the contract for it, only the first stage in the deal. *Brúðkaup*, 'bride-buy' and *bruðlaup* 'bride-transfer' were ways describing the wedding feast; and once she was bought by her husband, she retained rights to her *konufé*, woman's goods, or portion. *Brúðr* could be bride or any woman, *kona* could be woman or wife, and despite the strong emotional tie expressed on the rune-stones cited earlier, this formal cohabitation was 'essentially a commercial transaction between two families'[8], at least in christian Iceland, as in Anglo-Saxon England.

In the viking age more than one observer referred to concubinage of some kind as marriage *more Danico* 'under Danish rules', as when king Canute wed Ælfgifu of Northampton, daughter of a noble Englishman, in such a way that he was able to marry the dowager queen Emma three years later without preventing Ælfgifu's sons from

Ingefast and Jorunn, and when Ingefast also married Ragnfrid of Hagby, Jarlabanki was given Täby, perhaps to support his mother. But there could have been two Jarlabankis; see B. Sawyer 2000, 137–9.

8   Jochens in MESCA, 409.

becoming kings in Norway and England. The chronicler who wished to disparage one of these boys, Harald Harefoot, did not claim that Ælfgifu was not a proper or legitimate wife; only that Canute was not the natural father.[9] Ælfgifu herself went to Norway with the other boy, Sweyn, and seems to have governed there like a queen. Her arrangement with Canute was evidently full, but not exclusive marriage; a contract between families adjusted in the light of Canute's contracting with the more advantageous Anglo-Norman connexions of Emma.

Less formal contracts, like the famous one-night stands of Norwegian kings, or the sex-hospitality of hosts with slave women or nubile daughters, or the king's-woman-status of Álfhildr (see p. 19) were normal all over the West and further, and need not be confused with marriage, or attributed to Norse culture. As for the 'free choice of partner by women', there is no sign of it in the sources.[10]

Names

One way or another, families acquired women and supplied men to breed from, and stamped their offspring with names. In later Icelandic custom, these were pronounced by the father as an acknowledgement of paternity and a prohibition of exposure, and Snorri thought this had been the custom earlier in Norway. The rune-stones reveal that viking age fathers or mothers followed the older, pre-Migration system of most barbarian peoples, by reproducing name-elements in different combinations with each child: as with the seventh-century Bleking chiefs, Hathu-wolf and Hari-wolf; or by repeating the name of a recently dead kinsman, as with the Haralds, and Hemmings and Sigeferths of the eighth–ninth-century Danish royal dynasty, and the Ivarrs and Sihtrics and Godfreys of the Dublin kings. Both fashions conserved the characteristic worth or luck of the family; whether the second one involved a belief in reincarnation is unclear (see p. 297).

These were the ancient ways, but the naming was complicated by innovations after the eighth century:

1 The cult of Thor (and of Frey to a lesser extent) led to increase in the use of these names as elements, all over the North, so that by the

9 ASC, C and D, under 1035: 'Harold said that he was the son of Canute and the other Ælfgifu though it was not true'; E and F: 'it seemed incredible to many men' (EHD, i, 232), like 'Florence' of Worcester, later, who made him a shoemaker's son.
10 Old Germanist lore, refuted by Ebel 1993: rev. Jochens in *Álvissmál*, iii, 1994, 101.

eleventh century, Thorbjorn, Thorsten, Thorgrim, Thorgautr etc. and the shortened forms Toki, Tobbi, Tostig, Topi, were met with everywhere from Cork to Constantinople, regardless of religion or ethnic affiliation: the Norman Conquest of England brought in Tosten and Tustein from Calvados to dislodge Thurstan from the land he had won in Canute's day as a Norseman following in the steps of Thorsteinn who had sailed over from Denmark two hundred years before.[11]

2 The colonization of Iceland broke 'the restrictive bonds imposed by inherited naming principles' and let settlers 'give rein to their linguistic imagination',[12] if the names in *Landnámabók* are genuine. They started a new naming tradition, which seldom involved varying combinations of hereditary name-elements, but reused full ancestral names, as when Snorri the historian got Snorri Goði's. It is not entirely clear how new this was, as we do not know the naming-customs of the sort of middling ninth-century families from which most of the settlers came. But here, as in the English Danelaw, new names were coined out of what seem to have been hitherto unassociated elements.

3 There was more random naming within families, as at Hunnestad in Scania (DR 282–6) where an array of at least eight stones proclaimed the sons of Gunni: Asbjorn, Tumi, Hroi, and Leikfrið; and as at Lund (1) and Grensten (DR 314 and 91) for a family of Thurkil, Ólafr, Ótur and Rifla, sons of Aski Bjarnisson; named like perfect strangers.

4 Some names, as well as name-elements, are more widely current; as are Sve(i)n, Assur, Toki, Bjorn, Eysteinn, Ulfr. Others are increasingly localized: Keira, Trionn, Ódinkaur, Illugi, and names suffixed-*fast*. No Sven, Bjorn, or Ulf appears in Gotland inscriptions.

These tendencies indicate various family policies, either to gain status (see Appendix A) through imitation (1, 3, and 4) or through retrospection (ii), rather than mere fancy; which is perhaps detectible in the simplification of compound names, by 'phonetic reduction' (Hróðulfr to Hrólfr) or by 'hypocoristic forms' (pet names: Askel to Aski) or by the preference for simple names to begin with (Alf, Bo, Dag, etc.).[13] Like Anglo-Saxons, Danes and other Northmen were

11 Twenty-three percent of the supposed viking-age names in Landnámabók contain the Thor compound; seven of the thirty-three Norse names on the tenth-century Manx crosses.
12 Fellows-Jensen 1994, 262; Boyer in *Gripla*, I, 1975, 26–9 on Danelaw personal names. See Snoedal in GV (2004) for rane Gotland names.
13 Short names have been called characteristics of 'ordinary Scandinavian peasants' by Karl Sandred (1987, 321), which would surprise kings Knub, Knut, Gorm, and

slow to adopt very foreign names, even after baptism. The story of how St Olave came to have a son called Magnus indicates, if not exactly, how this happened (king asleep, baby might die, poet remembers Charlemagne, king wakes, *fait accompli*) at least how strange it seemed, a century or more after the 1020s, that this should have happened in the homelands. Where Norse and foreigners mingled, in the colonies, hosts were more likely to borrow names than were newcomers, as if for them alien names might bring bad luck, or interrupt family identity. Some converts took christian names, but kept their own for normal use.

Kin-groups

Families were no less important in the North than elsewhere; unless they were subordinated, as many have imagined, to kin-groups. If it is true that 'the foundations of economic and social relations during the viking age were constructed round genetic ties' it might well follow that cousins were as important to each other as siblings, and that patrilinear kin-groups were the main social units.[14] These would be thumping generalizations, of the kind that increases in emphasis as the evidence thins. The Germanic Iron and Migration Ages are seen as periods in which war, trade, agriculture, religion and possibly law were organized by extended kin-groups, which had at some stage superseded or at least weakened the cohesion of tribes by establishing separate hereditary rights over tribal lands. From that or with that came a new land-law, a detribalized military force, led by kin-group chiefs, and a new form of political authority which could either be the ancestor of the state, or the heir of communalism; whichever it was (Marx, Engels and Maurer are the gurus), the kin-group was the key collective,[15] whether it be called clan, *sippe*, *fara*, *genelogia*, *slægt*, or *ætt*, to list some of the favourite misnomers or anachronisms. 'Everything is organized round the clan, *Sippe* in Germany, *ætt* in Scandinavia', wrote Ries in *HUG* (p. 239) of a period of time apparently extending from *c.*400 to *c.*1100.

Svein. There is no list of peasants' names from this period; only names for people rich enough to own villages, fight battles, or put up monuments. Those had all kinds of names: see Williams 1998.

14 Bäck 1999, 152, as a recent example, and Hedeager 1992 in English, or more fully in her *Danmarks Jernalder* (Aarhus 1990), esp. p. 177. But this is a hoary anthropological belief.

15 See Bazelmans 1991, 117–18 for post-Roman times, Harrison 1991, and Ausenda 1995.

The illusion was created largely by evidence of extended liability for compensation and contribution among the cousins and remoter kindred in the written Nordic law-codes of the twelfth century onwards; the more extended, in Iceland, were taken to represent the more archaic social system, of real kin communities organized to pursue quarrels and share landownership rather than *ad hoc* teams of interested parties in lawsuits. All signs of group activity among Germanic peoples were interpreted so. Place-names in *-ing* were signs of kin settlement areas; in *-lev* of land detached from the common stock and vested in the lineage;[16] in *kinda* (Götaland) of the same sort of thing (rather than places on the *kinnar* or slopes of hills and ridges). Lombard cemeteries in Pannonia, holding roughly a hundred adults; viking age cemeteries in Bornholm; some Frankish and Italian burial grounds holding more than one family; all have been called in evidence to support the existence of usually agnatic, or male-related collectives throughout non-Romanized Europe and well into the viking age. Despite the demonstration by A.G. Murray (1983) that most of these assumptions are groundless, they die hard; it is worth repeating that for the Norse, all kinds of associations larger than the family were possible, and the political theory of the time was couched in family terms; but of active social groups defined by descent from a common ancestor more remote than the father there is no trace.

Clientage, marriage alliance, fosterage, partnership, concubinage, religious cults and simple alliances were seven ways of reinforcing single families and combining them with others for which there is good contemporary evidence on the rune-stones and other written sources. Widespread mobility between all groups, by land and sea made co-resident cousinage impractical, even in Iceland, but of course there is no reason why it should not have been invoked among other family strategies. One possible kin-name, Rafnung, appears on Tofi's memorial in Denmark (Bække (i) and Horne, DR 54 and 34): 'descendant of Rafn'. But being proud of an ancestor does not mean membership of a genetically-defined clan. If the example of twelfth-century Iceland is relevant, the unlucky litigant had to bargain and plead for the support of his relations, and the cousinage had to be constructed according to circumstances. The *ætt* (which simply means lineage or lineages, not any specific group) was 'a complex structure based upon more or less contradictory

---

16 Bjerrum's view, in *Festskrift til... Hald* (1974); but Schönwalder 1993 shows that German *leben* PNN are often named after dispossessed Thuringian owners who had 'left' them to Franks in the 740s, and Albøge 1991 argues that for the Danes, *lev* just meant hereditary property.

principles' – descent in the male line, descent in the female line, allies by marriage and the 'ego-focus' of the defining member.[17]

Households

Families had to be carefully contrived and nourished, in the ways indicated above, which were those of the well-to-do. The family life of a slave, freedman or poor man may have been totally different, for all we know. Nevertheless, apart from the great halls, settlement archaeology over most of the Nordic world (see pp. 65–7, 208) points to the same kind of household, of family and dependents in one homestead and outbuildings, as a pattern followed quite far down the social scale throughout this period. Farms collected in villages or hamlets were separated by timber fences or stone walls from the fifth century onwards, but even the great halls, the 'rooms of leadership' used by the chiefs were not seriously defended against attackers, or closed against neighbours. These great families may have been thin on the ground (along the Norwegian coast, one every thirty miles; on the east coast of Jutland, one every fifteen; in Mälardal, one every ten); they were highly visible[18] and the ways they transmitted wealth and status were watched and if possible imitated. Large households for the rich; small for the poor.

Family Land

'The primary function of the Norwegian *ætt* was to defend its *óðal*';[19] is a frequently repeated and possibly accurate statement of how it was in the twelfth century and later. *Óðal* was land vested in families which could not be divided or sold to outsiders without the consent of the whole male kin-group, a restriction which applied to land by the same family over six generations in SW Norway, over four in the north. In Denmark, by that time, members of families with claims to share in the property as co-heirs of the owner would have to have their rights quashed by a ceremony (*scortatio: skødning*) before any sale would be accepted as valid; but then it would be. In

17   Hastrup 1985, 70–104 for a convincing analysis of the kinship arrangements of post-conversion Iceland and P. Hermann in VS xxiii 2004, 7–18.
18   As sites of feasts, rites, and assemblies.
19   Gurevich (MESCA 1993, 372–3) and Zachrisson 1994 see *óðal* as a mentality, or mystical notion; and see Clunies Ross 1994, 89, citing Vestergaard 1988, 180. For the origin of family tenures see Widgren 1983.

Iceland there were old estates entailed on immediate cognates of the owners, and known as *aðalból*, family properties; but no *óðal*. On Orkney, Udall has lasted until killed by Scotch lawyers and English politicians in our own day. Are these the remnants of a once universal Nordic–Germanic system of inalienable kin-group land-right? There is no evidence at all of how things were before the eleventh century; no sign, for example, in the English Danelaw that the ninth-century settlers had bequeathed inalienability to their tenth-century successors; they sold land for cash to bishop Ethelwold, and left their relations to quarrel with the new abbeys in the Fenlands and their patrons as best they could.[20]

Knut Helle has suggested that *óðal* was no antique tradition handed down from the viking age, but formulated later to protect family holdings threatened by pious donations to the clergy, or by an incipient land-market, stimulated by the profits of commerce and royal service.[21] The earliest reference to *óðal* is in Sigvat's *Bersǫglis-vísur*, 'straight-talking-verses', addressed to the young king Magnus of Norway *c.*1037. There, it means the private land of the thegns threatened by confiscation or damage; according to Sigvatr, and later poets, a king who interfered with *óðal* was a tyrant; which would account for the legend of how king Harald Harfagr had caused the emigration to Iceland by a general seizure of such estates in the ninth century. Other threats to property called for other tales, as when Sven Aggesen reported in the 1180s that Danish women had had no claim to inherit land at all, until they had ransomed king Sweyn Forkbeard from Slavs with their jewellry, and were rewarded with half-shares. Much earlier, Dudo of St Quentin had made his Normans emigrate from the North because a king coveted the allodial lands of his chief magnate, and drove him out: *allodium*, the family land holding of the Franks, was always under threat of usurpation or lordship by the powerful. In Scandinavia, at least in Denmark and Norway, the great halls, the great ships and the great land-holdings (such as those of the Uthinkaur family, which endowed the see of Ribe all over west Jutland) point to strenuous land-grabbing through-out the viking period, rather than a stable system of land tenure inherited from the Migration Period. Where there was danger to freeholders, their property could be protected by vesting it in a whole group of relations; where there wasn't, there was no need.

---

20 See Kennedy on 'Law and Litigation' in ASE, xxiv, 131–84 (1995).
21 Helle 1998, 250; Lars Ivar Hansen saw *óðal* in Norway as a 'strategy of social reproduction' for landowners not attracted by the newer strategy of accepting office from kings or bishops. Mats Larsson 1998 finds Swedish *ódal* in runic inscriptions, with estate boundaries and see Breen 1997 and 1999.

Mrs Sawyer has suggested that in tenth-century Denmark and eleventh-century Sweden anxieties over land-right were expressed in rune-stones, and the distribution of these stones is an index of royal interference in the pattern of tenure.[22] If so – it is an unverifiable hypothesis – the time to expect doctrines of inalienability among the landowners (whether old blood or parvenu) would be then, and there.

In Iceland, the lack of *óðal* agrees with the lack of true territorial lordship in post-conversion times (see p. 134n.) but in Orkney and the Isles there were greedy earls and other chiefs to keep at bay. In England there was an old mosaic of tenures, a conquest by West Saxon kings which gave security of title in return for political loyalty, and the subsequent intrusion of so many potential threats and reassurances – geld liability, clientage, vassalage, public duties, leases, bookland, mortmain – that no such system could have grown to maturity, if anyone had thought of it.

Not that family holdings in Scandinavia lacked protection before or during the development of *óðal*. Ancestors kept watch from graves, howes and stones, and were fed with beer, blood and incantation. Arguing from the common root of the words *erfi* (funeral feast) and *arfr* (inheritance) Grønvik derived heritability from the public entertainment at which the dead gave seisin to the living, as apparently commemorated on the B-side of the pre-viking age Tune stone:

THREE DAUGHTERS MADE A GOOD FUNERAL FEAST AS THE BEST LOVED OF INHERITORS.[23]

There were guardian spirits there already, in the grove, the tutelary tree, the rock and the hill, to keep the boundaries and patrol the outfields; domestic elves, nesting in the house; fetishes and fetches, and greater gods and goddesses allured to the family feasts; and eventually, inscribed rune-stones. In Sweden they were usually carved with the keep-off sign of the dragon, and in Norway there were plain boulders inscribed as *mærki* or landmarks. In view of these safeguards, a purely legal concept of inalienability will seem premature; for Nordic landowners, *blót* (offering) did the work of *boc* or charter among the English. Smaller holdings might have benefited

---

22 B. Sawyer 1991, 106–12; AB 2, 47 scholium 37 notes a big donation to Ribe, over an area in which there is a notable lack of rune-stones and high-status weapon-burials, if that area was in fact where bishop Othinkar's patrimony lay. See map 6, p. 151.

23 Grønvik 1998: Grønvik 1982 overstated the probable antiquity of the memorial feast, or *minni*. On the silver hoards see Staecker 1997b.

greatly from *óðal*, as they would have from the writ of *Novel Disseisin*, had they been so lucky. As things were, deposits of silver within the property for the ancestors, and over the boundaries, for the giants, seem to have been hopeful markers of title. Runestones were much more visible.

Feud

Thanks to the data in the sagas and laws, as interpreted in the schools of literature and anthropology, there is much written on how Nordic families, and Anglo-Saxons, competed and conflicted in the state of regulated private hostility known as feud, and derived from the kin-group system of ancient Germany. There is good evidence of how the Icelanders conducted such disputes in and out of law-courts in the twelfth and thirteenth centuries, but it is notable that there was no word for feud even there; the irascible families 'quarelled', 'waged war', 'fought', took 'revenge', apparently unaware that they were invoking an institution central to Germanic jurisprudence.[24] Go back three centuries; the evidence evaporates. The runes are silent. Attempts to read feud into the Rök inscription (see also pp. 236–7) founder on problems of translation. Sparlösa, pobably carved in the ninth century, tells of fighting and killing within a family, between rival kings,[25] but there can be no feud within a family, according to Germanist rules. Poets tell of hatred and enmity between peoples, rulers and heroes, not of contemporary families at war with each other, or the payment of compensation for injury under the threat of action by kinsmen. The deficit is usually made up by extrapolation from mythological feuds in the Eddas, by saga versions of Norwegian history, and from one narrative of a quarrel between families which disturbed Northumbria, on and off, over a period of sixty years in the eleventh century.[26] The gradations of kin responsibility for and entitlement to compensation payments, reaching to collaterals over four generations in the Icelandic *Baugatal*; the ethics and rules of engagement in unresolved disputes distilled from Njal's saga and shored up with analogues from Schleswig-

---

24 Lindow 1994a, 59–60, suggested that Icelanders locked their gods in kin-defined disputes because their own quarrels were conducted by temporary alliances (ibid., 64–5). See Boehm 1987 for anthropology and Thorláksson in CONIL 148–50 for saga feuds.
25 See now B, 238–55 for Sparlösa's inscrutability.
26 *De obsessione Dunelmensi*, now the subject of a monograph by Richard Fletcher: *Bloodfeud: murder and revenge in Anglo-Saxon England*, London 2002.

Holstein, Albania, and Merovingian Gaul, are contributions to a general theory of feud not based on the usages of the viking age.

Impressed by the meagreness of the evidence, Sawyer noted that even for medieval Iceland, the solidarity of the kin in pursuit of a quarrel 'has been exaggerated',[27] since quarrelers had a hard time of it enlisting support wherever they could. The viking-age evidence speaks of war within, not between families, like the Danish kings and kinglets, apparently all agnates (see p. 58) who led their nobles in intermittent civil war over the years from 812 to 864, until none was left. The McIver kings of Dublin were at each other's throats again and again from the 890s to the 990s, and to judge from Anscar's *Life* and Adam of Bremen Swedish rulers were no less unquiet inside the kin-stockade; the Orkney earls were wolves to each other. No doubt royal families were unrepresentative in this respect. No doubt other families had less wealth to fight over, more need to cling together to save what they had; but feud in the sense of rallying kinsmen to right or inflict wrongs ('performative kinship' in sociological jargon) was only one of several strategies in the more populous Baltic areas. To co-opt the local assembly, to get help from a chief, or cult-leader, or neighbouring family would do the job. Economics and geography and circumstances will have been the deciding factors in the pursuit of family quarrels, not a set of regulations recorded centuries later.

Enough has been said of natural families to show that the more successful ones were those able to transmit property and defeat competitors, as elsewhere. The less successful are invisible. In chapter 1, it was suggested that there were alternative, or supplementary groups like families; of which the most important were military households.

Military Households

It is no secret that when the Dane Alli died, about 900, his inscription (Glavendrup, DR 209) was the work of that Soti who called him HIS LORD (*trutin sin*); even if Alli's exact status as

SAULUAKUTHA   VIALITHSHAITHUIAR   THANTHIAKN

remains in dispute. *Kutha* may mean that he was a *goði* or cult-convenor and chief; one reading of the rest is that he had honour as *thegn* or leader of a military force. If that is how a great man was represented on Funen at the end of the ninth century, subsequent rune-stones in Götaland, Mälardal and the other parts of Denmark

---

27 'The bloodfeud in Fact and Fiction', TROG (1987), 27–38.

suggest an eclipse of *goðar* and a multiplication of *thegnar* over the next 120 years. The later inscriptions also display the companionship and mutual responsibility of the sort of men who would have served Ali, men described as *hemthigi, svenn, brothir, felaga* and *drengr,* whose relationship to their lords varied from clientage maintained at a distance, to living in the same household. There were also *skibara* (shipmates) who followed *styrismenn* (captains) and laid claim to a naval identity:

> BROTHIR ERECTED THIS STONE IN MEMORY OF ESBJORN HIS BROTHER WHO WAS A GOOD SHIPMATE.
>
> (Solberga, Scania, DR 275);

and

> AUSTAIN'S SONS ERECTED THIS STONE IN MEMORY OF SPARL THEIR BROTHER: SHIPMATE OF ASBIORN NAB.
>
> (Tangerup, Lolland DR 218)

are both late tenth century in style. Stones are rare before that; the lack of earlier inscriptions does not mean that the bond of comradeship in arms was a Late Viking Age development. All sources suggest that ninth-century armies were combinations of followings which on occasion could winter in separate *sodalitates* or companies.[28] The word used for the lord's household was *drótt,* whether in war or in peace, and this term included family, servants, clients and fighting men, all under the authority of the *truhtin.* There is no point in tracing this group back to the *comitatus* or war-band of the ancient Germans, which was an *ad hoc* selection of warriors to protect chiefs in war; or to conclude that when a new word appears in the eleventh century, *hirð,* a new institution has been born.[29]

To include a force of co-resident warriors, the *drótt* required a big house. Even the largest houses so far excavated (Borg, Lejre, Uppsala) would not provide living room or sleeping room for more than one hundred warriors, as well as other dependents; the feeding of even thirty *hemthigir* would tax the resources of more than

---

28   ASB 861.

29   Jochens and Harris maintain the Germanist view of *comitatus – drótt* continuity, and Lindow has argued (SS xlvii/3 1975, 323) for the drótt as matrix of skaldic verse and warrior-ethos, an intimate group expanded *c.*1000 into a larger, more open and structured *hird.* See Kristensen 1983 for a sceptical view of the *Germania,* and Hedeager 1992, 229–30 for the contrast between comitatus and *drótt,* already noted by Kuhn. After *c.*1020 poets refer to *inndrótt,* presumably for the inner circle of retainers.

one estate, and demand contributions from a distance. To man and equip three 30-oar longships would therefore mean reinforcing the 'hearth-troop' of the lord with less intimately connected braves, as had been tried among the Anglo-Saxons, at least since the seventh century.

1 Men could be hutted and fed, or at least supplied, outside the big hall but not far off. Along the Norwegian west coast, Knirk has found ring-shaped complexes of huts adjacent to the halls, either store rooms or lodgings or both, in use long before this period. Brink sees Swedish PNN such as Tegnaby as relics of the out-housing of retainers (see maps 2 and 4).

2 Men could be boarded out on compliant or complaisant land-owners, as in ninth-century Mercia, and as later in twelfth-century Norway.[30] There is no trace of this custom; it would be archaeologically invisible.

3 The household could move from hall to hall, consuming supplies and bringing the nucleus of armed retainers into regular contact with other dependents: the usual *iter* of western rulers, all the more necessary in the North, given the sparsity of resources and ease of sea transport in summer. *Veizla* was the name given to such a system in later west-norse sources, and the fixing of con-venient stages in Jutland, Viken, and Sweden may be revealed by *Hus(a)by* PNN. Rune-stones of the tenth century which com-memorate *Ármenn, Brytir, Landmenn*, (various kinds of steward) show the prestige of those who organized the entertainment of followers.

One poem seems to shed light on the early tenth-century Norwe-gian military household: the *Haraldskvæði* of Thorbjorn Hornklofi, a dialogue between two ravens about the court of the Rogaland king Haraldr, a contemporary and possibly ally of king Athelstan (924–39). The unconventional form and metre set these verses apart from the later skaldic poems, although their aim is also to praise the ruler and deride his foes. This could be a contemporary witness, or a historical reconstruction made to please one of the kings who later claimed descent from Harald, or a bit of both.[31] The strophes describing the king's court are the doubtful ones, as they depict

30 In *The King's Mirror* (c.1250) the *gestir* are half-pay royal henchmen sent out to visit 'the houses of many, although not always with friendly intent' (trans. Larson, 170).

31 Von See 1981 (311–17) accepted the first 12 strophes only as contemporary: see Fidjestøl in MESCA, 668–9 and NOHED 1991.

warriors, poets and entertainers in ideal terms, although in the present tense: as if from a distance, but in complicity. The warriors are both 'wolf-skins' and 'bear skins' (see p. 31); 'blood-drinkers' and shield-hewers, dressed in red furs with light-coloured stripes, silver-mounted swords with golden hilts, mail shirts, engraved helms and golden arm-rings, thanks to Harald's liberality. The ideal was domestic intimacy combined with rampant militarism and ostentatious wealth, and it was probably realized more fully in the Anglo-Saxon and Frankish households, even if the bloodthirstiness of christian retainers is somewhat emulsified in the western sources. Whether the last eleven strophes of *Haraldskvæði* are genuine or not, they represent a way of life common to knights, drengs, and samurai; there was no clear-cut distinction between cultures at this level. The Flemish monk who wrote *Encomium Emmæ* for Canute's widow *c*.1041 told his readers that Sweyn Forkbeard's retainers had been so loyal to him that 'not one of them would have recoiled from danger for fear of death, but out of loyalty and unafraid would have gone alone against innumerable enemies, even with bare hands against armed men, if only the royal signal should have been given to them as they went'.

The monk expects his audience to be favourably impressed, not dismayed by the barbaric bravado. Just as any father in Western Europe would have felt for the Swede who commemorated his son Bjorn on the Aspö stone:

[he] WAS KILLED ON GOTLAND. HE DIED BECAUSE FOL-LOWERS FLED, WOULD NOT WITHSTAND; GOD HELP HIS SOUL.[32]

Other poets attest the family feelings which prevailed inside the well-conducted *drótt* – *hirð* – retinue, sometimes even when the material rewards were meagre. Sigvatr, St Olave's poet, remembered his days in that king's service (1020s) sentimentally:

Man who loses woman's embrace longs for death
Love is bought too dear if we weep for the lost one.
But flight-hating king's man who has lost his lord
Sheds tears for his slaying, worse loss for us.

Sigvatr loved the 'gold', but he loved the cameraderie as well:

---

32 SR Sö 1974: Ruprecht, 92. The *Encomium* passage (trans. Campbell 1949) is cited by Frank in PAP 1991, 100, who argues for common ground between Norse and other Western cultures in the ideal of self-sacrifice.

I turn away from the king's men, from the games of the retainers
For I feel sick at heart and grow pale at what I see.
Then I remember how my far-famed lord
Often played with his men in their own hereditary fields.

Games and bonhomie bred solidarity, and emboldened some men, like Sigvat, to speak out, and give advice, as well as to die in battle. The nearer the lord, the intenser the love; never better expressed than in the story told after the Norman Conquest of how the ealdorman Byrhtnoth, on his way to the battle of Maldon, had refused the grudging hospitality of the abbot of Ramsey, offered to him but not to his followers.

I do not wish to dine on my own without these fellows, because I do not know how to fight on my own without them.[33]

Even a great independent chief, like earl Thorfinn of Orkney, was complimented (by Arnorr) as 'seat-companion of prince' (*thengil sessi*), and Sigvatr courted a lesser one, Ívarr the White, by reminding him

Ívarr, you were not seated very far from the glorious (king Olave)
When I brought words to our lord

(Mks, ch. 42)

So the glamour of comradeship with kings could be reflected afar. Olaf Tryggvason had been described by Hallfrǫdr *c*.1000, as

seat-companion to the whole people

despite the brutality and partisanship of his rule.
    Much of this was rose-tinted, or wishful thinking, because retinues could certainly be detached from their lords. This had happened to king Harald Bluetooth among the Danes *c*.986, when the men rallied to his son (the details are lost), to Hákon Jarl of Norway in 995, when he was left defenceless against Olaf Tryggvason, and to St Olave, when Canute bribed his men to desert (*c*.1027–8):

It honours not the body-guard that such should be heard of them
It were better for us that all were innocent of betrayal

---

33 *Liber Eliensis*, ii, 62. Jesch (2001, 299-30) dectects late eleventh century shift in the meaning of *drengr* from 'intimate of the leader' to 'henchman'.

was Sigvat's comment; but his lord had to flee Norway with a diminished household. One of the greatest praise-poems is by Bersi, to his ousted lord Sweyn the Jarl, defeated by St Olave c.1016; Bersi had been captured and chained after the battle, when he is supposed to have told the new king:

> *I humble myself, but not so low as to betray*
> *My loyal friends*
> *When I was young, I found your enemy*
> *To be among my friends.*

By this date, the ambitious chiefs were constructing larger and more contractual households (see below chapter 7) of paid warriors; but they could never dare relinquish the personal closeness of lord and men any more than could English or Frankish leaders of the same period.

The crew and the military household were like families serving the hall and the ship, even if they were paid. Could they not also have been age-sets, men and boys banded together to learn and train outside family structures, as among the Irish and early Germans?[34] In that case, their primary identity would be as initiates in some sort of extra-liminal lad-gang, or secret warrior society, or blood brotherhood, and their solidarity would have been reinforced by cult and ritual. They would become raving mask-dancers, in public communion with another world; they could indeed rush into battle naked or bear-furred, as legions of the damned, Jomsvikings jesting with fate, Odin's Own. These fantasies have sucked blood from anthropology and still walk upright, independent of evidence. Whatever may have been the system in the Migration Age or the Early Iron Age, there is no sign in this period that youths joined 'a named category of men who progress through the grades together', as among East African herding societies; or cults for men, like those of the Melanesians, with rites appropriate for each age. The name elements *Úlf* and *Bjorn* are not evidence of cult-associations in themselves, as they are far too widely diffused; nor can the interpretation of episodes in the poetic Edda as mythic archetypes of initiation rituals make such rituals any more factual than they were before.[35] As things stand, the Nordic

---

34 See McCone 1986 and 1987, and Breen 1997 for Irish *fénnidi* as autonomous bovver-boys.
35 See Mitchell in AUSA, ii, 117; and Nässtrom ibid. 163–9 for a reading of *Hyndluljóð*, a genealogical quiz, as a warrior's initiation ritual. Hufler, Slawik and Peuckert wrote much on Germanic *Geheimbünde*, more than might be expected of Dark Age secret societies. For archaeology see Price 2002, 369–78.

military household can be classified as a local variation of an institution found everywhere in the Carolingian west and elsewhere, and the vocabulary that goes with it is domestic, not tribal or cultic.

Dynasties

Dynasties were the most successful of the more successful families, in that their members inherited claims or rights to wield power as well as to hold wealth in moveables and farms. Whereas the descendants of Clovis, Charlemagne and Alfred could express this privilege in ethnic or national terms, as kings of the Franks, the West Saxons or English, Nordic rulers were hampered by the lack of equivalent terms (see pp. 121,123), or of mutually exclusive terms (Danes could be almost anyone in the ninth century) or of stable limits to their powers. These were expressed by the poets in a variety of titles, some just expressing leadership (*jǫfurr, stillir, gramr*) but mostly claiming descent from legendary dynasties (Ynglingar, Skjoldungar) and conjuring images of political power in terms of family inheritance to private property, even when large territories are meant. The various places terrorized by the big chiefs of the eleventh century become *ættlǫnd, ættleifð, erfð*, heritable estates. Thus, Thjóðolfr Arnorsson, of Harald Hardrada in the 1050s, at the end of *Sexstefjar*:

> May the high one, Ruler of retinues
> Cheerfully leave his inheritance and family estate
> To his sons: that is my wish.

What Harald had inherited from his father was a share in the estate of a small kingdom in the hills of Hringaríki. What Thjóðolfr meant by *arf ok odaltorfu* was the whole of Norway, which he had acquired from his half-brother Magnus and from the Danish king by buying one share with Byzantine gold, and winning the other by hard fighting.

Royal families of inherently kingly males and queenly females were found in these parts at least from the eighth century, when the kings of the Danes known to the Franks as hostages, allies and enemies all appear to be related, and to use characteristic names: three Sigifriths, two or three Guthfriths, three Haralds, two Halfdans, two Horiks, two Hemmings and two Angantyrs. Some of these names recur among the leaders of armies terrorizing the West: a Halfdan was king of Northumbria 876–77, and his successors include a Guthfrith (*c.*880–*c.*895) and a Sigeferth (*c.*895–7). There was a Guthfrith holding a stretch of Dutch coast for the emperor in 882, who was given a Carolingian princess as the price of his loyalty, and a Sigfrith who roamed the Rhineland until 891. These may have been scions of the one dynasty searching for inheritances abroad, while their cousins sat on the homelands; or, like the southern Norwegian kings with similar names, clients showing allegiance by calling their sons Harald, Halfdan, Sigfrǫdr and Eric. After *c*.900 new names appear: a Hardicanute rules at York, a Chnub in Jutland, then a Gorm, Olaf (Amlaibh), Ivarr (Imhar) and Sigtrygg (Sitriuc)[36] at Dublin, rulers of uncertain antecedents and, apart from Chnub, a bright future. From the 990s to 1034 all were brought into some sort of client or tributary relationship with Gorm's descendants, Sweyn Forkbeard and Canute. Only in 1042 was this male line broken, during a big Danish wedding at Lambeth, when king Hardicanute 'at his drink stood, and suddenly fell to the ground with a dreadful start, and those who were near caught hold of him, and he spoke not a word after that'.

Less fortunate families could intermarry, outside the christian ruling houses, and enhance their dynastic status by other means. In the ninth century, those who ruled in southern Norway called themselves kings, apparently in imitation of Danish overlords, and the habit spread over the mountains to the SW coast. By *c*.930 Harald of Rogaland called himself a king, and his sons and grandsons continued the practice down to the 970s; but meanwhile a similar hegemony over north Norway was established by the Hladir earls without benefit of kingship, and earl Hákon drove out or subjugated all the kings. He and his sons bid for dynastic status, and overlordship, through a various strategies:

1 by alliance with the Danish kings, to detach them from their links with Norwegian rulers in the south;
2 by employing several poets to advertise their claims to supremacy,
3 their encouragement of non-christian cults beyond Trondheim fjord, and
4 their symbolic marriage to all Norway; and if there is anything in the later stories of the sagas,
5 by Hakon's claiming sexual privileges over the wives and daughters of his subjects.[37]

36 See Appendix A for the repetition of these names at Dublin, and the 'aspirational' naming of the Orkney dynasty.
37 '... the report went far and wide that the jarl had the daughters of mighty men taken and brought home to him; he lay with them a week or two and then sent them home' according to the Hsk. Olaf Tryggvason saga, ch. 45 (trans. A.H. Smith); a

This could be described as a nativist approach to the task of dynastic enhancement. It won Hakon some thirty years of rule in Norway, with or without Danish help, and another sixteen for his Christian sons (1000–16), with the Northumbrian earldom after that; the last earl was accidentally drowned in the Pentland Firth en route to reclaim Norway in 1029. The shift in authority was typical; as with Dublin kings moving to York and elsewhere from the 890s to the 950s, as with the Orkney earls sailing up and down from Dublin to Shetland in pursuit of lordship and loyalty, as with the Danish kings all over the North. These dynasties began as families, but developed into large cousinhoods of military competitors, like the Danish kings of the ninth century, unable to secure in practice the transmission of power through one lineage except when relocated in western territories, and anchored to the durable institutions of the Franks (in Normandy) and the Anglo-Saxons. At the end of this period, the only Scandinavian ruler who could claim to represent a family royal for more than two generations was Emund of Sweden, the last of his line. Sweyn of Denmark was an earl's son; Harald Hardrada an up-country kinglet's.

Status

Status was transmitted through families, here as elsewhere. Slavery and freedom, certainly, but whether nobility as well is disputed. Among the Franks and Anglo-Saxons there was a hereditary status connected with but separable from wealth and property and public office, from which the medieval idea of nobility descends. Among Danes and Swedes commemorated on rune-stones ($c.950$–1050) the commonest honorific was simply 'good', and this could be applied both to the rich *búandi* or *thegn* (landowners) and to the brave *dreng*, or group-member, like Assur Saksi (on Aarhus 6) and Karl (on Hobro 2, DR 127). Sawyer has suggested that in Dk & S. Sweden it meant 'approved of by the king', but this is stretching, or rather contracting the meaning of a word normally used to show collective approval (as in Magnus the Good) or excellence of its kind (a good year, friend, dog). Something like 'respectable' would be a safer translation, if vague, and closer to the normal West European analogues: *vir bonus, nobilis*, if not *magnificus* or

baseless slander, no doubt, but polygyny and sexual hospitality were customary in thirteenth-century Iceland and twelfth-century Norway. According to one Frankish commentator, pre-Norse ninth-century Hebridean kings had no women other than their subjects' wives, in rotation (Chadwick 1955, PE ii 190–91).

generosus.[38] It was written of Gunulf Narfison on the Tryggevælde stone in Zealand that FEW ARE THAN HIM NOW BORN BET-TER, as if good birth were a real and valued asset *c.*900 and presumably earlier, whatever other ways of gaining status existed. But whether this meant birth into a family with property and wealth, or birth into a family with hereditary status is not clear. The tendency noted above (p. 12) to take non-heritable surnames commemorating a father or mother, rather than an ancestry, suggests the former; the archaeology is ambiguous.

The status wished on the dead by their families appears in the quality of graves and grave-goods, and the taller male skeletons are found in the best, as if genetic inheritance and better diet in childhood meant high status at death.[39] But richly-buried women were more often below average height. There was a gap between the very and the less grand throughout; between families which left large ship-settings, mounds and tall stones, and sent ostentatious goods with their dead, as at Mammen in Jutland *c.*970, and the ones content with cemetery graves or plain low tumuli; between women buried with single large brooches to hold their mantles of high rank at the throat, and women with two tortoise-backed shoulder-clips to fasten the straps of their rich, but less impressive dresses.[40] Such distinctions suggest that the people who were 'born better' let both worlds know it; the sequence of mound burials, presumably ancestral, found near high-ranking halls at the centres of local power showed the importance of lineage for those grandees at least.

Nevertheless, status could be achieved, as well as accepted, in the Nordic world, in order to pass it on to descendants, and the evidence points to three models of social promotion:

1   The Icelandic: in which colonization or migration raised families to an eminence based on the first-come-first-served principle: getting resources early which increased in value later, and building a social system to keep it so (see chapter 9).

2   The Danelaw: also colonial, but the way up was by assimilation – conversion, service, co-operation and reward from local rulers, English or Danish, with a foothold in the church hierarchy, as with the family of archbishop Oda of Canterbury from the 930s

38   B. Sawyer 2000, 107–11; and see now Herschend 1998. Ruprecht 1958, 113–24 reconstructed connections between several Swedish families over the 970–1050 period from rune-stones: a sort of squirearchy.

39   See Sellevold 1984: the usual formula then was 10 per cent environment, 90 per cent genes. The alternative deduction, that the genetic winners rose to the top in their own life-times, would imply social chaos.

40   Lønberg 1999.

to the 1030s. The Danes who submitted to Edward the Elder from 915 to 918 kept their land and rank, and begot lines of east-country thegns whose prosperity may account for the borrowing of that word by Scandinavian worthies before *c.*1000 (See Appendix D) One hundred and twenty years after the Dane Guthrum took the kingdom of East Anglia for himself, king Ethelred handed it to the Dane-descended Ulfketil as an office, without the title of ealdormen, which was reserved for the highest nobles. That reservation ended with Canute's conquest and distribution of spoils, the dinner-bell for ambitious warriors; by 1024 he ruled England with six Nordic earls.

3   The Mälardal: where loot from overseas and the profits of trade appear to lie behind at least some of the rune-stone families in the eleventh century. Call it the viking model, and it may apply to much of southern Norway in the eighth–ninth centuries, and to insular Denmark in the ninth–tenth centuries, as well as to Swedes; but in Jutland and eventually eastern Denmark this route was obstructed by the rival attractions of royal service. In Dublin, Man, the Western Isles and the Orkney earldom the viking way endured to the end of this period and beyond.

The question of whether royal land-grants created new nobilities, as Randsborg argued in 1980 for Denmark in the tenth century remains open. There is no direct evidence of such distributions, but the Anglo-Saxon system of rewarding attendance at the king's household with both office and estates, large or small, was in view during the tenth and eleventh centuries, and if Nordic kings had acquired large disposable land-reserves no doubt they would have copied it. However, only Canute managed this, in England; until then, tribute for kings and treasure for their men seems to have been the rule within Scandinavia, where there was no obvious royal right to authorize inheritances such as was offered by bookland (held by charter for a term, under conditions) in England. Objects of great virtue found in graves throughout this period, but mostly before 1000, may well represent status conferred by rulers: the plain, plaited, or twisted gold arm and neck rings, as at Høn, Tissø and Vester Vedsted, and other places in east and west Agder in Norway have been seen as badges of honour or noble vassalage in the ninth century; the very fine brooches of the Hiddensee type may be connected with the regime of Harald Bluetooth in Denmark from the 960s to 986.[41] Later come the packets of English silver, and the finds

---

41   The Hiddensee hoard could equally well have been hidden by Slavs (Ranians) as by Danes (see Filipowiak in SADO, 337–42), but the brooches meant the same.

of single pennies, and the references to geld on the memorials, which also point in part to the opportunities offered by royal service; and yet the most eloquent of the rune-stones, Yttergärde, shows clearly that two of the three gelds shared by Ulf were extorted by Tostig and Thorkell, neither of them kings. Ethelred's big geld of 994 went to three adventurers, of whom only one became a king.

Even at the end of the period, there were many ways of acquiring status other than by assisting the royal predators, as is shown by the inscriptions, graves, and new churches of the many parts of Scandinavia outside the effective reach of kings: Gotland, Småland, Bleking, Bornholm, Halland, Sweden north of the great lakes and Mälardal, Jämtland and Finland. Gotland's archaeology may hold the clue to how families throve elsewhere. The extraordinary number of ninth- and tenth-century hoards, buried inconspicuously three or four to a farm, were taken by Thunmark-Nylén to be the lost property of younger sons, killed overseas while trying to win silver for themselves, rather than for the family; so that the family benefited from having fewer mouths to feed,[42] or claimants for shares of land. This explanation of hoarding is not accepted by those who see the deposits as offerings, and remains one among many conjectures.

Graham-Campbell 'Rings and Things', VS, viii (1999), 53–64, and Trotzig 1991 for status-symbols in Birka and Gotland grave-goods. Moesgaard discusses single penny finds in VS, viii (1999), 22–3, as signs of lordly largesse. The distribution of similar brooches within ninth-century Jutland may also reflect the largesse of kings.

42 Thunmark-Nylen 1995 is the largest catalogue of grave-finds and hoards; the argument mentioned here is in Hårdh 'The function of silver', *Coins and Archaeology* (BAR Int. Ser. dlvi 1989) ed. H. Clarke and E. Schia, 43–51. See now Staecker 1997b, 94–101 for a telling criticism.

3

Communities and Associations

Settlements of men blazed
O prince, for you when young;
Often made householders
Sound furious war-alarm.

(Half-strophe (4) of Óttarr's *Knútsdrápa* in praise of king Canute, *c*.1030;
SkjD IB 273 version, rather than Kock i 140 and NN 734, who got 'hostility
towards houses' out of line 3)

Associations larger than households or similar groups, and smaller
than districts, could go by various names of which the commonest,
detectible in modern place names were *by/bœr, tuna, staðr, thorp*, –
each with a meaning which varied with geography.

This was also the period which began with a new sort of community
at Ribe, Hedeby and Birka, corresponding to what modern historians
call the *emporium, wic* or trading-town or *portus* on North Sea and
Channel coasts; it ends with Adam of Bremen's description of several
Baltic places as *urbes* and *civitates* as if their role as bishoprics or kings'
residences or densely settled sites qualified them for Roman names.
This comparatively sudden and irreversible development from market-
place to town was paralleled in the colonies formed in the British Isles,
but not in Iceland or Greenland, and connected in various ways with a
multiplication of rural communities in most of southern Scandinavia.
Since the 1960s, economic historians have been fascinated by these
changes, and have followed Hodges and Whitehouse in ascribing them
to new forms of economic life in Northern and Western Europe which
brought producers and traders into one system of markets from Samar-
kand and Constantinople to Dublin and Greenland.[1] This glorious

---

1 A much modified version of this theory is in the 'Concluding comments' by Peter
Sawyer to *hikuin* xxv, 1998 (on 'Town Archaeology in the Scandinavian and Baltic
Countries') and for Denmark see Näsman 2000.

sweep, and by implication, shaping of the local by the intercontinental community, will not be found here. Instead, six of the usual early medieval community-forming forces will be considered in turn, in their Nordic dress: (1) Settlement patterns (2) defence (3) economic co-operation (4) lordship (5) cult (6) aggression (7) confraternity.

Settlement

Settlement means both the deliberate act of colonization, and whatever way the land is lived in at a given moment, whether the houses are clumped together or, as in thinly pastured uplands, sparse but linked by social bonds. Most Nordic populations lived and live within one day's walk of the sea; nearly half, on islands (of which Norway alone claims 40,000), and many more than half in the western colonies. Rowing and sailing brought farms into neighbourhoods, even if not into villages, and what later became the parishes of these regions originate as associations of farms carrying out the functions of villages, in maintaining churches and paying priests. Whether these had a pre-christian past in some, if not all cases is doubtful. In twelfth-century Iceland there were *hreppar* or associations of 10–47 farms which co-operated in the care and feeding of the poor, and in insurance against loss of stock. They were administered in tri-annual meetings of elected leaders, and it is sometimes assumed that they go back to pre-conversion times: unwarrantably.[2] Scattered populations benefited from some co-operation, whether in Iceland or the interior forests of Scandinavia; where the ground supported more people, viking-age communities inherited a social past going back a thousand or two thousand years. Small units of interdependence – 'resource areas' of some $1\frac{2}{3}$ miles or 3 km in diameter – have been plotted by archaeologists from Bronze and Early Iron Age times as the habitats of shifting settlements; Reisborg (1988) finds 18 that cover the islands of lake Mälar, in a suspiciously schematic way. But there is no doubt that where and how the Nordic farmers lived *c*.800 was mostly decided ages before, and over a long course of adaptation to a sometimes hostile land and sea-scape.

In post-viking times, Scandinavia, like England, falls into two main divisions: village country, and farmstead or hamlet country.

---

2 Miller (1990, 19) and Stein-Wilkeshuis maintain the old view that *hreppar* were independent associations; of pre-Conversion origin, according to Byock 1988, 121–2; contra Cleasby-Vigfusson under *hreppr*, and see Sigurdsson 1999, 69–70 on their use to extend lordship in thirteenth-century politics, and Vésteinsson 2000, 80–4 on their link with tithe *Contra*, Karlson in CONIL 505–06.

Most of Norway, and the Swedish interior, the latter; Denmark and some Swedish coastlands, the former. Earlier, the distinction is not so clear-cut; but in much of Denmark, wherever arable soils were exposed, there had been larger collections of houses, periodically shifted within a resource-area, since Roman times. Vorbasse, in the middle of Jutland, is the best excavated and published of the Danish villages, and its history reaches from the third to the twelfth century, during which it was shifted eight times within half a square mile. During the viking-age shift the houses became halls, the cattle sheds were enlarged to hold up to fifty beasts each, and the largest farm was supported by twelve other buildings within its fence: not exactly the birth of the manorial village detected in the re-grouping of English rural settlement over the period from 850 to 950, but a concentration of larger households with one largest. From centres like this came the dependent settlements called thorps, in Denmark as in England, which would develop from farms or hamlets to more villages.[3] In Mälardal and Götaland there had also been villages since the Migration Age, and their numbers increased from *c.*750, despite the relative poverty of the soil; and in Norway there are traces of highly concentrated collections of farms in some southern districts, which probably date to this period.[4] Villages made economic sense either as units of exploitation by a lord, or as co-operative enterprises to reduce the risks and regulate the friction involved in homesteading; these factors will be discussed below. But even in low-lying Denmark, single or double-farm settlements lay between the villages as evidence either of the eminence or of the marginality of the owners.

In most of Norway the need for uphill pasture in summer and the impossibility of getting it in winter meant that settlement had developed along very different lines over an equally long, or longer period. Having a home farm on the shoreline or the valley-mouth, and a sequence of temporary dwellings far up into the mountains, with a seasonal migration or alternation of stock and hands between them, made community harder work: commuting, rather than staying at

3   Hvass 1979 and 1989 for 'the stable development of a community' at Vorbasse over a millennium, and Hvass 1985 for Hodde; DLU, 394–5 for a more recently found VA village at Sysvig (S. Jutland) of sixteen long-houses and twenty-seven sunken houses. Archaeologists find stable development where they have no idea at all of what actually happened to cause a shift of site.
4   Lillehammer maps the Norwegian clusters (Karmøy) in SAL 1999, 131–48. Runestone distribution implies that there were also villages within Mälardal, perhaps 50 by 1000, many more later; see p. 198 for the development, and Kaldal Mikkelsen 1998 on Danish single-farm settlements.

home was the norm (see pp. 199–200). There were distances of up to 30 miles between farms by *c*.800; but farmers were not land-lubbers, and the traditional measure of distance was by sea-leagues (*vika sjóvar* in the Middle Ages, or 8–9 English land-miles). Most settlements had their boathouse (*naust*) and landing-place of slabs (*stoð*), as well as their shieling (*setr*) far away in the hills: a two-way tug which contemporary Kentish communities would also have felt. Their long complexes of rights reach from the fishing hurdles in the middle of the Thames estuary to the grazing on the crest of the Downs and the swine-pasture of the Weald; but they had Roman roads and abundance all round them. The Norwegian Norse had mountain tracks and boats and herds as their inheritance from the past, and their resource-areas had to cover vast tracts in regions where the man-day was annihilated by winter darkness (see chapter 8).[5] The same sort of constraints shaped communities in the forested interior of the whole Fenno-Scandian peninsula, where the tug was between lake and river, as routes and fisheries, and the hunting–herding uplands round them: community meant connecting them in some way that enabled individual households to survive or prosper.

When it came to founding new settlements across the North Sea or the Baltic, the Scandinavian experience which had produced villages and dispersed settlement was of limited value both in long-settled areas where alternative models of community were well-established, and on virgin soil, where the natural constraints were different. They could bring basic skills and language with them, but they had to adapt: the subject of chapter 9.

Defence

Defence against man and beast is built into the name of the many *tunar* of Mälardal Sweden: it meant 'enclosed, fenced, or stockaded space', as with the Anglo-Saxon Kingstons, Nortons and Hamptons. To separate the house-plots (garths) from the fields, stakes were pounded in at common cost and maintained by the householders; as over most of Europe north of the Alps. The village fence at Vorbasse has been dated 720–34, and others were found at Nørre Snede, Mørup and Hodde, of the same type. Walls of peat or stone ring the infields of the dispersed hamlets of Öland and Gotland in the east Baltic, and Götaland is netted with ancient stane-dykes. These were not serious obstacles to armed assault, but property-markers and aids to husbandry in deterring deer,

5 See now Reidar Bertelsen 'Settlement on the Divide between Land and Ocean' in SAL, 261–7.

bear, boar, and wild cattle: unlike the ring-defences of villages along the German–Slav frontier, or English burhs. Nordic settlement plans do not suggest violent societies in most of Scandinavia; the danger of attack from outside was met by the many refuge forts near the coasts, and by the lookout places, or *varther*, which Ringtved has plotted in NE Jutland.[6] To maintain and appropriate such places would certainly have meant collaboration between homesteads, as between villages, but over areas more like districts than communities. True military collectives will be considered later, under *Aggression*; the defences of most communities suggest local consensus about landownership, common or private. How those field-walls could develop has been shown in Mälardal-Sweden, where from the fifth century, scrub was cleared and burnt in rows at the edge of the clearing, and then covered by stones.[7] Farm stockades, fences within villages, fences round villages, field boundaries, tillage-pasture divisions, pasture-wilderness markers have all been found in connection with pre-Conversion settlements; the regulations and responsibilities which served them all date from long after. As for the ideas which inspired them, the imaginative landscape-archaeology in our own time (as p. 322), makes the curving stone walls of Götaland and Iceland fuse with the snake-scroll on Swedish rune-stones and the dragons of mythology to represent a defensive principle round the female, the treasure, the home, the dead and the world.[8] So runs one reading of the walls, but many anthropologically-minded students now look on these limits as essentially religious: separating the living from the dead, the male sphere from the female, the normal from the abnormal. The case of Iceland, where twelfth-century law prescribed turf banks 5' 5' 3 and where some are four miles long, suggests that keeping stock off the pasture of other christians could also be an inspiration; and the great stress on the beating of village bounds (*rå* and *rör*) in fourteenth-century Swedish laws, and on the sanctity of *innangarð* (property inside the inner fence) can be connected with the introduction of tithe as a parish tax not long before, rather than with primal Norse cosmology.[9] 'Keep out' signs were probably backed by a host of unseen inhibitors in this period,

6   Ringtved in SAL 1999, 364–77.
7   Lindgren Hertz discussed Ögld. farms in VIPA, 46–53.
8   Johansen 1996, 93–100 for the transformative dragon; Andersson and Hållands 1997, 582–7 for Swedish bounds, with Roeck-Hansen 1991, 104–6 and Hedwall 1997, 609–12 on Åland and Östergötland.
9   See Lindow 1997b, 17, 29–30 on the mythical dimension, and Foote 1987, 60 on the Iceland turf-banks. Zachrisson discussed 'The Odal and its Manifestation in the Landscape' in CSA, ii, 1994, and Staecker 1997, 96–7 acknowledges the mystical element in settlement-geography, and Andren writes of 'Landscape and Settlement as Utopian Space' in SAL, 383–94.

since the visible defences were so meagre: even the new market settlements were not given proper ramparts until the later tenth century, and the first, Ribe, was merely marked off by a ditch 10′ wide and 5′ deep.

In Iceland there were land-keepers (*landvaettir*), spirits which had lived there before men, and continued to occupy wasteland and share the farms with the owners. An apparently tenth-century law (Úlfljót's, copied into Hauksbók (chapter 268) in the fourteenth century) made crews remove their ships' figureheads before landing 'and not sail towards land with gaping heads or yawning snouts, lest the *landvættir* be frightened of them' and presumably harm others on the island. Dead ancestors could usually be trusted to protect family holdings, from inside the fence, where they were buried; communities needed less private spooks, *disir* and small gods or large, who will be mentioned below (pp. 259–68).[10]

Economic Co-operation

Economic co-operation forms communities most obviously in 'areas with a low primary production per unit of area where only a very restricted number of cultivated plants can ripen' and the shortfall has to be met by concerted hunting, fowling, fishing and gathering by many homesteads. So it was in most of the Scandinavian interior and the whole subarctic region across to Greenland; sealing, whaling, trapping, inlet-netting used more hands than one farm could support. About the year 1000, at Gramsdalen in Oppland (Norway) they built a reindeer-trapping fence out of some 1700 pine logs, so well that it lasted to *c.*1280: a new scale of enterprise, which must have focussed the labour of about 100 square miles.[11] Where arable and pasture were more available the productive unit was not usually the village in this period, although it might serve production by imposing compatible rhythms of land-use on each farmer; but how it did this in the viking age is not recorded. The later allocations of strips to each inhabitant by the year (*solskifte*) have not been successfully traced to this period, except possibly at Gisstorp and Månstad in Västergötland, and were certainly not brought to Ireland or the English Danelaw by ninth-century settlers.[12] Danish and Swedish villages were to

10   In Iceland, rocks associated with elves are now protected by law, like antiquities, provided the association is traditional; in a recent case, a rock haunted only since 1970 was denied this protection, and moved: R. Traustadóttir in AF 1998, 151–64. Ulfljót's law was shown to be a learned reconstruction by Olaf Olsen in *Hørg, Hov og Kirke* 34 ff.
11   Mikkelsen 1994 and Myhre 1998, 16.
12   Weilgren 1989, 361; and see below, chapter 8.

become highly regulated concerns under the manorial regime of the twelfth and later centuries, but the archaeology of earlier settlements points to the personal lordship of the big farmers over the lesser, rather than to the organization of whole places by landlords.

Trade and marketing are held responsible for the forming of new communities everywhere, but especially here, by those who believe that the market economy is incompatible with the static, rural and hierarchical societies, and creates new 'social cadres' to function properly. This belief is poorly supported by evidence from the viking age, when there were indeed trading communities, trade, and much moving of goods and valuables over short and long distances, but no clear departure from the 'rural sector' as the main source of supply and demand. Contrary to the understanding of many students of the period, there was no lust for Baltic or North Sea goods on any large scale in the mediterranean world, the West or Islam, at least until the twelfth century; the demand was mostly the other way[13] (see map 8, p. 211).

The need to sell or allocate surpluses was met in the first instance and in parts, ultimately, by the seasonal beach-markets and trading places which have been traced all over Scandinavia from the eighth century onwards. One early example was a site in NE Scania, near the Helgeå, which was frequented until *c*.750, then moved to a village on the river, and only at the end of this period to a place which became the medieval borough of Åhus. Meanwhile, in west Jutland foreign traders reached the small village of Dankirke *c*.680–750, and then left its seven or eight households in peace, attracted to a new site of vacant lots at Ribe, nearby. Ribe had begun as a sandy site apart from a nearby village, divided into plots for summer trades; the market became a settled community only after 800. A recently found site at Sebbersund, an inlet on the south shore of Limfjord, N. Jutland, turned out to be genuine trading village of this period, but a very small one until *c*.1000, when it expanded into 150 small and two large households offering fish and made goods for Norwegian iron. It was similar round the Gotland coast; 30–50 small harbours brought producers and customers together without becoming communities of any size or permanence. Öland and Halland and the northerly Swedish coasts were similarily equipped

---

13 Finds of imported silver, gold and bronze of this period exceed finds of Nordic objects outside Scandinavia by at least 50 to one. Slaves would not be traceable, but most seem to have been captured elsewhere. On imported glass and pottery 700–900 see Näsman 2000, 35–48.

with 'dispersed markets' and 'trade annexes' to rural settlements or districts,[14] as was the Scanian coast, every forty miles or so.

These summer, or short-stay occasions were the springboard for commercial activity in the Baltic. They may have been set up by one or more interested landowners or chiefs, or have developed haphazardly on sites already consecrated by the distribution of prestige-goods from overlords to underlings, and have served both purposes. They were small-scale, but so numerous that the volume of business passing through them must always have exceeded that of the larger communities of traders, of which Ribe was the forerunner and Hedeby and Birka were the first true examples.

Hedeby is the Danish version of a name spelt Haithabu on one rune-stone, Hithabu on another, Haddeby in German, and known as *at haethum* to the Anglo-Saxons: it meant 'the heath-settlement', and has a file of chronicle evidence to itself[15] and a dendro-date for its earliest pier, of 726–50. According to the Frankish annalist, Hedeby gained a body of Slav traders moved by king Godofrid *c*.808 inside a frontier zone where the Franks could be checked by recent (*c*.787) extensions to the southern Danish ramparts now called Danevirke. It seems to have grown thanks both to the bad (805–12) and good (813–14, 816–34) relations between Frankish and Danish kings, and about 900 four older adjacent settlements were combined as a fortified manufacturing and trading community on a site of some sixty acres (24 ha) inside a high earth wall over $\frac{1}{2}$ mile long with a harbour and quay. It was big enough to be compared with the older Frankish and Anglo-Saxon emporia or wics, and to attract visitors from the Arctic Circle (Ohthere) England (Wulfstan, if he was not merely the reporter of what others knew), Russia and the Caliphate, as well as the Baltic coasts and Germany. The archaeology of the last fifty years suggests that during the tenth century there was a community of up to 1000 adults (more than 400) living directly or indirectly by trade and manufacture in

14   See Callmer in HØKO, 29–46, and Stig Jensen: 'Dankirke-Ribe', HØKO, 73ff; for summaries of the theories of the excavators at that date, 1991. Christensen and Johansen discussed Sebbersund in Aarbøger 1991, 199–229 and in SHAS (1995), 160–4; and see Lundström 1981 on the manufacturers of the Gotland port of Paviken (excavated 1967–73), and Fallgren 1994 on the twelve artisans working at Övra Wannberga on Öland. Carlsson 1991 is useful on the Gotland harbours, also in EUNO 1999. The theory that towns simply developed from beach-markets (*strand-stedsteorie*) is old, but unconvincing in view of their different functions. Myrvoll 1998 discusses the slow development of a town from a transit-centre in the Telemark; for Ribe, Hedeby and Åhus see Näsman 2000, 54–60.
15   ARF 808 tells how king Godfrey reacted to Charlemagne's interference with his Slav tributaries by moving merchants north to *Sliestorp*. See Müller-Wille in MESCA, 173–5 for a good summary of finds and literature down to 1988.

squalid conditions with a high standard of diet and dress). They were subject to what the Franks called a count (King's agent? local chief?), in the ninth century, and from the 830s there was sometimes a resident bishop or priest to serve the christians; apparently also a mint or two, and a well-founded quay and jetty. Much of Haithabu remains to be excavated, but more digging is unlikely to dispel the impression of intense and crowded productivity and chaffering revealed by Jankuhn from 1930 to 1980. It was a packed gateway of mixed population (Danish, German, Slav) and contested allegiance serving the whole Nordic region until its slow decline after *c*.1000. Something similar could be said of Birca, the emporium of the Swedish coast, situated on an island where Mälardal Swedes, Götar from the south, Frankish, Frisian, and East Baltic visitors found it convenient to do business from the 750s to *c*.1000, and where St Ansgar's mission also found christian residents or transients. This, too is a intensively but not completely excavated site, on which a population of several hundred aliens and Svíar made a living out of buying, selling and exchanging goods, in some kind of loose association with the Swedish kings.[16]

The viking-age development of Ribe, Haithabu and Birca was impressive, because exceptional and unprecedented. It has impressed economic and other historians so much, that even the roving raiders of the western seas have been credited with inherent proclivities towards urbanization and commercialization, and recent excavations at York and Dublin have been undertaken mainly on this assumption, and interpreted accordingly: an example of the hermeneutic circle (see p. 318). Vikings become economic apostles, Keynesian redistributors, city-boys with private vices which benefit the public, and a taste for high-density living which heralds various dawns. On this, a recently-published word from a survivor of the 1890s:

> The opinion that vikings were merchants is a new romantic conception, adapted to modern historians' general view of the role of trade in history.

And a word of sense from our own time, on the Irish experience: 'there never were any *viking* towns in Ireland'[17]

---

16 Who seemed to have owned the main farms on nearby islands. Burial customs suggest that nearly half the Birka people were foreign, but where from is unclear; see Ambrosiani in *Hikuin* xxv (1998), 12–13.

17 Clarke 1998, 335; on early Dublin see Ó Floinn 1998, 162–3 in the same collection, and Hines 1995, 101, on the non-Scandinavian aspects of York. The younger Weibull brother decried mercantile illusions in *Scandia* xl, iii/i. As Helliksen noted, within Scandinavia theories of town origins change with intellectual fashion about once a decade: see *Viking* lvi (1993).

because true vikings traded and raided from temporary encamp-
ments, and the populations which later crowded to, or near such
places was composed mainly of dealers, craftsmen, and merchants
from places nearer than Scandinavia, attracted or coralled by the
authority of the sort of rulers who hanged vikings in rows. There is
no sign that the prosperity of Danelaw towns in tenth- and eleventh-
century England, even York's, was the result of commercial acumen
by Nordic raiders. The actual economic effect of such raids is hard to
assess, as the only well-studied clues are ninth-century coin finds,
probably misleading, but all the signs of boom discovered so far (new
housing, rich deposits) belong to the 940s onward, the age of Wessex
empire.

York was already served by a trading community of Angles before
the Danish conquest, and the expansion of the town followed a
rehousing of manufacturers in a community nearer the walls of the
Roman city, apparently as a result of the entente between the invaders and the restored archbishop after 890. The archaeology of
Jorvik reveals that the basis of the ensuing prosperity was not the
long-distance exotic imports which the Nordic connection sometimes, but rarely, brought; it was a steady circulation of goods and
silver and agricultural products within Yorkshire, and to a lesser
extent, Lincolnshire and the Irish Sea coastlands. From 915 to 950
Dublin was a source of predatory kings, and a refuge for ejected
rulers, rather than a trading-partner; and it was only after 950 that
Dublin developed into a sizeable community, Irish-Norse in population, under the less turbulent rule of Olaf Cuaran and Sihtric Silk-
enbeard.

How far rulers planned and built such communities is not obvious
from the excavations. The Ribe evidence, of a regular or fairly regular
layout of plots on a base of wind-blown sand (as show by Mogens
Bencard in Stumann Hansen 2001) has suggested to its excavaters
planning by a leader, rather than by the traders themselves, who were
transients, or by local landowners; they would have been unwise to
invest so much labour in what proved rather a slow development. At
Hedeby, we know that king Guthfrith brought in the traders; at Birca
the Swedish king was an interested but not controlling power. It has
been suggested that such places were originally Frisian or even Frankish colonies; but within Scandinavia, the determination to ascribe
Ribe to state action, and make it a medieval town in embryo has
been relentless. English scholars have so far hesitated to attribute the
founding of Hamwich to the kings of Wessex or Mercia, because there
is no direct evidence of royal involvement; the excavators of Ribe are
less cautious. So in 1994 Feveile wrote of the few dozen ninth-century
denizens of the *vicus*: 'from what we know of later sources, the town's

laws, privileges, and obligations would have held good inside the ditched area. There the king's representative would guarantee market-peace and the tradesmen would pay tax in return'. Old hands will recognize this picture as the bureaucrat's daydream of Danish history, in which civilization is passed down through the proper channels; but there is no pressing need to apply it to early Ribe, which was unfortified until the troubles at the end of the tenth century, and could have run itself. Market-peace was not a royal invention. As Sawyer pointed out long ago, privileged times and places for markets and fairs have been established by agreement between all concerned at least since the Bronze Age; all kings could do was keep or break the pre-existing taboo on violence as it suited them. The origins both of these sites, and of craft-communities which eventually gravitated towards them long pre-date the viking age, and appear to lie in religious rather than bare economic thought; in suspending normal distrust where the ground and the season have been marked out in a particular way. So it is now suggested[18] that the rectilinear plots of the new *vici*, and of Ribe market were symbolic field-patterns, where farmers agreed to settle craftsmen in the hope of reaping symbolic harvest, in the shape of precious things from abroad; but it is not suggested how this can be verified other than by reference to the ways of other civilizations. It is worth remembering that none of the other *vici* of the late seventh or early eighth century (Dorestad, Quentovic, Ipswich, Hamwich) seem to have resulted from strong kingship, but rather to have benefited by weak control.

Lordship

Lordship (see map 2) nevertheless, has been a force in the forming of communities, and should be considered in a wider context than the urban dawn. It is inscribed over most of the Nordic world as elsewhere, in place-names, in rural archaeology and in writing. Three rune-stones in particular declaim lordship in the eleventh century: Jarlabanki's, in Uppland (U 212):

HE OWNED ALL OF TÄBY;

and Hromund's, up north at Malsta in Hälsingeland, who

GOT POSSESSION OF THREE SETTLEMENTS

18   Hed Jakobsson 1999, 46–9 and Callmer 1992b on the Nordic trading communities limited to serving the needs of small élites (142) see also Nielsen 2002.

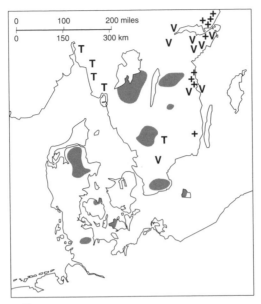

Place-names:

+ denoting *hersir* (lord)
V denoting *vísi* (chief)
T denoting *thegn* (local worthy)

Shaded areas cover the
rune-stones for thegns
and drengs; dotted areas
'cavalry graves'

Map 2   *Big men, c.900–c.1050*

and had five generations of his family included on the stone, in a frontier zone where few other memorials survive; and about 1000, at Skårby in more habitable Scania, some brothers recalled that Tummi OWNED GUSNAVA near Lund (DR 280). They and their like 'owned': but did they settle or make these communities?

The building of large halls before the viking age points to the affirming of local power; the reconstruction of some as 'multi-functional central place complexes' with 'nodal functions', has recently interested landscape archaeologists, especially in Sweden. Thus Gamla Uppsala, an ancient site dedicated to the dwellers in the famous grave-mounds, rather than to a resident community, had its one hall enlarged and rebuilt probably in the eighth century, and the hall, probably the king's, acquires dependent communities with specialized functions which Brink deduces from the place-names,[19] here

19 Brink 1994, 276–9, and 1996, 237–8, and 1997, 405; for Uppsala development Brink 1996, 268–71. The uncertain dating and interpretation of many Swedish PNN make these deductions conjectural; but see Map 4, p. 95.

as elsewhere. So in the parishes of Markim and Orkesta near Stockholm there is a typical spread of farm and settlement names which look to the royal manor, or *Husby*:

at Rinkaby and Karlaby, warriors were maintained or lived;
at Viby and Lundby, there were sacred places for offerings and sanctuary;
at Vivelsta, there was a pre-christian priest, or shrine-keeper

and in similar localities it is possible to deduce settlements named from horses, wheat, barley, assemblies, smiths and messengers, all of which might have served, and so been planted by viking-age lords, whose overbearing status alone is testified by the location of mounds, graves and stones near the halls (see map 4). This is lordship, if not quite on the contemporary Anglo-Saxon model (underpinned by royal or episcopal charter, a large semi-servile or servile peasantry, close links with ecclesiastical communities, and the legal rights of Toll, Team, Sake, Soke, and Infangenetheof); but remove the parchment and the clergy, and these 'good men', 'honourable men', 'men of the place', 'residents' 'householders' and 'thegns' (to select terms used on the 960–1060 rune-stones) were not less privileged than their English counterparts. One who acted as 'land-guardian', or *húskarl*[20] was clearly entitled to take the thief caught inside or outside the hall fence on his lord's account, or his lady's, and to ride armed about his duty. Such powers could be gained in a number of ways, in societies where endorsement by the kings was not all-important; the planting of dependent communities must have been one of them. This could be done

1   by leaving an old settlement with slaves or dependents and starting a farm and building shelters on new ground: some of the many Danish thorps (*strup* names) and Nybølle (new settlements) are examples;
2   by persuading a whole village to move to a better site, and directing the move so that neighbours become clients;
3   by developing existing resources.

How this might have happened in Mälardal was suggested by Sporrong in terms of environmental pressures.[21] The farm gets

20   DR 143 for the Egaa stone to Manni 'Land-warden of Ketil the Northerner'; whether 'land-men' were landowners or stewards is uncertain. But Assur, on Ravnkilde I, was definitely an estate-manager: *lanthirthir*.
21   Sporrong 1984, 200–11; Jørgensen 1987 for Danish PN evidence, and Callmer 1991–92, 203 for clear exposition of eight ways in which settlements might move in Scania.

overcrowded: the land is divided to allow a two-crop rotation, and smaller farms appear on the periphery, organized by the larger one in order to co-ordinate the rotation. Result: the makings of a manor. In Östergötland, by 1000, old farmsteads were claiming shares in what had been walled-off common land, and becoming enlarged *byar*. On Åland, a similar process of duplication and nucleation resulted in one-family households becoming *byar*, now named after their owners: Gunnar, Sibbi, Haraldr, Vigfast.

Any of these three social climbs could have been aided by foreign silver or slaves, at any time, but the transfer is only documented in the Swedish rune-stones which record 'taking geld' from raids on England from *c*.1000 to *c*.1016, or going to places on the eastern run to Constantinopole and the Balkans, via Ladoga or the Vistula, over a period from *c*.1000 to *c*.1125. From this evidence, Lindqvist deduces a continual transfer of alien wealth into the coffers of Swedish landowners, unable to maintain lordship on the yields of domestic agriculture;[22] but there is no way of quantifying the transfer. There are hundreds of English pennies found over Scandinavia and Finland and brought there from the 980s to the 1040s, and a wealth of Islamic dirhems before that, but how the silver was used is not deducible merely from evidence of wear and tear and peck-mark testing; that can show that a penny was current coin at one period of its existence, but not whether it made a lord out of a small land-owner. The case for social mobility within Scandinavia is bound to be patchy, but the coins don't help much, and the other archaeological evidence consists of precious exotic goods (Irish croziers, chalices, book-clasps, Frankish swords and ivories etc.) usually found near traditional seats of power, not in new settlements. New towns seem to have offered more visible opportunities to the producer, since in Jutland at least there is a notable shift in viking age settlements to the hinterlands of Aarhus, Hedeby and Ribe (see chapter 4, p. 92), and the demand for food and timber inside these places would be met by the villages, at least from *c*.900. Recent excavation at Winning, on the north shore of the Schlei, reveals a well-found tenth–eleventh century community of sunken huts, apparently serving as a link between the producers of Angeln district and the Hedeby consumers. Other Danish excavations reveal fairly sudden and uniform changes in the layout and land-allocation of villages,

---

22   Thomas Lindkvist 1988, 40–50, and see the extraordinary 'Runic-Varangian Who's Who' in Pritsak 1981, 587–640, which must include among 1,266 names at least some who transferred wealth from the East to the homeland. On Åland, see Roeck Hansen 1991, 101–3.

of which more in chapter 8; lordship was the most likely spur, if not the only one, but the pressures and inducements that were applied to ordinary farmers to get them to co-operate remain hidden. Emancipating them from slavery; controlling their supply of metal; lending them stock and seed after bad winters; acquiring by longevity hereditary status as law-finder or cult-leader: many possibilities, no facts.

Cult

Cult means ritual, celebration, games and shows, which bring communities together now, and were more intensely centripetal then, when they seemed to avert lethal misfortune, throughout the pagan and christian worlds. The traces of this in viking-age Scandinavia are the high mounds, long stone ship-settings, assembly places, and recognizable charms, amulets, and talismans among ornaments, as well as in place-names. All of which are more readily connected with individuals, families, and districts or territories than with village or hamlet communities; this level of cult has to be reconstructed out of sometimes late and ambiguous evidence: or from unambiguous signs of human and animal sacrifice

There were evidently local get-togethers among dispersled settlements which pre-figure the later parish feasts or *samburðaröl* of the Norwegian provincial laws. All over Norway they find cooking pits from two to six feet in diameter which are dated from the Bronze Age to *c.*1000; too large, mostly for single families, or too distant from houses, and so seen as sites for cult feasts. On Gotland, such occasions seem to have survived the conversion intact: the thirteenth-century Guta Laga has a word for those who seethed meat together, *suthnautor*, and the cooking pits found in Denmark and Germany are called *Kultfeuerstellen* by those who judge them to have been more than social cook-outs. *Seyðir* was the Norse term, which leaves the *Kult* to the imagination.[23] Similarily the games and games-meadows or playgrounds which leave traces in the place names of all Northern peoples (Leikvin, Leikvangr, Leikvöllr, in Norway, Levna Meadows in Shetland, Plaistow and Latchingdon in Essex etc.) are too widely

---

23   Or piety of those searching for the roots of the sacramental tone of festal eating found to this day in parts of Scandinavia; glorified in Bergman's *Fanny and Alexander*. On *seydir* archaeology see Narmo 1996, and on the possibility that some of these pits were for cooking human remains Oestigaard 2000, 53. The 'court-house' site at Bjarkøy (N. Norway) was ringed by thirty-two such pits; see plan in ISCEVA, 21.

diffused to be connected with any specific cult or size of community or social purpose.

In medieval Iceland they used to eat their ponies, and pit them against each other in public gatherings; in Denmark they seem in the viking age to have preferred other meats and to have raced their horses rather than watch them fight. Either pastime would bring people together, and might please Frey, if like Neptune he was concerned with horses, as Snorri later thought. But horses and gods go together, and horse-sacrifice was ubiquitous. Men competed with men in the many trials of strength fit for fighters: tugs of war ('rope-drawing'), wrestling (freestyle or catch-as-catch-can) jumping over fire, hockey (*knattleikr*), single-stick, swimming, oar-walking, and throwing clods (*torfleikr*). When tired of that, they could engage in competitive derision, versification and singing ('like dogs howling' at Hedeby, according to an Islamic observer); and then re-enact myths with masks, music and dancing. However, as a recent study[24] concludes, there is an 'absence of any contemporary account of such activities' as rituals or dramatic performances in the viking age: they have to be extrapolated from relatively modern folklore. The dialogues in some of the Eddic poems (satirical in *Lokasenna*, where Loki reviles the gods; competitive in *Hárbarðsljóð* between Thor and Odin, and comic in *Thrymskviða*, where Thor disguises himself as a woman) are not evidence of drama outside the minds of post-conversion poets and their modern interpreters. Nevertheless, at some point, villages and groups of farms must have joined in watching or doing some things like that, if not those things in that form.

Lindow raised the question of how exactly 'the important markers of group membership' were transmitted through time by 'tradition participants', and the answer for the ancient Norse is virtually inaudible. Where it happened is indicated by place-names and by the archaeology of house and farm sites, and there is a long history to this research. Until the 1960s it was believed that the conduct of rites, feasts and cults among the Norsemen was entrusted by communities to the owners of the older farms and halls which went by the name of *hof*, and kept this as their name or part of it thereafter. It was a view summed up by Magnus Olsen's *Hedenske kultminder i norske stednavne* (Kristiania 1915), which presented this and other 'sacral' place-names as a map of the religious life and organization of

---

24 Gunnell 1995, 15 and see 24–36; and 75–6 for the bit of felt with holes in it found in Hedeby harbour. It could have been a wolf-mask, according to Gunnell and Price 2002, 171–2; others may see a sheep-face. Gunnell argues for Eddic verse as a 'performance genré in CONIL 93–5, with bibliography.

ancient Norway; and demolished by Olaf Olsen's *Hørg, Hov og Kirke* in 1966, and by Laur 1968, at least as far as the automatic association of *hof* names with sacral functions goes. There are alternative derivations: from *hov*, a mound, hillock, howe, or farm, and archaeology has revealed not a single temple in any excavated *hof* after 150 years of effort to justify the sacral significance attached to the name. Olav Olsen 'released us from many misconceptions, misinterpretations, and romantic nonsense', as Wilson puts it, and began a beady-eyed desacralization of the Nordic countryside, which touched the other holy elements *horgr, vi, vangr* and *elgr*, supposed to be where people sacrificed, worshipped and feasted outside the *hof*. Topographers had multiplied such places by ignoring the likelihood that these words often describe natural features rather than cultsites, and by assuming that names with the element *goð*, good, must refer to priests or *goðar*. Nordic place-names are recorded far too late for pre-christian functions to be attached to more than some with confidence. So 'mythosophy' (coined by Jöran Sahlgren in the 1920s for reckless sacral PNN identifications) has been curbed, up to a point.[25]

But there is still theophoria down on the farm, and it is thriving on:

1 The irreducible minimum of PNN with sacred meanings where no other explanation suffices: in Norway, some 500 according to Sandnes (SANA, 16). Of the *vi* or *ve* names there are Odense (Odin's *vi*, or shrine) Viborg (shrine hill), Disvi (shrine of the female spirits, in Ögld), and combinations like Tyrved (*Tora-vi*, shrine of the Törn people, Sw.) or the seven *vi* PNN of Gästrikland coinciding with seven original parishes.

2 Current redefinitions of the sacral, to include work and social life of all kinds with the acts we classify as overtly religious: sacrifice, invocation, blessing and thanksgiving in places set aside for those purposes. Students of religion have been moving in this direction since Fustel de Coulanges re-sacralized the ancient city-state in the 1860s, and the pace has quickened in the wake of Dumèzil and Lévi-Strauss, so that recent work on the meaning of Nordic landscapes (e.g. Shepherd 1999 on Finland, Bradley 2000 on the North in general) finds or extends holiness well beyond places set aside for ceremonial use, into the home, the fields, the islands, the mountains

---

25 Vilmundarson 1992 is a good survey, and see Holmberg's bibliography in VC 12 (1994), 280–7; her 'Views on Cultic PNN in Denmark: a Review of Research' is in ONFRAC (1990), 381–93. The best is 'Mythologizing Landscape' by Stefan Brink in Stausberg 2001, 76–112; with bibliography.

and the wilderness. There was no escape; certainly not by conversion to christianity, a cult which in Scandinavia annexed or ate a hundred others. Thus the *Stavgard* PNN of Gotland refer to ring-fenced houses with no clear sacral function in the words; but half of them belong to places with Iron Age house-foundations and inscribed picture-stones of Migration or viking-age date, and all are singled out in Guta Laga as gathering places for parishes and districts. Swedish *hof* PNN are found between communities, as if they had originally acted as places for gift-exchange, rather than district shrines: but sacred, none the less.[26]

3 The continuing search for cult-place remains by archaeologists alert for votive deposits and vestiges of animal or human sacrifice in farms or workshops formerly treated as purely economic enterprises. There were no such vestiges at the great hall of Lejre, in Zealand, where they might have been expected, and Hofstaðir in Iceland stubbornly refused to live up to its name; but in a late viking age complex at Borg, near Norrköping in Ögld they have found a squarish outbuilding (19   24 , or 6   7 5 m) apart from the main hall, in a paved yard. It had no hearth, and no obvious economic use. It contained two rooms, with a row of flat stones against one wall. Inside it were found two rings; outside, a deposit of animal bones including ten decapitated dogs. The huts nearby were used for metal work. The excavator, A. L. Nielsen is convinced that here at last is a temple, shared by Frey and Freyja, and serving a lord's settlement down to the conversion. If so, the Gautar of Borg would have waited outside while the boss did something in the shed with his wife and the less fortunate family dogs.[27]

To judge by the remains of children and animals in pits and graves, under houses and near churches, all over the North, the place of sacrifice could be anywhere. They found charred child-bones thrown into pits with pigs, cows, goats and dogs on what was to be the site of Trelleborg camp in Zealand. At Repton, the young victims were laid away from the mass burial of adult bones round the dead chief; elsewhere lords and ladies and possibly seeresses were attended by sacrificed companions in their graves. Animals were any farmer's offerings. Human sacrifice could evidently go with high-ranking funerals, and by seasonal gatherings of whole peoples,

---

26 Vikstrand in SANA (1992), 127–30, and see Brink ibid., 107–20 on *ala* names, and Brink 1996, 261–2. For *høghr*-continuity in Östergötland see Selinge 1987.
27 Nielsen 1997, 373–92: the reconstruction is weakened by its debt to saga versions of pagan worship, but not implausible.

with armies giving back some of the prisoners gods had allotted them, even with crews launching a new ship: all very special occasions. The lowest level of *mannblót* could have been that of the village or group of farms fearful of disease or starvation, as folklore relates.

Aggression

Communities have often acted as military units, either spontaneously, as on the Saxon–Slav border in the twelfth century or by orders from above, as on the Hapsburg *militärgrenze* against the Turks in the Balkans; but the slightness of village defences in the viking-age Norse country shows that such communities were not habitual raiders of their immediate neighbours (pp. 67–8). Their aggression was channelled by selective recruitment into the military households classified in chapter 2 as families, and when these combined into the armies which roamed western Europe in the years between 830 and 930 they were mobile communities of sometimes long but limited duration. Their communal life has therefore left little trace on the ground or in the writing of their victims and hosts, who saw them as threats, punishments and transients rather than social experiments.

It is sometimes assumed that the fort-based jurisdictions of the Danes in England, ancestors of the east-Midland shires, and known as armies up to the time of Canute, represented methodical settlements by ninth-century raiders, who had halted, distributed land, and remained ready for service under their commanders, the jarls and holds.[28] In that case, many a By and Thorp may have begun as a warriors' village or hamlet; but this is unlikely. It implies a degree of central organization and control of tenure which is never found in medieval Scandinavia, and could hardly be improvised during the restless years from the 870s to 915 on alien soil. What the Danelaw rulers needed were gangs of full-time *drengs*, ready in the hall, not settler-militias. Something more like military communities may have been formed by those who went east into Estonia and Russia, although the hilltop villages excavated from Staraya Ladoga to Gorodische seem to have been populated *c.*750–900 in the same way as Scandinavian places, without serious defences, with similar proportions of men and women and with no heavy emphasis on

28 An old tradition, given weight and substance by the research of Sir Frank Stenton in the 1920s, virtually unchallenged until the 1950s, and maintained to the end by Cyril Hart.

military accountrements in the graves. That came later, and was concentrated in the larger stockaded towns of Novgorod and Kiev, where chiefs housed retinues and mercenaries to oversee large hinterlands.[29]

The best-known example of the Nordic warrior-community is fictional, the work of a romantic Icelander who wrote *Jomsvíkingasaga* probably in the 1220s. Not long before, the Dane Saxo had told of a viking colony established by king Harald Bluetooth in the tenth century to cow the Baltic Slavs, and he placed it in the town of Wollin on the estuary of the Oder, which a later Danish ruler, Valdemar I, had devastated in the 1170s. It was agreed that the Woliniane had been a powerful force in later viking days, and that both Slav and Nordic sea-raiders had been active along these coasts; the saga merges these not-unhistorical rumours into a society of Danish braves coming together under strict rules in the fort of *Jomsborg* to live as bachelor bandits by the highest standards of heroism, until a quixotic expedition to overthrow Hakon Jarl of Norway proved their nemesis. It is a good story, and some of it was borrowed by Snorri and used in his Olaf Tryggvason saga, in *Heimskringla*, and later elaborated in the Great Tryggvason saga, to become a main source of the viking myth. By a shotgun marriage between legend and archaeology, the pirates of Jom can still be described as one of several 'independent bands of warriors or freebooters based in the Baltic region'[30] and be allowed 'an important role in the reigns of Harald, Swein, and Cnut'; but there are no contemporary poetic references to this body, as distinct from other Baltic vikings, and the archaeology of Wollin tells a different story. There was a walled fort there from the ninth century onwards, overlooking a defended space of some twelve acres (5 ha) and a variety of small settlements inside and outside these defences along nearly two miles of river-bank, with a population supported by manufactures, trade and fishing rather than piracy. It was not a likely place for an independent viking colony, because Wollin's rulers played a leading role in the Veletian or Weltabian confederation of Baltic Slavs, and soon after 966 they were building a large new hall and stable apparently for religious purposes in the middle of the space by the fort, and so reaffirming their role as overlords of the delta. If they hired vikings to help, their hirelings left no distinct trace of

29   It is not yet clear how well-defended the Ladoga settlements were. Brisbane 1992 is the fullest guide to the archaeology of later towns.
30   Cited in Sawyer in Rumble 1994, 12; on the saga, edited and translated by N.F. Blake (1962), see Ólafur Halldórsson's outline of the MS tradition in MESCA, 343–4.

military encampment[31]; more suitable sites have been found on and off the east and south Baltic coast, but the finds of Nordic gear and ornaments are no longer taken as evidence of colonization by northern communities, rather than cultural assimilation, or contact.

In contrast to this fictional Fort Apache, there is the evidence of how Bluetooth's warriors actually lived in three of four ring forts which can be securely dated to the 980s, and have been partly excavated. These are the Trelleborg forts, named after the first to be identified, in the 1930s; laid out on a uniform system as four-house quadrangles and smaller buildings set in the four quadrants of a circular walled enclosure quartered by roads aligned with the points of the compass, and in two cases attended by more houses beyond the defences. The almost identical house-plans and building-techniques, the Aldershot aspect of the whole set-up, and the recorded militarism of the Danish kings led most excavators to assume from the beginning that these were army barracks, viking-packed holding-camps for the conquering hosts which subjugated England.

As more evidence came to light, the red mist receded. These formidable feats of military engineering were occupied by men, women and children in no great numbers who left little evidence of war-gear or conflict; many of the beautifully-constructed halls were used as smithies, storerooms, possibly as stables, and in no case were they arranged otherwise than similar buildings out among the villages and farms. At Fyrkat, the best-excavated, the finding of few weapons, little dirt or debris, and many whetstones suggested that some of the inhabitants were sanitary soldiers who left with well-honed arms; but no more than half of the 16 houses were lived in, and allowing space for women and children indoors, there would be room for no more than 20 men to a house; and some of those would have been gold-smiths, silversmiths and jewellers, to judge from the remains of their forges and workshops. The excavators Olsen and Schmidt concluded that the warriors were kept busy honing and cleaning equipment, and sweeping the ground between the houses, to pass the time (when they were not buying new jewellery from the makers, or riding out, over a rather empty NE Jutland district, to show it off). There was a cemetery outside the rampart, and the finest burial there was a woman's; she was laid to rest with her toe-rings, iron spit, bronze

---

31 Slupecki 1994, 83–9; see Jansson, Jonsson and Kazakevicius in Loit 1992 for short studies of cultural contact in Latvia and Lithuania. Fact and fiction about *Jom* are sorted in Filipowiak 1991, 38–9.

and copper vessels, and magical trinkets: henbane seed, an owl pellet, pendant like a chair, and pig-bones, things from the east Baltic rather than Denmark.[32] The colonel's lady, or a seer? But where was the colonel? In none of the camps is there a clearly identifiable head-quarters inside or outside the perimeter. These communities appear to have been leaderless in camp, but occupied places with authority stamped all over them. Why build so many fine houses, 93 feet long and 22 feet wide, with convex walls, porches, inner halls and end rooms, sustained and buttressed with up to 160 long oak posts; probably boarded in and out, possibly painted and decorated; and then use so many of them as workshops and storerooms? The sheer waste of resources is worthy of twentieth-century bureaucracies, with philosophies of state planning to justify their mistakes. Why import a load of high-quality rye from Eastern Europe to Fyrkat, while further north, Aggersborg made do with Jutland rye? Why bring barley from afar to Fyrkat, when it was the common local crop? Aggersborg on the Limfjord and the Scanian Trelleborg are close to important water-ways; why none of the others? Why the fearful symmetry of design, when earlier ring-forts in Frisia and the East Baltic had made do with more approximate geometry?

'Trelleborg problems' have not all been solved, least of all the big one: what were they for? 'To maintain law and order...to provide safe housing for mints' (Roesdahl)? To be refuges, in preparation for war with Otto II or Otto III? To bring Harald's rule to the outer reaches of his Denmark, as administrative or proto-urban centres? To distribute an over-large military clientage away from the royal house-hold (albeit available for concentration in emergency)? If they were for cowing Danes, they qualify as aggressive communities; if not, as defensive. It is certain only that mixed-sex groups lived in three of them for not many years, and were housed in lordly halls, on sites which only in the case of Odense (Nonnebakken) had been or would be places of any importance. Unlike the English *burh* forts which defended Wessex and later Mercia, none of these became market-towns, administrative centres or cities; they were all abandoned before they needed serious repairs, and two were burnt down. Per-haps it was an experiment that failed; perhaps a brilliant improvisa-tion which held the kingdom together after the king had retreated from Hedeby and sent tribute to the emperor. At all events, the all-

---

32 Roesdahl 1977, 91–2. The superb volumes on the Fyrkat excavations (volume i is edited by Olaf Olsen and Schmidt, volume ii by Roesdahl) include full English summaries and have not been superannuated by the dendro-dating of the site; note Helbæk on the grain in vol. i. On the camps' building techniques see Schmidt 1994(in English) 60–5, 94–104.

male community of fighting men cannot be found in these camps any more than in Jomsborg.[33]

Confraternity

As the evidence for wolf and bear brotherhoods in this period is so unconvincing, we are left with four 11th century Swedish rune-stones commemorating *gildar*: members of gilds. None reveals what these were except that two were for Frisians, or those who dealt with Frisians.

To judge from the Nordic gilds which appear from the 12th century onwards they could have been brotherhoods dedicated to feasting (*gildi* means a dinner in 10th century skaldic verse), veneration, trade, craft, or the mutual defence of alien residents. The runes show that some members were *drengjar* (companions in arms), and expected to be commemorated in this expensive way by their associates, without reference to their own families. The obvious parallels are English: St Peter's gild at Abbotsbury, founded by the Dane Urki (1024–58) for feasting, almsgiving, burial and prayers post mortem, and the Cambridge thegns' gild who pooled resources needed for loans, compensation-payments and care of the sick[34]. Those examples suggest that the early Nordic gilds were probably welfare clubs rather than trading companies.

33   The fifth ring-fort, at Trelleborg on the south coast of Scania was built over and slighted in the thirteenth century, but what survives differs somewhat from the others. The partly-moated rampart was slightly elliptical, built in two phases (vaguely dated) and the 65° outer slope was faced with boards; another reckless extravagance. See Bengt Jacobssen in *Hikuin* xxv (1998), 15–22. No trace of housing within the walls was found; Borring Olesen suggests that this was a precursor, not a Bluetooth camp (KUML 2000, 91–112).
34   See EHD i 559–60 and 557–78 for the gild statutes.

4

Districts and Territories

Far went the lord of the men of Vors
Through Halland with sword;
Hotly were fugitives followed,
Ruler of Hords burned houses.
Chief of Thronds burned
Many a district;
Viskardale lady lay awake,
Fires flamed in wind.

Bjorn Cripple-hand's verses on king Magnus Barefoot's raid on Denmark c.1093 resemble earlier war-poetry in linking rulers and their deeds to districts and territories rather than to realms and nations.[1] So the Norwegian king is merely lord of the dwellers in Voss, behind Bergen, and of the people from Hǫrðaland, just to the south. He attacks the Kattegat coast-lands south of the modern Gothenburg (then called Halland), as ruler of the northern country round Trondheim fjord, and his terrified victim is given an address in the valley-settlement on either side of the Viska river, rather than appearing simply as a Dane. In poetic idiom, Magnus' foray is not a matter of king against king or country against country; it is some localities versus others. This is a literary convention, 'part for the whole', as in Latin verse; but in the viking age it seems to reflect political reality.

Territorial units which refuse to merge into kingdoms or states have often been misunderstood, or dimissed as manifestations of 'separatism', 'backwardness', or 'the fringe'. No longer; the smaller units now seem as important to study as the greater, and here it is

---

1 Bjǫrn krepphendi's Magnussdrápa (ed. Kock, i, 200) was considered 'rather prosaic and in no way remarkable' by Finnur Jónsson, but it belongs to the tradition of itemized campaign – poems going back to fragments of Guthormr Sindri's Hákonardrápa (960s ?), if no further.

worth asking what was the contribution of the viking age to the territorial organization of Scandinavia and the western colonies; what exactly the Norsemen had inherited from previous centuries, and how they collaborated in spaces larger than those required by family and community.

In the middle of the sixth century, the historian Jordanes drew up a list of northern peoples. The names connected with the western coastlands of Scandinavia reappear 500 years later and some survive to the present day; but this continuity is more apparent than real, since Jordanes gives tribal designations without indications of the territorial boundaries.[2] As Svanberg (1999, 119) concludes: 'The "nations" of Jordanes were certainly not the same as Wulfstan's "lands", which in turn were not the same as medieval territorial hundreds and territories' – even if, like Hálogaland (N. Norway) they carried the name of the *Alogii*, or like Halland spoke of the old *Hallin*. The tribal names were not erased, like most of the mid-Anglian entries in the Tribal Hidage of the Anglo-Saxons; they were put to other uses, either attached to natural features (as with the *Theutes*, to a small Scanian river called Tjude Å) or to administrative jurisdictions serving rulers outside the district, or to regions of dispersed settlement of no particular allegiance but no surviving tribal organization (*Gythinge* in northern Scania is an example). In eleventh-century Norway it was natural to speak of Thronds, Vossings, Hords etc. as if these were tribal designations, but they were not; they merely showed where people came from, whether it were a *herað* (district), a *dal* (valley) or *land* (territory) or *bygð* (area of settlement). These could be even more ancient than the tribes,[3] and up to a point can be recreated from the spacing and pattern of archaeological finds combined with written evidence of boundaries in the later medieval or early modern period; neither entirely reliable guides to viking-age conventions (see map 3). In Scandinavia the study of these areas has been and remains hag-ridden by two misconceptions:

1   that they were essentially subdivisions, or subdivisions-in-waiting for the invigorating kiss known as 'the process of state formation';

2   that they were actually or nearly components of the Scandinavian nations of Danes, Swedes and Norwegians, of interest only in so far as they cohered in those patterns.

---

2   Svennung 1967, 9–4 for the texts; for the correspondences, Callmer 1991, 257–62 and Ramqvist 1991. Brink 1997 discusses the concept of Nordic territories.
3   Thrane 1991 reconstructed Bronze Age districts within the NW peninsula of Zealand (Odsherred) from groupings of settlements. Compare Burström 1991 on the archaeological detection of coherent settlements in deepest Sweden. See maps 1 and 12.

What follows is based on the opposite assumptions: that there are no fixed 'prerequisites of state formation' to be found in small-scale territorial associations, since overwhelming force can be generated suddenly and in mysterious ways, and leave the habit of obedience behind it; and that prehistoric nations (or whatever the viking age peoples are to be called) were not compiled from territories (see chapter 5).

Interactions between districts are sometimes simplified as links between core and periphery, between the distributors and the recipients of culture and material wealth. Archaeology suggests that in the Migration period the rulers of the Danes and Mälardal Swedes had sent precious things 'down the line' to their clients along the Norwegian coast or across to Finland and Estonia, by stages of distribution; Hyenstrand and Sawyer see this relationship continuing through the viking age and beyond, with the Danes as first served with the wealth, technology and ideas of the continent, and passing them on in ways which could underpin Danish overlordship, or be adapted to undermine it.[4] It is a convincing model up to a point, if it were not for the accessibility of most parts of Scandinavia to alien wealth and influence from different sources (western Europe, Byzantium, Islam) by fits and starts rather than in a steady and controllable seepage. The ports of entry (Ribe, Hedeby, Gotland, Birka) dispersed the imports round the Baltic in one way; native chiefs in another; and Frankish or Frisian envoys in yet another. More will be said of the nature of Nordic cultural dependency in chapter 11, but the impression given by viking age archaeology is that it was deep-rooted but too eclectic to create a permanent cultural ranking of territories. As well as absorbing influences from outside, each had a history and dynamic of its own, which is reflected in the localized distribution of types of artifact such as rune-stones, brooches and pots, and in cults and burials (see maps 8 and 11).

There were probably as many as four hundred districts within Scandinavia at this period, and sixty or so larger territories of various kinds (see map 4 for these). Here are some of the more important.

Scania

The south-western corner of the Scandinavian peninsula had been familiar to Roman geographers as the homeland of all northern

---

4 For maps and exposition of core–periphery in Roman times, see Jørgen Jensen 1982, 235–47; and Malmer (RER, 45–64) for erratic reactions of Nordic peripheries.

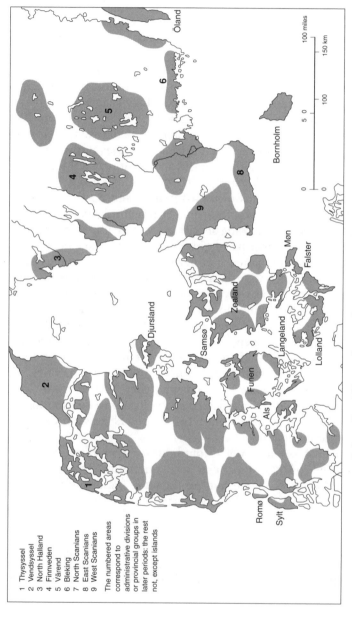

1 Thysyssel
2 Vendsyssel
3 North Halland
4 Finnveden
5 Värend
6 Bleking
7 North Scanians
8 East Scanians
9 West Scanians

The numbered areas
correspond to
administrative divisions
or provincial groups in
later periods: the rest
not, except islands

Öland

Bornholm

Mon

Falster

Djursland

Zealand

Samsø

Langeland

Lolland

Funen

Als

Romo

Sylt

100 miles

150 km

100

5 0

0

0

Map 3 *Hypothetical territories, c.750–c.1000*

The main concentrations of settlement in this period were within the shaded areas,
following Callmer in RER 1991. Further north, settlements were concentrated round Viken and
Lake Mälar, between Vätter and Väner, and along the larger Norwegian fjords.

barbarians: *Insula Scanza.*[5] Until the founding and development of Lund by Sweyn and Canute (990s–1030s) this was a geographical rather than a political term: an area of many districts, divided between the plains, low hills, and scrub-lands which drain west, and the forested hills which drain south, mainly by way of the 'holy river' Helgån. A belt of under-populated land came between, and before the 990s three territories are detectible: one in the south-west, looking to a centre at Uppåkra (3 miles South of Lund) and to Borgeby, with its coastal market at Löddeköpinge; one in the South-east, looking towards the island of Bornholm, and one in the north-east behind Vä, on the Helgån delta, where the woodlanders continued to cremate their dead long after the westerners had adopted inhumation.[6] In the east they formed *bo* or *bygðir* (settlement districts), put up few rune-stones, and imported few exotic goods. In the west, they kept some of the old tribal names for districts (*Liothidae* in Luggude, *Bergio* in Bjäre) and formed links with the western world through raiding and serving the Jutland kings; they embraced rune-stones, viking expeditions, trade, coinage and eventually christianity. First, *c*.900–*c*.980, some king or an ally built a ring-fort at Trelleborg[7] on the south coast; then by 995, a new town with a church dedicated to the Trinity and a mint was founded at Lund, presumably by Sweyn Forkbeard after his return from England; this was developed as Canute's 'new London' with more churches, defences and eventually a bishop, and became the central place for a royal and episcopal clientage; not for an administrative system of hundreds (*herreder*) until after this period. Western Scanians helped Toki Gormsson (presumably a brother of Harald Bluetooth) raid Uppsala (as on the Hällestad stones, DR 295–97), took part in the raids on England, and presumably fought for their lord when the Swedish king raided Helgån *c*. 1025; how far, and when, the eastern districts bowed to the new regime is unclear. In the 1040s Magnus the Good and Sweyn Estrithson (p. 36) fought over Scania, and each supported his own bishop and mint; but the handles of royal and episcopal power remained in the west, and the clear political antagonism between these halves is evident from Saxo's account of the events of the

5 One tenth-century MS of the tract *Origo gentis Langobardorum* derives Scanza from 'destructions' (scathe), an etymology sometimes linked to the dangerous shoals off Skanör; but according to Wagner (1994) it could well be linked to the skate-fish caught there. See Svennung 1963, 23–40; AB called it 'the most beautiful province in Denmark to look at, and named from that' (schön).
6 Larsson and Hårdh summarized the Uppåkra dig in Fornvännen 1997, 413; also Stjernkvist 1995, and for Borgeby, Svanberg 1998.
7 Bengt Jacobsson summarizes what has been found at this badly damaged site, in *Hikuin* XXV (1998) 15–22.

1180s, after 200 years of obedience-training. The home of the train-
ers, and of previous Danish kings was Jutland.

Jutland

Jutland was also well known to educated readers since Roman times
as the other 'womb of nations' and scabbard of the sword of barbarism: not a territory or a kingdom, but a region of very ancient
settlement embracing anything up to fifteen territorial groups of
districts. The natural separators were a central spine of sandy and
heathery geest, running from the Eider river to the north; the wide
arm of the sea called Limfjord, which at that period made an island
of the 'hat' of Jutland; and the North Sea tides, which rolled in to the
South-west coast and threatened an inhabited marshland over
1000 sq. miles larger in 900 than it is today. The whole peninsula
would have looked strange to its modern inhabitants; coastline, wet-
land, watercourses and lakes have changed, and the aurochs, bear
and boar have been exterminated, the central heathland reclaimed.
Distinct concentrations of settlement indicate territories ancient by
800: two north of Limfjord, corresponding to the later shires (*syssler*)
of Thy and Vend, and one across the eastern outflow, which disappeared. Five or six share the rest of North Jutland, beyond the 'King's
Water' (Kongeaa) and rather more between that and the Eider
marshes. Adam of Bremen presented Jutland in the 1070s as a land
of 'sterile, almost desert' soil except along the waterways, where
'there are very big cities'.[8] He wrote as travellers from Germany
saw it, riding the old road (Haervej) up through the middle heaths;
most Jutlanders lived off the beaten track, along the coasts. Their
heaths were not sterile, but had been created by regular burning over
the previous 3000 years for grazing livestock, and they still had 900
years of life in them for hunters, pastoralists and iron-winners. By
'very big cities' he may have meant 'large sees' since he was chiefly
interested in church organization; but in his time Hedeby, Ribe and
Aarhus had less than a thousand inhabitants each.

The development of these towns, and the building and maintenance of the southern defences *c.* 700, *c.*980 and in the 990s, had the
effect of concentrating population round the towns and emptying
the space between Danevirke and the Eider, while settlers moved to
the Schlei estuary in the east, and the North Sea coast islands in the

8   AB, 4: I; see Ringtved 1991, 49–61 for the political interpretation of pre-viking-
age archaeology in N. Jutland, and Andersen, Aaby and Odgaard (JDA, ii, 1983,
184–96) for the Jutland heaths.

west. *Sillende* (Schlei-land) was already mentioned by Wulfstan in the 890s, and despite the floods of 800 and 839, Danes and Frisians farmed the western marshlands from hillocks of ancient detritus, defended by ring-forts as refuges.[9] The motor for these changes was the seat of kings at Jelling, a centrally-placed residence already old when it was occupied by kings Gorm and Harald and made into the show-place of an aggressive new dynasty, monopolizing resources and manpower to buy off or resist the imperial claims of the Ottonian kings and Saxon dukes to the south. The new dynasty organized the adjacent lands into administrations, or *syssler*; the four nearest Jelling (Jelling, Almind, Barvid and Løver) set a pattern which was applied to other parts of Jutland without superseding previous territorial groups. The *herreder* into which syssler and other territories are found divided by 1085, west of the Sound, must also in many cases be a renaming of older district communities, and may be another reflection of Jelling authority, enforced in the period of the Trelleborg forts (map 6). The problem of *herred* origins has been discussed *ad nauseam* for over a century; not the most unlikely of the etymologies derives the word from *hiwa-rada*, a compound which (if it ever existed) meant 'jurisdiction of a household' and became 'administrative district with public obligations';[10] obligations which in the twelfth century were to include military service and the food, forage and money renders set out in king Valdemar's Land-register (1220s and 30s). In the viking age, neither syssler nor herreder operated in any way which left archaeological or documentary traces; how the great works of Bluetooth were executed and supervised remains a matter of conjecture. How and where the ninth-century Jutland kings had ruled is even more obscure, and whether their tenth-century successors really thought in terms of administrative structure rather than the piecemeal coercion of associations of landowners is doubtful. By 1050 the landowners had the last laugh; kings might look big, but the assembly of magnates at Viborg (an old holy place, now a bishopric and town with fort) decided who was to be king; as in 1042, when they chose Magnus of Norway, and 1046–7 when they preferred Sweyn Estrithson to Harald Hardrada.

9   See Jöns in *Offa*, liii (1996), 193–226 for a survey of finds on the SW borders, esp. the iron-working site at Rantrum; Kersten and La Baume 1958, 90–2 on Lembecksburg and Tinnumberg forts on Föhr and Sylt; Harck in SADO (1998), 127–34 and Hellmuth Andersen 1998 on Danevirke.

10   Albøge 1991, 58; see Kousgaard Sørensen 1978 for a demolition of the wilder origin-theories, and Nyberg 1985 for the Syssel–Jelling link.

Mälardal

Those two collections of territories were changed by kings in different ways. There was a comparable group of districts north and south of what is now lake Mälar and was then an estuary, much ramified, draining a fertile clay basin ringed by woodland; this was also the home of kings, and known as Svithioð (Suedia to Adam of Bremen). Mälardal is a modern term, used here to distinguish the Swedish heartland from the large semi-detached or unattached range of territories outside the basin, which Adam called Sueonia, and which occupies most of modern Sweden. The Sweden of those days was a rough oval, a hundred miles east–west and sixty miles north–south, a space later subdivided into three 'folk-lands': Uppland and Västermanland north of Mälar, Södermanland to the south, each composed of hundare, with Uppland's grouped into three 'lands' named after the number each contained. This orderly naming, by direction and number, means that administrators have been at work; unlikely much before the twelfth century, when the *hundare* were supplying kings with provisions and ship-service, assessed by parishes. In the viking age, as in the Vendel period, this basin was dominated by chiefs and landowners, rather than by kings, and the differences in burial custom between Uppsala (cremation and mound) and Vendel-Valsgärde (boat-graves) suggest a bipolar grouping of settlements rather than a row of territories; further reflected in the distribution of rune-stone types in the eleventh century. When the missionary Ansgar came here two centuries earlier he found a society ruled by a public assembly or assemblies, to which kings deferred in civil matters, although they led armies overseas and communicated with the Frankish emperor on behalf of their people; there is no reason to suppose that things changed very much after that, while kings 'sat at Uppsala' for ceremonial purposes, and fed themselves by moving round the estuary between *Husabyar*, as the halls to which supplies were rendered seem to have been called: an arrangement found in Britain, Denmark, Norway and Germany. Husby place-names are the only evidence, and they have been interpreted as military mustering points for the public levy, rather than as royal restaurants[11]; but the levy came later. As did the Mälardal *hundare*, or districts, in which the husbys were set, along with a recurrent pattern of place-names indicating essential services: a 'retinue farm', a 'warrior farm', a

---

11   Høilund Nielsen 1991 and Alkemade 1991 discuss *hundare*, B. Sawyer 1991, 109–9 outlines the runic divergences, and Larsson 1987 argued for the military function of *husbyar*, using Ambrosiani's method of imposing the PNN on a map of viking-age antiquities; and applying later tradition or fiction from Styrbjorn's *tháttr*.

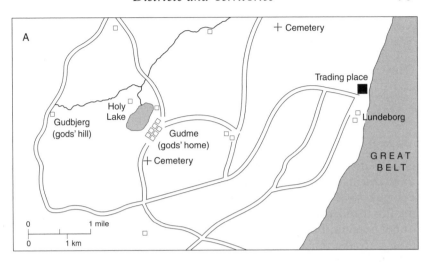

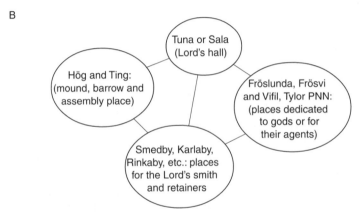

Map 4 *Viking-Age districts*
(A in Denmark, B in Sweden; after Stefan Brink)

'smith's farm', a 'lot-caster's farm' have been detected by Brink in many such districts, along with a husby, or a *sala*, all near an assembly-hill or howe (see map 4). As Brink argues, this pattern was a development rather than a stereotypical administrative district imposed from above; older districts, centred on the holy place, sacred well, or grove, were adapted to suit kings and chiefs, and renamed 'hundreds', as in England, to mark the change.[12]

12 P. Sawyer 1988 is the best guide. *Hundare* (first mentioned *c*.1050) seem to have been superimposed on Mälardal after an English model of Hundreds not long before 1050, but why and how is unknown.

Round Mälardal, within the hundred-mile wide nimbus where lands 'belonged to the Swedes', according to Wulfstan, but were not inhabited by them, territories reflected early settlement, and districts (whether häradar or bygdir) were not tied to rule from above.

Götaland

Götaland was always divided between Öster and Väster, and always to be distinguished from the island of Gotland, out in the Baltic. The Beowulf poet made this his hero's kingdom, and had a mourner predict its downfall after his death, thanks to the 'murderous hatred' of the Swedes. But there is no historical evidence of any such visitation; only the remarkable fact of a shared kingship between *Gautar* and the Swedes, who remained entirely distinct in laws and customs and administration for most of the Middle Ages. Modern Sweden is the result of this union; but how it originated is unknown. The Götaland territories and their inhabitants were named after a people known to Roman geographers and linked by later legend to the Goths, whose actual origins have been teased out by Heather in this series.[13] They were separated by lake Vätter, and the west shore of Vättern was virtually uninhabited in this period, as if taboo, or reserved for hunting; their outlooks followed their drainage, the Västergötland rivers to the Halland coast and the Kattegat, the Öster to the east Baltic. Most of the westerners lived within a forty mile (60 km) radius of Gudhem (seat of the gods?) and continued to do so after the conversion, when this became the see of Skara, centred on what had been the earls' place. Sagas later told much of these chiefs, but the only reliable information is that Ragnvald jarl Ulfsson was ruling over Gauts *c*.1016–1020s, and made a treaty with the Norwegian ruler St Olave so that each entertained the other's retainers; one of whom, the poet Sigvat, came trotting into Skara through the forests, and made verses about the journey.[14] The earlier history of the westerners can only be deduced from their archaeology; apart from one eloquent document, the inscribed stone of Sparlösa (*c*.850? 900?): copious, but largely unintelligible. It concerns kings or chiefs who 'sat in Uppsala' but were presumably born and buried west of Vättern. Why the family of Alrik scored this stone

---

13　P. Heather *The Goths* (1996) 10–50.

14　*Austrfararvísor* (*c*.1017–18); their number and order are uncertain but they indicate that this was a hard-riding journey among inhospitable heathens to reach their open-handed earl (ed. Kock, i, 114–16).

with strangely elongated runes, which remind some of Merovingian characters, and images resembling Frankish and Insular decoration on ivory crosses is unclear. It confirms the impression that this was an independent territory run by a dynasty with a wide outlook, from Uppsala to Zealand to Italy (see chapter 10), and the link with Sweden was contested after the end of this period: westerners had fought with Canute, and in 1100 their allegiance was claimed by the Bare-legged Magnus mentioned earlier (p. 87) as a Norwegian encroacher on Halland. In Östergotland stands the stone of Rök, raised in memory of Væmoð about the same time as Sparlösa, but different in design and content, more overtly religious. That territory was hilly pastureland, in which grazing rights brought communities into association at least from Roman times, and where these groupings were replaced by *hundare* after this period along the coast, but remained as identifiable settlement districts under the new name in the interior. Together, the Götalands filled a space about as big as Ireland, within which there were none of the easy lines of communication which held Jutland and Mälardal together, and could be used by rulers to extend their power. These territories were not self-sufficient in their economies, but they were generally able to accept exterior authority on their own terms, and formulate those terms in assemblies or by trading. Birka lay on the north edge, as their gateway to Mälardal, for most of this period, and the links that bound landowners to the Danish kings (*c.*1000–1030) seem to have been contractual.[15]

Hälsingland

Hälsingland – land of those who live on the narrow-necked bays is what it means, referring to the west coast of the Bothnian gulf – ran up from the north-east Mälardal, and represents a very different sort of territory: the seaward segment of a vast hunter–gatherer interior, used mainly by Lapps, but colonized by emigrants from Mälardal before 800, who mostly lived near the 'narrow-necked bays' but derived their wealth from the Lapp country. A Hälsing was a farmer with a fixed abode, who might in the eleventh century get rich enough to advertise lordship over six settlements, and set up runestones as at Rogsta and Sunnå; but the fur-trade, and his relations with the Lapps were what made him rich. His 'land' was boundless in this period, his territory a free backwoods society within what

15 On the detachment of Götaland from its neighbours see Hedvall 1997, 606–7, and on its survival as a commonwealth Sawyer 1988 B, 2–3, 36–9.

Adam of Bremen described as the 'head' or 'region' of the *Scritefinni* (Lapps, on whom see p. 126), but also as part of *Sueonia*. There is no sign of any political connection with the Swedish kingdom before the twelfth century, and in the thirteenth Snorri wrote that Hälsings had paid tribute to Norwegian rulers until St Olave had ceded his rights there to his Swedish father-in-law in the 1020s: another fiction to boost the pretensions of later kings, not to be taken seriously. The fur-barons who ran the country could have exported their wares either south or west without incurring an economic dependency in either direction; archaeology has revealed few imported goods of the kind that would tie a periphery to a core.[16]

A comparable backwoods community of communities could be found in the 8000 square miles of hill and forest north of lake Väner, Lapp country for the most part, with homesteaders, iron-winners and dairymen who spoke a Norse dialect and were called Værmar, 'dwellers on the warm river'. It is now called *Värmland*; was then pitted with reindeer traps and studied with auspicious rocks and stumps which indicate the religion of the trapper and hunter and lost none of their potency for centuries after the inhabitants had accepted christianity.[17] Like the Hälsings, they belonged to no one kingdom before the thirteenth century; and the great tract which lay to the north and west of these, in what has been called 'an extension of the Great Eurasian taiga' belonged to the outermost foresters, Norse and Lapp, who went by the name of *Jämtar*, an apparently Finnish word which recurs in the Russian for the people of central Finland: *Yam*. Lapps and immigrants from east and west had been settling round lake Storsjön (The Great Lake) since the sixth century and organizing the exploitation of the forest and iron-ore deposits, as well as the hunting and fishery. It was worth the effort, as the surplus could be carried west to the Thronds or east to the Hälsings, and the water of Storsjön moderates the climate and allows some farming. The viking age graves suggest to one interpreter that there was a strong sense of identity, or 'societal coherence' among the occupants, expressed also in a general assembly which later met on Frey's island (Frösön) in the middle of the great lake, where Austman's rune-stone still stands. This coherence, if it existed, seems to have been deduced from geography, the common elements in Nordic grave goods and graves (which excludes Lapps) and from later territorial arrangements, summed up in the word *Jämtland*, a province of mixed allegiance until the seven-

16   See Mogren in VIPA (1997) on the tenuous links with Sweden.
17   The absence of rune-stones suggests that this was later than 1050, although Adam of Bremen claimed soon afterwards that the *Wermilani* respected the Götland see of Skara: not their diocesan later, as they were poached by Uppsala *c*.1190.

teenth century. Snorri's St Olave saga (chapter 137) tells how this land was settled by refugees from tyranny both in Sweden and at Throndheim, and the grandson of the founder went on to colonize Hälsingland; either a reworking or a congener of the current foundation myths of Iceland and Norway. About 1110 king Eysteinn of Norway made Jämtar chiefs his clients through gifts, trading privileges, and a mutual defence pact: 'he proceeded by policy rather than by aggression' as the sagas put it.[18] But the churches already looked to Swedish bishops for ordination, and in the pagan period the Jämts may have delivered their wares as clients to the chiefs of the eastern coastland called *Medelpad*, at least before they began to thrive, as the sleighriding, burn-beating profiteers of Austman's generation.

Other free foresters peopled the tract to the west of Mälardal later called the dales: *Dalarna*. Wooded, uphill, but more arable than the northern lands, this became the immediate supplier of unworked iron to the Swedes, and was known in the twelfth century simply as the 'iron-bearing land': another link in the economic chain, of uncertain if any affiliation before that. The series of unattached polities continues to the south of Götaland where woodlanders had formed distinct societies separated by belts of forest and known later as *Niudhung, Finnveden* and *Värend*. Burström's study of the Iron-Age grave-types showed that before and during viking times the people of Finnveden (to the west) were buried under shallow mounds, in cemeteries, while at least the richer Värendians to the east honoured their dead with oval stone settings, and both kept their dead near the centre, away from the frontiers; a defensiveness and independence which survived the conversion, and their later appearance as components in a Swedish frontier zone called Småland: 'the small territories'.[19] The formation of all these lands beyond the reach of kings was a long series of fusions and clashes between immigrants and natives continuing from Roman times to the viking age and long after. From 750 to 1100 it was quickened by the economic stimulus and population pressure generated in coastlands, estuaries and islands. Not in all. Some coasts on the Baltic were less accessible and less fertile than others, and supported populations less interesting to the suppliers of forest products inland and to the coastal traders. East of Scania, beyond the rich peninsular district of Lister, lay *Bleking*, once the land of Hathuwulf's dynasty (see p. 44) and still

---

18 Morkinskinna ch. 64 and the Hsk saga of Sigurd the Hierosolymite ch. 15 tell the tale; and see Jakobsson, 1997, and Mogren 1997, 220–4 on the political orientations, *Jämtlands kristnande* (ed. Brink, Uppsala 1996) on religion.
19 Ersgård 1995 covers Dalarna; on Smaland, Ambrosiani 1988 and Brink 1997, 431–3. Burstrom 1991 was revised by Hansson 1998, and Svanberg 1999, 41–7 summarizes recent work.

independent, with remarkably uniform burial customs, down to the conversion (from Scania) in the 1050s. It had 'belonged to' Sweden in the ninth century, according to Wulfstan, and in the twelfth it obeyed the Danish kings; whereas *Möre*, the eastern coastland facing Öland, north and south of Kalmar, belonged to Sweden in Wulfstan's time, and seems to have remained virtually independent, and pagan, until the 1120s[20] In other cases (e.g. Scania, E. Jutland, Mälardal) the inhabitants of coasts, interiors and islands interacted in ways that enriched their owners and brought them into fierce competition.

Islands

Islands are natural territories, but the encircling sea brought danger as well as wealth. In the course of this period the islands east of the Sound remained more-or-less independent politically, as well-defended commonwealths, while to the west the warships of the Jutland kings were gradually annexing them to the Danish kingdom. Various fjord-based Norwegian chiefs kept hold of the thousands of offshore islands on some of which small North Sea polities had developed in the Migration period, as on Lofoten.

The chiefs of Funen (Fyn) had been great men in Roman times and later, as they were secure from land-attacks on a fertile island about the size of Majorca; but the straits are so narrow that as Adam of Bremen wrote of Funen 'it sticks to the region called Jutland' (AB,4,4). By 815 the place was under the rule of Jutland kings, who took refuge there when the forces of the emperor Lewis invaded without bringing boats. In the early tenth century chiefs called *goðar* set up stones at Glavendrup in the north of the isle, and Flemløse and Helnaes in the south-west presumably the leaders of the ten coastal districts which have been detected from the concentrations of viking-age finds. The king's man or under-king would then have ruled the settlements on either side of the fjord running from Odense north to the Kattegat, with Odin as his protector whichever dynasty ruled in Jutland.

This dependency cost dear: a Jutland king planted a ring-fort (Nonnebakken) outside Odense *c*.980, but his successors gave no security during the wars that followed the reign of Hardicanute, when there were frequent raids on the Danish islands from Norway.

20 Hsk. *Magnússonar Saga* ch. 24 tells of an expedition against the supposedly heathen Smålanders which he dates to 1124: it was led by a Norwegian ruler who had been to Jerusalem and back, but degenerated into a viking raid on Denmark and Kalmar.

Harbours had to be blocked with stakes (an ancient precaution) or sunken ships, and the Icelandic poets, crowing over the raids of Harald Hardrada from 1044 to 1064, give the impression that Funen was a soft target. So says Stúfr:

The raven was fed – Danes terrified each year: Island-Danes especially –

and they got no rest from contending kings, so that Arnórr Earl's poet could boast:

There were fewer dwellers in Funen after this

although enough to support the separate bishopric which Sweyn II established at Odense.[21]

Smaller islands to the south-east of Funen, Langeland and Ærø, felt the hand of the Jutland kings no less: they were militarized, as outposts against the Ottonian and Wendish warlords to the south. Fifteen well-equipped tenth-century 'military graves' have been found on Langeland, four with stirrups as well as arms, and they are spaced along a 30 mile axis as if to block approaches to the Great Belt and Funen, in collaboration with a similar distribution of warriors in SE Jutland.[22]

Zealand (Sjælland), according to the early verses attributed to Bragi, was the 'wide island of meadows' which had originally been ploughed from Swedish soil by the gigantic Gefion and her four ox-sons. She then married Skjold, and became the ancestor of all kings who claimed to be Skjoldungr: a later embellishment. The high literary profile of *Sjoland, Selun,* etc. reflects both a long political history and a strategic position between the Baltic and the western seas, where an island as big as Corsica, with good natural harbours and soils 'fertile in crops and full of brave men' (AB) could be a viable centre of power over other coasts, rather than an appendage. It was still heavily wooded, and the distribution of Iron-Age archaeology shows up the ring of some twenty-two coastal settlement districts, with a further eight either side of Roskilde fjord, separated quite clearly by forest belts. During the Migration Period, the main centre of power had been in the south-east, in the Stevns headland district, and whoever ruled here may also have dominated western Scania across the Sound;[23] but in the ensuing centuries other centres

21 For the Saxon Eilbert, who had lived in a hermitage on Heligoland frequented by North Sea vikings; he died in 1070 (AB 4, 3; 4, 9).
22 Pedersen mapped the graves in MASS 1997, 124.
23 Ringtved in ASSAH 1990, 52–9, for maps and references, and more in Svanberg 1999, 98–103. One interpretation of the Gefion myth is in Ross 1978.

emerged at Tissø in the west, where there was a great (158 feet) hall and a manufacturing high-consumption settlement until the tenth century: and at Lejre, in the middle, but connected by water to Roskilde fjord, where the great hall (excavated in the early 1990s) was evidently fit for a king and lasted to *c*.1000. In other parts of the island, rune-stones at Tryggevælde, Gørlev and Snoldelev commemorate magnates of the early tenth century: Gunulf the Clamorous, Thiaudi and Gunvald Rohaldsson the Prophet (*thuli*), all probable owners of other great halls with their own clients, craftsmen and warriors. Whether Lejre was meant by the Beowulf poet's *Heorot*, the seat of the Danish kings and prey of the unhuman Grendel and his mother; or whether the twelfth-century stories of a Lejre dynasty creating the Danish kingdom[24] reflect any real part of the past is unclear; equally so, the statement on the Rök stone, over in Götaland that at some period

TWENTY FOUR KINGS SAT ON ZEALAND

in sets of homonyms that baffle (see chapter 10) interpretation. At what period the Jutland fleets cowed these lords is unknown; the evidence only appears in the 980s with rapid assertions of king Harald's power. A ring-fort was built at Trelleborg, near the west coast, and the manor of Roskilde was boosted into a town, which by 1023 had a bishop and a mint and a market, and by the 1070s could be described (by Adam) as 'royal seat of the Danes' and in terms of the archaeology as a semi-urbanized area with concentrated settlement round the hall, cathedral, four churches and harbour. It had been saved from some but not all of Hardrada's raids by the ships sunk at Skuldelev across the fjord, and now resurrected and displayed in the museum; and according to Adam, it was now the turn of the Zealand *wichingi* (vikings) to terrorize the seas by arrangement with the king. The time was past, it seemed, when they could act as wholly independent predators; the transfer of kingship from Jelling to Roskilde (and Lund) was the immediate outcome of the Saxon-Slav threat in the 970s but in the long term committed the Danish rulers to constant itineration by sea from mainland to mainland by way of the Zealand polity they had annexed. In time, the districts here were renamed or rearranged into *herreder*, with fiscal obligations; but the freeholders, as in Jutland, met the interference by regular assemblies at Ringsted, an ancient site away from

---

24 As in the 'Lejre Chronicle' of *c*.1160 (SMHD, ii, 34–53) a Danish work, and whatever traditions lie behind the lost Skjoldunga Saga composed in Iceland *c*.1200.

Roskilde, where kings and bishops had to come to terms with the laws and customs of the islanders.[25]

To the south, the islands of Lolland, Falster and Møn (the last two reckoned very fertile by Early Modern tax assessments) had also supported chiefdoms in Roman and post-Roman times, and in the 890s Wulfstan found that 'they belonged to Denmark'. It appears from later rune-stones on Lolland (flat and featureless) that a Norwegian or Swedish chief called Krok, and one Toki Haklangsson, also probably a Norwegian, held power here, while another chief called Frathi was killed in Sweden on a raid, and won himself the second-tallest stone in Denmark, over eight foot (2.54 m). Combine these inscriptions with the sprinkling of Slavonic PNN (date uncertain), and the destiny of smaller islands is plainly written: to become the prey of pirate chiefs, or accept the rule of nearby overlords. Bluetooth seems to have annexed these islands, and he or his successors established two royal manors with churches at the two Kirkebys, and to have effaced pagan allusions from the surviving place-names.[26] On Falster the descendants of Sweyn Estrithson owned as much as 65 per cent of the properties at the end of the twelfth century; this, and the king's hold on dozens of small islands used as game-reserves, appears in king Valdemar's Land-Register (see p. 310) and was the end-result of a long series of naval intimidations which began before this period, when someone had a canal dug through the island of Samsø off the north-east coast (*c*.730). The intimidations came from chiefs active in the east Baltic and North Sea, from Slavs as well, and kept the little Danish islands in contention throughout this period and later. Large central earthworks on Lolland (Hejrede Vold) and Falster (Falsters Virke) secured less than two square miles (5 km^2) each for the harrassed islanders, while their villages crackled.

East of Denmark islanders met force with force and ruled themselves; as on Bornholm, Öland, Gotland and the Åland archipelago, to take the Norse-speaking islands first. *Bornholm* ('island of the Burgundians', although there is no archaeological link between the Migration Age remains and that people, rather than the Alemanni or Swabians) is only twenty miles (32 km) across at the widest, but it was home to a rich and distinctive civilization during the five or six centuries which preceded this period. Right in the middle of the

---

25　At what was said to be the mid-point of the island; the place of the *hringr* or protected enclosure.

26　Hald thought these Kirkebys were renamed pagan shrines, appropriated with 'temple lands' by kings: but see Kousgaard Sørensen in ONFRAC (1990), 399. For the stones of Tirsted, Bregninge and Sædinge, DR 216, 217, 219; and Løkkegaard Poulsen (1999) on Lolland–Falster earthworks.

southern Baltic, defended by granite cliffs and accessible only in few places, the island, so archaeologists say,[27] was ruled by rich nobles under the authority of some sort of priesthood or 'sacral kingship' located in the less populated north-east at Sorte Muld, where the discovery in 1986–7 of some 24,000 thin gold tokens suggests that the rulers wielded widespread influence over the sea. As Bornholm has no metal resources or salt, its Dark Age prosperity may have been based on cult as much as on aggression, and as the cult waned, that prosperity declined. By the beginning of the viking age there were no more gold tokens but *c.*900 Wulfstan found that 'Bornholm... had itself a king'. There were at least seventy-nine settlements, and one cliff-top fort (Gamleborg, at Almindingen) as a refuge, needed when Slav and other vikings began to raid in the tenth century; but there is no sign that the islanders came under foreign rule, or 'belonged' to anywhere else, until the 1030s, when the bishop of Dalby in Scania baptized them, perhaps on the orders of king Canute. Over the next century, the chiefs of the island responded to christianity by raising more than thirty pious rune-stones, with eloquent inscriptions and decoration of the Gautish-Swedish kind:

ASBJORN HAD THE STONE INSCRIBED IN MEMORY OF BUTIRTHU HIS WIFE: GOD LIGHTEN HER SOUL FOR EVER (Bodilsker 5, DR 378) and CHRIST HELP THE SOULS OF AUDB-JORN AND GUNILD AND ST MICHAEL IN LIGHT AND PARA-DISE.

(Klemensker I, DR 399)

are good examples. Rough seas, tenacious landowners of firm faith, and a growing market for dried salmon and herring preserved this as a semi-detached territory for a long time to come.

Gotland, a hundred and sixty miles to the north-east is an even better example of an island-territory distinct in most ways from its surrounding neighbours over at least a millennium. Not much bigger than Funen, the fifty-mile distance from the nearest mainland helped save it from conquest throughout this period, when it became the entrepôt for all Baltic peoples, with no one trading settlement like Birka or Hedeby but many small harbours.

Gotlanders enhanced their natural defences by maintaining an immense hill-fort (227 acres: 112.5 ha) twelve miles inland from the

---

27 See Watt and Jørgensen in HØKO, 125–89 for a résumé of the now abundant archaeological record; also Ringstedt 1992, 72–80, and Watt in MYWO 81–91, on the golden discs (*goldgubber*).

east shore. Torsburg was begun 500 years earlier; its $1\frac{1}{4}$ mile perimeter of timber-revetted limestone and earth wall was perfected at the end of this period and could hold the entire population (6000–9000 ?) if necessary. An all-round defence and warning system needed up to 1000 men, or fit women, to be mustered within a day; the solution to a perennial problem (which had left fifty-two smaller forts up and down the island as a reminder): how to keep out vikings. The families that created this polity left a series of carved stones unlike other Nordic memorials in style, but expressing images of the world and the gods like but not identical with those expressed in words by tenth-century skalds and thirteenth-century mythologers. In terms of developmental theory, Gotland was a paradox: open to all comers, the main importer of Islamic silver (from the 830s to the 880s, and 910–1010), seeded with rich graves and in direct contact (at least after 1000) with Courland (Latvia), Polotsk and Russia, the island has yielded few traces of coin in circulation, or silver fragments used as currency; no sign of a central town or market, and a rigid conservatism in the dress and ornaments worn by the wives of the landowners and farmers, with a prevailing equality of type and size in the excavated farms. The paradox is of course an illusion: a failure of modern interpretations that overstress the social impact of economic development. However they managed it, the Gotlanders remained independent, even after their need for Swedish markets led them to offer a small tribute (60 marks of silver) to the Uppsala kings in return for free access, possibly soon after this period.[28]

Öland, the long thin flat island which stretches for ninety miles along the Swedish coast was not so fortunate: ten miles of sea-water cannot deter raiders from hitting either vulnerable shore. From the Migration Age onwards, the Ölanders invested strenuously in building twenty-one forts (Eketorp, Ismantrop and Gråborg are the best known), some with interior housing for prolonged periods of refuge and all with districts to serve them. Deposits of treasure, tribute or loot, show how useful a lair this could be to predators, islanders or migrants, and at the end of the tenth century the famous stone of Karlevi proclaimed one such, Sibbi the Good (or the *Goði*: cult-leader)

WHO PERFORMED THE GREATEST DEEDS KNOWN TO MOST

---

28 Which led eventually to ship-service and closer ties. See GV 2004 for a recent survey of viking-age Gotland, especially Östergren on the Spillings hoard: 67kg (148 lbs av.) of gold and silver hidden 875–80. For Torsburg see Engström 1984, with English summary.

and lived or at least died near the south-west coast of the island, with a retinue of *lithsmen* to commission the monument and cut verse on it:

NEVER SHALL A MORE HONEST BATTLE-STRONG WAGGON-
GOD
ON THE MIGHTY LAND OF THE SEA-KING
REIGN OVER LAND IN DENMARK

which suggests that the old pirate (god of the sea-waggon) had made his fortune further west, as friend or foe of the Danish king. On the other side of the island, at Gårdby, a mother raised a stone to one son, Smithr, who had been a 'good dreng' or lord's retainer, while the other son, Halfburin

SITS IN GARDAR

(lives in Russia: Ö 28, Ruprecht 190)

The number of viking-age treasures found here (more than on Gotland) makes this an 'offshore island' in the modern sense; but it was an insecure hideaway in the long run, and the development of Kalmar on the mainland eventually brought in Swedish rule and an organization of the people into eight *härader* assessed at eighty *attungar* of 10 *hamnor* (rowing places) each: but not before the twelfth century.[29] Another 200 miles to the north–east lay a less troubled colony of islanders, on the Åland archipelago: 'land and water, sea and tarn, rock and island, hoisted and jumbled together',[30], stepping-stones between Sweden and Finland with sufficient arable and pasture to support a population estimated at *c.*6000 by *c.*1000: descendants of an eastward migration which began *c.*500.

Some 250 cemeteries of cremated bones under small circular mounds indicate that the four bigger islands were no nests of chiefs, but communities of farmers unprotected by forts because mainly bypassed by shipping en route to Ladoga and Novgorod up the Gulf of Finland.[31]

All round the Baltic, islands were polities in the balance, between invaders and predators on one tide, and wealth-bringers on the next; between exerting power over mainlands, like the insular Slav

29 On the forts: Näsman in MASS 1997, Wegraeus and Weber in *Eketorp* (ed. Borg et al., Stm 1976). Göransson 1978 predates the administrative arrangements, but see Fabech 1999, 44–6 on the Björnhovda central place.
30 R.E. Hughes *Two Summer Cruises* (London 1856), 65.
31 Nuñez 1995, and Roeck Hansen 1991 for survey and settlements, 500–1500.

commonwealths of Wollin and Rügen, like early Bornholm and Zealand, and bowing to those mainlands, as they all eventually did. But not yet.

North Sea Coasts

Different ecologies fixed territorial groupings for peoples living between the North Sea and the spinal mountains of the Scandinavian peninsula: deep fjords, steep slopes, diminished arable, shorter growing seasons and heavier snows sharpened competition between the farmers who had already settled the Norwegian coast as far north as the Lofoten islands in Roman times and earlier. Here, territories began as a long string of chiefdoms known collectively as *Nor-vegr*, the North Route, and therefore studied as the kingdom of Norway in embryo. This kingdom took shape as a 'hereditary possession' (see p. 48) of uncertain shape, fought over by rulers in and out of Norway over the second half of the period; but for most of it, the chiefdoms could better be described as the main slipways for colonists and vikings going west, sheltered by a line of offshore islands running 400 miles north from Stavanger fjord to Trondheim. Coastal shipping could go inside or outside this line, as weather allowed, and for the rulers of the fjords attack had long been the only method of defence; Myhre has shown how the distribution and concentration of boathouses (*naustar*) and large halls points to the centres of power.[32] All the way from Oslo fjord, south-west and round the cape, and then north as far as barley would grow (Malanger fjord), there was a pattern of dispersed settlements combined into cross-country communities of various kinds; and war and lordship had combined these into territories, each traversing four ecological zones: outer islands or skerries, inner coastlands, pastoral slopes, and high forest – sources of the timber and iron, meat, barley and seamanship that enabled war-lords to assert themselves in what all outside observers agreed was a poor country, blighted by rain, snow, acid soils and darkness. By 800 this was an ancient state of affairs, long exploited by Danish or other rulers who had managed the flow of prestige goods from Germany and Francia down the line to the waiting chiefs, but now it

32 Myhre 1985, 1993, 1997 and 1998 examine the boat-houses 'as indicators of political organization'; but as Christophersen points out (in *Hikuin*, xxv, 1998, 73–5) these polities were 'polycentric conglomerations of functions' – not centralized in one place, but looking to separate but common places for cult, law-meetings, marketing, and lordship.

was jolted by the arrival of Insular treasures – Irish jewellry, ivories, sacred silver-ware – which the raiders appear to have got for themselves.

In the course of the next two hundred years the number of independent chiefdoms round the Norwegian coast diminished, but there were still some thirty *c*.900, and the hegemony over the south-west wielded by Harald Harfagr of Rogaland in the next generation hardly reduced the total here, where Sogn, More (North and South), Romsdal, and Hǫrðaland continue to flourish as separate territories for centuries, under various overlords, despite westward emigration: see map 5. At the end of the tenth century, jarl Hakon's poet Einarr called the territories fighting under the earl's command as *folklönd*, 'lands with an armed population', and the other name *fylkir* has the same military connotation, rather than just 'people'. A hundred years later these were components of a Norwegian kingdom and contributors to a general Norwegian levy-fleet, the *leiðangr*, with local quotas of oarsmen, oars, cordage etc. equitably distributed up and down the coast and a new range of boathouses, all prescribed by laws; but there is no evidence of any such scheme in the viking age, despite its later attribution to Hakon the Good (*c*.960) or Harald Harfagr. At this period the chiefs launched their own fleets and chose whom they fought for.[33]

Within the northern district of Trondheim were the eight relatively small territories of 'Thronds', Inner and Outer, who followed the dynasty of Hakon jarl in the tenth and early eleventh century. The earls' hall and home farm lay at Lade (ON *Hlaðir*) 1½ miles east of Niðaróss on the south coast of the fjord, in a small temperate pocket where summer temperatures have been known to reach the 90s (35° centigrade) and the snow lasts only five weeks, as opposed to ten and more round about. Their political ascendancy may have cult-origins, but their wealth was based partly on the local farming, partly on the yields of their clients among the Lapps and the coastal farmers and fishermen. Other coastal chiefs, on Tjotta, Vaagen and Borg on Lofoten, men like king Alfred's friend Ohthere (Óttar), did well out of the commercial opportunities of this region north of the Trøndelag, called Hálogaland The earls led a far northern family of chiefdoms which outlived their departure in 1016–17 and the

---

33 To cut short a long debate on the antiquity of the levy system by accepting the arguments of Lund 1996 and 1997 and rejecting the use of skaldic references (by Malmros 1985 et al.) to *lið*, *leið* etc. as evidence of public levies, rather than raiding fleets. Map 7 attempts to reconstruct the bigger units of lordship round this coast and elsewhere in Scandinavia and map 5 the ethnic and local names in skaldic verse and thirteenth-century prose.

intervention of the southern king Olaf Tryggvason in the 990s. He set up the royal manor which became Trondheim, an 'urban centre'; but long after that, the Thronds told the southerners where to get off on many occasions. In 1030 they defeated and killed the ex-king Olaf Haraldsson, when he tried to regain his kingdom from the Danes; it had been said of Hakon Jarl by Thórdr Kolbeinsson, after his downfall, that

> No man forsook him
> For stubbornness marks the Thronds

and subsequent Norwegian history demonstrated this repeatedly. What created Norway was not a 'growing sense of unity' among the territories but a parallel development of economic interdependence and political rivalry; on which see chapter 6.

At the beginning of this period the chiefdoms of the south, adjacent to the big inlet called Víken, had a long prehistory. On the west side (Vestfold) the chiefs at Borre had been buried in high mounds with imported pattern-welded spearheads as symbols of power in the Migration period, and the east coast (Ostfold) was dominated by rulers living near Sarpsborg; by 800 these and other rival centres in the estuary lowlands (the whole region later called Borgartingslag) were under some form of Danish overlordship, which was being contested in 812–13 according to the Frankish annals, but was periodically reasserted throughout this period. The Oseberg lady in her burial ship may have been a high-living client of the Jutland king or not; it is said that when Harald Harfagr defeated the rulers of these territories, he secured his own hegemony by marrying a Jutland woman. Harald Bluetooth claimed that he 'won Norway', and from then overlordship was shared between various contenders in a highly unstable balance usually tipped by the weight of the Lade earls in the north.[34] Meanwhile the southern coastal territories benefited as intermediaries between the Jutlanders and the small mountain kingdoms established among the inland settlements of Opland and Tellemark; six or seven dynasties ruled these highlands until they were subjugated by Olaf Haraldsson in the 1020s, but the *fylkir* continued to prosper as producers of iron, furs and hides. Sea and rivers linked all

---

34 Bluetooth bought Hakon jarl by the gift of Vingulmark and Raumarike in the south (according to Hsk), Hakon's son Eiríkr regained power after 999 with Sweyn Forkbeard's help, and his brother Sveinn seems to have ceded power to Olaf Haraldsson in 1016. Meanwhile, Canute needed Eiríkr to govern Northumbria, and Eiríkr's son Hakon died before he could re-establish the family's power in Norway after Olaf's expulsion.

these territories to each other, but also to foreign overlords; overland they were connected by three ancient routes that followed the passes: From

1   Mälardal, through Jarnberaland and Jamtland to Trondheim
2   Ostfold – Raumarike – Gudbrandsdal – Raumsdal on the west coast
3   Vestfold – Valdres – Sogn, also on the west coast.[35]

This leaves the west-facing coasts of the Kattegat, defended by another long line of skerries out to sea, but backed by mountains less tall and interrupted by the mouths of a series of rapid rivers of which the Göta Älv (Stream of the Gautar) is the biggest. In the 890s the territory north of that river (listed in the sixth century by Jordanes as *Ragnariki*, later Ranrike) was described as part of Denmark, and *Halland*, the territory to the south (now Bohuslän in Sweden) remained so for the next 700 years. To an eighteenth-century lowlander, the uplands of Halland 'present only an hideous object to the eye, and fill the mind with ideas of some terrible devastation of nature'[36]; and of man, since the hills bristle with hill-forts, which had been the centres of power in the Early Iron Age. Since then, the chiefs had moved down to the less hideous coast lands, to lord it over a row of four dispersed valley settlements, connected by an inland track from ford to ford, and by the same maritime overlordship the Jutlanders established over all these coasts. North of Göta Älv, Harald Hardrada was ravaging Ranrike as a rebellious province in the 1060s, and it was to become the gateway for Norwegian probes into Götaland and Halland over the ensuing half-century. Before that, these often treacherous shores had become a frontier zone between the contenders for Canute's hegemony, and they remained lightly populated outposts of the kingdoms stabilized after this period.[37]

Enough geography. To conclude the show-and-tell: Nordic communities were gathered into districts throughout the north, but they were organized on different principles: some as contributors and

---

35   See Blindheim 'Itinerant trade in VA Norway' (UNHAVE 1987, 763–5) for the economic coherence of the *fylkir*.
36   A Dutch officer, trans. Radcliffe 1790, 29; and see Connelid and Rosén (VIPA, 28–9); for Lindqvist's study of Slöinge, VIPA, 179–97, and Svanberg 1999, 84–92.
37   Only five of the eight districts of Halland were listed as *herreder* in KVJ; it was, and remained a semi-independent prefecture, divided N–S by the Tvååker boundary which 'runs through history like a scarlet thread': see Connelid and Rosén in VIPA, 28–9.

potential refugees to island and hill-forts, some as undefended settlement areas within belts of woodland, some as feeding-grounds for itinerant rulers, some as independent lordships or associations of freeholders. These districts were the components, rather than the subdivisions, of territories; which again could be the open hunting-reserves of scattered settlers, as in Hálogaland and with the Jämts and Hälsings, or ancient kingdoms like Mälardal, or Jutland or Götaland or Zealand, or oligarchies of freeholders like Gotland, or submissive dependencies like the smaller Danish islands guarding the southern shores, or like Bornholm, which was not like anywhere else. The variety and vigour of these territories was the main story of viking-age Scandinavia, overlooked by those with eyes only for the deeds of kings, the pre-requisites of state formation, and the transforming effects of international trade. Kings were rulers of limited powers in the ninth century, intermittently powerful, and in the tenth increasingly so; but by 1050 they could only be said to control about half of Scandinavia, and their water-based empires had proved highly unstable. It may be that some had established, or were imposing patterns of local government such as the *hundare* in Sweden, and the *herreder* and *syssler* of Denmark; but while they were doing this, freeholders were finding a voice and a power of local resistance in all manner of gatherings, which gave backbone to all districts and territories and a long life to come.

5

Peoples

I was with the Syrians: and with the Chinese:
I was with the Greeks: and with the Finns:
And with Caesar.

The Anglo-Saxon *Widsith* poet set out his wares by peoples and their rulers, and drew no line between centuries, languages, stages of socio-economic development, religions, fact or fiction. He may have been a contemporary of Ohthere and Wulfstan, who also listed the peoples of the north, but in terms of geography, political affiliation, economy, culture and navigation, for the benefit of king Alfred, who believed that knowledge was power. Others, with less complicated agendas, classified all the northerners as unenlightened barbarians, sons of Belial or scourges sent by God (see p. 116). Led by the scholar and poet Alcuin, they set up a stereotype which survives to this day in the contrast between the Nordic peoples as vikings, and 'christian Europe'. At the end of this period it was expressed by Adam of Bremen, for whom it was an inherent missionary assumption; but he followed the equation through. Baptized northerners who respected the authority of the archbishop of Hamburg-Bremen were as good as, or even better than anyone else: 'having laid aside their natural savagery' the converts may say 'we believe that we will see the good things of the Lord in the land of the living'.[1] So, like the first Adam, he gave all these creatures their right names, and enumerated the species in the fourth book of his *History of the Archbishops*.

The capricious naming of Nordic groups by outsiders was noted earlier (pp. 2–4). Some names used locally are shown on map 5. It

---

1 Quoting Psalm 27:13: AB 4, 42. His optimism was not shared by Thietmar of Merseburg 50 years earlier. On king Canute's conquest of England: 'he who was formerly the invader and bold destroyer of that province, now remained its sole defender, as the basilisk in the desolate Libyan desert' (TM, 8, 7). He and his brother were 'of the generation of vipers'.

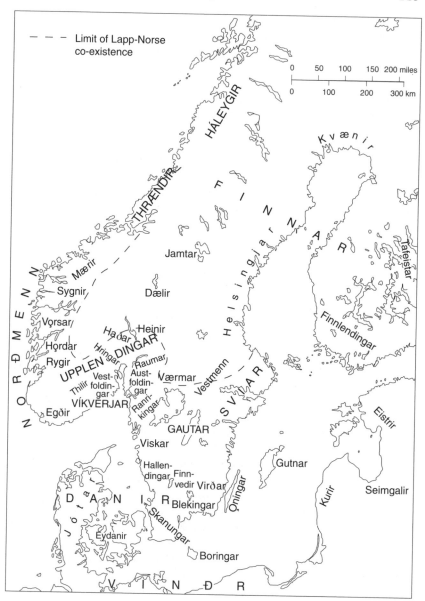

Map 5 *Scandinavian peoples, 750–1050*
As named by skaldic poets and medieval prose sources.
The larger groups are in capitals.

remains to ask whether they actually felt themselves to be nations or peoples, and what this meant. They never acted in such big masses during this period, and so the question may not seem particularly urgent; however, medieval ethnicity roused a feeding-frenzy among historians during the 1990s, and it would be discourteous to ignore the feast. It was an old topic, but new zeal was kindled by contemporary shifts in sensibility (the dwindling of some national loyalties and the revival of others); also by the bland assertion of non-medievalists[2] that all nations were artificial constructs created by the modern, or early-modern state, all in similar ways, to allow more efficient control of larger populations through a common culture and ethos. Stung by this slur on the nation-building efforts of pre-modern statesmen and scholars, their champions have responded by building on the ethnogenetic study which was patiently driven forward in German universities since the 1940s. Thanks to Wenskus, Lammers and Hauck there is at least a vocabulary for ethnic development north of the Alps in Late Antiquity and the Early Middle Ages. Smaller tribes (*Kleinstämme*) were either fragmenting into splinter-groups (*Teilstämme*) or expanding, through *Grossstambildung*, into large tribes (*Grossstämme*), which were populations held together by a nucleus of tradition (*Traditionskern*), often but not always embodied in a royal clan (*Königssippe*) which provided the sacral king (*Heilkönig*: on whom, see chapter 6). As with most technical terms in medieval historiography, these are theories masquerading as descriptions, and will therefore be avoided here. Besides, they don't seem to apply very neatly to Scandinavia or the Nordic colonies, where all these elements can be detected, but cannot be made to fit into the grand developmental pattern.

It would be better to begin by asking whether here or anywhere else, 'medieval names of human collectives refer to ethnic groups? that is, to peoples with the *wir-gefühl*, who thought of themselves as *us* in relation to the others, who were merely *them*?'[3] The asker, Wallerström, concluded that many such names used of people in the Baltic region referred primarily to the perceptions of outsiders, not to how they saw themselves. So *Finnar* were those walkers, 'finders' or itinerants of what we call the Fennic or Finno-Ugrian language-group who came into contact with Germanic agriculturalists: not exclusively Lapps or Finns, or Saami, but only the hunter-gatherers among them, and not all of them. The names multiply, and distinctions harden in the later middle ages; not because of any growth of ethnic consciousness in

2 Benedict Anderson (*Imagined Communities*) and E. Hobsbawm (*Nations and Nationalism*); *contra* S. Reynolds *Kingdoms and Communities* and 'Our Forefathers?' in *After Rome's Fall*, ed. A. C. Murray (Toronto 1998).
3 Wallerström 1997, 304; and see Hadley 1997, 83, and Heidenga and Gerrets on the discontinuity of Frisian identity in ASSAH, x, 1999, 119–26. Näsman (1999, 1–11) summarizes the developmental view of early Scandinavia.

Lappland, but because more outsiders get in there to do different kinds of business with the natives, who thus need to be called something.

If that was how it was as late as 1500 or 1700 in the subarctic region, was it the same for the more southerly Scandinavians before 1000? Are the Nordic peoples listed by Greek, Roman and Early Medieval geographers merely terms for small *ad hoc* associations which happened to impinge on warmer worlds as war-bands (like that of Chodochilaiacus-Hygelac-Hugleik, called Danes by Gregory of Tours, Geats in *Beowulf*, and eventually Dubliners by Saxo) slave-vendors or arms-buyers, but had no *wir-gefühl* with larger collectives? Something like this happened in the case of the *Rus*. The word seems to originate before this period, and was used by Balts and Fennic peoples to mean 'rowers', of no one ethnic group, but (as it happened) from Scandinavia. When the rowers moved into north Russia and formed settlements and associations of fur-dealers and raiders, the name went with them, and by 830 had been fitted by the officials and clergy of Constantinople into their mental encyclopaedia of gentile nations: they were *Rhos*. But when some of them were sent on from Byzantium to the Frankish court in 839, they were quickly identified as *Suiones*,[4] Swedes, a group of Baltic sea-raiders well-known in the West thanks to the mission of Ansgar to Birka. Eventually, Franks and Germans began to use *Russi* and *Rutheni* as ethnic terms, but only in the sense developed within Russia after the conversion to christianity: any people of any sort who accepted the rule of the princes who claimed descent from Rurik, and the Orthodox faith. Scandinavians were the last to adopt this term, since they had worked out others for the inhabitants along the 'East-way', of a coarsely functional kind: they were either *Gerzkr* 'fort-people', the bosses, or just Easterners, East-Wends. The Finns went on calling the Swedes *Ruotsi*. Thanks to the variety of such identifications, the written sources are full of ethnic confusion. *Rhos* might be Swedes to the Franks, but Swedes were often called Northmen; and Northmen were Danes; and Danes, to the poets, were usually Jutes; and Jutes, to Asser the Welshman, were Goths; and Goths, said Jordanes and Isidore of Seville, came from Scandinavia; and so on.

4 Franklin and Shepard 1996, 50–5 summarize recent speculation, now virtually sedated by Ekbo and Thulin's articles in MS xiii (2000). A view that in 839 the Rhos may have been acting for a king in Sweden, rates the power of such kings higher than Ansgar found it. Melnikova and Petrukhin 1990/91 summarized the case for Swedish descent. Another functional name which turned ethnic seems to be Lithuanian, from *leitis*, a military escort: (Bojtar 1999, 137); and another, Varangian, if *Væringjar* really refers to the *várar* or pledges given by members of a mobile association of traders or warriors. By 1200 it became a word for Scandinavians, in Russia (*varyagoi*).

Western observers of the Norse gave them collective names on different principles:

1 *Religion*

as in the Anglo-Saxon Chronicle, where the ninth-century invaders are called 'the heathen', which Asser translates *pagani*. The Irish annalists usually refer to them as *geinte* (gentiles, or unbaptized peoples) until the conversion of their Dublin Norsemen in the period 950–75.[5] Pagans and gentiles recur in continental writers down to the early eleventh century; ecclesiastical tradition demanded that after conversion, the gentile nations should become christian *populi*, led to salvation by their bishops, and by the end of this period some authors draw finer distinctions.

2 *Otherness*

(alterity, in troll's Latin). The *Gaill* of the Irish annals are just foreigners, 'them', although the term is qualified by time of arrival: the fair before 850, the dark ones after. Also by association with natives: *Gaill-goídil*, 'foreign-Irish' appear in the mid-ninth century as rootless marauders, but were sufficiently grounded in the tenth to give their name to Galloway. English and Frankish sources express the same shudder with the old stand-by *barbari*, spiced with 'unclean populace', 'plebs most filthy', 'squalid gangs' in the text of ealdorman Ethelweard's Latin chronicle of *c.*980, a time when a good crop of contemptuous vituperation was ripening in the more learned monasteries of the West, to range over the Nordic vices from moral nastiness to physical over-fastidiousness (bathing every Saturday).

3 *Whence?*

Northmanni was the commonest term for all Norse invaders and settlers in Latin sources, from the eighth century to the eleventh: it was not confined to those who settled in Normandy (*Normanni*) until later. Writers who lived nearer the north, like Adam of Bremen, eventually found this unsatisfactory; by his time the term was usually applied within Scandinavia to non-Danes, and he notes that, nevertheless, 'Danes and Swedes and the other peoples beyond Denmark are all called Northmen by the historians of the Franks' (AB 4,12) In the tenth century, the Wessex annalist called the Danelaw colonies to his east 'Northern', but the Dubliners who conquered them in 939–40 were called Northmen, as distinct from the Danes who 'had been subjected by force' to those intruders.

Other Norse intruders from the west were Irishmen (*Írar*) in the places named after them (Ireby, Irby, Ireton), because that is where

---

5 On which, see Ó Murchada 1992–3, and Ní Mhaonaigh 1998.

they came from; and in Normandy, Engelesque recalls settlers from the English Danelaw. When Northmen, who had been 'Irishmen' on occasions, stayed on in Dublin, they became 'Eastmen' to the more Celtic sort of Irishmen: the Ostmen of Oxmantown. This mutability suggests that when raiders were asked who they were, they replied in terms of territory, not of nation. As with the Dorset marauders of *c.* 790, who came from Hǫrðaland in SW Norway (p. 108), or the attackers of Brittany in 843, who were called *Westfaldingi*, or people from Vestfold, in Viken.[6] This seems to be how the Nordic invaders of Ireland got their more specific name of *Lochlannach*, 'people from Lochlann'; although its earlier recorded form, *Laithlind*, cannot easily come from 'Land of Lochs', or from Rogaland, two competing derivations.[7] Once the idea of Denmark as a country had been accepted in the West (after 900), it became more desirable to distinguish Danes who lived there from the many who didn't; so the Burgundian monk Ralph Glaber, in the 1020s referred to 'the kingdom of those people who are called Denmarks (*Danimarches*)' as if the place had made a new people out of an old one (RG 2,3).

4 *Function*

As in *pirati, wichingi, flotmen, scipmen* and the North German *ascomanni*: men who sail in ships made of or containing ash-wood. Terms applied to Nordic rather than other raiders because in this period there were more of them, and they seemed to 'haunt the tide' (Ermold). As argued in the introduction, these were not used as ethnic descriptions at the time, unless opprobriously, as by the Frankish historian Richer, of Normans.

Danes

Those four common perceptions of the Norse lasted throughout the viking age, slightly modified by the conversions. At the same time, there were apparently ethnic names which may have been given in answer to the question, Who are you? rather than supplied from books (like the Alans, whom Abbo of Fleury and Dudo of St Quentin included with the ninth-century invaders, or the Ishmaelites and

---

6 Higham 1995, 199–205 on the *Írar*.
7 Norse words beginning R do not become Irish loan-words beginning L; that is the only safe conclusion in the long and tendentious debate on the whereabouts of Laithlind/Lochlann, for which see ISCEVA, 62–6, 381–2, 424–5, and Ó Corráin 'The Vikings in Scotland and Ireland', *Peritia* XII 1998 296–339.

other biblical anti-types of gentile scourges); and the first and most frequent of these was Danes.

They had apparently been around for a long time. In the sixth century Jordanes described them as a people which had driven the Heruli from their homes in the far north; they were a nation as far as Procopius was concerned, and Gregory of Tours noted that they had raided the mouth of the Rhine in the 530s under a king. By the late seventh century they were seen as a *gens* ripe for salvation in the vision of the Northumbrian monk Egbert, and after their king Ongendus had rejected the offer of christianity in the early eighth, they acquired a set literary personality, as a fierce, uncouth and obdurate race typified by their awesome ruler Sigifrit, in the verses written by Charlemagne's Lombard follower, Peter of Pisa, in the 780s.

> If you look at the face of the grandiose Sigifrit
> (Now holding impious sway in a noxious kingdom)
> With a view to baptize that fellow from a holy font,
> You know that he'll rob you on sight of life and learning.[8]

After that, references to Danes are frequent and promiscuous in the West, and cannot apply to a single people or nation. Danes were (a) Northmen in general, from all over Scandinavia and the western colonies; (b) members of the armies which troubled Francia from the 830s to the 930s; (c) Normans; (d) Dublin Norsemen, but only after 986 in the Irish Annals; (e) settlers and their descendants in the English Danelaw, whatever their origin; and (f) inhabitants of Denmark.

From within Scandinavia there is almost complete silence on the ethnic question during this period, owing to the nature of the sources. What evidence there is gives no clearer idea of who was what than do the western sources. The poets used both Dane and Gaut to mean 'inhabitant', 'man', 'warrior'; they usually called Danish kings lords of the Jutes or Scanians – only twice in the whole corpus as kings of the Danes. King Gorm (died 958) of Jelling is not called king of Danes on his rune-stone, but his son Harald Bluetooth claimed to have 'made the Danes christian' and was evidently referring to the inhabitants of what he 'won': Denmark. But what was that?

---

8 Trans. from MGH Poet. Lat. Aevi. Car. i, 50–1; the reluctance of Frankish bishops and clergy to approach the Danes before 815 is well attested. In his reply to Peter's poem, Paul the Deacon declared that there was no point in bearding Sigifrid, because in due course 'he will arrive with his hands tied behind his back, and Thor and Odin will be no help to him'.

When in the 890s or earlier, Ohthere sailed south from *Sciringes hal* in Viken, along the east coast of the Kattegat he found *Denemearc* to port (on his left-hand side) all the way to the Danish islands, a stretch that would include all the later south-east territory of Norway, as well as Halland (on which see p. 110). On his starboard bow he had the open sea (the Skager Rack); but according to one school of thought,[9] he said he had Denmark on his left because he didn't have it on his right: at that date, Jutland was not in Denmark, because *mark* means 'frontier, outlying territory' and Jutland and Funen were centre, not periphery. Therefore when in the 980s king Harald claimed to be ruling Denmark, he meant that he had got control of the east Danes, and when he had called his mother 'ornament of Denmark' he meant that she had in some way brought this region in the east to be his inheritance.

Since no single source actually uses the word Denmark to exclude Jutland (Ohthere certainly doesn't), this distinction seems to be imaginary.

Shortly after 908, the annalist Regino of Prüm referred to Northmen raiding Holland 'from Denmark' (*ex Denimarca*), and as he was writing a long way to the south there is no reason to suppose that he tried to distinguish east Danes from Jutlanders. In 965 Otto I's diploma refers to bishoprics '*in marca vel regno Danorum*', as if for his chancery clerks, mark and kingdom were equivalent if not identical.

At some stage, the word probably did mean 'frontier of the Danes', but the most likely frontier is that on which Frankish and Danish envoys met and swore peace in 811 and 873, the river Eider which marked the northern limit of Saxon settlement. From there, the meaning stretched to cover all territories claimed by the Jutland dynasty[10] all the way up to Oslo fjord, and so to all lands inhabited by Danes east of the North Sea; which leads back to the question: who or what did they think they were?

Other medieval nations identified themselves by three myths: a real or feigned community of blood, through a notional descent from common ancestors; customs, laws and language held to be peculiar

9 Ekbom's idea, as in Skovgaard and Petersen 1977, and Sawyer in DADA, 22–3; but see Lund 1994 for the Orosius text and translation, and Lund 1991 for a summary. Sawyer (220–1) outlines the Thyra theory, which Mrs Sawyer elaborates in B. Sawyer 2000, 158–66, where Denmark 'border areas subordinated to Danish kings that were not yet fully integrated into the kingdom'.
10 On Otto's diploma see Refskou 1986, 173; and note the Skivum stone which commemorates a Jutlander as 'the best and foremost land-man in Denmark'. Examples of words for 'frontier' becoming names of whole peoples are found among Balts: Semigallians, Lettigallians, and Galindians all occupied areas called *gali*: boundaries.

to, if not shared by all members of, the nation; a common history, or core of tradition (as p. 114). These fancies can be found among the Franks, the Anglo-Saxons, and other civilized barbarians, because they were written down, at a comparatively early date. Not among the Danes or any other Nordic people of the viking age, because they wrote no books; national myths had to be laboriously invented or reinvented, beginning in Iceland in the early twelfth century. More of this in chapter 10; but there are modern myths of Danish development to fill the gap. The slogan 'From Tribe to State' carries nations along with it, as the social bodies created by that supposed evolution. There is a genealogy of the Danish state going back to the second or the fifth century,[11] in which Danes are defined by their liability to pay taxes in kind, construct earth-works, and obey a sort of evolutionary drill in line with the principles to be found in Classen and Skalnik's *The Early State* (1978) or W.G. Runciman's *Origins of the State* (1982): what was referred to earlier as the bureaucrat's daydream. More of this in the next chapter; for the time being it is enough to suggest that people called themselves Danes in the viking age because the events of the previous four centuries had given the name international currency. These events may have been highly unconstructive, anti-social and even suicidal; but if they impressed the Anglo-Saxon *Beowulf* poet as glorious, Scandinavians were unlikely to disagree.

In some cases, their national identities were improvised to meet the needs of the moment. The Northmen who came to the Lower Seine from various parts of the North had a Danishness defined for them by the Frankish historian Dudo of St Quentin after *c.*1000, as something created in Francia through a union of many 'birds' (English, Frankish, Breton, Danish, Alan, Norwegian) under the leadership of Rouen. Irish annalists who called the Dubliners Danes from the later tenth century, (not before) were perhaps referring to the supposed origin of their ruling dynasty, or just echoing the Irish word *dana* (fierce); another gift from foreigners, which was to have a long future in Irish folklore. The settlers of the English Danelaw were defined by their relations with an intrusive West Saxon king with of imperial leanings. Having been a ruling class under their own chiefs, from 915 they were subject to native authorities which respected their land-rights and customs in return for military service and taxation; they became components in a 'multinational empire', English by affiliation, Danish by status and law, alongside Mercians, Welshmen,

---

11   See Hedeager 1992, 83–7 and Axboe 1995, 225–33 and 1999 for this school, which dominated HØKO (1991); only Näsman's contribution questioned the title laid down by the editors: *From Tribe to State in Denmark*, 2.

Northumbrians and Kentishmen and other distinct groups under the hand of English kings.[12] Danes of Denmark could not be defined by difference in the same way, since they differed from each other as much as from other Northmen, and it was not until the end of this period that being a Dane, in the Baltic region, meant being subject to a Danish king: the Blekingar do not seem to have counted as Danes before they submitted to Sweyn II, perhaps in the 1060s, nor the Bornholmers. If 'the ethnogenesis of the Danes is beyond the reach of study',[13] their viking-age identity escapes clear definition.

At which point, archaeology comes to the rescue. It is commonly accepted that ethnic groups in prehistoric times identify themselves when similar grave-rituals, ceramics, settlement patterns, ornamental motifs, ornaments and weapons are found in one area rather than another. Such similarities become 'ethnic identifiers', and from them the prehistory of separate peoples is traced back to Bronze Age and Neolithic times, in Scandinavia as elsewhere, on what appear to be scientific grounds. The difficulty of telling Saxons from Angles and Britons in fifth-and sixth-century graves evaporates under this treatment, and the nameless tribes of the remoter past come to life as the exponents of particular cultures revealed by excavation. Such a method ought to reveal the ethnic map of viking-age Scandinavia without further ado. After all, it is used to distinguish Slavs from Finns from Swedes in darkest North Russia, and most pre-historians would be lost without it. However, there are at least two serious objections. One is the matter of verification: how do we know that shared burial rites and ceramic designs amounted to a 'we-feeling' when there is no other evidence of it? And the other is the very freakishness of ethnic designation when we do have evidence of that. As in the case of one odd sort of Dane or Northman which changed its name over this period.

Norwegians

Norwegians – people living along the coasts from the Kattegat to north of the Lofoten islands – was a term first recorded in the later tenth century and meaning 'North-Way dwellers'. In the 890s Ohthere had called himself the northernmost of Northmen, and

---

12 Williams 1986 cannot be bettered on the subject of Anglo-Danes.
13 Wood 1983, and see Ringtved 1999, Näsman 1999, 8; bearing in mind Komoroczy's description of ethnic prehistory as 'the wilful reflection of tribal consciousness back into the past' (cited in Bojtar 1999, 237). See Svanberg 1997 for a pure archaeological recreation of identity in Scania, and Barford, Czerniak, Webart,

Northmen continues to be used for Norwegians to the present day; but at some point a need was felt for a term which distinguished these from other sorts of Northmen, in Denmark and Sweden.[14] Norwegian historians connect this need with their own 'process of state formation', beginning with the interaction of North Sea chiefdoms in Roman times, and culminating about the end of the viking period; nearly a thousand years, during which the fjord-dwellers were 'a distinct people with their own territory' and had acquired 'something of an ethnic and cultural identity' or at least 'a budding identity of their own'.[15] There is no direct evidence of this whatever; it is a deduction from the general similarity of grave-goods and settlement patterns along the coast, a common dependence on seafaring which is a matter of ecology, not of ethnic identity. Others invoke political organization as the unifying principle. The trade-networks linking the far north with Kaupang, the transit-harbour in Viken, could have been 'administered' through a series of arrangements going back to 'an authority of some importance', resident at Huseby near Kaupang, so that 'around 900 AD the unification process was well under way'. If it was, nobody noticed; certainly not Ohthere, who mentioned no such authority. There had been a powerful chiefdom at Borre, in Vestfold, from the seventh to the time of Ohthere, but to call that 'an early phase...of a process towards a unified Norwegian state' (Blindheim) is only to repeat that small-scale organization may precede large; or follow, as in the case of fragmented empires. There is no beginning too ancient for *gamle Norge* if all that is needed is a row of rich burials, boathouses and a modest residuum from coastal trade. The historical record of the ninth and tenth century is of divergence rather than community along the North Way; a power-struggle in which earls of Hlaðir, kinglets of the south-west, and Danish kings set up contrasting systems of hegemony with no clear victor before the death of Canute (1035). The Norwegian kingdom which emerged under

Burström, and Hines, on the problems raised by this procedure, in *Archaeologia Polona* xxxiv (1996). Others attribute the flowering of animal art forms among the Norse to a wholly imaginary 'Scandinavian identity'.

14   The bigger Jelling stone (*c.*980) has NURVIAK, and the Egaa stone in Jutland (DR 143) refers to Ketil as NURUN, (Norron) which in that context means Norwegian; Dudo (*c.*1015) used *Northuigeni* for raiders of the 960s. The poem on king Athelstan which appears to call Harald (Fairhair) a king of the Norwegians was reworked at Malmesbury before being used by William in GR.

15   Helle 1995, 13–17; and 1998, 241. For the other theories, Blindheim ØPOLIS 1992, 137–50, and Myhre, passim, but esp. in Carver 1992, 201–13. Mundal 1997 argued that the use of provincial names by poets (as above, p. 87) is evidence of a 'concept of a greater national unity'. Or its absence?

Harald Hardrada was the product of military force applied both to its subjects and to its neighbours, a launching pad for Harald's wider ambitions to rule over as much of Britain Sweden and Denmark as he could get. International intimidation, from York to Constantinople was his aim, not national integrity. The emergence of Norwegian identity has no clear connection with the deeds of any of these warlords, but may have been a negative reaction to Danish overlordship; at first under Hakon Jarl in the 970s, when he defied Harald Bluetooth, and later in 1034 when a party of chiefs turned against the rule of Canute's son Sweyn and his English mother, and summoned a boy-king, Magnus Olafsson, to lead them (as p. 19). Even so, the distinction of Norwegians from other Northmen was no sharper than the lines between Norwegian law-districts. It may have meant more among the Norse colonists out west, who looked east for the mother-country.

Of these, the *Icelanders* had the largest and most viable new territory, a set of common institutions and a single place of assembly at which laws binding the whole colony were agreed. By 1050 they had one public religion and were ready for their own bishop, and had established a lead in the art of vernacular poetry; they were doubtless already fabulating about their unified past: see below, chapter 10, pp. 223–5. Tales of collectivity lit their long winters: such as when the poet Eyvindr the Plagiarist was rewarded for his verses in honour of the Icelanders with a large silver brooch, fashioned from silver raised by public subscription; and how he phrased his thanks:

The landsmen of sea's heaven
Sent it across to me.[16]

And how every Icelander was ordered to avenge an injustice by composing an insulting line against the Danish king Harald Bluetooth; and how St Olave decreed special privileges for all Icelanders trading or touring in Norway; and how English, Danish and Swedish kings had honoured individual Icelanders above other men, for their wit, their courage, and their metrical expertise.[17] Such narratives have a familiar ring. They resemble the myths and legends of American nationhood which partisans of the young republic foisted on their colonial and rebel past, and which have endured to the

16 For trans. Page 1995, 147–8. On the energizing role of saga heroes through Iceland's history, see Helgason 'Continuity?' in CONIL (1995) 64–81.
17 The connexion was made in modern times in Vilhjalmur Stefansson's *Iceland, the first American Republic* (1939) and in Richard F. Tomasson *Iceland: the first New Society* (Minneapolis 1980).

present day. Like the Icelanders, they claimed to spring from the 'best blood' of the Old World, rejected tyranny and illegality, and framed a governing assembly which bound all by its laws but left freeholders free. They, too, affirmed their nationality with anecdotes of civic responsibility and instances of native genius, drawn from as far back as the first land-taking. The resemblances invite the question: are these national myths equally unhistorical?

Although the islanders would seem, by 1050, to have met all three qualifications for medieval nationhood outlined above (p. 120) – a common body of law, a uniform vernacular language, a myth of foundation and descent – it is remarkable that the notion of ethnic separateness plays so little part in the early literature (1125–1225); all the attributes of nationality appear without it. So much so that a keen Iceland-watcher has concluded that here, ethnicity was invented in the twelfth century, and was largely invented by one family, the Oddaverjar descendants of Ari the Wise, to justify the social dominance of the ruling oligarchy of chiefs.[18] Hence the emphasis on noble descent, on the defence of property-rights, on the establishing of a General Assembly by the chiefs, on the pre-christian priesthood of those chiefs as *goðar*, on temple-taxes that foreshadowed tithe, on the succession of virtuous presidents who preserved the laws and customs in their memories, until they were codified in the winter of 1118. All these bullet-points of later tradition can be seen as rebutting slurs by native or foreign critics; by those who claimed (as a note in Landnamabok reveals) that Icelanders were 'descended from slaves and robbers' by those who resented the overweening land-claims of ambitious chiefs, by those who wished to enlarge the membership of the Althing, or who resented paying tithe to chiefs rather than clergy (after 1097). They asserted their dignity in this way because they were peculiarly dependent on what outsiders thought of them. Their only means of getting silver or timber was by employment as warriors or poets overseas, or by exporting woollens and hawks to Norway as favoured visitors, relying on the goodwill of kings. Ethnic separation played no part in this outlook, because they were trying to present themselves as good Northmen, true representatives of what the Norwegians and Danes of that period held dear, not deserving to be sneered at as colonial bumpkins, suet-landers, suet-fiends (*mǫrlendingar, mǫrfjandi*) or laughed at for preferring

---

18 Hastrup 1982, and 1990, 77–80; and see Weber 1988, 96. By 1200 the Odda-verjar owned some 48 farms. Mundal 1997 has Icelanders switching from a strong Norwegian to a new Iceland identity in the thirteenth century. On the dominance of chiefs see Vésteinsson in CONIL 18–19; on their goðorð authorities Ruthström ANF cxiv 1999, 89–102.

buttered porridge to decent food. None of these slights need have bothered them in the pre-conversion period, when different pressures were felt. More opportunities for getting land or a living on the island; more connections with Ireland and Britain; more shipping, and more mobility in general; more hope of better land out west, in Greenland or Vinland; more chances of dealing with or joining viking bands: no concern at all for ecclesiastical opinion, until a Saxon cleric started killing pagans, and Olaf Tryggvason threatened a trade-embargo in the late 990s.

In those days, and for long after, an identity as Northmen by blood, Icelanders by territory was quite good enough. Not even Ari, in the 1120s, presented the formulation of the local laws and customs as the birth of a nation. The focuses of loyalty remained firstly the family, secondly the patron or chief, thirdly the overseas ruler for as long as he remained a good lord. If it had been otherwise, Iceland would not have lost its independence in the thirteenth century. Patriotic Icelandic historians have tended to assume that this loss, or the preceding civil dissension, checked the growth of a long-established nation;[19] nurtured by consensual democracy: but the only contemporary evidence of how Icelanders saw themselves before the conversion is what survives of the satirical and encomiastic verse of the skalds, none of it patriotic in theme and most of it praising foreign kings and chiefs. There are no rune-stones or foreign visitors to fill the gap. Sayer's suggestion that the settlers were at least prone to 'passive xenophobia' directed against their Irish underclass is so meagrely supported by the evidence[20] that it can only be treated as a sally, waiting for reinforcements.

They are not to be found in the slighting references to dark-haired, swarthy characters in the sagas, which has been interpreted as the product of a strong Nordic racial awareness.[21] Any student of French or German medieval literature can skim off many similarily anti-saturnine scoffs; even if the Icelandic examples do relate in some way to the early history of the island, they would only show that in the thirteenth century, to be an Icelander was less important than being a blond Icelander. Ethnic identity is not in the picture.

19 For example, 'The Icelandic sagas tell the story of how Iceland separated from Norway, how it grew into its own, in short, how Iceland became a nation' (Andersson 1999, 932): a doxology among saga-critics, despite the balance of love and hate for Norwegians expressed in those texts; see Callow in SCEU, 323–31.
20 Sayers 1994: the argument rests mainly on the number of Old Irish loans in Old Norse which fall below what might have been expected if there had been as many Irish immigrants as Sayers assumes. See de Vries AEW, xx, 180–2 for the loans.
21 Jochens 1999, arraigning short personal names (Svartr, Hjalp, Kolr) and the nicknames Spoon-Nose and Sharp before the Race Tribunal.

Nor was it in Greenland, where the two outermost colonies of the Icelanders were established in the 980s and were apparently thriving by the end of the viking period. Adam of Bremen had heard of Greenlanders, as a piratical sea-green people, recent converts to christianity;[22] but Adam's idea of christianity was strict. It had to come from Hamburg-Bremen, the metropolitan see of the entire North. Nor were there many opportunities for piracy off the Greenland coast, since the land was mostly uninhabited at this date, and the waters cannot have attracted prizes worth having. According to the thirteenth-century versions of tales told in Iceland, the settlers began probing the American mainland about the turn of the century, and were ill-received by the Amerindians they called *Skrælingar* in a country they called *Vínland*, or Wine-Land. It was one of a series of otherwise unrecorded efforts to find raw materials or marketable products with which to maintain contact with Iceland and the Old World, and it seems to have failed in material terms, if the archaeology of L'Anse aux Meadows on the Newfoundland coast is all that is left. The inspiration behind these sagas was not Greenland patriotism but the pride of certain Iceland families in ancestors who had gone to the edge of the world and returned with alarming and amusing stories. The fate of the Greenlanders was to endure three or more centuries of hard work and danger as an outpost of Christendom, and to dwindle into neglected dependants of the Norwegian crown; the loyalty of the first settlers was to family and friends, rather than to any larger collective.[23]

The north-westerners of the Nordic world seem to have managed without any clear notions of ethnic identity, perhaps because they all spoke languages regarded as 'Danish' and were not in competition with ethnic groups for resources. But most of Scandinavia and the Fenno-Scandic region, from the North Sea to the Northern Dvina, was not inhabited by Norse speakers at this period: it was shared by the many peoples known to Othere, Wulfstan and Adam of Bremen mainly as huntsmen, herders and trappers, and so as potential competitors with the Northmen, or collaborators. Of the varous names they were given, *Finnar* is presumably the oldest, since *Phennoi*, *Fennaidi* etc. were known to the Roman geographers; and *Finnar*

22   AB 4, 37 (36); their green-ness reflects his.
23   See Bigelow 1990 for contrasting views of Greenland identity from Keller (126–41), who sees the settlers as primitive egalitarians on the Germanist model, and McGovern who detects a priest-ridden peasantry under the thumb of bishops, who inculcated such ultimately suicidal doctrines as the untouchability of the Eskimos, and regulated all contact with the outside world. Sayers pursues the persecution of the Celts all the way up here by deriving *skræling* from Old Irish and making Vinland a metaphor for Ireland (*Skandinavistik* 1993).

have reappeared since 1980 as a factor in viking-age and prehistoric history, in time with a new self-assertion by Lapps in Norway. They were able to present a moderate threat to the hydro-electric projects which disturb their pastures, and a slight shock to the complacency of social-democratic opinion, usually more interested in the wrongs of persecuted minorities in other continents. The do-gooders reacted by renaming their Lapps; Sámi, or Saami, was to be the new designation, and Saapmi their native land. Various opinion-formers then reopened a debate on the origins and identity of this people, which had been 'denied a prehistory' by 'the Norwegian archaeological establishment', and this debate touches all ethnic identifications of the Ancient and Early Medieval world.[24]

Odner argued that this whole region had once been used by a variety of families, tribes and working-teams, until they were separated into hunter-gatherers and agriculturalists by 'a process of differentiation and specialization in the Finnish Gulf area around the time of Christ'. After that, a third group, of man-hunters and territorial aggressors, responded to the demand for slaves and northern produce outside the area. Each group needed the other for the exchange or appropriation of goods; the hunter-gatherers were the Lapps (*Finnar* to the Northmen), the agriculturalists were the Kainu (*Kvenar* to the Northmen, *Cwenas* to the Anglo-Saxons, which also meant Women), and the militarists were the Northmen, if that is what they called themselves about that time. The identities came not from language, political organization, or group awareness, but from economics; the names are trademarks, misinterpreted as tribal or national by geographers and clerics itemizing the inhabitants of the outer world on lines that made sense nearer the Mediterranean. A proposition which prompted a cyclostyled discussion by Schanche and Olsen on the theme: 'Were they all Northmen?', and was challenged by those who see the archaeological evidence of settlement along the Bothnian and north Norwegian coasts as clear evidence of cultural and ethnic distinction, not merely of economic specialization. A 'stiff Norse ethnic self-consciousness' set up an 'ethnic territorial frontier from Viken to Malangen as a defensive ideological strategy', keeping Norsemen out of the hinterland until after the viking age, and receiving its produce through formalized exchanges with the Lapps: the gifts Ohthere described as tribute.

---

24 Odner's *Finnar og Terfinnar* (Oslo 1983) revived this debate, which has been continuous since medieval times; the book was condensed into an English article in NAR, xviii, 1985, 1–13. In reply, see Urbanczyk 1998, 214–15, and David Loeffler, *Contested Landscapes / Contested Heritage* (Umeå 2005).

Lapps may have been 'denied a pre-history' in Norway, but for the last 300 years they have been closely or superficially studied by travellers, ethnographers, anthropologists and all kinds of parsons, religious and secularist. By some, their religion and culture has been used as a guide to the beliefs of the Norsemen, supposedly borrowed and put on ice; their languages are sieved by philologists for loan-words in order to reveal what some early North German might have muttered in the Age of Migration, before migrating.[25] Lapps continued to oblige their observers by keeping reindeer, beating ritual drums, setting up wooden idols, and performing small sacrifices almost down to the present day. Many look different, dress differently, and talk a different language, so that it remains difficult to view them as just another sort of Norsemen by descent, disadvantaged by the processes of history. Nevertheless, most Lapps don't keep reindeer, worship idols, dress in Lappish costume, or talk Lappish. All have long been subject to definition by the bureaucrats of four governments (Norwegian, Swedish, Finnish, Russian) with quite different views on the subject, and historians have followed suit.

Zachrisson attempted to establish cultural criteria by which to sort out 'Scandinavian Ethnicity' from 'Saami Ethnicity'. On the one hand, agriculture and stock-raising, sledges, permanent dwellings. On the other, herding, hunting, skis and impermanent *kaatar*. Leaving aside her invention of something called Scandinavian ethnicity, she ignores the abundant evidence that *Finnar* occupied every kind of terrain north of Mälardal and Viken in the middle ages, and they could not all have lived by subarctic pastoralism; they were divided into sea-Finns, fell-Finns and farming Finns, and lived accordingly. Some could indeed be called representatives of a circumpolar Eurasian–American hunting–herding culture, like the Iroquois and *Skraelingar*, but they were none the less Scandinavian for that.[26] As for their history in the viking age, there is only conjecture, often based on the assumption that these peoples have always been victims. Their folklore and jokes usually involve outwitting the strong and the sinister intruders, the tall *stallo*; therefore they have always been under-dogs, 'have never conquered others' territory, have never engaged in systematic warfare against other people', according to

<hr />

25 Jorma puts the time of first Fennic-Germanic contact at 1500/500 BC; Koivulehto (1986) aligns the loan-words in Lappish with the supposed date of the Germanic sound-changes they anticipate. It is blind man's bluff of high intellectual calibre. See Rydving in ONFRAC, and on Lapp cults Kjellström in SAAR, and Olaus Magnus (OM 3, 2). On Lapp and Nordic belief and magic, Price 2002 ch. 4.
26 Zachrisson in VC 12; Odner and Inger Sörli have traced early Lapp presence far to the south of Norway, and for Lapp burials in Jämtland see Haasson in *Fornvännen* lxxxxix. Hultkrantz in SAAR (1987), 110–21, for kindred Amerindian-Lapp beliefs.

one sympathizer.[27] This is true for the last 500 years, but before that the hunter-gatherer herdsmen and the Norsemen were not so unevenly matched. The traditions and inventions embedded in Icelandic literature are not contemptuous of Lapps, who appear as outlandish hunters of surpassing toughness and skill, and as the possessors of magical powers which make them invisible, invulnerable and omniscient. Earlier on, the skalds say little about them. Ohthere told king Alfred that his Lapps paid him a tribute in kind per head, of skins, feathers and manufactured goods; how often, and why, he left unsaid, but the tribute was proportional to the rank of the payers. It would make sense if this were in exchange for barley-bread, beer, steel arrowheads and some of his valuable beef; otherwise, it is impossible to see how he could have compelled payment, with the vast open spaces into which the Lapps could have melted.

Archaeology has found few traces of viking-age Northmen in those spaces, beyond the enigmatic stone-and-turf walled hunting camps distributed widely from north Jämtland to Varanger fjord, and called *stalo*, like the grim intruders of folklore.

A change came when the right to enter Lappland and trade, while collecting a general tribute called *finnskat*, became a privilege granted to friends or agents of the Norwegian king. The Heimskringla saga of St Olave included a detailed narrative of how this privilege became a contentious issue between the king and the northern chiefs in the 1020s, on the assumption that it already existed at that date in its thirteenth-century form, a regalian right. If so, it may have been taken over from the earls of Hlaðir, who had ruled the north down to *c.*1017; or this could be a reflection of an early royal intervention in what was still a local matter between northern magnates and their Lapp clients. Until then, and for long after, Lapps and Northmen were as much united as separated by their economic lives, and there can be little doubt that Norse ethnic self-consciousness was not so stiff that they did not intermarry: the popularity of the name-element and name Finnr was lasting and is difficult to explain other than by amicable relations.[28]

The people called Finns in English call themselves Suomi, after the inhabitants of SW Finland in post-viking times, the corner first settled

---

27 Saressalo 1987. Lapps fought in hunting-groups and clans for the occasional use rather than the ownership of territory, and this was how war was conducted by all who lived in the subarctic region down to the end of the Middle Ages.

28 In contrast, no names seem to have been formed from *Vindr*, meaning Slav, although Wends were close neighbours of the Danes from the seventh century onwards: Janzen 114. For a good summary of the theories of Saami development see Bjørnar Olsen. 'Belligerent Chieftains', CCC, 9–31.

by Swedes, and so classified as a land, or territory. *Finlont* appears on a rune-stone, and *Finnlendingar* in a verse of about the same decade, round 1030[29]: evidently an imposed identity, reflecting a Norse outlook rather than a Finnish one? The archaeology of the previous two centuries suggests otherwise. In the districts called Lower Satakunta and Salo, a clearly defined horseshoe running round the angle of Finland for 250 miles (400 km) with a width of up to thirty-five miles lie the relics of a 'strongly armed civilization' similar to that of the Northmen. Large chamber-graves held the bones of richly dressed males with horse-gear, spear, swords, iron tools and distinctive brooches. Grave 348 at Luistari (*c.*950) held not only arms, but weights, purses, six kufic coins, a star-spangled blue cloak and imported brooches – attributes of high status over the water in Sweden; and the odd distribution of these graves corresponds with the growth-zone of a kind of rye which grows after ordinary ploughing, rather than after the burn-beating usual elsewhere in the region. The grave-goods connect with central Europe, Mälardal, Gotland, Öland, the upper Dnieper, Ladoga and the upper Volga. These people certainly had connections, although they shunned the south coast; the similarity of their precious things to those of Swedes is remarkable, but it is unlikely that they were Swedes, rather than Suomi who made themselves into a nobility on the nearest available model.[30] By language, they were *Finnar*; by civilization, Northmen or Swedes; what they called themselves may have been Suomi. They would certainly deserve a place in a book about Norsemen, if only there was anything to say about what they did.

Relations between Northmen and their eastern neighbours involved both economic interdependence and competition for resources. The Kainulaiset, or Cwenas, who lived on the lowlands round the north end of the Bothnian gulf were raiding across the mountains to the north-west into Halogaland, in Ohthere's time; they carried their boats over what seems an impossibly long distance, if they pushed up the Torneå, but the prize of Lapp tribute must have been worth it. Ohthere was wary of the people further north, on the White Sea, known as Biarmians, and they too claimed a share of what the Northmen wanted; according to the poet Glúmr Geirason, they were raided by the Norwegian king Harald Grey-Cloak about the middle of the tenth century, on what must have been either a summer expedition by sea from Norway past the North Cape or a

---

29 Pritsak 359 for the inscription; Sigvat was the poet.
30 Which Schaumann-Lönnqvist (1997, 70) takes as evidence of a client-relationship with the Uppsala king, from Merovingian times onwards. See also Lehtosalo-Hilander 1990, Solantie in FENSC v 1988, and Engelmark *et al.* ibid. x 1993, 70–5.

winter ski-run from a camp among the Lapps or Cwenas. Over a century later, king Sweyn II of Denmark told Adam of Bremen of stocky, muscular raiders from the eastern mountains who would appear 'either once a year or every three years' and rob the Swedes, but he gave them no tribal name; if he had, it might have been Karelians, or they could have been a more widely recruited viking partnership.[31]

Swedes (Svíar) and Gautar

Swedes bore the name of an ancient people (mentioned by Tacitus), and early in this period were considered a *gens* by the Frankish clergy who served the christians of Birka from the 830s to the 860s. Thirty years later, Wulfstan drew a distinction between the *Sweon*, of Mälardal, and people who 'belonged to' them in what is now southern Sweden. Adam of Bremen spelt out the difference: there were *Suedi* in *Suedia*, and a large ring of *Sueones* or Swedish satellites, and an outer world of raiders and trappers and herdsmen which surrounded that. There was a long history to this situation, which includes the wealth of the Mälardal chiefs in the Vendel period, and the terror roused by the sea-raiding Suiones mentioned by Tacitus in the second century. By 830 the emigration to NW Russia was under way, and the Mälardal freeholders were attending an all-Swedish assembly to which their kings deferred; from the Life of St Ansgar it appears that Swedish identity involved the right or claim to collect booty or tribute from the eastern Baltic coastlands; to debate public affairs in the assembly; to maintain a close relationship with gods, in war and peace, even by the attempted association of dead kings with them in the next world. This could be described as a territorial identity boosted by overlordship into something more, but restricted by the nature of the hegemony: the *Gautar* to the south[32] (pp. 96–7) accepted it, without becoming Swedes, and when the Danish king Canute or the Russian princes offered better rewards to Swedish or Gautish warriors they went where the pay was. By 1030 Canute could call himself king of 'part of the Swedes', and the unity of cult among them, if it had ever really existed, was split by

---

31   AB 4, 25. Karelians (*Koreloy*) are first mentioned in Novgorod birchbark document no. 590, a letter of about the same date as AB. Sweyn knew about these distant wars because he had served the king of the Swedes, Anund, for twelve years, when he was young; or so Adam says he said.
32   AB 1, 60; 4, 14; 4, 24; and see Nyberg 1987, and Sawyer 1991, 24–6 on the belated recognition of Gautar by ecclesiastics.

the steady increase in conversions to christianity, led by king Anund, but not followed by all. New forms of identity, as vassals of the Sigtuna king; as believers subject to the bishop there; as dwellers within a defined territory larger than the Mälar basin; as rulers of the east Baltic islands; were waiting for the Swedes by the end of the period, but blocked or delayed by unfavourable circumstances, in particular by the resilience of the former ring of tributaries and clients. Swedes had no monopoly of violence in the east Baltic; nor did Northmen in general. Swedish identity, like the others, remained one among several for eastern Scandinavians.

Swedish kingship was part of it, but the kings could not and did not unite the Swedes. They ruled where they felt secure: Olof Skötkonung at Sigtuna (994–c.1015) then in Västergötland; Anund Jacob at Sigtuna again, Emund in Uppland during the 1050s, and the new family of Stenkil mainly in the west again, leaving parts of Uppland to Thor, Odin, Frey and their partizans. Then a civil war broke out, two Erics were killed, and there were competing kings to the 1090s. The only contemporary source (down to c.1075) is Adam of Bremen, who naturally emphasized the christian–pagan division among the Swedes and Gautar; he presented the most renowned temple of Uppsala (of which no archaeological trace has been found) as the power-house of paganism, and clergy not authorized by Bremen as mere troublemakers. Things may have looked quite different to the natives, who, on the whole, were adopting christianity at their own pace, under various influences, by the decisions of local oligarchies or individual landowners. 'The process that eventually united the Götar and Svear to form the medieval kingdom'[33] was apparently the encroachments of Danish and Norwegian kings from the 1090s onwards; so, not a process at all, but the outcome of competition between leaders within those groups whose loyalties remained uncertain through much of the 12th century.

---

33 Sawyer 1993, 60; and for a new conspectus of the conversion, Brink's 'New Perspectives on the Christianization of Scandinavia' (SCEU 163–76) is brief and helpful.

6

Politics

Be warned in advance: it's serious
When all the senior men
(I heard some of it) intend
To stand up to the ruler;
It hurts when men at meeting
Put heads together and
Bury noses in cloaks...

So the poet Sigvat told his lord, the young king Magnus of Norway, towards the end of the 1030s,[1] in the course of a political dispute between a rapacious court and an indignant gentry: the sort of quarrel which was common in medieval and early modern times all over western Europe, and needs no heavy gloss for modern readers. Evidently it could happen in early eleventh century Scandinavia as well; but for the rest of the viking age the poets concentrate on battles rather than domestic disputes, and for the period before c.950 there are only hints of wars between rival warlords from foreign sources, and a brief glimpse of Swedish and Danish politics from the Life of St Ansgar, from a missionary point of view. This has not deterred historians from proposing schemes of political development for the whole age, both inside and outside Scandinavia, and from interpreting archaeology accordingly.

For some, the *process of state formation* has become the main theme of this period and of the previous 700-odd years.[2] Lindqvist

1   The king's retainers were damaging property and threatening hereditary possession, and Sighvat's 'Plain- speaking Verses' (*Bersǫglisvísur*) suggest that revolt was imminent. They were cited in Ágrip, the earliest Olaf saga, Fagrskinna and in the Heimskringla Magnus-saga, so they had not lost their sting 200 years later; see Kock, i, 123 for a version of this strophe (no. 12).
2   For example, 'If one poses the question of whether the development of Viking Age pottery can illuminate the early stages of the state-formation process in Denmark the

argues that any system of exploitation by which a surplus is appropriated by a minority 'requires' a state to 'supply ideology' in support of this inequity; others simply assume that big concentrations of authority grow out of little ones through military expansion or economic development. In such schemes, the day-to-day conflict of interest groups is subordinated to the emergence of a future political structure, which in turn is outdated as soon as emerged. Those who examine the 'pre-state' society of the Swedes of Mälardal (before *c*.1000) can say little of the politics, as the evidence is missing; instead they present the 'changing nature of traditional production' or the tectonic friction of mainly-imaginary social structures as what the Swedes were up to; never the wrangling of mortals. The only interesting question is when these people achieve their state: *c.750*? *c.1000*? *c.1100*? *c.1250*? The question of what such states are, and what the preconditions for their existence is answered by reference to theorists (Perry Anderson, Lord Runciman, Elman Service) whose conclusions are based mainly on pre-digested summaries of Dark Age history, like this one. It is a circuit closed against verification. Another approach, solely through the words of contemporary poets, leads to the conclusion that pagan Norwegians lived under a regime in which resources were controlled for the public good by a chain of delegated authorities leading from the gods to the army of freemen. Another theory, it seems.[3]

Intimations of statehood can be found in many or most early medieval societies, but that was not necessarily the most interesting thing about them. Medieval Iceland was virtually stateless, down to the 1280s. Its laws were not enforced by any public body, private and public were not distinct categories, there was no administration, army or king: it would be absurd to present the first 400 years of Icelandic history as the slow development of an institution that was not needed. The distribution, rather than the concentration of power, did the job of maintaining property, social order and religion.[4] But Iceland was Iceland; not much like king-infested, war-ready Scandinavia, where kingdoms and states are supposed to have been generated. As they were, in profusion, with Danish kings wielding

answer must unfortunately be rather negative' (Madsen 1991, 234); but note Høilund Nielsen on 'The Animal Art of Scandinavia as the Basis for the Study of Early State Formation' in vol. vii of the York Conference *Medieval Europe 1992: Art and Symbolism*. Note also Staecker's opinion that hammer-pendants 'were not capable of fulfilling the requirements' of state- builders.

3 Bäck in VIPA (1997), 184, invokes the changing nature of production; Malmros recreated an ideal skaldic state from the verses.
4 Durrenberger 1992 81–95. Chieftaincies eventually began to look like embryonic states, but only towards 1200; see Vésteinsson 2000, 8–9.

hegemony and lordship over a range of tributaries and tribes and provinces, Frisian, Frankish, English, Swedish, Irish, Scots and other chiefs trying the same thing with temporary success. The outfitting and control of amphibious military expeditions is what was going on; migration to foreign lands; constant challenges to authority. Those things happened: to study the underlying state-formation process there would be like drinking wine for the calcium content, and will not be attempted here; although it is quite possible.

Instead, the nature of viking-age politics will be sketched in terms of who held power and what they did with it: mainly kings, chiefs, lords and freeholders in assemblies. Kings and kingship have been studied the most, since more is known about them; and as a result no less than nine kinds of king have been detected in this region, and each endowed with a different sort of power.

Kings

Sacral

The daddy of the sacral king idea was the social anthropologist Frazer, who concluded that in primitive societies all over the world there were rulers who connected their tribes with the dead and the divine, and were responsible for public welfare; if things went badly, they were sacrificed.[5] This notion has been extended to include all holy men with kingly attributes and all kings with priestly functions, and was applied to the Germanic peoples early and often, but with most effect by Wenskus; in *Stammesbildung und Verfassung* (1951) he argued that such kings emerged among the ancient Germans as leaders of the cult-communities on which the tribes were based. Hauck (1955) and Baetke (1964) followed suit, and the proposition was modified to fit Nordic conditions in Boyer's *Yggdrasill* and Steinsland's *Det hellige bryllup og norrøn kongeideologi* which derived the mystique of kings from their supposed descent from a holy marriage between a god and a giantess, re-enacted in ritual and by the idea that the ruler marries the country. Most sacralists are happy to identify the king's cult with that of Odin, although Hauck built up a case for Freyr; they see the king as 'transmitter of an

5   See Gunnell 1995, 5–6 for Frazer's influence on Scandinavian scholars. Dowden (2000, 106) describes the king- sacrifice theory as based on 'grotesque garblings' of Strabo's tourist-guide of ancient Greece merged with a selective trawl of kingship rituals reflecting various religious outlooks. See Fleck 1970 for the oral examination, and Schjødt in MAMMEN 1991, 305–10.

extraordinary psychic power' (Taylor 1994) through his eyes, hands, knees, emblems, words, dreams, and as an adept in occult knowledge, who achieved his status by passing an oral examination after acquiring 'numinous' information by which to safeguard the harvests, health and luck of his people through regular sacrifice, to avert or postpone his own.

Alfred Smyth persuaded generations of students that such kings were regularily sacrificed to appease Odin and improve the weather,[6] and that when they led campaigns in the British Isles, the chosen victims were captured English and Irish kings. By contrast Steinsland doubted whether sacral kings were victims as well as sacrificers, and Thomas Lindqvist sees the office as kingship with cult duty, rather than divinity; Ringtved thinks it evaporated long before this. Olof Sundqvist is probing the subject full-time at Uppsala, and McTurk has attempted to clarify the issues on the basis of evidence (taken almost entirely from sagas). In 1974–5 he concluded that some Nordic kings were held to be descended from divine beings, and acted, not as gods, but as intermediaries between men and gods; but that some people may have thought that they were gods, by reincarnation; and that they were therefore 'marked off from other men by an aura of specialness which may or may not have its origin in more or less direct association with the supernatural'.[7] This was drawing it mild, too mild for most, and twenty years later he replaced the 'may or may not have' with 'has', but let the 'more or less' stand. As a definition this might exclude king Louis Philippe from the club, but few others; and in any case, the argument really concerns texts and assumptions which belong to the twelfth and thirteenth centuries, not contemporary evidence. As Martin has pointed out, the attempt to specify the sacral king merely fuses the unrelated religious attributes of ordinary kings into one imaginary being.[8] There is good evidence that at various times and places kings have been descended from gods, gods incarnate, agents of gods, priests of cults, objects of cults; even Chaney's *Cult of Kingship* (a best-selling sacralist thesis) would be a title that made excellent sense if it referred to Queen Elizabeth I or Louis XIV, for whose cults there is abundant contemporary evidence, rather than to Dark Age rulers

6 'The sacrifice of kings was an established procedure in pre-Christian Scandinavia'; 'a society which indulged in the ritual slaying of its own kings could not be expected to deal kindly with the kings of its enemies', Smyth 1977, 219–20.

7 McTurk 1974–5 and 1994; also his article on *Kingship* in MESCA 353–55, with bibliography down to 1990. Also Ringtved in SAL (1999), 376, Lindqvist in KRIS (1994), 236, and on inauguration rituals: Stausberg 2001, 620–50.

8 Martin in PISMA 1990, 377–8, and note Lindqvist's conclusions in *Freyr's Offspring*, Uppsala 2000.

for whom there is almost none. It can be assumed that kings were regarded as exceptional beings in viking times as in all other times, everywhere. All rulers need legitimacy, and will get it where they can. If in a world infused by supernatural power, then by absorbing such power, whether conceived of in christian or pagan terms, conferred by anointing with oil or by sitting in a tub of stewed horseflesh. As for Nordic rulers, there are are three questions to be answered: (1) Were they sacrificed? (2) Were they regarded as gods before or after death? (3) Were they priests, or intermediaries between their people and another world?

(1) No, there is no evidence whatever that any king was ever sacrificed either among or by the Nordic peoples. The justification for this long-cherished delusion lies mainly in the problematic verses in *Ynglingatal*, which tell of a prehistoric Swedish ruler called Domaldi:

> *It happened long ago – That sword-carrying men – Reddened earth – With their lord – And the host of the land – Bloodied their arms – In the lifeless corpse of Domaldi – When the race of the Swedes eager for crops, would slaughter – the foe of the Jutes.*
>
> (Turville-Petre 1978–9 (MS xi, 48–67) slightly altered)

This is one of a 'series of terse, riddling statements about mythical Swedish kings who died in various strange and ignoble ways'; the verses were given a prose gloss in Ynglinga Saga, and incorporated into Heimskringla by Snorri, who may have seen Domaldi as a 'pagan ruler destroyed by bad religious practises'[9], although the verses make no clear mention of famine, or of sacrifice, and seem to allude to a king's murder by his warriors. Lönnroth believes that the original tale had him sacrificed for good harvests, as the desperate act of a hungry people looking for a high-status victim, rather than as a ritual procedure. But this is a fiction, from a post-conversion source, not a story of every day life in pagan Uppsala. Similar tales were told in ninth-and tenth-century Ireland.[10]

9   Lönnroth in SMEOL, 92, who remarks that these stories are 'the ideal objects for post-structuralist deconstruction' such as in Krag 1991. *Historia Norvegiæ* (*c*.1200?) interpreted Domaldi's exit as a sacrifice to 'Ceres', by hanging, despite the weapons in the verses: Ceres as personification of harvest, rather than goddess.
10   The threefold death by spear, drowning and burning accounted for three rulers, and was celebrated in a poem by Fland Mainistrech; which is interpreted in Aitchison 1998 (VISO, 108–25) as a warning to unjust kings that their inauguration rituals (by arming, bathing, and fire-lighting) could be reversed. He further suggests that the many regicides noted in the Annals of Ulster over this period were actually such

Smyth's version of the killing of king Edmund of East Anglia in 869 as a sacrifice to Odin by the rite known as the blood-eagle (breaking the victim's neck and extracting the lungs through the ribs backwards) was based on his reading of the account in Abbo of Fleury's *Passio*, which (a century later) gave Edmund a martyr's death conflated from the hagiography of St Stephen, St Sebastian, St Oswald and others, without specifying this most strange method.[11] One eleventh-century verse refers to the capture of York in 867 as the time when *Ivarr cut eagle on Ella's back*; and as Ella was one of the two Northumbrian kings who were killed in the battle for the city, he cannot actually have been sacrificed, nor is it likely that the poet thought he had been, even if it is not clear what exactly he meant by this metaphor. From this ambiguity a whole legend of the butchering of Ella for the snake pit death he had inflicted on Ragnar Lothbrok was elaborated in the twelfth and later centuries;[12] but the twentieth-century legend of king-sacrifice after battle is impossible to square with the many kings and nobles who collaborated with and employed these invaders, presumably not at the risk of being sacrificed like slaves or animals, the victims for which there is reliable evidence (see p. 82). As for kings sacrificed by their own people for domestic purposes, the questions: which kings? when? remain unanswered.

(2)   According to the Life of St Ansgar (*c.* 865–75), Swedes opposed to the christian mission of Birca had believed that a former king Eric had joined the gods after his death, and was being reverenced with a shrine and offerings. There is a story in Flateyjarbók of how Odin tempted the future St Olave, and how a former king Olaf communicated with him from his burial mound at Geirstad, as if to be reincarnated in him.[13] And there are various later genealogies deriving kings and other rulers from gods and giants;[14] and it is possible to interpret the inscriptions on the Rök, Sparlösa and Malt rune-stones

---

reversals, 'a recrudescence of archaic social practises, possibly including ritualized regicide', spurred by the 'political stress' of the times. A possibility, but frequency says nothing of cause.

11   Smyth 1977, chs xiv and xvi.

12   And weighed down with modern comment and controversy, as well as graced by Mr Heaney's fifth flock of stanzas in *Viking Dublin: North* (London 1975, 15) and by the careful glossing in McTurk 1991.

13   See Heinrichs 1994 for an investigation and analysis; and note Krag 1999.

14   On which see Faulkes in MS, xi, 1978–9; on the descent of rulers from giants and giantesses (chthonic beings) see Steinsland 1991 for a full development: with interruptions from Motz 1994 and 1996. North 1997 shows how Odin's role as ancestor was borrowed from Anglo-Saxon descents from Woden; probably long after the mid-tenth century date he proposes.

as evidence of divine kingship, failing all else. But none of these interesting fragments suggest that kings were seen as gods in their own lifetimes, however 'special' their gifts and their destinies; nor that their joining gods after death actually made them into gods. The two great verse apotheoses of Norwegian kings, *Eiríksmál* and *Hakonarmál*, both pagan, present a future life in Valhalla, or among gods, as the reward for fighters who feed Odin's birds with corpses on earth (see chapter 12, p. 294); but there is no suggestion that they become gods, simply because they were kings, or that this was the usual destiny of kings. In Icelandic literature Odin is the guide, philosopher and fiend of certain unlucky kings, as in Saxo Grammaticus. In *Grímnismál*, an Eddic poem, he fosters, selects and sends a young man overseas to kill his brother and become a king. He teaches king Harald War-Tooth the art of war, disguised as the counsellor 'Brown', only to betray and kill him in the final battle. None of which sheds light on what was the actual connection between kings and Odin in pagan times. The Gotland stones and the skaldic verse suggest that this god was associated with death, poetry, magic, battle and runes, not with kingship in particular.

(3) Scepticism about the sacrality of Northern kings has not been welcomed by Schjødt or by Steinsland or by many others with anthropological sympathies. For them, the lack of positive Nordic evidence cannot outweigh the almost-universality of this idea among other peoples; there is an a priori case for it which ought to be the starting-point for inquiry.[15] However, there have been societies where the king was not high priest of his people; where Moses led and Aaron prayed; and there have been others, where priestly functions were so widely diffused among heads of families (as in ancient Rome and brahmin India) that a priest-king would be one among many, or superfluous. Why not start from there? Care of the shrines was a quality praised in two Norwegian rulers of the tenth century, Hakon the Good (supposedly a baptized christian) and Hakon Jarl: they pleased gods and got good harvests for the sacrifices the people offered. In good Hakon's case this can hardly have meant more than toleration of the status quo; in bad Hakon's, his poet Einarr said it was because he restored what his predecessors, the sons of Eric Bloodaxe had 'defiled', that is, he was a responsible patron, rather than a pontiff. In any case, he was not usually known as a king, and the numinous qualities found in those

15   See Schjødt in Mammen 1991, and Steinsland 1991 and GR (1992, 736–51); *contra* Lindqvist in KRIS (1994) 236, and the demolition of Frankish 'sacral kingship' as a Germanist fiction by A.C. Murray in his *After Rome's Fall* (Toronto 1998): '*Post vocantur*'. Lindqvist compares rulership ideologies of the Swedish Ynglingar and the earls of Hlaðir in Erkens 2005.

who were have no necessary link with specific sacral functions. References to the glittering and fearsome eyes of Norwegian kings may well point to superhuman properties, as in christian countries: Eric Bloodaxe and St Olave shared this optical voltage with Notker's Charlemagne and Widukind's Otto I, and all who have to face down strong men and women, and read their hearts. To claim that Bloodaxe's 'terror-helmet' (*ægishjalmi*) was not so much a poetic embellishment by Egill, as a sacral Coppergate-style head-piece, adorned with snake or dragon reliefs or crest, is adding fantasy to rhetoric; fearful helmets are found buried and were sometimes worn by anyone who could afford them, but the only sacred helms we can be sure of are those imitated from Roman images and stamped on the pennies of English christian kings.[16] As with the good harvests brought by the good king; the connection is so common in both christian and pagan contexts that it can have no particular meaning for Nordic kingship. Whether the king was supposed to embody the luck (*heil*), or, as Steinsland claims both the good and the bad luck of his people, is a question, but whatever the answer, the actual politics of such responsibilities are obscure. If we cannot show that any king was sacrificed, even in well attested periods of famine,[17] or behaved as a high-priest, or was treated as a god, or was praised by poets for his numinous knowledge, there is nothing left of Nordic sacral kingship in the viking age, other than a long-cherished fancy of those who read paganism as christianity through the looking-glass.

Both pagan and christian rulers hedged their kingship with divinity as best they could, but the multifocal and diverse character of Nordic religions, combined with the constantly changing geography of kingship, made a royal priesthood impractical. Drawing strength from cults, from ancestors, from sacred objects and places, was policy rather than the discharge of a sacred office, or at most a magnified version of the religious duties shared by all good men and their wives. It has been argued[18] that sacral kingship survived in Norway

16 Egill's *Arinbjornarkvida*, st. 4 and 5 liken Eric's eyes to stars, the moon, and snake's eyes (Kroesen 1985); Sigvatr's *Erfidrapa* to St Olave recalled his sepentine gaze; like the smith Weyland's, in *Völundarkvida*, and of course Sigurd Snake-Eye. See Marold 1998 for the helmet.

17 King Horik 1 of the Danes (813–54) survived the famines of 823, 825 and 850. Harald Bluetooth outlived notably bad years in 962, 970 and 975; Hakon Jarl, friend of the gods, came through 970 and '75 and the droughts of 988 and 992 unsacrificed. In the end, according to the legend in *Ágrip* (c.1180) he asked his slave to cut his throat for him, but this was to avoid capture by his enemies, not to improve the weather.

18 Fidjestøl 1991, using one strophe of Haraldskvædi; see Turville-Petre 1976 for text and trans. on p. 14. Ringtved (SAL 1998, 376) assumes that Danish sacral kingship must have died out much earlier, with the dissolution of tribal society.

under the patronage of the earls of Hlaðir, when it was rejected by the ambitious Harald Harfagr, who according to his poet was ready to hold Yule at sea, rather than on land. His son may have been fostered by a christian king, Athelstan. And so in Sweden, when king Olof Eriksson neglected the sacrifices of Uppsala, and became a christian. But these rulers would never have been more than participants in the sacred feasts of their peoples, and there is no evidence at all that they ceased to participate. At the end of the period, with king Sweyn II of Denmark sending his son to the pope for some kind of consecration, and the cult of the martyr-king Olave already attracting devotion all over the Northern world, sacral kingship had a great future in these regions; not much of a past.

Fighting

The evidence for fighting kings is more abundant, both in the Western annals and in the verses of the kings' own poets; even in the runic inscriptions, such as that to Ful, of Aarhus, who

MET DEATH WHEN KINGS FOUGHT

(DR 66: M 220)

about the same time (*c.* 1000) as Gunni of Råda in Västergötland who MET DEATH IN BATTLE WHEN KINGS FOUGHT, as did king Sweyn of the Danes, king Olaf of Norway and king Olof of Sweden in the sea-fight known to legend as Svöldr, but possibly in the Sound. The Frankish annals record immense bloodlettings among the Danes, when rival kings fought in 813 and 854 and 'the two parties wore each other down with killing, and countless common people were killed and of the royal family no one remained except one small boy' (AF, trans. Reuter, 36) The Anglo-Saxon chronicle related that at Ashdown in 871 the Danish kings led a separate division against king Ethelred I, and one was killed there; two more, or three, at Tettenhall in 910, and another at Tempsford in 917. In Sweden, in the 1060s 'all the powerful men... are said to have fallen in battle, and both the kings perished there, too. And so, from then onwards there was no-one left of the royal family...'.[19] Military kingship (Heerkönigtum) could not be better attested, from the beginning to the end of this age, even if most of the warlords came from the same few divinely-sanctioned dynasties.[20]

19   AB 3, 52.
20   Sawyer's 'Kings and Royal Power' in HØKO 1991 summarizes, contra McTurk 1996 and Axboe in JDA, x, 1991/2. Wormald detected a 'development' from sacral to

The poets who followed kings from the mid-tenth century onwards seldom used the word king (*konungr*) of their patrons before the 1020s: they preferred to flatter them with titles indicating military roles or qualities.[21] If Egill's praise of Eric Bloodaxe (in Hǫfuðlausn) be taken as a model, the laudable mid-tenth century king excelled in five ways, all military: (1) he breaks up and scatters gold to his warriors, regardless of expense; (2) he fights in person, with devastating effect, indifferent to danger; (3) he has a poet to advertise his fame and generosity and victories; (4) he holds his land 'in his talons', by force and fear; (5) Odin, the corpse-collector, approves of him; valkyries and ravens attend him. There is no mention of sacerdotal duties or even of the attention to shrines for which Hákon Jarl was praised in the 980s. The clichés of skaldic poetry are the eagerness of kings for war, for crossing the sea, for meeting foreign foes, for devastating the countryside, for feeding wolves, eagles and ravens with corpses; the achievements of any successful marauder, rather than a mirror for princes. The only social responsibilities the poets insist on is generosity to the retinue, and relentless hostility to vikings and thieves: kindness to accomplices, cruelty to rivals. Rather like inheritors of great business fortunes nowadays, these kings had to be seen as victors in competition, even if they were not. In reality, Canute and others were cold schemers who deployed heroic fame and military panache as one among several political weapons: the poets were not in the big picture.

Thus Canute's great coup of 1028, when he replaced king Olaf Haraldsson of Norway with his own nephew, earl Hakon, was celebrated by Thórarinn Praise-tongue (*loftunga*) in verses like those which traditionally listed battles fought by the patron. The Danish fleet set out from Limfjord, crossed the Skagerrack to Agder, sailed past Lister and Egersund, and Tjörnaglen, north to Trondheim, via Stadt and Stimshesten; then

brisk user of high-Jutes – there gave to his nephew the entire –
Norway;

military kingship (1982, 144–8), rather as the horse evolved from the unicorn. Ringtved (1999, 376) and most others would see the war- king as a break with the tribal system, rather than a development from it.

21 For example, *jöfurr*: lord of fighters, *all- valldr*: high commander, *gramr*: warlord, warrior, *harri* (after 1015): lord of men, *tyggi* and *hertogi*: army-leader, *mildingr*: giver, *skjoldungr*: shielder (rather than descendant of Skjold, in verse), *vördr*: defender, *vísi*: director, *dróttinn*: lord of retinue, *thengill*: ditto; *stillir*: silencer, controller. See G. Morris 1998, and forthcoming, on the use and development of these terms.

as if at the climax of a great conquest. But there had been no fighting. Canute had just paid off the Norwegian nobles and thrilled them with the sight of a big fleet. This was a lap of honour rather than a career of battles, but for the media old habits die hard.[22] Throughout this period, pugnacity is the quality no king can dispense with, at least in public, and even if Canute's hegemony was a short interlude of peace, the scramble for his dominions which broke out after 1035 proved once again that the ability to lead troops in battle could be the deciding factor in politics.

Feeding

Feasting and entertainment were the king's business all over the world; to eat, and to feed others, the most obvious manifestation of power. In Nordic countries at this period, royal administration was mainly concerned with the collecting and conserving of food and drink. This was because cooking and consuming held kingdoms together, as well as households.

The Swedish drunk who scratched THE KING IS GENEROUS WITH FOOD on a pig's rib recently found at Sigtuna probably lived in the twelfth century, but the words made sense at least from the fifth, when some lord handed out a gold medallion inscribed ALE – LEEK – INVITATION to broadcast his hospitality.[23] 'The king has fed us well. I am still fat round the roots of the heart' said St Olave's poet Thormoð, inspecting the gobbets on the arrowhead he had just extracted from his vitals; according to the anecdote in Olaf Saga (Heimskringla chapter 235). Up here, relative scarcity made food an even more valuable currency of power than in fruitful south Britain or Francia; more than just a symbol. At Borg, on the far northern Lofoten archipelago, the feasters at the chief's house were importing glass vessels and wheaten bread even in Roman times, to show who was who; in most excavated power-centres there is evidence of the frequent eating of boiled meat, and the malting of barley for beer. The rune-stones show that entertainment was the measure

---

22 Thórarinn's *Togdrápa* on Canute is in Skjd IA, 322–4 and IB, 298–301, and in Kock, i, 151–2, and Ashdown's translation is used in EHD, i, 312. Snorri cited the verses, and observed: 'Thórarin praises himself for being in king Canute's following when he came to Norway'. For discrimination in the choice of poetic epithets see Frank in SAG, i, 189–94.
23 *Fornvännen* lxxxvii for the rib, Arnold 1999 for a survey of the subject; on the medallion, Andrén 1991 shows the likeness to the Roman slogan: *Dominus-Pius-Felix*. It is not striking.

of worth among all landowners, like Bram of Sövestad in Scania, who was

THE BEST OF LANDLORDS AND THE MOST FREE WITH FOOD (DR 291)

To keep the loyalty of such *bumenn*, rulers had to outdo them in generosity, so that the poets might say, as did Kormak Ogmundarson of Sigurð Jarl (*c.962*):

> *Need no man bear cup – Nor casket's contents*
> *Nor vat's, with him – That way, to the wealth-wounder.*[24]

Feasting performed at least five useful political functions, apart from nutrition:

1   It redirected the surplus of a district or territory from potential rivals to docile and friendly guests, local or foreign. As host, the ruler was the major economic force of a wider area than he could intimidate or own: as with the 40 mile radius round the king's hall at Jelling, where the 13 rune-stones indicate a cluster of allied magnates. Similarly in Zealand, round Lejre.
2   It connected the great annual transitions (Yule, Spring, Midsummer, Harvest, Winter) which concerned everyone, with the power of the chief or chiefs; their wealth became the welfare of all, even if it only meant supplying victims for the deprecation of dearth, hard winters and sickness. Of course, believers in sacral kingship will prefer to rephrase this proposition.
3   It could also mark the importance of one family, by celebrating the inauguration of an heir or a ruler, or by commemorating the dead, or the betrothal of son or daughter. Some of the surviving verse may have been recited on such occasions, if not all the alleged 'inheritance-poems' (*erfidrápar*).[25] For the Tune stone, see p. 50.
4   It brought potential enemies and troublemakers together under the rule of conviviality: mimic war (horse-play, riddling, athletics, versification) to forestall the real thing, and a chance for the king to win in public without bloodshed: like the Norwegian ruler Harald Gunhildarson (960s) who

---

24   Cited in Hakon the Good's saga, ch. 14 by Snorri, who offered an imaginative reconstruction of the Hlaðir feasts and sacrifices. On Kormak's work: Holm-Olsen in MESCA 367.
25   Fidjestøl 1982, 193.

knew twelve different games, all kingly ones

according to his poet Glum Geirason. However, competition sharpened by alcohol made this a dangerous custom, especially when
retainers of the lord proved their virilities by bullying, mockery,
goading and bone-throwing: an incivility which reached murderous
depths in the Danish camp at London on Saturday, 19 April 1012,
when the drunken drengs pelted archbishop Elphege 'with bones and
with ox-heads' because he would not pay them more ransom-money,
and so made a martyr.[26]

5   It advertised rank. Nothing elaborate, by the standards of Hincmar of Reims, the hierarch who wrote of the hierarchy of the
Carolingian palace, but a great feast made it clear who was lord,
who was important, who was in service, and who didn't amount to
much. The archaeology of the halls is consistent with the literary
convention by which there was a high table to one side of the long
central fireplace, and a low table to the other, and the less favoured
sat nearer the door, where there was a doorkeeper to introduce guests
and keep out the unwelcome. By *c*.1020 the leaders of the retinue
were called stallers, from their right to places in the hall, so that
Sigvatr appealed to St Olave:

> *Now am I, your staller – Come home to this place … Say, king of
> people – Where you have decided to seat me Among the warriors.
> Your house – is dearest of all to me.*[27]

These favourites 'go before the knee of our lord' in Norway as in
England, at ordinary meals; feasts are when it shows.

Such advantages would apply where the king gave or assisted with
the feasting. At other times and places, as in eleventh-century Wales,
the ruler was the guest; a custom which enabled noble hosts to talk to
him on equal terms, unlike the providers of his own feasts. Nordic
rulers were certainly sometimes guests as well as hosts, but viking-
age evidence says more of the kings' own food-supplies than those of
others. If the place-names are to be trusted, food-renders were
brought by freeholders and tenants to royal manors, usually called
husabyar in Scandinavia and later in the Orkneys, for the ruler and
his retinue to consume on their rounds. This was *veizla*,[28] the Nordic

---

26   ASC C; trans. EHD, i, 222.
27   Skjd IB, 247.
28   Literally 'a giving'; Nyberg 1985 associated the Danish Husebys with the Jelling
monarchy, and the Norwegian ones with Danish overlordship. The earls of Hlaðir

equivalent of the *pastus, gistum, herbergum, gwestfa, fodrum* and *feorm* of other countries, and probably imitated from them at first by the Danes in Jutland-Funen (8 Husebys), then in Viken (22) and then in Mälardal-Sweden (40). Whether it began as a public subscription to a community feast, or was a tribute imposed by force, there is no means of telling; the impression given by thirteenth-century Icelandic sources is that chiefs competed for power through conviviality, and in that case kings would be likely to win.

The most complete reconstruction of the politics of feasting was included in the Heimskringla Olaf-saga (chapters 117–121) in a series of events involving the king's agent in the far north, and Ásbjorn Sigurðarson of Trondeness, a local magnate. Ásbjorn's father had dominated the district by giving the three main annual feasts, but now Ásbjorn was hampered by a harvest failure, and by the king's ban on the export of corn or malt from the south; that meant no beer, and a blow to prestige which drove the would-be host to defy the king, kill his agent and risk his own life.

The story is probably not an accurate reflection of the events of the 1020s, since it chimes too well with thirteenth-century views on kings, chiefs and royal officials, but it makes a credible political point about authority in the subarctic region. In the event, the king is persuaded to pardon Ásbjorn by his powerful kinsman Erling of Sole, provided he agrees to take on the job of king's agent himself. He agrees, but later spurns this office as beneath his dignity; and gets killed by another homicidal king's man, sent north to take over half the administration of Halogaland. Entertainment was a serious matter.[29]

Monetary

Monetary kings are a modern invention, but based on hard and abundant evidence: coins stamped with king's heads. None was like the Russian ruler Vladimir (*c.*978–1016), who took full resonsibility for the gold *zlatniki* he had cast, rather than struck, in the 980s, with inscriptions that read either VLADIMIR ON THE THRONE or VLADIMIR AND THIS IS HIS GOLD. A short-lived experiment

had eight of their own, at least: see Brink 1996, 248–50. Orkney earls had six, supplied by 13 *hollendr* or 'support farms': Schei 1998. See now Westerdahl and Stylegar in *Viking* 2004, 101–31.

29 On this episode see Bagge 1991, 40–2, 68–9; and see Braut 1996 on public feasting in general (English summary). Kentish kings had taken gold from any who killed their food- suppliers, and double compensation for any wrong done at the house where they were entertained: see Oliver 1998.

characteristic of the late tenth century, when the names and images of recently converted rulers appear on limited issues: Boleslaw of Poland, Olaf of the Swedes, Sweyn Forkbeard, Sitric of Dublin, perhaps Olaf Tryggvason as well. Other Nordic rulers may have been interested in the minting of bracteates (gold or silver discs stamped on one side) before that, since currency was kings' business elsewhere, a status symbol if not a source of profit. Frankish kings had inherited a monopoly of striking gold money from Roman emperors, and the Carolingians had authorized a reliable silver penny; some Anglo-Saxon kings had had their names on coins since *c.*705, and the Wessex kings later established a near-monopoly of coin, not by supplying moneyers with silver, but by banning them from minting any pennies other than those certified by a uniform image and inscription, obtainable only from the court.

Rulers eager for glory and already occupied with the getting and distribution of other people's silver naturally found this an attractive scheme, but it rested on supports which were not present in Scandinavia for most of the viking age. There had to be a widespread demand for coin as a medium of exchange and no easy way of satisfying it except through the authorized mints; there had to be means for the ruler to kill competition within the homeland; there had to be some form of taxation which would add to the weight-value of royal money as the sole or preferred medium of payment. Up in the Northern lands, from *c.*780 to *c.*950, the appetite for coined silver was more than satisfied by the import of Islamic dirhems struck by mints hundreds of miles away on the other side of the Caspian Sea, to a degree of purity and consistency in weight which could not be bettered anywhere in Europe, let alone in Scandinavia.[30] It is possible, but quite uncertain, that a Danish ruler may have had a say in the minting of *sceattas* (light pennies) at Ribe in the early eighth century, or in the bracteates of Hedeby a century later; if so, they were bragging rather than monetizing. Varenius has suggested that they were propaganda for pro or anti-Carolingian kings in so far as their images were Frankish or Nordic in inspiration;[31] but if they were for general use, why risk offending one or other party? There were no real substitutes for the dirhems, and when the supply faltered, as in the 830s and 850s, or ceased, silver could be fragmented and traded by weight, without asking anyone's permission: hack-silver appears in hoards wherever trading was brisk throughout the period.

---

30   Some 83,000 had been found in Sweden by 2000, 6,000 in the rest of Scandinavia, all struck between the 750s and the 960s; a lot, but as Lieber pointed out, a dozen silver dishes would weigh twice as much as all the coin hoarded on Gotland.
31   Varenius 1992, 143–4.

Settlers in England found pennies in continual demand and circulation, and appear to have supplemented king Alfred's heavy silver with the lighter St Edmund coins from the 890s onwards, and to have found continental craftsmen to make them. At York, the archbishop's mint seems to have minted money for Anlaf Sihtricsson (941–4) and his successors, using the images of raven and triquetra and cross. The steady increase in the output and quality of English mints from the 930s offered a temptation and another source of supply for the Norsemen in Scandinavia, who had imported very little Anglo-Saxon and Frankish money so far; but Norse kings were not in a position to become sole importers or imitators of English pennies, even when the slump in Islamic imports after the 950s would have made this an attractive prospect.[32] The infrastructure wasn't there; they couldn't ban the inflow from the West, or imitations by private silversmiths, or the use of money-substitutes. They could only announce their arrival in this competitive field by hiring an English moneyer to strike some SVEIN and ANLAF pennies after 995, as would-be christian monarchs rather than as economic developers. Olaf of Sigtuna's moneyer is estimated to have issued 'up to two million' coins, but the first batch were using a full mark of silver (208.5 g) for ninety-six pennies, and leaving the moneyer no rake-off, as he might expect in England. The weight was then reduced, but this seems to have made the money unattractive; so the mint had to resort to striking square blanks of silver, up to an acceptable weight, with round dies made for coin that wasn't.[33] Only in Denmark was the experiment in royal coinage sustained, or revived, and brought to a modest degree of success, perhaps as a result of Canute's need to hire troops on regular wages; but if, as Blackburn argues, his first Danish issue was struck while he was in England, and his brother Harald was ruling Denmark (1014–1018/19) we may well ask 'What was going on in the State of Denmark in the time of Harald Sveinsson?'[34]

Canute's main mints were in England and for England. His Danish ones are on map 6. The two and sometimes three weight-standards of his Danish pennies show the consequence of minting without firm control, even where there is demand, technical know-how, and a model to follow. Those (Becker and Bendixen) who claim that he introduced an organized coinage on the English pattern to Denmark,

---

32 The Late Second Hand (985–91) pennies of Ethelred II were reaching Scandinavia in gross before 997, but Long Cross was the type widely imiated there and at Dublin.

33 Following Herschend 1992 up to a point, Malmer 1989, 36.

34 See Malmer in HØKO (1991), 214; and Lawson 1993, 89–91 on the Harald-problem. He was left in charge of Denmark by his father in 1013, refused to share it with Canute in 1015, and was presumably dead by 1019.

admit that the three bases of English money, uniformity of weight at initial issue, of design, and of purity, were lacking. The hoards show a preference for English and German money even here, and a widespread use of hack-silver, rings, and ingots as tokens of value or money-substitutes. In Denmark the money announced the king's image, name, faith, and wealth; a whirling serpent on some Lund pennies, otherwise crosses, and 'elegant busts, but semi-literate inscriptions' (Malmer).

In England, at least since 1012, the king's pennies were not only propaganda, but the only legal currency and the only acceptable means of paying the annual land-tax to the collectors at the shire-town; they were minted there even when the commercial demand for such denominations was small, as in the west Midlands. No Nordic king levied regular annual taxation in coin, despite their evident greed for the wealth of others in the form of tribute or blackmail; as late as 1085 the only annual levy in Denmark (mentioned in the Lund charter of that year) was the Midsummer-geld, owed by house-holders in towns, not by the majority of freemen.[35] The way to get Nordic tax-money was long and hard: it was much more sensible to conquer England and use the seventy mints and existing tax systems over there, while defraying Scandinavian expenses with tolls on protected markets and harbours, and windfalls of loot and treasure. As the poets insist, the good king was a dissipator, not an accumu-lator: wealth-wounder, silver-foe, ring-tosser, was the winner, not the ruler who hid his winnings (as Eyvind the Plagiarist complained of king Harald Gunhildarson in the 960s) – least of all in a society where treasure belonged to gods, ancestors and graves, if not spent. These rulers took to striking money as one result of intenser compe-tition in spending and display, not as economic planners. In Norway and Sweden, when the supply of English silver ran out after the 1040s, the custom was discontinued; in Denmark it carried on.

State-builders

State-builders, in the guize of rulers who unify, centralize and urban-ize were generally given a pat on the back by twentieth-century historians, as if they planned more wisely and did better than the others. It is questionable whether these terms can be used at all of viking-age kings, even if some of them widened their dominions,

---

35   The legend of the Danish 'nose-tax' levied on Norwegians from 1030 to 1034 seems to be a twelfth- century horror-story, to scare those who still hoped for Danish overlordship; but see Syrett 2002, 130.

cowed their chiefs and helped to set up trading posts. War-lords and landlords tend to do such things, as temporary expedients and projections of their own personalities, not necessarily to change the political system. Harald Bluetooth's brag on the Jelling stone, that he

WON DENMARK ALL AND NORWAY AND DANES MADE CHRISTIAN

is not a sober record of unification, but a claim for glory on the strength of three magnificent 'wins', to counteract the more sombre story of how he had paid tribute to the Saxon emperor, had lost control of Norway, and was widely regarded by Danes as a tyrant – the black legend of Bluetooth lived on in Iceland (see p. 123). In the end, he lost control of his own household troops and had to flee. Such a ruler needed client kings, and chiefs, so that a poet might say of him, as Sighvatr of St. Olave *c.*1040:

> *The ruler took Upplondr (Opland) – from one end to other;*
> *Before that, eleven ruled them: – Now, men wisely give hostages...*[36]

He needed huge mounds of earth and rows of monoliths, glittering guards and figure heads, high halls and metrical masterpieces, not administrative structures or infrastructures. He wanted what all could see, not social development. Nordic rulers always show more zeal in robbing other peoples' kingdoms than in uniting or even defining their own. Modern Danes pick Bluetooth for the unification job, on the strength of the Jelling stone and the Trelleborg camps; but there is still the belief that the kingdom had been united long before, in the eighth century, and Sawyer has put in an eloquent plea for Harald's forkbearded son as the true founder. Sweyn, after all, installed bishops, struck coins (a few) probably founded Lund and Roskilde towns and conquered England: achievements he was able to hand on to his sons.[37] It was Hodges who euphemised his devastations of England in the unforgettable phrase (1982, 182): 'Svein was evidently seeking to build up his treasury in order to afford the urban process'

Urbanized or not, from the fourth to the fourteenth century the Danes were always coming together and falling apart, and the mili-

---

36 Second? stanza of the *erfidrápa*, re-using a praise of Hakon Jarl by Einarr in *Vellekla*, as earl of sixteen earls.
37 Sawyer 'Swein Forkbeard and the Historians' in *Church and Chronicle*, ed. I. Wood and G. A. Loud (1991), 27–40. See map 6 for the structure of the Danish kingdom in Canute's time.

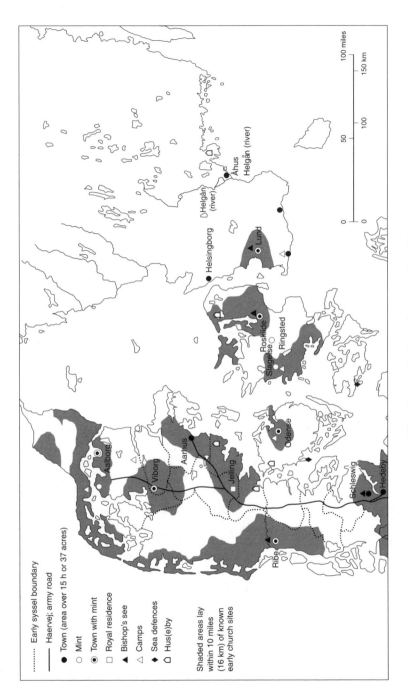

Map 6   *The Danish kingdom under Canute*

Legend:

...... Early syssel boundary
—— Haervej; army road
● Town (area over 15 h or 37 acres)
○ Mint
◉ Town with mint
□ Royal residence
▲ Bishop's see
△ Camps
◆ Sea defences
◻ Hus(e)by

Shaded areas lay
within 10 miles
(16 km) of known
early church sites

Aalborg
Viborg
Aarhus
Jelling
Ribe
Schleswig
Hedeby
Odense
Slagelse
Roskilde
Ringsted
Helsingborg
Lund
Helgån (river)
Åhus
Helgån (river)

0   50   100   miles
0   50   100 150 km

tary force established by kings in the eleventh century fitted in with both tendencies; driving the armed freeholders to oppose or exploit the perceived threat according to circumstances. Even within dynasties with monopolies of legitimate power, the competition between claimants continued to destabilize the state, such as it was. As in *c*.1075, when the chiefs had to choose a king from twelve brothers:

> *Strife swells in Denmark, Sweyn's sons out of joint when father died;*
> *Harald must defend by force land ... Against eleven brothers*

> (KS, ch. 27)

of whom, in due course, Canute IV was inspired to play the strong king, and in the summer of 1086 found himself hacked to pieces by his own subjects along with his agents of state control: seventeen brave but unfortunate men.

In Norway, unification mythology had an early start when twelfth- and thirteenth-century historians selected king Harald Harfagr of Rogaland (*c*.925) as the uniter, and ancestor of all subsequent kings; a position he gained in stages. First as a violent war-lord in the south-west who beat some chiefs from the south-east and sent his son to king Athelstan of Wessex; then as a convenient ancestor for the Olafs who seized the kingdom in 995 and 1015, so for their descendants, especially Harald Hardrada (died 1066, and known as Harfagr to the English Chronicler); then as an imagined descendant of ancient Swedish lineage (*Ynglingr*) with a heroic biography involving dreams of empire, the conquest of much of the North, a reign of seventy years, a height of $13\frac{1}{2}$ feet (from his grave-slab at Haugar) and parity of rank with the king of England; besides being responsible for the emigration of the Norse to Iceland, to escape his tyranny. This was written up in the course of the twelfth century and perfected in Snorri's saga (*c*.1230), and it has taken the last hundred years to dismantle the fictions and restore the history to stage one.[38] For the assembly of the territories of Norway, like that of the lands of the Svíar and Gautar, and of Denmark, was the slow-ripening fruit of convergent ambitions and chance, not the policy of any one king or dynasty, and the pace of

---

38 Helle 1998, 253–7 summarized what can and what cannot be known about Harfagr: handsome-, rather than blond-haired hero. His spurious descent from the Ringerike chief, Halfdan the Black, was exposed by Pesch 1997; his own descendants seem to have died out with Harald Grey-cloak in the 960s, and left room for the first, but temporary, hegemony over most of Norway imposed by Hakon Jarl, see Sawyer 1982, 107–8 on the development of the legend.

politics in the viking age joined and disjoined the component pieces (surveyed in chapter 4 and 5) as in a kaleidoscope, rather than a blender. The opposite view is put by Claus Krag in CHS 184–201.

Urbanizers

The six or seven towns established in Scandinavia by *c.*1000 are usually assumed to have been the work of kings able, in the words of Hodges 'to afford the urban process'. It was suggested earlier (p. 73) that before the late tenth century the connexion may have existed, but has not yet been proved or quantified, and so cannot be taken for granted. If royal power was one of the interests involved in Hedeby, Ribe, Birka, or the numerous coastal markets like Kaupang, it hardly made kings into urbanizers. Then and later, they lived on their estates (Lejre, Jelling, Borre) not in towns or *vici*;[39], and it could be said of Danish kings at least, that they had burned and sacked far more towns than they ever founded. However, by the 990s, possibly moved by 'the desire to monopolize exotic goods' (Hedeager), possibly by the itch to levy tolls on visiting merchants, possibly by the wish to get wealth from regions where there were few royal estates (Scania, South Jutland, northern Norway), kings seem to have woken up, and founded or helped to found new towns, some twenty-five all told between then and 1050, from Trondheim in the north to Schleswig in the south, as a rival to Hedeby. These have been described as '*points d'appui* for the new political order', planted by kings, bishops and magnates on foreign models, to act as minting-places, sees, royal residences and defensible administrative centres as well as markets and manufacturing centres. They repaid their founders with house-tax (as above: Monetary Kings), the profits of coinage, and tolls; but whether this was planned from the start by kings is not evident.

The earliest and most interesting case is provided by old Sigtuna, the Uppland town founded some twenty miles south of the ancient Swedish burial site of Uppsala. The 1988–90 excavations revealed a settlement of two rows of rectangular plots each approximately 7   35 m (23   114 feet) on either side of a 700 m (758 yards) stretch of road, with church and manor or hall in the middle. A dendro-date of *c.*975 may be too early for the whole complex, but the generous provision of

---

39 There was an ancient settlement south of the royal sites at Jelling, on Faarup Lake, which drained towards Vejle Fjord and the Baltic; the king's hall was at a deliberate distance, to be closer to old burials and lines of communication. See Hvass in PAP 1991 on Jelling, Christensen 1991 on Lejre (similar site), and Jensen and Watt in DIP (1993), 195–201 on 'Trading Sites and Central Places'.

space for about a hundred households has suggested that this was a deliberate plantation of royal retainers sent in to administer a district where kings were weak. Little sign of trade or manufacture has appeared in the earliest levels, so some rationale of a non-commercial kind is needed; but it is difficult to imagine what exactly a hundred administrative house-carls would be doing in a country without tax, or royal justice, or police, or written records, or many royal estates. It is not even known who was king of Sweden in 975: his resurrection as the great anonymous urbanizer seems premature, even though Sigtuna did become an important royal centre with a mint in the 990s.[40]

The development of the Danish metropolis of Lund in Scania, and of Roskilde in Zealand, is easier to envisage as the result of a deliberate policy of bringing royal power to bear directly on unreliable territories through an ostentatious reorganizing of the landscape and a concentration of houses and churches (see chapter 4, p. 91); some eleven had been consecrated in Lund alone by 1050, and the moneyers were busy issuing king Sweyn's money with the baptismal name MAGNUS, in an inscription stamped round the standing Christ.

Whether king or bishop had more interest in the founding of this and other towns is uncertain, but in either case the collaboration of magnates and farmers and merchants made it possible, and could not be taken for granted. The means by which these forces were brought together in the enterprise are lost from view, owing to the nature of the sources: see chapter 3, pp. 71–3. What kings wanted out of such places in the post conversion period was what their rivals and models in England and Germany got from towns there: tolls, a prior claim on exotic goods, military or naval manpower, rents, the profits of mints. What bishops wanted was an impressive church and residence, security for the training and feeding of clerics, and the 'work of god' (the performance of the liturgy) and a christian congregation willing (until tithing came in) to pay directly for services; a 'fort of god' (*kastra dei*) as the poets put it. What the magnates wanted is unknown, but traders wanted trade; and what they all actually got depended on circumstances beyond their control. In Norway, the earls of Hlaðir and later kings made spaces for trade outside the main settlement areas of the Thronds. By 1000 a site with fenced plots, for permanent occupation, was laid out at the mouth of the Nidelv; but Trondheim remained a market-place with a few houses and storage for goods, an adequate outlet for local produce, until

---

40 Until then, kings had probably lived in the 130 foot hall at Signhildsberg (Fornsigtuna'), a few miles west. See Peterson 1992 and Tesch 1992 on Sigtuna, and in general Andren, 'The Early Towns' in Randsborg 1989, 174–5, Hedeager in JEA 1994, 130–47 and Helle VC 12, 20–31.

after 1031, when the corpse of ex-king Olaf Haraldsson was dug out of a sandbank and brought to St Clement's church, where it was found intact, with hair and nails still growing. Within thirty years the king's burial-place had become the 'metropolitan city of the North-men' (AB 4, 32) goal of pilgrims from Dublin to Russia, and so full of wealth and shipping that to win it was halfway to winning Norway: a stone cathedral and a stone church would rise before 1100, and the great gild of St Olave could feast in splendour, unafraid. Olaf certainly turned out to be an urban king, if not in quite the way he would have wanted.[41] But by then he was credited with getting 'peace and plenty for all mankind'; see p. 275.

Convert kings

Convert kings are credited with mainly political motives for their choice of one god over many, which is now conceived of as one episode in the course of a socio-political revolution, or at least transition. So Mrs Sawyer sees the Jelling stone as 'a symbol not only of the transition from paganism to christianity, but also as the development of a new form of government' in which kings become sovereign; a contrast to Svialand, where the chiefs put up rune-stones to advertise their personal allegiance to the new faith, unconstrained by rulers.[42] In this perspective, the king's christening among Danes and Norwegians was a sort of coup d'état, winning him control of a cult previously shared out among all the rich and free of both sexes, and the service of literate males adept in administration and pregnant with future bureaucracies. This marked 'the decisive transfer of power from chieftains to king', and aligned the Nordic experience with that of other peoples, since this conversion-theory has long been applied as liberally as free paint to the Franks, the Anglo-Saxons, and all sorts of Germans, among whom paganism was 'a powerful agent of resistance to central authority' until they succumbed to the king of kings.[43]

41 Since according to his poet Sighvatr he burned more boroughs than he built: eight in *Víkingavísur*, on which see Fell *Speculum Norroenum* (ed. U. Dronke) and on Trondheim see now Soganes 1998, 316–35; Christophersen 1991 and 1994, with a brief summary (in English) in *Archaeologia Polona* xxxii (1994), 95–108.
42 See B. Sawyer in AUSA (1991), and Meulengracht Sørensen's summary of the power-transfer theory in HØKO, 243; Sandmark 2004 concurs.
43 Now a commonplace of Dark Age history, as in Bagge 2005, although he admits that there was 'no universal recipe for smooth state formation'.

Nevertheless, there are possible objections to this theory, and Mrs Sawyer noted one: it didn't happen quite like that in Sweden, whether because of the weakness of the king or the bifid nature of the kingdom (see p. 94). About 1015 the convert king Olof Eriksson made an attempt to destroy the 'temple of Idols' at Upsala, and was told by his subjects to retire to Västergötland and be a christian there. His son regained Uppland, and the Svíar became christian; but no strengthening of royal control ensued. It seems that a king must already have mastered his nobles for the new religion to be imposed; as in Jutland, where Gorm and Harald Bluetooth had a powerful support-group before the public baptism of the ruler. In those cases, the socio-political dividend of conversion was small. And the second objection is that it could be less than small, as with the first Danish convert-king, Harald (later known as *Klak*: the harmful, the blot?), a prize Carolingian satellite, baptized with full honours at Mainz in 826, but expelled from Jutland the following year and never able to rule there again. The second was Hørik II; at least he was ready for baptism in 864, when he made a vow to god and St Peter, but he is never heard of again. Among the Norwegians the baptised rulers (Harald Grey-Cloak in the 960s, Olaf Tryggvason in the 990s, and St Olave in the 1020s) met with constant and in the end successful opposition from their chief men, whether or not on the grounds of their christianity; if they were hoping for a decisive shift in the internal balance of power as a corollary of conversion, they were disappointed. The Olafs used the cross to cow enemies and consolidate support: Hakon, Athelstan's foster-son, was a less aggressive christian, and Hakon Jarl was a full pagan who ruled longer and more successfully than any of them. About the turn of the millenium, a Norse ruler weighing up his chances of bringing about a political shift to his advantage might have doubted whether christianity would help him. Thietmar of Merseburg tells of a Norse king's son called Gutring, who was being trained at the abbey of Verden in Saxony 'up to the rank of Deacon' (not as a priest) when his father died in 994. He fled, renounced christianity and was accepted as a king at home. He was still ruling there in the period 1014–17, still pagan;[44] perhaps the same as the Opland king called Hring in the Hsk. Olaf-saga. He was ousted by Olaf, and may have repented his apostasy; but he had had 24 good years by then. However, calculations in those terms seem unlikely. Christianity was not an exotic ideology, to be withheld or administered by rulers at will; it was a cult known and often respected and adopted by the Norse over this entire period, with or without royal assent. A would-be christian ruler is more likely to

44   Chronicon 7,38; trs Warner p. 334.

have assessed his prospects on four trembling scales, more delicate than the balance of power:

1   The spiritual: the fate of the king's own soul and body after death (evidently a great concern of Harald Bluetooth before he became a christian, to judge from the north mound at Jelling, his father's intended tomb), and the relative power of gods, which according to Widukind was much discussed in Harald's hall.

2   Reputation and status: how would this go with more or less powerful neighbouring rulers, with the foreign policy of the moment? Canute became 'dear to the emperor' but his convert grandfather, Bluetooth had antagonized Otto II and called in the pagan Hákon Jarl to help him, only to be expelled by his own followers, and defied by Hákon.

3   Domestic peace; how far heathen or uncommitted groups would react to the rewarding of christians. Zachrisson (1998, 149–54) suggests that this was why Sigtuna was founded, laid out in those numerous plots on either side of a church: each to be granted to a Swedish noble, to encourage and enlarge the christian community by offering coinage, rune-stone patterns, and masses, to be copied back on the home farms. Pure speculation, and if Adam of Bremen is to be trusted, the experiment failed for king Olof Eriksson; but the existing strength or weakness of christian groups inside the kingdom must always have been a weighty factor.

4   Immediate material reward, such as the gifts and silver which Alfred gave to Guthrum, Ethelred to Olaf Tryggvason, Lewis the Pious to Harald Klak, and the archbishops of Hamburg-Bremen to all Baltic rulers, when they could, following St Ansgar's example. Was it worth it?

Whatever the reading on these balances, this was a risky move, which could incur serious opposition; not an exercise in social engineering. Later ecclesiastical legend made the conversion of the Northmen entirely a matter of kingly will-power, guided by miracles, tribulations and teaching, irradiated by grace, and Mrs Sawyer has demonstrated the artificiality of this literature on all counts; it just couldn't have happened like that, and recent archaeology has shown how gradual, indecisive and ambivalent was the infiltration of christian culture.[45] There is no need to replace the hagiography of the conversion-legends with the pieties of socio-political evolution.

45   Discussions and articles in *The Christianization of Scandinavia*, ed. B. and P. Sawyer and I. Wood (Alingsås 1987) set a new standard in a short book; note Wood on Ansgar, and Birgit Sawyer on 'Scandinavian Conversion Histories'. See now Brink 'New Perspectives' in SCEU (2004) 163–75.

Sea-Kings

Sea-kings is a fair description of many northern rulers of this period, who spread themselves beyond their restricted land-bases by crossing the 'ugly land-fence', as one poet called the sea, in force, to levy tribute and win loot. The Rök inscription of *c*.800–50 refers to king Theodoric as 'governor of fleet-men', and Óttarr called Olaf Haraldsson 'chief of fleet-men' in the 1020s; but sea-ways had been the nervous system of the circum-Baltic lands for 3000 years, and their mastery had always been insecure, open to challenge by any chief who could put timber, men and (after *c.* 750) sail-cloth together. The cult of the longship involved both its use as a symbol of power – gilded, carved, painted, visible afar with raised mast and glittering wind-vane above the dyed sail – and a recognition of its fragility and treacherousness in the face of the elements: recognition in the form of sacrifice, omen-reading from the shore and sky, and continual pro-pitiation of misfortune by what survive as sailors' taboos, and unlucky landing-places. Add the making of stone ship-settings and ship-burials on land, and the symbolism branches out, well beyond the practical aim of getting marauders from A to B and back.[46]

Ship equals authority at Oseberg, S Norway, where a famous ceremonial 30-oar coaster was covered in clay to hold the elaborate burial of a great lady, or queen, in about 835. The whole west coast of Norway had by then been subject to naval chiefdoms for centuries, detected by the gathering of boathouses round early centres of con-sumption and wealth, one every 65 miles (104 km) or so,[47] and going back to the third century. Only two such boathouses (*naust*) have been found in Denmark (at Harrevig, on Limfjord), but PNN in *snekkja* (ship) do duty for the rest, and Canute's poets were to stress the naval basis of his kingship most fiercely, like Ottarr:

> *Wind blew over you, chief;*
> *You set all prows out to sea*
> *Westward, on course to make*
> *Your name notorious*

with the nautical bluster of a

> *liberal fancy-rigger of the sail-cloth of the spit-river reindeer*

(i.e. of a ship), and Sigvatr followed suit with

46 See p. 303n.
47 Myhre MASS (1997), 179–82 for Norway; and Crumlin Petersen 1991, 185 for Denmark. Danish *snekke* place-names may include some war-ship docks, but in general apply to anywhere with any ship-connexion over the Middle Ages.

bore on the breeze
dark sails on yards land-ruler's dragons

and the merging of power, ship and charisma reached a climax in
Arnorr's *Hrynhenda*, a eulogy addressed to king Magnus of Denmark
and Norway about 1045:

> *It seems to me, as the ruler makes ocean-ski skim sea-king's slopes,*
> *just as though, skimming the wave with him, were the angel-host of*
> *the skies' prince.*

> (trans. Edwards 1979, 100)

Opportunities for gain and glory overseas tended to detach these
rulers from their own countries, and raised the problem of how to
stretch authority over cruel seas; to which the answer was more
ships, and some kind of regular plying of the intervening distance,
preferably with the ruler on board. The solution worked tolerably
well in keeping England and Normandy together over the period
1066–1204, with Channel crossings of up to 70 miles, as with the
transbaltic hegemony of the Danish kings from 1168 to 1240; but
the North Sea was a different proposition. Nordic rulers skirted
round it to raid and sometimes get new lands to rule as emigrants
from the 800s to 1013, when Sweyn Forkbeard seems to have
assaulted England with a view to keeping it within his family, along
with Denmark; and left Canute this project to complete. He could
not do so without an armament far beyond the means afforded by
Danish royal manors, geared to food-production: he needed supplies
of timber, sailcloth, awnings, cordage, iron nails as well as trained
oarsmen which only his chiefs and Norwegian allies could deliver.
The ambitions of the sea-king gave chiefs a political importance
magnified rather than diminished, and their reward was the wealth
of England, and the earldoms distributed after 1017. Canute's was a
tax-system that kept his fleet in service and spared him the need for
continual warfare for gain, even if he had to put to sea every three
years or so. When English magnates resumed control of England in
1042, the sea-kingship was suspended, or relocated to the Baltic
where it remained geographically feasible, if smaller-scale, for centuries to come.[48]
   These eight varieties of king do not exhaust the list by any means,
which in a more patient world would include legislators (even if there

---

48 A concept most fruitfully developed by Tore Nyberg of Odense. Norwegian
hegemony in the northern British Isles linked countries less desirable to other rulers
and so less costly to keep: Orkney, Shetland, the Hebrides, Faroes, and Man.

weren't any within Scandinavian self-help, collective-memory legal arrangements); patrons of artists and poets; and pilgrims, following in the footsteps of Canute (1027); and exiles, in the tradition of the Halfdan who was some kind of hostage at the court of Charlemagne before 807. But eight are enough for now, enough to show that the politics of this age allowed fearful manifestations of royal power, but no steady development of institutional kingship at the expense of other lordly powers. Kings domineered as far as their ships would reach, but had no monopoly in any of the activities listed: even the privilege of striking coins was modified by the abundant supply of money from foreign sources, and domestic money-substitutes. 'The historical figure of the king dominates the forces that are shaping the future' wrote Joseph Harris[49] of saga-narratives of conversion, and modern narratives often give the same impression; but not contemporary sources, even when focussed on rulers. There is too little evidence of government and royal presence in most of the north, too much competition between armed chiefs and angry freeholders. Kings were winners who by 1050 were only beginning to find the means of consolidating their victories beyond the up-phase in cycles of depredation and distribution. Harald Hardrada's reign in Norway (1046–66) is typical: twenty years of strenuous warfare against his neighbours and subjects, financed by a dwindling stock of Byzantine gold, ending in a bid for the only card worth having: a reliable tax-base overseas. He avoided the fate of his half-brother St Olave: he was not driven out and then killed by his own subjects; but he failed to escape from the traditional pattern of sea-kingship.

Chiefs

Chiefs (see map 7) or magnates enjoyed a status which appears in the archaeology of graves and dwelling-places, and in the runic inscriptions. They upheld or dislodged kings, cults, rivals; fitted out fleets and dominated districts; they maintained military households, and could count on freeholders as clients. Men like Ruulf of Flemlose (Funen, Dk: DR 192) the *goði* or cult-leader of the *Nura*, commemorated on two rune-stones *c.* 900, who might live in 260 foot (80m) long halls, like the big one at Vorbasse, with traces of dependent work shops and imported goods, and stalls for 100 cattle; or those buried under ship-settings, or in boats under conspicuous mounds, or in chambers like that of Mammen in North Jutland (*c.*980), the sort

---

49   SMEOL, 203; but see Jakobsson 1997 on the christian origins of all the saga king-portraits (rev. Jochens SS (1999), xxxi).

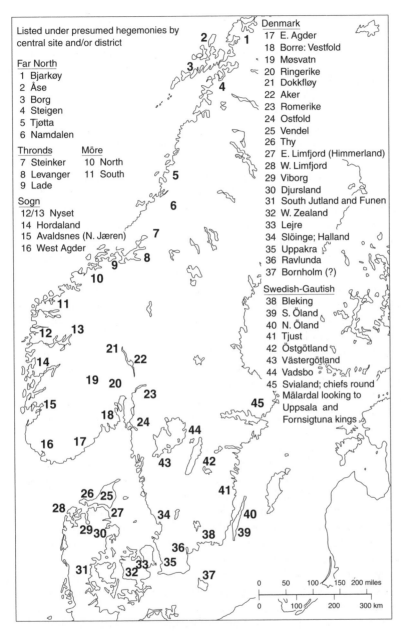

Listed under presumed hegemonies by central site and/or district

Far North
1 Bjarkøy
2 Åse
3 Borg
4 Steigen
5 Tjøtta
6 Namdalen

Thronds
7 Steinker
8 Levanger
9 Lade

Möre
10 North
11 South

Sogn
12/13 Nyset
14 Hordaland
15 Avaldsnes (N. Jæren)
16 West Agder

Denmark
17 E. Agder
18 Borre: Vestfold
19 Møsvatn
20 Ringerike
21 Dokkfløy
22 Aker
23 Romerike
24 Ostfold
25 Vendel
26 Thy
27 E. Limfjord (Himmerland)
28 W. Limfjord
29 Viborg
30 Djursland
31 South Jutland and Funen
32 W. Zealand
33 Lejre
34 Slöinge; Halland
35 Uppakra
36 Ravlunda
37 Bornholm (?)

Swedish-Gautish
38 Bleking
39 S. Öland
40 N. Öland
41 Tjust
42 Östgötland
43 Västergötland
44 Vadsbo
45 Svialand; chiefs round Mälardal looking to Uppsala and Fornsigtuna kings

0   50   100   150   200 miles
0   100   200   300 km

Map 7   *Chiefdoms and kingdoms, c.800*

These are indicated by big halls, central places, concentrations of finds, burials and monuments, with sparse or no settlement in between.

of *hǫfðingi* who could boast, like Austman, son of Guthfast, that he 'erected this stone, and made this bridge, and had Jämtland christened'; to whom a king might offer a warship to buy support,[50] or the name of *jarl*, but little less. In Iceland, the colonial versions of such chiefs were able to establish both individual and collective authority over the free population without competition from kings. In Norway the competition was fierce, but magnates were the arbiters of kingship, as were Gudbrand of the Dales and Erling Skjalgsson of Sole near Stavanger in the 1020s. Both were affronted by St Olave, and Erling was killed; but that was the end for the king, who was ousted and eventually killed by a combination of other magnates.

Such combinations or factions were the essence of high politics in Scandinavia as in England or Francia. They set up kings, by violence or peacefully, and supported them for as long as the rewards lasted: more than a generation in the case of king Horik of the Danes (813–54) but usually much less. Until the 890s the Danish chiefs would back rivals from the same cousinhood; from then to the 930s there was an ill-recorded succession, and thereafter Gorm's family established the hold on kingship which lasted to 1042, strengthened by a large personal following of household warriors, which became a paid army in England. Competition between would-be inheritors of this regime restored magnates to their political pre-eminence in Denmark: they took Magnus of Norway as king in 1042, and Sweyn II five years later. The middle range of politics involved competition for social power between chiefs – the top range in Iceland; a competition which flourished well outside the normal range of kingly power, in northern Norway (p. 146) Götaland and the Baltic Islands (for Sibbi of Öland, see p. 106) and northern Sweden. The lower range was when chiefs established or asserted their power with or against other freeholders, either in open confrontation or by the exerting of the pressures outlined earlier in chapter 3 pp. 74–8.

There is no clear picture of how such families gained their advantages over others in the first place, only a priori assertions of how they must have exploited the known wealth-producing forces of the age. There were lucrative raids; therefore the chiefs become a 'new viking military caste', in which members achieve 'total power of life and death over their immediate retinue': a caste, because the ninth and tenth-century graves show that the women were honoured as highly as the men, life-and-death because 'grave-companions' have

---

50   According to the Hsk saga of St Olave (*c.*1230, chs 52, 75, 128), the chief Ketel of Ringanes was given a thirty-man warship by the king for his support against earl Sweyn; after he had betrayed his own kings to Olave, he got the king's half- sister as well, in this late but probably not baseless version of events.

been found in a few graves, and the Encomiast of Emma wrote that Sweyn Forkbeard's men were ready to die for him.[51] Control of the resources and raw materials needed by the warmongers was another possible source of power, especially for Austman, the boss of Jämtland mentioned above, and the back-country chiefs; or promotion to the care of royal manors and the patronage of the more successful dynasts, which Randsborg thought he could detect from the sudden appearance of post-Jelling rune-stones in Scania, and Swedish historians from the later raising of stones carved with royal lions in Uppland. It is unlikely that any king in this period had the resources and prestige to create a chief out of nobody; but he could favour those who favoured him. So could the poets, as in Bjarni Hallbjarnarson's verses to the king-making regicide Kálfr Árnason, who was to be killed raiding Denmark in the 1050s with the connivance of Harald Hardrada. He was the great Thrond who had organized resistance to St Olave, and helped enthrone both Sweyn Alfífason and king Magnus; he was praised in the same terms as a warrior-king, but also as the recipient of a land-grant from Canute; and as the one who deposed his son. A verse from the 1040s attests his power before king Magnus exiled him:

I need the high-commander's help
Half the kingdom's under Kalf.

His career suggests that it was still possible to play off rulers against each other, if dangerous, and that people like him were the natural leaders of the territories uneasily yoked into kingdoms, thanks to their armed retinues.

Freeholders

Freeholders were players at all the three suggested levels of Nordic politics. The *buandar, bu-menn* of the districts, would be the richer of these people, some of them called *thegnar* in the poems and the rune-stones, like their counterparts in England; but there is no connotation

---

51 EE, 9; Wamers 1995, 156 for the new caste, and of Erik Lönnroth's view of the eleventh-century Swedish nobles as viking profiteers, opposed in Gräslund (ØPOLIS 1993, 181). Others have attributed changes in settlement patterns and land-ownership among the Danes *c*.950–1000 to a move from common to private ownership imposed by 'central élites' – king and nobles: see Ulsig and Sörensen in HT (D) 1985, 110–18, Hahnemann 1997 and Thurston 1999, who detects (p. 669) 'élite-sponsored false consciousness' among the Scanians who underwent this course of treatment.

of royal service in either source.⁵² Both Sigvatr and Arnorr referred to the thegns of Norway and the Orkneys as unruly and obstinate opponents of kings, not as vassals, although lords and kings needed their support for effective rule, and could not rest easy when they grumbled together at assemblies, as at the head of this chapter. There were hundreds of freeholders who cannot have been thegns or *bumenn*, and their sons made up the rank-and-file of the armies and the military households and so reinforced the power of lords and kings; but it stretches the evidence to make such service into a social revolution, a transition from rank defined by status to rank defined by function, in which, between 950 and 1050, military *drengir* and administrative *landmenn* and *brytir* (stewards) rose to form a new squirearchy among the Danes and Svíar.⁵³ As there is no clear indication of what made status in the ninth century (not enough runes, no poems), or of the function of any but a small minority of those commemorated on eleventh-century runestones, the case for a significant social transition cannot be compelling. The military graves of tenth-century Denmark need not mark a new crop of landowners, rather than the old gang reacting to military pressure from the Ottonian empire and the Jelling kings by rallying to Jelling, as Eisenschmidt suggests.

The probable course of how these landowners got hold of their farms and villages, their arms and slaves, in the viking period remains purely conjectural, and has been noted before, in chapter 3; to say that it involved the repression of non-freeholders and the unfree is to state the obvious. Their relations with chiefs and kings may seem too narrow a definition of politics, and there have naturally been attempts to widen it by introducing the idea of class-conflict. After all, the total number of kings, chiefs and freeholders at any one time in the viking age cannot have been a majority and may have been a small minority of the population; the regrouping of farms and aggrandisement of halls suggests friction between an elite of exploiters and a declining 'gentry', and the presence of slaves offered a reserve of potentially subversive manpower, such as the lower orders which were bribed to revolt against the freemen of Saxony in 842, and were crushed in two bloody battles. But any such interactions among the Norsemen are unrecorded. The condition of slaves, paupers and poor farmers can be traced faintly in the archaeology, but whether there was any kind of class-consciousness among them can only be inferred from their smaller shares of well-being and lack of

52   See Jesch 1993 for a shrewd analysis of the poetic evidence, and Christophersen 1981–2 for a processual reading; also Morris 1998, 146, and see Appendix D below.
53   Petersen in MASS, 123–35.

status, or from much later law-codes, sagas and incidents: which is a dead end. Discussing the post-Roman period, Ausenda maintains that 'a clear dichotomy between rich and poor does not exist in real society, because wealth distribution is more like a continuum' in which the rich lose and gain status without direct contact with the poor, and the poor focus their attention on the slightly less poor who are close, rather than on the distant rich.[54] However, the rich would be more visible to the poor in the relatively small viking-age societies, where the free assembled to confer and quarrel at regular intervals, in the open air, wearing their wealth, if they had any, and the slaves were the silent spectators, or left at home. Class-war would probably be the wrong term for the antagonisms expressed there, or in violence between masters and slaves on isolated farms, unless stretched as Geoffrey de Ste Croix stretched it for the ancient world. The conflict noted at the head of this chapter was between court and country, in the cruder sense; we would know nothing about it, but for Sigvatr's verses, and he was a courtier who sympathized with the countrymen.

Assemblies

Assemblies were an alternative to the battle field for the expression of grievances, and sometimes their resolution, and the siting of such meetings has been discussed, in chapter 4. Any notion we have of the procedure followed, beyond the sinking of noses into cloaks, comes from sources too late to represent viking-age reality; the more detailed and convincing (like *Thinga-saga* in Morkinskinna, chapter 70), the less so. For example, the famous adoption of christianity by the Icelanders assembled at Thingvellir, about midsummer 999.[55] It was mentioned by Ári in the 1120s, who gave the gist of a speech by the law-speaker, Thorgeirr, proposing a compromise solution in the interests of political harmony; all were to be baptized, but pagan customs could continue in private. So it was decided, according to Ári, and his version was elaborated in several sagas, with much corroborative additional detail, like the story of how pagans in geysir country would only accept baptism in hot water. There is no contemporary evidence of these events, and the evident shaping of these

---

54   Ausenda 1995, 140; cf. Hodges 'Archaeology and the Class Struggle' in Randsborg 1989, and Olaussen 1997.
55   1000 in Ari's chronology, but as his new year began on September 1 the synchronism with Olaf Tryggvason's death (September 9) by which the conversion was dated, would be in our 999: Einarsdottir 1964, 107–26.

narratives to suit the politics and religion of later centuries has made them prime candidates for reinterpretation and deconstruction. At one extreme there is Jónas Gíslason's traditional parliamentary history, in which the 52 voting chieftains are broken down into parties, and an anti-heathen coalition (16 christians plus 8 time-servers plus 2 turncoats) achieves a 26–26 tie with the heathen die-hards, and the speaker adjudicates in the public interest; at the other, G.W. Weber takes all the narratives to be fictions based on 'the ingenious application of a missionary topos', by Ári, who had learned from Bede, Adam of Bremen and the Life of Anscar that valid baptism must come from the free choice of the individual.[56] In between come those who stress the possible contribution of outside pressures from Norway, or inside from a putative Irish-christian underclass, but the fact is that all our notions of parliamentary procedure in Iceland post-date the writing down of the 'Assembly Procedures Section' in the *Grágas* collection[57] no earlier than 1117, and can only relate rather vaguely to viking-age custom, here or elsewhere.

Assemblies may have developed during this period from what had been mainly religious festivals, into mainly legal and political forums, but if so this hardly justifies the view that law and politics were in essence affirmations of the unity of the cosmos and the solidarity of the folk in the middle of it.[58] The practical and the religious reasons for meeting need not be child and parent, or expressions of an underlying consensus among participants. Sacrifice, invocation and feasting took care of the future, and therefore must not be missed; but the prosecution of grievances and group-interests by appeal to the public, or open consultation, was practicable in assemblies of the dispersed independent farmers simply because, for most, this was better than fighting. On the whole, for most of this period, kings had the military manpower to win fights of this kind, but Sigvat's

---

56 Gíslason ONFRAC (1990), 222–5; Adalsteinsson 1978; Strömbäck 1975; Weber 1987, 116–17; Cusack 1998, 116n; all present divergent views, while Jochens 1999 affirms that the conversion 'followed time-honoured Icelandic principles' as if this had never been questioned. According to Vésteinsson (2000, 18–19) Ari's account 'tells us more about the preoccupations of high-powered churchmen in the early twelfth century than what was happening at the time'. In 1856, the yachtsman Lord Dufferin was given an entirely different version of events 'carefully preserved', which he re-told as 'a characteristic leaf out of the Parliamentary Annals of Iceland'. *Letters from High Latitudes* (London 1857), 98–100.

57 Trans. Perkins and Foote (Winnepeg 1980), 53–138.

58 Dowden 2000, 276–90 restates the case for a pan- European concept of *thing* as centripetal cosmic force and replay of creation; and see Adalsteinsson 1992, 88–9 on the oath-taking provisions of medieval Icelandic law as evidence of thing-sacrality. Frense 1982 is the fullest modern development of the case.

verses show that by the 1040s assemblies had the political muscle to check them, even outside Svíaland, where kings had deferred to the assembly in the 830s.

It is right to tell princes everything that their people wish

said Halli the Stiff of a meeting in the 1060s when Danish and Norwegian kings were forced to make peace by their followers.[59] However, there is no reliable contemporary evidence about assemblies within Scandinavia between the 830s and the 1020s. Later sagas claim that Norwegian public meetings debated and sometimes decided who should be king and whether christianity should be accepted; the assembly of the Swedes decided questions of war or peace, foreign policy, and misgovernment. Such accounts reflect the assumptions of 13th century Icelanders, for whom parliamentary procedure was all-important, and need be no more historical than the oratory of generals and heroes in histories by classically-educated authors. Nevertheless, the fact that all Norse colonies and settlements looked to public assemblies of freemen to settle political and legal business in the 12th century suggests that the custom came from the homelands in the ninth and tenth. The gatherings and procedures developed in different ways in different places: in Iceland, to take on the functions of government and reinforce the power of oligarchy, in Scandinavia to maintain local law and custom against overbearing rulers, at York to co-operate and consult with earls and archbishops. No *thing* attracted regular participants from more than 120 miles away except the *Althing* at Thingvellir in SW Iceland; a geographical constraint from which kings and their retinues were free.

---

59 Poole 1991, 73–5; for Halli, Skjd. A, 401, B, 370–1; Kock, i, 184–5.

7

War

FADER HAD THESE RUNES CUT IN MEMORY OF ASSUR HIS
BROTHER
WHO MET DEATH IN THE NORTH ON A VIKING RAID.

The words on the stone at Västra Strö in Scania (DR 384, M 278, 355–6) meet modern expectation of how a Norseman should be remembered, but they are exceptional: 96 per cent of Danish and 90 per cent of surviving Swedish inscriptions are for people who died at home. The viking is rarely mentioned, and the military virtues seldom emphasized. For these, see the poems, monotonously bellicose, or such tales of mythical fire-eaters as the Ingjald of *Ynglinga saga* chapter 36, who promised 'that he would double the size of his kingdom towards every corner of the earth or else he would die'; or the record of Nordic raids in the annals of the West. They occurred somewhere or other almost every year from the 790s to the 1020s, and it has been suggested (see p. 6) that if the viking age has any coherent theme, this was it. It was not as if Norsemen had been peace-loving householders before the 790s, and then exploded; but the archeology of fortifications shows a very warlike state of affairs in Jutland and the eastern Baltic before 500, and an apparent reduction in violence thereafter, so much so that Brink has suggested that Scandinavia was more peaceful than Anglo Saxon England. There were raids round the Baltic before 790, all the same, and the intimidation of Slavs, Balts and Finns, by Northmen. The change came when raiders undertook an extra three or four hundred miles of rowing and sailing to pillage not only the north-west but eventually the whole of western Europe down to Africa.

Why they did this is a question with many answers.[1] How they did it will be considered next.

---

1 Usually materialistic and economic, as if the desire for *Lebensraum* and silver were peculiar to Nordic societies rather than shared by all societies; or techno-determinist,

The obvious answer is by banding together in large amphibious armies which remained active over long periods, living off enemy territory until the leaders' demands were satisfied, or scaled down, or negated by defeat. Such armies survived for years, winter and summer; they were led by groups of commanders, but seldom disintegrated even after repeated defeats in battle; they included women, children, slaves, livestock and foreign auxiliaries. As they were mobile, their archaeology is meagre: objects which might have been dropped on the march, fortifications which might have been occupied. The story of the great armies must still be told as it was by the Frankish, Irish and Anglo-Saxon annalists. Repton, a rampart and burial-site discovered in 1982, and apparently connected with an occupation by a Danish army in 874, seemed like a breakthrough, but remains a puzzle. An earth-wall was dug to enclose a space between the river Trent and the Mercian royal monastery, and perhaps a wide trench for docking ships; but the camp was not lived in, and the burials were so strange that a long silence has followed the closer analysis of the bones. Why should some 260 men and women have died all at once, or near the same date, then remained unburied for a year, for animals to pick at, and then have been carefully arranged in a mass grave apparently centred on a single chamber tomb? Whatever the answer, it may shed little light on how the Danish armies operated, or even on their size and composition. Some of the corpses were those of big, muscular males, but only one was obviously killed by violence, and the lack of grave-goods makes it uncertain whether they were Danes or Angles.[2]

It is clear from the written sources that these armies were combinations of retinues or household troops led by lords obedient to senior chiefs, whether earls or kings, and that until the eleventh century they were held together by the distribution of rewards rather than by payment of regular wages. How big they were, or could be, is a problem in quantification which has been answered or approached in many ways, none of them conclusive.

However, something can be said of the shipping, horsing, camping and strategy of such armies, before moving into battle.

as if, in the words of Mrs Clinton, 'the Viking Longship was the Internet of the year 1000' (Preface to VINAS). On raids to the west, see now contributions to Stumann Hansen 2001 and VE (2005), chs 1–5.

2   Martin Biddle and Birthe Kjølbye 1991, 40–2, concluded that most of the males were of 'non-local' physical type, while the females (20 per cent) were possibly of Anglo-Saxon type; some bones were transferred from the Anglian mausoleum.

Shipping

The combination of abundant timber, iron and easy access to water in an enclosed sea had favoured the development of naval transport in the Baltic and along the Norwegian coast for hundreds of years before this period. By 800 the Gotland picture-stones and the Hedeby bracteates show that Baltic seamen had the use of sails, with complex rigging, a choice of four distict types of hull, and a tradition of oarsmanship in crews of up to 30 men. The shipbuilding represented by the Oseberg and Gokstad vessels consisted of nailing together and waterproofing a single thickness of planks on a loose framework of ribs, a technique which called for the least timber, specialized tools and work-space possible.[3] The conclusion that here was a technology and a weapon deliberately aimed at the vulnerable defences of western Europe would not be justified, all the same.

No ship actually or probably used by Norsemen in the raids of 790–990 has yet been found, and it is therefore not known whether the Gokstad model of 'viking-ship' (oars, sail, low freeboard, broad amidships, dragon prow) was typical, west of the North Sea. Foreign-built ships, more capacious and rigid, were certainly called for in 892, when an army crossed from Boulogne to Kent in ships 'provided' to carry horses and men together (ASC, A, C, D, and E, 892); presumably by Frankish builders. In armies made up of separate contingents uniform ship-design and length need not be expected. When Canute invaded England in 1015, according to Thórðr Kolbeinsson's *Eiríksdrápa*

> *Many ships of different sizes*
> *Steered up the river-mouth.*

The conditions of warfare in the west, where there were long defensible rivers, slaves and booty to transport, and hostile vessels constructed on different lines, cut the technological advantage of the Gokstad model down to size. From one point of view, such ships were essentially transports, delivering fighting units; from another they were symbols of authority (see p. 303n). How they were handled, and how they were decorated, seem to have been more important than the good points of their architecture. Experiments which have tested the sailing capacities of reconstructed longships cannot answer

---

3 To make a ship of that size. For smaller crews the Finnish five-part boat (hollowed keel and four side strakes lashed together with roots) was the most economical: see Taavitsainen in Huurre 1999, 307–12.

the question of how the fleets were sailed; what is needed are many reconstructed Norsemen in working order. Thirty or a hundred ships delivering warriors from the Baltic to the Seine cannot have been ruled by the same considerations as single craft, and their feats would be very expensive to re-enact.

The only contemporary sources which describe in detail what happened on sea-borne raids, rather than simply recording damage done, are the 896 annal of the Anglo-Saxon chronicle, about a fight somewhere in the Solent, and Alpertus of Metz's tract *On the Variety of the Times*, which records forays up the Rhine by Danish raiders in 1006 and 1007.[4] One later source is the Danish history of Saxo Grammaticus, where he describes raids undertaken against Baltic Slavs between 1158 and 1185 in ships similar to those of the viking age, most undecked, rowed and single-sailed. By putting these texts together, we get some idea of how they got men across the sea in a condition to fight and pillage; and the first thing needed was evidently high morale. This could easily be damped by prolonged rowing against a headwind, by rumour of enemy ambush or blockade, by fear of bad weather, by waste of time at anchor, by jealousy between rival crews, by mistrust of the council of captains, by any determined show of strength by enemy land or sea forces, or by mistrust of the leader. In this light, the safe arrival of so many fleets off the estuaries of Francia and Britain from the 790s and the small number of shipwrecks recorded is remarkable: a tribute to the caution of the captains, rather than to the wave-conquering impetuous launches of the poets. From 834 to 884, the Frankish annals record the coming of twenty-six or twenty-seven separate fleets; fewer reached England, but enough. The loss of a hundred Danish ships in the great storm of 877 probably did more to save Wessex than anything Alfred could do at that point. The leaders had to ensure that nobody put to sea in rough weather, or between August and April, or in cranky vessels; which meant constant repairs and refitting, as when Thorkell's fleet had to dock after six month's campaigning in 1010, or when Weyland halted for repairs after a year on the Lower Seine in 862.

How the men were trained to row as a crew, how their places were allocated, what they said or sang as they rowed, all that sort of detail is unrecorded; for the skalds, voyaging by sea was another chance for conflict, fortitude and display, not for sea-songs.[5] The sea was some-

---

4 For Alpertus see now *De Diversitate Temporum*, ed. H. van Rij and A.S. Abulafia, Amsterdam 1980. For Saxo's raiding details see SG (EC), 422–38, 444–7, 478–6, 490–3, 512–30, etc.

5 See Foote 1978 for the best sieving of the verse for nautical information, and for a detailed study of the vocabulary see now Judith Jesch *Ships and Men in the Late Viking Age* (Woodbridge 2001).

times deified, as Njorð or Ran, always seen as a threat, and never loved or celebrated; it was a food-source, a road, a barrier and a death-bed. Familiarity alone could have bred the seamanship of those who crossed it in large numbers, but cannot have prepared them for the difficulties they found on landing.

Ashore, most of them dispersed to get plunder, horses, cattle, slaves and fuel; their ships became lightly defended transports mainly confined to river routes, or were hauled up beaches. They became vulnerable to counter-attack, as the Danes discovered at Benfleet (893) and up the Lea (895), when they lost their fleets, and very nearly once again in 1004, when Ulfcytel of East Anglia sent orders that the ships docked at Norwich 'should be hewn to bits, but those whom he intended for this failed him'. When armies re-embarked, they could row out of danger or to find unprepared targets, as for example in 991, when 93 ships ravaged the Kent coast, then appeared at Ipswich, 100 miles to the north, then at Maldon 40 miles south-west; by land, such attacks would have been impossible, as the route would have been blocked by the strong defences of London, which were to repulse Olaf and Sweyn in September 994. There is no need to stress the obvious advantages of mobility; nor to overlook the cost of dependence on transport at the mercy of wind, fire, reefs, shoals, tides, leaks, rot and fog, the necessity of getting back to the fleet, the nuisance of protecting it through the winters, of manhandling and maintenance.

These ships may have had some technological advantages over others; but this is not the impression given by contemporary sources. What they liked to describe were big, ostentatious vessels, show-boats, like the one sent from Norway to king Athelstan 'which had a golden beak and a purple sail, ringed inboard with a close-packed row of gilded shields'; or like king Harald Hardrada's big ship in the 1050s. According to Thjóðólfr Arnorsson, it was 'resplendent', bore a 'bright dragon's mane', a 'decorated neck burnished with gold', and attracted the lingering gaze of 'fine ladies' because 'it was as if they saw an eagle's wings'. When king Magnus of Norway sailed to Jutland in the 1040s, Arnorr the Earl's Poet noted that the timbers were 'covered in red gold' and 'the tops of the masts gleamed there like fire'; as with king Sweyn Estrithson's Danish ships, 'gold-mouthed, high-masted beasts, all painted in fair hues' according to Thorleik the Handsome; and it was Thorleik who said that even in heavy seas, 'the slipway-bison gapes with gold-adorned mouth' as if the figure-head were still in place.[6]

---

6   Athelstan's ship was described in a twelfth-century reworking of a tenth-century poem, cited WM and translated EHD, i, 281; Thorleik's verses by Faulkes, in SnE, 142.

To risk so much wealth and glory in a sea-fight made little political sense, even when great chiefs were involved and honour demanded a showdown. King Sweyn Estrithson of Denmark endured fourteen years of harrassment from Harald Hardrada before confronting him with superior forces at the mouth of the Nissa river in 1062; and then he lost seventy crews and barely escaped with his life (according to Thjóðolfr). Those who had raided Francia or Britain in the ninth century and later always avoided sea-battles except when they had no choice, as when attacked by king Alfred in 875, 882, 885; and perhaps the fight on the mud-flats in 896 should be included, when Lucuman the king's reeve and his comrades crippled the stranded Danish raiders by the Solent. In 992, later invaders ran into one English flotilla while escaping from another, and this was the last time a Danish fleet had to fight an engagement in English waters. The conquests of Sweyn and Canute were accomplished without sea-battles, even when both sides were hiring navies of forty ships and more. These and other kings had good reason to be careful: from 1013 onwards, such fleets became the lifeline of hegemonies stretching across the North Sea: the Danish until king Hardicanute's last drink in 1042 (p. 59), the king of Norway's until 1468. A lost navy could mean a lost throne and from Canute's point of view the waste of an expensive standing army. The Anglo-Saxon Chronicle gave a famous calculation of the tax-liability for 1040 in terms of regular annual wages paid per rowing-room to the fleet;[7] presumably the system set up in 1012 for Thorkell's hirelings by king Ethelred.

The English king had already imposed a shipbuilding and armament duty on the whole country at a rate of one per 310 hides (land-tax units), for the great ship-levy of 1009. This turned out to be a disaster, and the beginning of two years of disasters, as the Chronicler points out more than once, and the idea of a regular public levy-system, if it was ever contemplated, ended there; hiring crews out of land-tax money was more cost-effective, as it seemed to offer a guarantee of the loyalty which was lacking in 1009, when twenty crews went off on a piratical spree and the loss of another eighty in a storm demoralized the remainder: the chief men deserted 'lightly'. Nordic rulers and chiefs have sometimes been credited with similar levy-systems, on the strength of the defensive obligations certainly in

---

7 The *hamele* is usually interpreted as one rower's rowlock, but this would imply an outrageous overpayment of 2s a week, more than a knight could expect in the 1150s. A pair @ 1s each is more likely; and as the pay-packets could go to any size of ship, calculations of the ship-total err: see Rodgers 1995, with full bibliography in the footnotes, and a correction by Jesch 2001, 156–7.

place by the thirteenth century, and known as *leidangr* or *ledung*: but Lund has shown how the evidence and the infrastructure for such systems are entirely lacking for the viking age.[8] Magnates, one-ship landowners, and partners (*félagar*) owned the ships, from first to last, and their gathering into fleets depended on the man-to-man tie of lordship or clientage, which at times failed Ethelred and generally held good under Canute.

The intenser military competition of the years after 1042 in Scandinavia was boosted by the arrival of Harald Hardrada with his chests of Byzantine gold, but gradually calmed as the kings ran out of resources and the chiefs lost interest in risking all to support fragile hegemonies. Harald was never able to re-establish his nephew Magnus' rule over Denmark, which ended when his body returned to Norway: in the words of a fine recessional:

> *Now travel home from south*
> *In dusk, past famous commonwealths,*
> *Ships downcast with this*
> *High-enterprizing leader dead.*

> (from Morkinskinna chapter 28, in Andersson and Gade's edition: not their translation)

Horses

A horse is a common simile for a ship in Scaldic verse (steed of the sea-leagues etc.) but seldom appears in its own right as a charger until later; some verse on the harrying of Scania by king Magnus in the 1040s includes horses 'hastening from the west' and the king spurring his, in Funen. But war-horses were no new thing: Swedish chiefs had been mounted like Persian or Roman heavy cavalry even in the seventh century, and had apparently trained lighter armed horsemen and infantry to follow them in probing enemy lines with spears and arrows.[9] Horses were included in the more elaborate burials of lowland Scandinavia, and at Stavrby near Middelfart they found a grave for two horses laid back to back between five dogs, perhaps a cenotaph for a dead lord. In 804, according to the Frankish Annals, king Godfred of the Danes was on the Schlei with his fleet 'and the whole *equitatus* of his kingdom', a phrase which presumably means 'chiefs with horses' rather than 'horse

---

8   Lund 1993 and 1994 were expanded in *Lið, leding og landeværn* (Roskilde 1996); and see his contribution on *leidang* in MIAS (1997), 195–9.
9   Tactics reconstructed by Engström 1997, with diagrams.

brigade', or cavalry. Whatever role mounted leaders had played in warfare before that was bound to diminish when sea-raiding increased; none of the earlier types of ship were built to transport horses, and even if they could have, it would have been a pointless additional risk.[10]

However, from the 920s to the 980s many leading Danes were buried with military honours and equipped with stirrups, harness, bits and spurs, in what are called cavalry-graves. They are found in north Jutland, mainly south-west of Limfjord, and near the Belts and southern islands. Whether these were vassals or opponents of the Jelling kings, their families presented them as knights by status, if not by training, although opportunities for profitable horse-borne raiding from Jutland to the south were virtually none. It has been suggested that these *herrenklub* cavaliers were merely parading equipment which 'in the previous century would have been won by direct participation in battle or intensive viking activity abroad';[11] but it is easier to believe that the models were the armies of the Carolingians and Ottonians, which had ridden into Jutland in 815, 936 and 974. From the 840s to the 860s, horsemanship and status were brought together most intensely at the court of king Lewis the German, the arch-enemy of the Northmen, from whose hard-riding regime at their own doorstep they could have learned the supreme importance of equestrian prowess[12] even before they embarked on raids overseas.

From the 850s onwards, getting horses became the means and one of the main ends of these raids. After an unmounted raiding party had been routed between Paris and Beauvais, the lesson was learned, and whole armies were horsed. The Danes who camped in East Anglia in 866 gave peace for horses, and rode to York the following year; the range, elusiveness surprise and general effectiveness of such forces was suddenly magnified both in Britain and on the continent. It is strange that their enemies failed to stop this happening, at least in the ninth century, but the casual nature of western stud-farming may have been a factor; mares allowed to roam freely in forests with the stallions must have been difficult to corral at short notice, to

10 ARF, 804; and DLU, 217 for the Stavrby grave; for analysis of the tenth-century horses at Süderbrarup see D. Heinrich in SADO (1998), 249–57. They stood thirteen hands on average. See map 12 for these burials.
11 Pedersen in MASS (1997), 132.
12 Goldberg 1999 contrasts east and west Frankish kings in this respect; and see Keefer 1996 on the horsing of the raiders, on which the English historian Ethelweard deserves a hearing: 'And now, with the equestrian apparatus denied them by nature, they forgot their fleet, and...ranged through fields and woods as swift as is the way of spies, or of the eternal god' (*Chronicle*, 4, 2).

forestall the rustlers. Besides, peace was worth a price, and a mounted army was quicker to move somewhere else. In 885 and 892, armies ferried horses over from the continent to Kent, to begin raiding without delay; and until 917 armies based in the Danelaw would ride across Watling Street for plunder. Frankish kings had forbidden the sale of steeds or weapons to Northmen, but the ban was ineffective. Even after a crushing defeat at Saucourt in 881, when 9000 mounted men are said to have been killed, 'the Danish army provided itself with horses' immediately afterwards' and 'went further into the Frankish realm' (ASC).

Whether they learned to fight as cavalry, from the saddle, is undecided. It would have been rash for recently mounted sailors to take on Franks trained from boyhood in combat on horseback both individually and in formation, and the great overthrows of Saucourt and Geule (891) may have been the result of such rashness; the breakthrough can only have come when Norse settlers got hold of the forests and downs of the Lower Seine, and the remnant of Carolingian bloodstock, and had time for schooling and training. Dudo of St Quentin, writing a hundred years later, described Rollo's men fighting as cavalry and infantry, but he is not to be trusted; it was probably the need for properly trained horsemen which made his son William recruit the Frankish retainers with whom he held Rouen against his enemies in the 930s.[13]

Meanwhile geography and economics slowed the development of horse-soldiering in Scandinavia; large mounted retinues were not much use at sea. Yet the raiding and conquest of England after 991 would have been impossible without horse-transport, and the ninth-century pattern was repeated. Horses were commandeered in West Kent in 999, and again in 1010, after Ulfcytel had been defeated at Ringmere Heath; that cost the English two years of rapidly-moving depredation. Sweyn Forkbeard got his mounts from Northern England in 1013, Canute his in Lindsey in 1014 and from the West Country in 1015. Most of the good horses in England must have been involved in the hard and bloody campaigns of 1016, but no contemporary source speaks of horsemen fighting in formation on the battlefield. To arrive, dismount, hammer, hew and slash, then ride off or in pursuit may have been the normal procedure for the Danes; but if so, it remains extraordinary that English thegns, with the fine horses mentioned in wills and charters, their stud-farms and chests of superlative weapons, did not manage to sweep the enemy from the field whenever they met.

13 Dudo, 3, 43; trans., 64–5.

Spades

Spades were the third indispensable weapon in this kind of warfare, which depended on the ability to instal loot and manpower rapidly behind all round defences in enemy territory, and to hold such bases at least through one and sometimes many winters. In this field, Norsemen had a long and impressive tradition visible in the many defensive fortifications of the East Baltic and SW Swedish highlands; see p. 105 for Torsburgen on Gotland and the Öland forts. Many of these were made and remade over centuries, and during the viking age they remained in use, while the other tradition of linear fortification cutting across landscapes reached a new peak in the extension and reinforcement of the rampart between the Schlei and the Eider, which came to be known as *Danevirke*, the work of the Danes. But what was needed on overseas campaigns was improvised or adapted fortification, preferably using earlier work (as at York, or London, or the Lympne fort, 'half-made' in 892) or natural defences: small islands were often occupied, or river-bends, as at Reading in 871 when the Danes 'made a rampart between the two rivers Thames and Kennet' (Asser) to cut off a defensible corner in which they defeated the West Saxons shortly afterwards, a plan repeated at Wareham, between Frome and Tarrant in 877. Minimal digging-in makes elusive archaeology: the Repton camp (p. 168) was a rare find in England, and the search for forts in Ireland (called *Dúnad* by the annalists if temporary, *Dún* if permanent, and in general *longphort*) continues: Dunrally on the Barrow in Co. Leix may be a surviving example, but the crucial base at Dublin seems to have been eradicated.[14] Those were all earthworks; but a very small stone ring-fort (23 feet or 7 m in diameter) has been found at Udal in South Uist and labelled 'viking' without much provocation. Most of the works attested in the sources appear as dots on maps, whether they were Udal size or elaborate, as when in 880 the Danes made their own wall round the Roman station of Nijmegen, and used the Carolingian palace there as a headquarters, or when they made a base on the Isle of Wight and remained there for much of the 990s – site unknown.[15]

14 Doherty 1998, 326; Ó Floinn 1998, 162–4, 'we have as yet no clear idea of what one (camp) looked like'. Now we have: the Dublin fort was an irregular tringular rampart between the Liffey and the Poddle, with the later castle at the SE angle: see Simpson 'Viking Dublin' VS xxiii 2004, 47–63.
15 Rouche 'The vikings versus the towns of North Gaul: challenge and response' in C.L. Redman (ed.), *Medieval Archaeology* (Binghampton 1989) has good maps of fortification on both sides; the Annals of Fulda describe the work at Niijmegen.

By that time, Danish kings had laid out carefully planned Trelle-borg forts in their own kingdom, on which see pp. 84–6; but there is no evidence to suggest that this plan was followed by the armies which terrorized England until Canute's conquest. They camped in English towns, and their hardest spadework was the digging of a canal round the south end of London bridge, to carry their ships upriver to Southwark; and then cutting off Southwark with another ditch, all within a few weeks of the summer of 1016, perhaps with slave-labour perhaps not. Neither London bridge nor Southwark fort were taken; but the army was free to move upriver, and the Lon-doners were pinned down. The poet who made the 'verses of the Lithsmen' describes how he saw the operation: *The army fought along-side the ditch, lady,* and *Out she will look, the lovely lady who lives behind the stone* (wall)...(to see) *how hard the Danish leader, eager for victory, attacks the men in the fort*...as if it were just an assault. But the sight of those ships bypassing the bridge must have outdone the hand-to-hand fighting around Southwark, which got nowhere. Nobody celebrates sappers, but the effectiveness of this spade-work over two centuries is notable. The Frankish annalist who reported of the Danes driven from their camp near Louvain in 891 that 'they had never been heard to have been conquered in any fortification' (trans. Reuter, 122) was exaggerating; the Londoners had taken the camp at Benfleet (Essex) in 893, when it was appar-ently defended only by women and children, and in 917 king Edward's host attacked and stormed the new Danish fort at Temps-ford, and killed or captured all the defenders. Other places lost to assault were long-term fortifications, not defences raised on the run or as temporary shelters; it was the short-stay works which the enemy were reluctant to test by assault, and preferred to surround or blockade,[16] because they were usually full of fighters.

Strategy

Ships, horses and spades enabled the roaming armies to afflict the West at various places and times from the 840s to the 920s, and the British Isles for a further century, until the whole northern world came under the direct or indirect rule of Canute. This long series of

16   or enter for trade, as in Francia and Ireland, when the red shield was hoisted at the gate. Very few spades of this period have survived; some, neither steel-shod or dished, could have been used as paddles. Engström, 62–3 shows examples from 3'2" to 5'3" long. The pit-falls which stopped enemy cavalry at Paris in 886 and in Poitou (S. Michel-en l'Herm) in 1018 add to their achievements.

victories, defeats and indecisive bloodlettings was not a conscious military strategy, or the pitting of one school of generalship (amphibious, mobile, predatory) against another or others, or a trial of strength between equally matched political complexes or states. The soldiering of the Norse served a shifting variety of purposes and paymasters, beginning with the units paraded earlier in this book: individuals bursting with ambition, like the earls Ottarr and Hroaldr who raided south Wales in 914, kidnapped a Welsh bishop, let him go for a mere £40 of silver and lost most of their men; but Ottarr survived and joined king Ragnal of Dublin.[17] Many of the invasions of the ninth century seem to have been by-products of family policy, the exclusion of brothers and cousins from power in Denmark, and in 1014 when Canute came home with his tail between his legs after failing to hold England, he was told by his brother Harald that he could not have a share of Denmark. Such dynasts could recruit followers like the Yttergärde Swede, who was getting geld to build up or defend his private property, an Uppland community. As more powerful chiefs would collect their clients to enforce wider lordships with the profits of war, or found new ones. The units composing roaming armies had various aims; only by forming a limited company on the joint-stock plan could they be realized. This never changed, despite the pretensions of Nordic kings after 1000. Olaf's army, the bane of Ethelred, was an association of three chiefs (Olaf, Josteinn and Guthmund) with a Danish king who had opted out before the others came to terms with the English king. Canute's army was a multifarious coalition of war-lords, not the instrument of a state. It is difficult to evaluate the strategy[18] when the war-aims are often unclear and the internal tensions of the armies hidden by the ignorance of the sources.

Terror

Military dominance was impossible to sustain in the face of the well-organized manpower at the disposal of Wessex kings and some Irish rulers and Continental magnates; negotiation, alliance and conversion to christianity were attractive alternatives, and frequently

17   Who let him be killed fighting Scots on Tyneside in 918; see Smyth 1975, i, 64–5 and 93–6 for this brief career.
18   Lund 1989 concluded that raiders were merely old-time predators with enhanced mobility; Griffiths 1995 stresses the ability to hit soft targets and escape counter-measures. Some did, some didn't; it is not clear that there was any 'viking art of war' involved.

offered. Guthrum got more by surrendering to king Alfred in 878 than by occupying his kingdom earlier in the year: great presents, recognition as a king and the peaceful occupation of wherever he wanted to settle outside Wessex.

Nevertheless, Nordic warriors are credited with military habits peculiar and abominable: surprise attacks on defenceless populations, the deliberate perpetration of atrocities, and the conduct of furtive and evasive manoeuvres. They are seen as terrorists, and credited or blamed depending on the attitude of the analyst to this way of fighting. There is a false assumption here.

All over the world, at all times, terror and surprise are the make-weights of forces at a disadvantage in open combat, or aiming to neutralize a hostile population. There is no need to except Nordic raiders from this rule, or their enemies. Bloodshed and cruelty were commonplace in war and peace, all through Christendom. It is surprising that Norsemen should have been seen as especially atrocious, or deliberately vile, when it is not recorded, for example, that they ever massacred over 4000 disarmed prisoners of war, as did Charlemagne in Saxony; or displaced an entire people, as did the same Charles from what is now Holstein; or perpetrated genocide, as did Cadwalla of Wessex on the population of the Isle of Wight in the 680s, according to Bede; or ordered the massacre of all foreigners in their country, as did king Ethelred of Wessex in 1002; or mutilated thousands of prisoners, as did the emperor Basil in 1014. No doubt they would have done so, if they had ever commanded the resources and the administrative machinery; king Hardicanute, who did, tried to extirpate the burghers of Worcester in 1014 (after they had violated holy ground to kill two of his Norse tax-collectors), but his earls lost heart, plundered instead, and 'killed few' (FlW). Others lacked the means; for all the harm they did in burning, enslaving and impoverishing westerners, the great killings were the prerogative of those thought of nowadays as the upholders of civilization and christianity. Our notion of humanity was alien to both sides. The realistic questions are:

1 Was Nordic atrocity calculated, in pursuit of military objectives otherwise unobtainable?
2 Or was it in excess of any strategical advantages it might have won, the result of inherent savagery or cult-inspired blood-lust?[19]

---

19 For example, 'There was a grotesque element in Norse barbarism which surpassed anything that had gone before' Smyth, in Smith 1984, 108, reinforced in Smyth 1999 and in Dumville 1997. On *berserkir* see above, p. 31, and for a defence of 'the conventional view' of Viking devastation, Dumville in Jesch 2002, 209–30.

To propose that viking ferocity was a rational strategy, like modern terrorism – a means of applying force so as to intimidate large populations and demoralize enemy forces – is to abuse the sources. These are nearly all the work of clerics, but represent a variety of attitudes, from the blank, laconic realism of the Anglo-Saxon chroniclers of the wars of Alfred and his son, from whom it would be hard to deduce viking savagery at any point, to the outrage of the Fulda annalist and Hincmar of Reims at the rampant bad faith and brutality of the Danes in Francia during the 870s and 880s. Those who denounce the invaders for their conduct find three aspects of it intolerable: it involved breach of sanctuary and the defiling of holy places and persons; it was marked by occasional indiscipline, breach of agreement, drunken insolence, and deceit; they enslaved and pillaged and sometimes recruited christian populations. The first kind of outrage was an offence against religion and the rules of war as understood, if not obeyed, within Christendom, but seems to have been incidental to the aim of seizing wealth or captives, not a policy of profanation, to demoralize believers. Alcuin's horror at the sack of Lindisfarne in 793 was roused by the refusal of 'St Cuthbert, with so great a number of saints, to defend his own'; and by the failure of the Northumbrians to lead the moral lives which would have spared them this affliction: it was not so much the Danes, as the Anglo-Saxons who were behaving badly.[20] The monks who were captured could be bought back, or saved by negotiations between rulers. Perhaps they were; but, as Halsall has pointed out, raiders from afar could sail away to the more profitable market without pausing to negotiate or bargain, or offer reparations. They were not accepting responsibility for their acts, in such cases; which was indeed hateful, but not an act of terrorism.[21]

The vile behaviour of armies under many commanders, living from hand to mouth, cannot have served any military purpose and may be seen as a prelude to disintegration. This happened soon after the drunken killing of archbishop Elphege in 1012, when Thorkell the Tall left his associates and went over to king Ethelred; it was, and remains, a common military weakness. Breaches of treaty and oath were not a Nordic speciality, either, and deception was endemic in warfare, as when in 882 the emperor Charles the Fat sent a task-force from his army to catch Norsemen unawares outside their fort at Asselt, and the Fulda annalist cites Prudentius: 'What do I care whether I win by force or tricks?' The third charge, of maltreating peasants, or

20 Alcuin's letters to the king of Northumbria and the bishop of Lindisfarne are translated in EHD, i, 774–9.
21 Halsall 1992.

recruiting them to serve against their masters, as archbishop Wulfstan complained in 1014, was no doubt justified; enslavement and
pillage were Norse objectives from first to last: 'often two seamen, or
maybe three, drive the droves of christian men from sea to sea, out
through this people, huddled together, as a public shame to us all'
complained Wulfstan in 1014, but goes on to say that this shame is
not felt; the English honour the pillagers, 'we pay them continually
and they humiliate us daily', and the fault lies with us. From first to
last, the slave business was one of connivance and common interest
between the raiders and the slave-purchasers and sellers of christian
countries; the clergy wrote as social critics, to remind nobles of their
duty, and their words lashed immorality rather than inhumanity.

Battle

In no case can Northmen be shown to have pursued a deliberate
strategy of terrorism in the modern sense, to check mass-resistance.
There was none to check.[22] Abhorrent for heathenism and for rap-
acity and aggression they were, but not, like Lenin, for calculated
cruelty. But cruelty there was, and the second question asks whether
this was a reflection of plain savagery or dedication to bloodshed on
religious grounds?

The case of the imaginary king-sacrifices was mentioned in chapter
6 (p. 136); there is no case at all for crediting Norsemen with the
sacred bloodlust of the Aztecs, who waged war to collect sacrificial
victims for the consolation of the cosmos. Had this been the objective, at least someone, somewhere, would have mentioned it at the
time; christian observers were schooled in the detection of holocaust
and human sacrifice, and the examples they give of the latter, which
certainly occurred, include captives, and slaves and freemen chosen
by lot, but always as a result of capture, never as a motive for it. The
god of the slain was usually Odin, and the poets make it clear that
Odin liked people killed in battle and consumed or excarnated by his
pets; virtual victims, as well as real ones. An Odin-cultist would do
well to kill in battle, and eventually to be killed himself; but aggressive ire was valuable in a row of men facing their peers with axes and
swords, quite apart from pleasing the war-god. The aim was the

22 Only two instances of peasant retaliation against the Danes occur in the ninth-
century Frankish annals; none in the Anglo-Saxon sources, although later versions of
events insist on popular indignation. Lawson and Nightingale bring the Londoners to
the boil over Canute's regime in the city, by stretching later accounts of the translation of St Elphege; at least a hundred rustics saved David Hemmings from the Danes
in the film *Alfred the Great* (1968).

same, in pagan as in christian societies: victory in hand-to-hand combat, against an enemy equally exalted.

Battle, the shield or weapon assembly, the parliament of edges, was the climax of human feeling and action for the Norse poets and presumably their audiences; but so it was for their enemies, who gave as good as they got, and usually won. It was a meeting of hearts and minds, as well as bodies:

> *It seems to me too poor a thing that you should go to your ships with our treasure, unfought, now that you have made your way so far into our land. Not so easily shall you win tribute; peace must be made with point and edge, with grim battle-play, before we give tribute.*[23]

said Ealdorman Byrhtnoth in the poem about his last battle, at Maldon in August 991, a defiance which the writer has charged with similar forms of irony, meiosis, antithesis and humour which a Nordic poet would be twisting into a very different prosody on the other side of the North Sea. Over there, battle-verse dwells on three ironies in particular:

1 Battle is a party: play, negotiation, social gathering, assembly. 'Valkyrie-sport', 'lads' get-together', 'weapon swapping', 'mail-coat meeting' and even a judicial process, as when Hallfreðr said of the fight of Svǫlðr:

> *The weapon promulgated the law Adequately for young men's death.*

So battle is not battle; but on the other hand

2 battle is not extremely pleasant. It is not 'as when a lovely woman with bent arms made a bed', or 'as when the maid serves men with leeks or ale' or 'as though mead were borne by modest maidens', or 'as when the maid bears the mead to the men in the king's halls'.

3 Battle is a transaction: a payment, a gift, or betrothal, an opportunity to get something even if it is a hail of spears or a death-blow, when 'the battle-strengthener engages himself to Hild' (a valkyrie) who 'prepares a bed for the harmers of most helmets'.[24]

---

23 Trans. Ashdown, EHD, i, no. 10. Compare Thjóðólfr's description of Harald Hardrada egging on his men at the Nissa river in 1064/65 as 'the peace-loving war-leader' (*friðvandr jǫfurr*: Poole 1991, 62).

24 SnE, 196; and see Niles 1989 and Harris 1986 for ON–AS parallels, and Edwards 1979, 90–1 for a convenient list of war and seafaring clichés in skaldic verse. For the clichés of sea-fights see Jesch 2001, 208–15.

Some of these phrases are ingenious, but as a whole they are not 'culture-specific', and they belong to a rhetoric already old when Homer used it. Convergences between Anglo-Saxon and Norse poetry have been noted by many scholars, and the fullest sympathy is delight in battle, as in the Brunanburh poem inserted in the Anglo-Saxon Chronicle to celebrate king Athelstan's great victory in 937. The poet deploys at least twenty-four phrases paralleled in skaldic clichés, some of them twice over, in seventy-four lines. 'It was natural for men of their lineage to defend their land, their treasure, and their homes in frequent battle against every foe' is a shared assumption, as is the notion of overweening confidence as the fighter's proper mood: Byrhtnoth's *ofermod* at Maldon, and Harald Hardrada's *ofrhugi* at Stamford Bridge, to cite two much-admired losers.[25]

Descriptions of how battles were actually fought in this period are seldom detailed, usually stereotypical, and never trustworthy. On the Frankish and Anglo-Saxon and Irish sides there are images of conflict and triumph derived from an education in biblical, classical and native lore, as betrayed when the Brunanburh poet assures his readers that 'never yet in this island before this by what books tell us,...was a greater slaughter...since the Angles and Saxons came hither from the east' – a literary context, which overshadows the narrative, such as it is, of an exemplary blood letting, rich in high-ranking casualties, but not in tactical information: even the site of the battle remains unknown. The poet left it to the three beasts which a Norse poet would also have mentioned: the raven, the eagle and the wolf; for like the other christian war-poets, this one had no misgivings at all about the cost of victory. It was the same in German, with the *Ludwigslied* praising God with a great Dane-kill at Saucourt in 881, and in Latin, with Abbo of St Germain exclaiming 'Hurrah!' (*evax*) at the feat of abbot Ebalus, who killed 500 Danes outside Paris, and gloried in heaped corpses. It was the same with the skaldic versifiers, who presented aggressive warfare in nearly all circumstances, from c.960 to c. 1160, as a sequence of four or five conventional actions:

1 Embarking and crossing sea: 'having out', 'bidding out', 'bringing out' in the fast and fearsome and fanciful vessels (mentioned previously, p. 171).
2 Embarking and moving inland: 'going up', 'carrying shield ashore' to meet the defenders, or devastate their country.

---

25 See Stúfr's encomium on the Stamford loser in SkjD. IB, 373. The notion that Byrhtnoth's arrogance was criticized in *Maldon* is well-established and ill-founded; it was the thegns who lacked the *mod* to stand and fight whom the poet scorned.

3 Fighting the defenders hand-to-hand, in 'shield-wall', or which
   ever of the three battle-images mentioned above seems metrically
   apt, but always with insatiable fury: 'like a maddened elk' is one
   memorable simile.
4 Driving away the fugitives, and leaving the dead in heaps for the
   wolf, the raven and the eagle to enjoy; whatever happens, they
   must get their rations of eagle-meat, wolf's yule-feast, raven's joy
   and she-wolf's breakfast, washed down with rook-beer, the
   watcher's warm ale. Scavengers are celebrated, not deprecated.
5 Being admired by, or at least avoiding the scorn of, women at
   home.

This year the fair Trondheim women
for we fought well
shall not jeer at us

said Sighvatr of the Nesjar battle of *c*.1016, and the lady of London
was watching Canute's charge over in England about the same time.
This is mostly poetical fustian, and it is not surprising that modern
historians have been eager to reconstruct the realities of this kind of
warfare, substituting their own sorts of infill from the stock-room of
military history. In the thirteenth century the writers of sagas began
this tradition, with apparently well-informed narratives of the tactics
and strategy employed by legendary and historical fighters from the
day when Odin invented the wedge-phalanx (*svínfylking*) to the day
king Harald Hardrada's men took off their mail-coats to catch their
breath in the hot September sun, and lost their lives at Stamford
Bridge:[26] all more-or-less intelligent fabulation suggested by the surviving verses, or family traditions, or folklore. It is not easy to work
out what happened from such a pungent gathering of inventions, and
as a result the period is starred with conjectural encounters such as
the great battle on the Holy River, which the Laud chronicle (E) puts
at 1025, when king Canute sailed from England to Denmark, 'and
Ulf and Eglaf met him with a great host, both a Swedish fleet and
army; and many men perished there on king Canute's side, both
Danes and Englishmen, and the Swedes held the place of slaughter'.
Both Ottarr and Sighvatr congratulated Canute on defending Denmark against the Swedes and Norwegians, despite the battle. Two
hundred years later this has turned into a fabulous and complicated

---

26 Narrated in Harald Hardrada's saga *c*.83–94, but better in Morkinskinna chs 49
and 50, trans. Andersson and Gade, pp. 267–76; and on the unreliability of the
military detail see Gelsinger 'The Battle of Stamford Bridge and the Battle of Jaffa',
SS, lx (1988), 13–29.

conflict, from which everyone emerged a winner, at least according to Hsk. Saxo, the Danish historian, tells of a desperate fight on a bridge, or causeway, built to reach an enemy on the island, while the Swedes are defeated elsewhere; none of which helps to discover what actually happened.[27] It can be assumed, without much confidence, that this was a war like many others, in which the more northerly war-lords tried their luck against the fatter south-lands and were seen off. Or it was a defiance by discontented Danish satellites, frozen out by Canute's monopoly of the old sources of wealth. The battle or battles were all important to the participants and their poets, but the real achievement was that many shiploads of warriors, selected from the paid army which garrisoned London, were induced to row and sail over 700 miles to the north-east to fight in defence of territory where most can have had no personal interest whatever: perhaps they were offered a bonus, or pay-rise, or feast at Lund, but no-one says what. The morale and logistics are what we find astonishing, rather than the almost-ritual test of manly courage on the battlefield which stopped the victors in their tracks. Nevertheless, battle was the crude index of leadership all over that world, and the contemptuous cleric who chronicled Ethelred's reign (a text reworked afterwards, under Canute) had no more patience with fight-shy captains than had Norse poets. Who can forget that dreadful day on the Wiltshire downs in 1003, when the ealdorman of Hampshire, at the head of his men, in full view of the enemy 'pretended to be sick, and began forcing himself to vomit, and said he had been taken ill; and so tricked the army he should have led'? The troops dispersed, and Sweyn Forkbeard led his men into Wilton opposed, to burn the king's stronghold.

Meeting the enemy head-on, unflinching, was sometimes more important than strategy, because it validated authority and rank. So it was in 871, when king Ethelred I of Wessex and his brother Alfred and the chief men fought nine major and many minor battles with the Danes; the same in 1016, when the two would-be English kings,

27 Gräsland (1986) suggested that this battle was actually fought over 300 miles away, on a stream also called Helgån in SE Uppland. There was once a village there called Holm, 'the island'; and a battle within Denmark could not have won Canute his supremacy in Sweden, attested by his letter of 1027 to the English. A classic abuse of evidence, but á-la-mode: the chronicle statement that the Swedes arrived 'from Sweden' and the poetic references to the defence of Denmark are brushed aside, as inconsistent with the gratuitous assumption that Canute's claim to be king 'of part of the Swedes' must result from a victory in Sweden. There is no reason why Canute should not have lost a fight in 1025, successfully defended Scania, and become king of certain Swedes. Gräsland was refuted by Moberg in Scandia lxiii (1987), but it was Moberg who rubbed the lamp by asserting that the English chronicler of the fight meant to say that Canute won: on which, see Campbell EE, 99, and on his Swedish troops, Syrett 2002.

Edmund and Canute, led their supporters into battle again and again, until 'all the nobility of England was destroyed', and the survivors made the peace of exhaustion.

Nevertheless, it is often asserted that Norse raiders adopted a guerillero strategy of hit-and-run devastation, deliberately avoiding battle and timing their movements to penetrate undefended territory when least expected. 'Vikings fought for money, not glory; they had no interest in seeking out particularily formidable opponents';[28] this would be true of robber-bands everywhere, and of vikings if the word were used in that sense; not of the roving armies in the West, or of the Thing-lith of Sweyn and Canute. Compare what the Anglo-Saxon chronicle (C version) tells of the army that sailed from Kent in 1010, 'and landed at Ipswich, and went straightway to where they had heard that Ulfcetel was with his army' – the commander who had mauled Sweyn's men at Thetford six years before, and was to stand up to Thorkell's on this occasion at Ringmere Heath: 'they themselves said that they never met worse fighting in England than Ulfketel dealt to them'. Four years earlier another army had ridden along the Berkshire Downs over Christmas, collecting supplies and 'always observed their ancient custom, lighting their beacons as they went'; they waited at Cuckhamsley Barrow 'for what had been proudly threatened, for it had often been said that if they went to Cuckhamsley, they would never get to the sea'.[29] Nothing happened; they marched on, and past the royal city of Winchester, 'proud and undaunted' to show themselves to the inhabitants. This was not furtive or elusive movement. The king of the English happened to be spending Christmas in Shropshire and the invaders challenged his thegns to come out and fight, near where Alfred had won his victory over the Danes 135 years earlier.

It was no different in the ninth century. Both in the British Isles and in Francia, armies avoid battle when they are likely to be defeated or when entrenched in strong positions (like the Danes besieging Paris in 886, 'who were well stocked with all things in their fortifications' and let a German relief-force wait for them to come out for $2\frac{1}{2}$ months before it retired; but they were ready for the next relief, 3 months later, with an offer of battle). The armies which campaigned in England from 892 to 896 were certainly more interested in gathering plunder than in challenging the forces of Wessex and Mercia; they only fought when they had to, at Farnham and Buttington in 893, and on the Lea in 895, and the whole war was a series of raids and chases, with livestock, loot and ships as the prize. Twenty years

28 Hill 1997, 8.
29 ASC (C) 1006, convincingly interpreted by Lund 1987, 258–9.

earlier, Danes had been fighting for territory or at least concessions of food-rights and silver for occupying forces; they had to humiliate Anglo-Saxon kings and ealdormen by defeat if preliminary offers of peace for supplies and horses were refused. As foreigners, without ready access to reinforcements, they had more to lose from an open fight than the defenders; but if this made them generally cautious, there were always times when they had to 'seek out particularily formidable opponents' or lose whatever advantage they had. The hit-and-run specialists got what they could carry, without confronting the local defenders; paltry gains, compared with what could be secured by braving and beating the proper authorities, or even by threatening to do so. Lund has argued that the main aim was a *frið* or treaty like those agreed between Alfred and Guthrum or between Ethelred II and the army of 994, which laid down terms of tribute, trade, litigation, compensation and residence: a permanent settlement, or at least security for a lifetime. Whether this package was in the minds of the chiefs or not, there were always those who extorted silver, gifts and moveables on the side, outside the treaty; entertainment and land-grants from kings and emperors; a place in the sun, or the chance to carry silver and glory home to the family, to prove the validity of the mental training in virile aggression which lay behind it all. As with the Greek hoplites who slaughtered each other for their cities' sake, the material gains of such warfare were secondary, however great; the mentality of the 'war-glad' came first, and it was shared by the Nordic invaders and their opponents.[30]

30 Following Runciman 1998, who isolates four 'memes' which kept the hoplites fighting: shared assumptions other than expectations of material gain. On the 'group ethos' among warriors and above all, not letting the group or comrade down by flight or treachery, see Jesch 2001, 216–61. The theory that their valour and ferocity was rooted in shamanistic sorcery, the Odin cult, and shape-changing, as components of a 'viking world view' has been revived in Price 2002 with much erudition. This world view enabled the warriors to fight as participants in an 'invisible battlefield' (ibid 393–4) or mystical concussion like that imagined by J.R. Tolkien in *The Lord of the Rings*. This insight cannot be examined here.

8

Work

The maids ground, exerted their strength. The young ones were in a giant fury. The shaft-poles shook, the mill-box shot down, the heavy stone burst apart in two.

And the mountain-giants' bride uttered words: We have ground, Fróði, so far that we must stop. The women have done their full stint at milling.

So ends *Gróttasongr*, the song of the grinder (SnE 106–9 for Faulkes' trans), sung by two captive women of superhuman power, who responded to king Fróði's productivity-drive by grinding out his death and destruction, and breaking the magic mill which had given him gold and peace and prosperity. These verses were copied out in the 1230s (certainly not handed down in this form from viking times)[1] but embellish a more ancient myth, hinted at when poets use 'Fróði's meal' as a kenning for gold. He was trying to get something for nothing, by abusing the wrong kind of women, whom it was unwise to enslave; but nothing was for nothing. Women ground the corn whether enslaved or not, as well as malting it for ale and cooking it for porridge, unless their rank and wealth required that they should merely supervise these tasks.

Analysis of words for work in Old Icelandic justifies few firm conclusions about the concept. The verbs are *yrkja* and *verka*, which could both be used for attempting, being engaged on or accomplishing any task, ploughing, rowing or making a poem; not easily to be disconnected from mental strife and making and doing in general. Poets spoke of their art as forging, brightening up, word-working, or building, and the rune-stone accreditations imply that

---

1   See Harris in MESCA 244–5 for a summary; and for a survey of early medieval concepts of work in the West see Ovitt's 'The cultural context of western technology' in *The World of Work*, ed. A.J. Frantzen and D. Moffatt (Glasgow 1994).

carving and colouring inscriptions was as good as composing prose or verse. Runes also show that smiths were highly honoured; and graves that work was divided between the sexes, at least in eighth-century Sweden. Women did the cooking, fire-tending, fur-dressing, tool-sharpening, and hair-dressing; fire-lighting, sword-wearing, preening, and gambling with dice was for men. Neither was usually buried with field tools, sickles and spades.[2] Rich graves reveal that highly-wrought, decorative and complicated things were for the powerful, as might be expected anywhere, but what this meant for the workers who made them, who might be slaves, like the smith on the Hørning rune-stone (p. 24) can only be guessed: a path to emancipation for that Toki, at least. A love-hate of technical skill can be detected in the story of Vǫlundr the smith (the Anglo-Saxon Weyland), who in the Old Norse poem uses his cunning for vengeance on the king who has lamed and imprisoned him. After beheading the king's young sons, setting their skulls in silver as cups for their father, and their eyes and teeth as jewels for their mother, he raped and impregnated their sister, and made wings to escape from his prison:

laughing, he rose in the air.[3]

The tale was common property in NW Europe through the middle ages, a possible warning to those lords who expected artificers to accept injury without retaliation, a corollary to Frodi's overworking of the big girls. Norsemen were as impressed with the importance of skills as social differentials as were Anglo-Saxon 'wisdom poets', but made the social differential of slavery or thralldom irrespective of skills; the condition of belonging to another depended on the accident of birth, capture, impoverishment or legal condemnation.[4]

Such generalizations are not supported by much evidence. There are no Nordic counterparts to the Ælfric dialogues in Latin and Old English, which give some idea of how work was ranked and seen in eleventh-century Wessex, or the classroom in which the busy serf recites the duties of his station ruefully but carefully to help the young masters learn their latin. For the viking age in Scandinavia

---

2 Ringstedt 1992, 152–7.
3 Trans. Larrington, PE, 102–8. McKinnell believes that the tale thus told comes from the English Danelaw, as there are five Weyland carvings in Yorkshire, and only one in Scandinavia (Ardre, viii); but there is no obvious reason why these verses should not have been made up in Iceland (SB, xxiii, 1990–3); and for a speculative survey of Weyland legends see Maillefer in HUG (1997).
4 See chapter 1 above, pp. 24–7.

there are no such records,[5] and attempts to wring workers' history out of *Rigsthula*, the tale of how king Rig met the people in their clearly marked stations of life, are negated by the dubiousness of the text, and by the artificiality of its social concepts. It could have been written by a social anthropologist. All the texts dealing with work are too late, because it is not a subject of much interest to the skalds or to the composers of runic inscriptions, hard workers though they were; the nearest approach to their philosophy of labour is found in the myths of the god Thor, who appears as a super-energetic opponent of natural forces – giants and giantesses – and expert wielder of the hammer, tongs and staff. He was undoubtedly the most popular god of this period, when his cult is attested by hundreds of hammer symbols in stone and metal, by personal names and place-names; and this popularity was despite a loss of authority to Odin, whom the poets fear more and invest with higher skills and a tendency to exploit Thor's readiness for work.[6] Their relationship changed from place to place over time, but it seems that a contrast between labour and cunning gave Thor a firm support among farmers which lasted well beyond the coming of christianity. For in Scandinavia and in all the Nordic societies to the West, as elsewhere, food-getting was the common work of all; by farming, hunting and gathering directly, or by way of trading skills or commodities. Each in turn:

Agriculture

Agriculture over most of the North followed systems already ancient at the beginning of this period, and which system to follow was decided by where you lived. Jacob and his pottage can thrive in the lowlands: Denmark, southernmost Sweden, Baltic coasts, Finland

5 Such as those which enabled Kuchenbuch to analyze *arbeide* in fourteenth-century Saxon texts. On the relationship between servitude and different kinds of work in Elfric's *Colloquies* see Ruffing in Frantzen and Moffatt (above, note 1). Among the Danes, the thirty-one places called Trelleborg (Thrall-fort) suggest that unfree (rather than communal) labour was notable in this period; see Knudsen in Nørlund 1948, 189–214.

6 Two pre-conversion Thor poems, by Vetrlidi Sumarlidason and Thorbjorn Dísarskáld, are more reliable than Snorri's versions of the myths in prose; the Eddic Thor-verse comes between. The many Thor-kennings used by nearly all poets are the best tribute; and see Lindow 1998b and 1994 on his work-ethic, and Wamers 'Hammer und Kreuz' (RBN [1997], 84–108) on the distribution of the symbols. Motz and Clunies Ross disagreed over Eilífr Goðrunarson's *Thórsdrápa* in SB, xxiii, 1993, 491–5. Doubts on the integrity of Rigsthula text are expressed by Karl Johansson in *Alvíssmál*, viii (1998), 67–92.

and in patches round the coast of Norway; all the rest is Esau's mountain, plateau and forest, for hunting, gathering, trapping, iron-winning and fishing. Even today, less than 10 per cent of the Fenno-Scandian land-mass is cultivated; in Norway, 1 per cent of the modern kingdom's area. Grain, deciduous trees and fruit will not thrive outside those enclaves. The deciduous forest line coincides exactly with the extent of the Danish kingdom *c.*1050, but there was mixed woodland to just north of Mälardal, and hazel, oak and bees to the head of Oslo fjord, close to the southernmost reindeer in those days. There was not much choice of technique; the landscape and the experience of $4\frac{1}{2}$ millennia, since southern Scandinavians switched from hunter-gathering to agriculture, decided the matter, with the help of the weather, which punished the unthrifty by starvation. The idea that Nordic farming over the first millennium AD offers 'a historical model of social continuity and steady growth'[7] is unduly smug; 'lacking the excessive demands of civilizations it was even ecologically balanced' say the modern *économistes*, floating on a concept (ecological balance) as arbitrary as the grain-and-population obsession of their eighteenth-century ancestors. What viking-age populations wanted was to satisfy a craving (also inherited) for barley and meat at any cost, not always obtainable through balanced husbandry, or by conserving rich tilth and pasture, in so grudging a climate, but always to be supplemented by getting whatever could be clawed in from the wild country, the heath and the mountain-side; or satisfied by emigration. The impressive residue of well-used soils over hundreds of years tells nothing of the regular cattle-plagues and harvest-failures which afflicted the region until modern times; it hides the painful fact that none of these farmers could make their land yield more than one winter's food at a time.

There were different ways of working different landscapes, and terms used to describe these must themselves be defined, before we look at these smiling scenes of near-starvation. Five stand out:

1   Burn-beating, Swidden, or *Brandwirtschaft*: the good old way of burning off areas of scrub and forest on a 21-year rotation, and sowing and raising one or two grain-crops in the ashes, with or without scratch-ploughing; then leaving the forest to regenerate, or not. It can be a preliminary to forest-clearance or a way of getting

---

7   End-note to Björklund and Hejll 1996. The best account of prehistoric agriculture in Denmark is still Jørgen Jensen 1982 (in English). On the Norwegian fishing-farming interplay see Reidar Bertelsen in SAL, 216–62, and Jakob Meløe *The Two Landscapes of Norway* (1990). For a recent survey of 'rural conditions' down to 1350 see Orrman in CHS 250–311.

small but regular harvests from uncleared land. The ash fertilizes well, and the soil recovers, but subsequent yields dwindle; it will only support one family (4–5 people) on 300 acres (120 ha) of woodland, and in the viking period it was found only on the fringes of forest and in the less favoured Finnish lowlands.[8]

2 Inland–Outland: using wilderness or upland areas for seasonal grazing so as to increase the stock-raising capacity of lowland farms. This could take the form of the Norse shieling, or *setr*, when the young men and women of the home farm (inland) drive the cattle uphill and camp in the mountains or up the valley for the whole summer, milking and defending the beasts; or among the Finns and farming Lapps, a long trip to game and fishing grounds linked to the homestead, the custom called *eränkäynti* in modern times. All detailed accounts of these methods are relatively recent, and the way they worked in viking times is only inferred from place-names and the archaeology of temporary shelters. The *setr* system should have yielded milk in summer, whey, curds and cheese later, meat after the November slaughter of cattle, and dung from the byre of the animals wintered in meadows or sheltered.

3 Infield–Outfield: raising crops and stock alternately on nearer and further fields, more and less intensely cultivated. Like Inland–Outland, this method was used throughout Europe; but it was relatively recent in Scandinavia, an innovation in Roman times. Fields near the homestead, (*akr*) were kept in 'perpetual tillage', and refreshed with loads of dung and straw left by the wintering of the livestock; or in part reserved as grassland, preferably irrigated in some way, for winter grazing (*eng*, *engi*, as in the ings which still appear in Yorkshire bottoms); in both cases lying within the magic circle of muck, the *mygi*, *tadl* or *tad* collected in the byre or the sheep-fold and raked out over the land each spring. Outfields lay outside that circle and were renewed by fallowing: letting them go unsown, if ploughed, or grazed sparingly if not. Walls and banks mark the difference on Gotland, the Götaland highlands and Norway, and line the droves that funnel cattle from in to out; it is a system found with variations all over cisalpine Europe in medieval times, and down to the nineteenth century.[9]

4 Open Field: the annual reallocation of village land in strips to householders with claims proportional to the size of their house-

---

8 Tvengsberg 1995 gives a brief survey of swidden in Fenno-Scandia.
9 SIDK 1984, 257 for evidence of early muck-spreading, and Jensen 1982, 223–4. For the antiquity of this in Jutland and on Gotland, Hansen, Hvass and Mikkelsen in HØKO (1999), 17–27; Widgren 1983 studies the Götaland evidence, from which he deduced a date of *c*.300 for the coming of Infield – Outfield and an expansion from

plots. The rearrangement of Infield – Outfield farming along these lines was one of the great economic and social revolutions of the middle ages, and has left its traces on huge swathes of the west-European landscape, as well as in parts of Scandinavia; but it was definitely not a feature of viking-age agriculture, and is listed here only because there are a few intimations of strip holdings, at Gisstorp and Månstad in Västergötland and in Småland, south of Götaland, which may date from then. A true open field system needs a large village, preferably with a court and by-laws, and this is found in lowland Scandinavia in the form known as 'sun-division' (*solskifte*) as the strips were allocated from east to west in rotation. Some Scandinavian historians see this as an import from England, and claim that the apportioning of strips to village crofts or tofts bears the stamp of Roman Law, introduced by the canonists in the twelfth and thirteenth centuries; there is no sign of it before then, and attempts to link its appearance in England to Danish settlers are therefore pointless.[10]

5 Outland Farming: the resort of the families living off inland and forest areas, but unable to make ends meet on burn-beating alone. Their minimal grain crops were supplemented by as much hunting and fishing, trapping and iron working as possible, and their link with the arable lands was through exchange or trade or clientage rather than by the regular transhumance of (2), and alternating between homes, which is how this system may have begun, in the early Iron Age.

In these ways, farmers might get a living from this difficult range of territories, blessed with life-giving seas on all sides, and cursed with altitudes, temperatures, soil-chemistry, and darkness in winter hostile to meat-and-barley consumers outside a few favoured lowlands. The pastoral tribes of the far north and interior, who lived on reindeer and slid through the winter on skis were the best adapted to the

c.700. See Ericsson 1999, 57 for the 'enclosure societies' of Möre (SE Sweden), and a very large field in Östgötland. On the origins of cattle-stalling, dictated not only by the need to accumulate dung, but to conserve trees in winter, see Zimmermann in SAL 1999.

10   Widgren 1989, 361 and Ericsson 1999, 57–8. A debate between Sørensen and Ulsig in HT (D) 1985, 110–18 touches on the dating of Solskifte among the Danes, which according to Hahnemann (ibid. [1997], 237–51) involved permanent field measurement and fiscal liability rather than the looser concept of *bol*: homestead and fields of any size, like the Anglo-Saxon hide in principle, but in practice no bigger than 25–30 acres. In some Halland villages there seems to have been continuous cultivation of infield over 3000 years, and strip allocation may be older there, but on what principle is unclear (Lindqvist (L) and Connelid and Rosen in VIPA, 28–9, 179–97). For maps of allocation at Borup see Steensberg 1983.

environment; but no-one could work hard enough to eat well in the bad years. It was well said by Eyvindr the Plagiarist, in the dearth of 970 (or 974) when he was in Norway:

Snow falls on the ground at midsummer. So, like Lapps, we have tethered The bud-gnawing deer indoors[11]

by which he meant goats. He proposed to row south, to catch herrings and try to sell them to 'my friends', for he had already sold his cloak-pin to buy livestock, and his arrows for herrings. It seems that the general European dearth of 1033–6 undermined the rule of Sweyn the Dane in Norway, and made people look back on the good harvests of St Olave with regret; as they had after Hákon Haraldsson died in *c.*970, and after Hákon Jarl's death in 995. There was indeed a slow cooling of northern temperatures from *c.* 970 to *c.* 1150, but the hard times had little to do with that. Weather did the damage, especially in marginal areas like the Halogaland where Ohthere made a good living off the Lapps in the 890s, but not by agriculture.

Sacrifice was the only insurance: the offering of blood and beer in the rituals of *blót*, ill-recorded but well enough to be accepted as an annual reality, propitiating higher powers in hopes of 'good year'[12] as it says on the seventh-century Stentoften stone in Bleking:

HATHUWOLAFR GAVE GOOD YEAR

to cite the more intelligible words of the inscription. Thietmar of Merseburg *c.*1018 and Adam of Bremen *c.*1075 mention Nordic sacrifices on a grand scale, held down to the 930s at Lejre in Zealand, and every nine years at Uppsala, apparently, down to the 1070s. In Iceland and Norway the right to sacrifice in private was said to have been preserved after the conversion, but the Uppsala holocausts must have been great public occasions and were offered to the images of three non-christian gods in the heart of a territory largely controlled by christian landowners. They, too, contributed; good years at Uppsala were worth scandal at Bremen. If this is unexpected, the survival of offerings by individual farmers and communities is not,

---

11 See Poole 1991, 12–14 for commentary, and Page 1995, 147: Snorri wove a context round these verses in Heimskringla, and ended the famine with an abundance of herring, suggested by Eyvind's verses.
12 Grønvik 1990 brought Odin into the inscription and the translations are comically diverse; see DR, 357 and B, 142 for dating and literature.

and accomodating these customs to the laws of the church cannot have been the hardest task of the clergy in the eleventh century, as it had all been done before in the British Isles and the Continent. It was conflict between the accomodators and the reformists of the twelfth and subsequent centuries which was bitter. As well it might be, since growth and generation could not be guaranteed by either set of customs, and when one failed it was natural to turn to the other. In the 1070s pope Gregory vii was told that Danes were blaming their clergy for the bad weather; and these were the people with the best soils, the best weather and the most daylight. Their farming methods deserve a closer look.

Lowland Farming

Lowland farming among the Danes has been revealed in detail by excavations at Vorbasse, Norre Snede, Morup, and Trabjerg in Jutland, Borup in Zealand. The great gas trench across the country, and further digs at Lejre and Todderup have drawn a settlement-profile for the whole region during the first millennium AD, which ends with 300 years of expansion in most of the north: the 'golden age of the primary producer' as Randsborg put it. The unit of production had become the farmstead, with the land worked on the infield – outfield plan; but here, from the sixth century, many farmsteads were grouped into villages, and from then onwards bigger settlements and more tools go together.

The most important, for arable farmers, was the plough; which for the viking age meant the soil-scratching machine we call the ard (ON (Old Norse) *arðr, haken* or hook in German), either a long crook harnessed to one or two oxen, or a pole with a handle at one end, and harness at the other, breaking ground with a 'stock-and-stilt' scratch or cutter (coulter) at the pulling end, and a share (blade) behind it. This was the thing that supported the civilizations of the temperate zone from the Bronze Age onwards, and it was superseded very gradually in most of that zone by the bigger wheeled plough: the heavy, mould-boarded earth-churner drawn by up to eight oxen, and used along the North German coast even in Roman times, for its greater efficiency in clay. There was plenty of that in east Jutland and the Danish islands, but there is no trace of deep ploughing here until *c.*700, the date of the furrows found at Borup; the Viborg harrow and the harrowing marks at Lindholm Høje suggest some wheel-ploughing there in the eighth – ninth century but this was the exception rather than the rule. There was more *c.* 1000 at the camps of Trelleborg and Aggersborg, but no discernible rush to copy the

Old Saxons, Anglo-Saxons and Celts in their plough-technology,[13] probably for good reasons. Wheeled ploughs and their big teams only worked well in big fields, where the turn came at the end of a long furrow (in Denmark, only $\frac{2}{3}$ of our furlong) and the overall acreage was large enough to justify the extra time and labour used on the job; the relatively small and independent farms common in Denmark down to the end of the period, and the lack of Open Fields made the ard a better tool, especially when reinforced with iron. It remained in use down to the twentieth century in parts of Denmark, long after the new plough had triumphed. By the tenth century, there was a story that Zealand had been divided from Scania by the goddess Gefion, with the four oxen who were also her sons: the poet Bragi had the steaming swift-pullers hauling their plunder off, and in Snorri's prose version of the story they detached it from Sweden by deep ploughing;[14] from which it would be rash to conclude anything about viking-age aration.

The real productivity-booster was iron; at first to shoe the ard, then (*c*.600) to lengthen the sickle into the scythe-blade for cutting hay (never corn), then to multiply the totals of tools at the farmer's disposal, and even (by 900) to tip some spades. Nails for cattle-sheds, bands for horizontal water-wheels (found at Ljørring) and the new sort of carts (swivel front axle) enabled farmers to feed more people than their predecessors, if not better. The main crop was always barley; after *c*.800 rye and oats were introduced, probably from the Slav lands to the south, to bring poorer soils into cultivation and compensate for the better land kept under grass for feeding bigger herds. Rye could stand cooler and wetter years, and gave better straw for thatching; but all these better yields could not keep pace, in Randsborg's analysis, with a growing population. In the ninth century, therefore, Danes had to emigrate or eat less; by the eleventh, the reorganization of a small-farm economy through the development of magnate-farms (such as Vorbasse) specializing in large-scale cereal production kept them at home unless they needed cash from England. How to verify this conclusion is a puzzle, since the archaeological evidence of inadequate production is entirely lacking, as is

13 Probably more evident after the tenth century than before. See Steensberg 1986, 143–8. The earliest remains of a wheeled plough found in the region (in a bog at Navndrup) cannot be older than 1120: KHL, xiii, 330–50. One VA ard-blade, like a broad spear-head, has been found in Denmark; the shares found on Samsø were cut from yew: Lerche 1995, 194–5.

14 A misunderstanding of the 'deep-wheel' (*djuprøðull*) the boys were pulling: Lindow 1997b, 15 translates 'gold' (the mill in the deep, again as above p. 189), Faulkes SnE 7 gives 'deep ring of land' (i.e. Zealand) and who will deny 'sun of the ocean'? Not a piece of agricultural machinery, anyway, whatever it was.

the evidence of general plenty thereafter. All that can be known is that the number of all settlements in this zone increased from *c*.700 to *c*.1050, and that the number of large farms in 1000 was greater than in 750. The purpose of the big farms was to feed owners and dependants, not the population at large; surpluses would fetch a profit at the new town-markets, to feed those people or foreigners, or be commandeered by kings for their food-stores. Small producers edged out by the lords may well have gone hungry, or sunk into servitude. In the earlier period, as throughout the middle ages movements of population were determined not so much by low overall productivity at home (no medieval agriculture prevented famine) as by the relative availability of land elsewhere: see next chapter.

The other nucleus of Lowland farming was in Mälardal, the Swedish basin 200 miles north-east of the Zealand which Snorri imagined had been extracted from it, leaving lake Mälar behind. The winters are long, and the soils thin; before this period, isolated homesteads were more common than villages, working properties which seem to have been barely adequate to support the glories of the Vendel chiefs. About 800, at Torstuna in Uppland they find bigger farms, each with an arable field of 35 acres (14 ha), and about 900, these farms tend to be concentrated into villages, each working a two-field system on 95 acres (38 ha) of arable, a gain made up of encroachments on pasture (out-field). Elswhere in the region, farmers ploughed no more than 15 acres of arable at a time, but built up the 'species-rich ecosystems' in-field and out, which are still there, by using iron-tipped ards, dung, and the rituals of Uppsala. Adam of Bremen called this a 'most fertile region'; which it is, compared with the rest of Sweden, described in the 1770s by a Dutchman as 'one continued rock of granite, covered in different places by a greater or lesser quantity of earth, which is for the most part badly cultivated'[15] Svíaland was a granary surrounded by forest and high ground, closer to the sources of iron and fur than Denmark, and able to offer wheat as well as barley in exchange. The plain of Östergötland was another lowland farming area to the south; it was also found to the west in Viken, on the coastal strips along Kattegat and Skagerrack, from which come the early (*c*.900?) verses by Thjodólfr known as 'All Through the Harvest' (*Haust-*

---

15 Radcliffe 1790, 4. See Göranson 1984 on Torstuna and Borgegård on the tilth in *Svensk Botanisk Tidskrift*, lxxiv (1990), 369–92. Ringstedt 1992, 120–4 estimates Migration-Age farm-size and productivity, and gets a living for 8–10 out of $7\frac{1}{2}$ acres of arable, seventy-four of meadow, seventy-four of pasture: (or =) 155 in all, as long as there was hunting and fishing beyond. Broberg 1990 comes to similar conclusions about north Uppland: minimal plough, maximal pasture and fishing – perch, pike, carp, cod and the *strömming* sort of herring.

lọng).[16] Some infield–outfield language was used in this: the ox was 'the whale of the rope', the 'yoke-bear', the 'dung-reindeer', and the 'harvest horse', and in the thirteenth century Snorri was able to list 46 synonyms, names and epithets for oxen, all but two complimentary. This was the tractor on which the early Norwegian chiefdoms were based, all round the coast to the Lofotens, all the more so where yields diminished and demand for them increased: not because the highlanders lived on bread, but because everybody lived on beer. As Olaus Magnus wrote in the sixteenth century, 'it is essential for those who live in most parts of these countries to look for their drink in the very seed from which they get their bread' (OM 13, 1; and see p. 146) However, in Norway, lowland is scarce, and could not be used for long, unless linked to highland pasture. The limits of lowland farming were here, and on the marshes of SW Jutland, which were being worked by larger populations of Danes and Frisians from the eighth century, and on the east Baltic islands.[17]

Upland Farming

Upland farming was adapted to the thin acid soils, heath, mountain, forest and winter darkness which cover most of Scandinavia. Small grain harvests were won as a by-product of a more extended use of natural resources and sheer space, developed over the previous millennium. The habit of summer migration uphill, to feed cattle on a *setr* (mountain pasture) was widespread in early medieval times; known in Northumbria in the eighth century, in the western Highlands, and on the Cotswolds and Wolds. Nordic settlers have left their names for the stages in the annual cycle all over the map of the northern and western British isles, but were willing to take over the Irish *airge* to describe spring as opposed to summer pastures, and to learn by their mistakes. On Faroe there is high ground, but not enough of it; excavations at Argisbrekka show that cattle were moved up to *setr* to begin with, on five of the islands, but overgrazing and overcrowding led to changes: sheep replaced cattle, and the bigger farmers established exclusive rights to upland pasture, bird-nesting sites, flotsam, seaweed and beached whales. On Coll and Tiree, *sæter* appear on the more sheltered eastern coasts, as *aergi*; on Orkney and Shetland such PNN may

16   Ed. and trans. in North 1997.
17   Malthus (*Essay on the Principle of Population*) noted that hay had precedence over grain in Norwegian home-fields, because 'if too much were taken into tillage, the number of cattle must be proportionally diminished, and the greater part of the higher ground would become absolutely useless'.

represent a development of earlier Pictish farming. On Man, the *eary* was a pasture no more than 6 miles from the home farm, not needing a whole summer's attention from the household. Smallish islands were not best suited to this system, modified or not, but those Norsemen who moved into Cumbria and on to the Pennines found the right conditions for north Scandinavian work-habits. In coastal settlements, all over these western colonies the great annual labour of springtime muck-spreading was reduced by the gathering of seaweed, which was and is easier to spread. As a result, house-sites slowly rose on mounds of waste to form the farm-hillocks (*gårdshaugar*) of which nearly 2000 survive in Norway. This negligence, which removed fertility from the natural cycle, proves how near the margin of subsistence these farmers worked; they could not throw over the chance of a small remission of time and energy when labour was stretched to the limit by the demands of fishing, fowling, pasturing and digging. Male muscle, timber and ox-power were spared; women seem to have scattered the seaweed.[18]

In Norway and in much of Jutland, grazing was found not only on uphill grass, but on coastal and sour-soil heathland. North of Bergen this was a period of winning heath from forest, and cutting it for winter fodder. A farm at Lurekalven could increase its pasture five or six times in this way, and survive on an arable base of only $2\frac{1}{2}$ acres (1 ha) enriched by bog-humus hauled into the byre and dunged and staled overwinter. It was dug in, each spring; effort was not spared here. Ingenious exploitation did not always pay off in the long run; heath needed regular burning, to encourage edible young shoots, and stock killed bushes and trees, and eventually lowered the total yield of the area. The balance had to be right, but archaeology suggests that in this as in other sorts of husbandry they had got the knack in the first century and kept it for the next twelve, and longer.[19]

Subarctic Farming

Subarctic farming fed Ohthere in Halogaland in the 890s or thereabouts: living like a lord nearly 500 miles north along the coast from Trondheim Fjord on the yields of minimal tillage and domestic stock-

18 Bertelsen and Lamb 1993. See Fellows-Jensen on the *airge* names in *Nomina*, iv (1980), 67–73, Fox in Thirsk 2000, 153–4 on English cotes, Quine 1992 for Man, and Sharples and Pearson 1999 on VA South Uist farming.
19 Kaland (VC 10, 1987, 80–2); on N. Sunnmore moors, Solbjerg in Kristiansen 1984, 155–69; and see Myhre in Indrelid 1984, 125–7. Holm 1999 suggests that Norwegian farmers depended so heavily on outland resources, even in the south-east, that the *gardr* must have included outland as well as infield – outfield; indeed, clearance-cairns in the wild show that crops were sometimes raised there.

raising,[20] supplemented by whale-hunting and the produce of pastoralists, who supplied him with furs, down, whale-bone and sealskin rope (in 117 foot, 36 m lengths from the more prosperous); and a herd of reindeer. How he got his tribute from the Lapps is undisclosed, but this was a form of colonial economy in which the linkman with the transport and connexions to markets could profit from the labour expended over a large hinterland. Grain could be grown in small amounts as far north as Malanger Fjord but no further, and then only for malting and beer (as above p. 198); to thrive was to know and trap both the wild animals and the people who also lived off them: beer helped. This precarious business could be carried on for hundreds of miles to the east as sedentary farmers found footholds and more ways of channelling Lapp produce south; but there is no sign that this was happening in these latitudes at this date. The new farming opportunities seemed to lie out west, in Iceland and ultimately Greenland.

Iceland was too good to be true. The first settlers found relatively mild winters, coastal wetlands with rough pasture for cattle, and a background of birchwoods reaching to the dire plateaux and mountains from which streams full of fish drained to the sea. There was game, but no bear or wolves to prey on stock; the woodland was easy to clear, and sun shone more often than further south in Shetland and Orkney. There were over 2500 sq miles of lowland to claim, and since the newcomers came mostly from south of Trondheim fjord, some even from Denmark, they ferried over cattle, sheep, goats and horses, camped in the wetlands, sowed barley, and began birch-clearing for fuel, and cutting winter fodder from scrub. The leaders struck inland, to be sure of the higher grounds as well as the coastlands; from the 870s to the 950s, at least, this was going to be an enclave of modified upland farming within view of the icebergs, the first of many experiments. But the woodland never regenerated, the scrub was grazed to the roots, the game died off, and the thin covering of humus was washed into the valleys. Overgrazing ruined the lowland pastures, and the deeper soils were needed for grass rather than barley, which in any case only ripened in the far south of the island. The interior could never become an abundant outland, only a dangerous no-man's-land occasionally convulsed by earthquakes and volcanic eruptions; the reliable resources lay in the fishing-grounds

20 Page 1995, 46–8 for trans. of Ohthere's relation; on the subarctic farm at Borg on Lofoten see Munch, Johansen and Larsen in VC 10 (1987). Kaland calculated that a coastal farm near Bergen in this period would support a herd of fourteen cows and ten sheep on 163 acres (66 ha) of land, which gives an idea of how much inland Ohthere would have needed for his twenty sheep, twenty cattle, and twenty pigs.

off the coast, already claimed or coveted by the chiefs. By 1000, the priority for hundreds of settlers was getting fuel, a boat and the protection of one of the first families, as a consolation for poor land held insecurely in less favoured sites. Nordal saw the main motive of the early settlers as the wish to live like lords on independent husbandry. If so, most were disappointed; the lords were the 1% who had the better farms, access to Norway, slave-labour, and coastal fishing and fowling.[21] Farming in Iceland supported some 25,000 people by the end of this period, no mean achievement on a habitable area about the size of Yorkshire within an island bigger than Ireland. The lessons of the viking age might have been less painful, had there been an earlier population of Lapps to teach the settlers how to conserve; as it was, the little groups of axe-men and dairy-women set about degrading their ecology and impoverishing their grandchildren in a social vacuum, to the music of their own voices, and the echo of dreadful farts inspired by indigestible food.[22]

Those who moved on to Greenland from the 980s were also confronted by delusive attractions, but not so great. There was grass, scrub, and easily worked stone, but evidently not the timber even in short lengths, or the humus to allow large herds and fields of grain; fishing and hunting were conditions of survival from the start, and the getting of walrus and narwhal teeth for sale overseas or to visiting Icelanders was the way to prosper. The Greenland that developed in the twelfth and thirteenth centuries consisted of two groupings of mainly 250–300 acre farms, where the decencies of life as understood in Iceland were maintained through an economy of substitution: bones and dung for fuel, conserved by thick stone and turf walls and roofs, driftwood and whalebone for timber, soapstone for the potter's clay, seal for mutton, and hunting expeditions as far north as Disko bay for the summer drove up to the *setr*. Even the milder Iceland winters could be mimicked at ground level by running irrigation channels through the home field (as at Sandnes) to take the edge off the frost.

Most of the archaeology dates from later centuries, and concerns the regime of christian bishops, installed after 1125. The early Greenlanders must have thanked their god or gods for the wide pasture, big game and abundant wild fowl, unaware that they were 'perched high on a food-web marked by long and short term instability'; but who wasn't, in the tenth century? Their earliest enterprise seems to have

---

21   For early farming see Sveinbjarnardottir 1992, 173–7, Einarsson 1994, 45 (map) and Rafnson 1990; the order of events is as proposed in Vésteinsson 1998.
22   On Icelandic farts see Gade 1995; Sayers SS lxvii/4; Motz 1996, 370 and Liberman SS lxviii/i 1996, 98.

been the probe to the American continent, to remedy the defects of their situation by finding a reliable source of timber and iron, and perhaps human contact or a market nearer than the thousand mile distance which separated them from Iceland.[23] It was a rational move, if they intended to sustain the hybrid hunting–fishing–grazing life on the traditional nordic plan of separate family farms; its eventual abandonment may have been due to the discovery that the difficulty of extracting raw materials from the continental land mass and its Amerindian population was greater than expected. What had driven this kind of farmer to the limits of agriculture and beyond was narrow margins of sustenance, the search for compensation in space, independence, virgin soils and untapped food resources for the wants inherent in the meat, milk and barley cycle of the homelands. So they stayed in a place where wood was gold and iron was silver.

Forest Farming

Forest farming was how the middle parts of Scandinavia were worked, from the evergreen swathe of taiga south to the woodlands of Norwegian Tellemark and Opland, right down to northern Scania. Hampered in their tillage by trees, or confined to burn-beating husbandry (p. 191), cut off from sea-transport, and condemned to deep snow in winter, they could still supply the islanders and shore-dwellers with everything that made them formidable: weapons, tools, long ship timbers and furs, and demand lowland surplus in return. It had been so before 500, and after a period of slacker interaction, coastal demand picked up in the eighth century and remained brisk. Traces of iron-winning in the backwoods have suggested a 'technological revolution' to some archaeologists; but there was nothing new in the process or the organization, only in the size of the output. Iron-production stayed in the hands of farmers, not of specialist iron-masters; their compensation for poor soils and intractable terrain. There are no detailed medieval accounts of this, but in these parts it remained a household industry until the nineteenth century, when it was studied in all the phases of the operation:

1   Prospecting; looking for places like bogs and shallow lakes where lumps of ore might lie underground, on the basis of knowing the lie of the land, or asking the Lapps, who knew it better.

23   McGovern 1992 surveys the archaeology since 1978, especially the Sandnes dig of 1984; and see Arneborg on 'the High Arctic Utmark' in OUTU 1998, 158–66. For recent work see Schlederman, Lynnerup, Berglund and Arneborg in VINAS (2000).

2 Probing with rods, finding, extracting and testing by colour, size, context and taste; drying the good ore, and storing it.

3 Preparing the site: building furnaces, burning wood slowly in half-dampened piles for charcoal, making sledges, cutting trails.

4 Smelting the ore with charcoal laid in beds; breaking it up; heated until molten, run off into moulds; a two-week job.

5 Hauling the pigs by sledge and water to the smithy.

6 Reheating, and working into rods, currency, or artifacts.

7 Carrying to market, by which time it would probably be out of the original winner's hands.

There were many jobs to do,[24] and the family or families that undertook them would have to camp away from home and take a month or two of the precious summer away from farming, trapping or hunting. That was how it was done in this whole woodland and in Jutland, where the bogs were still probed for ore in this period, although the farmers' needs far outran local production. Foresters like the Jämtar and the Värmlanders (p. 98) could get rich on this process, selling both to southerners and to Lapps; and in competition with Lapps, or co-operation, rob the wilderness of furs, reindeer hide, meat and antler. The demand increased from *c*.750, and is reflected both in the fur-trimmings found at Birka and in the reindeer pitfalls and fences of the interior.

So, from a starting-point with infield–outfield, the work of farming adapted to new physical surroundings in several ways, until it merged with more ancient hunter-gatherer systems at the extremities, and so allowed the spread of Nordic communities and homesteads over a cold crescent from Russia to Newfoundland. This was not an automatic if late consequence of the introduction of ploughing and reaping by Germanic or Celtic immigrants in remote antiquity, for there is no knowing the language group of those pioneers, and the value of their skills in these harsh latitudes depended on how well they could be combined with the old food-getting methods or with newer hunting and fishing techniques. Viking-age farming in Scandinavia involved an expansion of farmland and settlement almost everywhere so far investigated, thus a rise in population, and enough food to supply small towns by the end of the period. It also involved a decrease in the average height of men and women in the cemeteries where this kind of analysis is possible, and therefore a probably more

---

24 See Hyenstrand in Clarke 1979 for Sweden, and Johansen 1972 for Norway. The twelve axe-shaped iron blanks shafted with a spruce pole and found at Gjerrild Strand in N. Jutland were made in Norway for re-working overseas. Jottijärvi 1992, 185, maps Jutland iron deposits, and see map 8 in this volume.

inequitable distribution of the food than in the Migration period, at least in infancy, or a decline in the nutritional value of the produce. The latter is unlikely, given the variety of seeds and grains in samples of bread alone tested by palaeonutritionists; there was no sign of dependency on one or two degenerating grains. The sixty-four funerary loaves found in Birka graves were barley based, but also contain oats, wheat, emmer, spelt, rye, vetches, peas and flax; the rich staple food well known from the diet of English medieval peasants, in these climes the work of women, making large batches as seldom as once a year, and threading them to hang overhead. No leavening, no oven, but cooked on hearths like the ash-cake of pioneering America, and probably not eaten daily in most of Scandinavia at this date. Most of the barley harvested would be malted to make beer (more work for women), and most days farmers would live on grain crushed, soaked and heated with butter or whey to form *grautr*, the dish Icelanders were supposed to find irresistible, and others unavoidable.[25] The archaeology of food and drink has revealed an impressive range of homegrown, gathered and imported foods on most sites excavated, with evidence of the rearing and slaughter of animals on a new scale: clung from more cattle wintering at Ribe *c.* 720 than were needed to feed the population, and this was on the mutton side of Jutland; beef, pork, and sometimes horse were the meat of the east Jutes. Some farmers and some consumers were doing extremely well, which in a world where self-sufficiency was the norm and where resources such as land and manure were restricted, was not necessarily good for everyone. However, this was not a zero-sum equation; apart from farming, or in conjunction with it, there were skills to compensate for low yields, in industry and commerce.

Industry

Farms depended more and more on metal tools, and the smith's work has been thoroughly examined by archaeologists, who have found complete sets of iron-working tools at Tjele in Jutland and in Halleby river, Zealand; the Mästermyr set is later. The careful farmer could have a wealth of metal utensils: shears, lamp-stands, lighters, spits, keys, knives, locks, choppers, cauldrons, pans, pins, nails, sickles,

25 See Hansson 1997 for survey of palaeonutritional research since 1927; on baking KHL, ii, 405–6 and Graslund in KHL, i, 307–11, Campbell in *Saga och Sed* 1952 on bread-culture: there is early evidence of the hard flat-bread in Norway and Shetland. Cahen 1921 for the social and religious importance of beer.

scythes and many axes, as well as his plough-share. A Närke household of this period, if fully equipped, would be using nearly a
hundredweight (48 kg) of metal, when half of that would suffice for
a whole Flemish manor of the ninth century, to judge from the
Annapes list.[26] Add the deep deposits of mould-cast jewellery and
ornament (25,000 mould fragments were found in one Birka workshop) and there is good reason for Clarke and Ambrosiani's description of a 'distinct technical and typological change to mass-
production' beginning at Birka in the 760s, when the workshops
are many and permanent. The older settlement at Helgö was a
market with workshops, but apparently used by a shifting population
of craftsmen and merchants; the output was much smaller, as was the
population, so that if volume and concentration be the criteria, Birka
was a break through.[27]

Nevertheless, metal-working had been highly productive in Jutland
and the Danish islands since Roman times, on a scale which has only
been revealed by recent metal-detection, and it is not necessary to
explain the weight of worked metal in use by the workshops brought
together at Birka or Ribe. These were convenient gateways for foreign buyers, but utensils, ornaments and tools, of iron, bone, wood
and soap stone changed hands at small markets round the coasts,
reached by travelling craftsmen and vendors, or at the halls of the
chiefs, where a smith could be a member of the household. According
to the stone he had erected to his brother KILLED OUT EAST (DR
108) Tosti, of Kolind was 'Asvith's smith'. There is no sign that these
or any other kinds of skilled worker formed a new class of urban
producers in this period, since their work could be done anywhere
and combined with farming; as on Gotland, where some of 5000
tortoise-backed bronze brooches were produced in an island as yet
free of towns or large settlements. Specialization is a big step towards
what we see as industrialization, but it seems that the Norsemen and
their wives were taking it very slowly, and developing skills without

26 Graham Campbell's *Viking Artifacts* (London 1980) remains the indispensable
register, fully illustrated and explained. Hansson 1989, 63–9 and 72–3 on the Närke
(east Sweden) households. Here, the quantity of metal was more important than
quality. Nordic iron was not sufficiently hardened to make durable coin-dies until
after 1000, and its production has been called 'low-technical': The art of pattern-
welding rods into superfine sword-blades had been understood in the West since the
fifth century, but did not reach Norway until the tenth. Quantity rather than quality
was the aim.
27 Ambrosiani and Clarke 'Birka and the Beginning of the Viking Age' is in SADO
(1998), 36–7 and see Lundström 1988 on Helgö, which Hyenstrand saw as a
Frankish trading-post. Callmer 1995, 29–49 discusses another early manufacture
and market site migrating down the Holy River in Scania to become Åhus in the
eleventh century.

detaching them from farm-work or the local market. Ship building, sail-weaving, and house-building were clearly the leading labours of the age, far exceeding in input and consequence the smaller handcrafts; but they remained within the competence of domestic workers. No permanent shipyard has yet been discovered in the Baltic region. The site at Paviken on Gotland (excavated 1967–73) was a busy one, at which boat repairs and possibly building were carried out each summer, but not over winter; the yard at Fribrødre (N Falster, Dk) was in use from I050 or thereabouts for breaking up old ships and possibly building new ones in the Slavonic way, with wooden nails;[28] but the usual way was for farmers or chiefs to make vessels with any labour to hand, and for kings to maintain a shipsmith to plan and oversee the making of big warships. Most of the work was done with long-handled axes and wedges, for getting planks from logs; short-handled axes for shaping and finishing, and hammers, for nailing it all together. The raw materials – long logs, iron and walrus-hide for ropes – were more abundant in Norway and Sweden than in Denmark, but the difference was not enough to concentrate ship building north of the Skagerrack, or anywhere else.

One small longship's sail would cover 650 sq. feet (62 sq. m), and would need nearly 80 miles (126,000 m) of yarn, as much as four women could spin in a winter, and Ottarr's verse makes it clear that women were the spinners; but there are no archaeological traces of weavers' weights or of long sheds for specialist spinners and weavers.[29] Loom-weights and spindle-whorls are found everywhere, especially in sunken-floor houses and surviving samples make it clear that women continued to weave the cloths and patterns already popular before c.750 without succumbing to unnecessary innovations.[30] Their work was essential to aggressive warfare; whether as wives, daughters, or slaves, they must nearly all have spent much of

28 Lundström 1981 on Paviken; Skamby Madsen in ASMA (1991) on Fribrødre.
29 Recent excavations at Næs, on Avnøfjord (SE Zealand) have revealed a large-scale linen manufacturing complex, carried on c.750–c.900 from 79 sunken houses dependent on one long house and serviced by a canal for soaking and fermenting the flax, heated drying pits, and forges and craft workshops producing trade-goods for cloth-buyers. A new fashion (linen shifts and shirts) and a new weed made a living for perhaps a hundred families where ten would have struggled; see Møller Hansen and Højer in KUML 2000, 59–89.
30 Bender Jørgensen 1986 is indispensable on early Norse weaving: from which it appears that Syrian and British patterns appear among the 250 fragments analyzed, but the majority were old favourites. Recent finds of weaving huts and weights in Denmark appear in DLU, 242–3 (Ejstrup) and 253–4 (Dalgaard); Guðjónsson 1989, 186, fixed the meaning of the terms for parts of looms, with diagram. Poole 1991, 116–56, discusses the macabre weaving poem *Darraðarljóð*, recited by valkyries predicting a bloody battle while employed at a loom weighted with men's heads.

the year clothing, equipping and beautifying the men and their ships.

Housebuilding was the same; largely the work of people building their own homes with as much labour as they could find out of their own resources. This is easy to see in the structure of the sunken houses, where most lived: wallposts rammed into roughly rectangular ground-plans, thatched roofs on rough-hewn or uncarpentered rafters, stone hearths and two rooms at most. The splendour of the great halls reflected far greater command of labour by owners, and the excavation of Lejre (South-west of Roskilde, Dk) shows how this increased through the centuries. The aisled hall already standing there with adjacent buildings *c.*650 was rebuilt for the fourth time in the 890s to a length of 156 feet (48 m) and a width of 34 ($10\frac{1}{2}$ m) in the middle section; it tapered towards the ends in a characteristic viking-age fashion also found at Nørre Snede and Trelleborg. There were five interior rooms in the new Lejre, four doors, a cellar and a long central fireplace in the west room. A presumably massive roof needed the support of two rows of interior columns, the bowed walls and forty-seven external buttress-posts; there was enough room indoors for two lawn-tennis courts, or twenty-five of the largest sunken-houses yet found. The hall was served by a storehouse or stable two-thirds as big, a smithy, kitchen, grain-dryer and stalls, but was sinking into decay a century later; all these big houses used forests of timber, and needed constant repair, but until 1000 they grew longer, and taller and more numerous, and were increasingly imitated by middle-range houses of 50–75 feet (20–30 m). Three-aisle buildings (the Sædding type) gave way to buttressed houses with one central and two end-rooms within very convex walls (Trelleborg and Vilslev types); in all, five types[31] were tried within the 300 years, but no attempt to solve the underlying problem of damp appears until a priest, probably English, had the first Lund church raised on ground-sills supported by stones, towards the beginning of the eleventh century. The abundance of timber, and of metal to work it, and of wood-carving skills to adorn it made rot seem lesser evils than draughts, and cold, and sparks from the central hearth.

What these examples of energetic ingenuity suggest is not an industrial revolution, but a more and more prodigal use of resources by a wider range of people of all sorts, but principally by the chiefs and landowners who needed ships, fine clothing and big houses and could exploit the general diffusion of skills and tools.

31 See the house typology chart in Bender Jørgensen 1995, 19, and 214–15 for these. It was calculated that the houses, board-walks and fences at Trelleborg in Zealand used 8,000 tall trees, or 200 acres of woodland (85 ha) for a useful life of 5–15 years: Nørlund 1948, 202.

Trade

Trade, if long-distance, has been seen as the defining characteristic of the age, the economic activity by which Northmen put life into the whole of Northern Europe: the motor not only of a commercial boom but of state-formation, urbanization and social changes.[32] A rebuttal from the marxist camp by Tom Saunders asserts that trade was secondary, a reflection of social changes described by the mantras of 'kinship or clan into feudalism' and 'the emergence of the state from tribute hegemony'. Whereas fifth- and sixth-century Scandinavians had exchanged local produce, or received exotic status symbols in small ports at Dankirke (Jutland), Lundeborg (Funen) and Helgö (SW), the eighth/ninth century markets at Ribe, Hedeby and Birka attracted imports from afar in bulk: pots and glass from the west, whetstones and querns from the Rhineland, silver *sceattas* from Frisia, jugs from Saxony, dirhems from Asia, to be exchanged for the furs, iron and slaves demanded by the consumers of the fat cities of the south. The reason for these changes could either be that Nordic or other middlemen saw an opportunity and took it, plugged northern economies into the international trade-routes, and jerked them into expansion; or that the chiefs and kings of the north reached a degree of control over their societies which enabled them to expand their previous privilege of importing rarities into the founding of markets and then towns and getting revenue out of them. Either way, after or before, trade and social transformation are hitched together in ways which lead to strange conclusions. As when the trading post of Kaupang on Oslo Fjord 'had to vanish' *c*.900, because 'it was in fact too early for the Norwegian society, based as this was on a rural structure'; or when one commentator claims that 'the basic prerequisites of a capitalist economic system already existed in the Mälar valley during the early part of the viking period' but functioned in a state of 'anachronistic system shock'. That is, the Svíar were on one time-level, when the hillbillies brought in their furs and antlers with a view to part-exchange, part tribute-payment; while the sophisticated foreign merchants sailed in with silver and exotica to pay for goods and re-sell on the Frankish market,[33] like regular proto-capitalists. Timing is everything in this kind of analysis, as in a modern world where it belongs; but that

---

32 As argued by Sawyer and Hodges up to a point: see discussion in NAR, xxviii, 1995, i and ii, by Saunders, Andren and Bertelsen; and Näsman in *Hikuin*, xvi (1990), 'Om fjärrhandel'. The theory is much older.
33 Schia in Addyman 1992, 111 and Bäck in VIPA (1997), 153: worth reading, despite everything, as is Brather in PZ, lxxi (1996), 46–82 on the different systems of

anachronism is deduced from a contrast between two unknowns (the mentality of Frisian and Frankish traders, and that of Nordic suppliers) complicated by a third: the exact terms on which commercial dealings were conducted (see map 8 for some of the results).

The moving of goods, whatever the purpose (gift, barter, 'administered trade', fixed-rate exchange, fixed silver-value exchange, hand-out to clients, renders to lords, open sale) was hard work. Not only the transport, but the bargaining with competitors who might take what they could not afford to buy and customers who tried to pass bad silver and weighed their receipts on accurate scales with unpredictable weights, (see Appendix C) all counting as ores and half-marks, somewhere. In the ninth century an honest slave-dealer would have to contend with sudden flooding of the market after successful raids on Irish or English monasteries, so that men and women bought for pounds would fetch pence; in the eleventh, packets of Danegeld silver would lower the value of coin at unpredictable intervals, when they reached Scandinavia; and on all journeys at all times, trade goods were only secure when protected by superior force. If shipwrecked or stranded, the trader lost both goods and life on most (but not all) Baltic and North Sea coasts; if he docked safely in a port, he had to pay for moorings and selling-rights. It is usually assumed that viking-age traders reduced such risks by forming associations and partnerships, but the evidence is slight: four references to gilds on late Swedish runestones (which are 'Frisian' in two inscriptions); it is only certain that they sometimes travelled in convoys.

Rare things, delightful luxuries, mundane commodities and human workers were nevertheless successfully ferried long distances in ships of increasing capacity, so that by 1050 forty-ton cargoes could be stowed in sailed vessels built for the purpose, from Lake Ladoga to Greenland. Well before this, the westward traders had accomplished their great work of selling back to christian landowners the slaves the Danish armies had captured in the first place, if they could not get the captives down to Spain for a better price; but it was the long-distance commerce of the easterners which is best recorded. In the 940s, the Byzantine emperor Constantine Porphyrogenitus described the 'agony and fear, hardship and danger' of the Rhos fur-traders from Kiev, for the education of his successors[34] and so of us. What

distribution for high and low value goods within Scandinavia. The custom in twelfth century Iceland, by which chiefs fixed prices (Gelsinger 1981, 38) is a good example of an apparently archaic system fully in tune with local needs and perhaps recently set up to meet them.

34 *De Administrando Imperii*, of which this section appears translated in Page 1995, 94–7; and see Howard Johnston 1998 for the beginning of the demand for furs in the eastern empire.

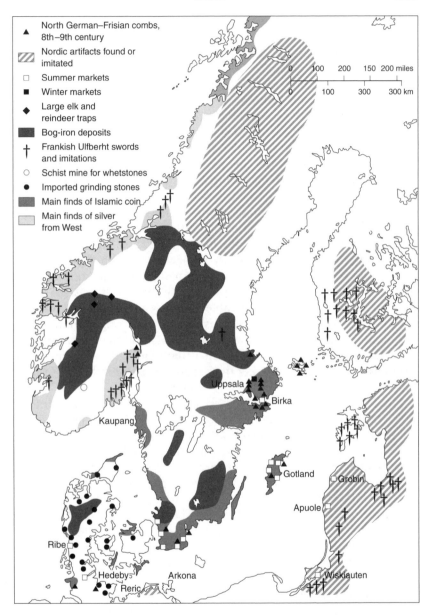

Map 8   *Import–export, 800–950*

we learn is that these Norse-speaking colonials were not professional traders at all, or pioneers of commercialization or promoters of social transformation. They were transporters of goods collected as tribute from an extended hegemony imposed over various Balt, Slav and Finnish peoples, in which the Rhos or Rus were the rulers, not the trappers or *voyageurs*. Their food was supplied by their tributaries during November; after a drunken Yule, they bought planks prepared by the same tributaries and made flat-bottomed boats on the Dnieper, to carry furs and wax and slaves on a laborious down-river voyage to the Black Sea. This involved manhandling vessels and cargoes round or over seven cataracts, and slipping past predatory bands of Pechenegs on the Steppe; then along the Bulgarian coast, held by khagans of variable sympathies, down to the great city of Constantinople. There, by the treaty of 907, the emperor gave them baths and monthly rations and equipment for their return journey the following spring; provided they had their cargoes registered and sealed by the officials, in groups of no more than fifty, and resided in one suburb, and entered the city by one gate, and bought no more than a fifty gold piece quota of silk per man, and went straight back to Kiev without wintering again on the Black Sea. It was the usual bureaucratic wonderland, tolerable only because the emperor was very powerful and there was no easier way of getting gold and silk; although the laughing waters waiting for them on the return journey must have made them doubt this. It is hard enough to imagine how they got their goods to market over those thousand miles;[35] but how they got the gold and silks back to Kiev is harder.

No Norsemen can have worked more strenuously. The Roman officials classified them as merchants, because they brought goods and were not envoys; but the treaty of 912 allowed them to enlist as soldiers in the emperor's army, and they would have passed as warriors anywhere up to the outskirts of the city. Control of imports exalted their regime in Russia, but they were cocks of that walk only because they could skim the produce of a vast forest hinterland and pay little or nothing for it, and so retard the development of any sort of free market or trade from the Vistula to the Volga. The passing of silver coins through their territories to Scandinavia is sometimes attributed to the fur-trade, as if this were an opening-up of the dark forests by pioneers and dealers active along defined routes. It was probably more like what Samson has called 'fighting with silver',[36] establishing clientage and dominance by the handing out of bullion; only indirectly connected with fur-dealing, since Scandi-

---

35   One who didn't, Rafn, was remembered south of the worst Dnieper cataract (*Rufstain*) by one stone, and on Gotland by another, brightly painted: Pritsak 1981, 326.
36   SAP (1991), 193. On the variety of concepts of silver-value, or money see Engeler 1991, esp. 121–7, 180–5 (in German) and T. Zachrisson 1998, ch. 2.

navians and Rus had all the furs they needed at home, and there is no sign of any greedy western market before the eleventh century.

A survey of these three activities – farming, industry and trade – at this distance of time, is bound to be inaccurate, but one thing seems to be clearly visible in all three, as in warfare: the unstinted expenditure of energy by men and women. To stay alive in Scandinavia was harder work than in warmer parts of Europe, and demanded fiercer exploitation of natural resources: iron, timber, and a vast reserve of forest and upland wild life, surrounded by seas full of fish. More than the Anglo-Saxon or the Frank or the Irishman, the Norse farmer or retainer was offered a choice: to live strenuously at home, or embark in the hope of reaching the sources of the gold, silver, wine and luxury goods which the laborious economy of Scandinavia, for all its variety, could procure only for a very few. If this was their hope, most emigrants were to be disappointed.

9

Emigration

Day after day was the killer's front door (shield)
Raddled with blood, when we first
Went raiding with the chief,
My goddess;
Now, since hard fighting
Has just stopped, we can rest,
Shoreline of day's plenty,
In lovely London.

Liðsmannaflokkr, Verses of the Soldiers, *c*.1020.

From *c*.725 to *c*.1025 people left Scandinavia for various purposes
and settled far and wide, from the Black Sea to America. The contemporary northern sources, rune-stones and skaldic poetry, say
nothing whatever about any large-scale emigration, although some
stones refer to individuals who died overseas after *c*.1000. Where
the emigration resulted in the transfer of Nordic languages and
customs, it can be traced with some uncertainty in place-names and
later vernacular languages, and in very broad outline by DNA sampling and other forms of physiological analysis (see p. 316) of the
living and of the dead. Archaeology provides patterns of culture and
settlement which can connect overseas societies with the homelands,
although not necessarily as a result of emigration. Contemporary
eastern sources say nothing of the Nordic emigrations (although
much of the after-effects); the western references are meagre, and
concern only the settling of armies. Later reconstructions of what
happened are abundant and fanciful and too deeply embedded in the
outlook and emotions of much later societies, especially if they
have been woven from family traditions. The most impressive is
the *Landnámabók* ('property-claim-book') of thirteenth-century
Iceland, which lists the events and characters of the original settlement, 300 or more years earlier, and provides a perfect mirror of

how the rulers of the island saw their past, and a snare for later historians, if they don't step through the looking-glass. But they must, and they have, and the apparently minutely-recorded peopling of Iceland sinks back into the shadows which shelter all the colonizations.[1]

There have been many attempts to quantify and explain these movements, but all that can be attempted here is a review of some instances of migration.

1 For *Eastward Migrations* the lack of written evidence leaves the story almost entirely to archaeologists and numismatists, and the vast areas involved still hide many clues. It now appears that at some date not far from 750 families of east Scandinavians began living on the shores of Lake Ladoga and its tributary rivers, especially the Volkhov, which flows north and drains an area Finns had left as a hunting-reserve or cultivated by burn-beating.[2] Grave-goods found in the thirteen 'find-complexes' east of Staraya Ladoga suggest a relatively peaceful occupation by the newcomers, similar to that of the land to the south, round lake Ilmen, by Slavonic immigrants shortly before. By some means, these Slavs, and the Finns who had occupied the region since Neolithic times, became the tributaries of the Norse settlers as they moved up the Volkhov, occupying hill-tops for over-wintering and using the river in summer. After a century of infiltrating the valley from lake Ladoga to lake Ilmen, at some date after 940 one group set up a stronghold at what they called *Holm*. It became the Old Town district of Novgorod, and the central place of a large territory. During this early period, the population of the new country was apparently supplemented by further Nordic immigration, and by more Slavs; but it was not to become a Minnesota (rural reservation for Big Swedes).

Soon after 800, Norse chiefs (*Rus*) began pushing east towards the Volga and south to the Dnieper, as traders and predators rather than settlers, building forts at strategic points within a vast triangle

---

1 On the difficulty of identifying any prehistoric migration anywhere from archaeological evidence, see Burmeister (S) and critics in *Current Archeology* xli/4, 2000, 539–67.
2 The Volkhov valley void was deduced from pollen-analysis by Possaert and Hammar in *Tor* 1997. In 1994 an eight-oar sailing-boat, the *Aifur*, covered the 746 sea-miles between Sigtuna and Novgorod in 130 days, to show that the trip was feasible for families with boat-building skills and light loads; see Edberg in *Fornvännen*, xc (1995), 147–57. However, they had to haul the boat overland for over 250km: see Sindboek in *Fornvännen* 2003, 179–93: 'Varagiske vinterruter'.

between Ladoga, the Upper Volga, and Kiev, covering half a million square miles. How the initial settlement by Swedish farmers had turned into this extended network of economic exploitation is not entirely clear from the archaeology, or the Arabic and Greek sources. The early immigrants were not drawn in by a thirst for silver, since not much reached the north-west until the end of the eighth century, and their land-hunger seems to have been satisfied with little; the decision to become the Mafia, and eventually the overlords of the Russian river-basins, was not the continuation of the agricultural colonization of the Volkhov valley but a reaction to the greed of distant southern markets for slaves and furs.

The late ninth-century Rus described by the Islamic traveller Jarhani (as reported in Ibn Rusteh's geography) were non-agricultural marsh dwellers, who waged war on Slavs for the purpose of selling their captives to the Chazars; they were shipmen and dealers, gleaming with gold and the coin stuck into their belts, flashy but hygienic predators under the rule of their own Khagan; unclean, is how the Baghdad envoy Ibn Fadlan found them in 922, when he reached the city of Bulghar and visited the Rus trading-huts.[3] By this time such operations had reached Constantinople as well (see p. 211) and the hegemony behind it needed reinforcing with military muscle; there were jobs in the retinues of Rus chiefs for more Nordic emigrants, selling military skills in a market where the top buyer was the Byzantine emperor, offering 40 gold pieces a year to Chazar and Varangian guardsmen. That emigration is easy to understand, and it continued to flow until the fall of Constantinople in 1204; and perhaps the original inflow of Swedes to Ladoga makes sense also, as a farming opportunity. Whether the ninth-century drive, or explosion, was generated by forces among the Rus (as is often assumed: hunger for silver, confidence in techniques of river transport and warfare are given as the motors) or by the policy of the Chazar khans, a thousand miles away down the Volga but manipulators of a vast hinterland of tributaries is still unclear. This would not be the first case of a grandiose imperial policy which went wrong, if the khans hoped to quell Slavs and warn both Islam and Byzantium by encouraging these versatile Norsemen in such hare-brained schemes as the attack on Constantinople in 860 and the expedition to Baku in Azerbaijan in 912. The khan let them loose on the Caspian for a half-share of the loot, which he got, but his muslim subjects wiped the raiders out on their return to the Volga.

---

3   There is an English translation of Ibn Fadlan by Smyser in *Franciplegius* ed. J.B. Bessinger and R.P. Creed, New York / London 1965; and see Ellis Davidson 1976, 64–7 and 109–10 on Ibn Rusteh.

The map, and the story of Nordic immigration to the east is changing too fast for a survey to catch. Much of the archaeology was inadvertently destroyed by nineteenth-century excavators and suppressed by Stalinists; new data bring theories to heel,[4] for the time being.

2   Russia turned out to be a land of opportunity, the high-road to Caesar's golden city, and it was to shimmer for centuries in Icelandic legend as a mirage of hospitable kings, seductive queens, opulence and danger.[5] Western Europe was different, and nowhere more so than in the *Faroe Islands*, which lie in the North Sea, half-way between Norway and Iceland. The seventeen habitable ones offered no rich soils, no broad plains, no chance of wealth either from mineral resources or trade, no subject population and no easy farming. According to the Irish geographer Dicuil, writing in the 840s, some islands which were probably these had been used as retreats by Irish hermits until the vikings had driven them away, leaving only sheep and seabirds behind. So far this statement has not been supported by archaeology, and there is no clear evidence of habitation much before c.900 (the Totanes farm excavated in the 1980s). Johansen has deduced much earlier colonization by analyzing the pollen in peat-samples containing carbon, the chemical which sometimes means human habitation; but as these conclusions have not been accompanied by traces of huts or houses, they remain hypothetical. Totanes has been called 'the typical North Atlantic settlement': four rectangular houses and an infield between a beach and a wide amphitheatre of hill-pasture. Artifacts from the deposits round the houses show that even in the viking period 'daily life seems to have been virtually impossible without imports', which were probably got by the sale of wool and fleeces in the British Isles or Norway. If the hermits left the sheep, they left a strong hint which the Norse were slow to pick up. As in Iceland (see p. 201) they tried cattle and goats, and only c.1050, when the cows had spoilt the grazing and the goats had cropped the juniper that sheltered the game, were the islands fully resigned to the sheep after which they were named. Thereafter grazing was allocated in proportion to the size of the infield of the coastal farmers who owned them. The original Scandinavian immigrants may have hoped to live by seal-hunting and wild-fowling on the cliffs and trapping game in the birchwoods, as Rafnsson suggests; the islands had evidently been familiar sea-marks from the eight century onwards, en route to better

4   Nosov 1998, 65 summarized the state of research, and the revival of pre-Soviet ideas on the birth of trading towns.
5   Ellis Davidson 1976, 150–63 discussed these novelistic sources.

places.[6] The few families that moved there may have based their decision on disappointed hopes in Shetland, 100 miles south-east, or on the shorter and so safer distance for ferrying cattle from Norway. The history is unrecorded. Narratives combined in the 1830s to form a synthetic Faereyinga Saga tell of a first settler called Grímr Kamban, but these are thirteenth-century fictions of little relevance to the ninth.

3 *Shetland*'s first Nordic settlers are equally unknown to archaeology and narrative sources. Intermittent excavation at the site named Jarlshof, which was occupied from the Bronze Age to the sixteenth century, revealed many phases of building and repair during viking times, and a wealth of finds too complex and jumbled to allow secure dating. At some date near 850 a group of stone buildings was erected next to a 70 20 foot hall, which was divided into a kitchen and a living space. This could be the house of an emigrant Norse chieftain, taking advantage of the local stone to announce his lordship over the south end of the big island, Mainland. There was evidently something here to be lord of, more than the gulls' eggs of Faroe: an ancient and flourishing Pictish culture, attested by the hoard of silver hidden on St Ninian's Isle about 800–25, and other jewellery and sculpture. The Picts had apparently obeyed an authority at the place the Norse called the king's fort (Cunningsburgh), and others at the settlements named after *papar* or clergy; when and how the immigrants arrived and took over remains a mystery. Nicolaisen worked out a chronology of settlement based on putting the three common place-name elements, *staðir*, *setr* and *bolstaðir* in a sequence, when there is no reason at all why they should not have been contemporary. Other students have floated imaginary answers to the questions raised by the wholly Nordic character of the islands in the thirteenth–fifteenth-century documents, when they had evidently been entirely Pictish, or at any rate not Nordic in the early ninth century. Attempts to pre-date the Norse arrival to the eighth or seventh centuries were founded on tenuous philology and have been abandoned, along with the view that the Picts were simply exterminated or expelled; but that many were dispossessed and enslaved by a small immigrant elite, or sidelined by a large immigration either from Norway or Orkney, or merged with the immigrants and adopted their language and customs remain possibilities in

6   See Johansen 1971 and 1985 on the early settlement theory, and Debes 1993 on the archaeology; also Stummann Hansen 1993, and EXTRA (1992), and Mahler 1998 on farming. Rafnsson is cited from OXVIK, ch. 5. A compact and scholarly survey of the archaeology by Símun V. Arge, 'Vikings in the Faroe Islands' will be found in VINAS, 154–63.

play.[7] No sign of a clear break with the past appears in the archaeology of Pictish sites, but that means nothing, given the fewness of
the thorough excavations; large halls and lordships, like Strom in
Whiteness, and the many small farms with cattle and barley liveli-
hoods could be continuations and adaptations of what was there
before, or a fresh start by the newcomers. The destiny of Shetlanders
to be fishermen with farms lay far in the future, after the cattle had
failed, and the fish-trade had expanded. It may have been the soapstone quarry at Cunningsburgh which first attracted the Norsemen,
or the mild winters compared with Norway, or whatever the Picts
had built up; the fog has not lifted.

4 *Orkney* was richer; there was fertile, long-cultivated soil, and a
population which worked metal at the Brough of Birsay and looked
to some sort of authorities there, and at Skaill, Deerness and Pool on
Sanday. Excavation has revealed round cell-buildings thought to be
Pictish as well as longhouses and farmsteads of the Norse type, all of
roughly the same period, possibly ninth century; but as in Shetland,
the place-names formed over the next 300 years are very Norse
indeed. The pagan burials at Pierowall (on Westray, the north-west
island) contained many valuable things, such as keys, combs and
brooches, as well as weapons and sickles, along with the bones of
horses and dogs: here lived a rich Nordic community of family
groups, probably *c.*850–950, but at Pool there are artifacts radio-
carbon dated as early as *c.*800. As the Life of S. Findan (see p. 26)
reveals that there was a bishop on Orkney in the 840s, and as the
Westness cemetery is shared by christians and pagans with no sign of
desecration, the immigrants and the native Orcs may have reached an
understanding which allowed christianity to survive. Places named
after clerics (*papar*) enjoyed tax exemptions in the Later Middle
Ages, which would be significant if the names really indicated places
where priests survived, rather than had lived. 'Some Ideas about
what may have happened' by Lamb include (1) the defeat of Pictish
nobles by Norse warriors *c.*800; (2) the rule of the islands by Nordic
chiefs with native priests as their administrators in the ninth century;
and (3) the creation of an earldom by the chiefs *c.*900, who steal
church lands to support the earl, and install Norse settlers on these
estates. The ideas are consistent with the archaeology in the sense
that they are not patently inconsistent; they certainly run counter to
the scheme Marwick worked out from the place-names, which was

---

7 Graham-Campbell summarizes the archaeology in VISC (1998), 155–60, and
63–7. For Nicolaisen's place-name theories see TV (1982), 95–115, well-mapped;
see Bigelow in AA, lxi (1990), Morris and Rackham 1992, and Smith in SSNB 1995
for further contributions to the settlement problems.

only concerned with rural settlement by Norse-speakers, and collapses with the artificial dating of names on which it was based. It seems clear that there was never a peasant migration from Norway, small farmers teeming west in the hope of a better living on unoccupied land; if they wanted unoccupied land they could go to the Faroes, or Iceland, and their landing on Orkney, whenever it was, depended on the goodwill or need of the chiefs who had fought for it, or possibly just bought it. Agriculture here was not such a pinch-gut business as on Shetland, and the wild life was richer; the chiefs on Birsay and Sanday could hunt the otter, the hare and the red deer, and strengthen their position by offering farms to shipowners and livestock-carriers as they became available. Lamb's theory of the foundation of the earldom by the suppression of the monasteries fits the subsequent collapse of Pictish culture and language; but as that happened everywhere in North Britain, the fit is loose.[8] The Norse-speaking Orkney of the twelfth century, which had the king of Norway as its overlord, and a historical myth about relations between those kings and its own dynasty of earls, came into being by stages which remain very obscure, and need not have included or excluded settlement from Norway or back from islands further west at any time.

As with the traces of other settlement in *Pictland* (NE Scotland), where the Orkney earls had authority over Caithness and Sutherland in the eleventh century and later. There are a few graves and isolated finds of Norse character from the pagan period, but not a single identifiable settlement, despite many place-names pointing to a Norse-speaking population at some period: a concentration of *bolstaðar*, *ergi* and *setr* names (52 in all) appears in north and west Caithness. This may result from migration post 1000 from Orkney, encouraged by earls interested in straddling the Pentland Firth, or hunting the red deer with people who spoke their language. The remains of a nine-foot cod, found in a viking-age midden at Freswick in Caithness, indicates serious fishermen among these settlers.[9]

5 *NW Scotland and the Hebrides* were more inviting to the Nordic farmer than those wind-blasted heavy clay lands to the east. There was a Gulf-stream climate, light but limy and fertile soils on the west coasts of the outer islands, with shell and seaweed as dressings for tillage; less cruel wind, less heavy rain than on Orkney. Irish emigrants had settled the coastlands from Loch Fyne to the Great Glen since Roman times,

8 Smith in SSNB 1995; Bigelow in AA, lxi (1990); Morris and Rackham 1992; Thomson SSNB 1995; Hunter, Bond and Smith VACON 1998, 272–8 for résumé of settlement evidence; Morris in ISCEVA 1998, 84–8, Lamb 1993.
9 Norris in TV (1982), 70–94; Graham Campbell and Batey 1998, 67–70, 140–2 and 125–7; and see now Barrett 2000, and his forthcoming work on Norse settlement and diet.

and there is at least a date for the conquest of the rest of the west by Northmen in the contemprary Annals of St Bertin, kept at the West Frankish court, under 847:

After the Irish had been under attack by Northmen for many years, they were made to pay tribute; and they also got control of the islands round Ireland, and stayed, meeting no resistance from anyone.

This is usually taken to mean the western isles of Scotland, since Ireland's offshore islands reveal few traces of Norse settlement. There are many, on most of the Isles: over ten 'pagan' graves on the Outer Hebrides south of Lewis, eleven on Colonsay and three on Eigg, with little more than a square mile to dig into. The graves and treasures do not correspond with the concentrations of Norse place-names on Lewis (79%) and NE Skye (66%), which suggests that the denser sort of settlement, which supports a non-indigenous language, was not the aim or immediate result of the conquest of the islands by pirate chiefs, but possibly a backwash from the settlements in Ireland which were checked by the expulsion of the Dubliners in the 890s. The place-names also show that the Gaelic and Norse languages (neither indigenous to the Outer Hebrides) developed separately until the thirteenth century, when Gaelic prevailed[10]; in contrast to Shetland and Orkney, where it never entered. The chiefs who ruled the islands after 847 seem to have compensated for their setback in Ireland by encouraging farmers, both Irish and Norse, to live in these parts and man their ships: taxation came much later. Seven *papar* names in the Outer Hebrides may mean that priests were left undisturbed; the mixed Norse-Celtic ornaments in the grave at Valtos on Lewis suggest some cultural fusion before 900, but the whole chronology of settlement is uncertain. It is possible to distinguish earlier from later place-names by the soil-quality, area of arable, nearness to coast or chapel, but this only produces a sequence within the range of years from 850 to 1266. The case for settlements from Ireland organized by baffled predators is purely hypothetical; future archaeology will help.

10   On Lewis PNN and language see Cox in Ureland 1991, 479; Barnes, in VIRE 1992 ('Norse in the British Isles') found little borrowing between the languages; Cox, much. Sveaas Andersen (1991, 131–47) and Olson discuss the loans, and conclude that Norse adopted *ergi* for their own *setr*, Gaels adopted *bolstaðr* and *boer* for farms, over a long period. Recent excavations on South Uist have revealed many (21) Norse settlements, mostly close to previously occupied sites and apparently continuous with them; new sorts of pots and house- plans did not mark a break with old patterns of land-use or the arrival of an entirely new population; see Sharples and Parker Pearson, NAR, xxxii (1999), 41–62, and Kruse in SCEU (or PNN).

6   Settlement in *Ireland* is usually seen as a military occupation by ruthless predators which dwindled into four or five new towns spaced out along the coast from Dublin to Limerick, where Black and White Foreigners lived on trade, tribute and loot. If that is how it was, it was not like other colonizations in the British Isles, with their seizure of wide rural spaces, their merging with local political structures, and deep contamination of local language. All that appears, by *c.*950, is a short list of small fortified townships under the erratic overlordship of a dynasty called the sons or descendants of Imhair, alias Ívarr in Old Norse: the McIvers of Dublin and York. The great changes which Binchy attributed to these Foreigners (in 1959) were urbanization, monetization and disruption of the old political structure of Ireland, a community of small kingdoms under kings and highkings: changes made by warriors and traders, not by immigrant farmers. Trade, war and seamanship were the forces that counted in the transformation of the Irish from a regulated, traditional society under multiple authorities, lay and clerical, into a militarized war-zone between competing dynasties with wider hegemony in mind. This contrast was overdrawn and left the nature of Norse immigration uncertain.

Since 1988, when Bradley drew attention to the links between the towns and the hinterlands which supplied their food and much of their population, Norse colonies no longer seem peripheral. It is now suggested that colonists penetrated deeply into the countryside to aid the stimulation of economic life by the rulers of Dublin; perhaps on the model of the Wessex-Mercian burhs, or those forts which became towns, so the argument runs.[11] But the only evidence in support of this is in ON place-names, which are not in themselves evidence of settlement, and are anyway infrequent. Thanks to the Wood Quay excavations, the growth of Dublin into a city from the 950s onwards is well known, when the increase of population came from Ireland and the west of Britain, rather than from Scandinavia. Thanks to recent excavation in the Liffey valley more is also known of the original immigrants of the 830s and 40s, the several hundred men and a few women who were found buried upstream in the Nordic way: 'a military elite engaged in commerce' according to Ó Flóinn. These people[12] lived along the river, with a fort at Dublin founded in 842 as their refuge and trading place, and their settlement was dispersed with the

---

11   Bradley 1998, 63–70: the development of Dublin's hinterland on English lines in unlikely, because the McIvers did not actually control it. See Clinton 'The Souterrains of Co. Dublin', DAB, 117, for the strong native presence just north of the city, and the sparse signs of Norse settlement to the south.
12   For cemeteries at Kilmainham and Islandbridge, a mile above Dublin, see O'Brien, 'A Reconsideration', DAB (1998), 35–44.

capture of this early Dublin by an Irish king in 902. Where they came from is revealed neither by the archaeology nor by later Irish texts (see p. 117) and opinion is divided between the western isles of Scotland, and some part of Norway, preferably the south-west.[13] Norway was the original source, in either case; the presence of Irish objects in ninth-century Norwegian hoards, and the nature of the pagan burials in Ireland establishes the link; but Ó Corráin has argued for an intermediate kingdom of the Norse within the British Isles as the *Lochlann* from which Irish sources derive their vikings. In that case their predatory and mobile conduct, geared to looting, blackmail and enslavement, would be easy to explain: they had secure bases outside the country. If they were fresh from Norway or Denmark, looking for places to settle and farm, they had a strange way of going about it. Had any of them such bucolic ambitions, they were thwarted by the vigorous reaction of Irish kings from the 860s to 900; the tenth-century revival of the Norse had to be based on fortified bases and alliances with Irish rulers.[14]

The other insular settlements, or traces of Norse intervention, in the Isle of Man, Cheshire, Wales, Lancashire, Cumbria and SW Scotland are alike in two ways: none of them can be securely dated to the century of intense piracy, 790–890, and none of them can be linked to Scandinavia in ways which suggest that these were the goals of a planned emigration. They came in from the Hebrides, from Ireland, from England and from the Continent after failing or succeeding at the viking game, either by invitation from their own or other chiefs, or by conquest; these landfalls would often be the last refuge of scoundrels, for centuries to come. A big enterprise, the subjugation of Ireland, had failed; a big business, slave-trading, had succeeded; as the colonies come in the aftermath of the failure, it seems that they result from it.[15]

7 *Iceland* was different, in that its later chiefs produced a settlement legend so powerful and detailed that it survives as popular history to this day (see p. 123). In the *Landnámabók* story, the island was

13 On whom see Ó Floinn 'The Archaeology of the Early VA in Ireland', O'Brien 'Viking Burials at Kilmainham and Islandbridge' and Clarke 'Proto-towns and Towns' in ISCEVA (1998).

14 Ó Corráin's insular Lochlann, or Greene's rather, reaffirmed in ISCEVA, 424–5, is resisted by Wamers and Myhre on archaeological grounds: too much Irish stuff found in Norway in ninth-century contexts. How it got there is unclear, and its connexion with Early Irish geography more so. See Ní Mhaonaigh on Irish–Norse relations, also in ISCEVA, 381–402 and for a new survey VE 80–117.

15 On which, see Graham-Campbell 1998a, 106–12, and ISCEVA 104–30; for SW Scotland, Crawford 1987, 25–7, 98–100. For Manx evidence: Tarlow 1997, and Moore in RRIM 1999, 171–82.

colonized from 870 to 930 by hundreds of separate immigrations mainly of respectable or noble Norwegians in search not only of a livelihood but of secure hereditary freehold tenure, threatened by the tyranny of king Harold Fair-hair. The 'property-claim book' circles the coast, giving brief anecdotes of some 430 settlers, among the 3500 named people and their 1500 farms; most of them flattering to the kin of the in-comers: like Ketil Trout, who

> went north to Torgar, where he burnt the sons of Hildirith to death in their own house...their slander had brought about the death of Thorolf (his kinsman)...after that, Ketil decided to go to Iceland.[16]

Evidently a great grandfather worthy of The Godfather. The book tells of how they moved, what they transported, why and how they selected the sites of their future farms, how they established their boundaries and placated the land-spirits, what gods they worshipped, what laws they brought, and made, and who was descended from them. With data so abundant, the historian's prayers in the darkness of the age seem to be answered; but this was no Domesday Book. It was a compilation of family traditions formed over centuries to uphold the oligarchy of chiefs which ruled the island from the eleventh century onwards; a regime based on prior land-rights. Rafnsson's *Studier i Landnámabok* (Lund 1974) showed that the emphasis on property secured by supposed ancestors of the big men of the twelfth century means that this is not an accurate record of the actual settlement, even if it holds many edited and rearranged fragments of it. Families do not tell the truth about their history: compare the Domesday record of who held England in 1086 with the hundreds of claims by families convinced that their ancestor 'came over with the Conqueror'. Besides, archaeology has not been kind to the *Landnáma* legend in all its details.

It began with Irish monks or hermits, living in the island before 870, but departing on the arrival of the Norse, and leaving books and crosses behind them. This is perfectly credible, but no trace whatever of any such occupation has been found, even in places named after *papar*. Instead, some archaeologists have made radiocarbon and

---

16 LN, 344; trans. Pálsson and Edwards, 130. No surviving version of this book can be older than *c*.1250; see Benediktsson in MESCA, 373–4 for a summary of the problems and literature, and *The Book of Settlements* (H. Pálsson and Edwards) Manitoba 1972 for a complete translation. The five surviving MSS may derive from an early twelfth-century work, possibly Ári's, but now lost. They are a valuable source for post-viking-age history, and for Jesse Byock's *Viking Age Iceland* (Penguin 2001). See now Vesteinsson in CONIL 7–26 for a summary of the archaeological evidence of the actual settlement.

palaeobotanical tests at Gásir, in the north, in the Vestmann islands and near Reykjavik and have concluded that the first farmers were active as early as 700, 170 years before the Norse even claimed to have set foot there. These findings have been generally rejected as unsound, but the re-examination by Theodórsson found them satisfactory insofar as the dating technique could be relied on.[17] This remains an open question, since the quantity of early evidence is not overwhelming, yet. If there was such a population it could have been Irish or Norse; the eighth- and seventh-century Irish and Norse left easily detectible traces of their houses elsewhere, and they should be found here.

Ári claimed that Iceland was peopled by Scandinavian emigrants and their Irish slaves, in unstated proportions; subsequently, the Irish immigration was overlooked (unless a queen or princess came in) because it could make no difference to later property rights in land. Slavery lived on, but the masters and mistresses only wanted to hear what happened when the first slaves had killed and run for it. They did not get far. Yet Ári also reveals that in his day (*c.*1100) foreigners accused all Icelanders of being descendants of slaves; he, and most Icelanders until quite recently, were interested only in Scandinavian ancestors, preferably of royal descent. Blood-group and genetic testing have been used to quantify the Irish component in the modern population, and some tests reveal blood-groups and gene-patterns closer to some Celtic models than to some Norwegian ones; which reveals little about who came from where *c.*900, if much about the sex-life of Icelanders since then. Palaeogenetic estimates of the Celtishness of the early population vary between 14 per cent (Wijsman) and up to 75 per cent (Saugstad); a large gap, between milestones made of ice-cream, and statistically worthless. There is as much genetic evidence of Lapps as of Irish: the so-called Tydal race look Saami, and East Baltic ornaments have been found in early sites. Traits in blood, such as the frequent O allele, can result from mutation and adaptation over time, rather than from the original composition of the test-group's remote ancestors: so far,[18] Ári has the last word: many Iceland settlers came from Norway, some from the British Isles.

---

17   Hermann-Auðardottir 1989; Theodórsson in NAR, xxxi (1998), 29–38. Ahronson 2000 deduces pre-870 settlement from 'Columban' crosses incised on cave walls, supposedly Irish-inspired.

18   Sigurdsson 1988, ch. 2 reviewed the evidence, as had Bjarnarsson et al. (1973); it was firmly rejected by Vilhjálmsson 1991 and 1993; Urbańczyk takes the archaeology of sunken huts to indicate a Slav presence (CM xv 2002, 155–65).

Landnámabók indicated SW Norway as the commonest source (47%) of located emigrants, and there is no scientific objection to this; it is only strange that there is an entire absence of cremation-graves in Iceland, when they form 90 per cent of the SW Norwegian total. Shortage of wood is the obvious explanation, but these were special occasions, and it took a few decades for the birch to be cleared. Perhaps they wanted to dig themselves into virgin soil, literally; or felt that they had already arrived where cremated people went. The impression that *Landnáma* gives of hundreds of quite separate landfalls is not supported by the archaeology of the earliest phase, which has revealed clusters of buildings shared by two or more families, the lucky ones, who later separated and took the best sites; a more calculated and seigneurial plan of settlement than was assumed, consistent with the need for sound and seaworthy transports, fit to carry cows, bulls, rams and horses. However, these were not the chiefs and captains of men imagined by their descendants; not one of the 300 pre-christian graves found on the island contains the luxuries and weapons which went with upper-class corpses in contemporary Scandinavia, cremated or not.

These were farmers with a few clients and poor relations, owners of one or two sailing-boats, at least if they came from Norway; but some at least must have come direct from Ireland or the Scottish islands with their slaves, in ships they had used for raiding. Their treasure, if they brought any, was not buried with them, and perhaps it was bequeathed and spent by the families. There is a coincidence between a group of four Iceland and four Lewis place-names which suggests that some immigrants from the Hebrides had no wish to forget their time there.[19] If they brought Irish or Picts or Gaels with them, they need not all have been slaves; but if there was a free Celtic immigration it is remarkable that the written culture which developed and flowered after 1100 should afford so little clear evidence of it; not in place-names, personal names, loan-words, or traditions is there proof of a literate Irish community among the Norse. Norse interest in and contact with Ireland is well attested, and Irish influence on Norse literature and oral tradition is at least detectible if not obvious; but it is hard to believe that it came from within the population of Iceland. The Celts within that population evidently lacked the status which it was the burning ambition of literate Icelanders to maintain and boost. Free land and the illusions of

---

19 Leiruvági, Esja, Kjós and Laxá in Iceland echo Leirabagh, Eshaval, Ceose and Lachassay, alias Liurbost, Ceos, Lacasaigh, south of Stornoway. See Einarsson 1994 and Herschend 1994 on patterns of settlement; on the cramping effect of *Landnámabók* on archaeology see now Friðriksson and Vésteensson in CCC, 139–61.

something for nothing (as noted previously, p. 200) were a strong pull on many families within an 800 mile radius of the Iceland coast, (1280 km), but that sickening voyage with stock, wealth and dependents evidently ruled out any disorganized rush of homesteaders. Those who could afford it, came to set up the little lordships which Herschend and others have detected in some places; others might join with neighbours to pool the cost. That would explain why, for example, so many thirteenth-century Icelanders claimed forbears from the one territory of Sogn (north of Bergen): 32 per cent of the whole south-west contingent, from an area of which Sogn occupies less than 10 per cent; and why most of them settled in SE Iceland. Neighbours helped each other and stayed together.[20]

8   *Greenland* also had a foundation legend, rooted in the pioneering work of Ári. In the 980s, when Iceland was becoming overcrowded, one chief and his family led colonists to the south-west coast of this vast white island, and in the course of the eleventh century two stretches of that coast were populated by further immigrants, in the so-called east and west settlements. In Landnámabók and the sagas, the west settlement is the work of the red Eiríkr, sailing a convoy of 14 ships to Brattahlið; allowing room for cattle and cargo, this would mean up to 150 people, or 30 to 35 families. To go so far with such uncertain prospects (the seal, deer, caribou, and abundant soapstone were joys to come) was not for small groups or single families; this migration is only conceivable as the work of a lord with clients who trusted or feared him. The adaptation to utterly alien circumstances, which makes these colonies so interesting, had only begun in the viking age, and the first reaction of the settlers to their surroundings may be judged by the speed with which many of them struck west and south in search of some better source of whatever they needed, if not of a better place to live. Vinland voyages are the subject of thirteenth-century sagas, and of many imaginative reconstructions since then. One saga, the *Grænlendinga*, composed *c.*1200, relates that a large party of colonists went to these parts under Thorfinn Karlsefni. After two or three years, men, women and children were driven out by natives; and a subsequent party was mostly marooned or murdered by Eiríkr the Red's daughter, Freydis. There is no way of sifting fact from fiction in these narratives; wherever Vínland was thought to be, such probes have left no mark on the landscape visible today. What did was the mainly male groups in Newfoundland about the turn of the millennium, and their brief stay at the site now called

---

20   Herschend 'Models of Petty Rulership' in *Tor*, xxv (1993), 175–99; but all such schemes, including the one above, are based on saga and Landnama evidence, or on place-names, and may well be misguided.

l'Anse aux Meadows in houses built of turf laid round timber frames. Winter lasts 6–8 months in this damp, desolate, windswept place, and grain will not grow; but these pioneers worked bog-iron at a small forge, span, sowed and made things of bone, wood and soapstone. They kept at least one pig, as the Ingstads discovered from the debris; but this was a short-lived enterprise, with no future as a self-supporting settlement. It must have served some other purpose (a rendez-vous with Amerindians, where metal could buy something? a lookout on the route south, to warn intruders off Eiríkr's seigneury?) or simply have been a mistake, a miscalculation based on a run of unusually mild years.[21]

In all such small outposts the bleak hopelessness of the enterprise seems more obvious now than it can have at the time, to people accustomed to feeding themselves on whatever they could catch, and sitting out winters in hungry isolation. The thought of the next move would keep them warm, and that thought remains hidden. Thus on St Kilda, a small now uninhabited island 60 miles west of the Hebrides, one Norseman of rank was buried in the tenth century with the full panoply of war, and another left a hoard of coins; here, where the appalling seas make landing dangerous even in summer. No warrior could have lived there without intending to leave, if only to one of the inner Hebridean islands, Coll, Tiree, Eigg, where piracy would have been profitable. But some people stayed, on what they called *Hirta*, and their descendants were reconciled to fish and gull's eggs and rain.[22]

9   The English *Danelaw* is the conventional term for the whole eastern side of England from the Tees to the Thames estuary, in which, according to twelfth-century jurists, customs and laws other than those of the rest of the country were to be found; the word is in the early eleventh-century text called *Edward and Guthrum*, but not in a geographical sense. This was the big arena over which Danes had achieved some kind of political authority during the years from 866 to 950, and in some parts of it they had settled in numbers sufficiently large to maintain their own language and customs, and so, eventually, by the accident of London's absorption of east-country immigrants, to affect the development of modern English. Within the Danelaw, place-names and personal names and dialects survive as evidence of a Nordic presence, and for more than 150 years philologists have studied this evidence and have sometimes attempted to deduce the

---

21 Wahlgren 1986, 121–33 summarizes, and see Barnes 1995 and Wooding 1995 for the Vinland ventures; Sigurðsson discusses the historicity of the saga evidence in 'Orality and Literacy' CONIL 285–300, and Perkins argues that Norse visits to the American mainland remain unproved: SB XXVII 29–69.
22 Graham-Campbell and Batey 1998, 77, 87, and 92 for the archaeology.

extent, volume, date and nature of the Nordic immigration which lay behind it (see p. 310), or behind most of it. All that the Anglo-Saxon Chronicler has to say on the subject is that in 874, 876, 880 and 896 invading armies halted and settled down: they 'settled there and shared out the land' or 'began to plough and provide for themselves' and on these phrases hang all we know about what Anglo-Saxon witnesses thought was going on.

Modern interpreters have imagined that 'dealing out land' meant a survey and apportionment involving an obligation to pay tax and owe military service; and that 'ploughing' meant acquiring several hundred ploughs, hitching them to stolen oxen or horses, and getting down to a spell of honest work, as 'peasant farmers'. A ninth-century annalist would have associated ploughing with 'no going back' (as in Luke 9: 62), a determination to stay put rather than migrating and living off pillage and blackmail; and 'sharing out land' with leaving some to the Anglo-Saxons, certainly not with any administrative exercise: the phrase was a cliché of subjection and conquest. In all these cases, the Danes came into ancient habitations, vacant where the landlords had fled[23] or had been killed, and the newcomers were fattened by years of depredation and extortion. The terms on which they got land are unrecorded, but need not have differed from the terms on which it was held before, unless it had been held in perpetuity, from God, by monks; but even then, the monks had leased or loaned such land to lay tenants. Personal ties between lords and men had been the force that kept these armies going, and these would have continued to bind land-holders to the chiefs; the habit of raiding was not cured by these settlements, and it was that more than anything, which led to the West Saxon conquest in the following century.

Behind these events lay the inevitable loss of impetus within the roaming armies, and the collaboration of Anglo-Saxon host-kingdoms. It was certainly no plan of territorial acquisition hatched within Scandinavia, or wave of colonists misinterpreted as armies by western sources; for these forces, settlement temporary or permanent, was one of a range of possible outcomes wholly dependent on the military and political situation of the moment. What actually happened in Northumbria, Mercia and East Anglia during the first phase of Nordic occupation is unknown, and it has been the misfortune of placename students that so many historians have expected them to find out. Place-names are the work of time, during which many are eroded, disguised, renovated and multiplied, so that

---

23   As at Partney abbey in Lincs, and Whitby in north Yorkshire, according to Sawyer 1998, 98.

the place-name map of 1086 (which can be reconstructed from Domesday Book) could not possibly reveal the colonization of the 870s through the Norse or partly-Norse names. All the place-name virtuosi can do is show what the names mean in the contexts of where they lie, collect types, analogues and variants, and speculate. The results are vital for the social history of the Danelaw over the 200 years before 1086, and can be supplemented by the many Anglo-Scandinavian names which appear during the following 200 years, old and new;[24] but the three fundamental questions about the immigration (when? where? volume?) are not answered by this means. ON PNN reflect diffusion and diffraction and fusion of one language over 400 years, through all kinds of experiences other than conquest and settlement, and it is time to roll up that map of *Bys and Grimston-Hybrids* which masquerades as a map of Scandinavian settlement in so many text-books. It is an impostor, which has survived only because the archaeology of settlement has so far had such meagre results.

Ignoring, for the moment, the toponymists and archaeologists, it is possible to offer four main types of colonization which appear in the early middle ages all over the world:

1 by starting new farms on virgin or unintensively worked land;
2 by taking over working farms as owners or lords;
3 by living as household members at the cost of others;
4 by building a fort or town and living off its market or the proceeds of raiding or renders from a subjugated country round about.

There are other ways, but these are the ones which have left traces in England, although the traces can rarely be pinned even approximately to datable events such as the demobilization of Danish or Dublin armies. Thus the remote hill-farms excavated at Ribblehead and Simy Folds, on the upper Ribble and the upper Tees are reckoned to be Nordic, from the rectangular shape of the houses, and post 850–75 from one coin find; but that any less-than-desperate immigrant would choose to live in these places is hard to believe. Halfdan's army of 874 could do better than that; these farms, like the thorps round Wharram Percy in Yorkshire and the poorly-sited

---

24 As in Fellows-Jensen 1995, which deduces social interaction between Danes and English from personal names. See now Townend 2002 for a convincing demonstration of the mutual intelligibility of ON and OE in this period, contra Gneuss 'Anglicae Lingial interpretatio' Proc. British Academy, Lxxxii 107–48.

Irebys and Irby of the north-west are not testimony to a great immigration, but to its lean aftermath, if there was one.[25]

The taking of manors and farms in working order would be the first choice of immigrants, and there is enough overlap of Norse remnants (hog-back tombs, Scandinavian utensils and ornaments) with English place-names (Middleton, Yorks is the best example) and of Anglian remains with Norse place names to make it likely that this often occurred. Some thirty or forty Anglian religious communities attested before 850 seem to have disappeared before 950, and would have left such estates at least available to Danes; but the entire lack of documentation, and the inability of place-name virtuosi to date or characterize those bys and thorps except within broad limits makes the map of ninth-century colonization impossible to draw. Danes would always prefer to own what was there, rather than make new; these were ancient, well-worked landscapes, chartered, or at least registered in gospel-books, held under time-honoured rules, in no immediate need of fragmentation or altered land-use; all that would come about over time, not through a big Nordic influx. If it occurred, it would be employed in the manning of the military households and forts which proved such a nuisance to West Saxon rulers before they were subjugated in the tenth century. Even after that subjugation, Danish landowners remained in possession, under the supervision of English ealdormen, and so prolonged the period during which places were given Nordic names, and obscured the frequency and type of the early ones. In Lincolnshire, most of the many such names may result from the Wessex conquest, when dependable Danes were allowed to keep their estates, and the estates kept their names: a record of title rather than sod-busting.[26]

If the Scandinavian and part-Scandinavian English place-names are the result of the diffusion of landownership and Norse speech over two hundred and more years, rather than of one immigration, there is no point in trying to calculate the one from the other. A narrative can only be inferred from a sparse record of events composed from the Wessex point of view. That means that there is a large hidden factor, in the dealings of the invading armies with the Anglian population, which was of no interest to the chroniclers; and yet the

25 Coggins 1992, for the finds; Higham SSNB 1995, 199–205 for Irebys.
26 Higham 1995, 198 and Fellows Jensen 1995, 172–5 on hybrid names; Watts 1988–89 (*Nomina* xii) on the lateness of Co. Durham ON PNN, and Sawyer 1998, 110–14 for a summary of current conventions in Lincolnshire place-name analysis which reveals their flimsy foundations. See Hadley in ANS, xix (1997) for a full and fair review of evidence and controversies and for an assessment of the borrowing of ON words into OE and ME see Wollmann 1996; into Scotch, Kries 2003; into Norman, Ridel 2004.

readiness of natives to collaborate with Danes is evident, even in unsympathetic sources.[27] The newcomers of the 860s–890s arrived in military formations, but with wives and children; they did enough damage, directly and indirectly to make the main task of rulers and landowners that of restoration. By the mid 870s there were bare farms, empty halls and burnt barns all over the midlands and the east; as on the large estate at Beddington (Surrey) which was let to the bishop of Winchester in the 890s 'quite without stock and stripped bare by heathen men'. The bishop restocked with minimal herds of oxen, pigs and sheep, sowed a mere 90 acres (out of many hundred) with seed, and put in seven slaves; which is the sort of thing the heathen men who had stripped Beddington[28] would be doing east of Watling street in other depleted farms, on a smaller scale. Places named after Danes may indicate where this happened, over a generation or two; but there is no need for one explanation, when several would do. Danes continued to settle in England over 150 years, as occasion served; as conquerors until the 890s, as allies of the English kings to the 1020s, and the survival and spread of their idioms points to a remarkably successful infiltration or merger despite outbursts of furious fighting. Wherever they came from (mostly from the Continent, rather than direct from Denmark or Norway, until the tenth century) they were able to adapt to the social structure, economic arrangements and religion of their unwilling or willing hosts in eastern England, and kept their gains by transferring allegiance to the all-conquering rulers of the west country.

10 *Normandy* carries the name of settlers to the present day. It was the sole survivor on the Continent of a century of occupations (840–944) during which Nordic armies won a hold on various Frankish or Frisian territories: on parts of the North Sea coast from 830 to the 880s, Loire valley districts from the 850s to 920s, islands on the Seine and round the coast, Brittany 918–36. The others came to their ends in defeat and expulsion, unable to reach a long-term accomodation with the local authorities as had the Danish settlers in England; the Normans survived because the kings and dukes of the West Franks in the tenth century needed allies at the mouth of the Seine to defend this gateway against other Northmen, Bretons and disloyal Franks, and the leaders of the Rouen army agreed to accept baptism for land. These were old campaigners, survivors of

27 For example, the alliance with Ceolwulf II of Mercia and four of his chiefs, later with the Mercian prince Brihtsige and the West Saxon etheling Ethelwold, with kings Egbert II and Ricsige of Northumbria, with the archbishops of York from 900; these were leaders of many more.
28 Charter, trans. EHD, no. 101.

the raid to England in 892–6, no doubt reinforced since then, but thoroughly tamed by a defeat at Chartres in 910; the leader, Hrolfr, was Rollo to the Franks, but christened Robert, and came to terms with the archbishop of Rouen in the same way as the York kings reached agreement with their archbishop. Later legends told of an orderly hand-out of shares in an almost deserted country to Rollo's warriors, with a restitution of church estates at the same time, but there is no contemporary evidence of this at all. The colonization of Normandy was a series of land-seizures and grants over the period 900–70, not the prompt demobilization of Rollo's army following his baptism; that army, as a fighting force, was his reason for being there, and he continued to lead it to war through the 920s. In 916 and 966 this region absorbed other armies, from England and Scandinavia, and its military manpower outgrew the modest but useful purpose of the original settlement. Rollo's grandson Richard was generally recognized as a count, a christian ruler among a hybrid piratical population of uncertain loyalties, and chief shareholder in the new riches of Rouen. His family had acquired large estates of their own, and had rewarded followers with others: Toki got Tocqueville, Manni got Manneville, Aki Aqueville, and so on; but the very uncertain hold this family had on any territory to the west of the Seine until *c.975* means that their part in organizing settlement was strictly limited.[29]

They seem to have been more interested in inviting Franks to serve them than in preserving any kind of Nordic nucleus or colony, and in civilizing the Norsemen along Frankish lines. After the 960s there were no more recorded Norse settlements here, but until then the prospect of owning land in the Seine valley, rather than merely raiding and leaving, was evidently magnetic to many Scandinavians (mostly from Denmark, to judge by the place-names) with military skills, ships and retainers.[30]

These ten examples can be grouped into varieties of colonization: by the seizing of strong points and staying there, by occupying armies, which win control of districts by force or negotiation and survive long enough for some of their component members to gain rural estates, by shipping livestock and goods from Scandinavia or

29 A short but useful summary of devastations and settlements in Francia is given by Niel S. Price in VINAS (2000), 116–26, who contrasts the Breton and Norman settlements with undue confidence. On Normandy, Jean Renaud *Les vikings et la Normandie* (Rennes 1989) is not bad, and in English David Bates *Normandy before 1066* (1982) is sound, as is Musset's 'Essai sur le peuplement de la Normandie' in Galinié, 1989 97–102.

30 Outline of settlement in Bates 1982, 2–23.

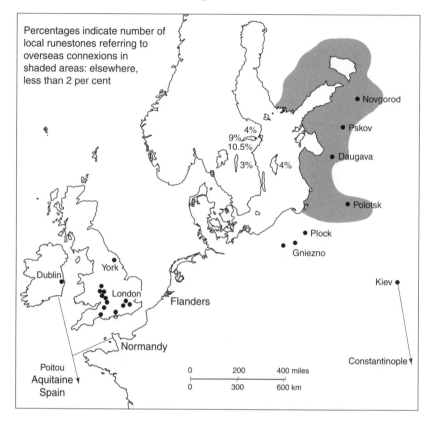

Map 9   *Migration, 950–1050*

Places where there is archaeological or other evidence of Nordic
emigrants (using Melnikova 1998).

from plundered countries to unoccupied land, by purchase, by flight,
by diplomatic concession. None of the affected regions fits exclusively into one of these categories, nor did Norwegian, Swedish and
Danish colonizations differ in some ethnic way from each other;
political circumstance and geography were the differences. The political factor in the eastern settlements was the foreign policy of the
Chazars and Bulgars on the Volga, which is a mystery, and the
counter-moves of the Byzantine state, which become clear in the *De
Administrando* of Constantine Porphyrogenitus. In the west it was
the Carolingian policy of protecting frontiers by letting Danish kings
have jurisdictions on the Frankish side, and sending missions far into
the Baltic on the other. No Norsemen attempted to settle perma-
nently on their own account, rather than occupying bases to raid

from, until after 850 on the Continent and Ireland, 870 in England and Iceland. Colonization was one possible by-product of raiding, a course open to those who had done well out of it, or who had found unoccupied land for the taking. There was no peasant migration of surplus families who could not be contained in the homelands; rather, the predatory armies reached a point at which they stopped, or split up. After 975, rulers outside Scandinavia offered regular employment to emigrants as guardsmen in their retinues. The problem of the roving Norse was solved by the demand for mercenary manpower in Byzantium, Russia, Poland and England, where mostly unviolated graveyards shelter the armed remains of people who had been taught to uphold rather than threaten the authority of christian rulers.[31]

Postscript : Settlements in England

See now Halsall, Evison, Richards and Hall for a through reassessment of settlement evidence in *Cultures in Contact* ed. Dawn Hadley and Julian Richards, Turnhout 2000. A perceptive essay on 'Ethnicity, Migration Theory and the Historiography of the Scandinavian Settlement of England' (17–39) points out that the subject has now been 'stuck in an impasse which is some forty years old', mudfast in obsolete concepts and methods. The impasse has now been broken through by Townend 2002 which argues that the Norse and the English could understand each other's speech, and that Norse continued to be spoken in England to the twelfth century. The strong influence of that on English says nothing of where, when, and by how many; but suggests that settlers and natives lived close together. For an eleven-zone division of settlement in the West, see Fellows-Jensen in SCEU 2004:137–49 'Scandinavian settlements in the British Isles and Normandy'.

---

31 See map 9. On Scandinavian burials in Poland, see Kara in DEBU (1992); all near centres of Piast power.

10

Past

THAT I SAY THIRTEENTHLY WHO WERE TWENTY
KINGS SAT IN SEALAND FOUR WINTERS BY
FOUR NAMES SONS OF FOUR BROTHERS:
FALKIS FIVE RATHULFSONS, HREITHULFS FIVE RUGULFSONS,
HAISLAR FIVE HARUTHSSONS, GUNMUNDS FIVE
BIRNARSONS.

So it says among the many runes carved into the great stone of Rök in Östergötland, which most authorities date to the ninth century[1]; and despite long and painful research going back 150 years or more, none of them has established what it means, or what it is, other than a reference to one old tale among many more which have been lost. Rök gives the impression of how the past seemed to one group of Gautar in the viking age, for the purposes of commemorating Væmoð, son of Varinn, who died before his father: it was MOG-MINNI, which seems to mean 'powerful memory', summoning bits of the past to help the present, in this case to be summarized and inscribed but usually to be recited from memory. As a result, we are mostly in the dark about the epics and episodes which inspired the old Norsemen themselves, before they became semi-legendary characters in Icelandic literature. Rök and Sparlösa are fragments of an iceberg which has melted; but given the importance of the past in the lives of most pre-modern societies, it is worth asking what part it played in this one? The Norse have had various pasts imposed on them, and the viking age is a good example (see pp. 4–6); and another would be the Germanic Tradition, or the Germanic-Nordic Continuum in which the culture of the Germanic family of languages forms a unity reaching from Roman or earlier times to the end of the

---

1 Gade 1995, 235 for dating; for brief bibliography, Kratz in MESCA 558–9 (to 1979); since then, Grønvik 1990, and Meulengracht Sørensen 1990.

middle ages, and includes a single pre-christian world view. The intellectual effort needed to support this Romantic concept exceeds its value as a way of looking at the evidence; at any rate, it will not be used in this study, which only concerns concepts of the past demonstrably current among the Norse before *c.*1050[2]

But was there one? Here there is an initial difficulty in the view that 'the modern conceptual categories of past, present and future were completely unknown to medieval people, who were in many ways without history... there was a ritual perception in which the past was present in the present. In this respect there was no difference between past and present'.[3] Presumably the reference is not to literate medieval people, who had learned about time from the bible, or from St Augustine, but to those who repeated the same rituals of song, dance, and sacrifice every year, so as to blur the distinction.

They did what they had done, and would do; therefore 'Germanic culture was dominated by its conception of its own past', which was all that actually happened. Bauschatz illustrated this statement with a diagram in which the non-past (present and future) is a stream constantly rushing into a box, or well, labelled PAST; a 'binary time-system' of past and non-past, like an ever-rolling stream which cannot bear all its sons away because it rolls in a circle. In support of this idea, he pointed out that there is no future inflexion in Germanic verbs: in Old Norse, *skulu* (need to), *vil* (want to) or *munu* (have a mind to) are added to the verb 'to love' to translate the plain *amabo*, 'I will love'.[4] Others prefer to use Snorri's prose Edda to construct an Icelandic world-view in which time is the cosmic ash-tree Yggdrasill, a vertical suspended in the horizontal created by tensions between the gods and giants, and rooted in a well or spring tended by women called Norns, who by the thirteenth century were named Past, Present and Future (*Urðr, Verdandi, Skuld*) – probably a recent rationalization. This tree occurs in the Prophecy of the Seeress (Vǫluspa) in different aspects, from seed to tremulous age, and was there interpreted by Steinsland as 'the image that expresses the process the poet wanted to describe: history'. The seeress certainly speaks of the passing of time in many ways, but not once of what we call history; the history of mankind. It is all about gods, monsters and giants, and therefore relevant to this chapter only in so far as people envisaged history as myth. Which they did, up to a point (see p. 241); but the

---

2 For a concise summary of the Germanic concept see Gutenbrunner in GEDI 1986, 173–97, and Jochens 1996, ch. 1, applies it to Iceland.
3 Carelli in VIPA (1997), 397; compare Bradley 1987 and Malmer 'On Objectivity and Actualism in Archaeology', CSA, v (1997), 13.
4 Bauschatz 1982, 180–7; and see Poole 1991, 147 on the historic present and auxiliary *mun* in *Darraðarljóð*.

kings mentioned on the Rök stone were not gods or giants, and the idea of a human past will bear investigation first, as discernable in other kinds of evidence. Gods go in and out of human time in most mythologies, and the fusion of past, present and future makes sense for their careers, whether finite or infinite; less so for mortals, who in the viking age knew a past of MOGMINNI, a present of activity captured in the vivid diction of verse, and a future in this world as fame, in the next as a better or worse or similar life, but different; at least, some of that is true for some of them. Where and how did they find their past?

Sagas

Not in sagas, which survive as written prose texts with verse embellishments written between the 1170s and the fifteenth century for the amusement of educated Icelanders, male and female, or for the Norwegian court. They concern a range of subjects and episodes, from the creation of the world (*Veraldar saga, c.*1189) to the reign of king Magnus Hákonarson of Norway (1263–80) and those about the pre-viking age mainly concern Jewish, Greek and Roman antiquity, the past of learned catholics. The saga versions of viking-age events, often detailed and apparently realistic read more like historical novels than any sort of narrative Guthrum or Sweyn Forkbeard may have listened to in that period. They were written with great skill for a different audience, in a different world, and to claim that they 'incorporate' ancient techniques of narrative, heroic echoes, syncretic truth etc.[5] is beside the point; the concerns of thirteenth-century Icelandic authors were tied closely to thirteenth-century priorities, not to the accurate representation of what had seemed important four hundred years back. Comparison between different versions of the same saga in different MSS, or between different sagas on the same topics (as with those in Morkinskinna, Fagrskinna and Heimskringla on Norwegian kings) show how inventive and selective these writers were, and how seldom dependent on a firm oral tradition like that behind the Rök stone inscription, above. A good example is *Ragnars saga loðbrókar*, written perhaps *c.*1230 about the life and family of a hero with hairy breeches who was supposed to have lived in the

---

5 For the 'saga mind' see Steblin-Kamensky 1973 and Hallberg in MS, vii (1974), and for the unhistorical character of historical sagas Durrenberger 1992 and Clunies Ross 1998, 13 and 50: 'Literature became history for them'; Sigurðsson 1993 and Jochens 1996 continue to mine thirteenth-century texts for tenth-century archetypes. Mundal deals with the complexity of the VA–saga connexion in TROG (1987), 15–25. Fix on variation between MSS is in NOWELE xxxi, 105.

ninth century and had already been incorporated, at length, into the Danish history of Saxo Grammaticus; he survives as a pseudo-historical character to this day.[6]

An analysis of the evidence by McTurk (1991) has revealed Ragnar to be a wholly synthetic figure, made up of five elements:

1 a pirate chief called Ragnar who died after raiding Paris in 845 and was remembered in the abbey of S. Germain-des-Près.
2 *Lothkona* or *Lodbroka*, a female spirit of some kind; or possibly the human mother of
3 a family of marauders active in Britain and Francia in the 860s and 70s, and known by *c.*1100 as the 'sons of Lothroc';
4 stock episodes of dragon-slaying and seduction, applicable to any hero;
5 an actual invasion of Northumbria in 867, when king Ella died:
6 death in a snake-pit, like Gunnar's in the Volsung stories.[7]

Put all these together, add various imperial conquests, law-codes and political conflicts, and the result is the great Danish king Regnerus of Saxo's ninth book; put them together another way, without so much politics, and the result is Ragnar's saga. In neither case is there any viking-age Nordic tradition behind them: the sources are Norman historians, Icelandic pedigree-fakers, stories about other people, and one remarkable poetic soliloquy called *Krákumál*, composed by a late twelfth-century Icelander in a spirit of heroic revival: Ragnar himself, writhing in the Northumbrian snake-pit, speaks of his many achievements in war, and of his contempt for death and confidence in the vengeance of his sons. This became the crucial text for the invention of the viking ethos in the eighteenth century; it may not have been read by the author of the saga, but they thought along the same lines, to celebrate an imaginary past in a modern idiom. The point has been hammered home by too many text-critics to need further emphasis here: the post-conversion date and character of the 'antiquity-sagas' (*fornaldursǫgur*) however pagan in subject and treatment they may seem, rule them out as sources for what was in the minds of real pagans, and real converts of the viking age. This also true of the

---

6 For example, Smyth 1977, 1–53.
7 McTurk's arguments are summarized in MESCA, 519–20; the female Lothbrok appears in graffiti among the Maeshowe runes of *c.*1150, some of which are facetious (Barnes 1993, 353, 58, 62), and she may be no more accurately gendered than MS BATMAN on a lavatory wall. She was certainly a He to William of Jumièges in the 1060s, and *Lothkona* seems to be a very dubious deduction from a Swedish place-name; Hairy-breeches has inspired many such, as McTurk shows.

saga-narratives of the conversion itself; they follow a five-step, predetermined plan, which a large christian literature had established as appropriate – not regardless of what actually happened, since the events of 990–1030 in Iceland and Norway must have left many memories behind, but shaping it to the pastoral and political needs of the twelfth and thirteenth centuries.[8] These tales belong to the category known as Icelanders' Sagas, which include those best known to the outside world: Njal's saga, Grettir's, and *Laxdæla*, and are usually taken to be fictions woven round the memories or names of people who actually lived, rather than oral traditions[8]

Epic Verse

Epic verse is the usual history of warrior societies, and it would be reasonable to assume that long poems about heroes in action would have been current in Scandinavia during the viking age, as entertainment for the diners in the long halls. The English author of Beowulf certainly thought so, when he made a Danish thane compose a 'skilful narrative' of the hero's fight with the monster Grendel, and added the story of Sigemund the dragon-slayer; later the Danish revellers fall silent, for a poem about Hengest and Finn and more fighting. This tale of tales has been made to stand for heroic culture of the pre-conversion period, both in Britain and in Scandinavia, although it comes from a literate christian world and is consciously distanced from the old days. What the Norse actually listened to then can only be reconstructed, not with confidence, from texts much more modern than *Beowulf*, of which the 'Battle of the Goths and the Huns' in Hervara Saga was long considered the most archaic,

8 The case for their representing a historical genre going back two centuries or more has recently been re-stated, on the grounds that (1) sagas by different authors often deal with the same characters, (2) the accuracy of family traditions was guaranteed by the critical sense of the audience, (3) the survival of such traditions met the need to justify inherited wealth. Sigurðsson 1999, 25–35 develops this argument, which is helped by the proposition that social conditions in the VA and in thirteenth-century Iceland were not that different. So: 'it is much more difficult to argue that a group of authors living in the thirteenth century agreed to invent a glorious past for the Icelanders living in the period 870–1030...'; not that difficult, see below. Even if these points were taken, they hardly affect the question of what sort of historical outlook those early Icelanders had. On the conversion narratives see Weber 1981 and 1986 and in TROG (1988), 95–141 (in English); on the sagas about Icelanders Olason 1998. As for sagas about historical Norwegian kings, Krag (1998) demonstrates the uncritical way the verse and prose of the subsequent century were compiled *c*.1220 to form histories of Harald Hardrada (1046–66).

because of its *fornyrðislag* metre[9]: 'old-story-metre'. But metres have long lives, and all that can be deduced of this fragment, as of the many fine latin verses which Saxo Grammaticus attributed to the ancient Danes, but composed himself, is that they are about epic events which may have been of interest to the pagan Norse, or not. The Eddic poems are not epic; they consist of episodes and dialogues and references to stories which they never tell. These poets dramatize, soliloquize, itemize, allude, condense, improvise and avoid straightforward narrative. Since they refer to them, the old stories were there; but what form they had once taken is unclear, and need not have been tied to any one metre, or genre.[10] If the subjects of the Eddic poems represent some of the subjects of viking-age oral tradition, then it appears that much of their past was indeed a foreign country. It was a land-mass bounded by the Seine, the North Sea, the Baltic, the Dnieper, the Black Sea, the Danube, the Alps and the Rhone: the theatre for the operations of Sigurd the Dragon-slayer, Brynhildr the Valkyrie, Gunnar the Giukung and Atli the Buðlung, and other figures remotely connected with the wars of the Franks, Burgundians, Goths and Huns of long ago. The connection seems to have been the need felt by kings for glorious ancestors who would mean something to the neighbours they hoped to impress, Frankish, German, and Anglo-Saxon rulers of the viking and subsequent ages; highlights of the past lifted in the same spirit as the consumer-durables of the present. Just as the *Beowulf* poet adopted a Nordic past for his English audience, already quite at home among the ancient Jews and Greeks and Romans and Early Christians, and not all confined to the 'national' past dished up to some readers in the Anglo-Saxon chronicle so the Norse acquired epic ancestors from abroad, to tone up the days of old. This tendency was attested by the appearance of king Theodoric on the Rök stone, and may have begun even before the viking age; it certainly continued long after, while epics about Nordic heroes flourished overseas (Havelock, Ogier the Dane, Rollo) but tended to appear somewhat diminished and dulled in the written texts, or were altogether forgotten, like the kings of Sea-land on the Rök stone, and Heremod, and doers of the deeds which Saxo thought were inscribed on indecipherable boulders.

9   Pritsak's convenient summary of the poem and its problems is in MESCA, 286–7; it was translated by C. Tolkien in *Saga Heiðreks konungs in vitra; The Saga of King Heidrek the Wise* (London 1960).
10   Prose or verse? solo or duet? Some were praised to the music of the harp, as in *Edda* (Deutsche Harmonia Mundi : DHM 0 5472 77381), and the case for chant and drama is put by Gunnell in CONIL 82–100; but no VA harps have yet been found, and no later texts contain verses made for singing. Some Eddic poems (Skirnismal, Helgi poems, Fafnir's Lay) could be sung as dialogue.

Myth

Myth occupies the past more comfortably than history, since it is not
dependent on the memory of actual events and can be expanded or
contracted to occupy any vacant space left by the perception of
immediate surroundings. Snorri was very good at this: 'Gangleri
spoke: What were things like before generations came to be and the
human race was multiplied? Then spoke High...' (SnE trans.
Faulkes, 10) and Just-as-High and Third, with the myths of Ginnun-
gagap, Muspell and Ymir, the first man. The freedom of mythology
has not been allowed to pass unchallenged in these regions, by those
who think it reflects historical events of the remote past: the coming
of Indo-European pastoralists who conquered native agrarians is one
imaginable stimulant of the myth of two divine races, Æsir and
Vanir, and some other tool-using immigrants could have sunk their
arrival into the myth of gods and giants locked in perpetual opposition. A 'new upper class' has been found rising in the fifth and sixth
century, with anthropomorphic gods and goddesses pushing older
divinities (land-spirits, disir, elves etc.) into the back-seats they
occupy in later versions of Nordic mythology.[11] Such speculation
has been fermenting for the last 300 years, but the liquor is tainted,
because the ingredients depend too heavily on Snorri's one thirteenth
century compendium of myths, and on other post-conversion adaptations of what pagans believed. The Gotland picture-stones of the
eighth and ninth centuries give a more authentic idea of that mythology on that island; some 12 of the carved scenes can be related to
later written versions of myths or legends, but nine others cannot.
One stone, Ardre viii, carries seven episodes: Thor's fishing and
hook-baiting, Loki's capture and binding, creation, Völund's revenge,
and the story of Sigmund and Sinfjotli. If this stone had been lost,
like many others, the majority of these stones would be unintelligible.[12]
   The origin-myths of tribes and peoples form a special category to
our way of thinking, a bridge from myth towards, if not into history,
but that is not how they seem in oral cultures which do not separate
things in this way. So in the eighth century, old men told how the

11   On which, Motz ANF, xcix (1984) and *contra* Mundal 1990 and Steinsland
WOO 1986 ('Giants as Recipents of Cult') and Kroesen 1996; Nielsen in HØKO
(1991), 261 for the upper- and lower-class religions theory; Brown 1963 for myths
reflecting a historical invasion of Odinists, and Kroesen 1997 for the Valkyries as
indigenous collaborators in the conquest.
12   Althaus 1993, appendix 1 for list of subjects. A lost myth is on this cover.

Lombards (Langobards) had got their name from a practical joke played by Woden's wife on her husband as they lay in bed, or from a trick by which Lombard women made their hair look like long beards; and the ethnogeneses of the Norse were presumably more like that than elaborate fictions such as were later composed and written down in *Hversu Noregr byggðisk, Ynglinga Saga* and *The Chronicle of Lejre*. Even the wonderful Gotland genesis in *Guta Saga*, which incorporates all an ethnologist or social anthropologists could want of archaic thought, is couched in the language of the thirteenth – fourteenth century, and will hardly do as a relic of the viking-age.[13] The dominance of myth in ideas about the past among the Norse must be taken on credit, as a strong probability, rather than the richly-documented field of research which is sometimes the meat of well-attended conferences. What they actually discuss is the intellectual world of the twelfth – fifteenth centuries. When it comes to the human past, the only relevant texts are, as usual, the rune-stones and the scaldic verse.

Scaldic Verse

Scaldic verse hints at contemporary events, without much narrating, and with little reference to the remoter past, except in a sort of shorthand. A famous loose half-stanza about 'cutting eagle on Ella's back' has been interpreted as a reference to the conquest of York in 867 by a poet egging on Sweyn Forkbeard or Canute to conquer England; but almost any context will do, since Ella became a name synonymous with any English or other ruler. The *Liðsmannaflokkr* verses (*c.*1020) celebrate the conquest of England by Canute and earl Eric in 1015–16, and recall the wars of the previous decade; which is the usual attention-span of the praise poems, the battle honours of a single career.[14] There was room for a place-name, a personal or ethnic name, a combat-cliché, and another comment in parenthesis; no extended comparisons with the ancient heroes, or descriptive sequence.

Canute, you made out to Fljóta
(Bold guard glided over sea

13 Foulke 1906, 16–18 and notes for Langobard origins in Paul the Deacon's *History of the Lombards: Guta Saga* was translated into French by Maillefer in EG, xl (1985), 131–40, and ed. H. Pipping, Copenhagen 1905–7. See Blomkvist and Jackson 1999 for a pan-Germanic or Indo-European analysis.
14 'to recapture the moment of triumph in which a hero is illumined by glory, the end and justification of his life': Frank, cited by Lindow 1982, 106; Poole 1991, 86–115 on historicity, and Townend 2003 on gaps in scaldic memory.

Quick-to-resent, battle's flash)
Hard-mailed ship push

is how Hallvarðr told of the embarcation of the armada of 1015;
Fljóta was the Humber. The history is not so much in the verse, as in
what 'men say' already; as in the second strophe of Hallfreðr's elegy
on Olaf Tryggvason (*c*.999)

> *That speech shall be mentioned, that men say the active warrior spoke*
> *to his lads at the weapon-vituperation: the warrior forbade his lads to*
> *think of flight: bold words of the chief will live.*

So he told his men not to run away; hardly memorable as it stands,
but perhaps a reference to a more pointed Trafalgar-signal story, such
as the sagas later supplied.

In time – after an example apparently set inexpertly by the author
of the short Norwegian history called *Ágrip* (*c*.1190) – such verses
would become the 'documentation' of historical narratives, or the
corroborative footnotes; but during the viking age it seems that they
stood apart from narratives, whether prose or verse. Their purpose
was to encapsulate and circulate glory recently won.[15]

Genealogy

Genealogy, 'the history of the parvenu'[16] claimed the past for the
present in all societies, none more than Iceland in the twelfth century,
where the colonial magnates and clerics competed in terms of ancestry, and spun lineages which were later adopted or adapted in Scandinavia, to honour royal and other dynasties. But there is no reason
to assume that the viking-age Norse saw ancestry in the same way as
those who claimed to be descended from them; parentage and
immediate kinship are proclaimed by the rune-stones, very rarely
lineage. Skalds refer to chiefs by names which imply connexions
with the heroic past: Skjoldung, Buðlung, Yngling, and from these

---

15 Rather than preserving and modifying tradition, like the Irish poets described by
Richter (1994, 196 and 214) as 'the hinges on which society turned'; see also E.
Gurevich 1996, 64, on this contrast. See Jesch 2001, 217 on Olaf's words.

16 or 'an imaginative art', or 'metaphors for current situations and relationships'
(Ó Corráin, of the superabundant Irish pedigrees) or 'lists of names arranged in a
meaningful way' (Kleinschmidt 1999) or merely a 'chronological indicator' (Sigurðsson 1999, 27); for Norse descents see Faulkes 'Descent from the gods', MS, xi (1978/
9), Joan Turville-Petre 'On Ynglingatal', MS, xi (1978–9), and P. Sawyer on 'The
Background of Ynglingasaga' in Supphellen 1992, 271–5.

names genealogies were later to be fabricated. In the tenth century, they seem only to have been ways of saying 'ruler of high descent', and were virtually interchangeable.

This would change, with the influence of biblical, Anglo-Saxon and Irish models of linear genealogy; also with the fixing of freehold inheritance claims by descent from a common ancestor, as in the seven generation lineage on the Malsta stone in Hälsingland (Sweden) and the six generations cut on to the Sandsjö stone in Småland, both eleventh century. Icelanders had no rune-stones, but from the twelfth century they had a roll of real and imaginary ancestors in Landnámabók, and rights to farms and chieftaincies which could be defended at law by the recital of male lineages going back to the supposed first possessor. This practice could not have started for some generations after the settlement, and there is no reason to assume that 'most Norwegian settlers (in Iceland) carried long lists of forefathers in their mental baggage'[17] even if they could remember names out of which such lists would eventually be constructed by their descendants. Such as the author of the thirteenth–fourteenth-century 'Lay of Hyndla' (*Hyndluljóð*), in which the names of over seventy imaginary rulers and other beings are arranged into twelve or more descents by a giantess, in order to enlighten Freyja's lover Ottar the Foolish and enable him to win an inheritance from one Angantýr. No ordinary inheritance-suit would involve a genealogical quiz on this scale, but the idea may come from the law-courts, and the pedigree-faking which went on there.

By contrast, the ancestries of the period before *c*.1000 seem to have been asserted by recurrent names and name-elements within the family, and by retroactive adoptions of heroes and heroic dynasties, or previous rulers or owners (see Appendix A).

Pedigrees can function in many ways: to reveal real family ties, to reveal social status, to organize the past, to justify claims to territory, to link humans and gods, to create imaginary cousinhoods in the present, to repair a lack of suitable ancestors – these are seven of the commonest, which in most medieval societies worked most comfortably through lists of names. The Anglo-Saxon genealogical texts, as well as the Irish and the Welsh, performed all these duties admirably; except the first, which was better left to the older women's curiosity. Over the North Sea, the same functions had to be carried out by

---

17 Jochens 1999, 91, Mitchell 1991, 121–6, and Clunies Ross 1998, ch. 7 discuss the pedigree mania of the Icelanders, and Meulengracht Sørensen (1993, 213) the fixing of social status thereby. Sigurðsson (1999, 29) suggests that the dependence of ownership on descent guaranteed the accuracy of such records. A glance at any old *Burke's Peerage* suggests otherwise.

other means than the row or column of names written on vellum, and there is no clear indication of what these means were. Three have been suggested:

1   By memorizing or inventing lines of male ancestors in which each generation becomes connected with an episode and forms what Gurevich calls 'kinship-time';[18] which would explain the inscription on the Rök stone in so far as it is intelligible, but need not. Theodoric, the king in the second episode, lived

NINE MEN-AGES AGO

but there is no legible claim that he was an ancestor of Væmoð, for whom this was written. All the later lineages (*langfeðgatal*) are derived from written sources or new-made, so that if this tradition had existed it had been lost or discarded in favour of more attractive foreign models.

2   By affiliating or annexing the living to supernatural beings; not by descent from Odin or Woden, but by direct initiation into an Odin cult or Thor priesthood, or by symbolic marriage to a local goddess or giantess. This kind of sublimated genealogy has been detected in the man-woman icons stamped on pre-viking bracteates or goldgubber, and in one interpretation of the Rök inscription, as recording the reception of Væmod as a son of Thor, consecrated by his natural mother.[19] Again, the evidence is late and thin, mostly read back from origin legends and royal pedigrees of the twelfth and thirteenth centuries.

3   By deriving families from animals: a favourite topic of anthropology, with examples among Amerindian and African clans. Saxo derived the current (*c.*1215) Danish royal family from a bear, in the male line, and the earlier *Gesta Herewardi* and *Vita et Passio Waldevi* tell of bear-ancestry for the kings of Norway and Sigurd the Danish earl of Northumberland;[20] hints used to support theories of extensive animal-totemism among early Germanic peoples, with representations of fighting or gripping beasts on Migration-Age and

18   Gurevich 1969 argued that chronology and genealogy were merged into 'kinship time', so that *ǫld* could mean time, age, period or people; Whaley 1991, 353 adds the attractive idea that nicknames were remembered with the stories of why they were given. But the evidence is all post-conversion.
19   Grønvik's proposition in ANF, cv (1990); he also claimed that Hakon jarl's epithet 'offspring of Odin' (*Yggs niðr*: Vellekla 20) implied a similar cult-affiliation in tenth-century Norway.
20   See note in Saxo trans., i, 190. Bronze-Age beliefs in the descent of all humans from elks have been deduced by Bolin (1999, 152–4) from Swedish rock carvings.

Viking-Age metalwork as circumstantial evidence. Bears, wolves and eagles are fequently mentioned in viking-age and subsequent poetry, but never as ancestors, any more than pigs, deer or goats; leaders are called *jǫfurr*, which meant boar in Old English (*eofor*), but not in viking-age verse. Loki was made pregnant by a stallion, but no-one claimed descent from him.

These alternative genealogies are shadows, to fill the space left vacant once the Icelandic texts have been ousted.

Landscape

Landscape was the best record of the past, as Saxo Grammaticus understood in the thirteenth century,[21] when it was already usual to connect mounds, natural and artificial, with ancient kings; flat spaces with ancient battles; traces of cultivation and overgrown clearances with extinct populations; rocks with giants; unusual rock formations and fissures with lost writing; treasure troves with dead heroes and dragons; ruins with fabulous palaces. This way of thinking used to be called 'pre-scientific', as distinct from the 'science' of archaeology and settlement history; but with the recent recognition of 'metaphorical thinking', as the means by which past generations interpreted their environments, and of archaeology as equally subjective, the separation is less clear cut. Folklore and science intersect; they are cousins.[22] How viking-age people read the past from landscapes cannot be deduced from Saxo, or Snorri, or folklore, only from the evidence of how they used what they found; which stands out in three ways:

1 By *appropriation*; as with Ales Stenar, on Kaseberga ridge in SE Scania, which overlook the sea. These form the largest and most visible ship-setting of upright stones in the North, and have become a sort of cult-site for tourists; they were set up in this period on an older sacred area, with some of the Bronze Age stones reused, for no obvious purpose. Harald Bluetooth razed the great Jelling ship-setting, built a mound on a Bronze Age tumulus, then appropriated it for christianity with a church built to the south, and a corresponding

21 SG (FD) i; 7, 9, 14, 101 (Hamlet's mound), 75 (Balder's), 261–2 (cairns and furrows in re-grown woods), 252.
22 On metaphorical thinking see Johansen 1996 and 1997, and Barrett and Hey-gardt 'Man the Interpreter' CSA viii, 2000. Barrett claims that 'the construction of monuments is always an interpretation of a pre-existing world' rather than 'a way of characterizing a particular period' (*Archaeologies of Landscape*, ed. Ashmore and Knapp, Oxford, 1999, 22).

mound exactly equidistant from the church along a north–south axis. On the crest of a hill near Vålsta in Södermanland (south-west) stands a rune-stone rising from a cairn of large boulders to commemorate Osmund, Rörik's son, who died in the eleventh century.

THE CAIRN WAS RAISED FOR RÖRIK'S SON

says the inscription. But it wasn't; the stones were piled at least 2000 years earlier, like others of that type.[23] Holy sites, whether cemeteries or hills or mounds were reused throughout the north; just as, in Blair's hypothesis, Angles and Saxons took over Romano-British sacred enclosures and reconsecrated them with pillars and fences. Places thought to have been seats of power, or close to the divine, were put to use and given histories accordingly.

2 By *imitation*; as with the large new tumuli, wood-lined burial chambers, horse or wagon burials, weapon and ornament burials which repeat and improve on patterns going back to the later Bronze Age, at least in southern Scandinavia. Viking-age chiefs looked back at Vendel chiefs who looked back at their precursors, for the way to be remembered. There are thirty-five Bronze Age ship-settings to set the trend for 950 more over the next 2000 years: new claims to land and luck announced in monumental mime.

3 By *rejection, or slighting*; as in the breaks in burial patterns over the first millennium: from wetlands to dry land (*c*.300–*c*.400), from more to less elaborate interments (*c*.750–850); with the custom of unaccompanied burial near churches not becoming general until the twelfth century in most of Scandinavia. The move from bog burial and cult was never total, but it marked a general relocation of the sacred to sites nearer the seats of social power,[24] and some scholars are tempted to find an echo of this shift in the violence and tension between families of gods and giants in the later Nordic myths; pointless conjecture, because there is no way of testing it. Gods without cults – Loki, Heimdall, Forseti et al. – had a thousand years in which to lose them before anyone wrote down their names. Nevertheless, some of the past was less acceptable to the

---

23 See Burström 1994 and 1996, and Pedersen 1997, 126, for other mounds in Jutland (Hald) over neolithic and bronze age burials, and for continuous use as burial place and residence over 2000 years Lejre in Zealand (Dk) is a good case; Dünhof 1997 reviews evidence for connexion with dead, also Reichert in RUQUIF 1998, 74–6. For ship-settings, Roslund in *Fornvännen* 1995, 139–45.
24 Fabech ('Sakrale pladser', SANA 1992) emphasizes the permanence of this shift, through the conversion to modern times; and see Pedersen 1997a and b on burials connected with that conversion.

Norse, and may account for some of the taboos over places and people which survived into modern times.

Apparently more obvious rejections took place overseas, in land-scapes already rich in imagined pasts, both oral and written: the fabric of christianity, buildings and monuments and treasures was damaged or desecrated all over the British Isles and Northern France in the ninth century (the loss cannot be quantified) and had to be patiently and selectively repaired after that. But the repairs took place and connected the past to the post-viking present architec-turally and in words; the great revivals of Rouen, St Wandrille, Jumièges, York and Durham and the surprisingly frequent survival of pre-viking-age building or stonework in eastern England suggest that the devastations were acts of pillage and war rather than attempts to efface the christian past.[25] Whether the great heathen burial at Repton was meant to desecrate or share the holiness of of the Mercian minster remains uncertain; St Wystan's church was defiled, but one chief and many skeletons were carefully stacked in a small chapel or bone-house to the west, and others decently laid out round the east end.

By these means, some Norsemen constructed pasts for themselves and others which were not coherent or made to fit any particular cosmic time-scheme. The evidence is mostly lost, but by probing what isn't, we can find at least three different pre-christian uses of history.

1 *Publishing land right*: monumentally in the rune-stones, and per-haps by recitation in meetings and at feasts, to judge from the later Icelandic custom. Not a cue for long pedigrees, but only for the minimum ancestry needed for hereditary tenure; what that was, before the twelfth century, is unknown.

2 *Reinforcing authority*: asserting links with gods, heroes, primeval rulers, giants, local spirits, animals, through tales, ceremonies, sym-bols, burials, buildings and choice of sites.[26] Not only rulers but all with households to manage could exploit these 'mechanisms', and continued to do so after the conversions with the added resources of book-culture. The poem *Rígsthula* (translated as The List Of Rig by Larrington in PE 246–52) is an example of how the new learning

25 Contra Foot 1999, 189–92, who stresses the blanking of the Anglian memory after the dispersal of religious communities and record keepers.

26 Ritual re-enactments and woven or carved scenes were frequent reminders of past times. The early poems about scenes on shields (Thjoðolfr's *Haustlǫng*, Bragi's *Ragnarsdrápa*) tell of gods and myths, rather than epic heroes, and the hangings Ulfr Uggason described in *Húsdrápa* were no different.

could explain economic inequality, rank, servitude, gender differences and the origins of the Danish kingdom in one fable of 50? stanzas, in which, as York Powell said (CPB i 516): 'it is interesting to note how the *spiritual life is confined to the gentlefolks*'. What the old learning was, on this topic, is not apparent from the pre-christian sources.[27] That historical justification was needed, both for political and for domestic authority, may be assumed, or deduced from the copying of foreign models (see next chapter) and from allusions to legendary and mythical figures in the skaldic verse. Eyvindr Finnsson the Plagiarist left the best evidence, in the fragments of his 'Enumeration of the Hálogalanders' (*Háleygjatal*), a poem on the ancestors of Hákon Jarl preserved by Snorri, in which *his descent in pot-liquid of gallows-cargo* (poetry, the hanged Odin's liquid) *we trace to gods* (trans. Faulkes, SnE, 72) possibly in 27 generations, going back to Odin and the giantess Skaði.[28] Hakon had risen to predominance over Norway in the 970s, and the poet offered him this *stone bridge* to carry his fame; either imitating, or setting an example to the rival chiefs who were trying to link themselves with the legendary Ynglingar rulers of the Swedes, and so to Frey-Njorð, another god. This annexation of convenient pasts was not peculiar to the Norse; their contemporaries on the continent and in the west were busy appropriating Troy, Rome, Scythia, Egypt, Israel and Scandinavia itself as ancestral homelands. The Norse did it without the benefit of book-learning, over a range of connections which we can only grasp in part, where they concern rulers named in the surviving verse.
3   *Explaining*: the landscape and sea-scape, the relics of past civilizations, the lie of settlements nowadays. The place-names, and what survives of local lore in medieval literature and later collections of popular tradition are all that is left of this elementary historification. As these stories change with each generation, the versions we have reflect viking-age tales only faintly, at best; and the place-names carry no stories with them, as a rule.

---

27 Any more than among the Irish, since there are none; see Ó Corráin, 'Irish Origin Legends and Genealogy' in *History and Heroic Tale*, ed. Tore Nyberg, Odense 1985.
28 Most of *Háleygjatal* is lost; the 27 generations are deduced from a thirteenth-century pedigree of the Hladir earls, which matches the 27 of Ynglingatal, and may owe more to that than to Eyvinðr's verses; see Marold in MESCA, 175–6.

11

Present

Have pity on this sinner, nor hold against me my previous disrespect nor the cruelty committed against you, unjustly and evilly, by my forbears. I confess you to be a most powerful friend of the eternal king, and henceforward for as long as I live I appoint you my advocate.

(Prayer of king Canute to St Elphege of Canterbury when he returned the murdered archbishop to his cathedral on 15 June 1023; according to the *Historia de Translatione* by Osbern. (ed., Wharton, ii, 143–47)

Canute's bloodthirsty and humiliating conquest of the English had turned out well for some, but needed a line drawn after it, to separate the bad times from the good, the viking from the virtuous Dane. So a Canterbury monk writes these lines for him, long after his death, and creates a historic moment to everybody's taste. The feelings of the dead about their day-to-day existences are hard to imagine, and easy to prescribe; very easy, it seems, in the case of the old Norse. Some of these prescriptions need examining.

Cosmic Order

Once upon a time, it was believed that all true Germanic peoples shared an outlook based on three concepts[1] (possibly four), and that with this outlook the Norsemen, among others of the right language-group, faced the world in a resourceful and spiritually satisfying manner for over a thousand years until they were slowly demoralized

---

1 Grønbech defined these as the inviolable peace between kinsmen, the maintenance of family honour at any cost, and the necessity of good fortune as an aspect of personality. *The Culture of the Teutons* distils these from a wide range of sources. R.L.M. Derolez *Götter und Mythen der Germanen* (1974) has yet to be translated.

or reeducated by christianity, the state, feudalism etc. Mythological-anthropological students filled in the background of these lives with a cosmos in which the Nordic present was squashed into a layer-cake: middle-earth, between upper and lower worlds, held together by the sacred tree and the coil of a world-serpent, and timed by an inexor-able destiny, represented by three Norns or one Urðr. This was the cosmic confection of Snorri eloquently upgraded into a philosophy by Carlyle (taking his cue from German authors), in the first of his *Lectures on Heroes* delivered in 1840. For him, it was a gospel of change: the consummation of centuries of Scandinavian intellectual development, representing 'the eager, inarticulate uninstructed Mind of the whole Norse people'. He is not much read nowadays, but this idea of pan-Nordic intellectual evolution lives on, despite protests.

Clunies Ross has appealed for 'much greater fluidity in the con-ceptualization of mythic space in medieval Scandinavian texts'[2] and has noted that even in the systematizing thirteenth century they do not really present a consistent view of the number of worlds, their geography, their ethnography, and the roles of their inhabitants. There is every reason to conclude that the surrounding world appeared even more incoherent in the viking age when these percep-tions hung on competing cults. Others argue that the search for underlying themes and 'blocks of cultural understanding' in that period is misconceived. In the few early poems the myths seem 'fragmentary enigmatic and changeable', not part of an agreed the-ology or cosmology. And others go further, and equate changing religious beliefs with changing social orders; society was the 'plausi-bility structure' of religion, and so by changing, changed it. Durkheim's glib equation frees the Norse from obedience to a rigid outlook on the world prescribed by tradition, in exchange for the equally dogmatic subjection of belief to social developments artifi-cially separated from religion and promoted above it.[3]

This separation is not found in a world where the supports of material life (agriculture, war, reproduction, transport) were seen to rest on the right kind of contact with other worlds, and other beings; it should not be applied here. At some point in the Roman period, or earlier, Germanic tribes began to pin hopes on personalized gods and goddesses, and ceased to offer wealth to the guardians of meres,

---

2 Clunies Ross 1992, and 1994, 51; see Lindow in ONIL, 49–52 for a résumé of current theories of pagan cosmology as advanced by Steblin-Kamensky, Gurevich, Meletinsky, Petruchkin.

3 See Nilsson 1992b, Solli 1996, 190, and Meulengracht Sørensen in OXVIK, 208; for the glib equation, P.L. Berger *The Sacred Canopy* (New York 1968), 47–8 will do, but for Durkheim, see his *The Elementary Forms of the Religious Life* (London 1915) and W.S.F. Pickering *Durkheim on Religion* (London 1975).

rivers and bogs. In the Migration period big halls became cult-centres, and remained so, in effect, through the conversion to christianity, when the landowners built the first churches near their own houses. The power of these people clearly affected the where and how of religious worship, but its impact on belief is lost beyond recovery; since this took different forms in different terrains, different social strata and different houses, perhaps between different sexes and individuals as well, the chance of a straight correlation between social and religious development is slight, and of a uniform pagan cosmology at any time, non-existent.

Ethics

Ethics are a different matter; they can transcend cultural and geographical boundaries, and afflict huge multitudes with the same ideas of right and wrong. It is, or was, commonly believed that viking-age ethics were contained in a thirteenth-century collection of proverbs and maxims attributed to Odin: *Hávamál*, or 'The Utterance of Him on High' published in Latin 1665, and known to some English readers since then in various versions.[4] A recent study defines this ethos as 'getting by with a dry skin'; expressed from prudential, unheroic and tedious gems such as:

> *To his friend a man should be a friend*
> *And to his friend's friend too;*
> *But a friend no man should be*
> *To the friend of his enemy.*

The taste for proverbial philosophy is perennial, but avid in the twelfth century when this collection was made: in England it might have been attributed to king Alfred, in Paris to Cato. The most famous stanza, no. 77, would pass anywhere:

> *Cattle die, kinsmen die*
> *The self must also die;*
> *I know one thing which never dies:*
> *The reputation of each dead man.*

If that was Nordic ethics, so was Ecclesiasticus and the Analects of Confucius; but as Amory has pointed out 'the equation of paganism

---

4   The one cited here is Larrington's, PEd, and see Larrington 1993, 22. On the dating of Hávamál: Evans 1989 and von See *Skandinavistik*, xvii, 1987, 133–4. On its later reception Wawn 1994 and on its debt to Solomon's wisdom Gislason in SAG, ii, 205–15.

with a specific code of ethics...is a scholarly fallacy of German and Scandinavian religious thought', and, he might have added, of social anthropology, social history and literary criticism all over the world. *Hávamál* was not an attempt to produce such a code, nor is there any sign that any one attempted this anywhere among the Norse at any time. From later Icelandic literature it appears that much importance was attached to *sómi* or *sœmð*, which (according to Lindow) meant 'the carrying out of proper actions in given social situations';[5] which would certainly separate the Icelanders from some advanced modern societies, but from none other in the last three millennia, at least. The word *siðr* covered the standards up to which they were expected to live, and it was extremely vague; it could mean custom commonly observed, or rarely, habit (personal or collective), and eventually religion or faith, as when the 'new siðr' (christianity) replaced the 'old siðr' (paganism); it slid between what you should do and what you normally did. Rigid rules of conformity would be difficult to enforce with words like that, and it has been suggested in chapter 1 that during the viking age the difficulty would have been greater; there was too much contact with foreign customs, habits, rules and laws; as in the English Danelaw, where king Edgar decreed 'that secular rights be in force among the Danes according to as good laws as they can best decide on', but at the same time king Edgar's new laws were 'to be common to all the nation, whether Englishmen, Danes, or Britons, in every province'. Meanwhile, the archbishop of York was confiscating land from the Anglo-Danish nobles of his province 'in compensation for illegal marriage', an act that would seem outrageous in Scandinavia before or after the conversion – and he a Dane himself, by descent. But it worked both ways: it was king Edgar, according to his obituary in the Chronicle, 'who did one ill-deed too greatly; he loved evil foreign customs and brought too firmly heathen manners within this land'; the sort of manners and customs complained of in the Old English letter to brother Edward, who was insulting English traditions 'since you dress in Danish fashion with bared necks and blinded eyes' (fringed and open-necked).[6] Dress, food, hairstyle and ethics were seldom seen as

---

5 Lindow 1975, 137, and Hastrup 1990, 73.
6 These documents are translated in EHD i: Edgar's Wihtbordestan code 2, i as no. 41, the York memoranda of Oskytel's acquisitions no. 114 and the brother Edward letter no 232, expurgated. The code known as 'Edward and Guthrum', which represents archbishop Wulfstan's programme for his Northumbrian diocese in the early eleventh century, put incestuous couples at the mercy of king and archbishop 'unless they make compensation...as the bishop shall prescribe'. This might take the form of a land-grant; but incestuous fornicators seem to have got off with a fine.

separable; the Danelaw was evidently a melting-pot which spilt over to the Wessex court in the west, and to Denmark in the east.

It has been claimed that here was a deep division between two incompatible systems. One in which gods were potent but not immortal or ethical, and could be scathingly satirized for their moral failings in a work like *Lokasenna* (probably twelfth century, but anticipated in the tenth by the verses disparaging Freyja as a bitch); the other in which ethics = religion = god, immortal and omnipotent and unique. This contrast was drawn between christianity and the polytheism of the ancient world, and was applied to the viking age by Paasche (*Møtet mellom hedendom og kristendom i Norden*); it would be valid in a theological debate conducted within guidelines drawn by the christian, or even a rationalist party, but not in a conflict of allegiances to old family friends. It is now more usual to credit the heathen (seen as a disparaging word by the more prissy historians of religion, as a source of pride by the less) with a concept of universe in which order (the gods) fights chaos (the giants), rather than good fighting evil. Good has to win in the end; but order and chaos are necessary to each other and their struggle will continue. So the christian and the pagan moral universes are equipoised. But they are not, because the christian one is well-attested by contemporary sources, and the pagan one is a twentieth-century deduction from a largely post-pagan mythology. Giants have been overworked by modern mythologers. Boyer took them to be an early attempt to personify natural forces, Motz as demoted gods from a pre-Germanic past, Dronke as enemies of the gods' power to regenerate themselves; but as Kroesen pointed out (ANF cxi 1996) they came in several shapes and sizes, and are shown leading far from chaotic lives; they marry, have families, social aspirations and reason. They were excluded from the society of gods, but one of them, Starkaðr, was able to lead a heroic life among men, and giantesses married royal ancestors. There is no justification for casting them as the negative pole in a binary universe, just because they live in the wild north and are continually assaulted and battered by Thor's hammer.

Ethics reinforced by religion were a speciality of the Anglo-Saxon kings and bishops who became lords of the Danelaw in the tenth century, and took money from those who broke the moral law as written and agreed. It does not follow that pagans followed custom uncontaminated by religion, or that christians were not mostly followers of custom rather than a religious ethic. How they interacted in England, Ireland and Normandy is not recorded in any detail, but there was evidently no head-on collision at ground level.

Over the North Sea, in the retinues of kings and chiefs, poets were celebrating an ethic fit for heroes; for them, life was conflict punctuated by drunken entertainment, and right and wrong were aspects of how far lord and man pleased or displeased each other. This moral oscillation turned on luck, mood, profit, loss and public opinion; it held sway in an exclusive world defined not only by wealth and military equipment but by the wit to know that

> *the tree of the flame of the storm of the paths of battle-beacons*

meant the man (tree) who carried the gleaming thing (flame) used in the fight (storm) to be expected in the direction of (paths) war-signals; which thing is a sword, and the man who carries it is a warrior.[7] Harsh fury towards foes, benign prodigality towards dependents are the poles of conduct in this verse, and its knowing audience teetered up and down the axis as long as raiding was in fashion. That code, as suggested previously (p. 16) for those people; others for others. Over there, there was no archbishop of York to bawl canon law at the gentry, and no legislating monarch to confuse matters with written codes and exhortations to do right as it was understood by learned men.

Law

The modern English word is an Anglo-Saxon loan of the Old Norse *lǫg*, which meant that which was laid down, or settled. Why borrow a word like this, from people like that, reputed lawless? And borrow it early, among the wreckage for which they were responsible, and let it pass as equivalent to time-honoured *riht* and *dom* and *æ*,[8] not reserving it for a law of the jungle, or a Dane-law? The questions come to mind because we tend to dissociate law from violence. They didn't; in Early Medieval societies it might interrupt violence or justify it, depending on circumstances, but the threat of force was always there, even God's vengeance in the case of moral laws. In these ways, the pagan Norse and the christian Anglo-Saxons were in agreement, and the consensus is written into the treaty agreed between kings Alfred and Guthrum at some date in the 880s. It depended on five common assumptions:

---

7 From the conclusion of Thórarinn's *Tǫgdrápa* on Canute, referring to the king himself; who gave 50 marks for it. Text: SkjD IB, 298–301, Kock, i, 151–2.

8 *Godes lage* was attributed to Moses in Athelstan's first code; *grið* (household security in Old Norse or truce) came to mean any kind of peace, even God's, in Old English: Fell 1982, 5 and Hofmann 1955, 150. See Fischer (A) 1989, 97–102, on this change. *Æ* was fading, anyway. See Wollman 1996 for English borrowing of ON words for injustice, oppression, discord, battle, and attack.

1 that each man shall have a legal value in silver, payable as compensation in cases of homicide to the victim's kin (A & G ii);
2 that the worth in silver shall depend on the status of the man: free, freedman, or slave (A & G iii);
3 that law-suits shall be decided by sworn testimony (like the treaties between Danes and Anglo-Saxons in the 870s, whether sworn on heathen rings (or swords) or christian relics;
4 that traders should be made to give hostages or warranty (A & G iv);
5 that he who cannot compensate those he injures is to be out-lawed: not in 'Alfred and Guthrum' but the word *utlah* appears in Edgar's reign and the custom of outlawry is mentioned in Ethelred's treaty with the army of 994. See above, 33–4.

These treaties between armies are not perfect representations of how law was understood in Scandinavia, but they are as near as we are likely to get, as there are no Nordic law-texts earlier than the twelfth century. Another way of filling the gap is to drive in a few of the sacred cows of Germanic legal history, and declare that Nordic law was 'sacred because instituted by the gods, who thus codified the will of destiny'; that it emanated from the spring of pure water which nourished the World Tree; that it was an interaction between widely extended kin-groups; that it was 'more or less synonymous with society'; that it was transmitted from generation to generation by song.[9] All of which is either obvious or very unlikely: until modern times all legal systems depended on divine sanction, invoked through oaths and prayers, but there was no disguising the fact that much of it was what humans agreed to or were compelled to accept by other humans. The skalds make it clear that in the tenth and eleventh centuries one meaning of law was 'what kings did and past kings had done'; and another was 'what people expected rulers to do'; and another was 'what happened between freemen at meetings'. That is how it was in most parts of western Christendom: law came at you from all sides, when counts, bishops, kaisers, landowners, sworn associations and public meetings were all in some sense legal authorities, as were village elders and sheets of vellum. Pagans may have had different sources, but not necessarily fewer, or more tolerant of

9 Ries in *Hugur*, 240 on destiny; Bauschatz 1982 on spring-water; Hastrup 1990, 73 on law as society; incantation of law (Schwartz 1973); has sometimes been deduced from the formulaic, alliterative and quasi-metrical wording of some medieval law texts, but see Foote 1977 on difficulty of tracing oral forms from written; and Fix in MESCA, 384–5. Fenger wrote of the legal system of the seventh century in HØKO (1991), 155–64; most scholars would be tongue-tied on any century before the eleventh. Not Frense (1982) or Brink in Jesch 1992, 87–117.

open violence. One text does suggest that there was a right of asylum, at least at Oklunda near Nörrköping in Östergötland during the tenth century:

GUNNAR CUT THESE RUNES AND HE FLED UNDER ACCUSATION
HE FLED TO THIS HOLY PLACE AND HE THEN GOT PROTECTION.

However, there is an alternative reading of the second line as:

AND HE HAS HELD THIS CLEARED LAND AND HE BOUND VIFINN

which takes some of the bloom off this particular right,[10] although there clearly were protected places, under *grith* in markets and assembly sites for limited periods.

Some ground was consecrated to violence, like the islands or makeshift arenas used for single combat; in later Icelandic tradition they were covered by a $7\frac{1}{2}$ foot (2.3 m) square cloth pegged at the corners, roped, and ditched. The fighting had to be there; to leave was to lose, and so the scope of violence was reduced. As also by the custom of offering compensation in silver for personal injury or killing, provided that the injured parties did not agree with Egill that 'it was shameful to sell his brother's body for money', or were not too high and mighty to ask for it. To offend the powerful was to risk death, here as elsewhere, but by spreading the obligation to pay, and the right to receive, the odds were somewhat evened. We know how this system worked once it had been formalized in written tariffs both in Iceland and Norway, but that was in the twelfth and thirteenth centuries: what happened earlier can only be imagined.

However, some procedures found both in home and colonial Nordic countries may date from early settlement days. For example, both in twelfth-century Norway and in Iceland the first recourse of litigants was not to a court or assembly but to a twelve-man panel of arbitrators called a *dómr*. Six were nominated by each party to hear witnesses and decide or refer the case to public courts: see Karlsson in CONIL 504, 507–9. This could be a survival from the Viking age; but the recourse to arbitration is allowed in all medieval legal systems at some level, even where, as in England, the right of the ruler to punish tended to hustle perpetrators of some misdeeds into courts

10 Ruthström 1988 and Lena Peterson in SAS xi 1993, 33–40; B 285 prefers Salberger's version.

rather quickly. The relative weakness of Nordic kings in this period did permit the survival and development of self-help legal systems over most of the north until the seventeenth century.

Gods

Gods – humanoid but superhuman, polymorphic but individual, strong but not invincible – were the chosen defenders against the immediate threats of nature and man. Their cults, with images and temples, had been brought to the margins of the northern world by the Romans, and probably by Greeks before that, and spread north from there, like runes[11] and radishes, but adapted to a world where divinity lived in mountains, rocks, woods, bogs, rivers and wildernesses. The viking age can be seen as the time when one god outdid the others through a combination of stronger supporters and superior theology and theodicy: the slow triumph of christianity, jerked forward, towards the millennium, by royal conversions. Or it can be seen as a time when multiple gods, who had been jostling each other since the third or fourth centuries, were gradually reorganized into an order with a christian or a pagan trinity at the top, and the traditional local cults at the bottom, immutable until the Lutherans started work on them in the seventeenth and eighteenth centuries. Or it can be seen as the period of cultural assimilation, when the church came in with the silver pennies and the wine and the over-mighty kingship and the walnuts, infiltrating the mother lands with the skills she had learned in taming the colonies. Christians naturally picked on the other gods as old enemies, whom they had been trained to combat on all levels by centuries of practise; they had already lined them up as days of the week in lieu of old Mars, Mercury, Jove and Venus, and dispersed or demoted their cults on most of the Continent and the British Isles. But the battle was far from over by 1050, and the long afterlife of the old gods in christian Iceland[12] shows what the literature of conversion conceals: they had much in common with the christian god, more

---

11   The theory that runes were brought to the Baltic by Germanic veterans of the Roman army in the second century A D has been challenged by Bernard Mies, who restates the case for 'The North Etruscan Thesis of the Origin of the Runes' in ANF CXV 2000 33–82. Both the similarity of the letter forms and the idiosyncratic order of the runes are consistent with his argument, which implies a diffusion from NW Italy in the last centuries B C, via the Alpine region.

12   Not as objects of cult or worship, but as members of a reorganized mythology, actors in a cycle of myth and legend deliberately equated with that of classical authors by Snorri in *Skaldskaparmal*. According to Boyer (1975) this was a literary revival, instigated by broad-minded clerics, after the narrow-minded ones had eradicated the living religion; McKinnell (1994) stresses the freedom to invent within 'Late Norse Heathenism'.

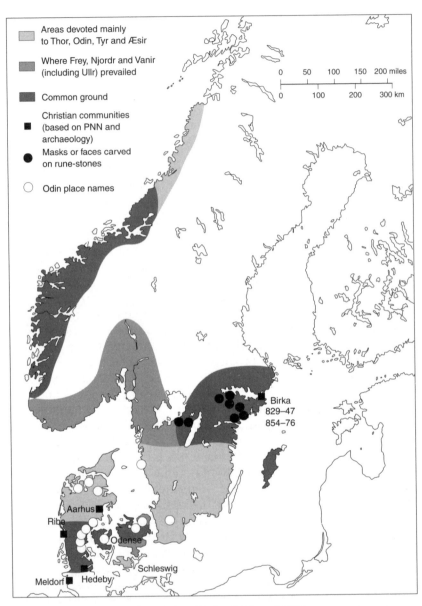

Areas devoted mainly
to Thor, Odin, Tyr and Æsir

Where Frey, Njordr and Vanir
(including Ullr) prevailed

Common ground

Christian communities
(based on PNN and
archaeology)

Masks or faces carved
on rune-stones

Odin place names

Birka
829–47
854–76

Aarhus

Ribe

Odense

Meldorf   Hedeby

Schleswig

Map 10   *Cults 800 – 1000*

than with the older deities who were tied to places and peoples and possibly genders. In an age of migration and travel and displacement they could move; they could say, with Jehovah, 'the Lord thy God is with thee, whithersoever thou goest' to the warrior in the mobile retinue, the professional poet and fur-dealer, without also demanding obedience to a moral code. They could demonstrate, in myth, command of wind, fire, inspiration, thunder, health: explain themselves, and take part in a dialogue with the poets and the farmers.

Ælfric of Eynsham, Wulfstan of York, and Dudo of St Quentin all agreed; round the year 1000, Thor was the favourite god of male Danes. Every other kind of source agrees: place-names, runic inscriptions, personal ornaments, personal names make it clear that from Greenland to Finland and beyond, this was the god of the moment, the one you could trust, the one to placate. He was invoked on sticks and stones as helper of all men, but especially fishermen, herdsmen, mountain men and farmers. His hammer, club, or pestle was the most widely diffused religious symbol, and he alone had verses addressed directly to him, to celebrate his herculean victories over giants and giantesses. He alone kept the loyalty of his followers for centuries after they had accepted baptism, and still cherished him in folk-tales as a sort of Desperate Dan. The surviving verses of Eilífr Goðrunarson's *Thórsdrápa* portray him on one of his most famous missions, destroying the giant Geirroðr and his daughters:

> *Their hostility-acorns* (hearts) *did not fail . . . the Danes of the distant flood-rib* (rock-giants) *sanctuary had to bow . . . the driver of the hull of the storm's hover-chariot* (Thor) *broke each of the cave women's age-old laughter-ship-keels* (backbones).[13]

Knotty phrases, retelling more vividly an old story which had changed slightly in each version for centuries. The other favourite was his accidental catching of the world-serpent on a fishing trip, when the beast was not supposed to emerge until the end of the world; with a bull's head as bait on the eighth-century Gotland stone Ardre viii, breaking through the bottom of his own boat on the tenth-century Gosforth stone in Cumbria, and about that time Gamli Gnævaðarskáld's verse had him destroy the serpent with his hammer; the incident could be joke or apocalypse or both. His crashing and smashing of the giants (Vetrliði named two male and two female,

---

13 Cited in *Skaldarskaparmál*; trans. Faulkes in SnE, 72–3, and 73 for Gamli's verses. See SS, lx (1988), 119–36 for Lindow 'Addressing Thor'. If the face with the turned-up moustaches cut on some Södermanland rune-stones is Thor's, and the droopers are Christ's, there was a war of whiskers among some eleventh century Swedes; see Hultgård 1992 and map 10.

Thorbjorn six female and two male) has been interpreted as the battle of the farmers against boulders in the arable, or the annihilation of women's rights, or the struggle of order against chaos, or of agrarians against hunter-gatherers, or of the present against the past; none of which would be much use to cult members, who seem to have drawn strength from his strength, however, it was used.

All of which runs counter to the impression given in Snorri's and many modern mythologies that Odin was the top god, the father of the other gods, the lord of their world, the all-wise, the all-powerful. Even Saxo Grammaticus (*c.* 1215) who reckoned that he had been merely a fraud, an impostor, (and that Thor had once been beaten in battle by a Danish king) had to acknowledge that the imposture had been remarkably successful: he had been 'credited all over Europe with the honour of godhead' and the kings of the North had made a golden statue of him to worship, and sent it to Byzantium, and after an exile he came home and made all the other gods abdicate. His cult was certainly ancient: as Woden, in late Roman times, he had been given the day named after Mercury, the trickster, traveller, trader, guide and educator. Soon afterwards, according to a theory which has become well-entrenched,[14] he appeared as focus of an esoteric warrior-cult, which entered Scandinavia (or left it, according to Hedeager) on the wings of hidden knowledge, shamanism, transvestism, male-bonding and ancestor worship. But the Anglo-Saxons made him the common ancestor of their royal dynasties, and the Lombards thought he had named them and given them victory through his wife's duplicity. The development of this cult is a mysterious subject which has been successfully appropriated both by the advocates of sacral kingship (see chapter 6) and by those who see him as essentially the god of the ruler, (sacral or not) and of the upper classes. Thus Axboe writes of the ambiguous images which appear on the golden discs of the pre-viking period that they 'can be seen as a projection of the political ideas of the élite into the religious sphere, so that the promotion of a heavenly lord could legitimate wordly princes' efforts to establish and maintain their power in Scandinavia';[15] but the same could be said of almost any religious imagery, if decipherable, and this is open to many interpretations, not necessarily political.

---

14 Expounded in the *Festschrift* by Hagen, Keller and Strombach: *Iconologia Sacra* (Berlin 1994) and in HIHO (1992), and for a survey of Danish bracteates, clearly illustrated see GUM (1998), 238–68. On Höfler's view of Odin as patron of warrior-clubs see Lindow in ONIL (1985), 48–9. On the 'Odinism' of the eighteenth and nineteenth centuries see Thor S. Beck: *Northern Antiquites*, New York 1934: a very strange tale.

15 Axboe 1995, 232. But the iconologists supply the evidence, and they are a skittish herd. In 1970 Hauck saw amulets depicting a nude man touching his chin and genitals as representing a primeval hermaphrodite ancestor of mankind. By 1985 he had become a man in a state of regenerative ecstacy, invoking spirits; by 1992 he

The remarkable thing about Odin's cult in the viking age is how little impact it had on place-names, personal-names, rune-stones, and foreign observers, and how specialized are the functions assigned to him by the skalds, who owed their poetic gift entirely to his talent for theft. In the surviving verses of this period, there are seventeen or eighteen allusions to his abstraction of the mead of poetry; one by Kormakr to his seduction of Rind, one by Ulf Uggason to the pyre of his son Balder, and a description of his reception of dead fighters in Valhalla both in *Eiríksmál* and *Hakonarmál*. At the end of this period, *c.*1050 Arnorr the Earl's poet, a good christian, called him All-father, and was presumably not the first to think of him in that way; the pagan poets, like Glum Geirason (*c.*960) called him victory-god, and claimed that he appeared on earth to help men in battle, as well as merely collecting the corpses from valkyries. The poets had him as their patron, and it may have been their professional interest which kept on promoting him; but Egill Skalagrimsson's lament for his sons puts their esteem in perspective:

I was on good terms with the lord of the spear*
I grew truthful, believing in him,
Until the friend of chariots*, the prince of victory*,
Broke friendship with me.
I do not sacrifice to the brother of Vikr*
Because I am eager to do so;
And yet the friend of Mímir* has given me
Recompense for my harms, if I count better.[16]

Egill's son had been drowned, and Odin had not saved him, but the poet is still grateful for his god's gifts:

that skill devoid of faults; and such a spirit that I unmasked deceivers as open enemies,

i.e. flawless versification and psychological insight. Even a flawed Odin deserved sacrifice for that. Hallfreðr the troublesome poet (*c.* 1000) agreed:

symbolized the shaman's ordeal, in which he was about to be eaten by monsters; see Wood 1995, 253, on the obscurity of these images. Motz 1994, 8–10 made the man into a transvestite doing a perverted dance. Depictions of men with spears, horses, long hair and birds do not become Odin simply by applying the words of Snorri Sturluson written five to seven hundred years later. See Starkey 1999 for an exposure of the inconsistency and unreliability of the Hauck school's Odinism.

16   trans. Turville Petre 1976, 39–41 and 72; and see Marold GR (1992), 693–6 on the elusiveness of Odin mythology. The phrases marked with asterisks refer to Odin; Snorri gave twenty-four other kennings for him in *Skáldskaparmál*, and he was known by the names of other gods: Tyr and Gaut. The English chronicler Ethelweard (*c.*980) recognized the prevalence of Odin worship among Danes, Northmen, and Swedes, but he was himself a direct male descendant of Woden.

I remembered the highly-valued practice of people, my ancestors, and reluctant I turn my hatred on the first husband of Frigg because I serve Christ, for the rule of Odin pleased the poet well:

but he decided to make a clean break, all the same:

let the trolls do homage to Odin

More will be said later (chapter 12) of Odin's special relationship with dead fighters. His connexion with kings has been deduced partly from the Anglian genealogies of the eighth and ninth centuries, which systematized Anglo Saxon kings' ancestry by deriving them all from Woden, their version of Odin, and partly from the proximity of Odin place-names in Denmark to supposed centres of royal power: Odense, Oddense, Vojens, Onsved, Onsbjerg, Onsild.[17] From that, it has been suggested that royally sponsored Odin-cult amounted to a state religion in tenth-century Denmark, set up to combat christianity and exalt the king. The theory is unsound, because the place-names are undatable except within very broad limits, and could easily have been formed like other theophoric names, to indicate shrines with strong local followings. Kings would have to come to terms with several cults: in Denmark with Tyr and Thor, as well as Odin, in Svíaland with Thor as well as Frey-Njord, in SE Norway with Ullr as well as Thor. Kings are not known to have claimed descent from Odin before the twelfth century; or rather, it was then that Icelanders began to claim descent from kings, whom they derived from Odin because they knew that Anglo-Saxon rulers came from Woden; Scandinavian rulers were slow to take the hint (the Danes, very), which is not surprising considering the disrepute into which his cult had fallen by then, outside the poetic circles of Iceland. Before the conversion, he was evidently seen as one of the three main male gods, with particular responsibility for warfare, poetry and one form of life after death; worth cultivating for people in high-risk occupations and word-smiths. A pendant recently discovered at Old Ladoga (tenth century?) may serve as a reliable witness to what one Norseman thought of him:

THOR HAS COURAGE RUNES
LET NOT THE RUIN OF THE GIANTS TAKE ME
ODIN GRANT
MERIT'S something HORSE[18]

---

17 Hald 1963 developed the argument from place-names; it is now well established among archaeologists of the Jutland warrior-graves and advocates of the state-development approach to Nordic history. See map 6.
18 I cannot translate DATHAR NAKI FAK, nor can the runologists; see Kumenko in NOWELE, xxxii (1997), 181.

evidently the nag Sleipnir on which Odin carried dead men to his corpse-hall, or hole: Thor now, Odin later. There were goddesses too, but all attempts to discuss the cults of Frigg. ('beloved') and Freyja ('Lady') run up against the dearth of evidence from this period. They are important figures in Snorri's mythology, actresses in the group-conflicts between giants, Aesir and Vanir; but they are not well-represented in place-names, or given clearly defined authority over human concerns: sex, childbirth, pregnancy, marriage, weaving, cooking, for example. Both were mothers, both promiscuous at times, both married, both beautiful; they came from different families in the mythology but it could be that they began as aspects of the one goddess, Frigg the German, Freyja the Nordic, and that Frigg came north with the cult of Odin, only to find that her role as Venus was taken by her double. It was Freyja who was defamed by the poet Hjalti Skeggjason in the 990s as a 'bitch', and he was outlawed for blasphemy by the Icelanders. But neither goddess was credited with an annual festival or a particular public shrine, or a mythological role apart from their relations with male gods. Their rites may have been exclusively for women, and if so the male-dominated myths have undervalued them; or it could be that they were less successful than the male gods in competing with older feminine spirits, rooted in the landscape and the locality: the *dísir* or spirit-women cultivated in the great winter festival of Svíaland, and in Norway, the giantesses whom Thor never quite managed to eliminate, whose descendants became kings; and whatever lay behind Thorgerðr Hǫlgabruðr and Irp, a West Norwegian fertility goddess and her dark opposite.[19]

Place-names show that the divine helpers of the viking age were sometimes thought of as a group, accessible at places now known as Gudme, Gudum, Gudhjem and Gudbjerg in Denmark, and the six Gudvins of Norway; which is certainly how ninth-century Swedes envisaged them (in the *Life of Anscar*), as gathered in a *collegium* to which favoured mortals could be admitted after death. Adam of Bremen, 200 years later, wrote of the 'multitude of gods which they worship', from which they select one for help, when hard pressed in battle: 'after a victory they are devoted to him in future, and put him before the others' (AB 4, 22). This relatively free market in divinity raised questions about the relations between all superhuman beings which the myths attempt to answer, long after one god has been promoted above the rest on a permanent basis.

---

19 See now Mc Kinnell on 'Thogerðr Hölgabrúðr and Hyndluljoð' in MYWO, 265–90, and Näsström 1995 on Freyja.

No Nordic society can have been ignorant of christianity during this period; it was the religion of the Franks and the Frisians, of the Anglo-Saxons and the Irish, of the Saxons and the Greeks, and missionaries had approached a Danish king as early as the beginning of the eighth century. By the millennium, the date round which later authors grouped the conversion of the Icelanders, and the Norwegians and Danes, this was one of the old Nordic religions, even unsupported by any firm church organization, or clear presentation of monotheism. The archaeology of burials reveals a century of christian influence in Norway before the 950s, when the last obviously pagan graves were prepared in East Agder (south-west), and even the great heathen statements at Mammen and Jelling in Jutland did not exclude christian symbols from the burial chambers: rolled wax candles, the famous axe-head inlaid with triquetra and tetragram in silver; and to the south, at Thumby-Bienebeck, a many-chambered grave held a lady with cross and hammer pendants together. Cremation was giving way to inhumation in many districts; cultural contamination was preparing the ground for the christian god by making his apparatus less and less alien, more compatible with domestic cults.

Some historians have imagined that this conjunction of cults was a cause of stress, even a trigger for viking aggession. Nothing is less likely. The stark opposition between the two systems of thought existed in the minds of christian theologians, but had in practical terms been modified by centuries of interaction between christians and non-christians before 800. Norsemen presented the church with three intolerable patterns of conduct: human and animal sacrifice, disrespect for christian persons and places, and respect for false gods. Everything else was negotiable, and had been negotiated between the clergy and other barbarian peoples from the fifth century onwards.[20] Christianity adjusts to circumstances, like other religions, and the heathen who settled in the West adjusted to christianity; but the crucial transformation of the one god into a guarantor of civil authority and victory in war had taken place long ago.

A Norwegian rune-stone[21] sums up the Nordic conversions:

20   This is not to agree with Russell (1996) that Germanic thought and custom had so deeply infected christianity from the fifth century onwards that it became 'Germanized'. Romanized, perhaps; acclimatized elsewhere, certainly. Nor to claim that the Danes and Svíar who wore hammer-amulets in the period 920–1020 were not loyal to Thor rather than Christ; only to suggest that the sudden change to cruciform bangles (1000–1015) traversed a bridge rather than a chasm (see Staecker 1999). For a reassessment of the *Kulturkampf* see now Thomas A. Dubois *Nordic Religions in the Viking Age* (Philadelphia 2000).
21   Galteland, Irje: Birkeli 1973, 99–101.

ARNSTEIN ERECTED THIS STONE IN MEMORY OF BJOR
HIS SON.
HE MET DEATH IN THE ARMY WHEN CANUTE
ATTACKED ENGLAND.
GOD IS ONE.

The boy's own faith cannot be assumed from this, but his family were evidently christians, and all the Swedish stones commemorating those who attacked England in 1000–16 are christian. This god was not averse to large-scale devastation and bloodshed, any more than were Odin or Thor. He had armies of martyrs and saints ranged in his city, as well as stores of wisdom and rewards after death and the service of rulers on earth. His ascendancy over the other gods could hardly have been a shock within societies used to judging gods by their efficacy and 'putting one before the others' on the basis of the result, as Adam of Bremen reported. In the 960s this one was adopted by a very powerful Danish king, but the archaeology reveals no direct threat to other cults over the next generation, only a very slow provision of timber churches in some places connected with kings or leading noble converts.

With the Nordic communities overseas, it has been said that 'Christianity... may have been less a factor which distinguished the native population from the Scandinavian settlers, than a force for their integration' since the landscapes they claimed, and the societies into which they intruded were already committed to a god and his saints who gave victory in battle, fertility on the farm, and security of title to land. In the English Danelaw the situation is summed up by the Norse cemetery at Ingleby, overlooking three shires, and apparently serving Danes settled in that district in the ninth century. They were pagan enough to raise small mounds over the graves, but only a few were actually buried there; most of the mounds are cenotaphs, memorials to the dead, who are presumably lying near the church. In Rouen, the great chief Rollo is apparently resting in the cathedral; but the transition may have been less discreet. According to the historian Adhemar, writing a century later, 'as his death drew near he went mad and had a hundred christian prisoners beheaded in front of him in honour of the gods whom he had worshipped, and in the end distributed 100 lbs of gold round the churches in honour of the true god in whose name he had accepted baptism'.[22]

---

22 Hadley 1997, 92; on assimilation; the Adhemar is translated from the better text edited by Bourgain (*Ademari Cabannensis Chronica*, Turnhout 1999) rather than from later versions, as in PL cxli, 37, which are less clear. On Ingleby see Richards et al. 1995.

Imitations

The uneven, gradual and imperfect acceptance of the new god side-by-side with vigorous cults of the old ones is easily explained by the fragility of the Nordic political units (kingdoms, chiefdoms, lordships) through which christianity had to be implanted. Or would be, if it were certain that such organizations were obviously stronger in seventh-century Anglo-Saxon Britain or Ireland, or among the Bavarians or Saxons in the eighth; but it isn't. That horse has had a good run, and needs a rest, both from those Nordic scholars who have invented potent unitary kingdoms at impossibly early dates, and from those who imagine that christianity has to wait for the right moment in 'state-formation' to catch on. Let them dismount, and look round the landscape.

Unlike post-Hamlet Scandinavians, those of the viking age do not seem to have been introspective to a fault. They were not islands unto themselves, not even the Greenlanders and the St Kilda crusoes who had geography against them. They saw the outside world not only as a store of loot and luxury, but as the bright pattern of life, to be imitated as well as plundered. The chiefs of the Svíar were already under the spell of Frankish civilization in the sixth century, the so-called Merovingian period of Baltic archaeologists; and before that the rulers of the Danish islands had treasured the silverware and glass of the Roman empire. Buchholz referred to 'a Germanic eagerness to take over foreign elements and conceptions in the religious sphere', but the Norsemen imitated in every sphere.

Imitatio Imperii meant aping the authority and high living of the two successive western empires of the Carolingians (750–900) and the Ottonians (919–1024), especially by the Danes, their near neighbours and sometime tributaries (936–83). Frankish and Saxon influence in their dress, swords, belts and harness is obvious, down to small details. Acanthus leaf decoration found its way to the back of Norse trefoil brooches by 850, and spread through Denmark, just as the gripping beasts, or asymmetrical style had come the same way in the previous century. The elongated and convoluted creatures that clasp themselves and each other in the woodwork of the Oseberg ship can be traced to the decorative forms of christian Franks and Bavarians[23]; the Vivian bible, the Lothair Gospel (of Tours) and the

---

23 HUG 224 for Buchholz; Wamers in Freeden 1999, 198–228, for Oseberg. Acanthus leaf was followed by vine-scroll, as developed at Metz, 826–55; see Skibsted-Klaesøe 1997, 80–1. For a study of the wide distribution in the North of Carolingian metalwork and ornament with plant-motifs from *c.*830 (some 50 finds) see Lennartson in *Offa* liv/lv 1997–8, 431–620.

Drogo sacramentary were ninth-century Frankish achievements which shared motifs with Norse brooches and sword-hilts. The chamber and boat-graves near Hedeby (*c.*840) which housed three mules and three horses, as well as a chief and two males armed with Frankish equipment have been interpreted by Ellmers as the tomb of a Danish king, his cup-bearer, marshal and retainers, imitating the pomp of his Frankish overlord, but practising a 'very peculiar form of suttee' with his retainers.[24] At any rate, he had adopted a very selective form of christianity, if this was the Harold baptized at the court of Lewis the Pious in 826. Whoever it was, he was following a trend, or possibly leading it; the Ladby ship-grave, a century later, included eleven horses and a pack of hounds, the full parade of a Frankish lord. The twenty Frankish forts built on the Lower Rhine *c.*850–900 seem to have been the model for the Danish ring-forts, just as the top-quality Ulfberht swords of Francia were expertly copied in the North. Ceremonial washing bowls (before meals) appear at Ribe, and copper food and drink cans from the Rhineland at Birka, with sets of silver cups for exclusive drinkers. Harold Gormsson the convert king commissioned a unique composite rune-stone, unlike any before or since, because carved to read like an Ottonian gospel-book, with images in relief as in England, and among them a lion gripping a serpent which Fuglesang derives from an Ottonian war-banner.[25] The big Jelling rune-stone was never copied entirely, but some of its features (the serpent, and animal and plant decoration) spread eastwards over the next 50 years, in token of the same cultural prestige which had brought them to Jelling. Imitations of the politics and ideology of western rulers, a conscious desire to share their glory, reached a climax with Canute's journey to the imperial coronation of 1027 at Rome. *Dear to the emperor – friend of Peter's* was the highest praise Sigvatr could give his patron, who was also *chief and foremost ruler* in his own right, a king of kings, and according to Óttarr of peoples as well:

> Let us so proclaim King of Danes Irish and English
> And Islanders, That his renown Continue travelling
> To all lands With heaven's power

24 Hellmuth Andersen 1985; Ellmers 1986.
25 Fuglesang 1989, 190, 207; inventive looting of Widukind. See Malmer 1966 for Frankish influence on bracteate-images, with Varenius in CSA ii 1994. In FESTOL 1988, 93–104 Ørsnes traced style C brooches of N. Jutland from an equestrian motif on a seventh-century Frankish altar-rail. Hanssen 1990, 222 discusses the Frankish shore-forts' link with Trelleborg, und Steuer in Kunst und Kultur ed. C.Stiegemann (Mainz 1999), 317–22 on Frankish horses and swords.

Byzantium's influence as a model of imperial ideas and symbols was felt by the Rus from *c*.850 and reached Scandinavia well before 1045 and the return of Harald Hardrada and his varangians with their golden gratuities. The eastern empire was one source of the exotic goods found at Birka, Valsgärde, and Uppsala and of the cross-pendants, ringed crucifixes and combs, or at least their patterns, found widely in eastern Scandinavia and Finland. Attempts to connect these finds with early and unrecorded christian communities are unconvincing, since they could be used by anyone, like Islamic silver money.[26] Byzantium evidently worked on the imagination of Nordic pagans in ways which may be hidden or camouflaged in what was later to appear as their mythology; by Snorri's time it was thought that Odin had once lived there, with the 'divine senate' of gods (as Saxo called them), but there is no sign that anyone had thought this before the conversion to christianity. Direct contact between the eastern emperors and the Baltic regions has been deduced from the finding of a lead byzantine seal at Hedeby; it belonged to a Theodosios who may have been the envoy sent to the emperor Lothair I in 840, but there are too many ways it could have got there to link Byzantium and the Danes diplomatically.

Borrowings from *Ireland* were many, as might be expected with a continuous Norse presence round the island from the 840s onwards and contact through raiding from the 790s. Loot got back to SW Norway and was put to new uses; holy-water cans became food-bowls in the graves of dead pagans, rings became pendants, pyxes became ale-cups, ink-horns became drink-horns. Clasps were ripped off books to decorate Norse women as brooches; their dresses were fastened with Irish ringed pins, made for that purpose, and animal-headed rings circled their arms; the mixing of motifs is summed up in the description 'Hiberno-Norse'. Ireland was a country of many kings, a few high-kings, warlike nobles, and wealth reckoned in herds of cattle, slaves, and food-stores; a familiar scene to the Norsemen, enhanced by the unfamiliar concentrations of wealth and power in monasteries inadequately defended. Cultural assimilation was to be expected in small Norse communities dependent on a large Irish hinterland for food, manpower and profitable alliances. King Olaf Cuaran, ruler of York and Dublin (consecutively, at various times between 927 and 981) has been seen as a deliberate imitator of Irish

---

26 Salo (1995 and 1998) deduces cells of believers in Finland from the eighth century onwards, Latin or Greek according to the shape of their crosses. Duczko and Fuglesang review these theories in Müller Wille, AWLM 1997; but see Staecker's attempt to derive Anglo-Saxon missions from pendants, ibid. On the Hedeby seal see Shepard 1995.

high kingship, who employed an Irish poet to sweeten his reputation among native speakers,[27], and the question of how much later Icelandic literature borrows from Irish remains open. Themes such as the visit to the underworld, crazy warriors, superhuman powers of hearing, weird women and miraculous dogs are common to both in the twelfth century and later, but there could be other reasons for this than a borrowing by eighth or ninth-century invaders. They made a 'Hiberno-Norse' western world which kept in touch with Scandinavia and Iceland for some time. The case for deriving skaldic versification from Ireland rests on six resemblances: strict syllable counting, internal rhyme, consonance, syllable-chopping, four lifts to the line and end-line stress. These satisfied Turville-Petre as evidence that the Irish metres inspired Norse poets to break from the simple heroic metre, which is preserved in Eddic verse, and take the skaldic route to *dróttkvæðr* or 'retinue poetry'. It is difficult to imagine this happening if the Nordic poets had not overcome the language barrier, and learned how to appreciate Irish verse, at a date early enough to let them set an example to Icelanders and Norwegians in the early ninth century, when the earliest examples of skaldic metre appear (on the Rök stone); and if the raids on Ireland began in the 790s there was hardly time for this to happen. Nor is it clear why the new metres should have appealed so strongly to Scandinavians; nor why there is no trace of a Hiberno-Norse school of poets at Dublin among the surviving samples. It is tantalizing to have good reasons for a Norse cultural debt to the Irish, and so little hard evidence of it, at least in the viking age; it remains an invitation to students in all fields, to follow in the steps of Rooth, who showed quite convincingly (in 1961) how the myth of Balder, the invulnerable god killed by mistletoe thrown by his blind brother has Irish origins; and then to find the same myth indicated in bracteates struck in Germany centuries before there could be any question of Irish influence. But who can say it was not the Irish who taught Norsemen the way to Iceland, and the power of the saints? The unbaptized Icelanders who nevertheless believed in St Columba (LB 24) need not be fictional.

The power wielded by Danes in *England* during the ninth and eleventh centuries robbed the Anglo-Saxons not only of silver but

---

27 On this, Doherty in ISCEVA 1998, but see Ní Mhaonaigh's doubts ibid. 399–400. The poem 'Amlaib of Dublin the hundred-strong' is in AU for 974. Turville-Petre's argument was modified but upheld by Sveinsson 1975, McKenzie 1981 and Arnason 1991; Sigurdsson 1988 gives the six resemblances, but see Gade 1995, 8–12. On the borrowing *c.*1040 of the Latin trochaic dimeter see Foote in *Aurandisla*, 252. For the borrowing of the cults of female saints from Ireland to Norway see Rekdal 'Vikings and Saints', Peritia xvii–xviii (2003–4), 256–75.

of words, techniques and ideas. The settlers began imitating East Anglian pennies by 890, with the help of Frankish moneyers. The York coinages followed, and in c.918 they struck a penny with the Frankish king Charles the Bald's monogram on the obverse. Ten years later they were minting York money with a sword and hammer on one side and in one case a cross on the other. In the 990s imitations of king Ethelred's pennies were being struck in Denmark, and at Dublin by king Sitric (Sigtryggr), and moneyers are transferred from Gloucester (or Watchet) to Dublin, from York and Lincoln to Lund, and even to the pirate chiefs on the Isle of Man by c.1025; by when the English penny had replaced the Islamic *dirhem* as the token of wealth in Scandinavia and far into the east. The Anglo-Saxons' patterns of decoration were imitated from the beginning, and inspired a whole international style, the Ringerike (see Postscript, p. 317n); first (800–50) the spiralling scrolls they had themselves got from Syria long before, and the animals crawling up stone crosses. By 1000 four foundations of Norse power were known by words borrowed from the English:

hird   had joined *drótt* as a usual word for the lord's household or following; from OE *hired*, any sort of household;

thegn   became the usual word for substantial landowners;

harri   became one word for 'lord' (OE *Heorra*) and

langskip   was borrowed for long ships.[28]

There is no need to labour the point. Throughout this age, the Norse were remodelling themselves on patterns they found among the people they pillaged and tormented, in so far as these patterns were useful to them. They did not rush in to fill a vacuum, but were adopted to reinforce what was already there: kingships, lordships, the cult of war, festivity, funerals and poetry. Norsemen did not become less Nordic or more European as a result; all that had happened was an acceleration, temporary and spasmodic, of a toing and froing which had been going on since the last Ice Age, and would continue. In matters of religion it affected pagans quite independently of christian missions and deliberate assimilations; there was a convergence of ideas which delayed and blurred Nordic conversions within Scandinavia and wherever church authority was weak and under-represented: virtually everywhere. Widukind of Corvey, a well-informed contemporary source (c.970) reported that 'the Danes had been christian of old, but

28   Rarely: see Jesch 2001,123. Hofmann 1955 was the indispensable study of ON loans from Old English; note pp. 79–97 on the Anglicisms in the vocabulary of one poet, Sigvatr, who cannot have spent long in England.

all the same they used to serve idols with gentile ceremony', because they believed that 'Christ was indeed a god, but there were other gods greater than he...'[29] If Widukind was right, the conversion of king Harold Bluetooth by one Poppo (*c.965*) was not a transition from heathenism to christianity, but from a state in which Christ was not the most powerful god, to one in which he was; the stage at which other gods ceased to be gods would come much later, just as the stage at which they were the only gods was very much earlier. The reception of the new god was slow and discriminating, as with the other imitations (see map 6).

'The pagan mental strife' which accompanied the conversions 'has gone unrecorded';[30] but hints of it are in skaldic and eddic poetry, and in the cryptic archaeology of material symbols. For skaldic verse, like classical verse, depended on allusions to heathen mythology, and the poets (like Egill, see p. 263) looked to Odin for inspiration, and as the originator of all verse. This verse could ridicule and discredit the new religion, as in Iceland; it could only be purged of its paganism very slowly. And yet, by 1000, all the most generous patrons of the poets had been baptized, and it was only a matter of time before they would expect poets to advertise the fact. Not earl Eric Hakonsson, apparently; Canute's deputy in christian Northumbria until 1024, himself a christian, was praised at length in Thórdr Kolbeinsson's *Eiríksdrápa* in entirely traditional terms as a *raven-plenty-giver* who *frequently diminished the Englishmen's army* so that the *wolf pack got many corpses to eat*. If he referred at all to god, the strophe has been lost; but at the same time Eric's ally and lord, Canute, was being firmly connected to the christian firmament by Thórarin:

Canute protects land as guardian
Of Greece heaven's kingdom

and by Hallvardr hareksblesi:

Within earth's fence...no noble hero
Nearer monks' ruler than you.[31]

---

29   Rerum Gestarum Saxonicarum, 3, 65.
30   Carver 1995, 122 of Anglo-Saxons mainly.
31   SkjD IA, 317–18, IB, 293–4; Kock, i, 149–50; Fidjestøl 1982, 125, for Hallvardr, SkjD IB, 300–1, Kock, i, 152–3 for Thorarinn's *Glælognskviða* (see below); this is a loose refrain, in which *himinríki* (heaven's kingdom) is borrowed from Old English *heofonrice*. For *Eiríksdrápa* SkjD IB, 203–6, trans. EHD, i, 307; the first half of st. 14 is entirely about wolves, corpses and blood.

The ideas that god was a sort of king and the king a sort of god were easily assimilated from the ceremony of courts like those of Lewis the Pious, Otto I and Ethelred the Unready, of whom Gunnlaug Serpent's Tongue declared, apparently with his tongue unforked:

> *All army is in awe, agog*
> *At England's prince as at god*[32]

The new theology seems to have stuck there until the end of the eleventh century, when poets begin to justify the ruler's god-man status in more subtle terms; but meanwhile a synthesis of many views of divinity and kingship had been created round the corpse of St Olave, at Trondheim. His cult began as the project of an English bishop, familiar with the royal martyrs of his own country, and the devotion they inspired, and in England the commemoration of the slaughtered Óláfr Haraldsson went through the normal channels: in one pontifical before 1050, then in calendars more generally, with a liturgical celebration drawn wholly from stereotypes. In Norway, the living Olafr had terrorized and badgered his subjects, until they drove him out; not because he was a zealous christian, but because he was a tyrant, impatient of other chiefs within Norway, and unable to expand his own clientage widely enough to support government over the territories.

> *Each king fled far away from you, prince,*
> *And all such knew that you cut out the tongue*
> *Of the one who lived northernmost*

so that by 1028 he had to flee an exasperated country with a devoted clique of poets, god-children, and gangsters. In the years soon after his death (29 July 1030) there was a powerful voice from his retinue, Sigvatr's, proclaiming that he had been a great and glorious ruler; but few will have agreed with this premature historical revisionism. The change came when the corpse took on a life of its own, as described in the poem called Sea-Calm Lay (*Glælognskvida*) ascribed to Thórarinn, which declared that

> *The people-king has now arranged for himself a throne in Trondheim.... there where Óláfr settled and where after being king-man he was buried alive*

---

32 Lines sometimes seen as suspect by those who assume that Ethelred was not feared by his enemies or admired by his friends. The variant versions in two MSS of Gunnlaug's saga suggest an early and authentic original, and Ethelred's record as a paymaster, treasure-dispenser, and Dane-killer supports the attribution, as well as his overtly Christocentric kingship: SkjD IA, 194 and IB, 184 for texts.

not literally, since he had been truly slain at Stiklestad, but as a spirit resting within a corpse on his way to heaven, 'won' by his death:

Thus the glorious prince lies there, pure, with his body intact, And there on him as on a living man his hair and nails increase. There do bells ring of themselves over his wooden-walled bed, And every day do the people hear clangour of bells above king-man.

Here is christianity speaking to the public in terms that a pagan can understand and respect. One who was at least a great fighter, furious in death, now lies, sits and grows hair, suspended between heaven and earth under a canopy of unearthly clanging, and

He obtains from god himself year's plenty and peace for all men

just as pagan leaders like Hákon jarl had hoped to obtain in the previous century. But unlike them

There comes an army where the holy king himself is, kneeling for help. And the dumb and the blind apply to the prince and go healthy away.[33]

The miracle stories accumulated from the 1040s onward. The cult spread through the entire Nordic world, from Dublin to Novgorod (not at first to Iceland) nourished both by an international taste for and belief in royal martyrs, and by an urgent local demand for an intermediary between the new god and the realities of the Nordic world. Olave had lived the life: sailed, raided, plundered, fought, fornicated, murdered, plotted, versified and played games more recently and notoriously, in familiar places, than had the other great intercessors, SS Mary, Michael, Peter, and Clement, none of whom had done more than half of these things. However, Olave's human frailty or vigour had nothing to do with his sainthood; it was enough that he had authority while alive, had been brutally killed and worked miracles afterwards.

Communications

Communications by sea with the outside world were all too good; by land, within Scandinavia, confined to the one heavily-defended track

---

33   The Sea-Calm Poem text in Skj. 1B 300–01 was amended by Kock i 152–23, and by Magerøy in *Glælognskviða ar Toraren Lovtunge* (Oslo 1948), and its context was discussed by Hellberg in ANF 1984 XIX, who concluded that it could date from the 1030s or the 1020s. On the liturgical development of the cult see Iversen 'Transforming a viking into a saint' in *The Divine Office in the Latin Middle Ages* ed. M. Fassler and R. Baltzer (Oxford 2000) 401–29.

which led past Hedeby from Saxon and Slav country and to the many paths threading through Lapland to the east. The mental communication between the Norse was mainly by word of mouth, or gesture, or image (the painted shield, or tapestry, or carving) and is therefore mostly lost. We tend to reconstruct it from the one vernacular literature later to appear in the abundant book-learning of Iceland, and so we have probably been led very far astray. Which is the less convincing: an elaborate fiction about the viking age composed three hundred years later by a monk in an Icelandic monastery, or a statistically based reconstruction by an ideologically wired-up research student today?

They might agree, however, that the development of Runes and runic literacy by the pagan Norse was an impressive intellectual achievement, which supplemented oral culture and left some witnesses to what it was like, as well as creating an epigraphic literature, and at least the possibility of communicating by inscribed slats of wood or birch bark.[34] Not many of the surviving rune-epistles can be dated before 1050. The theory that there was frequent runic correspondence is still unconfirmed by any finds comparable with the post 1100 deposits at Bergen and Novgorod; the early yields from York and Dublin are meagre. Lines like those found at Nursak in Greenland are memorable not because they indicate widespread Nordic literacy, but because they communicate a passing thought, or wish, we cannot fully understand:

> *In the sea, sea, sea, is where the gods lie in wait:*
> *She is called Bibrau, the girl who sits in the blue.*[35]

In this we hear the ephemeral; that is the present. In the inscribed memorial stones there is more concern with the future (see next chapter), the prolongation of fame and title, and sometimes the curse or spell on the malevolent. To work, they needed a reading public, which at least in eleventh-century Svíaland must have been numerous, and responsive to the conventions and formulas which sometimes seem obscure now. Even a stone-cutter could sometimes give an immediate and unconventional sense-impression, as in the verses on a stone found in a mound on the farm at Hønen in SE Norway, which are dated *c.*1040:

---

34 The written and spoken word fed each other, and flourished together, whether the writing was runic or Roman or both; the stage at which 'society and its institutions could not operate without the support of written texts' (Derolez, cited by Jesch in RUQUIF 1998, 467) was far in the future; such a dependency would have been counter-productive at this period.

35 Stoklund : 'Greenland Runes' VACON (1993), 528–43.

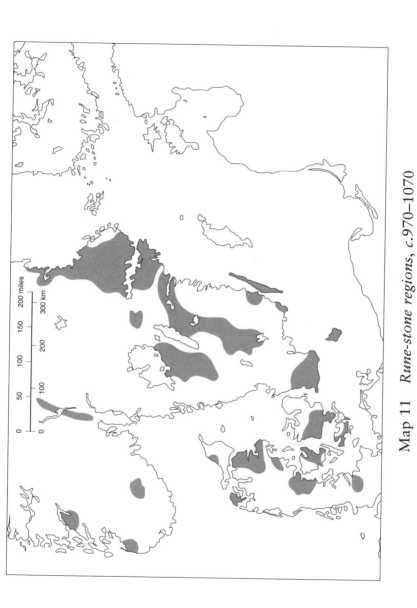

Map 11 *Rune-stone regions, c.970–1070*

Runic memorials are concentrated in the shaded areas, which can be divided into
18–20 runic districts with distinctive styles and types: Palm 1992 analyzes.

OUT AND FAR AND LACKING TOWEL AND FOOD
WIND-COLD ON ICE IN THE UNINHABITED.
ILL MAY SUCCEED GOOD FORTUNE, TO DIE EARLY.

Which is one attempt at a translation, among many others made since the 1820s; none satisfactory, since the Hønen poet, master of two metres (*Málaháttr* and *fornyrðislag*), was cryptic in his diction. But he and his audience had the gift of literacy; he, the more precious one of knowing when to stop.[36]

36 NIY, ii, 23–36 for Magnus Olsen's discussion and dating; he took the *uninhabited* to mean East Greenland, and the victim to have been a nephew of Harald Hardrada, Finn Fegir. For the geography of rune-stones see map 11. On the two metres see Russell Poole 'Metre and Metrics' in CONIL (1995), 256–6 and 268; on the echoes of literary forms in runic inscriptions see now Larsson ibid. 403–26.

12

Future

Tell me the news from hell: I know what's happening in the world.
(Balder's Dream, st. 6, trans. Larrington PEd, 244; but *I will (tell) about home*
would do for the second line)

Even a man or woman lacking inflected future tenses may still have a future, and hack it out in stone; like the Swedish lady Ingerun, of Broby near Täby in Uppland: *Hon vill austr fara...*

SHE WILL EASTWARD TRAVEL AND AWAY TO JERUSALEM

and the three baptized brothers who built a bridge for their father's memory at Sälna, not far away:

ALWAYS WILL LIE
WHILE AGES LIVE
THE BRIDGE FIRM FOUNDED
(and) WIDE AFTER THE GOOD (man)

or the lady of Runby, whose quay and rune-stone in honour of her husband and sons:

SHALL STAND IN MEMORY OF THE MEN
AS LONG AS MENFOLK LIVE

and so far, it has.[1] These hopes were carved after the viking age in an idiom developed during it. The expectation of a christian heaven gained by good works and a lasting if finite fame on earth run through them; and for the heathen, it was not so different. Both the

---

1 Jansson 1962 (trans. Foote) has a good section on these and similar inscriptions (85–2), and see 104–9 for the evidence of a competition in pursuit of future fame

future in this world and in the next inspired hope and fear, and the evidence for each will be considered in turn.

Hopes

The future in this world was foreseeable in so far as it repeated the past: famine or dearth at least once a lifetime, a lifetime lasting some forty years for women and also for men (although women who got past thirty would outlive men), some dreadful winters, many drownings, and for the fortunate the importation and display of bright and fascinating artifacts from the south. The hope of personal survival would be reinforced by the hope of descendants and a good name after death. As with farming, there were ways of safeguarding fertility in humans; some spectacular like the rites at big public assemblies, some local, like whatever happened at the fifty or so stumpy white phallic stones which survive along the south-west coast of Norway, older than this age, but in use to modern times,[2] and some domestic: strokings of the tanned horse-pizzle, feedings of the smooth-snake in the byre, dancing with the straw-man called Bó or Bú. In Snorri's mythology there is no sign of the cult of the conceiving and childbearing mother-goddess as a dominant religious force; it seems that the divine family called Vanir (Njorðr, Freyr, Freyja) were concerned with sex and procreation, while the Odin family took care of war, politics and wisdom. But the sex-life of this civilization cannot be reconstructed from family sagas about randy Icelanders, nor from the archaeology of detachable phalluses, nor from tales of the seductions of Odin and Frey, or Freudian fantasies about Thor's hammer. All that emerges is an impression that in all matters of fertility, offerings brought luck, and that dancing and singing[3] pleased or perhaps merely woke the luck-givers at certain times. In arable country, plough-ceremonies with garlanded ards, and the eating of porridge and bread saved from the previous Yule

---

between Jarlabanki of Vallentuna and the former chiefs of the district, Ulfr and brothers, who had put up an obtrusive pillar in the assembly-place. Jarlabanki moved the thing-place.

2 See Solberg 1999 on these Holy White Stones, which she dates to the late Roman and Migration period: only one example among many of the generous provision of fertility symbols left by previous generations. The collared and capped stone shaft at Grebö in Östergötland is still painted red, white and black to preserve the farm's prosperity.

3 Not the 'effeminate gestures and clapping of mimes' at Uppsala which Starcatherus condemned in Saxo (HD, i, 172); these were professional entertainers, unwelcome in public ritual (Gunnell 1995, 14).

continued down to the twentieth-century at Shrovetide, and may have started when the plough first appeared. The furrows found under mounds and market sites of the viking age were not there by accident, but broke ground in hope of a good outcome. How exactly farmers ensured their own progeny in those days is not recorded, but there is a good story in *Landnámabók* about 'a famous man in Sogn called Geir, and he became known as Végeir, because he was a great sacrificer. He had a large number of children' and they are listed as Vébjorn, Véstein, Vémund etc. (LB chapter 149; trans., 70–1). *Vé* meant holy place, and so begot this thirteenth-century gloss; but it shows how the connexion was thought to have worked.

Hope of future worldly fame is easier to detect, as there are several thousand runic inscriptions and monuments to produce in evidence; the use of writing is perhaps a sign of less optimism than prevailed in societies where 'hero-stones' were uninscribed foci of oral tradition; but no sign of less greed for admiration among men. Whatever their unexpressed purpose, the stones and settings declare themselves to be AFTER: AFT : AUFT : AFTIR : AIFTIR : EPT : EPTIR : IFT : IFTIR : EFTIR: UFT somebody or other; whatever the spelling, the preposition of commemoration[4] – imitated from Northumbrian gravestones – fixes a name for the forseeable future to admire, AS LONG AS THE WORLD EXISTS or at least VERY LONG, or LONG. The eleventh-century Thor-worshippers in Södermanland called their inscriptions 'runes-everlasting' (*Sírun*), and the favoured stone was granite, even when more workable stone was available and used now and then.[5] This was a wise investment. The long needle stone of Ågersta (Trögd, Uppland) is still erect and legible:

HERE WILL STAND A STONE BETWEEN TWO FARMS

and it did, for 700 years down to 1856, when they changed the boundaries. The viking age began with perhaps less than a hundred inscribed stones in place; by 1100 there may have been 100 in Norway alone, 500 in Denmark and 3000 in Sweden, allowing for the destruction of half in subsequent centuries by desecrators, builders, road-menders and dry-stone wallers, as well as by subsidence through neglect. It was a bet on the future which christianity seems

---

4   DR, i, 741–4; 11 of the 16 variations given.
5   Hultgård in KIKOT (1998), 90–2, and Jesch in RUQUIF, 464. Hagenfeldt and Palm (*Sandstone Runestones*, Stockholm 1996, 12) give 66 per cent of all Runestones as granite or gneiss, 17 per cent as limestone, and 14 per cent as sandstone; but sandstone was used only after *c.*1050 in Sweden.

to have made more attractive, even as it offered a spiritual afterlife; but it was mainly confined to more prosperous areas of Scandinavia. The inscribed posts erected elsewhere have all perished, and the alternative ways of commemorating the dead in the British Isles kept the number of rune-stones low, outside the Isle of Man. There are none in Iceland earlier than the fourteenth century, despite the abundance of hard lavas to work with; there, as elsewhere, future fame rested on oral transmission, of which the only authentic survivor is some of the skaldic poetry, since most of it has proved less perennial than bronze.

However, the poets seem less concerned with the future than with the immediate renown of their patrons, perhaps going as far as a future-perfect:

> *Few ring-showering rulers will thus have measured the southward path with feet* boasted Sigvatr of Canute, after his journey to Rome in 1027.

Being better than contemporaries or predecessors is usually good enough for these war-lords, but Arnorr went further in his 'mighty poem' to the young Magnus of Norway and Denmark (Hrynhenda I *c.*1046):

> *every prince is far worse than you; may all your success be greater than theirs, until the sky is riven.*

The hope of fame everlasting for the patron was linked to the poet's own hope of being remembered for the quality of the verse. It is strange that more did not follow the lead of the Rök sculptor, and inscribe full strophes on stone, but some did, notably at Högby, and at Hällestad and at Gripsholm, for the brother of the Swede Yngvarr who led an expedition to Russia and beyond in the 1030s or 40s, and died there

> *Far to get gold*   *Fared they manfully*
> *And out east*   *Gave to the eagle;*
> *Died southwards*   *In Saracen-land.*

That disastrous venture was remembered on thirty of the surviving Swedish stones.[6]

---

6 There is a bibliography of the Yngvarr problem by Haakon Stang in MESCA, 558, and for text and trans. of Gripsholm, Jansson 1962, 41. 'Saracen-land' in this context meant the southern coasts of the Caspian Sea.

Stones and mounds stood still while verses were forgotten, houses fell into ruin after a generation or two, settlements moved or divided, and many families emigrated. To assert and announce a hereditary freehold was as much as most farmers could do for their posterity in this world, and Bjorn Finnviðarsun took the opportunity of doing so when he commemorated his treacherously slain brother on the stone at Nora (Uppland):

IS THIS ESTATE THEIR HEREDITARY (odal) AND FAMILY PROP-
ERTY, THE SONS OF FINNVIDR AT ÄLGESTA

Hundreds must have expressed in other ways this confidence in a propertied future for their families, as did their charter-holding contemporaries in England and Francia.

Temporal Fears

The huge stone of Björketorp (Bleking, south-west) was raised two or three hundred years before this age, but the dire word cut into the B-side: MISCHIEFPROPHECY[7] holds good for the fears of subsequent centuries. Mishap due to risky navigation, foul weather and arduous work, as well as human violence, was inevitable; the cemeteries show that the healthy had good reason to fear sickness, not more than elsewhere overall, (although the earliest burials at Lund, (990–1020) include the remains of five lepers, and by 1100 there were forty more) but with more chance of catching it in the undisturbed filth of the new towns and from transient seafarers. The Thor's hammer pendants worn by men and women, and often buried with them all over the North, were charms against misfortune, like crosses, as well as anti-christian symbols.[8] The whole range of Nordic jewellery can be assumed to have had virtue of this sort, and acted as insurance, as well as a visible display of wealth. Broken bits of ecclesiatical metal-work had not lost power by rapine or by their reuse as brooches on Norse women's shoulders.

The fear of harm from natural causes was accompanied by fear of sorcery, fear of the dead, and fear of defamation, as almost everywhere else in the world, christian or pagan, and the three dreads were

7 Reading UTHARABASBA as ú-tharfa-spá: DR, 360. M, 134–6 dates this 700–750, B 120 to the 590s. Looijenga 2003, 178–9 discusses and construes.
8 Roesdahl 1982, 160 has the Trendgaarden jeweller's mould with both cross and hammer; Wamers in ISCEVA (1998) on amulets, and Arcini 'Leprosy in Lund' PONO (1993), 267.

interconnected. The resentful or hungry dead could suck away prosperity, like the witch or wizard who could use the art of *galdr* inependently, or enlist the help of the dead and the divine through *seiðr*, to bind and kill; and the satirist could use spells or libels to blast the fame of men and women in this life and forever, and undo the hard work of poets and rune-carvers.

Defamation

I'll not indict him   *I'll just indicate him:*
The rascal with the hook-nose   *Whose treachery drove*
King Sweyn from the country   *And Tryggvason lured*
                               Into a trap.[9]

These lines, attributed to Stefnir Thorgilsson *c*.1000, were preserved nearly 200 years later in Oddr Snorrason's saga of Olaf Tryggvason, with a neat Latin translation, and may be judged effective, since there is no other contemporary evidence to straighten Earl Sigvaldi's nose and acquit him of treachery, and the sagas weave complicated plots to justify the charges. The Icelanders had laws against verse like this, one of several forms which *nið* (defamation) could take, and the most durable; a weapon which a poet could not draw lightly. The impetuous Egill Skalagrimsson was said, nevertheless, to have uttered *nið* against a king, Eric Bloodaxe, and his queen, a would-be wedge between Eric and the Norwegian nobles and gods:

So gods may pay back
Powers expel prince
Gods and Odin be enraged
With him, for ravaging what's mine.
Frey and Njorð! make
Oppressor flee from his lands;
Be the noblemen-harmer, shrine-desecrator,
Loathed by land's god.

According to the saga Egill reinforced these verses with a horse's head set on a 'pole of defamation' and left the king to his fate; which turned out to be exile and dispossession, a coincidence which makes the whole

9   Skj. IA, 153, IB, 146 for text, and Dronke PE, ii, 204, 220 for a fanciful reading of 'hook-nosed' as socially derogatory. The earl was supposed to have ruled the Jomsvikings, who were supposed to have kidnapped Forkbeard, who was also haunted by defamation: 'it was whispered by the lowest of the low that on account of this he ought to be addressed as slave', Thietmar 7, 36 (26).

story incredible: fable to show how a mere Icelander could undo a king with words and gestures. At all events, the slander was effaced by Egill's later praise-poem, if the so-called 'Head-ransom' is genuine. Others were less forgiving than Bloodaxe. The priest Thangbrand was slandered by pagans in Iceland in the 990s, and replied by killing them, as had the so-called bishop Fridrekr and his acolyte Thorvald, when they heard verses that went:

> *Has children borne*
> *Bishop nine;*
> *Of all of them*
> *Is Thorvald father.*

The poet died, the verses live; and they and their like have been connected with formulas of execration, 'scathing incantations' and magic.[10] Simple sexual abuse seems to have done the trick in Iceland, whether it moved the gods or public opinion, and there was a story that the Danish king Harald Bluetooth and his steward in Norway were proclaimed sodomites in verse by Icelanders given no redress for goods shipwrecked in Jutland:[11] a contrast with the English king Edgar, who avenged the stranded Danish merchants of York by devastating the beachcombers of Thanet (969 or 974): 'he despoiled all of them of their possessions and even deprived some of life'.

The Dead

The dead could prejudice the future in most parts of the world, by walking. The Nordic and Latin undead-traditions recorded later are different in that the northern dead could return in the flesh or in dreams at any time, however carefully they had been buried or cremated, while further south the unburied, the suicide, the murder-victims and tenants of desecrated graves were much quicker to rise; but this difference may lie only in the sources from which the beliefs come. No peasant society trusts the dead entirely. Their feeding, coaxing and propitiation was necessary, since they were a force to be harnessed if possible; if not, to be kept down and under. Optimists

10 See Almqvist 1965 for the best study of *nið* poems. Against Thangbrand, pp. 55–112 of vol. i, pp. 89–118 on Egill's; also ed. and trans. in Turville-Petre 1976, 22. Several were probably first collected in the lost Ólafr Tryggvason saga by Gunnlaugr Leifsson (*c.*1200).

11 Almqvist 1965 ch. 3 accepts the Bluetooth verses as genuine. The slander is a good contrast to the self-glorification on the big Jelling stone and to Adam of Bremen's making him out to have been a saint: see Lund in Jesch 2002, 303–20.

hoped that ancestors would guard the family property and luck if properly housed, entertained and remembered, as when in 958 or 959 the Danish king Gorm's corpse was laid in an oak-boarded chamber, double-walled, with tongue-and-groove joins, accompanied by a large treasure of all kinds of utensils (mostly lost) and sealed within a huge reinforced mound of turves. A few years later he was dug out by his convert son, and buried in a church nearby, where holy ground would hold him tighter, while his spirit soared. The theology differed, but the aim was the same, and many christians assumed that the dead lived in their graves until resurrection, if not to the full: 'asleep'. While Gorm's great-grandson Canute was feasting at Wilton Abbey, and grossly reviling the former English king Edgar and his sanctified daughter Edith, his archbishop opened Edith's tomb. The veiled corpse sat up, unveiled, and reproved the Dane, who fell to the floor, a believer. She had heard everything; she was listening, and Canute should have known better; his father had been killed by a chance arrow shot from Bury, while he was defaming St Edmund the Martyr. Dead saints were notoriously dangerous when roused, and dead pagans no less.[12]

About five hundred years earlier this was acknowledged in the words on the Flistad stone, in Västergötland:

BEWARE THE DEAD DESTROYER

– the *aptrganga* or *draugr* in Icelandic literature. Offerings and celebrations could sedate the dead, but if those failed, exhumation and disintegration were tried, or just the head and feet were severed, as in the Kaupang inhumation cemetery, and with two skeletons at Kalmargården in Sweden. The great lady in the Oseberg ship-burial, laid to rest with such opulence, was dug out of her mound, her bed chopped to pieces and her bones scattered, not merely for loot; her rich goods were untouched. At Ladby, in Denmark, they broke into the ship-burial and did remove the goods; which they then broke into 500 fragments, and shovelled back into the excavation, and remade the barrow. At Balladoole on the Isle of Man fifteen out of sixteen christian graves were violated, and some emptied, before Norsemen put their own dead in the boat and mound above them, whether as assertive parvenus, or simply newcomers fearing the old owners.[13]

12 See William of Malmesbury *Gesta Pontificum*, ed. Stubbs p. 190 for the Edith tale, and Demidoff in MS, xi, 30–47 on 'The death of Sweyn Forkbeard – in reality and later tradition'.
13 Brøgger 1933, 100; Eriksen 1991, 188–91; Bennike 1985, 107; for Ladby, Sørensen in BUSO (1997), 165–70; also Bennike and Christoffersen on the headless man of Lejre in *Skalk*, iii (1981). On Balladoole: Tarlow 1997.

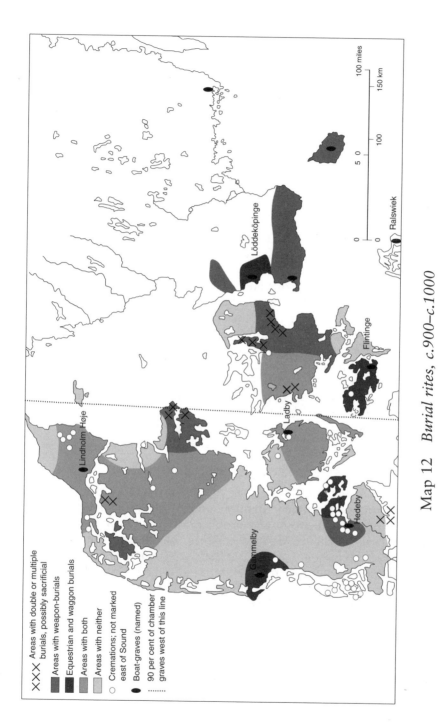

Map 12 *Burial rites, c.900–c.1000*

(After Eisenschmidt 1994 and Pedersen in MASS (1997); Näsman in MAMMEN 166–7; and Voss in Offa 1973, 113)

Legend:

XXX Areas with double or multiple burials, possibly sacrificial

Areas with weapon-burials

Equestrian and waggon burials

Areas with both

Areas with neither

○ Cremations; not marked east of Sound

● Boat-graves (named)

.... 90 per cent of chamber graves west of this line

Labels on map: Lindholm Høje, Gammelby, Ladby, Hedeby, Löddeköpinge, Flintinge, Ralswiek

Scale: 0   100 miles
0   150 km
5 0
0   100

Bogs had been good places to put corpses since the Bronze Age, and in Jutland for some time to come; but bog was not in itself a sedative, since 10 per cent of the prehistoric sleepers had been staked down,[14] and precautions recur in dry soil. One tall elder in the Danish Ottestrup cemetery had a large stone laid on the lid of his coffin to make sure: 'Rest in Peace' was no empty formula, whatever the religion. If the dead had to be kept from harming the living, so must the living be deterred from harming the dead and so wounding the repute and honour of their families.

Unsuccessfully, in the case of Harold Harefoot, one of Canute's sons. He was proclaimed king and ruled from 1037–40 in England, and so slighted the authority of his half-brother Hardicanute in Denmark; he expelled Hardicanute's mother Emma. He was buried at Westminster, then a small abbey on a bushy island in the Thames; but when his brother arrived from Denmark he sent an archbishop, earl Godwin 'and other men of high position' and had the body dug up, thrown into a marsh, hauled out and launched into the river. It was picked up two miles downstream near the Danish camp at Southwark, and given burial in St Clement Danes, in the Strand; William of Malmesbury insists that it had also been thrown into a privy, but at any rate king Harold I had been degraded and punished in a way that made sense both to christians and pagans, and separated him for ever from his father's royal family. Such treatment was what his grandfather Sweyn's body would have suffered at the hands of Ethelred in 1014, if an English lady had not sent it back to Denmark.[15]

The Unforseen

The unforseen demanded attention, and got it, through augury, lots, magic, ritual, shamanism and prophecy, and the sources show that the appeal to chance decided matters which educated christians usually left to reason. Usually, but there are so many cases of prelates (like archbishop Adalbert of Hamburg-Bremen) consulting sooth-sayers and dice that the distinction may be false. Abbot Ælfric drew the line in his *De Auguriis*: 'a man may cast lots...without witchcraft, so that he may allot himself pastures if men wish to divide them'; but one thing leads to another. Among the Norse, bunches of

---

14   None so thoroughly as 'Queen Gunnhild' of Haraldskjær, *c.*490 BC; see Boyer 1994, ch. 1 for later examples; and Rudolf and Angela Simek in HUG (1997), 65–71 for 'Bog People Revisited'.
15   EE, 2, 3; which also makes Sweyn pray Canute not to return to Denmark without his body (1, 5). He did, but the lady embalmed it and delivered it to his sons.

sticks were thrown down 'to clarify the intentions of supernatural forces thought to direct personal fate'.[16] Ninth-century Danes decided the fate of captives the choice of sacrificial victims, the conduct of war, and which god to appease through this method. 'I dare not support this mission of yours' said the Swedish king to St Anscar (*c.*830) 'before I have consulted our gods by lot casting', and the same source relates that Danes eager to plunder Birka changed plans when the lots advised them to plunder somewhere else, across the Baltic.

Dangers could be deprecated by asking gods and others to drink and dine in the great or lesser feasts, where the humans offered blood, human and animal, and hoped for luck in future. There is a contemporary witness to the bargain in the same Life of St Anscar, which cites a reprimand sent to the Swedes by the gods 'with our support you have held this most fertile land... in peace and prosperity for many years. On your part you have performed sacrifices and rendered us your votive offerings... if you want to keep us friendly to you, increase the neglected sacrifices and offer greater votive gifts'. The language is too biblical to pass as verbatim communication from Asgard, but the ideas behind it were shared by christians and pagans. Future success would come to king Alfred of Wessex when he began to send alms to Rome, and gave half his time to god; Canute, on his way to Rome in 1027 was seen depositing a cloak-full of silver on the high altar of St Omer's abbey, and 'passing no altar, small though it might be, without giving gifts and pressing sweet kisses upon it'.[17]

But where luck is seen as a finite good, a total distributed among mankind (as in many parts of the world today, but most notoriously in the witch-burning villages of South Africa) steps had to be taken against its appropriators and its diminishers. A future marred by dwindling health or wealth could be averted by practising magic against the known or suspected enemy; either *galdrar*, the use of spells or signs to harm others immediately, or *seiðr*, the achieving of similar objectives on the basis of communication with the unseen through a medium or a trance. These are the terms used in later law-texts, where both are proscribed as diabolical; but their long survival in Iceland and Scandinavia indicates that many found them socially

16   Clunies Ross 1998, ii, 138ff; and see Seebold 1986, and Flowers 1986, 48–61; Ellis Davidson 1988, 152–4 discusses briefly; for the *Vita Anscarii* trans. Page 1995, 229. Casting lots is so rational and common a way of reconciling conflicting opinions that it needs and needed no religious sanction or 'rune-magic'. The *lytir* or augur remembered in Swedish place-names was evidently a leading man in each district.
17   EE, 2.21; trans. Campbell, 37.

useful, if not essential services and so they got reward or punishment depending on circumstances. The man with the hole in his head, cased in bark, naked, and staked down in Thames mud between high and low-tide below London walls (c.900?) may have earned his fate in this way, like the widow arrested and 'drowned at London Bridge' for driving iron pins into an effigy in the 950s.[18]

After Death

After death lay another future to provide for. Some spent their all on it; according to Wulfstan, in the OE Orosius, there were Balts among whom the dead man's possessions went entirely on drinking and games at the wake over a month or two; any left over were divided into prizes to be won by strangers in a horse-race and the clothes and weapons were cremated with the body, which had been 'ripening' meanwhile.[19] This was not the way among the Norse, where sometimes rich deposits of worldly wealth were included both with the buried and the burnt over this whole period, in patterns which vary greatly between graves, dates and districts. The rites of burial within Scandinavia were not recorded by Wulfstan or anyone else, and can only be reconstructed in part by archaeologists; but if their remains reflect concepts of death and after life, it seems that there are many different opinions on the subject. This diversity appears in the later written sources, and inspired a memorable book by Hilda Ellis Davidson nearly sixty years ago; since *The Road to Hel*[20] was 'A Study of the Conception of the Dead in Old Norse Literature' there is no need to go through those sources here. Archaeology has confirmed the impression that rites varied, but their meaning in terms of life after death need not have reflected the variations closely; some may have been seen as better ways of getting to the same goal as the others.

Thus cremation followed by interment with burnt or unburnt treasure and sacrifice was introduced after the Migration period and remained common throughout southern Scandinavia from c.750 to c.900; less so, thereafter, except in Finland, but never entirely abandoned until the conversion. The only witness to the idea behind it is the report of Ibn Fadlan, on the boat-cremation of

---

18   EHD, i, p. 519 for trans. of S 1377; *The Independent* 24 May 1991 for report of Bull Wharf Lane burial. See Tolley 1995 on useful spirits and Price 2002, 224–6.
19   Wulfstan, trans. Fell, 32; and see Bojtar 1999, 18–19.
20   Cambridge 1943; reprinted 1968. Mauled by philologists and precisians, but illuminating to generations of students.

Future

a Rus chief and a strangled slave on the Volga about 921. He claimed that the girl-victim claimed that she had had a glimpse of another world: green, and populated by family and friends. Rus bystanders scoffed at muslims for letting their own dead lie in earth to be eaten by worms, presumably because cremation sent theirs directly, uneaten, to a better place; and yet they must have known that paradise waited for muslims, too. There must have been something about rotting underground which repelled them, more at any rate than becoming crow's meat above it; and this may account for the careful assembly of bones picked clean by animals at Repton in the 870s, and then buried. The burning of an entire boat with corpses was not usual in Scandinavia, or so it seems from the archaeology, but there was a later tradition that at one period ships had been filled with dead men and weapons and firewood, and launched with hoisted sail, to float rudderless, in flames until they sank:[21] the 'viking funeral' of modern romantics. Naturally there would be little trace of it, if this ever happened.

Most of the burials in the crowded cemeteries of Hedeby, Kaupang, Birka and Lindholm Høje contain the ashes of men and women with uncremated grave-goods: for use after death, in a future world, or as tokens of the care and respect of the survivors? The things said and done at funerals are lost, but were more significant than the burials which ended them. Sigvallius analyzed 488 cremations in a district just north of Stockholm, where the farmers were slow to change their funerary customs over the first millennium. During the viking age they laid fewer livestock on the pyres than earlier, but still slaughtered horses and cats (for Freyr and Freyja, possibly). There was no sign of human sacrifice or suttee as far as the evidence goes, but it is incomplete; 90 per cent of the cremated bone is missing, or minutely fragmented. At a more cosmopolitan site like Birka there were three main cremation procedures:

1 burning the dead with goods on a boat, and leaving or burying the ashes on the site;
2 burning the dead with goods, and then separating the bones from the burnt goods and burying them apart;
3 burning the dead without goods, on a sort of *ghat*.

Bones from east and south Norwegian cremations reveal that there were four different heats to which these corpses were exposed: 200°,

---

21   King Haki of Sweden was supposed to have been cremated in this way (Ynglinga Saga, chapter 23) and Sigurðr Hring in the lost Skjoldunga Saga embarked on the fire-ship and 'at the same time slew himself with his own hand', Ellis 1943, 43, discusses, and Lindow 1997, 84–6.

400°, 700–800°, and 1000–1100°. The 48 per cent cremated at low temperatures were merely baked, smoked or heated, on rather than in pyres; in these and other cases flesh was often carved or scraped off the bone beforehand, as if to be eaten, and the bones later served up on plates or in cauldrons. It seems that that is exactly what was happening; corpses and bone were offered to gods as meals, to avert misfortune. High temperature cremations could also be accompanied by sacrificial victims; in both cases the dead were transformed, rather than annihilated, and in some places (as in the Isle of Man burials) cremated animals could be buried with the unburnt corpses of chiefs and their sacrificed women[22] (see map 12 for geography of tenth-century burials).

Others believed that the dead stayed in their graves and remained formidable even decomposed; as mentioned previously, pp. 283–4. Well-furnished inhumations, made as domestic as possible with stone slabs for walls and ceilings, earth piled above, and inside, weapons, artifacts, tools, ornaments, food and sometimes human or animal companions, were not for the utterly inert. Such graves appeared long before this, all over Europe, in the Bronze Age, and persisted in Sweden down to c.600; then reappear, with the decline of cremation after the 890s, notably at Birka and Hedeby, and reach a high point in Denmark in the second half of the tenth century. Such preparations may refer back to the ancient mounds, as a way of joining immemorial land-watchers, or to the contemporary christian belief in the resurrection of the flesh, or merely be a recruiting of the dead to protect the family's new title to land. Christian clergy were irrevocably opposed to cremation, but not to richly-furnished graves, at this period, or to the concept of the restless dead; what they believed of the unbaptized corpse appears in the story of the Norse raider cursed by archbishop Lievizo of Bremen c.996; he returned to Norway and died, but his corpse would not decay for 70 years, until a bishop went north and absolved him.[23] Elaborate inhumations, like elaborate cremations, are evidence above all of the need to impress family status on the beholders, rather than to make a statement about a particular sort of afterlife. Nevertheless, it is hard to believe that the great chambered mounds were purely commemorative; and the ample folklore of the living-dead tenanting these mounds throughout the north at all periods must be conclusive. The future existence of many viking-age people was held to be sentient, passionate, vindictive and subterranean, at least part of the time.

22 Oestigaard 2000 argues for cremation as cooking with much theoretical accompaniment, using P. Holck, *Cremated Bones* (Oslo 1987) as evidence. For a concise survey of grave-types see Müller-Wille in MESCA, 237–40.
23 AB, 2, 33 (31) and scholium 67 (68); christian literature is rich in similar examples of the 'St Erkenwald baptism'.

Bo Gräslund (1994, 18–19) has suggested that there were only two contrasting views of death in early times: one in which the soul was free either to remain in the body, or leave it and wander, and another in which the soul was ejected with the last breath, either to be reincorporated in another world or submit to a prescribed post-mortem regime of purification or reamalgamation with the creator. The first view was held by believers in the Norse and Germanic gods, by the societies which took trouble to pacify the freed soul with burials and communication and propitiation, sacrifice and celebration. The second was the christian and islamic view, but it was also the faith of the 'wilderness religions' of Fenno-Scandia: of 'Arctic shamanism'[24] and of whatever non-theists lived among the hunting, gathering and servile populations of the Baltic coastlands. There is certainly evidence of attempts to placate the free soul, archaeological in this period and direct in the folklore of peasant communities all over Europe down to the present day; and it would of course imply a wholly different afterlife from that of the wilderness-religions, in theory. Yet it is not so in practice; the beliefs mingle and converge, and are confused in three ways at least. Shamanism (ecstatic communication with the dead or the spirits) thoroughly permeated the whole Nordic and Baltic world; Lapps and Finns allowed the dead to be house-guardians, beasts or vampires apparently at their own discretion, as if free; and medieval christianity included so many ceremonies for the wellbeing of the dead and the warding-off of their malevolence that only a theologian would know that this was not a fairly free-soul religion.

The word for soul most commonly found on christian rune-stones (SIOL: *sála, sál* in OWN) was borrowed from Old English and used for the sort of immaterial personality which might or might not ascend to the christian heaven; if properly 'helped' by Christ, or by St Michael, then to heaven. Alternative words were indigenous, and show that the concept was not new: ATA, ANTA, (*andi*) was breath (even bad breath) and life and used for the christian's soul as well, and the Holy Ghost. There were three other non-denominational words for out-of-body personalities: *hugr* (see p. 311) *hamr* and *fylgja*, each with a long future in Icelandic literature; not to mention the *geð* and *moðr* which inspired the body from within.[25] Pagans

---

24 On shamanism see part of *Northern Religions and Shamanism* ed. M. Hoppál and J. Pentikäinen (Budapest 1992), and for a detailed survey of 'circumpolar religion and... ON Shamanism' Price 2002, ch.5.

25 As Samson points out, at this period the christian afterlife was more firmly material than the pagan, owing to the doctrine of the resurrection of the flesh, in white robes as at burial: 1999, 129 and 137.

could evidently survive death in their own terms, whether free or not. The question was, where? For those who did not remain underground in their graves, there were at least seven possibilities, even if each was not open to all comers.

1 *Living with the Gods*: 'If you want to have more gods, we are ready to admit to our society Eric, once your king, so that he may take his place among your gods'; so ran the often-quoted invitation of the gods to the Swedes *c.*830, according to the *Life of St Anscar.* This is too close to the conventional gibe at all polytheists: 'those whom pagans declare to be gods are found to have been men in former times'[26] to be be trustworthy, and the divine-kingship theorists have dined too well on this passage, which is ironical in tone. Yet the hope of joining the gods, or at least the group called Æsir, cannot be ruled out. The most grandiose mound-burials (as at Adelsö near Birka) over cremated remains seem to bid for status in heaven as on earth. The burning or interring of so much wealth, in slaves, livestock and precious objects makes little sense as an application to join Odin's zombie army of *einherjar,*[27] and the king Hakon celebrated in Eyvindr's poem as bringing his slain warriors to Odin's hall, in 'the green home of the gods' was to be 'given the house-peace of the einherjar' but drink ale with the gods themselves, all of whom turned out to welcome him. Humans could be deified even without the benefit of christian polemics; Bragi Boddason, supposedly the first skald, was in Asgard, along with the ex-king of the Danes Hermóð, in *Hákonarmál*, which appears to date from the later tenth century.
2 *Valhalla*, the hall of the slain, was a product of the cult of Odin, a place where the casualties of war were assured of sex, drink, pork and battles every day until they joined in the great final war of gods against monsters; or so it was in Snorri and two of the Eddic poems, although the details vary. Carvings on Gotland stones usually dated to the eighth century[28] reveal that this was a current belief in the east Baltic at that time, and the symbols of resurrection carved on the Sparlösa stone (*c.*800) in Västergötland include a hall and a rider which may refer to it. Later sources put together the hall, valkyries and horse, which make up the earlier myth, with the battle that brings the current world to an end and a daily routine of warfare. The place eventually becomes an antithesis of christian paradise,

---

26   Isidore, *Etymologiæ* 8, 11, 1.
27   Roesdahl on 'Princely Burial in Scandinavia' in Kendall and Wells 1998 for other examples, supposedly Odinic, and Nielsen in HØKO, 248–50 for counter-arguments.
28   Lillbjärs (iii) has the welcoming woman, Tjängvide (i) has a woman and Odin and a domed hall, Ardre (viii) has Odin and a hall; on later ideas see Steinsland, 'Eros og død', MOR, 152–3 and Marold 1992, 700–1.

where there is neither rest nor spiritual solace, nor room for ordinary women or non-combatants.

Valhalla has been connected with tenth-century ship, waggon and weapon graves by Roesdahl and Eisenschmidt, on the grounds that the vehicles would get the dead to the hall and the weapons be used there. But ships and carts could go anywhere or nowhere: the Oseberg ship was moored in its mound by a cable; and the careful and varied arrangement of weapons points to their use as status-symbols rather than as equipment for perpetual war. Many shields were buried, few helmets or mail-coats; an omission strange even for fighters whose wounds healed every evening before dinner. Why the generous rations given to richer Danes (game, ham, venison, buckets of beer and mead) when food was never scarce in Valhalla? Why the greater variety of weapons in Norwegian than in Danish graves, why so few in east Jutland? How would decapitated grave-companions fit into the next world? There are too many unanswered questions about these graves to let them all lead to the same concept of afterlife; the theory is based on the assumption that the unified challenge of christianity demanded a unified response, when there is no reason to believe that christianity was seen in that way, or that belief in Valhalla was spurred by that, rather than by a variety of competing afterlives.[29] It was an opportunity for those who trusted Odin to serve him after death; never more than a small minority of inveterate fighters and war-lords whose corpses had been left on the battlefield to rot, or feed Odin's pets: the eagle, the raven, the wolf, alias the gore-swan, the hostility-gull and the watcher. The Lapps exposed their dead freely, the Norse only the corpses of enemies, as at *Assandun* in 1016; for them, Valhalla was compensation for a painful and even anonymous death away from the family farm.

3 *Hel*, the deep, dank repository of the dead was the place the *einherjar* avoided; the word is found among the Goths and Old Saxons and Anglo-Saxons, but what it actually meant in the viking age is not clear. A goddess called Hel appears in Egill's verse, but above ground; much later, in Vǫluspá (st. 43) she has a high hall underground and a 'sooty red cock' to waken the dead. In Balder's Dreams she has a watch-dog, with a blood-stained chest, who barks at Odin; but by that time the concept had been overlaid by the christian *inferus* or *Hades* or *Orcus*, and continued to be embellished

---

29 See Roesdahl 1983 and 1997, and Eisenschmidt 1994, and Anne Pedersen in BOSO 1997 and MIAS 1997 for a view of these graves as reactions to Ottonian display, and Crumlin-Pedersen 1995 for a survey of possible meanings of boat-burial.

with macabre details and geography appropriate to a place of punishment:[30] rivers of ice and fire, perilous bridges, impaled bodies, snake-houses, foul smells. All that is too close to Irish and Anglo-Saxon visions of the other world to be of purely native growth, but if the viking-age Hel was anything like that (although not a place of torment) why would anyone want to go there? The later tradition that it was open to all who had not died in battle or been chosen by valkyries is difficult to square with the care and concern for the dead revealed in the graves; why prepare them so competitively for a college with no entrance qualifications and precious few amenities? Hel remains a mystery; even more so the place.

4   *Under the Sea* Where Egill Skalagrimsson (see p. 262 above) thought his sons were kept by the giant, Ægir. Other poets gave other souls to Ægir's wife, Rán, with her fish-net.

5   *An earthly land of the dead*: Ódáinsakr, the field of the immortals is mentioned in some sagas and by Saxo (book iv) as a refuge 'unknown to our people'. Saxo also described the 'shining fields' somewhere in northern Russia, ruled by the brother of the king of hell, with his twelve noble sons and twelve lovely daughters, where unwary travellers were entertained with fatal banquets, luscious fruit and enthralling sex. Whether any of this was believed in the viking age is unknown, but there was a world wide custom of setting aside tracts of land for the use of the dead, and Ellis Davidson found that both Icelanders and Lapps of a later date knew of holy mountains or hills where ancestors lived.

6   *With the poor, Over the stream*; where the modest burials are, bone and charcoal under a stone slab, accompanied by a knife, glass beads or a cheap brooch, some distance from the well-appointed cemeteries and mounds; usually opposite settlements and across streams. What kind of afterlife was connected with these graves is not clear; the conjecture that this was a survival from the early Iron Age, before the Æsir and the upper classes got the upper hand is no more than that.[31] But it would be preferable to stay near the village and watch, rather than sinking to Hel or attempting to gatecrash selective afterlives; or becoming the grave-companion of a master and continuing to serve after death. Who-ever contributed the ten pit-fulls and many grave-fillings of burnt bone in Ottestrup cemetery on Zealand (Dk) may not have done so from choice; according to Ibn Fadlan only the free were cremated

---

30   Outlined in Simek 1993, 137–8, and see Dronke's comments on Vafthrudismál, 43, Skírnísmál, 35, 3 and Vǫluspá, 2, 5 in PE ii, 109 and 412. Ellis Davidson 1943, 84–7 discussed the geography of Hel.
31   Nielsen 1991, 251.

among the Rus on the Volga, and the slave girl sacrificed on the pyre apparently saw this as a privilege.

7 *Reincarnation* was a further possibility: that is, a posthumous life in this world with a different body. There is no evidence whatever of such a belief in the viking age, but a gloss on the Eddic poem *Helgakviða Hundingsbana* states that 'there was a belief in the pagan religion, which we now reckon an old wives' tale, that people could be reincarnated'. The protagonists of that poem 'were thought to have been reborn': Helgi as another Helgi on earth, Sigrun as a valkyrie. The tales of Olaf, the elf of Geirstað, a long-dead king who hands on regalia (through a third party) to the future St Olave has been interpreted by Heinrichs as a repudiation of pagan ideas of reincarnation; the old Olaf asks that his corpse be beheaded in the grave-mound, presumably to free his soul and let it enter the new-born Olave, who dismisses the idea as a popular misconception when he grows up. It is not clear what lies behind this; a christian apologist, *c.* 1200, editing a story about a saint so that he can both be a re-born king and a witness to the truth that such re-birth is impossible? A strong local tradition legitimizing Olave's rule in a way that distinguishes him from other kings, rather than invoking a commonly-held belief? A revelation about how kingship had once been seen in that part of Norway? In any case, the anecdote as it survives[32] is post-conversion by a long way. There is only a strong likelihood that the transmission of power and property in pagan times was sometimes reinforced by the idea that the current holder was in some sense stronger than metaphorical a previous holder 'come again'; a strong likelihood because it was found throughout Christendom despite the disapproval of the orthodox, and under a 'free-soul' dispensation – why not?

Seven lives beyond death, or at least beyond the tomb, were not all; nor by any means a choice open to all the living. They were destined by rank, place, gender and accident (drowning, death in battle) to one of doubtless more than seven final or at least posthumous homes. Some of these were influenced by the encroaching image of the christian heaven, just as the christian hell became a sort of heated Hel's kingdom. Graves with christian symbols and connotations recur throughout Scandinavia in tenth-century and even earlier contexts: cross-pendants, chalices, candles and east–west orientations. The new heaven was proclaimed on eleventh-century

---

32 In the Legendary Olaf saga, and in Landnámabók: versions retold in Turville-Petre 1964, 193–4, with little comment; much in Ellis Davidson 1943, 138–47; and see Heinrichs 1994.

Swedish rune-stones. It was LIGHT and PARADISE, attainable with the help of four great patrons: God, God's Mother, Christ and St Michael. It was the HOME BEST FOR CHRISTIANS, even those like the dead of Eggeby, Brössike and Lilla Lundby (in Uppland), for whom it was BETTER THAN HE DESERVED or KNEW HOW TO DESERVE, even.[33] The poets fill in some of the details. For Hallvarðr it was 'the hall of the hills' (*sal fjalla*), guarded by God as king Canute guarded his lands. For Thorleifr Rauðfeldarson it was 'sky's radiance'; for all, a kingdom where souls and bodies would be reunited. The runes declare three ways in which the rich could get there by their own efforts:

1   by building bridges or causeways, mentioned in 160 Swedish, 5 Danish and 2 Norwegian stones; praised in verse at Sälna (Uppland);
2   by building the church, or, in Norway, erecting a stone cross;
3   by commissioning memorials inscribed with christian symbols or formulae, even for men who had died at war, or overseas, or with pious self-advertisement like that of king Harald Bluetooth who MADE DANES CHRISTIAN, or Ingerum of Almarestäket the would-be pilgrim (above p. 279). In the Northern Isles of Britain, apparently by sponsoring 'Christian sculpture'; see Christopher Morris 'From Birsay to Brattahlið' SCEU 187–95.[34]

But why should they exchange a non-christian afterlife, which was not explicitly punitive, for a paradise which carried with it the risk of eternal damnation, and in any case the society of social inferiors? If such a question was ever put to a priest, he might have pointed to the selective character of six of the seven afterlives mentioned above, or to the words Bede gave to the Northumbrian counsellor, who saw man's life as a sparrow's flight through the king's hall: 'of what follows and what went before, we know nothing at all' (HE 2, 13). The variety of pagan after-lives may have caused a similar doubt, and enhanced the certainty of christian teaching; or the assurance that those who led others to baptism, or endowed churches, would be saved.[35] With access by burial in the angels'

---

33   Herschend (1994b, 16–20) attributes the sixteen examples of this formula to a period of christian revival or fervour, but B. Sawyer (2000, 141) thinks they may commemorate very late converts, or the unconverted.
34   Hagland 1998, and B. Sawyer 'Woman as Bridge-builders' in PEPO 1991, 211–17, and now ch. 6 of B. Sawyer 2000.
35   In Sweden, the rune-stone fashion spread with christianity; and yet as Herschend points out (1994b, 26–7) the christian did not need the rune-stone to survive death. It showed how the family hoped things would go.

white robes, by works before death, by the prayers of others after death, the christian heaven was never unobtainable at this date; or incompatible with the communication between living and dead which was socially vital, and continued uninterrupted until the Reformation or later.

Ragnarǫk

Ragnarǫk means 'fate of the gods', rather than 'twilight', and is a term found in Eddic verse, not in any viking-age source; as explained by Snorri, it meant a comprehensive mutual destruction of gods, giants, and monsters in a final cataclysm which would end the world and presumably, mankind. After that, a new immortal world would appear, inhabited by six divine beings, including Balder. Wagner made opera out of this, and in the eleventh or twelfth century it inspired the poem *Vǫluspá*, the Prophecy of the Seeress, which could either be a pagan response to christian ideas of the world's end, or a christian poet's use of pagan myths to proclaim the death of the old gods.[36] There are references to some of the episodes in the diction of the skalds and on tenth-century and later inscribed stones: Gosforth, Thorwald's Cross, Skipwith in Britain, Hørdum in Denmark, Altuna in Uppland Sweden; but none, (possibly the binding of Loki on Ardre viii) on the eighth-century Gotland stones. It seems that at some point before the end of the viking period various unrelated elements involving gods in danger (Odin and the wolf, Thor and the world-serpent, Loki unbound, Tyr losing a hand) were organized into a coherent eschatology not inconsistent with the christian apocalypse, or the version of it called *Mutspelli* in Old Saxon. If so, *Vǫluspá* could have been the first news of *Ragnarǫk*, rather than the last gasp of pagan theology. For most of the viking age, the 'victory-gods' were triumphant: it is difficult to believe that eager followers of Odin and Thor expected their gods to be eaten alive or poisoned, and not rise again. The *Vǫluspa* poet or poetess showed how this would happen, but only at the end of this world, as the preliminary to the rise of a second world, where the Æsir live together in harmony and 'enjoy pleasure throughout eternity', remembering past times and playing backgammon or fox-and-geese with golden pieces. The gods of the heathen occupy a christian paradise on earth; whoever thought of this attractive and self-

---

36 Strophes 44–58. See Dronke 1988, 122, and VIRE 122–5 and PE, ii, 98–104 for analysis, and restatement of non-christian authorship; a claim which involves too many difficulties to be accepted here.

contradictory idea stood somewhere between christianity and paganism, which must have been where most northerners were.

The end of the world was a periodic obsession among laity and clergy in western Christendom; as when the millennium from the Passion, 1033, coincided with the ending of a long famine and a highly visible eclipse of the sun. Soon after 1064 the christian poet Arnorr was lamenting the dead earl Thorfinn of Orkney by claiming that his better would not appear before the 'world would be engulphed, the sun turn black, earth sink, sky be split and sea swell over the mountains' as if this apocalypse would be familiar to his hearers. The gods lived on, as heroes, devils, kings, comic characters, and symbols; and *ragnarǫk*, describing their deaths, was one of the ways in which they were to survive.

Postscript

Modern Research

Over the last 25 years so much has been published on this period, and so much excavated, that it may seem that we know twice or three times as much about it as in 1981. But we don't. The mountain of new data gives birth to 'scientific overload', and the endeavour to apply new solutions to a reliable historical framework has been disturbed by the current devaluing of all historical knowledge into an adjunct of theory. The situation is common to most branches of learning in which methods of evaluating and criticizing data have lost the status they enjoyed from c.1850 to c.1960, while the technology of research has been developed to an almost magical pitch of refinement. Viking research used to be summed up every decade or so by syntheses or surveys like those of Brønsted, Almgren, Gwyn Jones, Foote and Wilson, and Sawyer. They were criticized as partial and programmatic, but they did the job. They made sense of the viking age in terms respected and shared by most specialists and by the public. They, and their readers, wanted to know more about the past as it was.

Those were the days when truth was something specialists could issue to ignorant amateurs. As Christine Fell said of the mere historian: 'in areas where he does not control the methodology it is unwise to deploy the results...though there is room for the private scholar there is no room in universities now for the amateur...we must be seen as professionals'.[1] 'Be seen as' is rather sad, but the rest is the authentic voice of old-time philology, chilling the inexpert, untroubled by the question of who controls the controllers of the methodology. This faith in pure expertise lives on, but has been undermined both by the inane abundance of information technology, with the sheer volume of viking/Old Nordic information available on the internet sweeping over the scholars, and by the preference among

1 'Norse Studies' in *Norse Revaluations*, ed. R. Samson 1995 (VIRE) 28.

younger experts for historical theory over fact finding. As the Nor-wegian archaeologist Solli puts it: 'For me, historical archaeology does not exist, only the writing of archaeologies exists... influenced by general cultural and social theory'; she wishes to escape from 'the prison of precision' and fly away with the post-processual post-modernists.[2] Others zoom in to the ideologies of the viking age, or try to construct one which will explain artifacts, technology, build-ings, events, politics and the lot. They too escape from the prison of precision and enter the holiday-camp of paradigm, that set of assumptions on which the thought of any period is grounded. Nordic research is no longer dominated by an intellectual priesthood: the traditional disciplines survive with difficulty in universities and museums and institutes, rumpled and sometimes outmanoevred by new philosophies, new science, and discontented students. It is a rich and rewarding scene, which the bystander can merely itemize under three headings: (a) old schools; (b) new or rejuvenated techniques; and (c) new philosophies.

The Old Schools

Archaeology has been the royal road to the understanding of the Nordic past for nearly two centuries, and it still is. Journalism, television and large exhibitions confirm the archaeologist as guardian and guide of the viking age, and star of wonder to a profession involving thousands of employees in state-funded departments com-mitted to 'administering and preserving a cultural heritage'. He or she demands and sometimes gets a lot of money, if not usually a job for life. The money is never enough, but that holds good for hospitals and day-care centres and police-dogs; the great thing is to connect the pump to the petrol tank, and that has been achieved, for diggers into the viking past, over much of the northern hemisphere. When gov-ernments get stingy, public support is keen enough to justify corpor-ate and private generosity; the science is blinding, the yield fabulous. If old hands like Randsborg and Wilson doubt whether the quality of interpretation matches the quantity assembled, and if young ones doubt the validity of the whole enterprise (see below, *New Philoso-phies*) most of the diggers remain true to the old progressivist formula: more = better. They, more than most, can be said to 'control their methodology'; they can show and tell to millions, even if their expensive methods raise the question of cost-effectiveness more

---

2   Solli 1996, 89, and below pp. 27–8; and Varenius 1991, 137–8 on the hermeneu-tic approach.

acutely for the unspectacular work. Loss of coherence and certainty within the ranks has not yet shadowed the public face. Certainly not, in the salty world of *Marine Archaeology*, where spectacular finds (Roskilde Fjord, Graveney, Hedeby) refined techniques of excavation and preservation, international co-operation, and a high profile go together. Accurate replica-building and sailing offer quasi-factual data by which to test theories of Nordic seamanship and, naval architecture. Formerly, shipbuilding was identified as the technological cutting edge, the secret weapon that gave the Norse a military advantage and a communications network, the equalizer; the work of Crumlin-Petersen over three decades has modified this well-established doctrine[3] by showing the variety of problems and solutions which all Baltic and North Sea shipbuilders faced and attempted, without the benefit of a single model of viking ship for all purposes, but in touch with comparable Frisian, Anglo-Saxon, Frankish, and Slavic design. At the same time the launching and testing of replica vessels has virtually become an international sport, vicariously enjoyed by everyone and transcending the ordinary limits of research so as to approach the ideal of the Romantic inventors of the whole viking mystique: to make history live.

Other subdivisions of archaeology move in the same direction: town and village archaeology in particular, and even if they never get beyond the sideshow or Alton Towers effect the replica settlements confirm the primacy of archaeology as the hotline to the viking age and the early medieval period in general. It is easier to sell than the other kinds of research because it incorporates some of the main prejudices of our time: that the hidden must be revealed, that technical innovation is the key to success, that teamwork makes truth. More will be said under *New Techniques*, because they have become the lifeblood of this powerful organism, which not only finds out new things in new ways, but presents and interprets them to a far wider audience than any other form of Nordic research.

---

3   Varenius (1992, with English summary, 134–46) rejects the idea that ships change shape because craftsmen think up better ways of overcoming problems of seamanship, because the ship was a symbol as well as a vehicle, and a response to the demands of social development on land. Why else have a dragon at the prow and gilt at the mast-head? Westerdahl (SHAS 1995, 41–50) agrees: ideology shaped the ship. If only we could be sure what it was. He has suggested that mast and sail involved gods (wind) in campaigns powered by human rowers; Varenius that ships on coins symbolized Nordic opposition to Frankish influence (CSA, ii, 185–6) and Carver sees ships as 'transferable icons' used for the political legitimation of the current deity' (Carver 1995, 120). It is hard to believe that christians buried in boats, as at Sebbersund, were legitimating theirs. For the long view: Røstad in *Viking* lxvi 2003, 31–48.

Anthropology, social and economic, and *Sociology*, its twin, get second place among the old schools, if only because they contribute more and more to archaeology and the others. Thus Polanyi's theory of the essential difference between modern and pre-modern concepts of trade was formulated in 1957 and still dogs interpretations of viking age economies.[4] The belief that 'sentiments are socio-cultural constructs that can best be understood within their specific context' has opened ways into the inner life of Nordic peoples for all confident enough to construe that context with the help of socio-anthropological theory. The belief that dead societies can be reassembled by comparison with others 'at a similar stage of development' has broken the silence of the less communicative northern peoples, and attempts to reconstruct Nordic life in general rely heavily on anthropological concepts: the chiefdom, the kin-group, gift-exchange, age-banding, polygyny, patriarchy, peer polity interaction and gendering are the bricks of which the viking age has been rebuilt. The pervasion is summed up in the title of a book by Hastrup: *Iceland: Island of Anthropology* (Odense 1990). It concerns post-conversion Iceland, rather than the earlier period, and even so, it has been well said that 'we do not know medieval Iceland as it actually was, only the world created by the sagas...we have no empirical basis for saying that something was important that they did not recognize as important'[5]; at the most, 'we see levels invisible to them but present nevertheless'. Such misgivings are rare. Systems of social organization and thought have been imposed on the viking period as if the cryptic nature of the evidence justified a holiday from verification. So the application of gender theory to the creation myths found in the thirteenth-century prose Edda yields (in Linke 1992) 'mythological images' which reveal 'early North Germanic assumptions about sexual procreation'. Diagrams help, but whether a triangle with the words FIRE (male) ICE (female) and *Anthropo-Cosmic Giant* at the angles represents another peep at the sex-life of the Early German, or anything at all, is unknowable. 'And if anyone ever thought this thought, where did the system of thought exist until the anthropologist discovered it?' asked Gunnar Karlsson of a Hastrup insight, but the question

---

4 See Thorláksson on profit in thirteenth century Iceland (FROSA 1992, 231), and for the Nordic inner life, the work of Gurevich, Steblin-Kamensky, Hastrup and Jochens. It was Steblin-Kamensky who wrote: 'I think I understand Iceland and its culture, but perhaps I've invented my own image of it' (*Myth*, 1982, 105). A moment of truth unparalleled in the influential work of Dumézil, who fitted up his Norsemen with a trifunctional social order and a predetermined Indo-European cosmology and mythology spun from dubious sources, and *ne regrettait rien*.
5 Karras 1992, 303–4, referring to the free Icelanders' sleeping with slave-girls: no big deal in sagas, but crucial in a gendered anthropological analysis.

concerns a whole new generation of anthropologically minded Nordic researchers, on whom see p. 318. As similar analyses of other societies multiply and discriminate, such concepts change, and it turns out that current theories of social development in the viking age rest heavily on ideas and concepts such as chiefdoms, states, hierarchies, urbanization and craft specialization which are no longer as firm as they looked, at least among the anthropologists from whom they were borrowed. They talk now of the segmented and the decentralized state, the heterarchy, the temporary chief, and the co-existence of types of economic organization formerly placed in sequence.[6] Despite her fickleness, we are married to this tart; but now must turn again, in sorrow, to the mortal ruins of a great queen who once ruled us with a rod.

Philology, the study of language and literature ('to read the past through words' – Roberta Frank's definition) is the oldest route to early Nordic times. Once proud and omniscient, with the prestige of a science, and a hundred university chairs to sit in, she still keeps her head up, but she has lost weight, and her authority has been bypassed. Some of the fat went with the habit of reading the viking age back from the thirteenth century and later Icelandic narratives called sagas, and from the corpus of mythological poetry known as the Elder (Poetic) Edda, and from the guide to myth, legend and poetic diction composed by Snorri in the 1230s: the Prose Edda. This habit was formed two hundred years ago, when it was held that such works represented traditions passed down from generation to generation as records, however distorted, of what happened in the remote heroic age. It can still be claimed that the praise-poems within these texts are mostly authentic heirlooms preserved in this way; even that the collection of proverbs called 'The Utterance of Him on High' (*Hávamál*) is 'very much what one would expect of a poem composed in the Viking Age and orally transmitted for a century or two' (Evans 1989 but see p. 253); others find these utterances perfectly consistent with much later dates of composition. A revolution in the assessment of source-value announced in Scandinavia and Iceland towards the end of the nineteenth century has worked its way through the study of Old Norse (and Latin) texts, and saga-study has ceased to be used as a telephone to the vikings in most Old World universities. These texts are now used to unravel the mental world of the Iceland in which they were written, or as problems in palaeography. They are not irrelevant to the realities of earlier times, but there is no agreement on what the relationship was. It is claimed that

---

6 Stein 1998 summarizes new trends in the concepts of power, and Magnusson Staaf (1994, 5–53) noted the mismatch of systems-theory and archaeology.

in combination with runic inscriptions, sagas and other medieval
tales can reveal the pre-christian world; North believes that Anglo-
Saxon paganism 'can only be uncovered...through an Icelandic
literature four centuries younger,' and has written *Heathen Gods in
Old English Literature* (Cambridge, 1997) to prove it.[7] This is still a
busy workshop, but its products are not used here; the reader cannot
be expected to take on trust source-interpretations which are invari-
ably speculative and unverifiable, even if they happen to be perfectly
sound. Instead, there are four specialized branches of philology
which come with some kind of rules.

Runology first. Inscriptions in the runic alphabet, or futhark, are
the only authentic literature of this period to be preserved in its
original, or near-original form. These are not dumb things with
inborn sense, like most artifacts; they talk. The zeal of Page in this
cause over the last thirty years has convinced many in the British Isles
that these texts do not merely 'confirm' history derived from other
sources: they are historical events in themselves, more authentic than
any other writing. Nevertheless, 'the fact that the Vikings speak
directly to us only in their runic inscriptions has seldom been found
relevant to serious study of the Viking Age';[8] the new day is slow to
dawn over here. In Scandinavia, runology has had its 400th birthday,
and the task of compilation and reading inspires many articles a year,
the *Runrön* series of monographs, and the circular *Nytt om runer*
published at Oslo. Most work is on the letters cut into memorial
stones; the majority of these belong to the period 960–1100, and 90
per cent of those are to be found within the modern boundaries of
Sweden: over 50 per cent in Uppland. Despite the thousands of
survivors, it appears that rune-stones were rare events, or unknown
in much of Scandinavia and all of Iceland – extremely rare until after
the conversion to christianity, and therefore always liable to produce
skewed results if used for quantitative analysis in the field of viking-
age social history; as they must be. Such memorials were a local

---

7 Lönnroth 1977 and Mitchell 1991 argued for the extraction process, and Mitchell's introduction offers a concise survey of the main schools of saga-criticism. Price
2002 shows that it is still possible to take, or skim, ON literature as evidence of a
single 'world-view' among Nordic heathens.
8 See Page 1997 for a look at the lastest research (in French). There are said to be
90 full-time runologists at work in the world, but 'only a handful' study ON runes.
Historians who have used their work in recent years include A. Christophersen
(1981–82), B. Sawyer (1991 onwards), A.S. Gräslund (1986–7), C.F. Hall Hallenk-
reutz (1982) and A. Hultgård (1998). On the Rune-text Data-base, privately funded
and in progress since 1993, see L. Petersen in VC, 12, 305–9; and for rune-based
social history B. Sawyer 2000 and Herschend 1994b offer contrasting studies. Note
Syrett 2002 on political implications.

fashion, possibly inspired by Irish or Anglo-Saxon epitaphs, although using a Nordic writing system (on which see pp. 276–7). The thirty-three surviving inscriptions on the Isle of Man are the earliest dense concentration of such memorials in the Norse world (*c.950–c.1020*). There were also runes on weapons, ornaments, walrus ivory, bracteates (stamped coin-like discs), coins and wood. The deposits of inscribed birch found at Bergen and Novgorod belong to a later period, but two examples found at Hedeby have been dated to the tenth century, and more early letters may be uncovered if they are lying in the right kind of mud. Potentially, there is a continuous record of changes in language and culture for over a thousand years during which, historians claimed until recently, there were 'no written sources from within the Nordic world'. The question now is: at what point did literacy become widespread among these unlettered barbarians?[9]

There is one little difficulty. Historians want to be sure of what the inscriptions mean, before they use them; and with most of the earlier ones, and many of the later, there is a wild diversity in interpretation and dating. Lerche-Nielsen has listed six different readings of the Glavendrup stone, the most important early Danish example, and has been convinced by none: and these are only the more recent. They are all distorted by preconceived notions of viking age politics or religion; and see p. 235, for the Babel of translations rising from the great Gautish stone of Rök. The most interesting find of recent years, the stone of Malt, in Jutland, with its run of 137 runes apparently cut before 900, has so far defied clear interpretation.[10] Runology rests on other branches of learning: linguistic theory, phonetics, art-history, archaeology; so that it is never quite secure as a philological discipline, despite the intellectual edge of its adepts. In 1990, a wonderful paper 'On types of argumentation in Runic Studies' was addressed to the third runic symposium at Grindaheim, and according to one listener it 'could have dampened the spirits of a much larger conference';[11] while at the other extreme, the cryptographers, numerologists and occultists reach a wide and credulous public with hilarious rune-magical sallies to embarrass as well as depress the experts. Björn Andersson (author of *Runor, magi,*

9   Most of the runes in Scandinavia and the British Isles have now been published, and the former are now collected in a single computerised corpus, which will include a semantic analysis of poetic and runic vocabulary: see L. Petersen 1989 and VC 12, 305. For early runes see Looijenga 2003.
10   See Stoklund in MOR (1994), 168–70, Grønvik in ANF cvii 1992, B, 361–72, and Barnes, as Boadicea, in *Scandinavica*, xxx (1991) and SB xxiv/2, 156.
11   Liberman of Barnes, in his review of Knirk's edition of the *Proceedings* in *Scandinavica*, xxxv (1996), 269.

ideologi (Umeå 1995), where the magical theories are discussed) laments the lack of a comprehensive modern theory of runes. All the same, this is the space to watch; they find new material every year.

Which is to slight the contribution of *skaldic studies*, the reading of thirteenth-and fourteenth-century texts which purport to include verse composed and committed to memory by viking-age poets. These 'court metre' strophes have always been the hardest nuts to crack in the whole field of Norse literature, but students now have the advantage of guides by Frank, Gade, Lindow, Bately, Jesch and Clover, to select only the English-language authors.[12] The texts were all edited and roughly translated into Danish by Finnur Jonsson at the beginning of the twentieth century, with all MSS readings and a lexicon of poetic usage: a giant's work with flaws which have occupied dwarfs ever since, so that until the whole corpus is finally computerized, work on these poems has meant continual cross-reference between Jonsson's *Skjaldedigtning* (Skj), Koch's *Den norsk-isländska skaldedikningen*, Koch's *Notationes Norroenae* (in which the irascible Swede rejected hundreds of FJ's readings), most of the post-1900 editions of sagas in which the verse occurs, and for light relief Vigfusson and York Powell's *Corpus Poeticum Boreale*, a monument of capricious emendation. The fundamental problems with this material remain unsolved: how, when and why did Nordic poets begin composing in this way? How exactly was their work transmitted over two centuries to the first scribes? Were there inter-mediate texts, now lost, or was it pure oral transmission? How were the verses performed?[13] And since some of the poems are undoubt-edly later concoctions on viking-age themes, how genuine are the rest? At best, their authenticity can only rest on strong probability, established by source criticism; but that is good enough for most historical purposes, and Frank, Poole, Marold, Malmros, Foote and Meulengracht-Sørensen have used these texts for vigorous historical reassessments. In this survey, none of the verse attributed to the period before the 950s has been accepted as contemporary. Some of it may be, but it is too problematic in its present form to support propositions about the early viking age. Poems associated with

12 On skaldic studies see the review article by Jesch in CM, xi (1998), 105–16. Marold's 'Der Skalde und sein Publikum' (AUSA 1991, ii, 54–66) is a good analysis in German of how the praise-poem is constructed, but the indispensable study is Gade's The *Structure of Old Norse Drottkvæð Poetry* (Cornell 1995). On Snorri's Edda see Faulkes 1991.

13 Recited theatrically, with gesture, or deadpan; shouted; chanted unaccompanied; chanted to some kind of beat? The last is highly unlikely, but all modes have advocates; see Gade 1995, 23–7 and 224–6.

Hákon jarl, and chiefs and rulers of the generations that followed form solider evidence: it has been assumed that we have many of the actual words of Eyvindr the Plagiarist (*Skaldaspillir*: 960s–980s), Egill Skallagrímsson (hero of a highly fictional saga, about a real poet active from the 950s to the 70s), Glum Geirason (960s), and Eilífr Guðrúnarson (980s and 90s). These men and their female rivals (see p. 23) perfected a difficult art, but their work defeats translators and leaves most modern readers cold. Attempts have often been made to use it to confirm historical statements based on other sources, as in Ashdown's versions included by Dorothy Whitelock in *English Historical Documents* vol. i; but this is uphill work, given the uncertain date and stylized format and often ambiguous intent of the verses. As guides to the mentality of the most important Nordic group, the military retainers, in the period 950–1050 they are by contrast the indispensable source, and have been used accordingly.[14]

Why not the Eddic poetry as well? This collection of eleven mythological and eighteen legendary (or 'so-called mythical and so-called heroic': Motz) poems gets its name from one book, known also as Codex Regius, written in Iceland *c.*1270, lodged in Copenhagen from 1666, and now back home. As Jochens says, 'this small MS, not much larger than a hand, is the unique black diamond that has irradiated pagan mythology and Germanic heroic legend through the ages'. Adaptations of some of the poems had made them familiar to readers throughout Europe and North America by 1900, and some historians still use them for insights to the religion, ethics and general carrying-on of pagan Scandinavia: the vikings' bible, so to speak. As the immediate source and audience of Codex Regius was the educated christian squirearchy (clerics and landowners) of Iceland, this won't do; they were writing to entertain each other, not to forward a parcel of ancient lore in prime condition, untampered with, to posterity. There is older stuff among the verses, which may survive as evidence of a debate between christian and pagan or syncretist poets which continued through the tenth and eleventh centuries, but detecting it involves too much glossing and sifting to fit into a work such as this. As Martin (1988, p. 79) puts it, the writers of these poems lived at a time when paganism was in one sense, past: the religion of the ancestors; in another sense, present, as superstition at home and heathenism abroad; and in another sense, internal, in the risky 'gentile' philosophies of scholars, and in the deviant soul. They wrote of Odin, Thor and the old days with those things in

---

14 Clunies Ross and four other editors announce a new edition of the skaldic corpus in book and electronic form, which will be a godsend to all scholars alive in 2007. The verse has been used most successfully in Jesch 2001, see esp. pp. 15–33.

mind; but none of those senses would have meant anything to the viking-age pagans. See now Gunnell and Whaley in CONIL 82–100, 479–502, for surveys and analysis.

The third useful type of philology is the study of *names* of *places* and *people*. Toponymics is a pursuit which offers clues to the way Late Iron- and viking-age societies saw, used and altered the countries round them; to their social organization; and to their colonization. After nearly 150 years of trial and error, it flourishes in the British Isles, Scandinavia and Germany, nourished on growing collections of place-names of all kinds and dates, from the great English Domesday corpus of 1086–7 to the field and stream names now being snatched from oblivion by taxing the memories of living farmers. Interpretation has grown more and more meticulous throughout the last century: Cameron, Gelling, Fellows-Jensen (working in Copenhagen), Watts, Thompson, Cox, Mary Higham, and Insley have batted for England and Scotland with notable results. The view that Scandinavian elements in place-names are simply evidence of rural colonization by Nordic settlers in the Viking Age has been superseded; a more complex and interesting range of possible contacts over a longer period has been proposed, and the connections with settlement and invasion revised. Fellows-Jensen 1995 was not the same as Fellows-Jensen 1991, or 1972; and for the overthrow of Marwick's chronology of Orkney farmnames, see Thompson in SSNB (1995) 42–63. This is a volatile subject in the British Isles; in Scandinavia, where the earliest fat file of place-names is from King Valdemar's Estate Book (*Jordebog*), compiled in Denmark *c.*1230, such studies are attached to public bodies, but remarkably lively, thanks to a general tendency to use place-names (in lieu of the non-existent documents) as first-hand evidence of early social and administrative structures, and as pointers to the cultic landscape. For an introductory survey of Norse toponymics see Fellows-Jensen in MESCA (1993) 501–4, and for controversy, sample Holmberg 1990 and 1994, Mundal 1990, and Sigmundsson 1992. For place-names that illuminate wholly unrecorded settlement, e.g. in Åland, see Hellberg 1987 and Roeck Hansen 1991. Similarily, the study of personal names reveals patterns of family cohesion, inheritance, religious affiliation and historical consciousness. Thanks to the runes and to the chroniclers, there is a good supply of viking age nomenclature, both names and nicknames, and fine printed collections: von Feilitzen's for Domesday Book, Björkmann for all English sources, Adigard de Gautries for Normandy, Janzen for Scandinavia.

The fourth contribution of the philologists lies in *linguistics* generally, especially in the study of language development and diffusion, which makes it possible to trace the contact between the Norse languages and the Irish, Welsh, Old English, Frisian, Saxon and Fennic tongues. What the colonists in the British Isles spoke, and for how long, and when it changed has been a troubled topic over the last fifty years; Danelaw speech was discussed in a long debate in NOWELE iv 1984, and its character convincingly delineated in Townend 2002. For the British north-west, see contributions to LACON (1991).

So philology remains indispensable; archaeologists and anthropologists who have ignored this approach, have stumbled. What word-study can and cannot do was sketched by Frank (1997 502–12) in her discussion of the word *hugr*, vital in Old Norse, apparently even in viking times. By the thirteenth century it had acquired at least thirty different meanings, ranging from 'love' to 'hostility' by way of 'mind' and 'thought', and was commonly paraphrased by the dark expression 'wind of the giantess' in poems. Why? No clear answer is found in the contexts or from parallel kennings. We can only conclude that these were people who were not as nice about the distinction between thinking and feeling, internal and external, as we are; but would be entirely on the same wavelength in these matters as the Anglo-Saxons.

Among the other old firms still in business, one of the oldest is that kind of *Religious History* or cultural research which concerns cult, mythology and divinity. Its long history is very briefly summarized in Simek 1993 (148–50), and blessed with a full bibliography by Lindow (New York and London 1988) and Lindow's further survey in MESCA 1993 423–6. This research has in the past been overshadowed by systematizers – e.g. Höfler, Gurevich, and Dumézil – who have spun overarching thought-patterns from late texts which turn out to be representative of almost anything but the religion of the viking age, or from pictures and artifacts uncritically interpreted in the light of e.g. Jungian psycho-philosophy. So it was, so it is, and will ever be; but close study of strictly contemporary evidence combined with the fruits of religious anthropology, rather than too heavy a reliance on the literary mythologies of Snorri Sturluson and Saxo Grammaticus offers an alternative. For example, Lindow's *Murder and Vengeance among the Gods* (Helsinki 1997) discriminates between the more and the less likely notions of Balder, the 'god without a cult' whose myth has brooded over this whole branch of learning for too long, as an antetype of Christ the redeemer, the resurrection and the life. Comparative religion has breathed life into the study of Nordic paganism, and the Nordic conversions (see chapter 11); but 'the myth of perpetual recurrence' is the title of a famous book by Eliade, and may serve as the epitaph for much of twentieth-century mythography: the same texts, the same techniques and the same conclusions come round rather too often. But see now Orton 'Pagan Myth and Religion' CONIL 302–19.

The study of *Folklore* has long been the crutch to the study of Nordic religion, social life, and thought, since the lack of contemporary evidence cripples investigation. As long as the soul of the nation was sought in peasant custom, this custom was held to preserve the beliefs of an ancient pre-christian world: the corn-dolly was Freyja. The theory may have been wrong, but the result of it was a mass of evidence collected from the conservative peasantry of Scandinavia and the Northern Isles over the last 200 years. Recent attempts to bring some rational criteria of relevance to this mass have borne some fruit, if not much; for example, Perkins 1999 on the land-spirits of Norway, and Gunnell 1995 on viking-age drama. Without this material, the nature and power of land, house, mountain and sea-spirits could only be guessed, and the beliefs of subarctic Scandinavia, the Lapps and the Western Isles would be entirely lost. The folklore of finding, and not finding, buried treasure has recently been used as a guide to the mind of the viking age depositors of treasure: see Zachrisson 1998 chapter 8 on the Uppland hoards. A short but absorbing summary of Scandinavian research into folk-tales and beliefs is to be found in Lindow 1978, 17–56.

None of these routes to the past can be described as a mainly historiographical technique, but with them and through them runs the edge-tool of historical research: *source-criticism*. All kinds of unlikely texts were held to be sound evidence for the viking age until the twentieth century, and their authority yielded slowly to critical assault. The critics prevailed. Most of the written evidence, whether contemporary or not, is now seldom treated as factual narrative. The task of reinterpreting these sources, finding out what they were meant to mean, now occupies the time of many students and impels some to very high levels of scepticism, and imaginative deconstruction. Thus *Ynglingatal*, a verse genealogy of the supposed Swedish ancestors of Norwegian kings, has been reinterpreted as a twelfth-century satire on pagan kingship in general (Krag 1991); *Rígsthula*, a fable of rank and degree once held to encapsulate either pagan political theory or tri-functionalist Indo-European social theory, has reappeared as a tract in favour of 'the modern image of Christ-centred kingship' (Dronke in VIRE (1993) 127); Adam of Bremen's vivid description of the temple at Uppsala, with its gilded roof, golden chain, three idols, holy well and sacrificial grove (a cornerstone of traditional Scandinavian historiography) has been read as a metaphor of Gregorian churchmanship as seen from the anti-Gregorian camp (Janson 1998), a satirical fiction. It may seem perverse to mention these brand-new stylings under the heading of

Old Schools, but they are all continuing a revaluation of the sources begun in the 1890s by Erslev and the Weibulls, in Denmark and Sweden; or, rather, smuggled in from Germany by various unguarded passes. Less swingeing treatment of the texts remains the inescapable task of all researchers; the old *Quellenkritik* lives, as in Ó'Corráin and Etchingham's work on the Irish Annals which concern viking raids, and Dumville's on the Insular and Irish sources relating to Northern Britain in the earlier part of the viking age, which has led him to reject most assumptions about the origins of Scotland;[15] or when Sawyer pointed out that *naufragium*, in Alcuin's famous letter on the Lindisfarne raid of 793 (trans. EHD i p. 776) means 'disaster', here as elsewhere, not 'raid from the sea', so that the long-held idea that the Northumbrians had never thought a viking attack possible evaporates: they had simply not expected any harm at all. Sawyer's vigilance has also unfastened the date of the fall of Eric Bloodaxe and the kingdom of York (952 not 954), and has freed the reign of the Danish king Sweyn Forkbeard (988–1014) from the incubus of misread or misleading or posterior sources in a poignant reprise of Weibull's original charge.[16] The question is, how far do you go? Source criticism is apt to lose its edge in the world of deconstruction, where it becomes what has been called 'suspicionism': the routine assault on the credibility of primary sources in the interests of social theory. As when Ingimundarson insists that Iceland's sagas and charters must be treated as 'indexical' to the 'class position of the lower peasants' although they seem to be by and mainly about the upper classes and to reveal the plight of the less fortunate only obliquely. Hastrup blew the trumpet for the new learning when she announced that 'source criticism evidently is important but on the other hand most of it rests on a fundamental logical error: it takes "reality" for granted, while only the sources can be'.[17] Nevertheless, when we hear

---

15 Ó Corráin 1998; Etchingham 1996; and Dumville 1997, who denounces 'the comprehensive unwillingness of most twentieth-century historians to engage clearly and critically with the written sources for this period'; hence their failure to notice that the Norsemen did not overthrow the Pictish kingdom, or speed the triumph of the Dalriatan Irish over the Picts, or ally with these Scots to subjugate others.
16 See his contribution to *Church and Chronicle in the Middle Ages*, ed. I. Wood and G.A. Loud (1991) – 'Sweyn Forkbeard and the Historians', and 'The Last Scandinavian Kings of York', *Northern History* xxxi (1995), 39–44.
17 FROSA (1992), 225 for Ingimundarson, and Hastrup 1986, 12. Sources cannot be 'taken for granted' either. The collection of kings' sagas called Heimskringla, usually attributed to Snorri and dated *c.*1230, now appears to be a compilation made fifty years later (Berger in ANF, cxiv (1999), 5–16); if so, everything changes but the texts; the greatest historian of the Middle Ages dwindles into the greatest mythographer. Downham rejects all sources which make Eric Bloodaxe king of York in MS XIV, 51–.78

a story about a dead friend, we cannot help wondering: did that really happen? even if it was a good story.

It is time to leave the Old Schools, with apologies to the *numismatists* and the *art historians* and the *agrarian historians* and the other well-established guides to the viking age who might have been found at work *c.* 1950, as they are today, and to consider

New Methods

New Techniques are usually associated with archaeology. Over the last 30 years they have raised expectations to a point at which the entire material world, especially of the remoter Nordic settlements, seems to lie within our grasp. It is easy to select a dozen innovations which have laid bare the lives of populations once thought to be beyond the reach of modern curiosity:

Palaeoclimatology, armed with pollen analysis, lava, and ice-core sampling, offers a reasonably clear picture of the changes and constant features of the northern climate over the first millennium A D, and the discovery that for most of the viking age temperatures and rainfall were not dramatically different from what they are today has had a sedative effect on theories inspired by thermal determinism, the freezing up of the Norwegian hill-farms and the vision of a lush and sunny Iceland.

Palaeo-ecology, -biology, -botany, and *-entomology* have filled in stretches of the settled and the unsettled landscape so minutely that the very fleas in the hair of Harald Harfagr have been numbered and weighed. There is no escape. What they wiped their arses with in tenth-century Viborg (moss) is now public knowledge, and the diet they shared with their whip-worms can be itemized: fine-milled barley, rye, oats, bran, field-beans, wild strawberries, hazelnuts, blackberries, raspberries, elderberries and fish. From such data, relations between settlement and surrounding country can be calculated. First at Ribe, now at Dublin, the size of animal bones has revealed, or suggested, large hinterlands busy with stock-raising; *landscape archaeologists* (on whom see p. 322) and others use these techniques to reconstruct the economies of large areas, and fit them into patterns of control, cult and status which used to be conjured from the evidence of burial sites alone.[18]

18   See Robinson and Boldsen's report on Viborg Søndersø in AA lxii 1991, 71. If the latrines had never been found, *Stable Carbon Istotype Measurement* of bone fragments would still have revealed the source of the protein in the diet: see Liden and Nelson in *Fornvännen,* lxxxix (1994), 13–21. For flora and fauna of the northern isles, see Anderson in VIPA (1997), 15–17 and VACON (1993), 522–3; Hansson 1997 analyses VA diet.

Precise dating techniques (*Feinchronologie*), first through tree-ring measurements (Dendrochronology, invented in 1949), has been applied to finds from Nordic sites with zeal since the 1970s. Tage Christensen's dendro-dating of the Trelleborg timbers (the slides delivered by a despatch-rider in leathers to the maestro, in front of a conference of intimidated date-guessers in 1981), ended forty years of inconclusive speculation on the context of such fortifications. The Jelling mounds surrendered their birth-certificates soon afterwards, and the buried ships of Oseberg and Gokstad were freed from a century of historiographical palpation by the dating of their timbers. Material not ring-datable has been fitted into wider time-bands by *Tephrochronology*, using layers of volcanic ash associated with datable eruptions in Iceland, and by the ice-sampling mentioned above; and Radio-Carbon dating, with its large margins of error (plus or minus 140 years) has been refined by *Accelerator Mass Spectrometry* into a more accurate tool.

Where is as interesting as when, and it is now possible to find the source of jet ornaments by *X-Ray Fluorescence Spectroscopy*, which analyzes their elemental composition. Metallurgical science now includes a chemistry which reveals the source of silver, and so settles long-standing debates about the movement of bullion over the northern world, whether coined or not, and iron and steel have been traced to their approximate birthplaces by a new kind of slag and phosphor analysis (on which see Jouttijäævi in Aarbøger 1992, 182–89). This was an age remarkably rich in tools and weapons, by the standards of other parts of Europe, and it helps to know where they came from. But the new gadget which has transformed all metal-finding, and enriched numismatics beyond measure, is the *Metal Detector*, commonly wielded by those amateurs banned from the universities by Professor Fell (p. 301). Since the mid-eighties, these hunter-gatherers have discovered so many single coins over parts of Britain and Scandinavia once thought to be coinless that the daily use of money in this period now seems to be firmly established, whatever it was used for. Economic historians now accept that viking age consumers (a) accumulated and transported coin in gross; (b) deposited it in accordance with what was probably religious practise, in hoards and graves and thank-offerings; (c) hid it in times of emergency; (d) circulated it through small transactions over wide areas south of the latitude of Trondheim; and did all these things at the same time, not in a sequence governed by any law of development. It clears the air a bit.[19]

19 See Metcalf's tribute to the 'metal-detectorists' in VC 12, 196–214; 'The Beginnings of Coinage in the North Sea Coastlands: a Pirenne-like Hypothesis'.

Another scientific break-through of interest to archaeologists and others trying to fix the nature of migrations and ethnic affiliations is *DNA sampling*; also tempting to medical historians and anthropologists. This relatively new science (in combination with the old blood-group and pigmentation surveys) offers broad hints on the population movements and mixes of the viking age in so far as they have not been effaced or distorted by subsequent contamination. That is, if the samples are taken from living populations, as has been the case in Orkney, Iceland and Norway; dead bone and tissue of the right date are better witnesses. However, thanks to the disciples, colleagues and rivals of Sir Walter Bodmer, it now seems improbable that Nordic immigrants wiped out or expelled all the natives of Orkney and Shetland, or imposed a race-bar on the settlement of Iceland: some kind of Celtic-Nordic merger is indicated in both cases. Racial purity is no longer a concept used by Nordic historians, and it is easy to forget how important it used to be, in the days when vikings were forgiven their barbarism for their contribution as sperm-donors to Old Europe; but that is another story. Modern anti-racialists are eager to get in ahead of the geneticists' swabs, and proclaim the extensive intermarriage of their forebears with Lapps, Finns and West Slavs; how a migration of early Swedes turned into Russians is already established, and preliminary sampling certainly suggests a mixed genetic background linking Nordic populations with all the circum-Baltic stocks. Where DNA analysis is more immediately relevant to this period is in the deduction of gender, diet, pathology and kinship from human and animal remains. When these methods have been fully tested in the collaborative project called *Svealand*, the future of these methods will be clearer.[20] Meanwhile bone and tooth scrapings from burials are revealing how far skeletons belonged to the same families, and what, if any, reliance can be placed on the traditional picture of the kin-based Nordic society (see pp. 46–8).

If the history of viking-age art is a branch, or separatist movement of archaeology, it should be noted here as a reborn topic also spurred on by new technology, especially by *Computerized Correspondence Analysis*, which entrusts to a machine the detection of links between motifs and of developments in style which were formerly left to the subjective judgement of experts. A more stringent methodology and a more reckless spirit of interpretation have joined hands, so that the style-despots have been given a new lease of life in the realization

20   Liden and Götherström 1999 provide a bibliography. See now Milman in VS xxiii (2004) for an attempt to derive the modern frequency of the C 282Y mutation of the HFE gene from Viking Age emigration.

that what used to be called 'Viking Art' was not a self-sufficient development but a variation on themes common to Western, Irish, Mediterranean and Eastern craftsmen. The conventional sequence of Nordic styles[21] was challenged and modified by Fuglesang in the 1980s, and she has since refined the reading of ornament on Swedish rune-stones into what she considers a firm dating scheme running for a century after the 990s; firm enough, apparently, to challenge the Icelandic dating of Yngvarr's expedition from Uppland to Russia, even when linked to the Georgian chronicle (*c*.1040.) The style of the monuments put up to commemorate the men who did not return is anchored to the early 1020s: somebody has got it wrong. German scholars have been very active in this field: Karl Hauck, on bracteate design, Michael Müller-Wille, on cross-cultural inflences, and Egon Wamers (on Insular metalwork found in Scandinavia) have leavened their rigorous analysis and assembly of the material with bold re-interpretations of its meaning; while Lang's work on the fragments of early tenth-century sculpture found at York Minster has shown so many links with the Jelling style that the case for its Anglo-Danish origin, and so for other English influences on the Jelling kingship, is strengthened.[22]

Philology has not been transformed by new methods to the same extent, but *computerization* has speeded and standardized research in all fields, particularily in lexicography; it has pandered to the hoard-ing instinct which has always possessed some scholars, and has fed the urge to continuous publication which has inspired others. Brigaded into great projects, the servants of the word have become a global army of the cutting edge, employed on machine-based enter-prises of which the computerized database of all the sagas at the university of Iceland is the HAL. Meanwhile, there have been

---

21 It used to go: *Broa* (from the gripping-beast motifs noted there and at *Oseberg*), followed by *Borre* (symmetrical ring-chain patterns), followed by *Jelling* (asymmet-rical ornament, as on Gorm's silver cup), followed by *Mammen* (inlay of tendrils on the axehead buried there), followed by *Ringerike* (Anglo-Saxon and Ottonian influ-ence, deeper relief) and finally the fearful delicacy of *Urnes*. Now see Skibsted Klaesøe (1997), on the various overlaps between syles, and Høilund Nielsen (1999) on the precarious foundations of all Nordic archaeological dating when not aligned with continental dates of similar finds.
22 EYM½ (1995), 433–67 for Lang, and Fuglesang's 'Viking Art' in MESCA (1993), 694–700 for short survey and bibliography; also her 'Ikonographie der Skandinavischen Runensteine' in ZPDB (1986), 183–210, and more in Düwel 1998 and RUQIF, 197–218. Gräslund's attempt to organize the Swedish material is in VC 12, 117–31. For the British Isles see Fuglesang and Lang in Szarmach 1986; and for cross-cultural ideas, Helmut Roth (ed.), *Zum Problem der Deutung frühmittelalter-licher Bildinhalte* (Sigmaringen 1986).

some genuinely helpful innovations in critical method. The *clause arrangement analysis* of Reichardt and Edwards (*Arkiv* xcviii 123–75) seems a more reliable indicator of the consistency and dating of skaldic verse, even when it survives in fragments, and unattributed; thus a vital contribution to historians exasperated by the uncertain status of these sources. *Psycholinguistic theory* may even uncover 'lexical and semantic networks linking words in the mind of the skald' unconsciously, and so partly reveal how this verse was composed.[23]

Any survey of new methods will be obsolete before it is written, and incomplete. Those whose research lies in demography, religious history, folklore, the history of childhood, economics, food, agriculture, building, war and transport will understand why they are not specified in this context as pioneers in new techniques of research. There isn't room: and they owe more to new ideas than to new procedures. It is time to mention a few.

New Philosophies

New philosophies have inspired archaeologists above all, and as they hold the gates to knowledge of the old Nordic past their receptiveness affects all.

Processualism was a philosophy of the New Archaeology of the 1960s, which sought to discover systems of social order from more comprehensive excavation, by linking finds to theories of social change, usually marxist or post-marxist or more-or-less determinist. The archaeologist's duty, or pleasure, was to connect things with social evolution, which in Nordic archaeology meant using viking age finds as evidence of transitions: from tribe, to chiefdom, to state; from Iron Age to Medieval; from pre-feudal to feudal. Some of the old hands still do this,[24] and are derided as 'positivists' by the young turks for their lingering nineteenth-century prejudice in favour of establishing fact through scientific inquiry, unaware that they are merely wandering blindly within the *Hermeneutic Circle*.

That means the closed system in which we believe that the past explains the present, and at the same time explain the past in terms

---

23 Also see Sundqvist 1998 on the authenticity of the poems attributed to Kormák.
24 Moberg, Welinder, Christophersen, for example; and some young ones. Jakobsson 1992 was a memorable interpretation of variations in viking-age sword distribution and type in terms of the power symbolism of class struggle. Criticized by Staaf 1994, 60–4. See also Randsborg 1989, 178–9 for 'Archaeology and the Class Struggle'.

which only reflect the present, so that neither explains the other in any objective sense. How could anyone fall into such a pit of error? In the 1980s many continental archaeologists came to agree with the Norwegian Arne J. Johnsen that archaeology cannot be objective because it only finds what is already defined by the criteria of later ages: towns, cemeteries, cult-sites. Then Shanks and Tilley proposed that 'the meaning of the past does not belong to the past but to the present', and a few years later Påvel Nicklassen advised his colleagues that 'the other old comrade you have to get rid of is truth'; for round about 1988, according to Herschend, 'reconstructions of the past became uninteresting in themselves. Prehistory lost its artless charm when understanding the present instead of the past became the final aim of the archaeology'.[25] The hot air specialists have got out of hand. This shift has been explained in terms of psychology: processualism derived from the left hemisphere of the brain, which organizes sense-data, and post-modernism comes from the regulator, a brain function which 'creates the illusion that our individual selves are at centre stage, directing the play through our conscious decisions';[26] however, post-processualism is here.

In Scandinavia, as in Great Britain, the doctrine of *Post-Processualism* has strong democratic implications, in the form of *Collaborative Inquiry*, in which 'the researcher and the researched undertake project activities and decision making together' (Adams and Brooke 1995, 101); not so easy, when the researched are dead, but in that case 'those directly affected by the research goal' (local people, students, the district authorities, the television audience et al.) can stand in for the deaf-and-dumb Danes, and make it possible for the excavators to 'discard the passive view of data which is still prevalent' and challenge 'the dominant scientific paradigm' which has robbed the people of their past by its inveterate 'fact-fetishism'. The slogan inspires many who publicize and finance the digs; dancing with the dead has never been so popular a theme since the sixteenth century. The interpretation of the past thrives on its abolition. Hodges claimed archaeology as 'the weapon with which to join the ranks of the Romantics,' because it 'makes it possible to rewrite history, engineering the romantic view of the past', and Solli (see p. 302) claims full poetic status for the archaeologist: only imagination can free her both from 'the general cultural and social theory of the day, and from a dependence on the cult of fact'. Not unlike the

---

25 NAR 1998, 76–7; and see the pro-hermeneutic Hegardt in CSA, viii.
26 Flannery 1999, 3; alias Thorfinn the Skull-Splitter, earl of Orkney *c*.950.

anthropologist Hastrup's ambition 'to arrive at a general theoretical understanding that resonates with my own experience'.[27]

Few in Scandinavia wish to be entirely fact-free and ego-centred; many put their research at the service of contemporary trends and movements. As Myhre wrote in 1991: 'the critical-political aspect of archaeological theory has come further in Scandinavia than in most other Western countries'; so, for example, Herschend commends Hedeager for publishing *Skygger* in her own language rather than English, because by enlightening monoglot Danes about Iron-Age matters it may 'counteract fascist tendencies among Scandinavian Germanists, or rather extremists with intellectually biased views on such things as democracy, labour market legislation, integration or ethnicity'.[28] Old processualist professors can come up smelling of roses under this regime, since their marxist, feminist and internationalist predilections are not seen as flawed by their penchant for fact-based knowledge; that has been abolished. Tom Saunders maintains a rear-guard action in defence of marxist history as a 'more fruitful conceptual basis for research' than no theory at all; and Dommasnes pointed out in 1992 that 'without the optimistic belief that true knowledge was possible' women's history would never have got started; since nineteenth-century pioneers would not have been content to fight one set of fictions, male history, with another. But in general, post-processualism has 'increased awareness that archaeology is more subjective than objective'. Sir David Wilson sees this as a passing phase. 'There is now in much of Scandinavia a return to our proper archaeological roots – the study of material...we are more cautious of pure theory', he wrote in 1996, when he was more concerned with the decline in literacy than the lure of the immaterial. But the two things go together. In overcrowded archaeological departments, ignorance makes theory all the more enticing; ideology smooths the brow of incompetence[29] and amuses the leisure of genius.

---

27 Hastrup 1998, 203; Solli in *Meta* 1992/3, 22–35 and NAR, xxix 1996, 89, and in general Karlsson's dialogue advocating 'contemplative archaeology' in CSA vii (1999), 55–64. In 1991 Hegardt had concluded that 'archaeology that is thought to describe a prehistoric reality is impossible'; he proposed a 'humanistic and ethnocentric approach' involving analogy and anthropological philosophy, instead (*Tor*, xxiii, 55–85).
28 NAR 1998, 76–7. Nordic committment to the repression of fascism was shown when Liestøl the runologist led a group of delegates out of a conference in Italy because it was defiled by the presence of a South African, Peter Buchholz, author of 'Your ancestors and mine – reconcilation through research', Hugur, 219–29. The bewilderment of the hosts was courteously expressed.
29 Høilund Nielsen found that 'the theoretical development of archaeology' has led to 'a decline in the attention paid to typological analysis...a deterioration in the knowledge of the basic material' (ASSAH viii 1995, 1). The recent convergence

Two new theoretical approaches, the *archaeology of gender* and *women's archaeology* have reached the stage of institutionalization in Scandinavia as elsewhere, and have broadened scrutiny of the viking age. KAN (Women in Archaeology in Norway) was founded in 1985 as a ginger-group, and its members will rise within state-funded archaeology until they 'will have the opportunity and responsibility of deciding 'what is important to learn about the past' (Dommasnes in NAR xxv 1992), which may turn out to be what they thought in 1985, and so entrench what has been called the second phase of feminist archaeology, which looks for prehistoric female supremacies, the cult of the mother, etc.; for which this is not a very promising period. Others have moved into the third phase, in which binary (he–she) gendering is no longer the assumption on which the reconstruction of social life is based; for which see Gilchrist 1999 56–68, Bayliss Smith 1999 371–5 (the gendered cultural landscape) and Lillehammer 1987 (gender-bias in heritage-concepts). Something is said of viking age gender-bending in chapter 1, and of the impact of feminist theory on other fields.[30]

Liberation from 'the prison of precision' came in these climes about the time that Russian investigators of the viking age emerged from a more stringent system of incarceration. The Soviets had inherited from Russian nationalists and from Slavophiles the belief that theirs was essentially Slav country, and always had been, regardless of the Nordic transients whom the Russian Primary Chronicle (*c.* 1115) had presented as the chosen founders of the Russian state: a stance on one side of a controversy which has celebrated its 250th birthday, and has many grandchildren. By the 1980s, archaeologists in Novgorod had reached conclusions about the chronology of this period which differed from those bequeathed to the school of Kiev by Grekov, the commissar of Early Russia; Novgorodian archaeology had revealed sporadic but in places dense settlement in the Volkhov – Ladoga basin by Scandinavians, not long after the arrival of similar numbers of Slavs in what had been a Fennic wilderness – then the emergence of towns secondary to the building of forts by Nordic chiefs – and extension of their tributary system southwards, apparently without Slav political models to follow. In time, this version of

---

between processualists and post-processualists behind the banner inscribed 'Archaeology For All' was noted by Berglund in NA, xxx/2, 105–15.

30 In a recent collection of feminist contributions (Caesar 1999) Rundqvist calculated from the titles of Swedish archaeological papers of the 1990s, that women were more likely than men to depreciate their own work, and less likely to announce it in humorous or irreverent tones: an imbalance 'indicative of patriarchal repression', even in Sweden.

the past won converts even inside Russia;[31] this is by the way, but shows what can be achieved by scholars who sense the difference between voluntary and involuntary imprisonment, precision and piety.

In the West there have been other new philosophies to unsettle the archaeologists, but the most productive for Northern Research has been the thinking behind Landscape Study; in particular *Spatial Analysis*, which sounds like a technique, but also involves the free interpretation of the configuration of the settled and unsettled earth in a metaphysical as well as a physical sense. It has now 'swept to a commanding position in the practise and teaching of archaeology' in Great Britain (according to Ucko and Layton), but it has deep roots in Scandinavia: see Kristiansen 1984 for Carlsson, Göranson, Solberg and Sporrong on investigations into viking-age landscapes. A recent compilation, SAL 1999, contains 53 contributions on this theme in 499 pages, and its editor, Fabech, offers a definition which expresses the strength and weakness of the landscape approach: 'The spatial study of human interaction in which the landscape is primarily a social scene and the subsistence-production merely a backdrop' i.e. more like Millais than Millet. A fair survey of the Danish approach is given by Fabech in ASSAH x 1999: 'Organizing the Landscape', and in some of the examples given below in chapters 3 and 4, it may seem that the organization is as much in the mind of the observer (e.g. Brink) as in the viking age; at least, to the superannuated fact-fetishist. Reading landscape is a healthy outdoor pursuit, not confined to any one discipline, or unduly constrained by professional rules. It has opened up the understanding of the Late Iron age as of earlier times, beyond the foci of village, cemetery and cult-site.[32]

Post-structuralism, *Feminism* and *Postmodernism* have invaded the non-archaeological avenues to the past in fairly predictable ways, with benign results where their advocates have stopped short of the landmark inscribed by Hilda Kress: 'I am not seeking historical truth: what really happened, where and when,... but rather (I seek) the meaning of the feminine within the text, according to the theories of Irigaray, Kristeva, and Cixous'.[33]

---

31 Nosov 1998 summarizes the trials of Soviet archaeologists in this field; and see Sne 1999 for the effects of marxist orthodoxy on Latvian scholars. But Barford estimates that in Poland, after 1966, the amount of Marxist archaeological work published was less than one-twentieth of the whole: AP, xxxi (1993).

32 see Andersson in VIPA, 645–70, and Kirkinen in FENSC, xii (1995), 65, on Geographic Information Systems in general and Brink 'Mythologizing Landscape' in Stausberg 2001.

33 *Mattugar meyjar* (Reykjavik 1993), 9; reviewed in English by Larrington in *Alvíssmál*, v (1995), 117.

The Future

For many years, Scandinavian historians believed that their countries had developed in ways that differed radically from those taken by continentals and natives of the British Isles: from tribal communities to quasi-democratic nation states. By stressing their inheritance from the viking age (freehold agriculture, the people in arms, the all-powerful assembly, the unwritten law, the elective kingship) they claimed to have evolved without benefit of feudalism and hierarchy; and so gained the label of 'particularists' and risked being written off as old-fashioned nationalists out of touch with the main currents of modern thought. Then from the 1950s they switched horses, and began the avid reinterpretation of the past by borrowed light. Who can forget the cult of history as retold by the marxist Perry Anderson, which gripped Nordic students in the 70s? Then the light began to flicker and fade.

Now in the postmodern strobe light, Northern Research is more tentacular, more co-operative, and more productive than it was thirty years ago, and less detached from other medieval fields of study. The old Nordic peoples have entered the mainstream, as respondents to impulses and ideas which ran in various directions through Early Medieval Europe. The research itself has spilled out from its North European and North American cradles, where it began as the study of ancestors, and caught hold in France, Italy, Mexico, South Africa and Australia, as part of the study of human culture in general. Outside Germany and France, English has become the common language of Nordic scholars, and the whole business has been saturated with the rhetoric of contemporary professional scholarship.

As delegates conclude their conferences, symposia and colloquies, no matter what they came to discuss, they disperse to the strains of the same Nunc Dimittis, viz. that their eyes should see:

1 interdisciplinary co-operation, extending outside university departments if possible towards collaborative enquiry with the whole of society;
2 vaster and vaster accumulations of evidence 'preferably in machine-readable form', using Automatic Data Processing;
3 international co-operation on all levels; and
4 more rigorous application of more standardized standards of research, publication and training.

God is omniscient; God is in the machine; God is global: God is metrical. These platitudes issue from the more institutionally minded fellow-workers in the field; and the language is infectious, even if what goes on behind the scenes is another matter. In 1988, a Committee on Archaeological Heritage Management promulgated the Stockholm charter, for the guidance and compliance of archaeologists unsure of their raison d'être. It began: 'it is widely recognized that a knowledge and understanding of the origin and development of human societies is of fundamental importance to humanity in identifying its cultural and social roots'. Tautology rules, up there, but elsewhere root-identification usually means putting scholarship at the service of politics, especially when it is supported by public funds to the extent hoped for by the barons of the Stockholm charter; so that for Europhiles, for example, the project is to replace national with proto-European prehistory, because 'an integrated Europe needs a specifically European heritage-interpretation'.[34] In Northern Research, this means emphasizing the cross-cultural currents rather than the local, the particular and the parochial; spreading Charlemagne all the way to Lapland, or Byzantium to Bergen. But that jars with the heavy funding of historical and archaeological work by states and nations and unregenerate national tax-payers, eager to identify their own roots in their native soil. Which in turn is at odds with the belief of most archaeologists that there is no such thing as a European or as a national prehistory. There were too many distinct cultural groupings within modern state-boundaries, even in viking-age Scandinavia and Britain, for the modern nation to be anything more than a convenient fiscal supplier.[35] And then not all politicians are keen on roots; some regard these fibres that 'net the dreamless head' as impediments to progress and the 'Enlightenment Project' of the rootless cosmopolitan. There is little danger of consensus. We can breathe again.[36]

34   Cited in Pluciennik 1996 from *Building a New Heritage* (Routledge 1994) and see Burström 1991 for the rejection of national history (English summary, 147–9). The notion that Charlemagne's *Reich* was the EU in embryo, and the viking age a 'process of Europeanization' for the Nordic peoples has been touted by Gidlund, Sörlin, Hyenstrand, and Linnér in Sweden, but has been resisted in the British Isles, where the viking age is something done to the natives, rather than vice versa.

35   Randsborg (2000, 218) spots the 'sharply increasing role of adminstrative archaeology' in Scandinavia as a perpetuator of 'nationism': who pays for data-banks, site-protection, and PR, calls the tune. At the Old Uppsala Heritage-Site it was called by local business; Birka was left to the central government: see Trotzig, AP, xxxvii (1999), 157–67.

36   For a serious and incisive analysis of the intellectual problems facing archaeology and Viking studies, see Price 2002 ch.1, which introduces a book distinguishable by 'a moratorium on explicit theory'.

Appendix A

Dynastic Identities

(to illustrate p.245)

1 Rising by Descent in Orkney

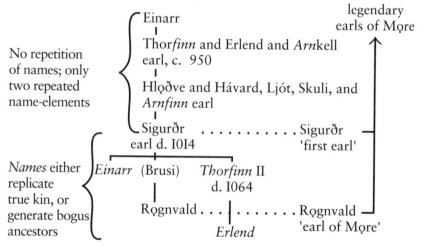

2 *Repetitive Naming in Dublin:* dynastic identity preserved by five key-names over seven generations (see p. 59)

	IVARR	OLAFR	SIGTRYGGR	GUTHFRIDR	RǪGNVALDR
1	d. 873	d. 871	–	–	–
2	two: d. 896	d. 896	d. 896	d. 896	–
3	d. 904	d. 896	d. 927	d. 934	d. 921
4	–	d. 941 / two: d. 980	—940—	—981—	d. 944
5	d. 977	—977—	two: d. 960	d. 963	d. 980
6	—1000—	d. ? / two:	d. 1042 / d. 1022	d. 1035	d. 995
7	d. 1046	d. 1034	d. 1073	d. 1036	d. 1035
8		—1050—		d. 1075	

Note: These are lists of names, not lineages. The dates are from Irish annals. All claimed descent from the first Ivarr (Ímhair), who was later affiliated to some imaginary kings in Scandinavia with appropriate names. For a detailed history of this dynasty see Benjamin Hudson *Viking Pirates and Christian Princes* Oxford 2005.

Appendix B

Dates

	Inside Scandinavia	Outside Scandinavia
c. 710	St Wilbrord's mission to the Danes. Trading place laid out at Ribe; quay at Birka.	
726	Canal cut through Samsø, off NE Jutland. Work on S. Jutland defences	
730s–750s	Wheel-turned pots made at Ribe	Nordic settlements around lake Ladoga. Franks conquer Frisians.
750s	Ribe and Birka expand.	
760s	Mass-production of metal-work begins at Birka.	
770s–80s		Charlemagne subdues Saxons.
787–8	Danes dig more defences on Schlei and negotiate with Charlemagne.	
790s	Islamic silver coin reaches Denmark	Raids on British Isles and Ireland.
800	growth of Hedeby	Charlemagne orders defence of northern coasts.
804–12	Charlemagne and Danish kings compete for power over Western Slavs and Frisians; war averted by death of king Guthfrith. Peace.	
815	Jutland cowed by Frankish army.	Raids on Ireland continue; Blathmac martyred at Iona (825).

826	Bracteates (anonymous halfpence) struck in Jutland.	Harald the Danish king baptized at Mainz with his followers and given land.
829	St Anscar's mission to Birka.	
831		Hamburg made archbishopric of the North.
834–50	Hørik rules the Danes. Lady's ship-burial at Oseberg.	Hit-and-run raids on Frankish coasts and river valleys; camp at Dublin.
850s	Civil war among Danes.	Winter camps in Francia and Britain; Danegeld paid, and defences reorganized.
860		Rus raid Constantinople.
864	Impending conversion of Danish king?	Hamburg see merged with Bremen.
864–934	No information on Scandinavian events from any outside source; Danish hegemony collapses?	Most of eastern Britain, northern Francia and Loire valley, the Low countries and N. German coast invaded, plundered and occupied by Norsemen; others infest Ireland and the northern Islands, and settle in Iceland, the Danelaw and NW England.
*c.*900	Poets: Thjoðölfr? Bragi Boddason?	Reports on Scandinavia by Ottarr and Wulfstan copied into translation of Orosius.
900–10	Danish chiefs and warriors adopt 'cavalry grave' rituals. Gokstad ship-grave in Norway.	Magyars terrorize Germany, and Danelaw armies raid Wessex. Norse expelled from Dublin 902–14.
910–20	Arabic and Western silver imported to Birka reaches peak and Danish silver hoards increase.	Northmen of Rouen submit to king of West Franks and accept baptism. Danes in England submit to king Edward and to invaders from Dublin.
	Gyrd and Chnub rule Danes at Hedeby.	Loire Danes occupy Brittany.
920s	Poets: Thorbjorn Hornklofi?	Ibn Fadlan visits Rus on Volga. Old Ladoga walled.
930s	Harald Harfagr dominates SW Norway; sends ship to	Northmen driven from Loire Valley and Brittany,

	Athelstan? Chnub and Sigtrygg kings at Hedeby.	but stay in Normandy; no geld payments recorded after 927.
934	After raiding Frisia, Danes subjugated by king Henry and the Saxons and pay tribute. Christians visited by archbishop Unni.	937 Norse in Britain defeated by king Athelstan but regain York in 939.
940s	Bishops appointed for Ribe, Aarhus and Schleswig-Hedeby, but king Gorm remains unbaptized.	Rus attack Constantinople and Azerbaijan. Novgorod established.
	Hakon the Good king in Norway.	Eric Bloodaxe king of Northumbria.
c.950	*Poets*: Guthormr Sindri, Egill Skalagrimsson, Kormákr, Jórunn	Olaf Cuaran retires to Dublin: Thorfinn Skull-splitter rules Orkney.
952		Eric killed on Stainmoor; York submits to king Eadred.
958	Gorm the Danish king buried in the North Mound at Jelling; Harald Bluetooth succeeds.	
c.960	Harald Eiriksson succeeds Hakon the Good in Norway.	Dublin Norse begin raiding Wales.
c.965	Harald Bluetooth baptized by Poppo, completes South Mound at Jelling, reburies Gorm in a new church?	Norse raiders reinforce Normans in war against Chartres.
c.968	Hakon Jarl becomes ruler of Norway.	Viking raids on Moslems and Christians of W. Spain, 966–71.
970–1	Mound burial at Mammen, N. Jutland	
974	Harald raids Saxony, and Otto II, the emperor takes Hedeby and reimposes tribute on the Danes.	
c.975	*Poets*: Eyvindr the Plagiarist, Glum Geirason Eilífr Goðrunarson, Vetrliði.	

978–81	Round forts built in Denmark; Sigtuna founded in Sweden.	Irish Norse subjugated by king Mealseachlainn; vikings active in the Channel and Wales.
983	Harald Bluetooth and Slav allies regain Hedeby from the Empire with Hakon Jarl's help. Hedeby longship I (100 feet, 30.9 m) constructed.	
*c.*985	More English and German coin imported than dirhems.	First settlements in Greenland. Christians active in Iceland.
986	Harald Bluetooth driven from Denmark and dies: Sweyn Forkbeard king.	
991–3	Eric the Victorious of Sweden invades Denmark? Influx of coin to Sweden and Gotland in '90s.	Sweyn and Olaf Tryggvason raid England.
994	Olof Eriksson king of Swedes issues pennies at Sigtuna.	Olaf makes peace with king Ethelred and returns to Norway.
*c.*995	Lund founded; Olaf T. king in Norway; Hakon Jarl dies.	Coins minted at Dublin for king Sihtric.
999	Olof and Forkbeard defeat and kill Olaf Tryggvason, and share Norway.	Icelanders adopt christianity, with reservations.
*c.*1000	*Poets*: Hallfreðr Ottarsson ... Halldor the Unchristian ... Steinunn ... Thorleifr Rauðfeldarson ... Úlfr Uggason First named royal coinages. Uppland Swedes begin raising rune-stones; last Danish waggon-burials, at Hørning and Onsvala.	Greenlanders begin visiting American coast: settlement at L'Anse aux Meadows.
1003–14	first native bishop appointed: Odinkar of Ribe. Bishop Thorgaut at Skara.	Raids from Scandinavia lead to the eventual submission of the English to Sweyn Forkbeard; after his death, his son Canute is expelled.
1015		

Canute and Eirikr Jarl invade England, and wage war;
five battles in five months.
Olaf Haraldsson returns
to Norway

1017–18	Harald, king of Danes. Olaf Haraldsson wins Norway.	Canute, now sole king of England, marries Ethelred's widow Emma and accepts English laws at Oxford.
1019–24	Canute secures Denmark and introduces bishops and mints; Olaf Haraldsson imposes Christianity in Norway; Anund king of the Swedes.	Eric Hakonsson earl of Northumbria. Earl Thorfinn of Orkney swears loyalty to king Olaf Haraldsson of Norway.
c.1025	*Poets*: Sighvátr... Óttarr...Thórarinn Thormoð...Thórðr Kolbeinsson... Bjarni Gullbrárskáld... Hallvarðr Háreksblesi	
1025–6?	Battle on Helgån. Canute's enemies checked	
1027	Olaf Haraldsson has his rival Erling killed.	Canute attends the imperial coronation at Rome and sends an open letter to the English.
1028	Olaf Haraldsson driven from Norway; Canute sails to Trondheim.	Canute dominates Norwegians, Scots, Dubliners and Welsh.
1030	Olaf Haraldsson (St Olave) is killed at Stiklastad. Canute's son Sweyn accepted as king of Norway.	
1035	Magnus Olafsson king in Norway. Massive hoarding of coin in Finland.	Canute dies in England. 1025–40 Ingvarr leads Swedes and Gauts to disaster in the east.
1036	Canute's daughter marries the emperor Conrad's son.	
1040–2		Hardicanute king in England: decrees heavy tax
1042	Magnus Olafsson accepted as king in Denmark	Edward the Confessor succeeds Hardicanute in England.

1043?	Slavs defeated at Lürschau by Magnus. Rebellion of Sweyn Estrithson.	
1044–6	War of Sweyn, Harald Hardrada and Magnus the Good	English fleet ready for Norwegian invasion.
1046–7	Sweyn king in Denmark, Harald in Norway; hostilities to 1062.	English refuse to help Sweyn.
1050	First mint at Trondheim; first bishop at Skara	Most of Edward's fleet disbanded.
c.1050	*Poets* Arnórr Thórðarsson Jarlaskald, Ormr Steinthórsson? Valgarðr, Thorleikr Fagri.	
1053	Leo IX's privilege lays the whole north from Greenland to Finland under the metropolitan authority of archbishop Adalbert of Hamburg-Bremen.	
1056		First bishop of Iceland
c.1060	Three more sees in Jutland	
1062	Sweyn II defeated by Harald at the Niså	
1066	(?) king Stenkil dies and two Erics fight for Sweden	Harald of Norway killed invading England at Stamford Bridge; Olaf the Quiet succeeds.
1069		Sweyn II invades England and takes York
1070	*Poets*: Steinn Herdisarson, Stufr the Blind, Halli.	Sweyn sails back to Denmark with plunder and geld.
1072		Abp. Adalbert dies and Bremen goes to Liemar.
1075	Sweyn II dies? and his sons raid England with 200 ships. Adam of Bremen finishes his *Gesta* about then.	
1080	Temple of Uppsala destroyed? Canute IV king of the Danes	Godred Crovan founds kingdom of Man and Suðreyjar.
1085	Canute prepares to invade England, & endows Lund.	
1086	Canute killed at Odense	

Appendix C

Weights and Measures

Weights: The common Nordic weights of this period were the mark (mǫrk) and its subdivisions, which were compatible with several other systems. A mark of *c*.205 g (7 ⅕ ounces) was equivalent to:

1 four times the Islamic and Permian (North Russian) trade weight of 51 g; and 48 times the Islamic gold weight (*mitgal*) of 4.23 g, which was the weight of the *dinar*, and of the basic unit on Gotland in the tenth century.
2 half the Carolingian pound of 408 g (six Frankish ounces or 120 pennyweight);
3 two-thirds of an Anglo-Saxon pound at eighth-century weight; and
4 eight times the older North Germanic *ora*, which was possibly the value of a sheep in silver at one stage (at 28 g; but 24 g later).

However, hundreds of Nordic weights from this period have been found, and they show a wide range of denominations and variations, with units of 4.23 g on Gotland, 4.1 g at Hedeby, 4 g at Birka, half-marks between 90 and 100 g, and marks from 180 to 216. An *ora* could be 29.7 g (as at Fyrkat *c*.1000), or 26.8 g or 24.5 g (as all over the North Atlantic countries and in the Danelaw). The Danelaw mark of 192 g was superseded after *c*.1016 by a heavier unit of 214–216 g. Attempts have been made to derive the mark and its fractions from Islamic weights (by Sperber), from a confraternity of Baltic traders (by Steuer) or from the monetary experiment of Swedish kings (by Gustin).

Units of length: The ring-forts built on Jutland *c*.980 were planned with a 29.6 cm (11 ⅔ ins) 'Roman' foot, but the Trelleborg foot on Zealand varied between 27.6 and 31.6 cm. Buildings in Sweden were planned with an ell (*aln*) of *c*.47 cm (18½ ins), but it was longer on Gotland, and reached 63 cm in Jutland, where it coincided with the pace used in Iron Age field measurements earlier. Distances at sea were reckoned in variable *vika* (about 13 km in the later Middle Ages), on land by the *rǫst, rastar*, of about $5\frac{1}{2}$ km or 3–4 miles. (See Sperber 1996, Gustin in VIPA (1997) and Hårdh in VS viii 1999.)

Land measurements: There seem to have been no purely area measures for spaces larger than ground-plans for houses, settlements, and camps. The word *ból* meant a farm in Denmark and Norway and was used by 1085 as an indication of value rather than size. It reached Iceland, the Hebrides, Orkney, and Shetland as *bóstaðr*, in the - bister settlement names. In the English Danelaw the bovate or oxgang of 10–18 acres is the usual estimate, eight of those to the ploughland or carucate, for arable only. It sounds Nordic, and *plogs-land* also occurs on Orkney; but within Scandinavia, the plough (aratrum) appears (after 1200) as a tax-unit rather than a measure-ment of area. In legend, the goddess Gefion (see p. 197) was pro-mised a ploughland, meaning as much as oxen could plough in a day and a night; it was evidently a very rough measurement of work. The acre appears in twelfth-century Norway and Iceland as a term for any arable land; in Denmark the *ager* became a ploughed strip of fairly constant width and variable length, like the medieval English acre but much smaller: less than a fifth in some places. The *bol* could cover only 25 of our acres. (See 194n.)

Appendix D

Thegns

(See map 2 on p. 75)

There are places called *Tegneby* or *Tegnaby* (thegns' manor or farm) in the coastlands north of Gothenburg, and there are eleventh-century rune-stones referring to thegns: sixteen survive in Västergötland, ten in a small area of North Jutland, eight in Södermanland, four in SE Scania, two in Småland, and one each in Funen, Lolland, Bornholm and Östergötland. They are shadowed by stones erected in memory of *Drengs*, also found in Västergötland, NE Jutland and Scania; the inscriptions suggest that drengs were bold, brave, useful, fit, reliable men, but only one is remembered as a householder; thegns were 'good', landowners and householders, powerful and paternal. Drengs could have been thegns in the making, but only in England are there places named after them; whereas in Sweden and Denmark there are several places named after *rinkar*, who appear to have been military retainers lodged in, maintained by, or rewarded with *byar*.

The distribution is so odd that no clear picture of how, when and why men were described in this way emerges. State-formation addicts have readily linked them to the 'new order' of powerful rulers in the tenth and eleventh century, in which royal vassals and retainers become 'officials' promoting central authority down in the provinces, with hypothetical 'administrative duties'. If the word *thegn* was borrowed from England, the idea behind it is unlikely to have been 'royal official'; English thanes could become officials, at court, but were usually landowners with local public duties (in the shire courts, the shire armies, and many parishes) inherited with their status. To Nordic intruders, they can only have appeared as local bosses, district defenders; which is how they appear in the skaldic verse of *c*.1030 onwards. Sighvatr and Arnorr use *thegn* as a description of independent landowners in Norway and Orkney; not of officials or royal retainers, but sometimes of their opponents.

As the incidence in place-names and runic inscriptions of the designations thegn, dreng, visi, hersir (and stýrir) reflects local commemorative fashion at different dates, rather than the distribution of power at any one date, map 2 is thoroughly misleading. See Strid 1987, Randsborg 1980, Sawyer (B) in VS v 1986 and 2000, Stoklund 1991 and Jesch 1993A for conflicting views; Peter Sawyer identified all rune-stone thegns as 'under the lordship' of Canute (*The Making of Sweden* Alingsås 1988, 34), who claimed to be 'king of part of the Swedes', in his second letter to the English. This conclusion awaits closer dating of the evidence, such as the stones in North Jutland and Västergötland which both commemorate Karl the Good, 'Thuri's partner, a right well-born dreng' (DR 127: M.379–80). For a recent summary of the evidence and arguments see 'Drengs and Thegns again' by M. Syrett in SB xxv/3 2000 243–70 and Syrett 2002 108–110.

References

Abels, Richard, 1997: 'English Logistics and Military Administration 871–1066: the impact of the Viking wars', MIAS, 257–65.

Adams, Max and Carole Brooke, 1995: 'Unmanaging the Past', NAR, xxviii/2, 93–104.

Adalsteinsson, Jon Hnefill, 1978: *Under the Cloak*, Uppsala.

——,1992: 'A Piece of Horse-Liver and the Ratification of Law' in *Snorrastefna*, ed. U. Bragason, Reykjavik, 81–98.

——,1999: 'Religious Ideas' in *Sonatorrek* SB, xxv/2, 159–7.

Addyman, P. and Roskams, S., 1992: *Urbanism*, York.

Ahlbäck, Tore, see SAAR and ONFRAC, K. Ahronson, 2000: 'Evidence for a Columban Iceland', NAR, xxx/2, 117–24.

Aitchison, N.B., 1998: 'Regicide in Early Medieval Ireland', VISO, 108–25.

Åkerman, Sune, 1978: 'Towards an Understanding of Emigrational Processes', SJH, iii, 131–54.

Albøge, Gordon, 1991: *Stednavne i Hanherred* (Dansk Stednavne, xxi), Copenhagen.

Alkarp, Magnus, 1997: 'Källan, lunden och templet', *Fornvännan*, 154–61.

Alkemade, M., 1991: 'A History of Vendel Period Archaeology' in *Images of the Past*, ed. N. Roymans and F. Theuws, Amsterdam, 267–97.

Almqvist, Bo, 1965, *Norrön niddiktning*, 2 vols, Stockholm.

—— 1991: (with Seamus Ó Catháin, ed.), *Viking Ale*, Aberystwyth.

Althaus, S., 1993: *Die Gotländischen Bildsteine: ein Programm*, Göppingen.

Ambrosiani, Björn, 1988: 'Lika och ändå olika' in FESTOL, 9–14.

—— 1994: ed. with Helen Clarke, VC 12, Stockholm.

Amory, Frederick, 1987: 'Second Thoughts on Skaldskaparmal', SS, lxii/3, 331 ff.

—— 1982: 'Norse–Christian Syncretism', *Gripla*, vii, 264 ff.

—— 1992: 'The medieval Icelandic Outlaw', FROSA.

Andersen, Harald, 1988: 'Gaaden om Gorm', *Skalk*, ii, 18–28.

—— 'The Graves of the Jelling dynasty', AA, lxxi, 281–300.

Andersen, M. and Birebæk (eds), 1993: *Vikingernes Rusland*, Roskilde.

Andersen, Per Sveaas: see under Sveaas.

Andersen, S.T. et al. 1983: 'Environment and Man', JDA, ii, 184–96.

References

Anderson, Atholl, 1985: 'The Scandinavian Colonization of the North Swedish Interior' in S.L. Dyson (ed.), *Comparative Studies in the Archaeology of Colonialism* (BAR, ii, NS ccxxxiii), 38–50.

Andersson, Björn, 1995: *Runor, magi, ideologi*, Umea.

Andersson, C. and Hållans, A-M., 1997: 'No trespassing', VIPA, 588–602.

Andersson, Eva, 1995: 'Invisible Handicrafts', LAR I, 7–20.

—— 1999: *The Common Thread* (Lund Institute of Archaeology Report, lxvii).

Andersson, Gunnar, 1997: 'A Struggle for Control', VIPA, 353–72.

Andersson, Hans: see VIPA.

Andersson, Theodore and K.I. Sandred, 1978: *The Vikings*, Uppsala.

—— 1994: 'The politics of Snorri Sturluson', JEGP, xciii, 55–78.

—— 1989: 'The Viking Policy of Ethelred', ASCEN.

—— 1999: 'The King of Iceland', *Speculum*, lxxiv/4, 923–33.

Andersson, Thorsten, 1991: 'The Origin of the Tuna-names reconsidered', PAP, 196–204.

—— 1992: 'Orts und Personnamen als Aussagequelle', GR 508 ff.

Andrén, Anders, 1985: *Den urbana scenen. Städer och samhall i det medeltida Danmark*, Lund.

—— 1989: 'State and Towns in the Middle Ages', *Theory and Society*.

—— 1993: 'Doors to Other Worlds' Scandinavian Death Rituals', *Journal of European Archaeology*, i, 33–56.

Antonsen, Elmer, 1998: 'On Runological and Linguistic Evidence for Dating Runic Inscriptions', Düwel 1998, 150–9.

Árnason, Kristján, 1991: *The Rhythms of Drottkvæd*, Reykjavik.

Arnold, Bettina, 1999: 'Drinking the Feast', CAJ, ix, 71–93.

Aronsson, Kjell-Åke, 1991: *Forest Reindeer Herding* AD *1–1800*, Umeå.

Arrhenius, Birgit, 1982: 'Snorris Asa-Etymologie und das Gräberfeld von Altuppsala' in *Tradition als historische Kraft*, ed. N. Kamp and J. Wollasch, Berlin/New York.

Askeberg, Fritz, 1944: *Norden och Kontinenten i gammal tid*, Uppsala.

Aström, Berit, 1998: 'The Creation of the Anglo-Saxon Woman', STN, lxx, 25–34.

Ausenda, G., 1995: 'Segmentary lineage in contemporary anthropology and among the Langobards' in *After Empire*, ed. G. Ausenda, Woodbridge.

Axboe, Morten, 1995: 'Danish Kings and Dendrochronology: Archaeological Insights' in *After Empire*, ed. G. Ausenda, Woodbridge.

—— 1999: 'Towards a kingdom of Denmark', ASSAH, x, 109–18.

Bäck, Mathias, 1999: 'No Island is a Society', VIPA, 129–61.

Bagge, Sverre, 1991: *Society and Politics in Snorri Sturluson's Heimskringla*, Berkeley.

—— 2005: 'Christianization and State Formation in Early Medieval Norway', SJH xxx107–34.

Bartlett, Robert, 1998: 'Reflections on Paganism and Christianity in medieval Europe', *Proceedings of the British Academy*, ci, 55–76.

Bapty, Ian and Tim Yates, 1990: *Archaeology after Structuralism*, London.

Barnes, G, 1995: 'Vinland the Good: Paradise Lost?', *Parergon* NS, xii/2, 75–96.

Barnes, Michael, 1993: 'The Interpretation of the Runic Inscriptions of Maeshowe', VACON 1993, 349–69.

—— 1994: *The Runic Inscription of Maeshowe*, Uppsala.

—— 1998: *The Norn Language of Orkney and Shetland*, Lerwick.

—— 1997: 'How Common was Common Scandinavia?', NOWELE, 29–42.

—— 2004: 'The Scandinavian Languages in the British Isles', SCEU 121–36.

Batey, Jesch and Morris: see VACON.

Barrett, James et al., 2000: 'The Viking Age and When did it Happen?', NAR xxxiii, 1–39.

Bayley, Justine, 1992: 'Viking Age Metalworking – the British Isles and Scandinavia compared', TEIN, 91–7.

Bazelmans, Jos, 1991: 'Conceptualizing Early Germanic Political Structures: a review of the use of the concept of Gefolgschaft', IMPA, 91–130.

Beck, H., 1994: 'Skandinavische Landnahme im atlantischen Bereich aus literaturhistorischer Sicht' in Müller-Wille, 197–211.

Bekker-Nielsen, Hans, 1987: 'Runelitteraturen og andre skriftlige kilder til Danmarks ældste historie', TROG, 65–9.

Becker, C.J., 1998: 'Danske mønter som historisk kildematieliet i 1000-tallet', FESTOL, 123–36.

Bender Jørgensen, Lise, 1995: (and Eriksen, P.): *Trabjerg*, Aarhus.

Benedictow, Ole Jørgen, 1993: 'Demography', MESCA, 122–7.

Bennike, Pia, 1985: *Palaeopathology of Danish Skeletons*, Copenhagen.

Berglund, M.H., 2000: 'Consequences of Styles of Thinking', NA, xxx/2, 105–15.

Bersu, G. and D.M. Wilson, 1966: *Three Viking graves on the Isle of Man*, London.

Bertelsen, R. and R.G. Lamb, 1993: 'Settlement Mounds in the North Atlantic, VACON, 544–54.

Bertilsson, Ulf, 1989: 'Space, Economy and Society: The Rock Carvings of North Bohuslän', ASP, 287–321.

Besteman, Bos, and Heidinga, see MAIN.

Beyschlag, Siegfried, 1981: 'Die Reichseinigungen der Beiden Olafe', GEDI, 9–42.

Bibire, P., 1986: 'Freyr and Gerð', *Sagnaskemmtun*, ed. R. Simek, Vienna.

Biddle, Martin and Birthe Kjølby, 1992: 'Repton and the Vikings', *Antiquity*, lxvi, 36–51.

Biezais, Haralds (ed.), 1972: *The Myth of the State*, Stockholm.

Bigelow, Gerald, 1990: *The Norse of the North Atlantic* (AA, lxi).

Birkeli, Fridtjov, 1973: *Norse steinkors i tidlig middelalder*, Oslo.

Birkmann, Thomas, 1995: *Von Ågedal bis Malt: die skandinavishcen Runeninschriften*, Berlin.

Bjarnason, C. et al., 1973: 'The Blood Groups of Icelanders', *Annals of Human Genetics*, xxxvi, 425–5.

Björklund, E. and L. Hejll, 1996: *Roman Reflections in Scandinavia*, Rome.

Blackburn, Mark, and D. Dumville (eds), 1998: *Kings, Currency, and Alliances*, Woodbridge.

Blindheim, Charlotte, 1978: 'Trade Problems in the Viking Age', VIK, 166–76.

Blindheim and B. Heyderdahl-Larsen, 1995: *Kaupang Funnene*, ii.

Blok, D.P., 1978: 'De Wikingen in Friesland', Naamkunde x, 25–47.

Blomqvist, Nils, 1999: 'Common People in Common Places', EUNO, 31–30.

Boehm, C., 1987: *Blood Revenge*, Philadelphia.

Bojtar, Endre, 1999: *Foreword to the Past*, Budapest.

Bond, Julie M., 1998: 'Beyond the Fringe? Recognizing change and adaptation in Pictish and Norse Orkney', *Life on the Edge*, ed. Mills and Coles, Oxford, 81–90.

Borg, Kaj, 2000: *Eketorp III* (Lund).

Bornholdt, 1999: 'Myth or Mint?', RRIM.

Boyer, Regis, 1975: 'Paganism and Literature', *Gripla*, i.

—— 1981: *Yggdrasill: La Religion des anciens Scandinaves*, Paris.

—— 1983: 'On the composition of Völuspá', in *Edda: a collection of essays*, ed. R.J. Glendinning and H. Bessason, Winnipeg.

—— 1991: 'Vikings, Sagas, and Wasa Bread', AUSA, 43–6.

—— 1994: *La Mort chez les anciens Scandinaves*, Paris.

Bradley, J., 1987: 'Time Regained: the Creation of Continuity', JBAS, xcl, 1–17.

—— 1988: *Settlement and Society in Medieval Ireland*, Kilkenny.

Bradley, Richard, 2000: *An archaeology of Natural Places*, London.

Brady, Niall, 1994: 'Labour and Agriculture in Early Medieval Ireland', WW, 245–45.

Braut, A.T., 1996: *Samburdarøl og gjestebud*, Bergen.

Breen, Gerard, 1997: 'Personal Names and the recreation of berserkir and úlfheðnar', SAS, xv.

—— 1999: 'The Wolf is at the door', ANF, cxiv, 31–43.

Breisch, A., 1994: *Frid och fredlöshet*, Uppsala.

Brink, Stefan, 1990: 'Cult sites in North Sweden', ONFRAC (1990), 458–89.

—— 1990: '*Sockenbildning och sockennamn*, Stockholm.

—— 1994: 'The PNN of Markim-Orkesta', VC 12, 277–9.

—— 1994: 'En vikingtida storbonde i södra Norrland', *Tor*, xxvi, 145–62.

—— 1995: 'Forsaringen – Nordens aldsta lagbud', VS, xv.

—— 1996: 'Political and Social Structure in Early Scandinavia', *Tor*, xxviii, 235–81; part 2 in *Tor*, xxix (1997), 389–438.

—— 1999: 'Social Order in the Early Scandinavian Landscape', SAL, 423–37.

Brisbane, M.A., 1992: *The Archaeology of Novgorod: Recent Results*, Lincoln.

Broberg, Anders, 1990: *Bönder och samhälle i statsbildningstid*, Uppsala.

Brothwell, D., D. Tills, and V. Muir: 'Biological Characteristics' in Berry and Firth (eds), *The People of Orkney* (1986), 54–88.

Buchholz, Peter: 'Shamanism', MS, iv, 7–20.

Buckland, P.C., Sadler and Smith: 'An Insect's Eye view of the Norse Farm', VACON (1993), 501–27.

—— (et al.): 'Twig Layers, Floors and Middens', VC 12 (1994), 132–43.

Burmeister, Stefan, 1998: 'Ursachen und Verlauf von Migrationen', SSF, xi.

Burström, Mats, 1991: *Arkeologisk samhallsvergränsning*, Stockholm.
——, 1994: 'Forntidabruk af den förflutna', *Fornvännen*, lxxxiv.
—— 1996: 'Other Generations', Interpretations of the Past', CSA, iv, 21–40.
Byock, Jesse, 1988: *Medieval Iceland*, University of California.
Caesar, Camilla, et al., 1999: *Han Hon Dem Det* Lund Institute Report, lxv.
Cahen, Maurice, 1921: *La libation*, Paris.
Calissendorf, Karin, 1964: 'Helgö', *Namn och Bygd*, lii, 105–52.
Callmer, Johan, 1991: 'Platser med anknytning till handel', HØKO, 29–47.
—— 1991/92: 'To Stay or to Move', MLUHM.
—— 1992a: 'Interaction between Ethnical Groups in the Baltic Region Region', CONBA, 99–107.
—— 1992b: 'Exchange and Trade in the Baltic Region and beyond', EXTRA.
—— 'Territory and Dominion in the Late Iron Age in Scandinavia', RER 1991.
—— 1994: 'Urbanization in Scandinavia and the Baltic Region *c*.700–1100' in VC 12 (1994), 50–90.
Cameron, Kenneth, 1996: 'The Scandinavian Element in Minor Names and Field Names in NE Lincolnshire', *Nomina*, xix, 5–27.
Capelle, Torsten, 1986: 'Schiffsetzungen', PZ, lxi, 1–63.
—— 1995: 'Bronze-Age Stone Ships', SHAS, 71–5.
Carelli, Peter, 1987: 'Thunder and Lightning', VIPA, 393–417.
—— 1993–94: 'We are not all equal in the Face of Death', MLUHM, NS ix, 43–59.
Carlsson, Anders, 1983: *Djurhuvudformiga spännen och götlandske vikingatid*, Stockholm.
—— 1988: *Vikingatiden ringspännen från Gotland*, Stockholm.
Carlsson, Dan, 1984: 'Change and Continuity in the Iron Age Settlement of Gotland' in Kristiansen 1984, 129–53.
—— 1991: 'Harbours and Trading Places on Gotland', ASMA, 145–58.
Carver, Martin, 1995: 'Boat Burial in Britain', SHAS, 110–24.
Cassel, K., 2000: 'Where Are We Going?', CSA, viii, 33–49.
Chesnutt, Michael, 1989: 'The Beguiling of Thórr', in McTurk and Wawn 1989, 35–63.
Charles-Edwards, Thomas, 1998: 'Alliances, Godfathers, Treaties and Boundaries', KICU 1998, 47–62.
—— 1993: *Early Irish and Welsh Kingship*, Oxford.
Christensen, Aksel E., 1969: *Vikingetidens Danmark*, Copenhagen.
Christensen, Tom, 1991: 'Lejre Beyond Legend', JDA, x, 163–85.
Christophersen, A., 1981–82: 'Dreng, Thegn, Landmen and Kings', MLUHM, 114–34.
—— 1989: 'Kjøbe, selge, bytte, gi' in *Medeltidens fødelse*, Lund.
—— 1991: 'Ports and Trade in Norway during the Transition to Historical Time', ASMA, 159–70.
—— 1994: (with S.W. Nordeide), *Kaupangen ved Nidelva*, Trondheim.
Cinthio, Maria, 1997: 'Trinitätiskyrken i Lund – med engelsk prägel', *Hikvin*, xxiv.

Clarke, Helen, 1979: *Iron and Man in Prehistoric Sweden*, Stockholm 1998.

Clarke, H.B., 1998: 'Proto-Towns and Towns in Ireland and Britain', ISCEVA, 331–80.

Clausen, Berthe (ed.), 1993: *Viking Voyages to America*, Roskilde.

Clunies Ross, Margaret, 1992: 'The Mythological Fictions of Snorra Edda', Snorrastefna, 204–16.

―― 1994: *Prolonged Echoes: Old Norse Myths in Medieval Northern Society*, vol. i.

―― 1998: vol. ii of *Prolonged Echoes*.

Coates, R., 1999: 'New Light from Old Wicks: the progeny of Latin vicus', *Nomina*, xxii, 75–114.

Coggins, D., 1992: 'Aspects of Early Settlement in the North Pennine Dales' in *Medieval Europe* (York Conference), viii, 95–9.

Coles, John, 1990: *Images of the Past*, Uddevalla.

Coupland, Simon, 1990: 'The Rod of God's Wrath or the People of God's Wrath?', *Journal of Ecclesiastical History*, xlii, 535 ff.

―― 1998: 'From poachers to gamekeepers: Scandinavian warlords and Carolingian kings', EME, vii/i, 85 ff.

―― 1999: 'The Frankish Tribute Payments to the Vikings and their Consequences', *Francia* xxvi/i, 57–75.

Crawford, B.E., 1987: *Scandinavian Scotland*, Leicester.

―― 1992: 'The Cult of S. Clement of the Danes' in *Religion and Belief*, ed. J. Grenville, M. Carver et al., vol. vi of the York Conference *Medieval Europe*, 1–4.

―― (ed.), 1995: SSNB.

Crosby, Alfred W., 1995: 'Afterword', AGMA, 337–42.

Crumlin-Pedersen, Ole, 1986: 'Aspects of Viking Age Ship-building', JDA, v.

―― 1991a: 'Ship Types and Sizes A D 800–1400', ASMA, 69–82.

―― 1991b: 'Søfart og Samfund i Danmarks Vikingetid', HØKO, 181–208.

―― 1991c: 'Aspects of Maritime Scandinavia', ASMA Roskilde.

―― (ed.), 1995: *The Ship as Symbol*, Copenhagen; in which is 'Boat-Burials at Slusegaard', 87–99.

―― 1997–8: 'Skipsfundene fra Hedeby', *Kuml*, 161–8.

―― 1997: *Viking Age Ships and Shipbuilding in Hedeby and Schleswig*, Roskilde.

Cusack, Carole M., 1998: *Conversion among the Germanic Peoples*, London/New York.

Damgaard-Sørensen, Tinna, 1991: 'Danes and Wends: a Study of the Danish Attitude towards the Wends', PAP.

Damsholt, Nanna, 1987: 'Kvinderne i Ansgars liv', TROG, 71–87.

Davies, R.H.C., 1987: 'The Warhorses of the Normans', ANS, x.

Debes, Hans, 1993: 'Problems concerning the Earliest Settlement in the Faroe Islands', VACON, 454–64.

Derville, Alain, 1998: 'La population du Nord au Moyen Age', *Revue du Nord*, lxxx, 501–30.

Diinhof, Søren, 1997: 'The Custom of Sacrifice', BUSO, 115 ff.

Doherty, Charles, 1998: 'The Vikings in Ireland': a Review', ISCEVA, 288–330.

Dommasnes, Liv, 1992: 'Two Decades of Women in Prehistory', NAR xxv/i, 1–14.

Dowden, Ken, 2000: *European Paganism*, London/New York.

Dronke, Ursula, 1968: 'Beowulf and Ragnarók', SB xvii, 302–25.

—— 1978: 'The Poet's Persona in the Skald's Sagas', *Parergon*, xx–xxii, 23–8.

—— 1989: 'Marx, Engels and Norse Mythology', *Studies in Honour of H.L. Rogers* (Leeds Studies NS xx), 37 ff.

Dumville, David, 1997a: *Three Men in a Boat*, Cambridge.

—— 1997b: *The Churches of North Britain in the First Viking Age*, Whithorn.

Durrenberger, E. Paul, 1992: *The Dynamics of Medieval Iceland*, Iowa.

Düwel, Klaus, 1985: *Das Opferfest von Lade*, Vienna.

—— 1986: 'Zur Ikonographie und Ikonologie der Sigurdarsstellungen', ZPDB, 221–71.

—— 1987: '*Handel und Verkerhr der Wikingerzeit nach dem Zeugnis der Runeninschriften*: vol. iv of *Der Handel der Karolinger – und Wikingerzeit*, ed. Düwel et al., Göttingen.

—— 1994: *Runische Schriftkultur*, Berlin.

—— (ed.), 1998: *Runeninschriften als Quellen interdisziplinärer Forschung*, Berlin/New York.

Earle, Timothy (ed.), 1991: *Chiefdoms, Power, Economy and Ideology*, Cambridge.

Ebel, Else, 1993: *Der Konkubinat nach altwestnordischen Quellen*, Berlin.

Edwards, Diana, 1982–85: 'Christian and Pagan References in 11th century Norse Poetry', SB, xxxi, 34–54.

Einarsdóttir, Ólafia, 1964: *Studier i Kronologiske Metode*, Lund.

Einarsson, Bjarni F., 1994: *The Settlement of Iceland: a Critical Approach*, Gotheburg.

Eisenschmidt, Silke, 1994: *Kammergräber der Wikingerzeit in Altdänemark*, Bonn.

—— 1998: 'Grabfunde der Wikingerzeit in Nord und Süd Schleswig', VS, vii, 55–75.

Ellis, Hilda R., 1943: *The Road to Hel*, Cambridge.

Ellis Davidson, H.R., 1976: *The Viking Road to Byzantium*, London.

—— 1983: 'Insults and Riddles in the Edda Poems', *Edda*, ed. R.J. Gendinning and H. Bessason, Manitoba.

—— 1998: *Myths and Symbols in Pagan Europe*, Manchester.

—— 1998: *Roles of the Northern Goddess*, London/New York.

Ellmers, Detlev: 'Fränkisches Königszeremoniell auch in Walhall', *Beiträge zur Schleswiger Stadtgeschichte*, xxv, 115–26.

—— 1986: 'Schiffsdarstellungen auf skandinavischen Grabstein', ZPDB, 341–72.

Engeler, Sigrid, 1991: *Altnordische Geldwörter*, Frankfurt.

Engfield, Roy, 1972: 'Der Selbstmord in der germanischen Zeit', *Seminar*, viii, 1–14.

Engström, Johan, 1984: *Torsburgen: tolkning av en gotländsk fornborg*, Uppsala.

—— 1997: 'The Vendel Chieftains: a study of military tactics', MASS, 248–54.

Ericsson, Alf, 1999: 'The Rural Landscape of Medieval Möre', EUNO, 55 ff.

Erkens, F.-R. (ed.) 2005: *Das Frühmittelalterliche Königfum*, Berlin/New-York.

Ersgård, L., 1995: 'The Change of Religion and its Artifacts' (MLUHM 1993–4), Lund.

Ersson, Per-Göran, 1974: *Kolonisation och ödeläggelse på Götland*, Stockholm.

Etchingham, C., 1996: *Viking Raids on Irish Church Settlements in the Ninth Century*, Maynooth.

Evans, D.A H., 1989: 'More Common Sense about Hávamál', *Skandinavistik*, xix/2, 127 ff.

Fabech, Charlotte, 1992: 'Sakrale pladser i sydskandinavisk jernalder', SANA, 141–67.

—— 1992: Skåne – et kulturellt og geografisk grænseland', *Tor*, xxv, 201–45.

—— 1999: 'Centrality in Sites and Landscapes', SELA, 455–74.

Fallgren, J.-H., 1994: 'En vendel – och vikingatida grobhusbebyggelse', *Tor*, xxvi, 107–4.

Faulkes, Anthony, 1978–79: 'Descent from the Gods', MS, xi, 92–125.

—— 1993: *What was Viking Poetry For?*, Birmingham.

Faulkes and Perkins: *Viking Revaluations*, London, VIRE.

Fell, Christine, 1981: 'Vikingavisur', SPEN, 106–22.

—— 1993: 'Norse Studies', VIRE.

Fellows-Jensen, Gillian, 1984: 'Place-name Research in Scandinavia', *Names*', xxxii, 267–324.

—— 1991–92: 'Place-names in Thorp', *Nomina*, xv, 35–52.

—— 1991: 'Of Danes and Thanes and Domesday Book', PAP, 107–21.

—— and Bente Holmberg (eds), 1992: *Sakrale Navne*, Uppsala; including her 'Cultic PNN: A View from the Danelaw', 263–72.

—— 1993: 'Tingwall, Dingwall and Thingwall', NOWELE, xxi, 53–67.

—— 1995: *The Vikings and their Victims*, London.

Fenger, Ole, 1988: 'Gammeldansk Ret', Viborg. 1991: 'Germansk Retsorden', HØKO, 155–64.

Feveile, Claus, 1994: 'The latest news from Viking Age Ribe', VC 12, 91–9.

Fidjestøl, Bjarne, 1991: 'Skaldediktning og trusskiftet', NOHED, 113–31.

Filipowiak, W., 1991: *Wolin-Jomsborg*, Roskilde.

Finnestad, Ragnhild, 1990: 'The Study of the Christianization of the Nordic Countries', ONFRAC, 256–72.

Fischer, Andreas (ed.), 1989: *The History and Dialects of English*, Heidelberg.

Fitzhugh, W.W. and E.I. Ward (eds), 2000: *Vikings: the North Atlantic Saga*: VINAS.

Fix, Hans, 1997: 'Text editing in Old Norse', NOWELE, xxxi, 105–17.

Fjeld, Ellen, 1992: 'Sentrum og periferi... på Hedemarken' in *Økonomiske og politiske senra i Norden*, ed. E. Mikkelsen and J.H. Larsen, Oslo.

Flannery, Kent, 1999: 'Process and Agency in Early State Formation', CAJ, ix, 3–21.

Fleck, J., 1970: 'Konr-Óttarr-Geirrødr: a knowledge Criterion', SS, xlii, 39–49.

Flowers, Stephen, 1986: *Runes and Magic*, New York/Berne/Frankfurt.

Fonnesbech-Sandberg, E., 1987: 'Vægtsystemer i ældre germansk jernalder', Aarbøger.

Foot, Sarah, 1991: 'Violence against Christians?' *Medieval History*, 1/3, 3–16.

——— 1999: 'Remembering Forgetting and Inventing', TRHS, vi/9, 185–200.

Foote, Peter, 1977: 'Oral and Literary Tradition in Early Scandinavian Law' in *Oral Tradition and Literary Tradition*, ed. Bekker Nielsen et al., Odense, 47–55.

——— 1987: 'Reflections on *Landabrigdisthattr* and *Rekatháttr*', TROG, 53–64.

Frank, Roberta, 1989: 'Did Anglo-Saxon Audiences have a Skaldic Tooth?', ASCEN.

——— 1991: 'The Ideal of Men dying with their Lord', PAP, 95–106.

——— 1994: 'King Canute in the Verse of his Skalds', Rumble 1994, 106–24.

——— 1996: 'Hand Tools and Power Tools in... Thórsdrápa', SMEOL, 94–109.

——— 1997: 'The Unbearable Lightness of Being a Philologist', JEGP, xcvi, 486–513.

Frankis, John, 1999: 'From Saint's Life to Saga: the Fatal Walk', SB, xxv/2, 121–35.

Franklin, S. and J. Shephard, 1996: *The Emergence of Rus 750–1200*, London/New York.

Freeden, von, Koch, U. and A. Wieczorek (eds), 1999: *Völker an Nord und Ostsee und die Franken*, Bonn.

Frense, Bo, 1982: *Religion och Rätt*, Uppsala.

Fridriksson, Adolf, 1994: *Sagas and Popular Antiquarianism*, Aldershot.

Fuglesang, Signe H., 1983: 'The Relationship between Scandinavian and English Art from the Late 8th to the Mid 12th century', in Szarmach, 201–41.

——— 1986: 'Ikonographie der skandinavischen runensteine', ZPDB, 183–218.

——— 1998: 'Swedish Runestones of the 11th century: Ornament and Dating', RUQUIF, 197–218.

Gade, Kari Ellen, 1985: 'Hanging in Northern Law and Literature', *Maal og Minne*.

——— 1995: *The Structure of ON Drottkvaett Poetry (Cornell Islandica, xlix)*.

Galinié, Henri (ed.), 1989: *Les mondes normands*, Caen.

Gelsinger, Bruce, 1981: *Icelandic Enterprise*, Columbia.

Gilchrist, Roberta, 1999: *Gender and Archaeology*, London/New York.

Gilmore, Carroll, 1988: 'War on the River', *Viator*, xix.

Goldberg, Eric, 1999: 'More Devoted to the Equipment of Battle', *Viator*, xxx, 41–78.

Göransson, Eva-Marie, 1999: *Bilder av kvinnor och kvinnlighet*, Stockholm.

Göransson, Sölve, 1999: 'Medieval Changes in Field Division . . . on Öland', EUNO, 43–54.

Görmann, Marianne, 1990: 'Nordic and Celtic Religion', ONFRAC.

Graham Campbell, James, 1980: *Viking Artifacts*, London.

Graham Campbell, James, 1991: 'Anglo-Scandinavian Equestrian Equipment' in *The Battle of Maldon*, ed. D.G. Scragg, Manchester.

—— 1994: *Cultural Atlas of the Viking World*, Abingdon.

—— 1998a: (with Colleen Batey): *Vikings in Scotland*, Edinburgh.

—— 1998b: 'The Early Viking Age in the Irish Sea Area', ISCEVA, 104–30.

Gräslund, Anne-Sofie, 1993: 'Lokala bebyggelse-sentra i Oppland', ØPOLIS, 181 ff.

—— 1996: 'Kristnandet ur ett kvinnoperspektiv', KRLS, 313–34.

Gräslund, Bo, 1986: 'Knut den store och Sveariket', *Scandia*, lii, 211–38.

—— 1994: 'Prehistoric Soul Beliefs', PPR, lx, 15–26.

Greene, David, 1978: 'The Evidence of Language and Place-Names in Ireland', TV.

Griffith, Paddy, 1995: *The Viking Art of War*, London-Pennsylvania.

Grønvik, O., 1982: *The Words for Heir, Inheritance and Funeral Feast*, Oslo.

—— 1988: 'Om Eggjainnskriften', ANF oiii, 37 ff.

—— 1998: 'Enda en gang om Tuneinnskriften', *Maal og Minne* 1998/i, 35.

Guðjónsson, Elsa 1989: 'Járnvárdr yllir', Ancient and Medieval Textiles, ed.L. Monnas.

Gunnell, Terry, 1995: *The Origins of Drama in Scandinavia*, Woodbridge.

Gurevich, Aron Y., 1969: 'Space and Time in the *Weltmodell* of the Old Scandinavian Peoples', MS, ii, 42–53.

Gurevich, Elena, 1996: 'Observations on . . . Skaldic Training', CM ix, 57–71.

Gustafsson, Anders, 1999: 'Wiser than he himself', CSA vii, 27–35.

Gustafsson, Berndt, 1972: 'Durkheim on Power and Holiness', Biezais 1972, 20–30.

Gustin, Ingrid, 1997: 'Islam, Merchants or King?', VIPA, 163–77.

Hadley, D.M., 1997: 'And they proceeded to plough and support themselves: the Scandinavian settlement of England', ANS, xix, 69–96.

Hagberg, Ulk-Erik, 1999: 'From Pagan Cult Sites', EUNO, 39–42.

Hagland, J.R., 1998: 'Notes on Two Runic Inscriptions', *Scripta Islandica*, xlix, 34 ff.

Hagerman, Maja, 1996: *Spåren av kungens män*, Stockholm.

Hall, R.A., 1994: 'Vikings gone West?' VC 12, 32–49.

Hallberg, Peter, 1978: 'The Ship – Reality and Image', TV.

Hald, K., 1963: 'The Cult of Odin in Danish Place-Names', *Early English and Norse Studies Presented to . . . Smith*, ed. A. Brown and P. Foote, London.

—— 1971: *Personnavne i Danmark*, Copenhagen.

Halsall, Guy, 1992: 'Playing by whose rules? A further look at Viking atrocity in the ninth century?' *Medieval History*, ii, 2–12.

—— (ed.), 1998: *Violence and Society in the Early Medieval West*, Woodbridge (VISO).

Hansen, Bente H., 1984: 'The Scandinavian Element in English', NOWELE, iv, 51–95.

Hansen, Lars I., 1990: *Samisk fangstsamfunn og norsk høvdinge økonomi*, Oslo.

Hansson, Ann-Marie, 1997: *On Plant Food in the Scandinavian Peninsula in Early Medieval Times*, Stockholm.

Hansson, Martin, 1998: 'Graves, Grave-Fields, and Burial Customs', LAR, 49–66.

Hansson, P., 1989: *Samhälle och järn i Sverige: Närke*, Uppsala.

Hårdh, Birgitta, 1992: 'Silver hoards as a mirror of economic systems' in *Exchange and Trade*, ed. R. Hall, R., Hodges and H. Clarke: vol. v of York conference on Medieval Europe, 51–95.

Hårdh, Larsson, Clausson and Petré (eds), 1988: *Trade and Exchange in Prehistory*, Lund.

Harris, Joseph, 1986a: 'Saga as historical novel', SMEOL, 187–219.

—— 1986b: 'Brunanburh' in *Magister Regis: Studies in honour of R.E. Kaske*, New York.

—— 1993: 'Love and Death in the Männerbund' in H. Damico and J. Legerle, *Heroic Poetry in the AS Period*, Kalamazoo.

Harrison, Dick, 1991: 'Dark Age Migrations and Subjective Ethnicity', *Scandia*, lvii/i, 19–36.

Hasenfratz, Hans-Peter, 1982: *Die Toten Lebenden*, Leiden.

Hastrup, Kirsten, 1986: 'Text and Context' in *Continuity and Change*, ed. E. Vestergaard, Odense.

—— 1990: 'Establishing an Ethnicity' in her *Iceland: Island of Anthropology*, Odense, 69–86.

—— 1998: *A Place Apart*, Oxford.

Hauck, Karl (ed.), 1992: *Der historische Horizont der Götterbildamulette* (Abhandlungen der Göttinger Akademie der Wiss. Phil. Hist. Klasse 3rd series, cc), 1992.

Hed Jakobsson, Anna, 1999: 'Towns, Plots, Crafts and Fertility', CSA, vii, 37–53.

Hedeager, Lotte, 1988: *Danernes Land* (vol. ii of Gyldendal and Politikens Danmarkshistorie, ed. O. Olsen), Copenhagen.

—— 1992: *Iron Age Societies: from Tribe to State* (trans. J. Hines), Oxford.

—— 1994: 'Warrior Economy and Trading Economy', *Journal of European Archaeology*, ii/i, 130–47.

—— 1997: *Skygger af en anden virkelighed* Haslev (rev. in English by Herschend, NAR xxxi [1998], 76–7).

—— 1996: 'Myter og materiel kultur: Den nordiske oprindelsesmyte', *Tor*, xxviii, 217–34.

Hedvall, Richard, 1997: 'Boundaries in the Landscape', VIPA, 603–24.

Hegardt, J., 1990–91: 'Patrilateralt samhälle', *Tor*, xxiii, 55–85.

Heinrichs, Anne, 1986: '*Annat er várt eðli*: the type of the prepatriarchal woman in Old Norse literature', SMEOL, 110–40.

—— 1994: 'The Search for Identity: a Problem after the Conversion', *Alvíssmál*, iii.

Helgesson, B. and C. Arcini, 1996: 'A major burial ground at Fjälkinge', LAR, ii.

Hellberg, Staffan, 1984: 'Kring tillkomsten av Glaelognskviða', ANF, xix.

Hellberg, Lars, 1987: *Ortnamnen och den svenska bosättningen pa Åland*, Helsingfors.

Helle, Knut, 1994: 'Descriptions of Nordic Towns', VC 12, 20–31.

Helle, Knut, 1998: 'The History of the Early Viking Age in Norway', ISCEVA, 239–58.

Helliksen, W., 1993: 'Byutvikling og vareutveksling', *Viking*, lvi.

Hellmuth Andersen, H., 1985: 'Hedenske danske kongegrave', KUML, 11–34.

—— 1998: *Danevirke og Kovirke*, Aarhus.

Herrmann, J., 1982: *Wikinger und Slawen*, Berlin.

Hermann-Auðardottir, Margaret, 1989: *Islands tidiga bosättning*, Umeå.

Herschend, F., 1989: 'Vikings following Gresham's Law', ASP, 373.

—— 1993: 'The Origin of the Hall in Southern Scandinavia', *Tor*, xxv, 175–99.

—— 1994a: 'Models of Petty Rulership: two Early Settlements in Iceland', *Tor*, xxvi, 163–91.

—— 1994b: *The Recasting of Symbolic Value*, Uppsala.

—— 1998: *The Idea of the Good in Late Iron Age Society* (Uppsala Occasional Papers xv).

—— 1999: 'Ordering Landscapes, SELA, 331–5.

Higham, Mary C., 1995: 'Scandinavian Settlement in NW England', SSNB, 195–205.

Hines, John, 1991: 'Scandinavian English: a Creole in Context', LACON.

—— 1995: 'Egill's Hófuðlausn in Time and Space', SB, xxiv/2, 3 ff.

—— 1997: *The Anglo-Saxons*, Woodbridge.

Hjørungdal, T., 1991: *Den skjulte kjøn*, Acta Arch. Lundensia, xix.

Hodges, Richard, 1982: *Dark Age Economics*.

—— 1988: 'Charlemagne's Elephant and the Beginning of Commoditization in Europe', AA, lix, 155–68.

Hodnebø, Finn: 'Who were the First Vikings?', VC 10, 43–54.

Hoffmann, Dietrich, 1955: *Nordisch-Englische Lehnbeziehungen der Wikingerzeit*, Copenhagen.

Høilund Nielsen, Karen, 1991: 'Centrum og Periferi i 6–8 Århundred', HØKO, 127–54. Ibid 1997: 'From Society to Burial', BUSO 1997.

Holm, Ingunn, 1997: 'From Society to Burial and from Burial to Society?', BUSO, 103–10.

—— 1999: 'Gårdsbegrepet', UOA, 91–104.

Holm, Poul, 1988: 'Between Apathy and Antipathy: the Vikings in Irish–Scandinavian History', *Peritia*, viii, 151–69.

—— 1985: 'The Slave Trade of Dublin', *Peritia*, v, 317–45.

Holmberg, Bente, 1986: 'Den hedenske gud Tyr i Danske stednavne' in *Mange bække små*, ed. V. Dalberg and G. Fellows Jensen, Copenhagen, 109–27.

—— 1990: 'Views on Cultic Place-Names in Denmark: A Review of Research', ONFRAC, 381–93.

—— 1994: 'Recent Research into Sacral Names', VC 12, 280–7.

—— 1997/98: 'Da kom en snekke...', *Kuml*.

Holmqvist, W., 1986: 'Bilddenkmäler und Glaubensvorstellungen in der Eisenzeit Schwedens', ZPDB, 373–94.

Holtsmark, Anne, 1992: *Fornordisk mytologi: tro og myter under vikingatiden*, Lund.

Hoppal, M. and J. Pentikäinen (eds), 1992: *Northern Religion and Shamanism*, Budapest.

Hooper, Nicholas, 1984: 'The Housecarls in England', ANS, vii, 161–76.

Howard Johnston, James, 1998: 'Trading in Fur from Classical Antiquity to the Early Middle Ages', LEAF, 65–79.

Hudson, B., 1994: 'Knútr and Viking Dublin', SS, lxvi/3, 319–35.

Hultgård, A: *Ragnarök och Valhöll*, summarized as 'Ragnarók and Valhalla in VC 12, 288–93.

—— 1997: *Upsalakulten och Adam av Bremen*, Nora.

—— 1992: 'Religiös förändring', KIKOT, 149–54.

—— 1998: 'Runeninschriften und Runendenkmäler als Quellen', RUQUIF, 715–37.

Hultkrantz, Åke, 1978: *Studies in Lapp Shamanism*, Stockholm.

—— 1992: 'Aspects of Saami (Lapp) Shamanism' in Hoppal and Pentikäinen.

Huurre, Matti, 1999 edn: *Dig it all*, Helsinki.

Hvass, S., 1979: 'The Viking Age Settlement at Vorbasse', AA, 1.

—— 1985: *'Hodde: et vestjysk landsbysamfund*, Copenhagen.

—— 1989: 'Rural Settlement in Denmark in the first Millennium A D', in Randsborg 1989.

—— 1998: 'Jelling', SADO, 161–76.

Hyenstrand, Åke, 1974: *Centralbygd-randbygd*, Stockholm.

—— 1991: 'Iconography and Rune Stones: the Example of Sparlösa', PAP, 205–9.

—— 1996: *Lejonet draken och korset*, Lund.

Indrelid, Svein, and S. Ugelvik Larsen, 1984: *Sunnmøres Forhistorie*, Ålesund.

Ingimundarson, Jon H., 1992: 'Spinning Goods and Tales', FROSA, 217–30.

Ingstad, 1–5, 1987: The Norse Discovery of America, 2 vols, Oslo.

Insley, John, 1994: *Scandinavian Personal Names in Suffolk*, Stockholm.

Iversen, M., Näsman, and Vellev (eds), 1998: *Mammen: grav, kunst og samfund i vikingetid*, Højbjerg.

—— and Nielsen, B.H., 1992–3: 'Brandstrup iii', JDA, xi, 136–49.

Jackson, Tatiana N., 1991: 'The North of Eastern Europe in the Ethnographical Nomenclature of Early Norse Texts', AUSA, i, 228–37.

Jacobsson see Anna Hed.

Jakobsson, Ármann, 1997: *Í leit að konungi: konungsmynd íslenskra konungasagna*, Reykjavík.

Jakobsson, Mikael, 1991: *Krigarideologi och vikingatida svärdtypologi*, Stockhom.

—— 1997: 'Burial layout, Society and Sacred Geography', CSA, v, 79–98.

Jansson, Ingmar, 1987: 'Communications between Scandinavia and Eastern Europe in the Viking Age: the archaeological evidence', UNHAVE, 773–807.

Janzen, Assur, 1947: *Personnamn* (Nordisk Kultur vii), Stockholm/Oslo/Copenhagen.

Jaski, Bart, 1995: 'The Vikings and the Kingship of Tara', *Peritia*, ix, 310–51.

Jensen, Claus Kjeld, 1997: see BUSO.

Jensen, Jørgen, 1982: *The Prehistory of Denmark*, London.

Jesch, Judith, 1991: *Women in the Viking Age*, Woodbridge.

—— 1993: 'Skaldic verse and Viking Semantics', VIR, 160–71.

—— 1994: 'In Praise of Ástriðr Ólafsdóttir', SB, xxiv/i, 1–18.

—— 1998: 'Still standing in Ågersta', RUQUIF, 462–75.

—— 2001: *Ships and Men in the Late Viking Age*, Woodbridge.

—— 2002: *The Scadinavians from the Vendel Period to the Tenth Century: An Ethnographic Perspective*, Woodbridge.

Jochens, Jenny, 1998: 'Vóluspá: Matrix of Norse Womanhood', PISMA, 257–77.

—— 1992: 'From Libel to Lament', FROSA, 247–64.

—— 1995: *Women in Old Norse Society*, Ithaca/New York.

—— 1997: 'Gendered Trifunctionality: the case of Rígsthula', Hug, 111–22.

—— 1999A: 'Late and Peaceful: Iceland's Conversion', *Speculum*, lxxiv, 621–55.

—— 1999B: 'Race and Ethnicity in the ON world', *Viator*, xxx, 79–104.

Johansen, Arne, 1972: 'Iron Production and Settlement History', NAR v 84 ff.

Johansen, Birgitta, 1996: 'The Transformative Dragon', CSA iv, 83–102.

—— 1997: *Aspekter av tillvaro och landskap*, Stockholm.

Johansen, Johannes, 1985: *Studies in the Vegetational History*, Tórshavn.

Johansen, Olav Sverre, 1982: 'Viking Age Farms', NAR, xv, 45 ff.

Johansen, Øystein, 1980: 'Forhistorien, religionsforsknings grense?', *Viking*, xliii, 96–106.

Johnson, O.F., 1995: 'Euhemerisation versus Demonisation, PAC, 35–69.

Jones, Gwyn, 1968: *A History of the Vikings*, Oxford.

Jorgensen, Anne and B.L. Clausen, 1997: see MASS.

Jørgensen, Ove, 1985: 'Danmarks Geografi: en undersogelse af fire afsnit', NOWELE.

Jørgensen, Bent, 1980: *Stednavne og administrationsahistorie*, Copenhagen.

Jørgensen, Lars, 1991: 'Våbengrave og krigeraristokrati', HØKO, 109–25.

—— 1992: 'The Early Medieval Family', DEBU, 23–8.

Jørgensen, Liliane, 1986: 'Nybol' in *Mange bække små*, ed. Dalberg and Jensen.

Jørgensen, Lise Bender, 1986: '*Forhistoriske textiler in Skandinavien* (Nordiske Fortidsminder B, ix), Copenhagen.

Josephson, Folke (ed.), 1997: *Vikings and Celts*, Gothenburg.

Jottijärvi, Arne, 1992: 'Om muligheden for proveniensbestemmelse af jern', ANF, 183–91.

Julku, Kyösti, 1986: *Kvenland-Kainuuamaa*, Oulu.

Kabell, Aage, 1976: 'Der Fischfang Thórs', ANF, xci, 123–9.

Kaldal Mikkelsen, Dorthe, 1998: 'Single Farm or Village?', SELA, 177–93.

Kara, Michal, 1992: 'The Graves of the Armed Scandinavians . . . from the Territory of the first Piasts' State', DEBU, 167–77.

Karras, Ruth Mazo, 1990: 'Concubinage and Slavery in the Viking Age', SS, lxxii/2.

——1992: 'Servitude and Sexuality in Medieval Iceland', FROSA, 289–304.

Keefer, Sarah L., 'Hwar Cwom Mearh?', JMH, xxii, 1996.

Kendal, C.B. and Wells, P.S. (eds), 1998: *Voyage to the Other World*, Minneapolis.

Kersten, K. and P. La Baume (eds), 1958: *Vorgeschichte der Nordfriesischen Inseln*, Neumünster.

Kjølbye, Marie-Louise, 1989: 'Nyt syn på Balder-myten', *Danske Studier*, 47–68.

Kleinschmidt, Harald, 1999: 'The Fragmentation of the Integrated Process of Communicative Action', NOWELE xxxv, 77–114.

Knirk, James E., 1985: 'Recently Found Runestones', VC 10, 191–202.

Kolstrup, Inger-Lise, 1991: 'Ikonografi og Religion', NOHED, 181–203.

Kousgaard Sørensen, J., 1982: *Patronymics in Denmark and England*, London.

——1985: 'Gudhem', FMS, xix, 131–8.

——1990: 'The Change of Religion and the Names', ONFRAC.

Krafft, Sofie, 1956: *Tapisseries des temps des vikings*, Oslo lxviii.

Krag, Claus, 1989: 'Norge som odel i Harald Hårfagresætt', HT (N), 288–302.

——1991: *Ynglingetal og Ynglingesaga*, Oslo.

——1993: 'Hvem var Harald Hårfagre?' see Vea 1994.

——1999: 'Rane Kongsfostre og Olav Geirstadalv', HT (N) lxxviii/i, 21–47.

Kress, Helga, 1988: 'The Apocalyse of a Culture', PISMA, 279–302.

Kries, Suzanne, 2003: *Skandinavisch-schatische Sprachøeziehungen*, Odense.

Kristensen, Anne K.G.: *Tacitus' germanische Erfolgschaft*, Copenhagen 1983.

Kristiansen, K., 1984: *Economy in Settlement and Later Scandinavian Prehistory* BAR internat. series ccxi Oxford.

——and Michael Rowlands, 1998: see SOTIA.

Kristjánsson, Jonas, 1992: 'Heidintrú í forn qvæðum' in *Snorrastefna*, ed. Ulf Bragnar, 99–112.

——1998: 'Ireland and the Irish in Icelandic Tradition', ISCEVA, 259–76.

Kroesen, Riti, 1985: 'Hvessir augu sem hildingar', ANFC.

——1996: 'Ambiguity . . . between Heroes and Giants', ANF cxi 57ff.

——1997: 'The Valkyries in the Heroic Literature', *Skaldskaparmall*, iv, 129–61.

Krogh, K.J., 1993: *Gåden om Kong Gorms grav*, Herning.

Kroon, Sigurd, 1991: 'Hästkarlar, biskopar, kungar, Laurentiuskyrkor: Lund, 990–1145', *Scandia*, lvii, 37–63.

Kruse, Susan, 1993: 'Silver Storage and Circulation in Viking Age Scotland', VACON, 187–203.

Kuchenbuch, Ludolf, 1995: 'Links with the Village', AGMA, 138–62.

Kyhlberg, Ola, 1980: *Vikt och Värde*, Stockholm.

—— 1988: 'Spatial Patterns – Social Structures' in Lundström 1988.

Lamb, Raymond, G., 1993: 'Carolingian Orkney and its Transformation', VACON, 260–71.

Lang, James, 1986: 'The Distinctiveness of Viking colonial Art' in Szarmach 1986, 243–58.

Lange, W., 1958: *Studien zur christlichen Dichtung der Nordgermanen 1000–1200*, Göttingen.

Larrington, Carolyne, 1993: *A Store of Common Sense*, Oxford.

Larsson, Lars-Olaf, 1964: *Det medeltida Värend*, Lund.

Larsson, Lars, 1992: *Contacts across the Baltic Sea*.

Larsson, Mats, 1987: *Hamnor, Husbyar och Ledung*, Lund Report, xxix.

—— 1990: *Runstenar och utlands färder*, Lund/Stockholm.

—— 1996: 'Tvegifte i Täby?' Fornvännen, 143–51.

Larsson, Mats, 1998: 'Runic Inscriptions as a Source for the History of Settlement', RUQUIF, 639–46.

Larsson, T.B., and H. Lundmark (eds), 1989: *Approaches to Swedish Prehistory*, BAR Intern. Series D, Oxford.

Laur, Wolfgang, 1968: 'Theophore Ortsnamen' in *Studien zur europäischen Vor und Fnhhgeschichte*, ed. M. Claus et al., Neümunster.

Lawson, K, 1993 *Cnut*, London/New York.

Lecouteux, Claude, 1984: 'Fantômes et revenants germaniques', EG, xxxix, 227–50 and xl, 141–60.

Lehtosalo-Hilander, P.-L., 1990: 'Le viking finnois', Finskt Museum, 55–72.

Lerche, Grith, 1994: 'Radiocarbon Datings', *Tools and Tillage*, vii/4, 172–203.

Levesque, J.-M. (ed.), 1996: *Dragons et Drakkars*, Caen.

Liden, K., and A. Götherström, 1999: 'The Archaeology of Rank', ASSAH, x, 81–8.

Liestøl, Aslak, 1978–81: 'The Viking Runes: The Transition from the Older to the Younger *futhark*', SB xx, 247ff.

Lincoff, Gary, and D.H. Mitchell, 1977: *Toxic and Hallucinogenic Mushroom Poisoning*, New York.

Lindeblad, Karin, 1997: 'The Town and the Three Farms', VIPA, 491–512.

Lincoln, Bruce, 1995: 'The Ship as Symbol', SHAS, 25–33.

Linderoth Wallace, Birgitta, 2000: 'The Viking Settlement at L'Anse aux Meadows', VINAS, 208–16.

Lindow, John, 1982: 'Narrative and the Nature of Old Norse Skaldic Poetry', *Arkiv*, xcvii, 94–141.

—— 1998a: *Scandinavian Mythology: an annotated Bibliography*, New York/London.

—— 1998b: 'Addressing Thor', SS, lx, 119–36.

—— 1994a: 'Bloodfeud and Scandinavian Mythology', *Alvíssmál*, iv, 51–68.

—— 1994b: 'Thor's *hamarr*', JEGP, xciii, 485–503.

—— 1995: 'Nordic Legends and the Question of Identity', SS, lx.

—— 1997: *Murder and Vengeance among the Gods*, Helsinki and see SMEOL.

Lindqvist, Sune, 1941–42: *Gotlands Bildsteine*, 2 vols, Stockholm.

Lindqvist, Sven-Olof, 1961: 'Some Investigations of Field-Wall Areas', GA, xliii, 206–20.

Lindqvist, Thomas, 1988: *Plundring, skatter och den feodala statens framväxt*, Uppsala.

Löfving, Carl, 1991: 'Who ruled the region east of the Skagerrack in the eleventh century?', SAP, 147–56.

Loit, A., E. *Mugurevičs* and A. Caune, 1990: *Die Kontakte zwischen Ostbaltikum und Skandinavien im frühen Mittelalter*, Riga.

Lönnroth, Lars, 1977: 'The Riddle of the Rök Stone: A Structural Approach', *Arkiv*, xcii, 1–57.

—— 1986: 'Domaldi's Death and the Myth of the Sacral Kingship', SMEOL, 73–93.

Lønborg, Bjarne, 1994: 'Mærkevare', *Skalk*, 8–10.

—— 1999: 'Vikingetidens kvindedragter', *Kuml*, 259–68.

Looijenga, Tineke, 2003: *Texts and Contexts of the Oldest Runic Inscriptions*, Leiden/Boston.

Lund, Niels, 1987: 'Peace and Non-Peace in the Viking Age', VC 10, 255–71.

—— 1989: 'Allies of God or Man: The Viking Expansion in a European Perspective', *Viator*, xx, 45–59.

—— 1991: 'Denemearc, tanmarkar but and tanmaurk ala', PAP, 161–9.

—— 1993: 'Danish Military Organization' in *The Battle of Maldon: Fiction and Fact*, ed. J. Cooper, Cambridge.

—— 1994: 'If the Vikings knew a *Leding* – What was it like?', VC 12, 100–105.

—— 1996: *Lið, leding og landeværn*, Roskilde.

—— 1997: 'Is *leidang* a Nordic or European phenomenon?', MIAS, 195–9.

Lundström, Per, 1981: *De kommo vidd . . . vikingars hamn vid Paviken*, Uddevalla. Ibid. 1998: *Thirteen Studies*, Stockholm.

Lynnerup, Niels, 2000: 'Life and Death in Norse Greenland', VINAS, 285–94.

Mackenzie, Bridget, 1981: 'On the Relation of Norse Skaldic Verse to Irish syllabic poetry', SPEN, 377–56.

Madsen, Hans Jørgen, 1991: 'Vikingetidens keramik', HØKO.

Magnusson, Staff, Björn, 1994: *An Essay on the Theory of History in Swedish Archaeology*, Lund.

Mahler, Ditlev, L.D., 1993: 'Shielings and their role in the Viking Age Economy: New Evidence from the Faroe Islands', VACON, 487–505.

—— 1998: 'The Stratigraphical Cultural Landscape', OUTU, 51–62.

Maillefer, Jean-Marie, 1997: 'Essai sur Völundr-Weland', HUG, 331.

Malmer, Brita, 1989: *The Sigtuna Coinage*, Stockholm/Lund.

—— 1991: 'On the Early Coinage of Lund', PAP, 187–96.

—— 1997: *The Anglo-Scandinavian Coinage, c.995–1020*, Stockholm.

Malmer, Mats, 1991: 'The Mentalities of Centre and Peripheries', RER, 45–65.

—— 1997: 'The Objectivity and Actualism', CSA, v, 7–18.

Malmros, Rikke, 1985: 'Leding og Skjaldekvad', ANF, 87–139.

Marold, Edith, 1972: 'Das Walhallbild', MS v, 19–35.

—— 1986: 'Ragnarsdrapa und Ragnarssage', GEDI, 427–53.

—— 1992: 'Die Skaldendichtung als Quelle der Religionsgeschichte', GR, 685–716.

—— 1998: 'Die Augen des Herrschers', VS, 7–30.

Martens, Irmelin, 1985: 'Iron Extraction, Settlement and Trade in the Viking and Early Middle Age in S. Norway', VC 10, 69–111.

Martin, John S., 1988: 'Some Thoughts on Kingship in the Helgi Poems', PISMA, 215–26.

Martinson, Floyd M., 1992: *Growing Up in Norway*, Illinois.

McCone, Kim, 1986: 'Werewolves, Cyclopes, Dúberga and Fianna: Juvenile Delinquency in Early Ireland', CMCS, xii, 1–22.

—— 1987: 'Hund, Wolf und Krieger', Studien zum Indogermanischen Wortschatz, (Innsbruck), 101–54.

McDougal, 1996: 'Serious Entertainments: an Examination of a Peculiar Type of Atrocity', ASE, xxii, 201–5.

McKinnell, John S., 1987: 'Norse Myths and Northumbria', SS, lix, 308–24.

—— 1994: *Both One and Many*, Rome.

McTurk, Rory W., 1974–77: 'Sacral Kingship in Ancient Scandinavia: A review of some recent writings', SB, xix, 139–69.

—— 1994: 'Sacral Kingship Revisited', SB, xxiv/i.

—— 1991: *Studies in Ragnars Saga*, Oxford.

Matiushina, Inna, 1998: 'The emergence of lyrical self-expression in skaldic love poetry', *Maal og Minne*, 21–33.

Mattíasson, Haraldur, 1982: *Landið og Landnáma*, 2 vols, Reykjavik.

Melnikova, E.A., and V.J. Petrukhin, 1990–1: 'The Origin and Evolution of the name *Rus*', *Tor*, xxiii, 203–34.

Meskell, Lyn: 'The Somatisation of Archaeology: Discourses, Institutes, Corporeality', NAR, xxix/i, 1–16.

Metcalf, D.M.: 'The Beginnings of Coinage in the North Sea Coastlands: a Pirenne-like Hypothesis', VC 12, 196–214.

Meulengracht Sørensen, Preben, 1983: *The Unmanly Man*, trans. J. Turville-Petre Odense.

—— 1991a: 'Hakon den Gode og Guderne', HØKO, 235–44.

—— 1991b: 'Om Edddadigtenes alder', NOHED, 217–28.

—— 1992: 'Methodological Considerations', FROSA, 27–42.

—— 1993: 'The Sea, the Flame and the Wind', VACON, 212–21.

Michell, John, 1994: *At the Centre of the World*, London.

Miller, W.I., 1990: *Bloodtaking and Peacemaking: feud, law, and society in saga Iceland*, Chicago.

Mitchell, Stephen A., 1984: 'On the Composition and Function of Guta Saga', ANF, xci, 151–74.

—— 1991a: 'Heroic Legend, Parricide, and Istaby', AUSA, ii, 113–19.

—— 1991b: *Heroic Sagas and Ballads*, Cornell.

Morris, Carole, 2000: *Craft, Industry, and Woodworking in Anglo-Saxon and Medieval York*, York.

Morris, Christopher D., and D.J. Rackham, 1992: *Norse and Later Settlement and Subsistence in the North Atlantic*, Glasgow.

Morris, Christopher D., 1998: 'Raiders, Traders, and Settlers', ISCEVA, 73–104.

Morris, Guy, 1998: 'Violence and the Late Viking Age Scandinavian social order': *Violence and Society in the Early Medieval West*, ed. G. Halsall, Woodbridge, 1998.

Mortensen, Peder, and Birgit Rasmussen: see HØKO.

Motz, Lotte, 1973: 'New Thoughts on Dwarf-Names in Old Icelandic', FMS, ii.

—— 1991: 'The Poets and the Goddess', AUSA, ii, 127–33.

—— 1992: 'The Goddess Freyja', *Snorrastefna*, 163–73.

—— 1994: 'The Magician and his Craft', CM, 6ff.

—— 1996: *The King, the Champion and the Sorcerer: a Study in Germanic Myth*, Vienna.

Mulk, I.-M. and T. Bayliss-Smith, 1999: 'The Representation of Sami Cultural Identity in the Cultural Landscape of Northern Sweden' in Ucko and Layton, 358–92.

Müller-Wille, Michael, 1995: 'Boat-graves, Old and New Views', SHAS, 100–9.

—— (ed.), 1997: *Rom und Byzanz im Norden*, 1997.

—— and R. Schneuler (eds), 1994: *Ausgewählte Probleme europäischer Landnahmen*, Sigmaringen.

Munch, Gerd, O. Johansen and I. Larssen: 'Borg in Lofoten', VC 10 1987, 149–70.

Mundal, Else, 1987: 'Refleksionar kring historie, sanning og dikting', TROG, 15–25.

—— 1990: 'The Position of the Individual Gods and Goddesses in Various Types of Sources', ONFRAC.

—— 1993: 'The Orkney Earl and Skald Torf Einar and his Poetry', VACON, 248–59.

—— 1997: 'Framveksten av den islandske identitet', CM, x, 7–29.

—— 1998: 'Androgyny as an Image of Chaos', Maal og Minne.

Murray, A.C., 1983: *Germanic Kinship Structure*, Totonto.

—— 1998: 'Fredegar, Merovech, and Sacral Kingship' *After Rome's Fall*, ed. A.C. Murray (Toronto), 121–52.

Myhre, Bjorn, 1985: 'Boathouses as Indicators of Political Organization', NAR.

—— 1991: 'Theory in Scandinavian Archaeology since 1960': ch. 7 of I. Hodder (ed.), *Archaeological Theory in Europe*, London/New York.

—— 1993: 'The Beginning of the Viking Age', VIR, 182–204.

—— 1997: 'Boathouses and Naval Organization', MIAS, 169–83.

Myrdal, Janken, 1982: 'Jordbrugsredskap av järn före år 1000', *Fornvännen*, lxxvii, 80–104.

Myrvoll, Siri, 1998: 'Pre-urban Settlement: the Example of Skien', *Hikuin*, xxv, 23–34.

Narmo, Lars Erik, 1996: 'Kokekameratene på Leikvin', *Viking*, lix, 79–100.

Näsman, Ulf, 1991: 'The Germanic Iron Age and Viking Age in Danish Archaeology since 1976', JDA, viii (1989), 158–87.

—— 1997: 'Strategies and Tactics in Migration Period Defence', MIAS, no. 5.

—— 1999: 'The Ethnogenesis of the Danes and the Making of a Danish Kingdom', ASSAH, x, 1–10.

—— 2000: 'Exchange and Politics' in *The Long Eighth Century* ed. Hansen (Inge) and Wickham (C), Brill, pp. 35–68.

Näsström, Britt-Mari, 1995: *Freyja: the Great Goddess*, Lund.

Nicklasson, Påvel, 1995: 'Theory for the Sake of Theory', LAR, 53–63.

Nielsen, Ann-Lilli, 1997: 'Pagan cultic and votive Acts at Borg', VIPA, 373–92.

Nielsen, Leif Chr., 1990: 'Trelleborg', *Aarbøger*, 105–78.

—— 1991: 'Hedenskab og Kristendom: Religionskiftet afspeilet i vikingetidens grave', HØKO, 245–67.

Nielsen, Svend, 2002: 'Urban Economy in Southern Scandinavia in the Second Half of the First Millenium', Jesch 2002, 77–98.

Nightingale, Pamela, 1987: 'The Origin of the Court of Husting and Danish Influence on London's Development', EHR, ccciv, 559–78.

Niles, J.D., 1989: 'Skaldic Technique in *Brunanburh*', ASCEN.

Nilsson, Bertil, 1992: 'Till frågan om kyrkans hållning till ickekristna kultfenomen', KIKOT, 9–47.

Ní Mhaonaigh, Máire, 1998: 'Friend and Foe: Vikings in Ninth and Tenth Century Irish Literature', ISCEVA, 381–402.

Noonan, Thomas S., 1991: 'The Vikings in Russia', SAP, 201–6.

—— 1994: 'The Vikings in the East: Coins and Commerce', VC 12, 215–41.

Nørbach, Lars Chr., 1999: 'Organizing Iron-Production and Settlement', SAL, 237–47.

Nordal, Sigurður, 1990: *Icelandic Culture*, trans. V.T. Bjarnar, Ithaca.

Nørlund, Paul, 1948: *Trelleborg*, Copenhagen.

Norr, Svante, 1993: 'A Place for Proletarians?' CSA, i, 157–64.

North, Richard, 1991: *Pagan Words and Christian Meanings*, Amsterdam/Atlanta.

—— 1997: *The Haustlǫng of Thjóðólfr of Hvinir*, Enfield.

Nosov, Evgeny, 1998: 'The Varangian Problem', SADO, 61–6.

Novikova, G., 1992: 'Iron Neck-rings with Thor's Hammers', *Fornvännen*, lxxxvii.

Nuñez, M., 1995: 'Agrarian Colonization and Settlement of the Åland islands', FENSC, xii.

Nyberg, Tore, 1985: 'Nordiske Territorialindelinger og Nonnebakken', VS, iv.

—— 1987: 'Adam av Bremen och terminolgi' *Fornvännen* lxxxii, 115–26.

Nylen, E., 1988: *Stones, Ships and Symbols*, trans. Visby.

—— 1991, with J.P. Lamm: *Bildsteine auf Gotland*, Neumünster.

Ó Corráin, Donnchadh, 1979: 'High-kings, Vikings and other kings', *Irish Historical Studies*, xx, 283–323.

—— 1998: 'Viking Ireland-Afterthoughts', ISCA, 421–52.

Odén, Birgitta, 1996: 'Ättestupan-myt eller verklighet?' *Scandia*, lxii, 222–34.

Odenstedt, Bengt, 1992: *Runor och regionalitet*, Uppsala.

——1994: 'Who was Wulfstan'?' *Studia Neophilogica*, lxvi, 147–57.

Odner, K., 1985: 'Saamis (Lapps), Finns and Scandinavians in History and Prehistory', NAR, xviii, 1–13.

Oestigaard, Terje, 2000: 'Sacrifices of Raw, Cooked and Burnt Humans', NAR, xxxiii, 41–58.

Oexle, O.G., 1999: 'The Middle Ages Through Modern Eyes: A Historical Problem', TRHS, 6th ser., ix, 121–42.

Ó Floinn, Raghnall, 1998: 'The Archaeology of the Early Viking Age in Ireland', ISCEVA, 131–65.

Ólason, Vésteinn, 1998: *Dialogues with the Viking Age*, trans. A. Wawn, Reykjavik.

Olaussen, Michael, 1997: 'Politics, Warfare, and Architecture', MIAS.

Oldeberg, Andreas, 1966: *Metallteknik under vikingatid och medeltid*, Stockholm.

Oliver, L., 1998: 'Cyninges fedesl', ASE, xxvii, 31–40.

Olsen, Olaf, and Holger Schmidt, 1977: *Fyrkat: en jysk vikingeborg*, 2 vols, Copenhagen.

——(ed.), 1987: see DLU.

——1988: Royal Power in Viking Age Denmark', VS, vii.

O'Murchada, D., 1992–93: 'Nationality names in the Irish Annals', *Nomina* xvi, 49–70.

Ortman, Oscar, 1989: 'Problems and possibilities when working with the concept of ethnicity in archaeology', ASP, 167–77.

Ostmo, Einar, 1998: *Fra Østfolds oldtid*, Oslo.

O'Sullivan, Deirdre, 1992: 'Changing Views of the Viking Age', MH, ii, 3–12.

Ousager, Asger, 1994: 'Nationernes denationalisering', *Scandia*, lx, 45–63.

Page, R.I., 1983: 'The Manx Rune-Stones' in C. Fell *The Isle of Man*.

——1987: *Runes*, London.

——1993: 'Scandinavian Society 800–1100: the Contribution of Rubic Studies', VIR, 145–59.

——1995: *Chronicles of the Vikings*, London.

——1997: 'Les études runiques scandinaves aujourd'hui', EG, lii, 311–525.

Palm, Rune, 1992: *Runor och regionalitet*, Uppsala.

Pálsson, Gisli: see FROSA.

Pálsson, Hermann, 1996: *Keltar á Íslandi*, Reykjavik.

Pamp, B., 1974: *Ortsnamnen i Sverige*, Lund.

——1983: *Ortsnamnen i Skåne*, Stockholm.

Pedersen, Anne, 1996: 'Søllestad-nye oplysninger', Aarbøger 1996, 37–111.

——1997a: Weapons and Riding-Gear in Burials', MIAS, 123–36.

——1997b: 'Similar Finds-Different Meanings', BUSO, 171–83.

Pelteret, David, 1991: 'Slavery in the Danelaw', SAP, 178–88.

——1995: *Slavery in Early Medieval England*, Woodbridge.

Perkins, Richard, 1999: 'The Gateway to Trondheim', SB, XXV/2, 178–213.

Pesch, Alexandra, 1997: 'Wer war Hálfdan svarti?' FMS, xxxi, 70–95.

Petré, Bo, 1980: 'Bjornfällen i begravningsritualen', *Fornvännen*, lxxv, 5–14.

358 References

Petterson, Bjorn, 1992: Homes and Farmyards in... Sigtuna', *Urbanism*, 135–60.

Picard, Eve, 1991: *Germanisches Sakralkönigtum*, Heidelberg.

Pizarro, Joaquín Martinez, 1979: 'On Nið against Bishops', MS, xi, 149–53.

Poole, Russell G., 1991: *Viking Poems on War and Peace*, Toronto.

Price, N.S., 2002: *The Viking Way: Religion and War in Late Iron Age Scandinavia*, Uppsala.

Pritsak, Omelian, 1981: *The Origin of Rus*, vol. i, Cambridge, Mass.

Pulsiano, Phillip, 1997: 'Danish Men's Words be Worse than Murder', JEGP, xclvi, 13–25.

Purhonen, Paula (ed.), 1992: *Fenno-Ugri et Slavi*, Helsinki.

——1998: *Kristinuskon Saapumisesta Suomeen* (English summary), Helsinki.

Quine (Gillian), 1992: 'Medieval Shielings on the Isle of Man: Fact and Fiction' in *Medieval Europe* (York Conference), vol. viii, ed. A. Aberg and H. Mytum, 107–112.

Radner, J., 1978: *The Fragmentary Annals*, Dublin (FA).

Radcliffe, William, 1790: *A Journey through Sweden*, Dublin.

Ramqvist, Per H., 1983: *Gene*, Umeå.

Ramqvist, Per H., 1991: 'Perspektiv på regional variation och samhälle' in *Samfundsorganization og regional variation*, Aarhus.

Randsborg, Klavs, 1980: *The Viking Age in Denmark: the Formation of a State*, London.

——1989a: 'Archaeology in the 20th Century', AA, lx, 154–67.

——1989b: *The First Millennium* A.D. in Europe and the Mediterranean: an Archaeological Essay, Cambridge.

——(ed.), 1989c: *The Birth of Europe*, Rome.

——2000: 'National History, Non-national Archaeology', OJA, xix, 115–3

Rasch, Monika, 1988: 'Today's Beach – Yesterday's Harbour?', Hårdh 1988, 279–86.

Refskou, Niels, 1986: 'Den retslige inhold af de tre ottonske diplomer', *Scandia*, lxx/2, 167–210.

Reichert, H., 1998: 'Runeninschriften als Quellen der Heldensagenforschung', RUQUIF, 66–102.

Reisborg, S., 1988: 'Helgö before Helgö', in *Thirteen Studies*, Stockholm.

Reuter, Tim, 1992: *The Annals of Fulda*, Manchester.

Richter, Michael, 1994: *The Formation of the Medieval West*, Dublin.

Richards, J., M. Jecock, et al. 1995: 'The Viking Barrow Cemetery at Heath Wood, Ingleby', *Medieval Archaeology*, xxxix, 51–70.

Ridderspore, Mats, 1995: *Bymarker i backspegel*, Trelleborg.

Ridel, Elisabeth, 2004: 'The Linguistic Heritage', SCEU 149–59.

Ries, Julien, 1997: 'L'apport de Régis Boyer à l'étude du sacré', HUG, 233–43.

Rindal, Magnus, 1996: *Fra hedendom til kristendom*, Oslo.

Ringstedt, Nils, 1992: *Household Economy and Archaeology*, Oslo.

——1997: 'The Birka Chamber Graves', CSA v, 127–46.

Ringtved, Jytte, 1999a: 'Settlement Organization in Time of War', SAL, 361–81.

—— 1999b: 'South Scandinavia before the Danish Kingdom', ASSAH, x, 49–64.

Robinson, David, 1991: 'Plant Remains...from ...Lejre', JDA, x, 191–5.

Rodger, N.A.M., 1995: 'Cnut's Geld and the Size of Danish Ships', EHR.

Roeck Hansen, Birgitta, 1991: *Township and Territory*, Stockholm.

Roesdahl, Else, 1974: 'Jelling Problems', MS, vii.

—— 1982: *Viking Age Denmark*, London.

—— 1983: 'Fra Vikingegrav til Valhal', VS, ii.

—— 1989: 'Prestige, Display and Monuments in Viking Age Scandinavia' in H. Galinié (ed.), *Les Mondes normands*, Caen.

—— 1992: 'Princely Burial' in Kendall and Wells q.v.

—— 1993: 'Dendrochronology and Viking Study in Denmark with a note on the beginning of the Viking Age', VC 12, 106–16.

—— 1994: 'Vikingerne i dansk kultur', Fortid og Nutid 1995/2, 158–72.

—— 1997: 'Cultural Change and Religious Monuments in Denmark AD 950–1100', RBN, 229ff.

Rolfsen, Perry, 1981: 'Den sidste hedning på Agder', *Viking*, xliv, 112–28.

Rooth, Anna B., 1961: *Loki in Scandinavian Mythology*, Lund.

Rosell, Erland, 1981: *Värmländsk medeltid i ortnamnsperspektiv*, Karlstadt.

Roslund, Mats, 1997: 'Crumbs from the Rich Man's Table', VIPA, 239–97.

Ross, Hilda, 1993: *Mattugar Meyjar*, Reykjavik.

Ross, M.C., 1978: 'The Myth of Gefion and Gylfi', ANF, xciii, 149–64.

Roth, H., 1986: see ZPDB.

Rouche, Michel, 1989: 'The Vikings versus the Towns of N. Gaul', *Medieval Archaeology*, ed. C.L. Reman, Binghampton.

Rumble, Alexander (ed.), 1994: *The Reign of Cnut*, London.

Runciman, W.G., 1998: 'Greek Hoplites, Warrior Culture', *Journal of the Royal Anthropological Institute*, iv/4, 731–51.

Russell, James, 1996: *The Germanization of Early Medieval Christianity*, Oxford.

Ruthström, Bo, 1988: 'Oklunda-ristningen i rättslig belysning', ANF, ciii, 64–75.

Rydving, Håkan, 1990: 'Scandinavian-Saami Religious Connexions', ONFRAC, 358–73.

Sabo, K.S., 'Now the Peasants Want to Build a Village', VIPA, 671–95.

Salo, Unto, 1998: 'Kristinusko ennen kristianskoa Suomeria ii', SM 1998.

Samson, Ross, 1991: *Social Approaches to Viking Studies*, Glasgow.

—— 1992: 'Goðar: democrats or despots?', FROSA, 167–88.

—— 1999: 'The Church Lends a Hand', BOCO, 120–44.

Sandmark, A., 2004: *Power and Conversion*, Uppsala.

Sandnes, Jørn, 1992: 'Norsk stedsnavn og hedensk kultur', SANA, 9–21.

Sandberg-McGowan, Astrid, 1996: 'Viking Influence on Irish Weaponry and Dress?', CH, 215–31.

Sandred, Karl Inge, 1994: 'Viking Administration in the Danelaw', VC 12, 269–76.

—— 1987: 'The Vikings in Norfolk', VC 10, 309–24.

Saressalo, Lassi, 1987: 'The Threat from Without', SAAR, 251–7.

Saunders, Tom, 1995: 'Trade, Towns and States: a Reconsideration of Early Medieval Economics', NAR xxvii, 31ff.

Sawyer, Birgit, 1988: *Property and Inheritance in Viking Scandinavia: the Runic Evidence*, Alingsås.

—— 1991a: Women as Bridge-Builders', PAP, 211–24.

—— 1991b: 'Viking Age Rune-stones as a Crisis Symptom', NAR, xxiv, 97–112.

—— 1998: 'Viking Rune-Stones as a source of Legal History', RUQUIF, 766–7.

—— 2000: *The Viking Age Rune-Stones*, Oxford.

Sawyer, Peter, 1982: *Kings and Vikings*, London.

—— 1987: 'The Bloodfeud in Fact and Fiction', TROG, 27–38.

—— 1988a: see DADA.

—— 1988b: *The Making of Sweden*, Alingsås.

—— 1989: 'Ethelred II, Olaf Tryggvason and the Conversion of Norway', ASCEN.

—— 1991: 'Konger og Kongemagt', HØKO, 277–88.

—— 1991: 'Sweyn Forkbeard and the Historians', *Church and Chronicle in the Middle Ages*, ed. I. Wood and G. A. Loud, London.

—— 1995b: *Scandinavians and the English in the Viking Age* (Chadwick Memorial Lectures, v), Cambridge.

—— 1995: 'The Last Scandinavian Kings of York', *Northern History*, xxxi, 39–44.

—— 1998: *Anglo-Saxon Lincolnshire*, Lincoln.

Sawyer, Birgit and Sawyer, Peter, 1993: *Medieval Scandinavia*, Minneapolis.

Sayers, William, 1993: 'Vinland, the Irish, Obvious Fictions and Apocrypha', *Skandinavsitik*, xxiii/i.

Sayers, William, 1994: 'Management of the Celtic Past in Landnamabok', SS, lxvi/2.

—— 1998: 'The Ship heiti', *Scripta Islandica*, xlix.

—— 1995: 'Poetry and Social Agency in Egil's Saga', *Scripta Islandica*, xlvi, 29–62.

Schaumann-Lönnqvist, M., 1999: 'The West Finnish Warriors and the Early Svea Kingship', ASSAH, x, 65–70.

Schia, L.K., 1998: 'Huseby og Holland gårdene', HT (N) lxxvii/3, 316–35.

Schjødt, Jens Peter, 1991: 'Fyrsteideologi og religion i vikingetiden', *Mammen*, 305–10.

—— 1995: 'The Ship on ON Mythology and Religion', SHAS, 20–4.

—— 1999: *Myte og ritual i det forkristne Norden* (ed. MOR), Odense.

Schmidt, Holger, 1990: 'Viking Age Buildings', JDA, ix, 194–202.

—— 1991: 'Reconstruction of the Lejre Hall', JDA, x, 186–90.

—— 1994: *Building Customs in Viking Age Denmark*, Herning.

Schovsbo, Per Ole, 1987: *Oldtidens Vogne i Norden*, Copenhagen.

Schönwälder, Birgit, 1993: *Die – leben – Namen*, Heidelberg.

Schwartz, Stephen P., 1973: *Poetry and Law in Germanic Myth*, California.

Scott, Barbara C., 1996: 'Archaeology and National Identity: the Norwegian Example', SS, lxviii/3.

Seger, Tapio, 1990: 'Ten Thousand Years of Finnish Prehistory', FIMU.

—— 1991: 'Cemetery – An Archaeological Concept or a Prehistoric Reality?' RER, 205–16.

Selinge, Klas-Göran 1987: 'The Rune Stones . . . at Högby' *Runor och runinskrifter*, ed. Ambrosiani et al., Stockholm.

Sellevold, B.J., U. Lund Hansen, and J. Balslev Jørgensen, 1984: *Iron Age Man in Denmark*, Copenhagen.

Sharpe, Eric J. (ed.), 1973: *Man and His Salvation*, Manchester.

Sharples, N., M. Parker Pearson, 1999: 'Norse Settlement in the Outer Hebrides', NAR, xxxii, 41–62.

Sheehan, John, 1998: 'Early Viking Age Silver Hoards from Ireland', ISCA, 166–202.

Shepard, Jonathan, 1995: 'The Rhos Guests of Louis the Pious', EME, iv, 55–8.

Shepard, Deborah, 1997: 'The Ritual Significance of Slag', FENSC, xiv, 11–22.

—— 1999: *Funerary Ritual and Symbolism* (BAR Int. Ser. dcccviii).

Sigmundsson, Svavar, 1992: 'Atrúnaður og örnefni', SNA, 241–54.

Sigurðsson, Gísli, 1988: *Gaelic Influence in Iceland*, Reykjavik.

—— 2000: 'The Quest for Vinland in Saga Scholarship', VINAS, 232–87.

Sigurðsson, J.V., 1999: *Chieftains and Power in the Icelandic Commonwealth*, Odense.

Sigvallius, Berit, 1994: *Funeral Pyres: Iron Age Cremations in N. Spånga*, Stockholm.

Simek, Rudolf, 1993: *Dictionary of Northern Mythology* (Woodbridge), trans. by Angela Hall from *Wörterbuch der germanischen Mythologie*, Stuttgart 1984.

—— 1997 (with Angela Simek): 'Bog People Revisited', HUG.

Sjohölm, Elsa: 'Runinskrifterna som källa till svensk arvsrätt under aldre medeltid', *Scandia*, lvii, 121–6 and 327–31.

Skarin-Frykman, B., 1965–6: 'Eketorps Borg', *Tor*, ix, 198–229.

Skibsted Klæsøe, I., 1997: 'Plant Ornament: A Key to a New Chronology of the Viking Age', LAR, 73–88.

Slupecki, Leszek, 1991: *Wolin-Jomsborg: en Vikingetids Handelsby*, Roskilde.

—— 199AQ: 'Die slawischen Tempel und die Frage des sakralen Raumes', *Tor*, xxv, 247–98 (with bibliography).

—— 1994: *Slavonic Pagan Sanctuaries*, Warsaw.

Smirnickaja, Olga, 1992: 'Mythological Nomination and Skaldic Synonymics', SNA, 217–25.

Smith, L.M., 1984: *The Making of Britain: The Dark Ages*, Macmillan.

Smyth, Alfred P., 1977: *Scandinavian Kings in the British Isles*, Oxford.

—— 1999: 'The Effect of Scandinavian Raiders on the English and Irish Churches': a preliminary Reassessment' in *Britain and Ireland 700–1300*, ed. Brendan Smith, Cambridge.

Sne, Andres, 1999: 'Soviet Archaeology in Latvia' in *Inside Latvian Archaeology*, ed. Ola W. Jensen, Håkan Karlsson and A. Vijups, Gothenburg.

Solberg, Bergljot, 1985: 'Social Status in the Merovingian and Viking Periods in Norway from Archaeological and Historical Sources', NAR, xviii, 61–76.

—— 1999: 'Holy White Stones', VANO, 99–106.
Solli, Brit, 1995: 'Fra hedendom til kristendom', *Viking*, lviii, 23–48.
—— 1996a: *Narratives of Veøy*, Oslo.
—— 1996b: 'Narratives of Encountering Religion', NAR, xxix/2, 90–114.
—— 1997–8: 'Odin – the queer?', UOÅ, 7–42.
Sørensen, Anne Christina, 1997: 'Ladby: Ship Cemetery and Settlement', BUSO, 165–70.
Sørensen, John Kousgaard, 1978: 'Toponymic Evidence for Administrative Division in Denmark in the Viking Age' *The Vikings*, ed. T. Andersson and K.I. Sandred, Uppsala, 133–41.
—— 1990: 'The Change of Religion and the Names', ONFRAC, 394–403.
Sperber, Erik, 1988: 'How Accurate was Viking Age Weighing in Sweden?', *Fornvännen*, lxxxiii, 157–66.
—— 1996: *Balances, Weights, and Weighing in Ancient and Early Medieval Sweden*, Stockholm.
Sporrong, Ulf, 1971: *Kolonisation, bebyggelseutvekling och administration*, Lund.
—— 1984: 'A Model of Medieval Rural Society' in Kristiansen, 199–224.
Sprenger, Ulrike, 1992: *Die altnordische Heroische Elegi*, Berlin/New York.
Staff, Björn Magnusson: see Magnusson.
Staecker, Jörn, 1997a: 'Legends and Mysteries: Reflections on the Evidence for the Early Mission in Scandinavia', VIPA, 419–54.
—— 1997b: 'Brutal Vikings and Gentle Traders', LAR, 89–104.
—— 1999: 'Thor's Hammer', LAR, 89–104.
Starkey, K., 1999: 'Imagining an Early Odin', SS Lxxi/4.
Steblin-Kamenskii, A., 1982: *Myth*, Ann Arbor.
Steen Jensen: see FESTOL. Steensbergen 1986.
Steensberg, Axel, 1983: *Borup AD700–1400*, Copenhagen. 1986: *Man the Manipulator*, Copenhagen.
Stein, Gil, 1998: 'Heterogeneity, Power and Political Economy', *Journal of Archaeological Research*, vi, 1–144.
Steinsland, Gro, 1986: WOO.
—— 1979: 'Treet i Vǫluspá', ANF xciv, 120–50.
—— 1991a: 'see NOHED: 'Religionskiftet i Norden og Vóluspa 65'.
—— 1991b: *Det hellige bryllup og norrøn kongeideologi*, Oslo.
—— 1992: 'Die mythologische Grundlage für die nordische Königsideologi', GR, 736–51.
Steuer, Heiko, 1987: 'Gewichtsgeldwirtschaften', UNHAVE, 459–91.
—— 1994: 'Archäologie und germanische Sozialgeschichte' (in Düwel 1994, 10–55 with bibliography post 1980).
Stjernquist, Berta, 1981: *Gårdlösa*, Lund 1981.
—— 1995: 'Uppåkra, a central place in Skåne', LAR, 89–120.
Störli, Inger, 1993: 'Sami Viking Age Pastoralism – or the 'Fur Trade Paradigm' Reconsidered', NAR, xxvi.
Stoklund, Marie, 1991: 'Runestene, kronologi, og samfundrekonstruktion', Mammen, 285–97.
—— 1994: 'Myter, runer og tolkning', MOR, 168–70.
—— 1997: 'Runefundene fra yngre jernalder', VS vi, 25–36.

Strand, Birgit, 1980: *Kvinnor och män i Gesta Danorum*, Gothenburg.

Strausberg, Michael (ed.), 2001: *Kontinintäten und Brüche in der Rligions-geschichte*, Berlin/New York.

Strickland, Matthew, 1996: 'Military Technology and Conquest', ANS, xix, 353–83.

Ströbeck, Louise, 1999: 'On Studies of Task Differentiation', CSA, vii, 161–72.

Ström, Folke, 1986: *Nordisk hedendom* (3rd edn), Gothenburg.

——1974: *Nið, ergi and ON Moral Attitudes* (Coke Lecture) London.

Strömback, Dag, 1975: *The Conversion of Iceland* (trans. P.G. Foote), London.

Stumann Hansen, S., 1992: 'Cutural Contacts in the Faroe Islands in the Viking Age', EXTRA, 13–17.

——1993: 'Viking Age Faroe Islands and their southern Links', VACON, 473–86.

——2001 (ed.): *Vikings in the west*, Copenhagen.

Stylegar, Frans-Arne, 1997: '*Mos Teutonicus*: omkring Halvdan Svartes død', Viking, lx, 59–69.

Sundqvist, John, 1998: 'Clause arrangement in the Poetry of Kormakr Qgmundarsson', *Skandinavistik*, xxviii, 1–23.

Sundqvist, Olof, 2005: 'Aspects of rulership ideology', Erkens, Berlin.

Supphellen, Steinar, 1992: *Kongsmenn og Korssmenn*, Oslo.

Svanberg, Fredrik, 1999: I Skuggen av Vikingatiden, Lund.

Sveaas Andersen, P., 1977: *Samlingen av Norge og kristningen av landet*, Oslo.

——1995: 'Nordisk... innvandring på Isle of Man', CM, viii, 5–50.

Sveinbjarnardóttir, Guðrun, 1992: *Farm Abandonment*, Oxford.

Svennung, J. 1963: *Scadinavia und Scandia*, Lund/Uppsala.

Syrett, Martin, 2002: *The Vikings in England: the Evidence of Runic Inscriptions*, Cambridge.

Taavitsainen, Jussi-Pekka, 1998: 'Exploitation of Wilderness Resources and Lapp Settlement in Central and Eastern Finland', OUTU, 134–55.

Tarlow, Sarah, 1997: 'The Dread of Something After Death', in *Material Harm*, ed. John Carman Glasgow, 133–42.

Tesch, Sten, 1992: 'Sigtuna: the Town Plan', 189–96 of *Urbanism*, ed. P. Addyman and Steve Roskamo, York.

Theodorsson, Pall, 1998: 'Norse Settlement of Iceland', NAR, xxxi, 29–37.

Thirsk, Joan (ed.), 2000: *The English Rural Landscape*, Oxford.

Thomson, W.R.L., 1995: 'Orkney Farm – Names: a Reassessment of their Chronology', SSNB, 42–63.

Thrane, Henrik, 1991: 'Gudmeundersøgelserne', HØKO, 67–72.

——1998: 'Materialen zur Topographie einer eisenzeitlichen Sakral-landschaft', SADO, 235–47.

Thurston, Tina L., 1996: 'Reconstructing Local and Regional Landscapes in Viking Age and Early Medieval Denmark', META, i.

——1999: 'The Knowable, The Doable, and the Undiscovered', *Antiquity*, lxxiii, 661–71.

Tolley, C., 1995: '*Vórdr* and *Gandr*: Helping Spirits in Norse Magic', ANF, cx.

—— 1996: 'Snorri and Historia Norvegiae', *Maal og Minne*, 67ff.

Townend, M., 2002: *Language and History in Viking Age England*, Turnhout.

—— 2003; 'Whatever Happened to York Viking Poetry?', SB xxvii 48–90.

Trotzig, Gustav, 1988: 'Beads made of Cowrie Shells' in Hårdh 1988, 287–94.

—— 1991: *Vikingatida Gravkärlarkoppar*, Stockholm.

Turville-Petre, E.O.G., 1964: *Myth and Religion of the North*, London.

—— 1974: 'The Sonatorrek', *Iceland and the Medieval World*, ed. Turville-Petre and Martin, Melbourne.

—— 1976: *Skaldic Poetry*, Oxford.

Turville-Petre, Joan, 1978: 'On Ynglingatal', MS, xi, 48–67.

Tvengsberg, P.M., 1995: 'Rye and Swidden Cultivation', *Tools and Tillage*, vii/4, 131–46.

Twycross, Fiona, 1996: 'Politicizad Use of Norse Myth', NS xxxi, 69–93.

Ucko, P.J., and R. Layton, 1999 *The Archaeology and Athropology of Landscape*, London/New York.

Ulriksen, Jens M., 1990: 'Teorier og virkelighed i forbindelse med lokalisering af anløbspladser', *Aarbøger*.

Urbańczyk, Przemyslaw, 1992: *Medieval Arctic Norway*, Warsaw.

—— (ed.), 1997: *Origins of Central Europe*, Warsaw.

Ureland: see LACON.

Van Houts, Elisabeth, 1999: 'Countess Gunnor of Normandy', CM, 7–25.

Varenius, B., 1992: *Det nordiska skeppet. Teknologi och samhallsstrategi*, Stock.

—— 1995: 'Metaphorical Ships in Iron Age Contexts', SHAS, 34–40.

—— 1999: 'The Retinue and the Ship', CSA, vii, 173–82.

Vea, Marit (ed.), 1994: *Rikssamlingen og Harald Hårfagre*, Kopervik.

—— 2000: *The Christianization of Iceland*, Oxford.

Vésteinsson, Orri, 1998: 'Patterns of Settlement in Iceland', SB, xxv/i, 1–29.

Vestergaard, E., 1990: 'A Note on Viking Age Inauguration of Rulers' in J.M. Bak (ed.), *Medieval Coronations*, Berkeley/Oxford.

Vestergaard, Torben A., 1988: 'The System of Kinship in Early Norwegian Law', MS, xii, 160–93.

—— 1991: 'Marriage Exchange and Social Structure in Old Norse Mythology', SAP, 21–34.

Vibe Müller, I.H., 1991: 'Fra ættefelleskab til sogne felleskab', NOHED, 359–72.

Vierck, Hayo, 1981: 'Imitatio Imperii und Interpretatio Germanica vor der Wikingerzeit' in I.R. Zeitler (ed.), *Les Pays du Nord et Byzance*, Uppsala.

Vikstrand, Per, 1992: 'Ortnamnet Hov', SANA, 123–39.

Vilhjálmsson, Vilhjálmur Örn, 1991: 'The Early Settlement of Iceland', AA, lxii, 167ff.

—— 1993: 'Archaeological Retrospect on Physical Anthropology in Iceland', PONO, 198–214.

von See, Klaus, 1961: 'Studien zum Haraldskvæði', ANF, lxxvi, 96–111.

—— 1981: '*Edda, Saga, Skaldendichtung*', Heidelberg.

—— 1988: *Mythos und Theologie*, Heidelberg.

Wagner, Norbert, 1994/95: 'Scadinavia und Scandia', BzN, xxix/xxx, 137–59.

Wahlgren, Erik, 1986: *The Vikings and America*, London.

Wallace: see Linderoth Wallace.

Wallace, P.F., 1992: 'The Archaeological Identity of the Hiberno-Norse Town', *Journal of the Royal Society of Antiquaries of Ireland*, cxx, 35–66.

Wallerström, Thomas, 1995: *Norbotten, Sverige och medeltiden*, Lund.

—— 1997: 'On Ethnicity as a Methodological Problem', VIPA, 299–352.

Wamers, Egon, 1985: *Insularer Metallschmuck in Wikingerzeitlichen Gräbern Nordeuropas*, Neumünster.

—— 1994: 'König im Grenzland', AA, lxv, 1–59.

—— 1997: 'Hammer und Kreuz', RBN, 84–108.

—— 1998: 'Insular Finds in Viking Age Scandinavia', ISCEVA, 37–72.

—— 1991: 'Sorte Muld', HØKO, 89–107.

Watt, Margaret, 1988: 'Bornholm mellem Vikingetid og Middelalder', *Festskrift til Olaf Olsen*, Copenhagen, 105–22.

Watts, Victor, 1988–9: 'Scandinavian Settlement Names in Co. Durham', *Nomina*, xii, 17–64.

Wawn, Andrew, 1993: 'The Spirit of 1892', SB, xxiii, 213–52.

—— (ed.), 1994: *Northern Antiquity: The Post Medieval Reception of Edda and Saga*, Enfield.

—— 2000: *The Vikings and the Victorians*, Woodbridge.

Weber, G.W., 1986: 'Siðaskipti. Das religionsgeschichtliche Modell Snorri Sturlusonas', *Sagnaskemmtun*, 309–29.

—— 1998: 'Intellegere historiam'. Typological perspectives of Nordic pre-history', TROG, 95–141.

Weldinder, Stig, 1993: 'Pots, Females and Food', CJA.

—— 1998: 'The Cultural Construction of Childhood', CSA, vi, 185–205.

Wessén, Elias, 'Schwedische Ortsnamen und altnordische Mythologie', APS 1929–30, 97–115.

Westerdahl, Christer, 1995: 'Society and Sail', SHAS, 41–50.

Whaley, Diana, 1991: 'Nicknames and Narratives', AUSA, 341ff and ANF, cviii (1993).

Whitehouse, Ruth D., 1998: 'Feminism and Archaeology: an awkward relationship', PIA ix, 1–7.

Wicker, N.L., 1998: 'Selective female infanticide as partial explanation for the death of women in Viking Age Scandinavia', VISOC, 205–21.

—— 1999: 'Infanticide in Late Iron-Age Scandinavia', BOCO, 106–19.

Widgren, Mats, 1983: *Settlement and Farming Systems of Early Iron Age*, Stockholm.

—— 1989: 'Geographical Approaches to Field Systems', ASP, 353–66.

Wigh, Bengt, 1998: 'Animal Bones from the Viking Town of Birka', LEAF, 81–90.

Wiik, Kalevi, 1997: 'How Far to the South in Eastern Europe did the Fenno-Ugrians live?', FENSC, xiv, 23–30.

Williams, Ann, 1986: 'Cockles among the Wheat', *Midland History*, xi.

Williams, D.G.E., 1997: 'The Dating of the Norwegian *leiðangr* System: a philological approach', NOWELE xxx, 21ff.

Williams, Henrik, 1998: 'Runic Inscriptions as Sources of Personal Names', RUQUIF, 601–11.

Wilson, David, 1996: 'Fifty Years of Viking Age Archaeology: a Personal View', VS, xv, 7–26.

Wollmann, A., 1996: 'Scandinavian Loanwords in Old English', NOWELE supp. xvii, Odense.

Wood, Ian, 1987: 'Christians and Pagans in 9th century Scandinavia' in *The Christianization of Scandinvia* (ed. P. Sawyer et al., Alingsås), 36–67.

—— 1995: 'Pagan Religions and Superstitions East of the Rhine' in *After Empire*, ed. G. Ausenda, 253–79.

Woolf, Alex, 1998: 'Erik Bloodaxe Revisited', NH, xxxiv, 189–93.

Wormald, Patrick, 1989: 'Viking Studies: Whence and Whither?' in TV, 128–53.

Zachrisson, Inger, 1992: 'Can grave customs be taken over by one ethnic group from another?', Hoppal and Pentikainen, 108–14.

—— 1991: 'The South Sami Culture', SAP, 191–9.

—— 1993: 'A Review of Archaeological Research on Saami Prehistory in Sweden', CSA, i, 171–82.

—— 1994A: 'Saamis and Scandinavians – Examples of Interaction', VC 12, 173–9.

Zachrisson, Torun, 1994: 'The odal and its manifestation on the landscape', CSA, ii, 219–38.

—— 1998: *Gård, gräns, gravfält*, Stockholm.

Zeiten, M.K., 1998: 'Amulets and Amulet Use in Viking Age Denmark', AA, lxviii, 1–74.

Zimmerman, W.H., 1999: 'Why was Cattle-Stalling introduced?', SAL, 301–14.

Zvelebil, M., 1997: 'Hunter-gatherer ritual landscapes', *Analecta Praehistorica Leidensia*, xxix, 33–50.

Index

D: Danish K: King N: Norwegian Q: Queen S: Swedish

Aachen, 30
Aarhus: as focus, 77; population, 92
Abbo of St Germain, 21, 184
Adam of Bremen, 22, 33, 36, 42, 52,
    92, 94, 100, 112, 131, 157,
    165, 195, 266; as namer, 112,
    116, 131; on Uppsala, 312
administered trade, 72–4, 107; in
    Iceland, 209 n; in Norway, 122
administrative divisions: D., 91,
    92–3, 102, 111; N., 107–8; S.,
    94, 95 n, 106
Ægir, 296
Ælfric, abbot, 261, 288
Æsir, 41, 242, 294, 296, 299
Agdanes, 32 n
Agder (N.), 266; Canute off, 142
age-sets, 57
Aggersborg, 85
agriculture, 65–7; Faroes, 217;
    general, 191–205; Orcadian,
    220; Shetland, 219
Åhus, 70, 206 n
Åland isles, 77, 106, 310
Alcuin, 112, 181, 313
Ales stenar, 247
Álfhildr (Elfildis), 19, 44
Álfífa, 19, 43
Alfred, K. Wessex, 4, 10, 108, 127,
    157, 171, 173, 186; donor, 289;

fighter, 186; saved by extras,
    182 n
Alfred and Guthrum, law-text,
    256–7
Alpertus of Metz, 171
America, 1, 203, 227–8
ancestors, 12–13; dynastic, 244–50;
    epic, 241; vigilant, 50, 69
Ánlafr (Amlaíbh) see Ólaf(r)
Ansgar (Anscarius), St, Life of, 134,
    138–9, 157 n, 166, 289, 294
anthropology (contribution of), 57,
    68, 139, 304–5
anti-fascism, 320
Anund-Jacob, S.K., 132
archaeology: ethnic, 121, 169, 127;
    Hebrides, 221; heritage, 324;
    new trends, 318–22;
    Norwegian, 127; poetic, 319;
    Shetland, 218–19; survey of,
    302–3
Ári the Wise, 124–5; on conversion,
    165; settlement, 225
Arnorr, The Earl's Poet, 101, 263,
    300, 332; Hrynhenda, 159,
    172, 282
art history, 316–17
Ásbjorn Sigurðarsson, 146
Asgard, 41
Ashdown, 141, 186

Assandun, 295
Asselt, 181
assemblies (thingar), 111, 165–7;
Ringsted, 102; of scholars,
323–4; Swedish, 131; Viborg, 93
assimilation of colonists, 61, 120–1,
229–31
Athelstan, K. Wessex, 54, 152, 184
atrocities, 138, 145, 180–2
Aun, S.K., 41
Austman 98–9, 162–3
axes, 182, 204, 206

Balder, 272, 299, 311; his dream
295, 279; his pyre, 263
Balts, 84 n, 127 n, 290
baptism, 29; Bornholm, 104;
Frankish, 156; Iceland, 166;
naming, 116; Normans, 232,
268; postmortem, 290; rejected,
118
barbarity, 112, 116, 180 n, 181, 249
barley, 107, 129, 143, 192, 197;
Iceland, 201, 205
barter, 20, 70–2, 195
battle: ethos, 176–88; gods in, 266;
kings in, 142
bears, 31, 68, 92; ancestral, 246
Beddington, 232
beer, 50, 143, 146, 199, 205;
postmortem, 294; as bait, 201
Benfleet, 178
Beowulf, 102, 115, 120, 240–1,
306 n
berserkir, 31, 55, 57
Bersi, 57
Bersǫglisvísur, 133 n
Biarmians, 130–1
Birka: bones, 40; designs, 131; as
gateway, 64, 72, 97; work, 206
bishops, bishoprics, 37; Dalby, 104;
Funen, 101; Greenland, 202–3;
Iceland, 285; Jutland, 92; Lund,
154; Orkney, 219; rivals in
Scania, 91; Swedish, 98 n;
Winchester, 232
Bjarni Hallbjarnarson, 163, 331

Bjorn Cripple-Hand, 87
Bjorn Hitdælakappa, 28
Bleking, chiefs, 44, 99–100;
converted, 121
blood-eagle, 138
blood groups, 225
boat burials: map 12 and see burials
boat-houses: D., 158; N., 67, 107
Borg (Lofoten), 143
Borg (Ögld), 81
Bornholm, 103–4, 121
Borre, 109, 122, 153
boundaries, 67–9, 96, 101, 110,
193; field 68
Bragi Boddason, 101, 294, 328
bread, 205, 280
Brink (Stefan), 54, 75–6, 94–5, 168,
322
Brunanburh, 184
Buchholz (Peter), 320 n, 268
burials: Balladoole, 284; boat, 17,
109, 158, 291; bog, 288, 248;
Borre, 109, 122; Bull Wharf,
290; Danish, 40; Finnish, 9,
130; Fjälkinge, 40 n; Fyrkat, 19;
heathen, 266; interpretation of,
121; Kalmargården, 286;
Ladby, 286; Lund, 37, 283;
Mammen, 266; military,
weapon burials, 101, 175;
Orkney, 219; Oseberg, 109,
158; Repton, 81, 169, 249,
291; Stavrby, 174; Thumby
Bienebeck, 266; Visby, 40
burn-beating (swidden), 192–3
Byrhtnoth, ealdorman, 56, 183, 184
Byzantium, Rus and, 15, 210–13,
234; gold of, 160, 270; model
of, 270; Odin and, 262, 270

cairns, 248; clearance, 200 n
candles, 266
Canute (Knutr, Cnut), 36, 43, 142;
as basilisk, 112 n; coins of,
148–9; Danes and, 104;
emperor and, 157; England
and, 62, 170, 243, 267;

Norway and, 56, 142; praise of, 64, 112 n; prayer of, 251;

Canute (Knutr, Cnut) (*cont.*) St Edith and, 286; Swedes and, 131, 185–6, 336

capital punishment, 33, 37; of vikings, 2, 73, 76

Carlyle, Thomas, 3 n, 252

Caspian Sea, 216

cattle, 193, 200, 217, 219, 227; proverbial, 253; stalled, 160, 205; wild, 68

cemeteries, kinships in, 47; rites at, 291, 296; *otherwise see under the place-name: Lngleby 268*

Charlemagne, K. and emperor: court of, 160; cultural icon, 324; eyes of, 140; as killer, 180; name of, 46

Charles the Fat, emperor, 181

Chazars, 219, 234

chiefs, chiefdoms, 160–3; N., 107, 150–9; D., 101, 102; Iceland, 134 n, 224–6; *and see* maps 2 and 7

children, 38–40

Chnub, D.K., 45 n, 59, 328–9

christianity, farming and, 19, 195–6; heathens and, 266–8; kings and, 139–41, 259; theology of, 273–6

chronology, 5–8, 315; Ari's, 165; date-list, 327–32

churches, manorial, 63, 253, 298; Birka, 131; Falster, 103; Jelling, 286; Lund, 208; Repton, 249; Scanian, 154–5; Sigtuna, 154; Trondheim, 155

class conflict, concept of, 164–5

clans, 46

clientage, 54–5, 62–3, 174; emigrants', 227; Finns and, 130 n; Lapps and, 108

climate, 314

Clunies-Ross, Margaret, 21, 41, 252 n

Cnut *see* Canute

coins, round Baltic, 105; design, 272; kings and, 146–9; use, 315

collaborators, Anglo-Saxon, 232 n; Valkyries as, 242 n

collectivity, 10–11, 37; feeling of, 114; Icelandic, 123

colonization: of Åland, 106; general, 214–35; of Iceland, 45; of interiors, 61

comitatus concept, 53 n

communitarianism, 10, 27; *and see* collectivity

computers, 316–18

Constantinople, 77, 212

conversion, 260–1, 264, 268; Icelanders, 165–6; Jämts, 162, 298; kings, 147, 155–7; Norwegians, 267; of poets, 30; Swedes, 132, 156, 267

core–periphery interaction, 8 n, 89, 98

corpses: cooked, 291–2; dismembered, 37, 295; excarnated, 291; *and see* undead

cosmology, 237, 251–3

creation myth, 42

cremation, 17, 19, 25, 91; Adelsö, 294; Åland, 106; decline of, 266; Ottestrup, 296; and for rites, 291–3

cults, 260–6, 78–82; Bornholm, 104; S., 94–5; *and see* map 10

custom, 16, 253–6

Dalarna, 99

Danegeld, 77, 188

Danelaw: cultural influence of, 267 Edgar and, 254–5; landowners in, 49, 120–1; raiders, 82; settlements in, 228–33; social mobility in, 61; towns, 73

Danes, 58, 115; origins, 118; varieties, 118–21; and weather, 196

Danevirke, 92

defamation (slander), 29, 32, 224, 265, 284–5; of gods, 255, 265

defences: of Jutland, 92; village, 67–9; *and see* forts, fortification

dendrochronology, 315; of Hedeby, 71; of Trelleborg, 84
Denmark: defined, 119–20; the name 117; *and see* map 6
derision, 30, 79, 255
development theory, 4–8, 70–2, 88–9, 122; bureaucratic, 74; ethnic, 114
Dicuil, 217
dísir, 69, 265
districts, 87–111
DNA, 214, 225, 316
dogs (hounds), 81, 174, 269, 295
Domaldi, S.K., 137
dragons, 50, 68, 172, 239, 303 n; transformative, 68 n
drama, 79
drengir, 56n,57, 60
drowning: in Ireland, 137 n; life after, 297
Dublin, kings of, 52, 60, 179, 222, 314, 326; graves, 116–17, 222
Dudo of St Quentin, 49, 120, 176, 261
Dumville, David, 6, 180 n, 313
dung, 193, 200; heap, 37; 'reindeer', 199
Durkheim, Emile, 11 n, 252
dynasties, 15, 58–60, 325–6; Lejre, 102; magnate, 162–3

Edda, Eddic poems, 51, 72, 241n, 291, 297, 304, 305, 309–10
Edgar, English K., 254
Edith Land, 286
Edmund, K. and Saint, 138; coins, 148, 286
Egill Skalagrimsson, 27 n, 28, 38, 142, 263, 284, 309
Eider, river, 92, 119
Eilífr Goðrunarson, 191 n, 261, 309
Einarr, Orkney earl, 29
Einarr, 139, 150n
Einhard, 30
Eiríkr (Eric the Red), 227–8
Elphege, St (Ælfheah), archbishop, 145, 181, 182n, 251

elves, 50, 69, 242
emancipations, 24–5, 78, 190
emigration: to Francia, 120; from Norway, 108; to Russia, 131; in general, 214–35
Emma, English Q., 44, 55, 288
Englishness, 120–1
epic, lost, 28; *and see* 240–1
Eric (Eiríkr) Bloodaxe, K., 28; defamed, 284; his sons, 139
Eric, earl of Northumbria (Eiríkr Hakonsson), 73, 243
Erling, 24, 146, 162
eschatology, 299–300
Estrith (Ástriðr or Margaret), 36–7
Ethelred I, K. Wessex, 186
Ethelred II, English K., 173, 179, 180–1, 186–7, 274, 288
Ethelweard, chronicler, 116, 175 n, 263 n
ethics, 16, 253–6
ethnicity: archaeology and, 121; round Baltic, 112–22; of vikings, 3
eyes, 140
Eysteinn, N.K., 99
Eyvinðr the Plagiary, 28, 123, 149, 195, 250, 294, 309, 329

Falster, 103
families, 38–52; giants', 255; gods' *see* Æsir; Vanir; royal 58–9
famine, 140 n, 192, 195
farms, 67–9, 76–7; sizes of, 196–8; mounds, 200, in PNN 80
Faroes, 217–18, 199
farts, 202 n
feasts: inheritance, 50; parish, 78; royal, 143–46; Swedish, 94
fertility, 80–1, 192, 195–6, 280; kings and, 160; Mälardal, 198
feud, 51–2
Findan, St, 26, 219
Finland, 129–30; cremation 290
Finnar, *see* Lapps
Finns: their boats, 170; boys, 32; identity, 130; Lapps and, 127, 293

Finnveden, 99
fishing, 193, 198 n; Caithness, 220;
    on Limfjord, 70; Thor's, 262
fleas, 314
fleets, 135, 158–9, 170–4
folklore, 41, 82, 246, 261, 312
forest: clearance, 192, 200, 203–5;
    Gautish, 96; Scanian, 91;
    Swedish, 99
forts, fortification, 177–8; D.,
    82–6, 103; Dublin, 222–3; Frankish,
    269; Gotland, 104; Öland, 105
Franks: imitated, 268–70; in
    Normandy, 233; ships of, 170;
    scorned, 303 n; treaty with,
    119; war with, 175–6, 178
freeholders, 48–51, 163–5
'free souls', 293
Freyja, 40, 81, 241, 245, 264–5
Freyr (Njorðr), 44, 79, 81; and
    kings, 135
Fribrødre dock, 207
Frigg, 29, 41, 264–5; Woden and,
    243
Frisians, 92–3, 199, 210; identity,
    114 n; vikings, 2n, 3, 8
Funen (Fyn), 100–1
furs, 97–8, 198, 204
Fyrkat, 19, 84–5

Gaelic, 221
games, 79, 144–5, 299
Gamli Gnævaðarskald, 262
Gásir, 224
Gautar, Gauts, 96, 110, 118,
    131 n
Gefion, 101, 197
gender, 17–24, 304, 321
genealogy, 75, 138, 244–7
Germanicism, Germanists, 11, 22,
    35, 44 n, 46–7, 51–2, 126 n,
    236–7, 251–2, 254; in ethics,
    251–2; law, 257; vocabulary,
    114
giants, giantesses, 42, 138, 191, 246,
    249; anthropocosmic, 304;
    inscribed, 265; interpreted, 255

gilds, 86, 155, 210
Glælognskviða, 275
Glum Geirason, 145, 263, 309, 329
goats, 82, 195, 201
goðar, 52–3, 80, 100, 105, 124
Godofred (Guthfrið) D.K., 30, 174;
    and traders, 73
goddesses, 41–2, 265
gods, 259–68; collegiate, 96;
    patriarchal, 41–2; personal,
    252–3
Gokstad ship, 170
gold: coin, 149; on ships, 172; for
    silk, 212; sought, 16, 55, 189,
    190, 282; spent, 142, 160, 268,
    270; tokens, discs, 104, 263;
    wages, 216, 270
good, as concept, 16, 24, 61 n
good works, 298
Gorm, D.K., 93, 118; bones of, 36,
    286
Götaland, 96–7
Gotland, 104–5; agriculture, 193;
    brooches, 206, PNN 81;
    harbours, 70; picture-stones,
    24, 105, 242
graves *see* burials
Graham-Campbell, James, 6–7, 206 n
Greenland, 1 n; development,
    202–3; migration to, 227–8
Greenlanders, 126
Gregory VII, pope, 196, 312
Grettir, saga of, 33
Gnímnísmal, 139
Gudme (D.), 95, PNN 266
Guta Laga, 78
Guta Saga, 243
Guthormr Sindri, 23
Guthrum, D.K., 157, 180, 188
Gutring, N.K., 156

Hákon Eiriksson, earl of Hlaðir, 142
Hákon Haraldsson the Good, N.K.,
    108, 139; postmortem, 294
Hákon Jarl, of Hlaðir, 56, 123, 142,
    139, 157, 195, 246 n, 275; his
    death, 35, 56; poets, 108, 250

Halfdan, D.K., 160
Halfdan of York, 230
Halland, 87, 88, 97, 110; agriculture,
    194 n; allegiance, 119; marts, 70
Hallfreðr Óttarsson, 28, 29, 56,
    183, 244, 264, 330
Halli the Stiff, 167
halls, 48, 53–4, 75–6, 81–2, 85,
    145; building of, 208–9; chiefs',
    160–1; cults, 253; Lejre 101–2;
    Tissø, 101
Hallvarðr Háreksblesi, 244, 274,
    298
Hálogaland, 88, 108, 130;
    agriculture, 200; pedigree, 250
Hälsingland, 97–8, 99, 245
Hamburg–Bremen, see of, 112, 126,
    195; Adalbert 288; Lievizo 292
hamlets, 66–7
Harald Bluetooth, D.K.: conversion,
    157, 272; defamed, 285; defied,
    123; followers of, 56, 62, 109;
    mounds of, 247; sway of, 102,
    103, 118–19, 123; unifier? 150
Harald Greycloak Gunnhildarson,
    N.K., 130, 144, 149, 152 n, 156
Harald(r) Hardrada, N.K., origins of,
    10, 58; career, 21, 24; raids of,
    25, 101, 110, 123, 160, 172, 184
Harald Harefoot, Canute's son, K.,
    44; dishonoured, 288
Harald(r) Harfagr, N.K., 23, 122 n,
    31, 54–5, 59, 141; myth of,
    152–3, 224; poem about, 31,
    54–5, 122n, 141
Harald (Klak) D.K., 157, 269
Harald Sveinsson, D.K., 148
Harald War-Tooth, D.K., 139
Hardicanute (Hördaknútr), D.K.,
    59, 173, 180; finale, 288
Harris, Joseph, 53, 160
Hauck, Karl, 135, 263 n, 317
Hávamal, 253–4, 305
heaven (paradise), 297–9
Hebrides, 220–1; agriculture 199;
    Inner 228; and Iceland, 226
Hedeager, Lotte, 120 n, 153, 262

Hedeby (Haithabu), 25, 64, 71–2,
    85, 207, 270, 276
Hel, 290, 295–6
Helgån, Holy River, 91; battle of,
    185 n
Helgö, 206
helmet, 140; as prize, 29
Heremod (Hermoðr), D.K., 241, 292
hermeneutic circle, 318–19
Herschend (Frands), 24, 227 n, 319
Hincmar, archbishop of Reims, 145,
    181
Hjalti Skeggjason, 265
Hlaðir (Lade): earls of, 108, 91–2,
    126; feasts of, 141, 145 n;
    hegemony of, 59–60, 122;
    Lapps and, 129; Thronds and,
    154
hoards, 51, 312; Gotland, 63, 105n;
    Hiddensee, 62; Høn, 62; St
    Kilda, 228
homosexuality *see* sodomy
Hörðaland, 87, 108, 117
Hørik I, D.K., 162
Hørik II, 156
horses, 79; Iceland, 79, 201, 226;
    Odin's, 265; sacrificed, 291; war,
    174–6
households, 48, 52–4, 57
hreppar, 65
Hroaldr, earl, 179
Hrolf Ganger 23; *hugr*, 293, 311
Husabyar, Husbyar, 94–5, 145–6
Hygelac (Hugleik), 115
Hyndluljóð, 57 n, 245, 265n

Ibn Fadlan, 25, 35, 216, 291, 296
Ibn Rusteh, 216
Iceland: farming 201–2; landowners
    in, 49, 65; laws, 47, 51, 166,
    258; statelessness, 134, 69;
    walls, 68
Icelanders amusements, 79; derided,
    124–5, 226; ethnicity? 123–4;
    myth–makers, 120; names of:
    45; poetic, 28; politics, 162,
    165; settlers, 223–7

imitations, 268–72; of Danes, 89; of
  Franks, 97, 241; mounds, 248
individuality, concept of, 10–12
industry, 6, 71–4, 205–8
infanticide, 20, 39–40
infield–outfield, 193, 200 n
Ingjald, S.K., 168
Ingleby, 267–8
inheritance: feasts, 50, 144; female,
  20; of land, 48–51
Ireland: cultural model, 26–7, 245,
  270–1; forts, 177; regicide in,
  137 n; settlers in, 69, 117, 222–3
Iron: dating, 315; tools, 197, 203;
  winning and working, 203–4,
  228
Isidore of Seville, 115
Islamic silver, coin, 105, 147–8, 270,
  272
islands, 100–6
Ivarr the Boneless, 15, 138
Ivarr Guthfrithsson, 326; dynasty of,
  222, 326

Jämtar, 98–9, 204; Jämtland, 129,
  162, 298
Jelling, 93, 102, 144, 153 n; style,
  317; stone 150, 285n
Jesch, Judith, 23, 171 n, 308 n
Jochens, Jenny, 10, 21, 22, 27 n,
  53 n, 125 n, 309
Jom, Jomsborg, Jomsvikings, 83–4
Jordanes, 88, 115, 118
Jórunn, 23
Jutland, 92–3; defences, 68;
  farming, 196–98; iron, 204,
  206; markets in, 70;

Kálf(r) Árnason, 162, 163
Karelians, 131 n
Kaupang, 122, 209
keys, 19, 205
Kin–groups, 46–8, 316
Kings, 15, 59, 135; christocentric,
  274–5; coins, 146–9; epithets,
  142 n; islands, 100–3; markets,
  73–4; nobles and, 141–3; sacral,
  104, 114, 139–41; sea, 158–60

Knútr *see* Canute
Kormák(r) Qgmundarson, 24 n, 28,
  144, 263, 318 n,
Kvenir (Kainu, Cwenas), 127, 130

Landnámabók, 124, 214, 223–4,
  226, 281
landscapes, 247–9; archaeology of,
  75, 247 n; study of, 314, 322
Langeland, 101
Languages, 4, 310–11; migrant,
  214; N. Britain, 221; England,
  229–31; Fennic, 128; common
  Nordic, 126
L'Anse aux Meadows, 126,
  227–8
Lapps (Finnar, Saami), 22, 97–8,
  108, 114–15, 126–30;
  economy, 193, 190, 195,
  203–4; Icelandic? 225;
  postmortem, 295; tribute, 201
law, 33–4, 51–2, 256–9;
  Anglo-Saxon, 254; and
  kin–group, 46
legend, 236–41
leiðangr, ledung, 108 n, 173–4
Lejre, 81, 102, 144; hall, 208, 248 n;
  sacrifices, 195
leprosy, 283
Lewis the German, K., 175
Lincolnshire, 6, 231
Lindholm Høje, 196, 291
Lindow, John, 51 n, 53 n, 79, 253,
  310, 311, 291 n
Lindqvist, Thomas, 77, 133–4
linen (at Næs), 207 n
literacy, 276–8, Danish moneyers',
  149
Lithsmannaflokkr, 178, 214, 243
Lithuanians, 115 n
loan-words, 125 n, 231 n, 272
Lochlann (Laithlind), 117, 223
Lofoten Isles, 100, 108, 143
Loki, 41, 242, 248, 299; Lokasenna,
  255
Lolland, 103
Lombards, Langobards, 47, 243
London(ers), 178, 214, 290

lords, lordship: Anglo-Saxon, 76; of communities, 74–8; Icelandic, 226–7; sought, 202
Lund, 37, 91; burials, 283; church, 208; coins, 148–9, 154

McTurk, Rory, 136, 239
Maeshowe, 239 n
magic, 22, 284, 288–90; Lapp, 129; runic, 307–8
magnates, 101–2, 154
Magnus Barefoot, N.K., 87, 97
Magnus the Good, N. and D.K., 29, 49, 91; Danes, 93, 162; elegy, 174; his name, 46, 60
Mälardal, 94–6; chiefs in, 62, 131; economy of, 209; settlements in, 65, 67, 76, 198–9
Maldon, battle of, 30, 183
Mammen, 160, 266
Man, Isle of, 200, 282; burials, 286, 292; runes, 307
mannsöngr, 32
mark weight, 333
markets, 69–74, 209–13
marriage, 43–4; illicit, 254; sacral 42, 135
Medelpad, 99
metal detectors, 315
metaphorical thinking, 322
metres, 241, 271, 278
migration: archaeology of, 215 n; of cults, 262; to east, 215–17; to west, 217–35
miracles, 275
missions, 11–12, 234
Møn, 103
Möre (N), 108, 325
Möre (S), 100
Moriuht, 26–7, 32
Morkinskinna, 36, 99 n, 165, 174
mother goddess, absence of, 41–2
moustaches, 261n
Myhre, Bjorn, 107, 223 n
myth: gods, 262–3, 280; Icelandic 124–5; national, 120–1, 123–4

mythologies, 311

names: Danelaw, 229–30; Danish, 47 n, 42, 64; dynastic, 58–9; ethnic, 116–32; Hebridean, 220–1; personal, 13–15, 44–6, 129; place-names, 310; sacral, 79–82, 264, 266; Slavonic, 103; Swedish, 95
nations, 113–14; of Jordanes, 88
necromancy *see* magic
nið, 32, 284
Njorð, 172, 250, 284
Normans, Normandy, 45, 49, 118, 232–3; gullible, 27
Northmen, 4, 116, 122, 127
Norwegians: defined, 121–3; kings, 59; thegns, 335
Norway, 107–11; emigrants from, 217–27; halls of, 54; incoherent, 152–3; trade of, 122
Nursak, 276
nutrition, 204–5; of dead, 295; Icelanders', 124–5; study of, 314

oaths, 257–9
Oddaverjar, 124
oðal, 48–51, 68 n
Odense, 80, 85, 100; see of, 101
Odin (Oðinn): as ancestor, 245–6, 264–5; at Byzantium, 270; cult of, 242–3, 262–5; invoked, 284; patriarch, 41; queer, 32 n; and poets, 29; and the slain, 182; as trickster, 35, 191; tactician, 185; Wizard 22
Ohthere (Ǫttarr), 108, 112, 119, 122, 129, 195
Ólaf(r) Sigtryggsson (Amlaíbh Cuaran), Dublin K., 73, 147, 271
Ólaf(r) Eiriksson (Olof), S.K., 141; coins, 148; baptism, 156, 157
Ólaf(r) Haraldsson (St Olave), 30, 55–6; cult of, 141, 155, 195, 274–6; death of, 108; Gauts and, 96; Icelanders and, 123; Northerners and, 146; Opland

and, 109, 162; Swedes and, 98; and another, 138, 297

Ólaf(r) Tryggvason, N.K., 29, 56; elegy to, 244; Icelanders and, 125; Northerners and, 109; raids of, 172, 179; coins, 147

Öland, 105–6; markets on, 70

old age, 40–1

Olave, St *see* Ólafr Haraldsson

Ongendus, D.K., 118; (Angantýr), 58

Opland (N), 69, 109; kings of, 150, 156

Orkney: earls of, 52, 60, 145; settlers in, 219–20; thegns, 164, PNN 199

ornament, 7–8, 61; dating, 317; imitation of, 269, 271–2; point of, 133 n, 246–7, 283; sexing, 40; Torslunda, 31

Oseberg burial, 109, 158

Ostmen, 117

Óttarr the Black, 28, 64, 158, 207, 330

Óttarr Jarl, 179

Óttarr the Foolish, 245

Otto I and II: Bluetooth and, 157; court of, 269–70; eyes of, 140; Ottonians, 82, 164, 175; pressure, 85, 164

outlawry, outlaws, 11, 32–3, 257, 265

oxen, 198–9

palæogenetics, 225

palæopathology, 36

paradise *see* heaven

Paris, siege of, 21, 187

pasture, 191–200; Iceland, 201

patriarchy, 17, 41, 304; among S. archaeologists, 321 n

Paviken, 207

pedigrees, 25; male, 42, 244–5; not long, 249

periods of history, 4–8, 236, 317n

philology, 228–9, 305–11

Picts, 200, 218–20, 229

picture-stones (Gotland), 24, 105, 170, 242, 262, 294, 299

pigs, 5–6, 35, 228, 247

pilgrimage, 30, 155, 280, K. Sigurd's, 100 n

place-names *see* names

ploughs, 5, 196–7, 229; rites of, 280

poetesses, 21–3

poetry: Irish influence?, 271; kenning, 189–90; Odin's gift, 264, 273; skaldic, 243–4; what preserved, 30, 240–1

poets *see* skalds

politics: of Northmen, 133–67; of modern research, 323–4

polygyny, 42, 59 n

Poppo, 273

post-processualism, 319–20

priests, heathen, 76, 95, 102, 103

processualism, 318–19

proverbial philosophy, 253–4

quarrels, 28–9, 51–2; Thor's, 255, 258

queens, 17–19, 43

Ragnar Lothbrok, 138, 238–9

Ragnarǫk, 299–300

Randsborg, Klavs, 3, 62, 163, 197, 302

Ranrike, 110

ravens, 54, 142, 295

Reading, 177

Regino of Prüm, 119

reincarnation, 138, 297

reindeer, 69, 128, 194

religions: cults, 78–82; history of, 311–12; naming by, 116; tensions between, 259–61, 266–7

Repton burials, 81, 169, 249, 291

resource areas, 65

retinues, 11–12, 16, 52–8, 96, 106, 145, 162, 168–9

Ribe: mint 147; see, 49, 50; town, 69–73; trade, 209

Rigsthula, 191, 249–50, 312
Ringanes, 162 n
Ringsted, 102
roads, 92, 110, 276
Rogaland, 108, kings of, 152
Rollo (Hrolfr), 176, 233, 241; death
of, 268
Romsdal, 108
Roskilde, 102–3
Rügen, 107
runes, 276–7; origins of 259 n;
purpose, 281–2; runology
306–08; carving, 13, 189–90
rune-stones, inscriptions cited:
Aarhus 60, 141; Ågersta, 281;
Ålum, 38; Ardre, 20, 39; Aspö,
55; Bække, 47; Bällsta, 38;
Björketorp, 14, 283; Bodilsker,
104; Bro, 298; Broby, 279;
Fläckebo, 20; Flemløse, 100,
160; Flistad, 286; Frösön, 98,
298; Galteland, 267; Gårdby,
106; Gårdlösa, 14; Glavendrup,
14, 52, 307; Gørlev, 13, 102;
Grensten, 24, 45; Gripsholm,
282; Gummarp, 14; Gusnava,
75; Hällestad, 91, 282; Helnæs,
100; Hedeby, 35; Hønen, 278;
Horne, 47; Hørning, 24, 190;
Hunnestad, 45; Istaby, 14;
Jelling, 108, 155, 270; Karlevi
105; Kirkmichael, 3, 39;
Klemensker, 104; Kolind, 206;
Malsta, 74, 245; Malt, 307;
Man, 14, 39; Nora, 283;
Oklunda, 258; Oster Løgum,
13; Råda, 141; Rimsø, 38;
Rogsta, 97; Rök 13, 30, 51, 97,
102, 236, 241, 271, 282, 307;
Runby, 279; Sälna, 279;
Sandsjö, 245; Skårby, 75;
Skærn, 13; Snoldelev, 102;
Sövestad, 144; Solberga, 53;
Sparlösa, 51, 96, 236, 294;
Starup, 13; Stentoften, 14, 195;
Sunnå, 97; Täby, 42 n, 74;
Tangerup, 53; Tillitse 13;

Tryggevælde, 4, 61, 102; Tune,
50, 144 n; Vålsta, 248;Västra
Strö, 169; Yttergärde, 63, 179
Rus, 35, 82–3; Byzantium and,
210–13; etymology, 115;
money, 146; movements of,
215–16, 291
Russia (Garðar), 105, 106, 206;
archaeology of, 321–2
rye, 85, 197, 205
Rygir *see* Rogaland

sacrifice, 195–6; cat, 291; dog, 91;
horse, 291; human, 34, 41,
81–2, 268; of kings, 136–8,
289, 291
sæter, setr (shieling), 66–7,
199–200
sagas, 238–40; Hervara 239,
240 n; *and see* Jom;
Ragnar Lothbrok
sails, 170, 207
St Kilda, 228, 268
Samsø, 103, 327
Saucourt, 184
Sawyer, Birgit, 39, 43, 119 n, 155,
157, 306 n
Sawyer, Peter, 2 n, 5 n, 6, 52, 83, 89,
229 n, 301, 313
Saxo Grammaticus, 83, 139; on the
dead, 296; on gods, 270; on
heroes, 239, 241; on landscape,
247; on raids, 171, 186
Scaldic verse, 271, 308–9; *and see*
Skalds
scales, 19, 210
Scania (Skåne), 89–92; false
consciousness of, 160 n;
indiscipline of, 91–2; markets,
70–1; towns, 154
Schleswig (slesvig), 153
Scotland, 220–1, 313
seal (Byzantine), 270
seals, 201, 202, 217
Sebbersund, 70, 303n
secret societies, 57
seiðr, 22, 284, 289–90

sentimentality, 40, 55
settlement patterns, 65–7; Jutland,
    92–3; Sweden, 94–100;
    Zealand, 101
sex, 26, 31–2; of bones, 40;
    inscrutable, 280; of ruler, 59
shamanism, 22 n, 262, 288, 293
    and n, 312; Odin's, 263 n
sheep: English, 232; Jutland, 205,
    217, 333; value of, 333
Shetland, 218–19
ships: burials, 286, 269, 295;
    Canute's, 142–3; ideology of,
    303 n; kings and, 158–60; as
    rewards, 162 n, 172; stone
    settings, 248; war, 170–4
Sigifrit (Sigfriðr), D.K., 118
Sigiferth, K., 35
Sigtuna, 132, archaeology of,
    153–4; plan of, 157; rib from,
    143
Sig(h)vatr: and Canute, 268, 270,
    272 n; on lord, 55; and
    Magnus, 19, 49 et seq.; and St
    Olave, 28, 55, 96, 145, 185,
    275; on a ship, 159, 331
silver: coined, 146–9; distributed,
    51, 149, 289; sourced, 315;
    won, 182, 212
Sitric (Sitriuc, Sigtryggh) III Dublin
    K., 73,272.; coins, 147
Siward (Siweard, Sigurðr),
    Northumbrian earl, 246
Skaði, 250
skalds, 27–31; and kings, 142; not
    erotic, 32; not genealogical,
    244; patrons, 273; and sea,
    171; study of, 308, 318; their
    versification, 243–4
skis, 128, 194
Skrælingar, 126, 128
slander *see* defamation
slavery, slaves, 20, 24–7, 190; in
    Iceland, 225–6; Midlands, 232;
    Prices, 210; slave-hunt, 182;
    slave-trade, 70 n, 223

Slavs (Baltic), 83, 103–4, 129n;
    eastern, 215
Småland, 20 n, 25, 99
smiths, 24, 205–7
Smyth, Alfred, 136, 180 n
Snorri Sturluson, 22, 23, 28, 41, 42,
    45, 83, 98, 99, 137, 143 n, 237,
    242; his cosmology, 252;
    Heimskringla date, 313 n
social mobility, 61–2, 77, to
    earldom, 325; to elite, 162;
    from slavery, 24–5
sociology, 304–5
sodomy, 26, 32, 285
Sogn, 108, 110, 227
Solli, Brit, 32 n, 302, 319
Sorte Muld, 104
souls, 293–4
source criticism, 305, 312–15
spades, 177 n, 197
Sparlösa stone, 51, 96, 236, 294
stallers, 145
Stamford Bridge, 185
Staraya Ladoga, 82
Starkaðr, 255
state-formation theory, 8 n, 73–4,
    88–9, 111, 120, 133–5,
    149–53; conversions and, 268;
    cults and, 264 n
status, 60–3, 145, 162, 190–1, 245,
    250
Stefnir Thorgilsson, 284
Steinsland, Gro, 139–40, 237
Steinunn, 23, 330
Stockholm Charter, 324
Storsjön, 98
strip rotation, 69, 193–4
Stúfr the Blind, 101, 184n
suicide, 34–5, 291 n
Suomi, 129
Sveinn *see* Sweyn
Svíar *see* Swedes
Svǫlðr, 141, 183
Swedes, 131–2, 94–6; kings of, 141;
    laws, 68; literacy, 276; rune-
    stones, 155; as Rus, 115

Sweyn (Sveinn) Álfífason, N.K., 44, 163

Sweyn I Forkbeard (Sveinn Haraldsson), D.K., 35, 55, 148, 91; ambitions, 159; death of, 286; unifier?, 150; wars of, 186

Sweyn II Estrithson, D.K., 60, 172; bones of, 36–7; fugitive, 10; and Lund, 91, sons of, 141, 152; wars of, 172–3

swidden *see* burn-beating

synthesizers, 301

taxation: English, 120, 149, 159, 173; Danish, 74, 149; Orcadian, 219; Swedish, 43, 154

tephrochronology, 315

territories, 86–9; islands as, 100–6; Jutland, 92–3; North Sea, 107–11; Swedish, 94–9

terror, 21–2, 179–82

textiles, 19, 42 n; weaving, 207–8

thegns, 75–6, 335–6

Theodoric, Gothic K., 158, 241, 246

theophoria, 79–81

Thjóðolfr Arnorsson, 29, 58, 172, 198–9, 328

Thor (Thorr), 191, 242; cult of, 261–2, 281; names, 44–5

Thórarinn Praise-Tongue, 142, 273–4

Thórbjǫrn Dísarskald, 191 n

Thórbjǫrn Hornklofi, 54, 328

Thórðr Kolbeinsson, 109, 170, 273

Thorfinn, earl of Orkney, 56, 300

Thorgerðr Hölgabruðr, 265

Thorkell the Tall, 63, 171, 173, 181

Thorleifr Rauðfeldarson, 298, 330

Thorleik the Handsome, 172, 332

Thormóðr Kolbrúnarskáld, 28; death, 143, 331

thorps, 66, 76, 82

Thronds, 108–9, 163

Thumby-Bienebeck, 266

Thyra (Thyrwi), D.Q., 19, 119

timber, 68, 69, 159, 170, 208; substituted, 202

time, 237–8, 246

tithe, 65, 68, 123 n, 124, 154

toponymy *see* names/place-names

towns, 71–4; Jutland, 92–3; kings and, 153–5

trade, 72–4; kings and, 153–4; managed or administered, 89, 107, 122, 209 n; traders, 69–74; as work, 209–12; warranted, 257

transvestism, 21 n, 24, 263 n

trapping, 69, 126

Trelleborg, 81, 102; architecture at, 208; forts, 84–6, 178; ploughing at, 197; Scanian, 86 n, 91

tribes, 88–9

tribute, 62, 209; Lapp, 127, 129

Trondheim, 154–5; Canute at, 142; origins of, 108

Tyr, 264; and map, 260

Udal fort, 177

udall tenure, 49

Ulf Jarl, 36

Úlfr Uggason, 263, 330

Ulfberht swords, 269; and map, 8

Ulfcytel, of East Anglia, 62, 176, 187

undead, the, 285–7, 291–2

Uppåkra, 91

Uppland, 16, 20, 94

Uppsala (Gamla): kings and, 75, 91, 96; mimes at, 280n; raids on, 91; sacrifices at, 141, 156, 195

urbanization, 6, 64–5, 70–4, 150, 153–5

Uthinkaur, Odinkar, 49

Vä, 91

Valgarðr a Velli, 21, 25

Valhalla, 139, 262, 294–5

valkyries, 183, 242, 263; Brynhildr, 241; kings and, 142

vampires, 293

Vanir, 242, 280

Varangians, 115 n; wages, 216, 270

Värend, 99

Värmland, 98, 204
Västergötland, 69, 96–7, 194
veizla, 145–6, 54
Vendel period, 7, 248
versification: diction, 256; Irish
    influence? 271; metres, 241,
    271, 278; of skalds, 29–30
Vestfold, 109, 117, 122
Vetrliði, 262
Viborg, 93; harrow, 196; moss, 314;
    name, 80
Víken, 109, 117, 119, 122, 146;
    farming, 198; and viking, 2 n
viking (víkingr) concept, 1–6, 72–3,
    83, 117, 303; ethos 255–6
vikings: as caste, 162; commercial,
    72–3; funerals, 291; repressed,
    76, 142, 298; repulsing, 105
    Zealand 102
villages, 65–6; farming by, 193–4;
    Scanian, 70
Vínland, 11, 126, 227
violence, 28, 68, 82; cosmic
    balance?, 255; duels, 258;
violence (*cont.*)
    exaggerated, 168; kings and,
    141–3
Vladimir the Great, 146
Volkhov, R., 215
Vorbasse, 66, 67, 160
Vǫluspá, 23 n, 237, 295, 299

walls, field-, 67–8, 193
war-bands, 11, 52–8, 82–6, 168–9
warfare, 168–188; politics of 141–3
Warner (Garnier) of Rouen, 26–7
weapon graves, 101, 164, 172
weaving, 207
weights, 333–4
Weyland, myth of, 190, 242
Weyland (raider), 171
whale, 200–1, 202
Widsith, 112

Widukind of Korvey, 157, 273
Wight, Isle of, 177, 180
Winning, 77
witches, 22–3, 284, 286, 289
wizards, 22–3, 284
Wollin, 83–4, 107
wolves, 33, 184–5, 201, 273; alias,
    295; mask, 79 n
women: archaeology of, 321; to be
    avenged, 258; dress, 61,
    intimidated, 21–2; as observers,
    29, 178, 185; powerful, 17–19,
    84–5, 109, 286, rich old, 61;
    warrior-, 20–1, 104, 169; work
    of, 190, 200, 205, 207–8
Worcester, 180
World-Tree *see* Yggdrasill
work, 190–213; common, 69–74; of
    settlers, 229–32; Thor's, 261
Wulfstan, archbishop of York, 182,
    261
Wulfstan: on Baltic, 88, 96, 100,
    103, 112; on Balts, 290; on
    Swedes, 131, 261
xenophobia, passive, 125

Yggdrasill, 237, 252, 257
Ynglinga Saga, 22, 41, 168, 243
Ynglingatal, 137, 312
Ynglingar, 152, 250; as epithet,
    244
Yngvaldingar, 13
Yngvarr, 282, 317
York: archbishops, 232 n, 254 n,
    256; city, 72–3, 279; coins, 148;
    271; conquered, 138, 175;
    kings at, 271, 284; minster, 19
Yule, 141, 144, 212, 280

Zachrisson, Inger, 128, 157, 312
Zealand (Sjælland), 101–2; feasts,
    144, 154; legends, 101, 197,
    237